DRAMA CRITICISM: VOLUME I

A Checklist of Interpretation since 1940
of English and American Plays

DRAMA
CRITICISM

*

VOLUME ONE

A Checklist of Interpretation
since 1940 of English
and American Plays

*

ARTHUR COLEMAN

and

GARY R. TYLER

ALAN SWALLOW
Denver

To Tina and the Van Curens
—For more than a mere dedication
can express

TABLE OF CONTENTS

INTRODUCTION

This work is the fifth in a series of critical Checklists, and has been designed and compiled to answer an obvious need which has been recognized for some time by librarians, educators, and students. It is a Checklist of Criticism on American and British (including Irish, Canadian, Australian and New Zealand) drama appearing in periodicals and books published over the last quarter century (1940-1964).

The 1,050 periodicals which were researched for this work were selected from many different sources. All of the major "academic" periodicals, it will be noted, are included, as well as hundreds which are less well-known but no less legitimate.

The 1,500 books researched were selected with the assistance of the Library of Congress to capture all books published during this period which might even touch on drama. Monographs which are, in effect, "histories," or broad "surveys" have been excluded. Also not researched were books which can be located by referring to a library card catalog under a particular dramatist's name and which deal only with that dramatist and his works. (*Shakespeare's Tragedies: An Anthology of Modern Criticism* would not be included, for example.) Works which contain the name of a playwright in the title, but which might contain essays or critical materials on several playwrights have been researched. (Thus E. E. Stoll's *Shakespeare and Other Masters* has been researched to uncover essays on drama other than Shakespeare.)

Books orginally printed prior to 1940 but reprinted between 1940 and 1964 have generally not been researched. Researching this material could not be justified in a Checklist of Criticism representing an approach to drama which has emerged *since* 1940. As an aid for those who may wish to examine these monographs, a partial list will be found as a separate bibliography at the end of this Checklist. A few printed just prior to January, 1940 have been researched whenever "borderline cases" have existed. Dissertations have generally been excluded as less accessible and less professional efforts.

This Checklist is intended as a broad, nearly definitive, bibliography of all drama criticism—notable and obscure.* Therefore, when respectable critics have seen fit to devote their intelligent attention to any drama in the sources consulted, this information has been cited within the limitations set forth below.

---

*Needless to say, every conceivable critical "approach" to drama is represented. Of the five major classifications offered by Professor Wilbur Scott (*Five Approaches of Literary Criticism*, New York: Collier Books, 1962)—moral, psychological, sociological, formalistic, and archetypal—the formalistic approach (aesthetic, textual, ontological, or simply "new criticism") has emerged in this research as the most common critical approach.

In some cases, criticism of dramatic dialogues, operas, and masques has been included. Criticism of dramatic poems has been excluded.

Entries appear in this listing only when they are of some interpretive value, or are of a truly "critical" nature. It is sometimes difficult to draw the boundaries around *explication de texte*. The authors have been extremely liberal whenever there has been any doubt about how "critical" any given item might be. For example, biographical, source, genesis, plot, historical, and staging material have generally not been included. However, when this type of writing (either alone or combined with the more formalistic approaches) has had some critical value, or has added in some measure to the critical understanding of the play involved, it has been included. In this connection, an essay on the staging of a play can be very helpful when seeking the "meaning" where the drama is so complex that only through performance can the true intent of the playwright become apparent. Decisions of this nature have in almost every case been made favoring inclusion of this criticism. Study questions have also been included when they help to reveal meaning.

This liberal approach to the "depth" of the criticism has also carried over to its "breadth". Any of the "textual repairmen" represented in this Checklist would be aware that literary interpretation of details is only as sound as the text on which it rests. On the other hand, interpretation is included which may analyze only four lines of a play and do it in ten pages! This type of approach can clarify entire acts of a play by dealing only with a few lines. Therefore, it has been just a important to include interpretations of entire plays as it has to include lengthy considerations of "detail".

Where English or American dramatists have done loose translations of the plays of others, decisions were made regarding inclusion based on the direction the interpretation has taken. If the criticism has served primarily as explication of the original work, no entry would appear for the translator. Criticism of this type has been found very infrequently, and has been handled on an "exception basis". Criticism dealing with adaptations of other fictional forms has generally not been included.

Every entry in this Checklist has been examined at least once. Some have been read or skimmed by both authors.

Where essays have been reprinted in collections, etc., every effort has been made to note all such reprints. In the interests of uniformity, most periodical issues published as separate volumes will not be listed also as monographs.

Book titles listed in the body of the Checklist appear in some cases in shortened form. Full bibliographical information appears in the bibliography section. Unless otherwise noted, all book entries have been obtained from the latest edition of the work cited.

Where the authorship of certain plays has been questionable, or where plays are recognized by all authorities as "anonymous", they appear at the beginning of the listing under the heading *Anonymous*. The authors have not presumed to judge the authorhip of many plays for which, in some cases, disputes have existed for several centuries. Instead, where there has been doubt, the play involved will generally be found listed under *Anonymous* and cross-referenced under the playwrights to whom it is sometimes ascribed. Where authorities generally support the authorship of a particular playwright, but a dispute exists nevertheless, the main entry will appear under the dramatist's name with a cross-reference under *Anonymous*.

As with the listing itself, the bibliographical section following the Checklist proper, has been designed for maximum usefulness. Three separate bibliographies of books appear. The first is a listing of books in which drama criticism was found. The second lists books researched, but yielding no entries. The third is a partial list of those works printed between 1940 and 1964 which might contain drama criticism but which were not researched due to original publication prior to 1940.

Four listings appear for periodicals. The first is a listing of all periodicals researched, with those yielding entries listed in capitals. In addition, an appendix contains three charts ranking the periodicals in which entries were found—the first by the number of periodical pages of criticism which appear in the body of the Checklist, and the second by the number of separate entries included in the Checklist. The third chart is a combined ranking of the top 50 periodicals in the first two charts. This ranking leaves 40 periodicals which appear on BOTH lists. The resulting recapitulation presents a clear picture of which periodicals contain concentration (both in terms of the number of articles and their length) of drama criticism. They have been prepared to enable librarians, educators, and students to evaluate the "critical content" of commonly-used periodicals.

In connection with the compilation of this Checklist, a great deal of information has been gathered about the availability of, and research techniques best suited for, drama criticism. The authors would be most happy to share this information with others studying in the field of drama or drama criticism.

For assistance with that portion of the research done on the East Coast, we acknowledge with thanks the cooperation of staff members at the New York Public Library, and at the libraries of New York University, Columbia University, Fordham, Queens College, and C. W. Post College.

For assistance in research done on the West Coast, we single out the University of California's Research Library in West Los Angeles and the Library of the University of Southern California. To the staffs of these two institutions go heartfelt thanks. The courtesy and hospitality of their staffs, and the excellent facilities placed at our disposal, have contributed more than any other single factor, to the successful completion of this work. Four members of the UCLA staff deserve special thanks: Mrs. Ruth Berry, Reference Librarian, whose kind help has taken many forms over a long period of time; Mr. James R. Cox, Circulation Director; Mr. Walter M. Liebonow, Assistant Head of Circulation, for his unselfish devotion of time spent in locating research materials; and to Mrs. Elinore Friedgood, Catalogue Librarian, for her helpful advice on many matters within her field. Thanks go also to three members of the University of Southern California's staff: Dr. Lewis F. Stieg, University Librarian; Mr. Dale Jarvis, Head, Circulation Department; and to Brad Karelius.

We would like also to acknowledge the aid of Mr. Robert H. Land, Chief, Reference Department, General Reference and Bibliography Division, of the Library of Congress for his counsel in directing the authors to appropriate research material; James R. Hill, whose astute observations and novel suggestions have added immeasurably to the work; Clifford Shank, Jr.; Kenneth Shaffer; E. Norris Moran, Los Angeles Public Library; Tom Hartley, IBM; the Pacific Telephone and Telegraph Company for arrangements made to facilitate this transcontinental collaboration; and to many generous and helpful friends in several sections under the control of the Cashier's Department, at First Western Bank and Trust Company's Home Office in Los Angeles, whose contributions have been much to numerous and diverse to detail here.

Some of this research has been financed through grants awarded by Long Island University in New York. Both authors are grateful for their confidence and their support.

Special thanks must go to Mr. and Mrs. Robert P. Hoyle of Alhambra, California, for their kind encouragement for the duration of this project, and for the many hours spent assisting in the preparation of the manuscript. We thank them heartily.

Arthur Coleman   Gary Tyler
C. W. Post College   Los Angeles
of Long Island University
New York

PLAYS OTHER THAN SHAKESPEARE'S

ANONYMOUS

ABRAHAM AND ISAAC
Ellis-Fermor, Una. *The Frontiers of Drama,* 21-24.
Severs, J. Burke. "The Relationship Between the Brome and Chester Plays of *Abraham and Isaac,*" *Modern Philology,* 42#3: 137-151 (Feb, 1945).
Williams, Raymond. *Drama in Performance,* 41-45.

ADAM
Auerbach, Erich. *Memesis,* 143-151, 156-162.

ARDEN OF FAVERSHAM
Adams, Henry. *English Domestic or Homiletic Tragedies,* 100-108.
Cunningham, James. *Woe or Wonder,* 60-61.
Chapman, Raymond. "*Arden of Faversham:* Its Interest Today," *English,* 11#61: 15-17 (Spring, 1956).
Hanratty, J. "*Arden of Faversham,*" *The Use of English,* 11#3: 176-180 (Spring, 1960).
Jackson, Mac D. P. "An Emendation to *Arden of Faversham,*" *Notes and Queries,* 208: 410 (Nov, 1963).
Youngblood, Sarah. "Theme and Imagery in *Arden of Faversham,*" *Studies in English Literature 1500-1900,* 3#2: 207-218 (Spring, 1963).

BIRTH OF MERLIN, THE
See: William Rowley

BLOODY BANQUET, THE
Bowers, Fredson. *Elizabethan Revenge Tragedy,* 165-166.

BROME, THE
See: Anon—*Abraham and Isaac*

CAESAR'S REVENGE
McDiarmid, Matthew. "The Influence of Robert Garnier on Some Elizabethan Tragedies," *Etudes Anglaises,* 11#4: 299-301 (Dec, 1958).

McDonnell, R. F. *The Aspiring Mind,* 161-164.

CARDENIO

Muir, Kenneth. *Shakespeare as Collaborator,* 148-160.

CASTLE OF PRESERVATION, THE

Bevington, David M. *From Mankind to Marlowe,* 115-123.

Chews, S. *The Virtues Reconciled,* 44-5; 47.

Creeth, Edmund H. "Moral and Tragic Recognition: The Uniqueness of *Othello, Macbeth,* and *King Lear,*" *Michigan Academy of Science, Arts, and Letters-Papers,* 45: 385; 387-389 (1960).

McCutchan, J. W. "Covetousness in *The Castle of Perserverance,*" in *English Studies in Honor of James Southall Wilson,* 175-191.

Towne, F. "*Roister Doister's* Assault on the *Castle of Perserverance,*" *Washington State College Research Studies,* 18#4: 175-180 (Dec, 1950).

CESTUS, THE

Stroup, Thomas B. "*The Cestus:* Manuscript of an Anonymous Eighteenth-Century Imitation of *Comus.*" *Studies in English Literature 1500-1900,* 2#1: 47-55 (Winter, 1962).

CHRIST LED UP TO CALVARY

Frampton, Mendal. "The York Play of *Christ Led up to Calvary,*" in B. Maxwell (ed), *Renaissance Studies in Honor of Hardin Craig,* 6-12.

CLAUDIUS TIBERIUS NERO

Bowers, F. T. *Elizabethan Revenge Tragedy,* 158-161.

CLYOMON AND CLAMYDES

Bevington, D. M. *From Mankind to Marlowe,* 194-196.

Cope, Jackson I. " 'The Best for Comedy': Richard Edwards' Canon," *Texas Studies in Literature and Language,* 2#4: 501-519 (Winter, 1961).

COMMON CONDITIONS

Bevington, D. M. *From Mankind to Marlowe,* 191-194.

Cope, Jackson I. " 'The Best for Comedy': Richard Edwards' Canon," *Texas Studies in Literature and Language,* 2#4: 501-519 (Winter, 1961).

CONTENTION, THE—BETWIXT THE HOUSES OF YORK & LANCASTER

McManaway, James. "*The Contention* and *2 Henry VI,*" in S. Korninger (ed), *Studies in English Presented to Karl Brunner,* 143-145.

EDMUND IRONSIDES

Everitt, E. B. and R. L. Armstrong. "Six Early Plays Related to the Shakespeare Canon," *Anglistica,* 14: 103-106 (1964-1965).

Ribner, Irving. *The English History Play in the Age of Shakespeare,* 243-244.

EDWARD III

Everitt, E. B. and R. L. Armstrong. "Six Eearly Plays Related to the Shakespeare Canon," *Anglistica,* 14: 195-199 (1964-1965).

Koskenniemi, Inna. "Themes and Imagery in *Edward III,*" *Neuphilologische Mitteilungen,* 65: 446-481 (1964).

Muir, Kenneth. *Shakespeare as Collaborator,* 10-55.

Ribner, Irving. *The English History Play in the Age of Shakespeare,* 146-154.

Talbert, E. *Elizabethan Drama and Shakespeare's Early Drama,* 90-92; 110-112.

EVERYMAN

Adolf, Helen. "From *Everyman* and *Elckerlijc* to Hofmannsthal and Kafka," *Comparative Literature,* 9#3: 204-207.

Anderson, Mary D. *Drama and Imagery in English Medieval Churches,* 72-84.

Brooks, C. and R. Heilman. *Understanding Drama,* 100-111.

Cary, Joyce. *Art and Reality,* 154-159.

Ellis-Fermor, U. *The Irish Dramatic Movement,* 108-109.

Goodman, Randolf. *Drama on Stage,* 61-95.

Kaula, David. "Time in *Everyman* and *Dr. Faustus,*" *College English,* 22#1: 9-14 (Oct, 1960).

Kornbluth, Martin L. "A Twentieth Century *Everyman,*" *College English,* 21#1: 26-29 (Oct, 1959).

Ryan, Lawrence V. "Doctrine and Dramatic Structure in *Everyman,*" *Speculum,* 32#4: 722-735 (1957).

Tigg, E. R. *"Is Elckerlijc* Prior to *Everyman?"* *Neophilologus,* pp. 121-141 (Jan, 1941).

Thomas, Geoffrey. *The Theatre Alive,* 222-226.

Thomas, Helen S. "The Meaning of the Character Knowledge in *Everyman,*" *Mississippi Quarterly,* 14#1: 3-13 (Winter, 1960-1961).

Thomas, Helen S. "Some Analogues of *Everyman,*" *Mississippi Quarterly,* 14#2: 97-103 (Spring, 1963).

Van Loan, Thomas F. *"Everyman:* A Structural Analysis," PMLA, 78#5: 465-475 (Dec, 1963).

Williams, Raymond. *Drama in Performance,* 46-53.

Zandvoort, R. W. *"Everyman—Elckerlijc,"* Etudes Anglaises, 6#1: 1-15 (Feb, 1953).

FAMOUS VICTORIES OF HENRY V, THE
Clemen, W. *English Tragedy Before Shakespeare*, 194-197.
Ribner, Irving. *The English History Play in the Age of Shakespeare*, 73-74.

FIRST PART OF THE REIGN OF RICHARD II, THE; OR THOMAS OF WOODSTOCK
See: Anon—*Thomas of Woodstock*

FOUR CARDINAL VIRTUES, THE
Boas, Frederick S. *"The Four Cardinal Virtues,"* *Queens Quarterly*, 58#1: 85-91 (Spring, 1951).

GAMMER GURTON'S NEEDLE
Bevington, D. M. *From Mankind to Marlowe*, 33-34.

GISMOND OF SALERNE
See: Robert Wilmot

GORBODUC
See: Thomas Norton

HICKSCORNER
Bevington, D. M. *From Mankind to Marlowe*, 50-51; 138-139.

JOHN OF BORDEUX
Hoppe, Harry R. *"John of Bordeux:* A Bad Quarto That Never Reached Print," *University of Missouri Studies*, 21#1: 119-132 (1946).
McNeir, Waldo F. "Reconstructing the Conclusion of *John of Bordeux*," *PMLA*, 66#4: 540-543 (June, 1951).
————————. "Robert Greene and *John of Bordeux*," *PMLA*, 64#4: 781-801 (Sept, 1949).

KING DARIUS
Bevington, D. M. *From Mankind to Marlowe*, 175-178.

KING LEIR
Clemen, W. *English Tragedy Before Shakespeare*, 205-207; 285-286.
Law, Robert A. *"King John* and *King Leir,"* *Texas Studies in Literature and Language*, 1#4: 472-476 (Winter, 1960).
Everitt, E. B. and R. L. Armstrong. "Six Early Plays Related to the Shakespeare Canon," *Anglistica*, 14: 11-14 (1964-1965).

KNACK TO KNOW A KNAVE, A
Adkins, Mary. "The Genesis of Dramatic Satire Against the

Puritan, as Illustrated in *A Knack to Know a Knave,"
The Review of English Studies, 22#86: 81-95 (Apr,
1946).

Bennett, Paul E. "The Word Goths in *A Knack to Know A
Knave,"* *Notes and Queries*, 200: 462-463 (Nov, 1955).

LIFE AND DEATH OF JACK STRAW, THE

Adkins, Mary G. "A Theory About *The Life and Death of
Jack Straw,"* *Studies in English (University of Texas)*,
28: 57-82 (1949).

McDonnell, R. F. *The Aspiring Mind*, 156-158.

Ribner, Irving. *The English History Play in the Age of Shakespeare*, 74-79.

LOCRINE

Clemen, Wolfgang. *English Tragedy Before Shakespeare*, 92-
99; 258-262.

McDiarmid, Matthew P. "The Influence of Robert Garnier on
Some Elizabethan Tragedies," *Etudes Anglais*es, 11#4:
293-296 (Oct-Dec, 1958).

Ribner, Irving. *The English History Play in the Age of Shakes-
238-241.

LUST'S DOMINION

Bowers, F. T. *Elizabethan Revenge Tragedy*, 272-273.

Cross, Gustav K. "The Authorship of *Lust's Dominion,"*
Studies in Philology, 55#1: 46-47 (Jan, 1958).

Jones, Eldred. *Othello's Countrymen*, 60-68.

Wadsworth, Frank W. "The Relationship of *Lust's Dominion*
and John Mason's *The Turke,"* *ELH*, 20: 194-199
(1953).

MANKIND

Adams, Henry H. *English Domestic or Homiletic Tragedies
1575-1642*, 56-58.

MARRIAGE OF WIT AND SCIENCE, THE

Varma, R. S. "Act and Scene Divisions in *The Marriage of
Wit and Science,"* *Notes and Queries*, N.S. 10#3: (v.
208) : 95-96 (Mar, 1963).

MERRY DEVIL OF EDMONTON

Fiehler, Rudolph. " 'I Serve the Good Duke of Norfolk',"
Modern Language Quarterly, 10: 364-366 (1949).

MISERIES OF ENFORCED MARRIAGE, THE

See: George Wilkins

MUCEDORUS AND AMADINE
  Reynolds, George. *"Mucedorus,* Most Popular Elizabethan
    Play," in *Studies in English Renaisance Drama in Mem-
    ory of Karl J. Holzknecht,* 248-268.

NATURE OF THE FOUR ELEMENTS, THE
  Bevington, David. *From Mankind to Marlowe,* 45-47.
  Cliver, Leslie M. "John Foxe and the Drama *New Custom,"*
    Huntington Library Quarterly, 10#4: 407-410 (Aug,
    1947).

NICE WANTON
  Adams, Henry H. *English Domestic or Homiletic Tragedies
    1575-1642,* 69-71.

OF GENTLENESS AND NOBILITY
  See: John Rastell

OLD LAW, THE
  Price, George R. "The Authorship and the Manuscript of *The
    Old Law," Huntington Library Quarterly,* 16#2: 117-
    139 (Feb, 1953).

PARTIAL LAW, THE
  Parrot, T. M. "Two Late Dramatic Versions of the Slandered
    Bride Theme," in James G. McManaway (ed), *Joseph Q.
    Adams Memorial Studies,* 542-548.

PHILOSOPHER, THE
  See: Anon—*Wit's Triumvirate*

PLAY OF THE SACRAMENT
  Cutts, Cecilia. "The Croxton Play: An Anti-Lollard Piece?"
    Modern Language Quarterly, 5#1: 45-60 (Mar, 1944).

REVENGE FOR HONOR
  Bowers, Fredson T. *Elizabethan Revenge Tragedy,* 247-249.

REVENGER'S TRAGEDY, THE
  See: Cyril Tourneur

SECOND MAIDEN'S TRAGEDY
  Bowers, Fredson T. *Elizabethan Revenge Tragedy,* 166-167.
  Levin, Richard. "The Double Plot of *The Second Maiden's
    Tragedy," Studies in English Literature 1500-1900,* 3#2:
    219-232 (Spring, 1963).
  Schoenbaum, Samuel. "Middleton's Tragedies—A Critical
    Study," *Columbia University Studies in English and Com-
    parative Literature,* 168: 36-68 (1955).

SECUNDA PASTORUM
See: Towneley—Secunda Pastorum

SELIMUS
See: Robert Greene

TAMING OF A SHREW, THE
Everitt, E. B. and R. L. Armstrong. "Six Early Plays Related to the Shakespeare Canon," *Anglistica,* 14: 251-252 (1964-65).
Houk, Raymond A. *"Doctor Faustus* and *A Shrew,"* PMLA, 62#4Pt. 1: 950-957 (Dec, 1947).
———————. "Shakespeare's *Shrew* and Greene's *Orlando, PMLA,* 62#3: 657-671 (Sept, 1947).
Parrott, T. M. *"The Taming of A Shrew*—A New Study of an Old Play," University of Colorado Studies, 2#4: 155-165 (1945).
Shroeder, John W. *"The Taming of A Shrew and The Taming of The Shrew:* A Case Reopened" *Journal of English and Germanic Philology,* 57#3: 424-443 (July, 1958).

THOMAS OF WOODSTOCK
Clemen, Wolfgang. *English Tragedy Before Shakespeare,* 207-210.
Ribner, Irving. *The English History Play in the Age of Shakespeare,* 136-145.
Rossiter, A. P. "Prolegomenon to the Anonymous *Woodstock* (alias *1 Richard II),"* *Durham University Journal,* 37#2: 42-51 (March, 1945).

THE THREE MARIES
Williams, Raymond. *Drama in Performance,* 36-40.

TOM TYLER AND HIS WIFE
Bradbrook, M. C. "Dramatic Role as Social Image: A Study of *The Taming of The Shrew,"* *Shakepeare Jahrbuck,* 94: 135-138 (1958).

TRAGEDIE OF CLAUDIUS TIBERIUS NERO, THE
See: Anon—*Claudius Tiberius Nero*

TRAGEDY OF TIBERIUS, THE
See: Anon—*Claudius Tiberius Nero*

TRAVAILS OF THREE ENGLISH BROTHERS, THE
Schoenbaum, Samuel. "John Day and Elizabethan Drama," *Boston Public Library Quarterly,* 5:142-145 (July, 1953).

TRAIL OF TREASURE, THE
Bevington, David M. *From Mankind to Marlowe,* 153-155.

TROUBLESOME REIGN OF KING JOHN, THE (I & II)
Clemen, Wolfgang. *English Tragedy Before Shakespeare,* 199-202.

Elson, John. "Studies in the King John Plays," in James G. McManaway, *Joseph Q. Adams Memorial Studies,* 183-197.

Everitt, E. B. and R. L. Armstrong. "Six Early Plays Related to the Shakespeare Canon," *Anglistica,* 14:143-144 (1964-1965).

Law, Robert A. *"King John* and *King Leir,"* *Texas Studies in Literature and Language,* 1#4: 472-476 (Winter, 1960).

McDiarmid, Matthew P. "Concerning *The Troublesome Reign of King John,"* *Notes and Queries,* 202: 435-438 (1957).

TRUE TRAGEDY OF RICHARD III, THE
Clemen, Wolfgang. *English Tragedy Before Shakespeare,* 202-204.

Lordi, Robert J. "The Relationship of *Richard Tertius* to the Main Richard III Plays," *Boston University Studies in English,* 5#3: 139-142 (Autumn, 1961).

Talbert, Ernest W. *Elizabethan Drama and Shakespeare's Early Drama,* 66-67.

WARNING FOR FAIR WOMEN, A
Adams, Henry H. *English Domestic or Homiletic Tragedies 1575-1642,* 114-125.

Lewis, Arthur O. *"A Warning for Faire Women,* Line 143," *Notes and Queries,* 199: 18-19 (Jan, 1954)

Marshburn, Joseph H. " 'A Cruell Murder Donne in Kent' and its Literary Manifestations," *Studies in Philology,* 46#2: 134-136 (April, 1949).

WEAKEST GOETH TO THE WALL, THE
Everitt, E. B. and R. L. Armstrong. "Six Early Plays Related to the Shakespeare Canon," *Anglistica,* 14: 61-63 (1964-1965).

WILY BEGUILED
McDiarmid, Matthew P. "The Stage Quarrel in *Wily Beguiled,"* *Notes and Queries,* 201#9: 380-383 (Sept, 1956).

Maxwell, Baldwin. *"The Two Angry Women of Abington* and

Wily Beguiled," in B. Maxwell (ed), *Renaissance Studies in Honor of Hardin Craig,* 142-147.
ALSO IN: *Studies in Philology,* 20#3: 334-339 (July, 1941).

WIT'S TRIUMVIRATE
Schoenbaum, S. *"Wit's Triumvirate:* A Caroline Comedy Recovered," *Studies in English Literature 1500-1900,* 4#2: 227-238 (Spring, 1964).

WOODSTOCK
See: Anon—*Thomas of Woodtock*

YORKSHIRE TRAGEDY, THE
Adams, Henry H. *English Domestic or Homiletic Tragedies 1575-1642,* 126-132.
Blaynewy, Glenn H. "Dramatic Pointing in *The Yorkshire Tragedy,"* *Notes and Queries,* 202#5: 191-192 (May, 1957).

ABEL, LIONEL

ABSALOM
Mottram, Eric. "The New American Wave," *Encore,* 11#1: 32-34 (Jan-Feb, 1964).
PRETENDER, THE
Mottram, Eric. "The New American Wave," *Encore,* 11#1: 34-35 (Jan-Feb, 1964).

ADDISON, JOSEPH

CATO
Boas, F. S. *An Introduction to Eighteenth Century Drama,* 117-123.

DRUMMER, THE
Boas, F. S. *An Introduction to Eighteenth Century Drama,* 123-125.

A. E. (GEORGE RUSSELL)

DEIRDRE
Ellis-Fermor, Una. *The Irish Dramatic Movement,* 40-43.
McHugh, Roger. "The Deidre Legend," *Threshold,* 1#1: 42 (Feb, 1957).

ALBEE, EDWARD

AMERICAN DREAM, THE

Goodman, Henry. "Edward Albee," *Drama Survey,* 2#1: 76-78 (June, 1962).

Hamilton, Kenneth. "Mr. Albee's Dream," *Queen's Quarterly,* 70#3: 393-399 (Aut, 1963).

Mottram, Eric. "The New American Wave," *Encore,* 11#1: 28 (Jan-Feb, 1964).

Solomon, Jerry. "Edward Albee: American Absurdist?" *Western Speech,* 28#4: 230-236 (Fall, 1964).

Wellwarth, George E. "Hope Deferred—The New American Drama," *The Literary Review,* 7#1: 11-14 (Autumn, 1963).

THE SANDBOX

Cubeta, Paul M. *Modern Drama For Analysis—Third Edition* (1963), 598-604.

WHO'S AFRAID OF VIRGINIA WOOLF?

Chester, Alfred. "Edward Albee: Red Herrings and White Whales," *Commentary,* 35: 296-301 (April, 1963).

Dukore, B. F. "A Warp in Albee's *Woolf,*" *Southern Speech Journal,* 30#3: 261-268 (Spring, 1965).

Harris, Wendell V. "Morality, Absurdity and Albee," *Southwest Review,* 49#3: 249-255 (Summer, 1964).

Kerr, Walter. *The Theater in Spite of Itself,* 122-126.

Mottram, Eric. "The New American Wave," *Encore,* 11#1: 28-30 (Jan-Feb, 1964).

Schechner, Richard. "Who's Afraid of Edward Albee?" *Tulane Drama Review,* 7#3: 7-10 (Spring, 1963).

Schneider, Alan. "Who so Afraid?" *Tulane Drama Review,* 7#3: 10-13 (Spring, 1963).

Trilling, Diana. *Claremont Essays,* 203-228.

Wellwarth, George E. "Hope Deferred—The New American Drama," *The Literary Review,* 7#1: 14-15 (Autumn, 1963).

ZOO STORY, THE

Deutsch, Robert H. "Writers Maturing in the Theatre of the Absurd," *Discourse: A Review of Liberal Arts,* 7#2: 184-186 (Spring, 1964).

Goodman, Henry. "Edward Albee," *Drama Survey,* 2#1: 72-75 (June, 1962).

Wellwarth, George E. "Hope Deferred—The New American Wave," *The Literary Review,* 7#1: 8-10 (Autumn, 1963).

Zimbardo, Rose A. "Symbolism and Naturalism in Edward Albee's *The Zoo Story," Twentieth Century Literature,* 8#1: 10-17 (April, 1962).

ANDERSON, MAXWELL

BOTH YOUR HOUSES
Lawson, John H. *Theory and Technique of Playwriting,* 146-151.

ELIZABETH THE QUEEN
Knepler, Henry W. "Maxwell Anderson: A Historical Parallel," *Queen's Quarterly,* 44#2: 249-255 (Summer, 1957).
Rabkin, Gerald. *Drama and Commitment,* 274-275.
Wall, Vincent. "Maxwell Anderson: The Last Anarchist," *Sewanee Review,* 49#3: 343-349 (Summer, 1941).
Watts, Harold. "Maxwell Anderson: The Tragedy of Attrition," *College English,* 4#4 221-224 (Jan, 1943).

EVE OF SAINT MARK, THE
Rodell, John S. "Maxwell Anderson: A Criticism," *Kenyon Review,* 5#2: 272-277 (Spring, 1943).

HIGH TOR
Rabkin, Gerald. *Drama and Commitment,* 284-287.
Sievers, W. D. *Freud on Broadway,* 176-177.
Young, Stark. *Immortal Shadows,* 185-188.

JOURNEY TO JERUSALEM
Watts, Harold. "Maxwell Anderson: The Tragedy of Attrition," *College English,* 4#4: 228-230 (Jan, 1943).

KEY LARGO
Halline, A. G. "Maxwell Anderson's Dramatic Theory," *American Literature,* 16: 77-80 (March, 1944).
Healy, Robert C. "Anderson, Saroyan, Sherwood: New Direction," *Catholic World,* 151: 174-176 (Nov, 1940).
Rabkin, Gerald. *Drama and Commitment,* 286-288.
Rice, Patrick J. "Maxwell Anderson and the Eternal Dream," *Catholic World,* pp. 367-368 (1953).
Sievers, W. D. *Freud on Broadway,* 177-178.
Watts, Harold. "Maxwell Anderson: The Tragedy of Attrition," *College English,* 4#4: 226-228 (Jan, 1943).

MARY OF SCOTLAND
Watts, Harold. "Maxwell Anderson: The Tragedy of Attrition," *College English,* 4#4: 222-226 (Jan, 1943).

NIGHT OVER TAOS
>Robinson, Cecil. *With the Ears of Strangers*, 103-104; 109-111.
>Sievers, W. D. *Freud on Broadway*, 174-175.

STAR WAGON, THE
>McCarthy, Mary. *Theater Chronicle*, 6-7.

VALLEY FORGE
>Shirk, S. *Characterization of George Washington in American Drama Since 1875*, 39-43.
>Young, Stark. *Immortal Shadows*, 165-168.

—AND LAURENCE STALLINGS
WHAT PRICE GLORY?
>Steiner, Pauline and Horst Frenz. "Anderson and Stalling's *What Price Glory?* and Carl Zuckmayer's *Rivalen*," *Germanic Review*, 20#4: 239-251 (Nov, 1947).

WHITE DESERT, THE
>Sievers, W. D. *Freud on Broadway*, 171-172.

WINTERSET
>Abernethy, Francis E. "*Winterset:* A Modern Revenge Tragedy," *Modern Drama*, 7#2: 185-189 (Sept, 1964).
>Adler, Jacob H. "Shakespeare in *Winterset*," *Educational Theatre Journal*, 6: 241-248 (Oct, 1954).
>Boyce, Benjamin. "Anderson's *Winterset*," *The Explicator*, 2#4: 32 (Feg, 1944).
>Davenport, William H. "Anderson's *Winterset*," *Explicator*, 10#6: 41 (April, 1952).
>Dusenbury, Winifred. *The Theme of Loneliness in Modern American Drama*, 119-125.
>Halline, A. G. "Maxwell Anderson's Dramatic Theory," *American Literature*, 16: 67-68; 75-76 (March, 1944).
>Harris, Ainslie. "Maxwell Anderson: Poet and Playwright," *Madison Quarterly*, 6#1: 30-31; 40-44 (Jan, 1944).
>Kleger, Samuel. "Hebraic Lore in Maxwell Anderson's *Winterset*," *American Literature*, 18: 219-232 (Nov, 1946).
>Krutch, J. W. *Modernism in Modern Drama*, 120-122.
>Marx, Milton. *The Enjoyment of Drama*, 124-128.
>Pearce, Howard D. "Job in Anderson's *Winterset*," *Modern Drama*, 6#1: 32-41 (May, 1963).
>Prior, Moody E. *The Language of Tragedy*, 320-325.
>Rabkin, Gerald. *Drama and Commitment*, 268-270.
>Roby, Robert C. "Two Worlds: Maxwell Anderon's *Winterset*," *College English*, 18#4: 195-202 (Jan, 1957).

Sampley, Arthur M. "Theory and Practice in Maxwell Anderson's Poetic Tragedies," *College English,* 5#8: 415-418
(May, 1944).

Sharpe, Robert Boies. "Nine Steps to the Tragic Triumph,"
University of North Carolina Extension Bulletin, 36#3:
37-38 (March, 1957).

Wall, Vincent. "Maxwell Anderson: The Last Anarchist,"
Sewanee Review, 49#3: 349-362 (July-Sept, 1941).

Watts, Harold. "Maxwell Anderson: The Tragedy of Attrition," *College English,* 4#4: 226-228 (Jan, 1943).

ARDEN, JOHN

ARMSTRONG'S LAST GOODNIGHT
Morgan, Edwin. *"Armstrong's Last Goodnight,"* *Encore,*
11#4: 47-51 (July-Aug, 1964).

HAPPY HAVEN, THE
Gaskill, William. "Comic Masks and *The Happy Haven,"* *Encore,* 7#6: 15-19 (Nov-Dec, 1960).

Taylor, John R. *Anger and After,* 82-85.

SERJEANT MUSGRAVE'S DANCE
Brandt, G. W. "Realism and Parables (from Brecht to Arden)," *Stratford-Upon-Avon-Studies,* 4: 49-55 (1962).

Hall, Stuart. *"Serjeant Musgrave's Dance,"* *New Left Review,*
1: 50-51 (Jan-Feb, 1960).

Hunt, Albert. *"Serjeant Musgrave* and the Critics," *Encore,*
7#1: 26-28 (Jan-Feb, 1960).

Milne, Tom. "The Hidden Face of Violence," *Encore,* 7#1:
18-20 (Jan-Feb, 1960).

Rush, David. "Grief, but Good Order," *Moderna Sprak,* 58#4:
452-458 (1964).

Taylor, John R. *Anger and After,* 79-82.

AUDEN, W. H.

—AND CHRISTOPHER ISHERWOOD
ASCENT OF F-6, THE
Donoghue, Denis. *The Third Voice,* 62-70.

Maken, Ronald. "Power and Conflict in *The Ascent of F.6,"*
Discourse: A Review of Liberal Arts, 7#3: 277-282
(Summer, 1964).

Lechlitner, Ruth. "The Odyssey of Auden," *Poetry Magazine,*
66#4: 209-210 (July, 1945).

Maes-Jelinek, Hena. "The Knowledge of Man in the Works of
Christopher Isherwood," *Revue des Langues Vivantes,*
26: 349-350 (1960).
Stewart, Douglas. *The Flesh and the Spirit,* 60-62.
Williams, Raymond. *Drama From Ibsen to Eliot,* 251-256.

- - - AND CHRISTOPHER ISHERWOOD
THE DOG BENEATH THE SKIN
Prior, Moody E. *The Language of Tragedy,* 367-369.
Williams, Raymond. *Drama From Ibsen to Eliot,* 247-251.

ON THE FRONTIER
Williams, Raymond. *Drama From Ibsen to Eliot,* 254-256.

BAGNOLD, ENID

THE CHALK GARDEN
Weales, Gerald. "The Madrigal in the Garden," *Tulane Drama
Review,* 3#2: 42-50 (Dec, 1958).

BAKER, THOMAS

THE FINE LADY'S AIRS
Gagen, Jean E. *The New Woman,* 159-161.

BALE, JOHN

KING JOHN
Elson, John. "Studies in the King John Plays," in James G.
McManaway (ed), *Joseph Q. Adams Memorial Studies,*
191-197.
Johnson, S. F. "The Tragic Hero in Early Elizabethan
Drama," in *Studies in the English Renaissance Drama in
Memory of Karl J. Holzknecht,* 157-164; 169-171.
Miller, Edwin S. "The Roman Rite in Bale's *King John,"
PMLA,* 64: 802-822 (Sept, 1949).
Pafford, J. H. P. "Two Notes on Bale's *King John," Modern
Language Review,* 56#4: 553-555 (Oct, 1961).
Ribner, Irving. *The English History Play in the Age of
Shakespeare,* 37-41; 49-50; 52-54.

SIR JOHN OLDCASTLE
Adkins, Mary G. "Sixteenth-Century Religious and Political
Implications in *Sir John Oldcastle," Texas Studies in
Literature and Language,* pp. 86-104 (1942).

THREE LAWS, THE (I & II)
Bevington, David M. *From Mankind to Marlowe,* 128-132.

BANKS, JOHN

THE UNHAPPY FAVOURITE
Knepler, Henry W. "Maxwell Anderson: A Historical Parallel," *Queen's Quarterly,* 44#2: 249-263 (Summer, 1957).

BARKER, JAMES NELSON

POCAHONTAS; OR THE INDIAN PRINCESS
Earnhart, Phyllis. "The First American Play in England," *American Literature,* 31: 326-329 (Nov, 1959).
Peavy, Charles D. "The American Indian in the Drama of the United States," *McNeese Review,* 10: 71 (Winter, 1958).

BARNES, DJUNA

THE ANTIPHON
(n.a.). "A Daughter for Inquisitor," *Times Literary Supplement,* Page 182 (Apr 4, 1958).
Abel, Lionel. "Bad by North and South," *Partisan Review,* 25#3: 461-466 (Summer, 1958).

BARRIE, SIR JAMES M.

ADMIRABLE CRICHTON, THE
McGraw, William R. "Barrie and the Critics," *Studies in Scottish Literature,* 1#2: 117-118 (Oct, 1963).

BOY DAVID, THE
McGraw, William R. "Barrie and the Critics," *Studies in Scottish Literature,* 1#2: 129-130 (Oct, 1963).

DEAR BRUTUS
McGraw, William R. "Barrie and the Critics," *Studies in Scottish Literature,* 1#2: 124-127 (Oct, 1963).

KISS FOR CINDERELLA, A
Young, Stark. *Immortal Shadows,* 227-229.

MARY ROSE
Karpe, Marietta and Richard Karp. "The Meaning of Barrie's *Mary Rose,*" *International Journal of Psychoanalysis,* 38pt. 5: 408-411 (1957).
McGraw, William R. "Barrie and the Critics," *Studies in Scottish Literature,* 1#2: 127-128 (Oct, 1963).

PETER PAN
Karpe, Marietta. "The Origins of *Peter Pan,*" *Psychoanalytic
Review,* 43: 104-110 (1956).

Kingsnull, Hugh. "J. M. Barrie," *Horizon,* 4#19: 47-49 (July,
1941).

Lewis, Naomi. *A Visit to Mrs. Wilcox,* 145-149.

McGraw, William R. "Barrie and the Critics," *Studies in Scottish Literature,* 1#2: 119-120 (Oct, 1963).

Sternlicht, Stanford. "A Source for Golding's *Lord of the
Flies: Peter Pan,*" *The English Record,* 14#2: 41-42
(Dec, 1963).

TWELVE POUND LOOK, THE
Macgowan, K. *Primer on Playwriting,* 172-173.

WELL-REMEMBERED VOICE, A
Fulton, A. R. *Drama and the Theatre,* 83-88.

WHAT EVERY WOMAN KNOWS
McGraw, William R. "Barrie and the Critics," *Studies in
Scottish Literature,* 1#2: 122-123 (Oct, 1963).

WILL, THE
Millet, Fred B. *Reading Drama,* 87-90.

BARRY, PHILIP

FOOLISH NOTION
Sievers, W. D. *Freud on Broadway,* 205-208.

HOLIDAY
Sievers, W. D. *Freud on Broadway,* 197-199.

HOTEL UNIVERSE
Mizener, Arthur. "Poetic Drama and the Well Made Play,"
English Institute Essays, pp. 39-42 (1949).

Sievers, W. D. *Freud on Broadway,* 191-195.

IN A GARDEN
Sievers, W. D. *Freud on Broadway,* 188-190.

JOYOUS SEASON, THE
Sievers, W. D. *Freud on Broadway,* 199-201.

PARIS BOUND
Sievers, W. D. *Freud on Broadway,* 197.

PHILADELPHIA STORY, THE
Sievers, W. D. *Freud on Broadway,* 203-204.

SECOND THRESHHOLD
Sievers, W. D. *Freud on Broadway,* 208-211.

TOMORROW AND TOMORROW
Dusenbury, Winifred L. *The Theme of Lonliness in Modern American Drama,* 86-92.
Sievers, W. D. *Freud on Broadway,* 201-203.

BEAUMONT, FRANCIS & JOHN FLETCHER

BONDUCA
Wells, Henry W. *Elizabethan and Jacobean Playwrights,* 136-138.

CAPTAIN, THE
Ornstein, Robert. *The Moral Vision of Jacobean Tragedy,* 167-168.

COXCOMB, THE
Shaw, G. B. *Plays and Players,* 307-311.

CUSTOM OF THE COUNTRY, THE
Howarth, W. D. "Cervantes and Fletcher: A Theme With Variations," *Modern Language Review,* 56#4: 564-566 (Oct, 1961).
Wells, Henry W. *Elizabethan and Jacobean Playwrights,* 152-154.

DOUBLE MARRIAGE, THE
Waith, E. M. "The Sources of *The Double Marriage* by Fletcher and Massinger," *Modern Language Notes,* 64#8: 505-510 (Dec, 1949).
Wells, Henry W. *Elizabethan and Jacobean Playwrights,* 141-143.

FAIR MAID OF THE INN, THE
Maxwell, Baldwin. "The Source of the Principal Plot of *The Fair Maid of the Inn,*" *Modern Language Notes,* 59#2: 122-126 (Feb, 1944).
Sloman, Albert E. "The Spanish Source of *The Fair Maid of the Inn,*" in *Hispanic Studies in Honour of I Gonzales Llubera* (ed. Frank Pierce), 331-341.

KING AND NO KING, A
Knights, L. C. *Drama and Society in the Age of Jonson,* 292-295.
Mizener, Arthur. "The High Design of *A King and No King,*" *Modern Philology,* 38#2: 133-154 (Nov, 1940).
Ornstein, Robert. *The Moral Vision of Jacobean Tragedy,* 168-169.

Turner, Robert K., Jr. "The Morality of *A King and No King*," *Renaissance Papers*, pp. 93-103 (1960).

Wells, Henry W. *Elizabethan and Jacobean Playwrights*, 120-122.

KNIGHT OF MALTA, THE

Jones, Eldred. *Othello's Countrymen*, 80-82.

Wells, Henry W. *Elizabethan and Jacobean Playwrights*, 150-152.

KNIGHT OF THE BURNING PESTLE, THE

Liu, James. "Elizabethan and Yuan: A Brief Comparison of Some Conventions in Poetic Drama," *China Society Occasional Papers*, 8: 9-11 (1955).

Olive, W. J. "Twenty Good Nights," *Studies in Philology*, 47#2: 182-189 (Apr, 1950).

Wells, Henry W. *Elizabethan and Jacobean Playwrights*, 233-235.

LOVE'S CURE; OR THE MARTIAL MAID

Erickson, Martin. "A Review of Scholarship Dealing With the Problem of a Spanish Source for *Love's Cure*," in Waldo McNeir (ed), *Studies in Comparative Literature*, 102-119.

LOVE'S PILGRIMAGE

Wells, Henry W. *Elizabethan and Jacobean Playwrights*, 154-156.

MAD LOVER, THE

Cutts, John P. "Music and *The Mad Lover*," *Studies in the Renaissance*, 8: 236-248 (1961).

MAID'S TRAGEDY, THE

Berry, Francis. *Poet's Grammar*, 93-96.

Bowers, Fredson T. *Elizabethan Revenge Tragedy*, 169-176.

Danby, J. F. *Poets on Fortune's Hill*, 184-210.

Feldman, A. B. "The Yellow Malady: Short Studies of Five Tragedies of Jealousy," *Literature and Psychology*, 5#2: 46-49; 51-52 (May, 1956).

Leech, Clifford. *Shakespeare's Tragedies and Other Studies in Seventeenth Century Drama*, 87-89; 94-95; 107-108.

Masefield, John. "Beaumont and Fletcher," *Atlantic Monthly*, 199: 173 (June, 1957).

Ornstein, Robert. *The Moral Vision of Jacobean Tragedy*, 173-184.

Prior, Moody E. *The Language of Tragedy*, 101-104.

Ribner, Irving. *Jacobean Tragedy,* 15-17.
Wells, Henry W. *Elizabethan and Jacobean Playwrights,* 124-127.

PHILASTER

Adkins, Mary G. "The Citizens of *Philaster:* Their Function and Significance," *Studies in Philology,* 43#2: 203-212 (April, 1946).

Danby, J. F. *Poets and Fortune's Hill,* 162-183.

Davison, Peter. "The Serious Concerns of *Philaster,*" *ELH,* 30#1: 1-15 (March, 1963).

Masefield, John. "Beaumont and Fletcher," *Atlantic Monthly,* 199: 173 (June, 1957).

Ornstein, Robert. *The Moral Vision of Jacobean Tragedy,* 178-179.

Savage, James E. "Beaumont and Fletcher's *Philaster* and Sidney's *Arcadia,*" *ELH,* 14#3: 194-206 (Sept, 1947).

——————————. "The 'Gaping Wounds' in the Text of *Philaster,*" *Philological Quarterly,* 48#4: 443-457 (Oct, 1949).

Wells, Henry W. *Elizabethan and Jacobean Playwrights,* 122-124.

Wilson, Harold S. *"Philaster* and *Cymbeline,*" *English Institute Essays,* pp. 146-167 (1951).

SCORNFUL LADY, THE

Masefield, John. "Beaumont and Fletcher," *Atlantic Monthly,* 199:173-174 (June, 1957).

WIT AT SEVERAL WEAPONS

Savage, James E. "The Effects of Revision in the Beaumont and Fletcher Play, *Wit at Several Weapons,*" *University of Mississippi Studies in English,* 1: 32-50 (1960).

WOMAN'S PRIZE, THE

Bradbrook, M. C. "Dramatic Role as Social Image: A Study of *The Taming of the Shrew,*" *Shakespeare Jahrbuck,* 94: 146-148 (1958).

BECKETT, SAMUEL

(See Arthur Coleman and Gary R. Tyler, *Drama Criticism: Volume II. A Checklist of Interpretation Since 1940 of Classical and Continental Plays).*

BEDDOES, THOMAS LOVELL

DEATH'S JEST BOOK
Coxe, Louis O. "Beddoes: The Mask of Parody," *Hudson Review,* 6#2 : 252-265 (Summer, 1953).

BEHAN, BRENDAN

HOSTAGE, THE
Gilliatt, Penelope. "Brendan Beano," *Encore,* 5#4 : 35-36 (Nov-Dec, 1958).
Kerr, Walter. *The Theater in Spite of Itself,* 108-111.
Taylor, John R. *Anger and After,* 104-107.

QUARE FELLOW, THE
MacInnes, Colin. "The Writings of Brendan Behan," *The London Magazine,* 2#5: 58-61 (Aug, 1962).
Taylor, John R. *Anger and After,* 102-104.

BEHN, APHRA

FALSE COUNT, THE
Wilcox, John. *The Relation of Moliere to Restoration Comedy,* 149-150.

LUCKY CHANCE, THE—
OR AN ALDERMAN'S BARGAIN
Kronenberger, Louis. *The Thread of Laughter,* 110-113.

ROUND HEADS, THE ; OR THE GOOD OLD CAUSE
Mignon, Elizabeth. *Crabbed Age and Youth,* 88-93.

SIR PATIENT FANCY
Gagen, Jean E. *The New Woman,* 44-46.
Mignon, Elizabeth. *Crabbed Age and Youth,* 24-25 ; 87-89.
Wilcox, John. *The Relation of Moliere to Restoration Comedy,* 146-149.

TOWN-FOP: OR SIR TIMOTHY TAWDRY
Kronenberger, Louis. *The Thread of Laughter,* 106-110.

WIDOW RANTER, THE
Gagen, Jean. *The New Woman,* 112-114.

YOUNGER BROTHER, THE
Gagen, Jean. *The New Woman,* 124-125.

BEHRMAN, SAMUEL N.

BIOGRAPHY
Sievers, W. D. *Freud on Broadway,* 325-327.

NO TIME FOR COMEDY
Sievers, W. D. *Freud on Broadway,* 331-332.

RAIN FROM HEAVEN
Sievers, W. D. *Freud on Broadway,* 329-330.

WINE OF CHOICE
Sievers, W. D. *Freud on Broadway,* 331-332.

BETTERTON, THOMAS

THE AMOROUS WIDOW
Wilcox, John. *The Relation of Moliere to Restoration Comedy,* 23-25.

BICKERSTAFF, ISAAC

LIONEL AND CLARISSA
Boas, F. S. *An Introduction to Eighteenth Century Drama,* 288-291.

MAID OF THE MILL, THE
Boa, F. S. *An Introduction to Eighteenth Century Drama,* 286-288.

BLITZSTEIN, MARC

THE CRADLE WILL ROCK
McCarthy, Mary. *Theater Chronicle,* 23-26.

BOKER, GEORGE

FRANCESA DA RIMINI
Shuman, R. Baird. "A Note on George Boker's *Francesca da Rimini,*" *American Literature,* 31: 980-982 (Jan, 1960).

BOLT, ROBERT

A MAN FOR ALL SEASONS
Fosbery, M. W. *"A Man For all Seasons" English Studies in Africa,* 6#2: 164-172 (Sept, 1963).

BOOTHE, CLARE
   THE WOMEN
      Sievers, W. D. *Freud on Broadway,* 221-222.

BOUCICAULT, DION

   THE OCTOROON
      Enkvist, Nils Erik. *"The Octoroon* and English Opinion of
         Slavery," *American Quarterly,* 8#2: 166-170 (Summer,
         1956).
      Lippman, Monroe. "Uncle Tom and His Poor Relations: Ameri-
         can Slavery Plays," *Southern Speech Journal,* 38#3: 194-
         195 (Summer, 1963).

BOYLE, ROGER

   THE HISTORY OF HENRY THE FIFTH
      Burns, Landon C. "Three Views of King Henry V," *Drama
         Survey,* 1#3. 284-291; 298-300 (Feb, 1962).

BRANNER, H. C.

   JUDGE, THE
      Vowles, Richard B. "Bergman, Branner, and Off-Stage Dy-
         ing," *Scandinavian Studies,* 33#1. 1-2; 4-9 (Feb, 1961).

   SIBLINGS, THE
      Vowles, Richard B. "Bergman, Branner, and Off-Stage Dy-
         ing," *Scandinavian Studies,* 33#1, 1-2; 4-9; (Feb, 1961).

BREWER, ANTHONY

   THE LOVE-SICK KING
      Dent, Robert. "The Love-Sick King: Turk Turned Dane,"
         Modern Language Review, 56#4: 555-557 (Oct, 1961).

BRIDIE, JAMES (O. H. MAVOR)

   BAIKIE CHARIVARI, THE
      Luyben, Helen L. "Bridie's Last Play," *Modern Drama,* 5#4:
         400-414 (Feb, 1963).

   BLACK EYE, THE
      Luyben, Helen L. "James Bridie and the Prodigal Son Story,"
         Modern Drama, 7#1: 35-45 (May, 1964).

DAPHNE LAUREOLA
Worsley, T. C. *The Fugitive Art,* 69-72.

BROME, RICHARD

ANTIPODES, THE
Davis, Joe Lee. "Richard Brome's Neglected Contribution to Comic Theory," *Studies in Philology,* 40: 520-528 (Oct, 1943).

LATE LANCASHIRE WITCHES, THE
See: Thomas Heywood

BROWN, KENNETH

THE BRIG
Hunt, Alfred. *"The Brig,"* *Encore,* 11#6: 46-48, (Nov-Dec, 1964).
Mottram, Eric. "The New American Wave" *Encore* 11#1: 24 (Jan-Feb, 1964).

BROWNING, ROBERT

BLOT IN THE SUTCHEON, A
Prior, Moody E. *The Language of Tragedy,* 279-288.

IN A BALCONY
Stoll, E. E. *From Shakespeare to Joyce,* 328-338.

PIPPA PASSES
Ariail, J. M. "Is *Pippa Passes* a Dramatic Failure?" *Studies in Philology,* 37#1: 120-129 (Jan, 1940).
Faverty, Fredric E. "The Source of the Jules-Phene Episode in *Pippa Passes,"* *Studies in Philology,* 38#1: 97-105 (Jan, 1941).

STRAFFORD
Orel, Harold. "Browning's Use of Historical Sources in *Strafford,"* *University of Kansas Publications. Humanistic Studies,* 35: 23-37 (1962).

BULWER-LYTTON
(SEE: LYTTON, EDWARD G.)

BYRON, GEORGE NOEL

DEFORMED TRANSFORMED, THE
Steiner, George. *The Death of Tragedy,* 211-212.

MANFRED
    Evans, Bertrand. "Manfred's Remorse and Dramatic Tradition," *PMLA*, 62#3: 752-773 (Sept, 1947).

MARINO FALIERO
    Johnson, Edward. "A Political Interpretation of Byron's *Marino Faliero*," *Modern Language Quarterly*, 3: 417-426 (1942).
    Knight, G. Wilson. "Shakespeare and Byron's Plays," *Shakespeare Jahrbuck*, 95: 89-93 (1959).
    Steiner, George. *The Death of Tragedy*, 202-205.

SARDANAPALUS
    Knight, G. Wilson. "Shakespeare and Byron's Plays," *Shakespeare Jahrbuck*, 95 : 93-97 (1959).
    Prior, Moody E. *The Language of Tragedy*, 247-255.
    Steiner, George. *The Death of Tragedy*, 206-208.

CAREY, GEORGE V. F.

THE MARRIAGE NIGHT
    Bowers, Fredson T. *Elizabethan Revenge Tragedy*, 252-258.

CAREY, HENRY

CHRONONTONTHOLOGOS
    Boas, F. S. *An Introduction to Eighteenth Century Drama*, 194-196.

CONTRIVANCES, THE
    Boas, F. S. *An Introduction to Eighteenth Century Drama*, 191-193.

HONEST YORKSHIREMAN, THE
    Boas, F. S. *An Introduction to Eighteenth Century Drama*, 196-198.

CARLELL, LODOWICK

OSMOND THE GREAT TURK
    Bowers, Fredson T. *Elizabethan Revenge Tragedy*, 219-220.

CARPENTER, JOHN A.

THE BIRTHDAY OF THE INFANTA
    Young, Stark. *Immortal Shadows*, 1-4.

CARTWRIGHT, WILLIAM

THE LADY ERRANT
Gagen, Jean E. *The New Woman,* 167-170.

CARYLL, JOHN

SIR SOLOMON SINGLE
Wilcox, John. *The Relation of Moliere to Restoration Comedy,* 53-56.

CHAPMAN, GEORGE

ALL FOOLES
Goldstein, Leonard. "Some Aspects of Marriage and Inheritance in Shakespeare's *The Merry Wives of Windsor* and Chapman's *All Fools," Zeitschrift Fur Anglistik und Amerikanistik,* 12#4: 375-386 (1964).

BLIND BEGGAR OF ALEXANDRIA, THE
Kaufman, Helen A. *"The Blind Beggar of Alexandria:* A Reappraisal," *Philological Quarterly,* 38#1: 101-106 (Jan, 1959).
Rees, Ennis. "Chapman's *Blind Beggar* and the Marlovian Hero," *Journal of English and Germanic Philology,* 57#1: 60-63 (Jan, 1958).

BUSSY D'AMBOIS
Barber, C. L. "The Ambivalence of *Bussy D'Ambois," Review of English Literature,* 2#4: 38-44 (Oct, 1961).
Goldstein, Leonard. "George Chapman and the Decadence in Early Seventeenth Century Drama," *Science and Society,* 27#1: 33-37 (Winter, 1963).
Haddakin, Lilian. "A Note on Chapman and Two Medieval English Jurists," *Modern Language Review,* 47#4: 550-551 (Oct, 1952).
Higgins, Michael. "The Development of the 'Senecal Man.' Chapman's *Bussy D'Ambois* and Some Precursors," *Review of English Studies,* 23#89: 30-33 (Jan, 1947).
Leech, Clifford. *"The Atheist's Tragedy* as a Dramatic Commentary on Chapman's *Bussy* Plays," *Journal of English and Germanic Philology,* 52#4: 525-530 (Oct, 1953).
McCollom, William G. "The Tragic Hero and Chapman's *Bussy D'Ambois," University of Toronto Quarterly,* 18#3: 227-233 (April, 1949).

Muir, Edwin. "'Royal Man': Notes on the Tragedies of
George Chapman," *Orion,* 2: 92-100 (1945). ALSO IN:
Essays on Literature and Society, 22-32.

Ornstein, Robert. *The Moral Vision of Jacobean Tragedy,* 50-
60.

Prior, Moody E. *The Language of Tragedy,* 104-111.

Ribner, Irving. *Jacoben Tragedy,* 23-25.

——————. "Character and Theme in Chapman's *Bussy
D'Ambois,*" *ELH,* 26#4: 482-496 (Dec, 1959).

Roth, Robert. "Another World of Shakespeare," *Modern
Philology,* 49#1: 47-49 (Aug, 1951).

Schricks, W. "Mythological Patterns in Chapman's *Bussy
D'Ambois:* Their Interpretive Value," *Revue des Langues
Vivantes,* 18: 279-286 (1952).

Schwartz, Elias. "Seneca, Homer, and Chapman's *Bussy
D'Ambois,*" *Journal of English and Germanic Philology,*
56#2: 163-176 (April, 1957).

Simpson, Percy. *Studies in Elizabethan Drama,* 154-158.

Sturman, Berta. "The 1641 Edition of Chapman's *Bussy
D'Ambois,*" *Huntington Library Quarterly,* 14#2: 171-
202 (Feb, 1951).

Ure, Peter. "Chapman's Tragedies," *Stratford-Upon-Avon
Studies,* 1: 227-237 (1960).

——————. "Chapman's Tragedy of *Bussy D'Aambois:*
Problems of the Revised Quarto," *Modern Language
Review,* 48#3: 257-269 (July, 1953).

CAESAR AND POMPEY

Burton, K. M. "The Political Tragedies of Chapman and
Jonson," *Essays in Criticism,* 2#4: 405-406 (Oct, 1952).

Goldstein, Leonard. "George Chapman and the Decadence in
Early Seventeenth Century Drama," *Science and Society,*
27#1: 41-48 (Winter, 1963).

Ingledew, J. E. "Chapman's Use of Lucan in *Caesar and
Pompey,*" *Review of English Studies,* N.S. 13#51: 283-
288 (Aug, 1962).

——————. "The Date of Composition of Chapman's
Caesar and Pompey," *Review of English Studies,* N.S.
12#46: 144-159 (May, 1961).

Ornstein, Robert. *The Moral Vision of Jacobean Tragedy,* 79-
83.

Schwartz, Elias. "A Neglected Play by Chapman," *Studies in
Philology,* 58#2: 140-159 (April, 1961).

Ure, Peter. "Chapman's Use of North's Plutarch in *Caesar*

and Pompey," Review of English Studies, N.S. 9#35: 281-284 (Aug, 1958).

CONSPIRACY OF BYRON, THE

Hunter, G. K. *"Henry IV* and the Elizabethan Two-Part Play," *Review of English Studies,* N.S. 5#19: 238-239 (July, 1954).

Ornstein, Robert. *The Moral Vision of Jacobean Tragedy,* 60-64.

Parr, Johnstone. "The Duke of Byron's Malignant *Caput Algoe," Studies in Philology,* 43#2: 194-202 (April, 1946).

Ure, Peter. "Chapman's Tragedies," *Stratford-Upon-Avon Studies,* 1: 237-241; 244-247 (1960).

——————————. "The Main Outline of Chapman's *Byron," Studies in Philology,* 4#4: 568-588 (Oct, 1950).

EASTWARD HOE

Cope, Jackson I. *"Volpone* and the Authorship of *Eastward Hoe," Modern Language Notes,* 72#4: 253-256 (April, 1957).

Simpson, Percy. "The Problem of Authorship of *Eastward Ho," PMLA,* 59#3: 715-725 (Sept, 1944).

FOUNT OF NEW FASHIONS, THE

Wilkes, G. A. "Chapman's 'Lost' Play, *The Fount of New Fashions," Journal of English and Germanic Philology,* 62#1: 77-81 (Jan, 1963).

GENTLEMAN USHER, THE

Lacy, Margaret. *The Jacobean Problem Play,* 114-135.

Weidner, Henry M. "The Dramatic Uses of Homeric Idealism: The Significance of Theme and Design in George Chapman's *The Gentleman Usher," ELH,* 28#2: 121-136 (June, 1961).

Yamada, Akiriro. "Bibliographical Studies of George Chapman's *The Gentleman Usher* (1606)" *Shakespeare Studies,* 2: 82-113 (1963).

MASQUE OF THE MIDDLE TEMPLE
AND LINCOLN'S INN

Reese, Jack E. "Unity in Chapman's *Masque of the Middle Temple and Lincoln's Inn," Studies in English Literature* 1500-1900, 4#2: 291-306 (Spring, 1964).

NORTHWARD HO
> Nicoll, Allardyce. "The Dramatic Portrait of George Chapman," *Philological Quarterly*, 4#1: 215-228 (Jan, 1962).

REVENGE FOR HONOR
> See: Anon.

REVENGE OF BUSSY D'AMBOIS, THE
> Bowers, Fredson T. *Elizabethan Revenge Tragedy*, 144-149.
> Cohon, B. J. "A Catullian Echo in George Chapman's *The Revenge of Bussy D'Ambois*," *Modern Language Notes*, 60#1: 29-33 (Jan, 1945).
> Goldstein, Leonard. "George Chapman and the Decadence in Early Seventeenth Century Drama," *Science and Society*, 27#1: 37-41 (Winter, 1963).
> Higgins, Michael H. "Chapman's Senecal Man: A Study in Elizabethan Psychology," *Review of English Studies*, 47#83: 186-191 (July, 1945).
> Leech, Clifford. *Shakespeare's Tragedies, and Other Studies, in Seventeenth Century Drama*, 23-28; 195-196.
> —————. "*The Atheist's Tragedy* as a Dramatic Commentary on Chapman's *Bussy* Plays," *Journal of English and Germanic Philology*, 52#4: 525-530 (Oct, 1953).
> Ornstein, Robert. *The Moral Vision of Jacobean Tragedy*, 70-76.
> Wells, Henry W. *Elizabethan and Jacobean Playwrights*, 91-93.
> Wilson, E. E. "The Genesis of Chapman's *The Revenge of Bussy D'Ambois*," *Modern Language Notes*, 71#8: 567-569 (Dec, 1956).

SECOND MAIDEN'S TRAGEDY, THE
> See: Anon.

TRAGEDY OF BYRON, THE
> Burton, K. M. "The Political Tragedies of Chapman and Jonson," *Essays in Criticism*, 2#4: 406-407 (Oct, 1952).
> Gabel, John B. "The Original Version of Chapman's *Tragedy of Byron*," *Journal of English and Germanic Philology*, 63#3: 433-440 (July, 1964).
> Hunter, G. K. "*Henry IV* and the Elizabethan Two-Part Play," *Review of English Studies*, N.S. 5#19: 238-239 (July, 1954).
> Ornstein, Robert. *The Moral Vision of Jacobean Tragedy*, 64-70.

Parr, Johnstone. "The Duke of Byron's Malignant *Caput Al-goe*," *Studies in Philology*, 43#2: 194-202 (April, 1946).

Ure, Peter. "Chapman's Tragedies," *Stratford-Upon-Avon-Studies*, #1: 237-241; 244-247 (1960).

———————. "The Main Outline of Chapman's Plays," *Studies in Philology*, 47#4: 568-588 (Oct, 1950).

TRAGEDY OF CHABOT, THE—
ADMIRAL OF FRANCE

Burton, K. M. "The Political Tragedies of Chapman and Jonson," *Essays in Criticism*, 2#4: 400-401; 408-409 (Oct, 1952).

Haddakin, Lilian. "A Note on Chapman and Two Medieval English Jurists," *Modern Language Review*, 47#4: 550-553 (Oct, 1952).

Ornstein, Robert. *The Moral Vision of Jacobean Tragedy*, 76-79.

Ribner, Irving. *Jacobean Tragedy*, 35-49.

———————. "The Meaning of Chapman's *Tragedy of Chabot*," *Modern Language Review*, 55#3: 321-331 (July, 1960).

Sasayama, Takashi. *"Chabot, Admiral of France,"* *Shakepeare Studies*, 1: 15-32 (1962).

WIDOW'S TEARS, THE

Pearson, Lu Emily. "Elizabethan Widows," in *Stanford Studies in Language and Literature*, 134-135.

Schoenbaum, Samuel. *"The Widow's Tears* and the Other Chapman," *Huntington Library Quarterly*, 23#4: 321-338 (Aug, 1960).

Weidner, Henry M. "Homer and the Fallen World: Focus of Satire in George Chapman's *The Widow's Tears*," *Journal of English and Germanic Philology*, 62#3: 518-532 (July, 1963).

CHASE, MARY COYLE

HARVEY

Brown, Ivor and Athene Seyler. *"Harvey,"* *World Review*, pp. 17-20 (April, 1949).

Hornstein, Lillian H. *"Harvey:* Or Sanity in the Theatre," *College English*, 8#1: 37-38 (Oct, 1946).

Larson, Gerard. "From *Ten Nights* to *Harvey:* Drinking on the American Stage," *Western Humanities Review*, 10#4: 390 (Aut, 1956).

CHETTLE, HENRY

    HOFFMAN

        Bowers, Fredson T. *Elizabethan Revenge Tragedy*, 125-130.
        Simpson, Percy. *Studies in Elizabethan Drama*, 165-168.

CHETWOOD, WILLIAM RUFUS

    THE GENEROUS FREE-MASON

        Boas, F. S. *An Introduction to Eighteenth Century Drama*,
        205-208.

CIBBER, COLLEY

    CARELESS HUSBAND, THE

        Boas, F. S. *An Introdctiuon to Eighteenth Century Drama*,
        86-91.

    LOVE'S LAST SHIFT

        Kronenberger, Louis. *The Thread of Laughter*, 148-151.
        Parnell, Paul E. "Equivocation in Cibber's *Love's Last Shift*,"
          Studies in Philology, 57#3: 519-534 (July, 1960).
        —————————. "An Incorrectly Attributed Speech-Prefix in
          Love's Last Shift," *Notes and Queries*, 204: 212-213
          (June, 1959).

    NON-JUROR, THE

        Boas, F. S. *An Introduction to Eighteenth Century Drama*,
        91-96.
        Peterson, William M. "Pope and Cibber's *The Non-Juror*,"
          Modern Language Notes, 70#5: 332-335 (May, 1955).

    PROVOKED HUSBAND, THE

        See: Sir John Vanbrugh

    REFUSAL, THE

        Gagen, Jean E. *The New Woman*, 51-54; 74-75.

    RICHARD III**

        Kalson, Albert E. "The Chronicles in Cibber's *Richard III*,"
          Studies in English Literature 1500-1900, 3#2: 253-268
          (Spring, 1963).
        Takeuchi, Hideo. *"King Richard the Third* and Colley Cibber,"
          The Humanities (Yokohama), Section II #4: 1-7 (Oct,
          1955).
        Peterson, William M. "The Text of Cibber's *She Wou'd, and
          She Wou'd Not*," *Modern Language Notes*, 71#4: 258-
          262 (April, 1956).

_____

**Colley Cibber's Adaptation of Shakespeare's *Richard III*.

CLARKE, AUSTIN

BLACK FAST
Mercier, Vivian. "The Verse Plays of Austin Clark," *Dublin Magazine,* 19#2: 39-46 (April-June, 1944).

FLAME, THE
Mercier, Vivian. "The Verse Plays of Austin Clarke," *Dublin Magazine,* 19#2: 39-46 (Apr-June, 1944).

PLOT IS READY, THE
Mercier, Vivian. "Austin Clarke—The Poet in the Theatre," *Life and Letters Today,* 53#116: 14-18 (April, 1947).
——————. "The Verse Plays of Austin Clarke," *Dublin Magazine,* 19#2: 46-47 (April-June, 1944).

SISTER EUCHARIA
Mercier, Vivian. "The Verse Plays of Austin Clarke," *Dublin Magazine,* 19#2: 39-46 (April-June, 1944).

SONS OF LEARNING, THE
Mercier, Vivian. "Austin Clarke—The Poet in the Theatre," *Chimera,* 5#3: 31-32; 35-36 (Spring, 1947).
——————. "The Verse Plays of Austin Clarke," *Dublin Magazine,* 19#2: 39-46 (April-June, 1944).

CLOUGH, ARTHUR HUGH

DIPSYCHUS
Badger, Kingsbury. "Arthur Hugh Clough as Dipsychus," *Modern Language Quarterly,* 12: 39-56 (1951).
Bertram, James. "The Ending of Clough's *Dipsychus,*" *The Review of English Studies,* N. S. 7#25: 59-60 (Jan, 1956).

COFFEY, CHARLES

BEGGAR'S WEDDING, THE
Boas, F. S. *An Introduction to Eighteenth Century Drama,* 212-215.

BOARDING-SCHOOL, THE
Boas, F. S. *An Introduction to Eighteenth Century Drama,* 216-218.

COLERIDGE, SAMUEL TAYLOR
  OSORIO
    Fox, Arnold B. "Political and Biographical Background of
      Coleridge's *Osorio*," *Journal of English and Germanic
      Philology*, 61#2: 258-267 (April, 1962).

COLLINS, WILLIAM WILKIE
  THE LIGHTHOUSE
    S., L. C. *"The Lighthouse,"* *Dickensian*, 46#3: 144-145 (Summer, 1950).

COLMAN, GEORGE
—AND DAVID GARRICK
  CLANDESTINE MARRIAGE, THE
    Bergmann, Frederick L. "David Garrick and *The Clandestine
      Marriage*," *PMLA*, 67#2: 148-162 (Mar, 1952).
    Boas, F. S. *An Introduction to Eighteenth Century Drama*,
      328-332.
    Gerber, Helmut E. *"The Clandestine Marriage* and its Hogarthian Associations," *Modern Language Notes*, 72#4:
      267-271 (April, 1957).
  JEALOUS WIFE, THE
    Boas, F. S. *An Introduction to Eighteenth Century Drama*,
      323-328.

COLUM, PADRAIC
  THE LAND
    Ellis-Fermor, Una. *The Irish Dramatic Movement*, 189-191.

CONGREVE, WILLIAM
  DOUBLE DEALER, THE
    Fujimura, Thomas H. *The Restoration Comedy of Wit*, 170-176.
    Gagen, Jean E. *The New Woman*, 71-75.
    Holland, Norman. *The First Modern Comedies*, 149-160.
    Horton, Melvin. "Essays on Comedy in the Seventeenth Century," *Asides* (Stanford), 2: 27-28 (1941).
    Kronenberger, Louis. *The Thread of Laughter*, 122-128.
    Mignon, Elizabeth. *Crabbed Age and Youth*, 106-111.
    Wilcox John. *The Relation of Moliere to Restoration Comedy*,
      156-160.

LOVE FOR LOVE

Bateson, F. W. "Second Thoughts II: L. C. Knights and Restoration Comedy," *Essays in Criticism,* 7#1: 57-62 (Jan, 1957).

Brown, John Mason. *Seeing More Things,* 221-227.

Fujimura, Thomas H. *The Restoration Comedy of Wit,* 176-183.

Gosse, Anthony. "The Omitted Scene in Congreve's *Love for Love,*" *Modern Philology,* 61#1: 40-42 (Aug, 1963).

Kronenberger, Louis. *The Thread of Laughter,* 128-131.

Holland, Norman. *The First Modern Comedies,* 161-174.

Horton, Melvin. "Essays on Comedy in the Seventeenth Century Manner," *Asides* (Stanford), 2: 25-26 (1941).

Lyons, Charles R. "Congreve's *Miracle of Love,*" *Criticism,* 6#4: 331-348 (Fall, 1964).

Mignon, Elizabeth. *Crabbed Age and Youth,* 111-120.

Wilcox, John. *The Relation of Moliere to Restoration Comedy,* 160-163.

MOURNING BRIDE, THE

Avery, Emmett L. "The Popularity of The Mourning Bride in London Theaters in the Eighteenth Century," *Washington State College Research Studies,* 9#2: 115-116 (June, 1941).

Potter, Elmer B. "The Paradox of Congreve's *Mourning -Bride,*" *PMLA,* 58#4: 977-1001 (Dec, 1943).

OLD BACHELOR, THE

Fujimura, Thomas H. *The Restoration Comedy of Wit,* 165-176.

Holland, Norma. *The First Modern Comedies,* 131-148.

Kronenberger, Louis. *The Thread of Laughter,* 119-122.

Mignon, Elizabeth. *Crabbed Age and Youth,* 31-32; 95-106.

Wilcox, John. *The Relation of Moliere to Restoration Comedy,* 154-156.

WAY OF THE WORLD, THE

Alleman, Gellert. *Matrimonial Law and the Materials of Restoration,* 122-124.

Brooks, Cleanth and Robert Heilman. *Understanding Drama,* 389; 441-452.

Brooks, Cleanth. *Well-Wrought Urn,* 86-87.

Empson, William. "Restoration Comedy Again," *Essays in Criticism,* 7#3: 318 (July, 1957).

Fujimura, Thomas H. *The Restoration Comedy of Wit*, 183-196.

Gagen, Jean E. *The New Woman*, 152-154.

————————. "Congreve's Mirabell and the Ideal of the Gentleman," *PMLA*, 79#4Pt.1: 422-427 (Sept, 1964).

Holland, Norman. *The First Modern Comedies*, 199-209.

Knight, G. W. *Explorations*, 156-159.

Kronenberger, Louis. *The Thread of Laughter*, 132-145.

MacMillan, Dougald. "Speculum Consuetudinis: English Comedy of Manners," *University of North Carolina Extension Bulletin*, 29#3: 30-34 (Jan, 1950).

Meredith, George. "An Essay on Comedy," in Wylie Sypher (ed), *Comedy*, 18-22.

Mignon, Elizabeth. *Crabbed Age and Youth*, 120-131.

Murdick, Marvin. "Restoration Comedy and Later," *English Institute Essays*, pp. 111-115 (1954).

Nolan, Paul T. "Congreve's Lovers: Art and the Critic," *Drama Survey*, 1#3: 330-339 (Feb, 1962).

————————. "Congreve's Moment of Truth," *The Southern Speech Journal*, 25#2: 75-95 (Winter, 1959).

Styan, J. L. *The Eelements of Drama*, 106-107.

Van Voris, William. "Congreve's Gilded Carousel," *Educational Theatre Journal*, 10#3: 211-217 (Oct, 1958).

Wain, John. "Restoration Comedy and its Modern Critics," *Essays in Criticism*, 6#4: 383-384 (Oct, 1956).

Walley, Harold R. *The Book of The Play*, 260-261; 662-664.

Wilcox, John. *The Relation of Moliere to Restoration Comedy*, 163-166.

CONNELLY, MARCUS COOK

THE GREEN PASTURES

Eastman, Fred. *Christ in the Drama*, 103-111.

Ford, Nick A. "How Genuine is *The Green Pastures?*" *Phylon*, 20#1: 67-70 (Spring, 1959).

Garey, Doris B. "The Green Pastures Again," *Phylon*, 20#2: 193-194 (Summer, 1959).

Krumpelmann, John T. "Marc Connelly's *The Green Pastures* and Goethe's *Faust*," in Waldo F. McNeir (ed), *Studies in Comparative Literature*, 199-218.

Young, Stark. *Immortal Shadows*, 119-122.

COWARD, NOEL

BLITHE SPIRIT
Fulton, A. R. *Drama and Theatre,* 456-464.

CAVALCADE
Gupta, P. C. *The Art of Galsworthy and Other Essays,* 118-121.

DESIGN FOR LIVING
Marx, Milton. *The Enjoyment of Drama,* 166-170.

POST-MORTEM
Gupta, P. C. *The Art of Galsworthy and Other Essays,* 122-123.

PRESENT LAUGHTER
Brown, J. M. *Seeing More Things,* 200-208.

PRIVATE LIVES
MacCarthy, Desmond. *Humanities,* 94-96.

CRAWFORD, J. W.

THE DREGS
Nolan, Paul T. "J. W. Crawford's *The Dregs,*" *New Mexico Quarterly Review,* 33#4:388-408 (Winter, 1963/64).

CROXTON

PLAY OF THE SACRAMENT
See: Anon

CUMBERLAND, RICHARD

CHOLERIC MAN, THE
Boas, F. S. *An Introduction to Eighteenth Century Drama,* 306-309.

WEST INDIAN, THE
Boas, F. S. *An Introduction to Eighteenth Century Drama,* 301-306.

CUMMINGS, E. E.

HIM
Barzan, Jacques. "A Word About *HIM,*" *Wake* 5: 55-57 (Spring, 1946).

Bentley, E. *From the Modern Repertoire—Series Two,* 485-
494.
Margolies, Edward. "E. E. Cummings' *Him* and the European
Experimental Theater," *Southern Speech Journal,* 29#2:
107-114 (Winter, 1963).
Maurer, Robert E. "E. E. Cummings' *Him,*" *Bucknell University Studies,* 6: 1-27 (May, 1946).

SANTA CLAUS
Donoghue, Denis. *The Third Voice,* 70-75.

D., T.

THE BLOODY BANQUET
See: Anon

DANIEL, SAMUEL

THE TRAGEDIE OF CLEOPATRA
Michel, Laurence (and Cecil C. Seronsy). "Shakespeare's
History Plays and *Daniel:* An Assessment," *Studies in
Philology,* 52#4: 569-577 (Oct, 1955).
Norman, Arthur M. Z. "Daniel's *The Tragedie of Cleopatra*
and *Antony and Cleopatra,*" *Shakespeare Quarterly,* 9#1:
11-18 (Winter, 1958).
ALSO IN: *Modern Languagge Review,* 54#1: 1-9 (Jan,
1959).
Rees, Joan, "Samuel Daniel's *Cleopatra* and Two French
Plays," *Modern Language Review,* 47#1: 1-10 (Jan,
1952).
Schanzer, Ernest. "Daniel's Revision of his *Cleopatra,*" *Re-
view of English Studies,* N.S. 8#32: 375-381 (Nov,
1957).
Seronsy, Cecil C. "The Doctrine of Cyclical Recurrence and
Some Related Ideas in the Works of Samuel Daniels,"
Studies in Philology, 54#3: 392-397 (July, 1957).

PHILOTAS
Wilkes, G. A. "Daniel's *Philotas* and the Essex Case: A Reconsideration," *Modern Language Quarterly,* 23: 233-242
(1962).

D'AVENANT, SIR WILLIAM

CRUEL BROTHER, THE
Bowers, Fredson T. *Elizabethan Revenge Tragedy,* 202-204.

FIRST DAY'S ENTERTAINMENT AT RUTLAND HOUSE
  Cope, Jackson I., "Rhetorical Genres in Davenant's *First Day's Entertainment at Rutland House,*" *Quarterly Journal of Speech,* 45#2: 191-194 (April, 1959).

MAN'S THE MASTER, THE
  Elton, William. "D'Avenant's *The Man's The Master* and the Spanish Source," *Modern Language Notes,* 65#3: 194-197 (Mar, 1950).

PLAYHOUSE TO BE LET, THE
  Mandach, Andre de. "The First Translation of Moliere in the World," *Comparative Literature Studies* (Cardiff), v. 21-22: 2-9 (1946).
  Wilcox, John. *The Relation of Moliere to Restoration Comedy,* 127-128.

DAVENPORT, ROBERT

CITY-NIGHT-CAP, THE
  Olive, W. J. "Davenport's Debt to Shakespeare in *The City Night-Cap,*" *Journal of English and Germanic Philology,* 49#3: 333-344 (July, 1950).

KING JOHN AND MATILDA
  Ribner, Irving. *The English History Play in the Age of Shakespeare,* 295-299.

NEW TRICKE TO CHEAT THE DEVIL, A
  Olive, W. J. "Shakespeare Parody in Davenport's *A New Tricke to Cheat the Devil,*" *Modern Language Notes,* 66#7: 478-480 (Nov, 1951).

DAVIES, KITCHENER

STONES OF EMPTINESS
  Richards, Tom. "A New Direction for Welsh Playwrights," *The Welsh Review,* 4#4: 275-279 (Dec, 1945).

DAY, JOHN

BLIND BEGGAR OF BEDINAL GREEN, THE
  Schoenbaum, Samuel. "John Day and Elizabethan Drama," *Boston Public Library Quarterly,* 5: 148-149 (July, 1953).

ISLE OF GULLS, THE
  Schoenbaum, Samuel. "John Day and Elizabethan Drama," *Boston Public Library Quarterly,* 5: 145-146 (July, 1953).

LAW TRICKS
Schoenbaum, Samuel. "John Day and Elizabethan Drama,"
Boston Public Library Quarterly, 5: 146-148 (July, 1953).

PARLIAMENT OF BEES, THE
Schoenbaum, Samuel. "John Day and Elizabethan Drama,"
Boston Public Library Quarterly, 5: 149-151 (July, 1953).

TRAVAILS OF THREE ENGLISH BROTHERS, THE
See: Anon

DEEVY, TERESA

IN SEARCH OF VALOUR
Riley, J. D. "On Teresa Deevy's Plays," *Irish Writing,* 32:
33-34 (n. d.).

KATI ROCHE
Riley, J. D. "On Teresa Deevy's Plays," *Irish Writings,* 32:
35-36 (n. d.).

KING OF SPAIN'S DAUGHTER, THE
Riley, J. D. "On Teresa Deevy's Plays," *Irish Writing,* 32:
31-32 (n. d.).

STRANGE BIRTH
Riley, J. D. "On Teresa Deevy's Plays," *Irish Writing,* 32:
32-33 (n. d.).

WILD GOOSE, THE
Riley, J. D. "On Teresa Deevy's Plays," *Irish Writing,* 32:
33-35 (n. d.).

DEKKER, THOMAS

CUPID AND PSYCHE
Halstead, W. L. "Dekker's *Cupid and Psyche* and Thomas
Heywood," *ELH,* 11#3: 182-191 (Sept, 1944).

HONEST WHORE, THE (I & II)
Brown, Arthur. "Citizen Comedy and Domestic Drama,"
Stratford-Upon-Avon-Studies, 1: 69-73 (1960).
Lacy, Margaret. *The Jacobean Problem Play,* 60-84.
Turner, Robert K. Jr. "Dekker's 'Black-Door'd Italian': One
Honest Whore," *Notes and Queries,* 205: 25-26 (Jan,
1960).

Ure, Peter. "Patient Madman and Honest Whore: The Middleton-Dekker Oxymoron," *Essays and Studies (English Association)*. 19: 18-40 (1966).

IF IT BE NOT GOOD THE DEVIL IS IN IT

Ashton, J. W. "Dekker's Use of Folklore in *Old Fortunatus, If This Be Not A Good Play,* and *The Witch of Edmonton,*" *Philological Quarterly,* 41#1: 240-241; 243-245 (Jan, 1962).

Reynolds, George F. "Aims of a Popular Elizabethan Dramatist," in B. Maxwell (ed), *Renaissance Studies in Honor of Hardin Craig,* 148-152.

NOBLE SOLDIER, THE

Perry, William. *"The Noble Soldier* and *The Parliament of Bees,"* Studies in Philology, 48#2: 219-233 (April, 1951).

OLD FORTUNATUS

Adams, H. *English Domestic or Homiletic Tragedies* 1575-1642, 80-82.

Ashton, J. W. "Dekker's Use of Folklore in *Old Fortunatus, If This Be Not A Good Play* and *The Witch of Edmonton,*" *Philological Quarterly,* 41#1: 240-243 (Jan, 1962).

Bowers, Fredson. "Essex's Rebellion and Dekker's *Old Fortunatus,*" *Review of English Studies,* N.S. 3#12: 365-366 (Oct, 1952).

Lacy, Margaret. *The Jacobean Problem Play,* 48-60.

PATIENT GRISSEL

Greene, David Mason. "The Welsh Characters in *Patient Grissel,*" *Boston University Studies in English,* 4#3: 171-180 (Autumn, 1960).

Smith, William G. "Thomas Dekker's Welshman," *Dock Leaves,* 4#11: 47-52 (Summer, 1953).

SATIROMASTIX

Harrison, George. *Elizabethan Plays and Players,* 272-277.

SHOEMAKER'S HOLIDAY, THE

Brown, Arthur. "Citizen Comedy and Domestic Drama," *Stratford-Upon-Avon-Studies,* 1: 63-69 (1960).

George, J. "Four Notes on the Text of Dekker's *Shoemaker's Holiday,*" *Notes and Queries,* 194: 192 (Apr, 1949).

Halstead, W. L. "New Source Influence on *The Shoemaker's Holiday,*" *Modern Language Notes,* 56#2: 127-129 (Feb, 1941).

Hidden, Norman. *"The Shoemaker's Holiday," The Use of English,* 13#4: 249-252 (Summer, 1962).

Knights, L. C. *Drama and Society in the Age of Jonson,* 236-240.

Manheim, L. M. "The King in Dekker's *The Shoemaker's Holiday," Notes and Queries,* 202#10: 432-433 (Oct, 1957).

Nathan, Norman. *"Julius Caesar* and *The Shoemaker's Holiday," Modern Language Review,* 48#2: 178-179 (April, 1953).

Novarr, David. "Dekker's Gentle Craft and the Lord Mayor of London," *Modern Philology,* 57#4: 233-239 (May, 1960).

Thomson, Patricia. "The Old Way and the New Way in Dekker and Massinger," *Modern Language Review,* 51#2: 168-178 (April, 1956).

Toliver, Harold E. *"The Shoemaker's Holiday:* Theme and Image," *Boston University Studies in English,* 5#4: 208-218 (Winter, 1961).

Well, Henry W. *Elizabethan and Jacobean Playwrights,* 219-221.

SIR THOMAS WYATT
Shaw, Phillip. *"Sir Thomas Wyatt* and the Scenario and Lady Jane," *Modern Language Quarterly,* 13: 227-238 (1952).

WELSH AMBASSADOR, THE
Llyod, Bertram. "The Authorship of *The Welsh Ambassador," Review of English Studies,* 21: 192-201 (July, 1945).

WHORE OF BABYLON, THE
Pineas, Rainer. "Dekker's *The Whore of Babylon* and Milton's *Paradise Lost," English Language Notes,* 2#4: 257-260 (June, 1965).

Ribner, Irving. *The English History Play in the Age of Shakespeare,* 284-288.

WITCH OF EDMONTON, THE
See: John Ford

DELANEY, SHELAGH

A TASTE OF HONEY
Anderson, Lindsay. *"A Taste of Honey," Encore,* 5#2: 42-43 (July-Aug, 1958).

Ippolito, G. J. "Shelagh Delaney," *Drama Survey*, 1#1: 86-90
   (Spring, 1961).
Kerr, Walter. *The Theater in Spite of Itself*, 126-128.
Noel, J. "Some Aspects of Shelagh Delaney's Use of Language
   in *A Taste of Honey*," *Revue des Langues Vivantes*, 26:
   284-290 (1960).
Simon, John. "Theater Chronicle," *Hudson Review*, 14#1:
   83-84 (Spring, 1961).
Taylor, John R. *Anger and After*, 108-114.

DENNIS, JOHN

APPIUS AND VIRGINIA

Boas, F. S. *An Introduction to Eighteenth Century Drama*,
   144-149.
Cope, Jackson I. " 'The Best for Comedy': Richard Edwardes'
   Canon," *Texas Studies in Literature and Language*, 2#4:
   510-513 (Winter, 1961).

IPHIGENIA

Boas, F. S. *An Introduction to Eighteenth Century Drama*,
   137-141.
Wilkins, A. N. "John Dennis on Love as a 'Tragical Passion',"
   Notes and Queries, 203: 417-419 (Oct, 1958).

DENNIS, NIGEL

CARDS OF IDENTITY

Wellwarth, George E. "Nigel Dennis: The Return of Intellectual Satire," *Southern Speech Journal*, 27#1: 59-61
   (Fall, 1961).

MAKING OF MOO, THE

Wellwarth, George E. "Nigel Dennis: The Return of Intellectual Satire," *Southern Speech Journal*, 27#1: 56-59
   (Fall, 1961).

DICKENS, CHARLES
—AND WILKIE COLLINS

NO THOROUGHFARE

Morley, Malcolm. *"No Thoroughfare* Back Stage," *Dicken-
   sian*, 50#1: 37-42 (Dce, 1953).
Rosenberg, Marvin. "The Dramatist in Dickens," *Journal of
   English and Germanic Philology*, 59#1: 6-12 (Jan, 1960).

DIGBY, GEORGE

ELVIRA
Cordasco, Francesco. "Spanish Influence on Restoration Drama: George Digby's *Elvira*," *Revue de Litterature Comparee*, 27#1 : 93-98 (Jan-March, 1953).

DIXON, THOMAS

THE CLANSMAN
Da Ponte, Durant. "The Greatest Play of the South," *Tennessee Studies in Literature*, 2: 15-23 (1957).

DREISER, THEODORE

LAUGHING GAS
Ross, Woodburn O. "Concerning Dreiser's Mind," *American Literature*, 18: 239-240 (Nov, 1946).

DRINKWATER, JOHN

ABRAHAM LINCOLN
Burton, G. L. "John Drinkwater: The Dramatist," *Central Literary Magazine*, pp. 12-14 (Jan, 1940).

DRUE, THOMAS

THE BLOODY BANQUET
See: Anon

DRYDEN, JOHN

ALL FOR LOVE ; OR THE WORLD WELL LOST
Emerson, Everett. "Intention and Achievement in *All For Love*," *College English*, 17#2: 84-87 (Nov, 1955).
Hughes, R. E. "Dryden's *All For Love*: The Sensual Dilemma," *Drama Critique*, 3#2: 68-74 (May, 1960).
King, Bruce. "Dryden's Intent in *All For Love*," *College English*, 24#4: 267-271 (Jan, 1963).
Kossman, H. "A Note on Dryden's *All For Love*, v. 165 ff," *English Studies*, 31#3: 99-100 (June, 1950).
Levich, Martin. *Aesthetics and the Philosophy of Criticism*, 181.
Muir, Kenneth. "The Imagery of *All For Love*," *Proceedings of the Leeds Philosophical and Literary Society*, 5pt.3: 140-147 (Feb, 1940).

Nazareth, Paul. *'All For Love:* Dryden's Hybrid Play," *English Studies in Africa,* 6#2: 154-163 (Sept, 1963).

Price, Martin. *To the Palace of Wisdom,* 236-241.

Prior, Moody E. *The Language of Tragedy,* 192-212.

Starnes, D. T. "Imitation of Shakespeare in Dryden's *All For Love,*" *Texas Studies in Literature and Language,* 6#1: 39-46 (Spring, 1964).

Suckling, Norman. "Dryden in Egypt: Reflexions on *All For Love,*" *Durham University Journal,* 45#1: 2-7 (Dec, 1952).

Wallerstein, Ruth. "Dryden and the Analysis of Shakespeare's Techniques," *Review of English Studies,* 19#74: 165-185 (April, 1943).

AMPHITRYON

Kober-Merzbach. "The Third Source of Dryden's *Amphitryon,*" *Anglia,* 73#2: 213-214 (1955).

Wilcox, John. *The Relation of Moliere to Restoration Comedy,* 114-116.

ASSIGNATION, THE; OR LOVE IN A NUNNERY

Mignon, Elizabeth. *Crabbed Age and Youth,* 67-72.

Moore, Frank H. "Heroic Comedy: A New Interpretation of Dryden's *Assignation,*" *Studies in Philology,* 51#4: 585-598 (Oct, 1954).

Rundle, James U. "The Source of Dryden's 'Comic Plot' in *The Assignation,*" *Modern Philology,* 45#2: 104-111 (Nov, 1947).

AURENG-ZEBE

Jefferson, D. W. "The Significance of Dryden's Heroic Plays," *Proceedings of the Leeds Philosophical and Literary Society,* 5#3: 132-135 (Feb, 1940).

Kirsch, Arthur C. "The Significance of Dryden's *Aureng-Zebe,*" *ELH,* 29#2: 160-174 (June, 1962).

Le Compte, Edward S. *"Samson Agonistes and Aureng-Zebe,"* *Etudes Anglaises,* 11#1: 18-22 (Jan, 1958).

Prior, Moody E. *The Language of Tragedy,* 158-162; 170-177.

CONQUEST OF GRANADA, THE

Jefferson, D. W. "The Significance of Dryden's Heroic Plays," *Proceedings of the Leeds Philosophical and Literary Society,* 5#3: 125-132; 134-139 (Feb, 1940).

Loftis, John. "The Hispanic Element in Dryden," *Emory University Quarterly,* 20#2: 95-96 (Summer, 1964).

Price, Martin. *To the Palace of Wisdom,* 35-41.

Winterbottom, John. "The Development of the Hero in Dryden's Tragedies," *Journal of English and Germanic
Philology,* 52#2: 166-172 (April, 1953).

DON SEBASTIAN
King, Bruce. "Don Sebastian: Dryden's Moral Fable," *Sewa-
nee Review,* 70#4: 651-670 (Aut, 1962).
Moore, John R. "Dryden and Rupert Brooke," *Modern Lan-
guage Review,* 54#2: 226 (April, 1959).
————————. "Political Allusions in Dryden's Later Plays,"
PMLA, 73#1: 38-42 (Mar, 1958).
Price, Martin. *To the Palace of Wisdom,* 48-52.

DUKE OF GUISE, THE
King, Bruce. "Anti-Whig Satire in *The Duke of Guise,"
English Language Notes,* 2#3: 190-193 (March, 1965).

INDIAN EMPEROR, THE
Alssid, Michael W. "The Perfect Conquest. A Study of
Theme, Structure, and Character in Dryden's *The Indian
Emperor," Studies in Philology,* 59#3: 539-559 (July,
1962).
Fujiama, Thomas H. "The Appeal of Dryden's Heroic Plays,"
PMLA, 75#1: 39-45 (March, 1960).
Loftis, John. "The Hispanic Element in Dryden," *Emory Uni-
versity Quarterly,* 20#2: 96-98 (Summer, 1964).
MacMillan, Dougald. "The Sources of Dryden's *The Indian
Emperour," Huntington Library Quarterly,* 13#4: 355-
370 (Aug, 1950).
Perkins, Merle L. "Dryden's *The Indian Emperor* and Vol-
taire's *Alzire," Comparative Literature (Oregon),* 9#3:
229-237 (Summer, 1957).
Ringler, Richard. "Two Sources for Dryden's *The Indian
Emperour," Philological Quarterly,* 42#4: 423-429 (Oct,
1963).

MARRIAGE A LA MODE
Kronenberger, Louis. *The Thread of Laughter,* 88-92.
Wilcox, John. *The Relation of Moliere to Restoration Comedy,*
112-113.

RIVAL LADIES, THE
Wilcox, John. *The Relation of Moliere to Restoration Comedy,*
107-108.

SECRET LOVE
Gagen, Jean E. *The New Woman,* 142-143; 147-149.

SIR MARTIN MAR-ALL
Wilcox, John. *The Relation of Moliere to Restoration Comedy,*
35-36; 108-112.

SPANISH FRIAR
Kronenberger, Louis. *The Thread of Laughter,* 82-88.

TYRANNIC LOVE
Price, Martin. *To the Palace of Wisdom,* 45-48.

WILD GALLANT, THE
Mignon, Elizabeth. *Crabbed Age and Youth,* 62-67.
Wilcox, John. *The Relation of Moliere to Restoration Comedy,*
105-107.

DUNCAN, RONALD

THIS WAY TO THE TOMB
Speaight, Robert. *Since 1939,* 46-50.
Williams, Ray. *Drama From Ibsen to Eliot,* 260-261.

DUNLAP, WILLIAM

A TRIP TO NIAGRA
Glenn, Stanley. "The Development of the Negro Character in
American Comedy Before the Civil War," *Southern
Speech Journal,* 26#2: 142-143 (Winter, 1960).

DUNSANY, LORD EDWARD

THE GODS OF THE MOUNTAIN
Mierow, Herbert E. "The Greeks Started It," *Catholic World,*
166: 66-67 (Oct, 1947).

DURRELL, LAURENCE

ACTE (OR, THE PRISONERS OF TIME)
Durrell, Laurence. *"Acte; or The Prisoners of Time*—A New
Play in Three Acts by Laurence Durrell, With an Intro-
duction by the Author," *Show,* 1#3: 47 (Dec, 1961).

EBERHARDT, RICHARD

THE VISIONARY FORMS
Donoghue, Denis. *The Third Voice,* 223-235.

EDGEWORTH, MARIA

THE DOUBLE DISGUISE
Donner, H. W. "Echoes of Beddosesian Rambles," *Studia Neophilologica,* 33#2: 23-24 (1961).

EDWARDES, RICHARD
    CLYOMON AND CLAMYDES
       See: Anonymous.

    COMMON CONDITIONS
       See: Anonymous.

    DAMON AND PITHIAS
       Armstrong, W. A. *"Damon and Pithias* and Renaissance Theories," *Essays and Studies,* 39#5: 200-207 (Oct, 1958).
       Cope, Jackson I. " 'The Best for Comedy': Richard Edwards' Canon," *Texas Studies in Literature and Language,* 2#4: 513-519 (Winter, 1961).
       Jackson, James L. "A Use of Special Rhetoric in an Elizabethan Play," *Quarterly Journal of Speech,* 36#4: 540-541 (Dec, 1950).

ELIOT, T. S.
    COCKTAIL PARTY, THE
       Arrowsmith, William. "English Verse Drama: *The Cocktail Party,"* *Hudson Review,* 3#3: 411-430 (Autumn, 1950).
       ——————. "Transfiguration in Eliot and Euripides," *Sewanee Review,* 63#3: 420-442 (Summer, 1965).
       ——————. "The Comedy of T. S. Eliot," *English Institute Essays,* pp. 156; 164-165; 168-171 (1954).
       Bain, Donald. *"The Cocktail Party,"* *Nine,* 2#1: 16-21 (Jan, 1950).
       Barrett, William. "Dry Land, Dry Martini," *Partisan Review,* 17#2: 354-359 (April, 1950).
       ——————. "T. S. Eliot's *Cocktail Party,"* *Partisan Review,* 17#4: 354-360 (April, 1950).
       Barth, J. Robert. "T. S. Eliot's Image of Man: A Thematic Study of his Drama," *Renascence,* 14#3: 134-137 (Spring, 1962).
       Bateson, John. "The Collected Plays," *The Review* (Oxford), 4: 6-11 (Nov, 1962).
       Brandt, G. W. "Realism and Parables (from Brecht to Arden)" *Stratford-Upon-Avon-Studies,* 4: 44-49 (1962).
       Branford, W. R. G. "The God in the Machine: a Note on *The Cocktail Party,"* *Lingua,* 1#7: 7-10 (March, 1951).
       ——————. "Myth and Theme in the Plays of T. S. Eliot," *Theoria,* 7:105-106 (1955).
       Braybrooke, Neville. "Eliot's Search for a Lost Eden," *Catholic World,* 190: 152 & 155 (Dec, 1959).

Brooks, Cleanth. *The Hidden God,* 73-75.

Brown, Ray C. B. "Alchoholic Allegory," *Voices (Michigan),*
  pp. 33-40 (Summer, 1950).

Brune, Randall. *"The Confidential Clerk* and the Devil's Dialectic," *Thoth,* 1#1: 31 (Spring, 1959).

Carter, Paul J. "Who Understands *The Cocktail Party?,"*
  Colorado Quarterly, 2: 193-204.

Clurman, H. *Lies Like Truth,* 179-182.

Colby, Robert A. "The Three Worlds of *The Cocktail Party:*
  The Wit of T. S. Eliot," *University of Toronto Quarterly,*
  24#1: 56-69 (Oct, 1954).

Collins, Arthur S. *English Literature of the Twentieth Century,* 306-308.

Donoghue, Denis. *The Third Voice,* 114-137; 238-240.

Dutton, Geoffrey. "London Letter: A Measure for a Cocktail,"
  Meanjin Papers, 42: 204-206 (Spring, 1950).

Eliot, T. S. *On Poets and Poetry,* 91-92.

——————————. "Poetry and Drama," *Atlantic Monthly,* 187:
  36-37 (Feb, 1951).

Emery, Sarah W. "Saints and Mr. Eliot," *Emory University
  Quarterly,* 7#3: 129-142 (Oct, 1951).

Enright, Dennis J. *The Apothecary's Shop,* 206-212.

Fallon, Gabriel. "After the Party," *Irish Monthly,* 79#9:
  389-393 (Sept, 1951).

Fraser, George S. *The Modern Writer and His World,* 173-
  177.

Gardner, Helen. *"The Cocktail Party,"* *Time and Tide,* pp.
  284-285 (March 25, 1950).

Gassner, John. "T. S. Eliot: The Poet as Modernist," in *The
  Theatre in Our Times,* 271-281.

Glicksberg, Charles I. "The Journey That Must be Taken,"
  Southwest Review, 40#3: 208-210 (Summer, 1955).

——————————. "The Spirit of Irony in Eliot's Plays,"
  Prairie Schooner, 29#4: 232-235 (Fall, 1955).

Hallman, Ralph J. *Psychology of Literature,* 73-77.

Hamalian, Leo. "Mr. Eliot's Saturday Evening Service," *Accent,* 10#4: 195-206 (Autumn, 1950).

Hamilton, Ian. *"The Cocktail Party,"* *World Review,* pp. 18-
  23 (Nov, 1949).

Hanzo, Thomas. "Eliot and Kierkegaard: 'The Meaning of
  Happening' in *The Cocktail Party,"* *Modern Drama,* 3#1:
  52-59 (May, 1960).

Harding, D. W. "Progression of Theme in Eliot's Modern
  Plays," *Kenyon Review,* 18#3: 345-353 (Summer, 1956).

Hardy, John E. "An Antic Disposition," *Sewanee Review,* 65#1: 50-60 (Winter, 1957).

Heilman, Robert B. *"Alcestis* and *The Cocktail Party,"* *Comparative Literature,* 5#2: 105-116 (Spring, 1953).

Henderson, J. L. "Stages of Psychological Development Exemplified in the Poetical Works of T. S. Eliot (Continued)" *Journal of Analytical Psychology,* 2#1: 47-48 (Jan, 1957).

Henn, Thomas R. *The Harvest of Tragedy,* 225-228.

Heywood, Robert. "Everybody's *Cocktail Party,"* *Renascence* 3#1: 28-30 (Autumn, 1950).

Hobson, Harold. *The Theatre Now,* 5-12.

Hochwald, Ilse E. "Eliot's *Cocktail Party* and Goethe's *Die Wahverwandt-Shaften,"* *Germanic Review,* 29#4: 254-259 (Dec, 1954).

Holland, Norman N. "Realism and the Psychological Critic," *Literature and Psychology,* 10#1: 5-10 (Winter, 1960).

Hovey, Richard B. "Psychiatrist and Saint in *The Cocktail Party,"* *Literature and Psychology,* 9#3&4: 51-55 (Summer-Fall, 1959).

Howarth, Herbert. "Eliot and Hofmannsthal," *South Atlantic Quarterly,* 59#4: 507-509 (Fall, 1960).

Jennings, Elizabeth. *Every Changing Shape,* 168-170.

Kaplan, Charles. "Eliot Among the Nightingales: Fair and Foul," *New Mexico Quarterly Review,* 24#2: 227-228 (Summer, 1954).

Karlin, Ken. "Critical Notes," *Chicago Review,* 7#1: 52-54 (Winter, 1953).

Kenner, Hugh. "Possum By Gaslight," *Poetry Magazine,* 85#1: 47-53 (Oct, 1954).

Killinger, John. *The Failure of Theology in Modern Literature,* 196-199.

Kintanar, Thelma B. "T. S. Eliot's *The Cocktail Party,"* *The Diliman Review,* 7#4: 440-447 (Oct, 1959).

Kline, Peter. "The Spiritual Center in Eliot's Plays," *Kenyon Review,* 21#3: 471-472 (Summer, 1959).

Koch, Vivienne. "Programme Notes on *The Cocktail Party,"* *Poetry Quarterly,* 11#4: 248-251 (Winter, 1949/50).

Kramer, Hilton. "T. S. Eliot in New York (Notes on the End of Something)," *Rocky Mountain Review,* 14#4: 303-304 (Summer, 1950).

Lawlor, John. "The Formal Achievement of *The Cocktail Party,"* *Virginia Quarterly Review,* 30#3: 431-451 (Summer, 1954).

Lewis, Allan. *The Contemporary Theatre,* 150-169.

McCollom, William G. *Tragedy,* 239-241.

McElroy, Davis D. *Existentialism and Modern Literature,* 49-54.

McLaughlin, John J. "A Daring Metaphysic: *The Cocktail Party,*" *Renascence,* 3#3: 15-27, (Autumn, 1950).

Manning, Hugo. "Mr. Eliot's Strange Party," *The Norseman,* 9#2: 128-130 (Mar-Apr, 1951).

Melchiori, Giorgio. "Eliot and the Theatre," *English Miscellany,* 4: 228-233 (1953).

Monroe, E. Annette. "The Group Reading: Expression for Drama of Mental Action," *Central States Speech Journal,* 15#3: 172-175 (Agust, 1964).

Munz, Peter. "The Devil's Dialectic," *Hibbert Journal,* 49: 256-263 (Apr, 1951).

Murry, J. M. *Unprofessional Essays,* 162-172.

——————. "Mr. Eliot's *Cocktail Party,*" *Fortnightly Review,* 174: 391-398 (Dec, 1950).

Paul, David. "Euripides and Mr. Eliot," *Twentieth Century,* 152#906: 174-178 (August, 1952).

Pick, John. "Note on *The Cocktail Party,*" *Renascence,* 3#1: 30-32 (Autumn, 1950).

Quinn, I. T. *"The Cocktail Party,"* *Irish Monthly,* 79#6: 259-263 (June, 1951).

Rahv, Philip. *Image and Idea,* 196-202.

Reckford, Kenneth J. "Heracles and Mr. Eliot," *Comparative Literature (Oregon),* 16#1: 1-18 (Winter, 1964).

Robbins, R. H. "A Possible Analogue for *The Cocktail Party,*" *English Studies,* 34#4: 165-167 (Aug, 1953).

Russell, Peter. "A Note on T. S. Eliot's New Play," *Nine,* 1#1: 28-29 (Oct, 1949).

Schwartz, Edward. "Eliot's *Cocktail Party* and the New Humanism," *Philological Quarterly,* 32#1: 58-68 (Jan, 1953).

Scott, Nathan A. (ed). *The Climate of Faith,* 26-27; 35; 38-39.

Scott, Nathan A. "T. S. Eliot's *The Cocktail Party:* Of Redemption and Vocation," *Religion in Life,* 20#2: 286-294 (Spring, 1951).

Shuman, R. Baird. "Buddhistic Overtones in Eliot's *Cocktail Party,*" *Modern Language Notes,* 72: 426-427 (1957).

——————. "Eliot's *The Cocktail Party,*" *Explicator,* 17#7: 46 (April, 1959).

Spender, Stephen. *The Creative Element,* 189-190.

Stein, Walter. "After the Cocktails," *Essays in Criticism,* 3#1: 85-104 (Jan, 1953).

Styan, J. L. *The Elements of Drama,* 274-284.

Toms, Newby. "Eliot's *The Cocktail Party:* Salvation and the

Common Routine," *Christian Scholar,* 47#2: 125-138 (Summer, 1964).

Vassilieff, Elizabeth. "Piers to Cocktails," *Meanjin Papers,* 42: 193-203 (Spring, 1950).

Vincent, C. J. "A Modern Pilgrim's Progress," *Queen's Quarterly,* 57#3: 346-352 (Aut, 1950).

Weisstein, Ulrich. *"The Cocktail Party:* An Attempt at Interpretation on Mythological Grounds," *Rocky Mountain Review,* pp. 232-241 (Spring, 1952).

Williams, Ray. *Drama From Ibsen to Eliot,* 237-246.

—————————. *Drama in Performance,* 111-112.

Williamson, Audrey. "Poetry in the Theater: Eliot and Fry," *Chrysalis,* 4#5-6: 9-12 (1951).

Wimsatt, W. K. *Hateful Contraries,* 184-200.

—————————. "Eliot's Comedy," *Sewanee Review,* 58: 666-678 (1950).

Winter, Jack. "Prufrockism in *The Cocktail Party,*" *Modern Language Quarterly,* 22#2: 135-148 (June, 1961).

Wool, Sandra. "Weston Revisited," *Accent,* 10: 207-212 (Aut, 1950).

CONFIDENTIAL CLERK, THE

(n.a.). "Accepting Life's Terms," *Times Literary Supplement,* pg. 180 (March 19, 1954).

Arrowsmith, William. "Transfiguration in Eliot and Euripides," *Sewanee Review,* 63#3: 420-442 (Summer, 1955).

—————————. "The Comedy of T. S. Eliot," *English Institute Essays,* pp. 162-165; 168-171 (1954).

Barth, J. Robert. "T. S. Eliot's Image of Man: A Thematic Study of his Drama," *Renascence,* 14#3: 137 (Spring, 1962).

Bateson, John. "The Collected Plays," *The Review* (Oxford), 4: 5-6; 10 (Nov, 1962).

Branford, W. R. G. "Myth and Theme in the Plays of T. S. Eliot," *Theoria,* 7: 107-109 (1955).

Brooke, Nicholas. *"The Confidential Clerk,"* *Durham University Journal,* 46#2: 66-70 (March, 1954).

Brown, Spencer. "T. S. Eliot's Latest Poetic Drama," *Commentary,* 17: 367-372 (April, 1954).

Brune, Randall. *"The Confidential Clerk* and the Devil's Advocate," *Thoth,* 1#1: 29-34 (Spring, 1959).

Clurman, H. *Lies Like Truth,* 182-184.

Colby, Robert A. "Orpheus in the Counting House: *The Confidential Clerk,*" *PMLA,* 72#4: 791-802 (Sept, 1957).

Dobree, Bonanmy. *"The Confidential Clerk," Sewanee Review,* 62#1: 117-131 (Winter, 1954).

Donoghue, Denis. *The Third Voice,* 138-157.

Fergusson, Francis. "Three Allegories: Brecht, Wilder, and Eliot," *Sewanee Review,* 64#1: 562-573 (Fall, 1956).

Findlater, Richard. "The Camouflaged Drama," *Twentieth Century,* 154#920: 311-316 (Oct, 1953).

Glicksberg, Charles I. "The Journey That Must be Taken," *Southwest Review,* 40#3: 210 (Summer, 1955).

——————. "The Spirit of Irony in Eliot's Plays," *Prairie Schooner,* 29#4: 235-237 (Fall, 1955).

Harding, D. W. "Progression of Theme in Eliot's Modern Plays," *Kenyon Review,* 18#3: 353-360 (Summer, 1956).

Henderson, J. L. "Stages of Psychological Development Exemplified in the Poetical Works of T. S. Eliot (Continued)" *Journal of Analytical Psychology,* 2#1: 48-49 (Jan, 1957).

Hynes, Sam. "Religion on the West End," *Commonweal,* 59#19: 475-478 (Feb 12, 1954).

Jennings, Elizabeth. *Every Changing Shape,* 171-173.

Kenner, Hugh. "Possum By Gaslight," *Poetry Magazine,* 85#1: 53-54 (Oct, 1954).

Kirk, Russell. "Two Plays of Resignation," *The Month,* 9#10: 223-225 (Oct, 1953).

McElroy, Davis D. *Existentialism and Modern Literature,* 44-49.

Mitchell, John D. "Applied Psychoanalysis in the Drama," *American Imago,* 14#3: 263-268 (Fall, 1957).

Murry, J. M. *Unprofessional Essays,* 172-182.

Weightman, J. G. "Edinburgh, Elsinor and Chelsea," *Twentieth Century,* 154#920: 306-308 (Oct, 1953).

Williams, Raymond. *Drama in Performance,* 112-113.

CORIOLAN

Highet, Gilbert. *The Powers of Poetry,* 293-300.

Theall, Donald F. "Traditional Satire in Eliot's *Coriolan,*" *Accent,* 11#4: 194-202 (Autumn, 1951).

ELDER STATESMAN, THE

Barth, J. Robert. "T. S. Eliot's Image of Man: A Thematic Study of his Drama," *Renascence,* 14#3: 137 (Spring, 1962).

Broussard, Louis. *American Drama,* 89-90.

Donoghue, Denis. "Eliot in Fair Colonus: *The Elder Statesman,*" *Studies,* 48: 49-58 (Spring, 1959). ALSO IN: *The Third Voice,* 158-168.

Fleming, Rudd. *"The Elder Statesman* and Eliot's Programme for the Metier of Poetry," *Wisconsin Studies in Contemporary Literature,* 2#1: 54-64 (Winter, 1961).

Jennings, Elizabeth. *Every Changing Shape,* 173-175.

Kenner, Hugh. "For Other Voices," *Poetry Magazine,* 95: 36-40 (Oct, 1959).

Weales, Gerald. "The Latest Eliot," *Kenyon Review,* 21#3: 473-478 (Summer, 1959).

FAMILY REUNION, THE

Barber, C. L. "T. S. Eliot: After Strong Gods," *Southern Review* (Louisiana), 6#2: 387-416 (Autumn, 1940).

Barth, J. Robert. "T. S. Eliot's Image of Man: A Thematic Study of his Drama," *Renascence,* 14#3: 131-134 (Spring, 1962).

Battenhouse, Roy W. "Eliot's *The Family Reunion* as Christian Prophecy," *Christendom,* 10#3: 307-321 (Summer, 1945).

Blan, D. S. "The Tragic Hero in Modern Literature," *Cambridge Journal,* 3#4: 221-223 (Jan, 1950).

——————. "T. S. Eliot's Case Book," *Modern Language Notes,* 75#1: 23-26 (Jan, 1960).

Bodkin, Maud. *The Quest For Salvation in an Ancient and a Modern Play,* 1-54.

Branford, W. R. G. "Myth and Theme in the Plays of T. S. Eliot," *Theoria,* 7: 102 (1955).

Brooks, Cleanth. *The Hidden God,* 75-76; 88-89; 92-93.

Broussard, Louis. *American Drama,* 73-77.

Bullough, Geoffrey. "Poetry in Modern English Drama," *Cairo Studies in English,* pp. 37-42 (1959).

Carne-Ross, Donald. "The Position of *The Family Reunion* in the Work of T. S. Eliot," *Revista di Letterature Moderne,* 2#2: 125-139 (Oct, 1950).

Cornwell, Ethel F. *The "Still Point,"* 23-25; 31-32; 38-40; 46-47.

Eliot, T. S. "The Aims of Poetic Drama," *Adam International Review,* 200: 12-13 (Nov, 1949).

——————. "Poetry and Drama," *Atlantic Monthly,* 187: 35-36 (Feb, 1951).

——————. *On Poets and Poetry,* 87-91.

Emery, Sarah W. "Saints and Mr. Eliot," *Emory University Quarterly,* 7#3: 129-142 (Oct, 1951).

Evans, David W. "The Domesticity of T. S. Eliot," *University of Toronto Quarterly,* 23#4: 383-385 (July, 1955).

Floersheimer, Stephen. *"The Family Reunion:* A Reply to Mr. Murry," *Essays in Criticism,* 1#3: 298-301 (July, 1951).

Fraser, George S. *The Modern Writer and His World,* 169-173.

Gaskell, Ronald. "The Critical Forum," *Essays in Criticism,* 13: 106 (Jan, 1963).

—————. *"The Family Reunion," Essays in Criticism,* 12#3: 292-301 (July, 1962).

Gassner, John. "T. S. Eliot: The Poet as Modernist," in *The Theatre in our Times,* 271-281.

Glicksberg, Charles I. *Literature and Religion,* 140-144.

—————. "The Journey That Must be Taken," *Southwest Review,* 40#3: 206-208 (Summer, 1955).

—————. "The Spirit of Irony in Eliot's Plays," *Prairie Schooner,* 29#4: 230-232 (Fall, 1955).

Hamalian, Leo. "Wishwood Revisited," *Renascence,* 12#4: 167-173 (Summer, 1960).

Harding, D. W. "Progression of Theme in Eliot's Modern Plays," *Kenyon Review,* 18#3: 337-345 (Summer, 1956).

Hausermann, H. W. "East Coker and *The Family Reunion," Life and Letters Today,* 47#98: 32-38 (Oct, 1945).

Henderson, J. L. "Stages of Psychological Development Exemplified in the Poetical Works of T. S. Eliot (Continued)" *Journal of Analytical Psychology,* 2#1: 35-36 (Jan, 1957).

Henn, Thomas R. *The Harvest of Tragedy,* 222-225.

Horton, Philip. "Speculation on Sin," *Kenyon Review,* 1#3: 330-333. (Summer, 1939).

Isaacs, J. *An Assessment of Twentieth Century Literature,* 149-152.

Jennings, Elizabeth. *Every Changing Shape,* 164-168.

Kaplan, Charles. "Eliot Among the Nightingales: Fair and Foul," *New Mexico Quarterly Review,* 24#2: 223-226 (Summer, 1954).

Leaska, Mitchell. *The Voice of Tragedy,* 256-261.

Lightfoot, Marjorie J. *"Purgatory* and *The Family Reunion:* In Pursuit of Prosodic Description," *Modern Drama,* 7#3: 256-266 (Dec, 1964).

McCollom, William G. *Tragedy,* 236-239.

Melchiori, Giorgio. "Eliot and the Theatre," *English Miscellany,* 4: 219-228 (1953).

Muller, Herbert J. *The Spirit of Tragedy,* 296-298.

Murry, J. Middleton. "Note on *The Family Reunion,*" *Essays in Criticism,* 1#1: 67-73 (Jan, 1951).

—————————. *Unprofessional Essays,* 154-162.

—————————. "Mr. Eliot's *Cocktail Party,*" *Fortnightly Review,* 174: 391-398 (Dec, 1950).

Nicholson, Norman. *Man and Literature,* 196-199.

Palmer, Richard E. "Existentialism in T. S. Eliot's *The Family Reunion,*" *Modern Drama,* 5#2: 174-186 (Sept, 1962).

Peacock, R. *Poet in the Theater,* 16-17; 21-24.

—————————. "Public and Private Problems in Modern Drama," *Tulane Drama Review,* 3#3: 69-72 (March, 1959).

Peter, John. "*The Family Reunion,*" *Scrutiny,* 16#3: 219-230 (Sept, 1949).

Pierstorff, E. "T. S. Eliot, the Swedish Players and the Norwegian Public," *The Norseman,* 7#4: 263-271 (July-Aug, 1949).

Prior, Moody E. *The Language of Tragedy,* 360-367.

Ramsey, Warren. "The Oresteia Since Hofmannsthal: Images and Emphasis," *Revue de Litterature Comparee,* 38#3: 370-372 (July-Sept, 1964).

Rillie, John A. "Melodramatic Device in T. S. Eliot," *Review of English Studies,* NS13#51: 270-272 (Aug, 1962).

Scrimgeour, C. A. "The Critical Forum," *Essays in Criticism,* 13: 104-106 (Jan, 1963).

Stamm, R. "The Orestes Theme in Three Plays by Eugene O'Neill, T. S. Eliot, and Jean-Paul Sartre," *English Studies,* 30: 247-251 (1949).

Steiner, George. *The Death of Tragedy,* 327-330.

Styan, J. L. *The Dark Comedy,* 3-5; 181-185.

Thomas, R. Hinton. *German Perspectives,* 34-35.

Unger, Leonard. "T. S. Eliot's Rose Garden: A Persistent Theme," *Southern Review (Louisiana).* 7#4: 681-685 (Spring, 1942).

Waggoner, H. H. "T. S. Eliot and the Hollow Men," *American Literature,* 15: 113-122 (May, 1943).

Ward, Anne. "Speculations on Eliot's Time-World: An Analysis of *The Family Reunion* in Relation to Hulme and Bergson," *American Literature,* 21: 18-34 (March, 1949).

Williams, Raymond. *Drama From Ibsen to Eliot,* 232-238.

—————————. *Drama in Performance,* 110-111.

Williamson, Audrey. "Poetry in the Theater: Eliot and Fry," *Chrysalis,* 4#5-6: 6-9 (1951).

Wynn, Dudley. "The Integrity of T. S. Eliot," *University of*

Denver Publications. Studies in Humanities, #1: 71-73 (1950).

MURDER IN THE CATHEDRAL

Adair, Patricia M. "Mr. Eliot's *Murder in the Cathedral,*" *Cambridge Journal,* 4#2: 83-95 (Nov, 1950).

Adams, John F. "The Fourth Temptation in *Murder in the Cathedral,*" *Modern Drama,* 5#4: 381-388 (Feb, 1963).

Adelman, Janet Ann. "The Tragedy of *Murder in the Cathedral,*" *The Greycourt Review,* 4#3: 59-68 (May, 1961).

Barth, J. Robert. "T. S. Eliot's Image of Man: A Thematic Study of his Drama," *Renascence,* 14#3: 129-131 (Spring, 1962).

Beardsley, Munroe. *Aesthetics,* 139.

Bland, D. S. "The Tragic Hero in Modern Literature," *Cambridge Journal,* 3#4: 214-215 (Jan, 1950).

Bodkin, Maud. *Studies of Type Images,* 128-135.

Boulton, J. T. "Use of Original Sources for Development of a Theme: Eliot in *Murder in the Cathedral,*" *English,* 11#61: 2-8 (Spring, 1956).

Brooks, Cleanth. *The Hidden God,* 76-79; 85-88.

Brooks, Cleanth and Robert Heilman. *Understanding Drama,* 5-7 (Appendix—1961 ed.); 457-459 (1945 ed.).

Bullough, Geoffrey. "Poetry in Modern English Drama," *Cairo Studies in English,* pp. 34-37 (1959).

Clutton-Brock, Alan. "T. S. Eliot and Conan Doyle," *Times Literary Supplement,* pg. 37 (Jan 19, 1951).

Cornwell, Ethel F. *The "Still Point",* 32-34; 40-43.

Cubeta, Paul M. *Modern Drama for Analysis, Third Edition* (1963), 434-443.

Decleyre, J. "Thomas a Becket in West-Euroean Literature," *Revue des Langues Vivantes,* 19: 412-413 (1953).

Donoghue, Denis. *The Third Voice,* 76-93.

Eliot, T. S. "The Aims of Poetic Drama," *Adam International Review,* 200: 11-12 (Nov, 1949).

———. *On Poets and Poetry,* 83-87.

———. "Poetry and Drama," *Atlantic Monthly,* 187: 34-35 (Feb, 1951).

Emery, Sarah W. "Saints and Mr. Eliot," *Emory University Quarterly,* 7#3: 129-142 (Oct, 1951).

Fell, Kenneth. "From Myth to Martyrdom: Towards a View of Milton's *Samson Agonistes,*" *English Studies,* 34#4: 145-155 (Aug, 1953).

Fergusson, Francis. *The Idea of a Theatre,* 210-221.

———. "Action as Passion: *Tristan* and *Murder in*

the Cathedral," *Kenyon Review,* 9#2: 201-221 (Spring, 1947).

Garlick, Raymond. "On Murder Considered as a Fine Art," *Dock Leaves,* 2#4: 19-30 (Jan, 1951).

Gerstenberger, Donna. "The Saint and the Circle: The Dramatic Potential of an Image," *Criticism,* 2#4: 336-341 (Fall, 1960).

Ghosh, P. C. "Eliot's Drama of Martyrdom," *University of Calcutta Bulletin of the Department of English,* 4#3-4: 14-30 (1963).

Glicksberg, Charles I. *Literature and Religion,* 138-140.

——————. "The Spirit of Irony in Eliot's Plays," *Prairie Schooner,* 24#3: 222-230 (Fall, 1955).

Hawthorn, Richard Y. *Tragedy, Myth, and Mystery,* 195-216.

Henn, Thomas R. *The Harvest of Tragedy,* 220-222.

Hoffman, F. J. *The Mortal No,* 110-111; 127-128; 132-134.

Howarth, Herbert. "Eliot and Hofmannsthal," *South Atlantic Quarterly,* 59#4: 503-507 (Fall, 1960).

Isaacs, J. *"Murder in the Cathedral," Times Literary Supplement,* pg. 53 (Jan 26, 1951).

Jennings, Elizabeth. *Every Changing Shape,* 163-164.

Kline, Peter. "The Spiritual Center in Eliot's Plays," *Kenyon Review,* 21#3: 457-472 (Summer, 1959).

Knox, George. *Critical Moments,* 34-35.

Kornbluth, Martin L. "A Twentieth-Century Everyman," *College English,* 21#1:26-29 (Oct, 1959).

Leaska, Mitchell. *The Voice of Tragedy,* 249-256.

Martz, L. L. "The Saint as Tragic Hero. *Saint Joan* and *Murder in the Cathedral,"* in Cleanth Brooks (ed), *Tragic Themes in Western Literature,* 156-164.

Mueller, William R. *"Murder in the Cathedral:* An Imitation of Christ," *Religion in Life,* 27#3: 414-426 (Summer, 1958).

Murry, J. M. *Unprofessional Essays,* 152-154.

Nicholas, Constance. "The Murders of Doyle and Eliot," *Modern Language Notes,* 70#4: 269-271 (April, 1955).

Olson, Elder. *Tragedy and the Theory of Drama,* 251-254.

Peter, John. *"Murder in the Cathedral," Sewanee Review,* 61#3: 362-383 (Summer, 1953).

Peacock, R. *Poet in the Theater,* 20-21.

Prior, Moody E. *The Language of Tragedy,* 353-360.

Rillie, John A. "Melodramatic Device in T. S. Eliot," *Review of English Studies,* NS13#51: 272-275 (Aug, 1962).

Scott, Norman (ed). *The Climate of Faith,* 131-135.

Smith, Grover. "Mr. Eliot's New Murder," *New Mexico Quarterly Review,* 22#3: 331-339 (Aut, 1952).

——————. *"Murder in the Cathedral,"* *Times Literary Supplement,* pg. 117 (Feb, 23, 1951).

Spanos, William V. *"Murder in the Cathedral:* The *Figura* as Mimetic Principle," *Drama Survey,* 3#2: 206-223 (Oct, 1963.)

Styan, J. L. *The Elements of Drama,* 29-30; 232-233.

Waggoner, H. H. "T. S. Eliot and the Hollow Men," *American Literature,* 15: 119-122 (May, 1943).

Walker, David. "Thomas Beckett and Henry II," *Church Quarterly Review,* 162: 303-313 (July-Sept, 1961).

Warren, Phyllis. "Drama in the University," *Theoria,* 3:32-35 (1950).

Weisstein, Ulrich. "Form as Content in the Drama of T. S. Eliot," *Rocky Mountain Review,* 23#3: 239-246 (Spring, 1959).

Williams, Ray. *Drama From Ibsen to Eliot,* 227-231.

Williamson, Audrey. "Poetry in the Theater: Eliot and Fry," *Chrysalis,* 4#5-6: 5-6 (1951).

Wynn, Dudley. "The Integrity of T. S. Eliot," *University of Denver Publications. Studies in Hrmanities,* #1: 70-71 (1950).

ROCK, THE

Battenhouse, Henry W. *Poet of Christian Thought,* 168-170.

Bullough, Geoffrey. "Poetry in Modern English Drama," *Cairo Studies in English,* pg. 34 (1959).

Cornwell, Ethel F. *The "Still Point",* 56-60.

Melchiori, Giorgio. "Eliot and the Theatre," *English Miscellany,* 4: 210-213 (1953).

Waggoner, H. H. "T. S. Eliot and the Hollow Men," *American Literature,* 15: 104; 115 (May, 1943).

Williams, Ray. *Drama From Ibsen to Eliot,* 225-227.

Wynn, Dudley. "The Integrity of T. S. Eliot," *University of Denver Publications. Studies in Humanities,* #1: 69 (1950).

ETHERIDGE, GEORGE

COMICAL REVENGE, THE (OR LOVE IN A TUB)

Fujimura, Thomas H. *The Restoration Comedy of Wit,* 87-96.

Holland, Norman. *The First Modern Comedies,* 20-27.

Wilcox, John. *The Relation of Moliere to Restoration Comedy,* 71-77.

MAN OF MODE, THE; OR SIR FOPLING FLUTTER

Fujimura, Thomas H. *The Restoration Comedy of Wit,* 104-116.

Holland, Norman. *The First Modern Comedies,* 80-95.

————————. "Restoration Comedy Again," *Essays in Criticism,* 7#3: 320-321 (July, 1957).

Horton, Melvin. "Essays on Comedy in the Seventeenth Century," *Asides,* 2: 28 (1941).

Kronenberger, Louis. *The Thread of Laughter,* 49-54.

McDonald, Charles O. "Restoration Comedy as Drama of Satire: An Investigation into Seventeenth Century Aesthetics," *Studies in Philology,* 61#3: 527-531 (July, 1964).

Mignon, Elizabeth. *Crabbed Age and Youth,* 34-35; 41-47.

Sherbo, Arthur. "A Note on *The Man of Mode,*" *Modern Language Notes,* 64#5: 343-344 (May, 1949).

Wain, John. "Restoration Comedy and its Modern Critics," *Essays in Criticism,* 6#4: 378-382 (Oct, 1956).

SHE WOULD IF SHE COULD

Fujimura, Thomas H. *The Restoration Comedy of Wit,* 96-104.

Holland, Norman. *The First Modern Comedies,* 28-37.

Kronenberger, Louis. *The Thread of Laughter,* 44-49.

Mignon, Elizabeth. *Crabbed Age and Youth,* 38-41.

FARQUHAR, GEORGE

BEAUX' STRATAGEM, THE

Boas, F. S. *An Introduction to Eighteenth Century Drama,* 57-63.

Gagen, Jean E. *The New Woman,* 156-158.

Mignon, Elizabeth. *Crabbed Age and Youth,* 173-174.

Wilcox, John. *The Relation of Moliere to Restoration Comedy,* 175-176.

CONSTANT COUPLE, THE;
OR A TRIP TO THE JUBILEE

Boas, F. S. *An Introduction to Eighteenth Century Drama,* 35-40.

Kronenberger, Louis. *The Thread of Laughter,* 167-171.

Mignon, Elizabeth. *Crabbed Age and Youth,* 161-164.

Morton, Richard. "The Jubilee of 1700 and Farquhar's *The*

Constant Couple," *Notes and Queries,* 200: 521-525 (Dec, 1955).

INCONSTANT, THE   ----
Gagen, Jean E. *The New Woman,* 46-48.
Mignon, Elizabeth. *Crabbed Age and Youth,* 165-168.

RECRUITING OFFICER, THE
Boas, F. S. *An Introduction to Eighteenth Century Drama,* 51-57.
Hough, Roger L. "An Error in *The Recruiting Officer,*" *Notes and Queries,* 198: 340-341 (Aug., 1953).
——————————. "Farquhar's *The Recruiting Officer,*" *Notes and Queries,* 199: 474 (Nov, 1954).
Kronenberger, Louis. *The Thread of Laughter,* 175-179.
Mignon, Elizabeth. *Crabbed Age and Youth,* 170-172.

SIR HARRY WILDAIR
Boas, F. S. *An Introduction to Eighteenth Century Drama,* 40-44.

TWIN RIVALS, THE
Boas, F. S. *An Introduction to Eighteenth Century Drama,* 45-49.
Kronenberger, Louis. *The Thread of Laughter,* 171-175.
Mignon, Elizabeth. *Crabbed Age and Youth,* 168-170.
Rothstein, Eric. "Farquhar's *The Twin-Rivals* and the Reform of Comedy," *PMLA,* 79#1: 33-41 (Mar, 1964).

FAULKNER, WILLIAM

A REQUIEM FOR A NUN
B., J. R. "A General Introduction," *Faulkner Studies,* 1#1: 4-7 (Spring, 1952).

FERGUSSON, FRANCIS

THE KING AND THE DUKE
Bentley, Eric. *From the Modern Repertoire, Series Two,* 499-500.

FIELD, NATHANIEL

WOMAN IS A WEATHERCOCK
Blayney, Glenn H. "Field's Parody of a Murder Play," *Notes and Queries,* 200: 19-20 (Jan, 1955).

FIELDING, HENRY

DEBORAH
Roberts, Edgar V. "Henry Fielding's Lost Play *Deborah, or A Wife for You All* (1733)" *Bulletin of the New York Public Library*, 66#11: 576-588 (Nov, 1962).

DON QUIXOTE IN ENGLAND
Boas, F. S. *An Introduction to Eighteenth Century Drama*, 228-230.

FATHERS, THE
Goggin, L. P. "Development of Techniques in Fielding's Comedies," *PMLA*, 67#5: 773-781 (Sept, 1952).

HISTORICAL REGISTER, THE
Boas, F. S. *An Introduction to Eighteenth Century Drama*, 234-236.

INTRIGUING CHAMBERMAID, THE
Swaen, A. E. H. "Fielding's *The Intriguing Chambermaid,*" *Neophilologus*, 29: 117-120 (April, 1944).

LOTTERY, THE
Roberts, Edgar V. "Fielding's Ballad Opera *The Lottery* (1732) and the English State Lottery of 1731," *Huntington Library Quarterly*, 27#1: 21-38 (Nov, 1963).

LOVE IN SEVERAL MASQUES
Goggin, L. P. "Development of Techniques in Fielding's Comedies," *PMLA*, 67#5: 773-781 (Sept, 1952).

MISER, THE
Goggin, L. P. "Development of Techniques in Fielding's Comedies," *PMLA*, 67#5: 773-781 (Sept, 1952).

MODERN HUSBAND, THE
Goggin, L. P. "Development of Techniques in Fielding's Comedies," *PMLA*, 67#5: 773-781 (Sept, 1952).

RAPE UPON RAPE
Goggin, L. P. "Development of Techniques in Fielding's Comedies," *PMLA*, 67#5: 773-781 (Sept, 1952).

PASQUIN
Boas, F. S. An *Introduction to Eighteenth Century Drama*, 231-234.

TEMPLE BEAU, THE
Goggin, L. P. "Development of Techniques in Fielding's Comedies," *PMLA*, 67#5: 773-781 (Sept, 1952).

Rogers, Winfield H. "The Significance of Fielding's *Temple Beau*," *PMLA*, 55#2: 440-444 (June, 1940).

TRAGEDY OF TRAGEDIES, THE; OR THE LIFE AND DEATH OF TOM THUMB THE GREAT
Adams, H. H. and Baxter Hathaway (eds). *Dramatic Essays of the Neoclassic Age*, 300-306.
Boas, F. S. *An Introduction to Eighteenth Century Drama*, 222-225.

UNIVERSAL GALLANT, THE
Goggin, L. P. "Development of Techniques in Fielding's Comedies," *PMLA, 67#5*: 773-781 (Sept, 1952).

WEDDING DAY, THE
Goggin, L. P. "Development of Techniques in Fielding's Comedies," *PMLA, 67#5*: 773-781 (Sept, 1952).

FITCH, CLYDE

THE CITY
Downer, Alan S. *Fifty Years of American Drama*, 12-16.

FITZMAURICE, GEORGE

COUNTRY DRESSMAKERS, THE
Kennedy, Maurice. "George Fitzmaurice: Sketch for a Portrait," *Irish Writing*, 15: 40-44.

DANDY DOLLS, THE
Clarke, Austin. "Dramatic Fantasies of George Fitzmaurice," *Dublin Magazine*, N.S. 15#2: 9-14 (April-June, 1940).

MOONLIGHTERS, THE
Kennedy, Maurice. "George Fitzmaurice: Sketch for a Portrait," *Irish Writing,* 15: 40-44.

FLECKNOE, RICHARD

THE DAMOISELLES A LA MODE
Wilcox, John. *The Relation of Moliere to Restoration Comedy*, 46-48.

FLETCHER, JOHN
(See Also: Beaumont, Francis & John Fletcher)

BEGGAR'S BUSH, THE
Masefield, John. "Beaumont and Fletcher," *Atlantic Monthly*, 199: 174 (June, 1957).

BLOODY BROTHER, THE
   Bowers, Fredson T. *Elizabethan Revenge Tragedy,* 176-177.

BONDUCA
   See: Beaumont and Fletcher

CAPTAIN, THE
   See: Beaumont and Fletcher

FAITHFUL SHEPHERDESS, THE
   Masefield, John. "Beaumont and Fletcher," *Atlantic Monthly,*
      199: 174 (June, 1957).
   Wells, K. *Elizabethan and Jacobean Playwrights,* 167-175.

KING AND NO KING, A
   See: Beaumont and Fletcher

LOYAL SUBJECT, THE; OR THE FAITHFUL GENERAL
   Waith, Eugene M. "A Tragicomedy of Humors: Fletcher's
      The Loyal Subject," *Modern Language Quarterly,* 6#3:
      299-313 (Sept, 1945).

MAID'S TRAGEDY, THE
   See: Beaumont and Fletcher

PILGRIM, THE
   Mignon, Elizabeth. *Crabbed Age and Youth,* 150-152.

—AND PHILIP MASSINGER

THIERRY AND THEODORET
   Bowers, Fredson T. *Elizabethan Revenge Tragedy,* 168-169.
   Wells, Henry W. *Elizabethan and Jacobean Playwrights,* 139-
      141.

—AND WILLIAM SHAKESPEARE

TWO NOBLE KINSMEN, THE
   Edwards, Philip. "On the Design of *The Two Noble Kins-
      men,*" *Review of English Literature,* 5#4: 89-105 (Oct,
      1964).
   Kolkeritz, Helge. "The Beast-Eating Clown. *The Two Noble
      Kinsmen,* 3. 5. 131," *Modern Language Notes,* 61#8: 532-
      535 (Dec, 1946).
   Mincoff, M. "The Authorship of *The Two Noble Kinsmen,*"
      English Studies, 33#3: 97-115 (June, 1952).
   Muir, Kenneth. *Shakespeare as Collaborator,* 98-147.

VALENTINIAN

Bowers, Fredson T. *Elizabethan Revenge Tragedy,* 149-153.
Wells, Henry W. *Elizabethan and Jacobean Playwrights,* 133-136.

WILD-GOOSE CHASE, THE

Gagen, Jean E. *The New Woman,* 26-28.
Mignon, Elizabeth. *Crabbed Age and Youth,* 165-167.

FORD, JOHN

BROKEN HEART, THE

Anderson, Donald K. Jr. "The Heart and the Banquet: Imagery in Ford's *'Tis Pity* and *The Broken Heart,"* *Studies in English Literature 1500-1900,* 2#2: 209-218 (Spring, 1962).

Blayney, Glenn H. "Convention, Plot, and Structure in *The Broken Heart,"* *Modern Philology,* 56#1: 1-9 (Aug, 1958).

Bowers, Fredson T. *Elizabethan Revenge Tragedy,* 211-214.

Carsanga, Grovanni M. "The 'Truth' in John Ford's *The Broken Heart,"* *Comparative Literature (Oregon),* 10#4: 344-348 (Fall, 1958).

Davril, R. "Shakespeare and Ford," *Shakespeare Jahrbuck,* 94: 127-131 (1958).

――――――――. "John Ford and La Cerda's *Ines de Castro,"* *Modern Language Notes,* 66#7: 464-466 (Nov, 1951).

――――――――. "The Use of Physiology in the Elizabethan Drama With Special Reference to John Ford," in International Federation for Modern Languages and Literature, *Literature and Science (Third Trienniel Proceedings),* 129-131.

Eliot, T. S. *Essays on Elizabethan Drama,* 143-146.

Feldman, A. Bronson. "The Yellow Malady: Short Studies of Five Tragedies of Jealousy," *Literature and Psychology,* 5#2: 49-52 (May, 1956).

McDonald, Charles O. "The Design of John Ford's *The Broken Heart:* A Study in the Development of Caroline Sensibility," *Studies in Philology,* 59#2: 141-161 (April, 1962).

Ornstein, Robert. *The Moral Vision of Jacobean Tragedy,* 213-216.

Prior, Moody E. *The Language of Tragedy,* 145-152.

Ribner, Irving. *Jacobean Tragedy,* 156-163.

Sensabaugh, George F. "John Ford Revisited," *Studies in English Literature 1500-1900,* 4#2: 195-203 (Spring, 1964).

Ure, Peter. "Marriage and the Domestic Drama of Heywood and Ford," *English Studies,* 32#5: 211-216 (Oct, 1951).

Wells, Henry W. *Elizabethan and Jacobean Playwrights,* 127-129.

GREAT FAVOURITE, THE; OR THE DUKE OF LERMA

Sensabaugh, G. F. "Another Play by John Ford," *Modern Language Quarterly,* 3: 595-602 (1942).

LOVE'S SACRIFICE

Bowers, Fredson T. *Elizabethan Revenge Tragedy,* 206-211.

Kaufmann, R. T. "Ford's Tragic Perspective," *Texas Studies in Literature and Language,* 1#4: 527-532 (Winter, 1960).

Ornstein, Robert. *The Moral Vision of Jacobean Tragdy,* 216-221.

Ribner, Irving. *Jacobean Tragedy,* 162-163.

Sensabaugh, George F. "John Ford and Elizabethan Tragedy," in B. Maxwell (ed), *Renaissance Studies in Honor of Hardin Craig,* 253-257.

——————. "John Ford Revisited," *Studies in English Literature 1500-1900,* 4#2: 203-209 (Spring, 1964).

Ure, Peter. "Cult and Initiates in Ford's *Love's Sacrifice,*" *Modern Language Quarterly,* 11: 298-306 (1950).

Wells, Henry W. *Elizabethan and Jacobean Playwrights,* 67-69.

PERKIN WARBECK

Anderson, Donald K. Jr. *"Richard II* and *Perkin Warbeck,"* *Shakespeare Quarterly,* 13#2: 260-263 (Spring, 1962).

——————. "Kingship in *Perkin Warbeck,*" *ELH,* 27#3: 177-193 (Sept, 1960).

Eliot, T. S. *Essays on Elizabethan Drama,* 146-147.

Harbage, Alfred. "The Mystery of *Perkin Warbeck,*" in *Studies in the English Renaissance Drama in Memory of Karl J. Holzknecht,* 125-141.

Ribner, Irving. *The English History Play in the Age of Shakespeare,* 299-305.

——————. *Jacobean Tragedy,* 174-175.

Weathers, Winston. *"Perkin Warbeck:* A Seventeenth-Century Psychological Play," *Studies in English Literature 1500-1900,* 217-226.

Wells, Henry W. *Elizabethan and Jacobean Playwrights,* 104-106.

'TIS PITY SHE'S A WHORE

Adams, Henry H. *English Domestic or Homiletic Tragedies 1575-1642,* 177-183.

Anderson, Donald K. Jr. "The Heart and the Banquet: Imagery in Ford's *'Tis Pity* and *The Broken Heart,*" *Studies in English Literature 1500-1900,* 2#2: 209-213 (Spring, 1962).

Artaud, Antonin. *The Theater and its Double,* 28-31.

Bowers, Fredson T. *Elizabethan Revenge Tragedy,* 206-211.

Eliot, T. S. *Essays on Elizabethan Drama,* 139-143.

Hoy, Cyrus. " 'Ignorance in Knowledge': Marlowe's Faustus and Ford's Giovanni," *Modern Philology,* 57#3: 145-154 (Feb, 1960).

Kaufmann, R. T. "Ford's Tragic Perspective," *Texas Studies in Literature and Language,* 1#4: 522-524; 532-537 (Winter, 1960).

Millington, Gordon. "The Art of John Ford," *Mandrake,* 1#2: 5; 11-14 (Feb, 1946).

Ornstein, Robert. *The Moral Vision of Jacobean Tragedy,* 203-213.

Ribner, Irving. "By Nature's Light: *'Tis Pity She's A Whore,*" *Tulane Studies in English,* 10: 39-50 (1960).

—————————. *Jacobean Tragedy,* 163-174.

Sensabaugh, G. F. "John Ford and Elizabethan Tragedy," in B. Maxwell (ed), *Renaissance Studies in Honor of Hardin Craig,* 257-258.

—————————. "John Ford Revisited," *Studies in English Literature, 1500-1900,* 4#2: 209-216 (Spring, 1964).

Wells, Henry W. *Elizabethan and Jacobean Playwrights,* 49-52.

WELSH AMBASSADOR, THE
See: Thomas Dekker

— AND THOMAS DEKKER & WILLIAM ROWLEY

THE WITCH OF EDMONTON

Adams, Henry H. *English Domestic or Homiletic Tragedies 1575-1642,* 132-142.

Ashton, J. W. "Dekker's Use of Folklore in *Old Fortunatus, If This Be Not A Good Play,* and *The Witch of Edmonton,*" *Philological Quarterly,* 41#1: 240-241; 245-248 (Jan, 1962).

Wells, Henry W. *Elizabethan and Jacobean Playwrights,* 71-75.

FROST, ROBERT

A MASQUE OF REASON

Finnegan, Sister Mary J. "Frost's Masque of Mercy," *Catholic World,* pp. 357-361 (Feb, 1958).

Hatfield, H. C. "Frost's *The Masque of Reason,*" *Explicator,* 4:9.

Leyburn, Ellen D. "A Note on Frost's *Masque of Reason,*" *Modern Drama,* 4#4: 426-428 (Feb, 1962).

Stock, Ely. "*A Masque of Reason* and *J. B.:* Two Treatments of the *Book of Job,*" *Modern Drama,* 3#4: 378-386 (Feb, 1961).

Todasco, R. "Dramatic Characterization in Frost's *A Masque of Reason,*" *University of Kansas City Review,* 29#3: 227-230 (Mar, 1963).

Waggoner, H. H. "Frost's *The Masque of Reason,*" *Explicator,* 4:32.

FRY, CHRISTOPHER

BOY WITH THE CART, THE

Fay, Gerald. "The Theater of Christopher Fry," *World Review,* pp. 52-53 (March, 1950).

CURTMANTLE

Browne, E. Martin. "Henry II as Hero," *Drama Survey,* 2#1: 63-71 (June, 1962).

Merchant, W. M. "Lawyer and Actor: Process of Law in Elizabethan Drama," in G.I. Duthie (ed), *English Studies Today, Third Series* (1964), 113-114.

Parker, G. "A Study of Fry's *Curtmantle,*" *Dalhousie Review,* 43#2: 200-211 (Summer, 1963).

Scott, Norman (ed). *The Climate of Faith,* 62-63.

DARK IS LIGHT ENOUGH, THE

Alexander, John. "Christopher Fry and Religious Comedy," *Meanjin Papers,* 15#1: 77-81, (Autumn, 1956).

Becker, William. "Reflections on Three New Plays," *Hudson Review,* 9#2: 258-263 (Summer, 1955).

Donoghue, Denis. *The Third Voice,* 180-192.

——————————. "Christopher Fry's Theatre of Words," *Essays in Criticism,* 11#1: 44-49 (Jan, 1959).

Findlater, Richard. "The Two Countesses," *Twentieth Century,* 156#930: 179-183 (August, 1954).

Mandel, O. "Themes in the Dramas of Christopher Fry," *Etudes Anglaises,* 10#4: 341-342 (Oct-Dec, 1957).

Scott, Nathan A. (ed). *The Climate of Faith,* 27-29; 60-62; 123-124.

FIRSTBORN, THE

Mandel, O. "Themes in the Dramas of Christopher Fry," *Etudes Anglaises,* 10#4: 343-344 (Oct-Nov, 1957).

Spears, Monroe K. "Christopher Fry and the Redemption of Joy," *Vanderbilt Studies in Humanities,* 1: 20-22 (1951).

Stanford, Derek. "Comedy and Tragedy in Christopher Fry," *Modern Drama,* 2#1: 3-7 (May, 1959).

LADY'S NOT FOR BURNING, THE

Clurman, Harold. *Lies Like Truth,* 184-187.

Davis, Earle. "Christopher Fry: The Twentieth Century Shakespeare," *Kansas Magazine,* pp. 12-15 (1952).

MacNeice, Louis. *"The Lady's Not For Burning" World Review,* pp. 18-22 (June, 1949).

Mandel, O. "Themes in the Dramas of Christopher Fry," *Etudes Anglaises,* 10#4: 339-341 (Oct-Dec, 1957).

Spears, Monroe K. "Christopher Fry and the Redemption of Joy," *Vanderbilt Studies in Humanities,* 1: 25-28 (1951).

Stamm, Rudolph. "Christopher Fry and the Revolt Against Realism in Modern English Drama," *Anglia,* 72#1: 78-109 (1954).

Stephens, Peter J. "Mr. Fry, Your Rhythms are Showing," *The Poetry Book Magazine,* 3#2: 1-2 (Winter, 1951).

Styan, J. L. *The Elements of Drama,* 263-266.

Trewin, J. C. "The Plays of Christopher Fry," *Adelphi,* 27#1: 42-44 (Nov, 1950).

Williams, Ray. *Drama From Ibsen to Eliot,* 262-268.

Williamson, Audrey. "Poetry in the Theater: Eliot and Fry," *Chrysalis,* 4#5-6: 12-15 (1951).

Woodbury, John. "The Witch and the Nun: A Study of *The Lady's Not For Burning,*" *Manitoba Arts Review,* 10#3: 41-54 (Winter, 1956).

Worsley, T. C. *The Fugitive Art,* 79-83.

PHOENIX TOO FREQUENT, A

Cabaniss, Allen. "The Matron of Ephesus Again: An Analysis," *University of Mississippi Studies in English,* 2:41 (1961).

Mandel, O. "Themes in the Dramas of Christopher Fry," *Etudes Anglaises,* 10#4: 337-338 (Oct-Dec, 1957).

Spears, Monroe K. "Christopher Fry and the Redemption of Joy," *Vanderbilt Studies in Humanities,* 1: 23-25 (1951).

Stamm, Rudolf. "Christopher Fry and the Revolt Against Realism in Modern English Drama," *Anglia,* 72#1: 78-109 (1954).

Trewin, J. C. "The Plays of Christopher Fry," *Adelphi,* 27#1: 41-42 (Nov, 1950).

Worsley, T. C. *The Fugitive Art,* 119-121.

SLEEP OF PRISONERS, THE

Braybrook, Neville. "A Modern Religious Drama," *Irish Monthly,* 80#5: 196-200 (May, 1952).

Ferguson, John. "Christopher Fry's *A Sleep of Prisoners,*" *English,* 10#56: 42-47 (Summer, 1954).

Hobson, Harold. *The Theatre Now,* 82-85.

——————. "Christopher Fry's Newest Play in London," *The Poetry Book Magazine,* 3#4: 1-2 (Summer, 1951).

Mandel, O. "Themes in the Dramas of Christopher Fry," *Etudes Anglaises,* 10#4: 344-345 (Oct-Dec, 1957).

Styan, J. L. *The Elements of Drama,* 55-57; 232-3.

Worsley, T. C. *The Fugitive Art,* 227-228.

THOR, WITH ANGELS

Highet, Gilbert. *People, Places and Books,* 63-68.

Mandel, O. "Themes in the Dramas of Christopher Fry," *Etudes Anglaises,* 10#4: 338-339 (Oct-Dec, 1957).

Spears, Monroe K. "Christopher Fry and the Redemption of Joy," *Vanderbilt Studies in Humanities,* 1: 22-23 (1951).

VENUS OBSERVED

Donoghue, Denis. "Christopher Fry's Theatre of Words," *Essays in Criticism,* 11#1: 40-42 (Jan, 1959).

Elder, Walter. "Venus Attended by Muses," *Kenyon Review,* 12#4: 712-717 (Autumn, 1950).

Fox, Robert C. "Fry's *Venus Observed,*" *Explicator,* 16#8: 47 (May, 1958).

Hobson, Harold. *The Theatre Now,* 13-20.

Hope-Wallace, Philip. "The Theater of Christopher Fry," *World Review,* pp. 51-52 (March, 1950).

Mandel, O. "Themes in the Dramas of Christopher Fry," *Etudes Anglaises,* 10#4: 345-347 (Oct-Dec, 1957).

Metwally, A. A. "Christopher Fry as a Poet Dramatist," *Cairo Studies in English,* pp. 107-109 (1960).

Spears, Monroe K. "Christopher Fry and the Redemption of Joy," *Vanderbilt Studies in Humanities,* 1: 27-33 (1951).

Stamm, Rudolf. "Christopher Fry and the Revolt Against Realism in Modern English Drama," *Anglia,* 72#1: 78-109 (1954).

Williams, Raymond. *Drama From Ibsen to Eliot,* 262-268.

Williamson, Audrey. "Poetry in the Theater: Eliot and Fry," *Chrysalis,* 4#5-6: 15-19 (1951).

Worsley, T. C. *The Fugitive Art,* 116-119.

FULWELL, ULPIAN

LIKE WILL TO LIKE

Adams, Henry H. *English Domestic or Homiletic Tragedies 1575-1642,* 63-66.

Bevington, David M. *From Mankind to Marlowe,* 155-158.

GAGER, WILLIAM

OEDIPUS

Bowers, R. H. "William Gager's *Oedipus,*" *Studies in Philology,* 46#2: 141-153 (April, 1949).

GALSWORTHY, JOHN

JUSTICE

Bache, William B. *"Justice:* Galsworthy's Dramatic Tragedy," *Modern Drama,* 3#2: 138-142 (Dec, 1960).

Hallman, Ralph J. *Psychology of Literature,* 188-192.

Nethercot, Arthur H. "The Quintessence of Idealism: Or, The Slaves of Duty," *PMLA,* 62#3: 855-856 (Sept, 1947).

LOYALTIES

Eastman, Fred. *Christ in the Drama,* 70-71.

—————. "The Dramatist and the Minister," in Albert E. Bailey (ed), *The Arts and Religion,* 142-150.

Wilson, Asher. "Oscar Wilde and *Loyalties,*" *Educational Theatre Journal,* 11#3: 208-211 (Oct, 1959).

PIGEON, THE

    Eastman, Fred. *Christ in the Drama,* 69-70.

SILVER BOX, THE

    Choudhury, Asoke Dey. "Galsworthy's First Play," *The Visua-bharati Quarterly,* 26#1 : 21-23 (Summer, 1960).

    Worsley, T. C. *The Fugitive Art,* 199-201.

STRIFE

    Eastman, Fred. *Christ in the Drama,* 64-68.

    Nethercot, Arthur H. "The Quintessence of Idealism: Or, The Slaves of Duty," *PMLA,* 62#3: 855 (Sept, 1947).

GAY, JOHN

ACHILLES

    Boas, F. S. *An Introduction to Eighteenth Century Drama,* 188-190.

BEGGAR'S OPERA, THE

    Boas, F. S. *An Introduction to Eighteenth Century Drama,* 180-187.

    Bronson, Bertrand H. *"The Beggar's Opera,"* in Richard C. Boys (ed), *Studies in the Literature of the Augustan Age Honoring A. E. Case,* 14-49.

    Brustein, Robert. *The Theater of Revolt,* 260-261.

    Bushnell, Margaret. "Gay Satirical Method," *Asides,* 3 : 22-24 (1942).

    Hunting, Robert S. "How Much is a Cowcumber Worth?," *Notes and Queries,* 198#1: 28-29 (Jan, 1953).

    Mack, Maynard. "Gay Augustan," *Yale University Library Gazette,* 21#1: 9-10 (July, 1946).

    Price, Martin. *To the Palace of Wisdom,* 245-249.

    Sherwin, Judith Johnson. " 'The World is Mean and Man Uncouth," *Virginia Quarterly Review,* 35#2: 258-270 (Spring, 1959).

CAPTIVES, THE

    Boas, F. S. *An Introduction to Eighteenth Century Drama,* 178-180.

DIONE

    Boas, F. S. *An Introduction to Eighteenth Century Drama,* 175-178.

MOHOCKS, THE

    Boas, F. S. *An Introduction to Eighteenth Century Drama,* 167-169.

Stroup, Thomas B. "Gay's *Mohocks* and Milton," *Journal of English and Germanic Philology*, 46#2: 164-167 (April, 1947).

POLLY
Boas, F. S. *An Introduction to Eighteenth Century Drama*, 184-188.

THREE HOURS AFTER MARRIAGE
Gagen, Jean E. *The New Woman*, 78-81.

WHAT D'YE CALL IT, THE
Boas, F. S. *An Introduction to Eighteenth Century Drama*, 170-175.

GELBER, JACK

APPLE, THE
Abel, Lionel. *Metatheatre*, 128-134.
——————. "Living Theater," *Commentary*, 33: 331-334 (April, 1962).
Dukore, Bernard F. "Jack Gelber," *Drama Survey*, 2#2: 151-157 (Oct, 1962).

CONNECTION, THE
Abel, Lionel. *Metatheatre*, 122-127.
Bendetti, Robert. "Metanaturalism: The Metaphorical Use of Environment in the Modern Theater," *Chicago Review*, 17#2-3: 30-31 (1964).
Brook, Peter. "From Zero to the Infinitive," *Encore*, 7#6: 6-11 (Nov-Dec, 1960).
Dukore, Bernard F. "Jack Gelber," *Drama Survey*, 2#2: 146-152 (Oct, 1962).
Eskin, Stanley G. "Theatricality in the Avant-Garde Drama: A Reconsideration of a Theme in the Light of *The Balcony* and *The Connection*," *Modern Drama*, 7#2: 213-222 (Sept, 1964).
Hentoff, Nat. "Who Else Can make so Much out of Passing Out?: The Surprising Survival of an Anti-Play," *Evergreen Review*, 4#11: 170-177 (Jan-Feb, 1960).
Kerr, Walter. *The Theater in Spite of Itself*, 139-142; 182-185.
Kostelanetz, Richard C. "*The Connection*: Heroine as Existential Choice," *Texas Quarterly*, 5#4: 159-162 (Winter, 1962).

Markowitz, Charles. *"The Connection* and Beyond," *New Left Review,* 9: 46-48 (May-June, 1961).

Mottram, Eric. "The New American Wave," *Encore,* 11#1: 24-27 (Jan-Feb, 1964).

Vinaver, Stephan. *"The Connection," Encore,* 8#3: 33-37 (May-June, 1961).

Wellwarth, George E. "Hope Deferred—The New American Drama," *The Literary Review,* 7#1: 23-26 (Autumn, 1963).

GIBSON, WILLIAM

MIRACLE WORKER, THE

Weales, Gerald. "The Video Boys on Broadway," *Antioch Review,* 22: 216-218 (Summer, 1962).

TWO FOR THE SEESAW

Trilling, Lionel. "All Aboard the Seesaw," *Tulane Drama Review,* 4#4: 16-22 (May, 1960).

GILBERT, WILLIAM S.

GRETCHEN

Danton, George H. "Gilbert's *Gretchen," Germanic Review,* 21#2: 132-141 (April, 1946).

Pascal, Roy. "Four Fausts: From W. W. Gilbert to Ferruccia Busoni," *German Life and Letters,* 10#4: 263-265 (July, 1957).

—AND SEYMOUR SULLIVAN

PATIENCE

Berlin, Normand. *"Patience:* A Study in Poetic Elaboration," *Studia Neophilologica,* 33#1: 80-85, (1961).

TRIAL BY JURY

Hamond, John W. "Gilbert's *Trial By Jury," The Explicator,* 23#4: 34 (Dec, 1964).

—AND SEYMOUR SULLIVAN

YOEMEN OF THE GUARD, THE

Hall, Robert A., Jr. "The Satire of *The Yeomen of the Guard," Modern Language Notes,* 73#7: 492-497 (Nov, 1958).

GILDON, CHARLES

LOVE'S VICTIM; OR THE QUEEN OF WALES
Magill, Lewis. "Poetic Justice: The Dilemma of Early Cre-
ators of Sentimental Tragedy," *Washington State College
Research Studies,* 25#1: 29-30 (March, 1957).

PATRIOT, THE
Magill, Lewis. "Poetic Justice: The Dilemma of Early Cre-
ators of Sentimental Tragedy," *Washington State College
Research Studies,* 25#1: 30-32 (March, 1957).

GOFFE, THOMAS

ORESTES
Bowers, Fredson T. *Elizabethan Revenge Tragedy,* 188-189.
O'Donnell, Norbert F. "Shakespeare, Marston and the University: The Sources of Thomas Goffe's *Orestes," Studies
in Philology,* 50#3: 476-484 (July, 1953).

GOLDSMITH, OLIVER

GOOD NATURED MAN, THE
Heilman, Robert B. "The Sentimentalism of Goldsmith's *Good
Natured Man,"* in N. M. Caffee and T. A. Kirby (eds),
Studies for William A. Read, 237-253.

SHE STOOPS TO CONQUER
Hennig, John. "The Auerbachs Keller Scene and *She Stoops
to Conquer," Comparative Literature (Oregon),* 7#3:
193-202 (Summer, 1955).
Kronenberger, Louis. *The Thread of Laughter,* 187-190.
Sells, A. Lytton. "Oliver Godsmith's Influence on the French
Stage," *Durham University Journal,* 33#2: 90-97 (March,
1941).
Smith, John H. "Tony Lumpkin and the Country Booby Type
in Antecedent English Comedy," *PMLA,* 58#4: 1038-
1049 (Dec, 1944).
Styan, J. L. *The Elements of Drama,* 134-135.

GOW, JAMES E.
—AND ARNAUD D'USSEAU

DEEP ARE THE ROOTS
Dempsey, David. "Uncle Tom's Ghost and the Library Aboli-
tionists," *Antioch Review,* 6#3: 442-446 (Fall, 1946).

GRANVILLE-BARKER, HARLEY

FAMILY OF THE OLDROYDS, THE
Morgan, Margery M. "The Early Plays of Harley Granville-Barker," *Modern Language Quarterly,* 51: 329-331; 337-338 (July, 1956).

OUR VISITOR
Morgan, Margery M. "The Early Plays of Harley Granville-Barker," *Modern Language Quarterly,* 51: 334-338 (July, 1956).

WASTE
Norton, Roger C. "Hugo von Hofmannsthal's *Der Schwierge* and Granville-Barker's *Waste,"* *Comparative Literature (Oregon),* 14#3: 272-279 (Summer, 1962).

WEATHER HEN, THE
Morgan, Margery M. "The Early Plays of Harley Granville-Barker," *Modern Language Quarterly,* 51: 331; 337-338 (July, 1956).

GREEN, JULIEN

SOUTH
Meyer, John H. "Heat, Horror, and Mr. Green," *Renascence,* 7#2: 80-84 (Winter, 1954).

GREEN, PAUL

HOUSE OF CONNELLY, THE
Dusenbury, Winifred L. *The Theme of Loneliness in Modern American Drama,* 149-154.
Sievers, W. D. *Freud on Broadway,* 313-314.
Young, Stark. *Immortal Shadows,* 127-131.

IN ABRAHAM'S BOSOM
Sievers, W. D. *Freud on Broadway,* 311-312.
Young, Stark. *Immortal Shadows,* 88-90.

LOST COLONY, THE
Free, Willia J. and Charles B. Lower. *History Into Drama,* 99-175.

TREAD THE GREEN GRASS
Sievers, W. D. *Freud on Broadway,* 315-318.

GREENE, GRAHAM

COMPLAISANT LOVER, THE

Kerr, Walter. *The Theater in Spite of Itself,* 157-160.

Stratford, Philip. "The Uncomplaisant Dramatist: Some Aspects of Graham Greene's Theatre," *Wisconsin Studies in Contemporary Literature,* 2#3: 9-19 (Fall, 1961).

LIVING ROOM, THE

Cottrell, Beekman W. "Second Time Charm: The Theatre of Graham Greene," *Modern Fiction Studies,* 3#3: 249-251; 254-255 (Aut, 1957).

Cronin, Vincent. "Graham Greene's First Play," *Catholic World,* 177: 406-410 (Sept, 1953).

Findlater, Richard. "Graham Greene as Dramatist," *Twentieth Century,* 153#916: 471-473 (June, 1953).

Hortmann, Wilhelm. "Graham Greene: The Burnt-Out Catholic," *Twentieth Century Literature,* 10#2: 72-74 (July, 1964).

Hynes, Sam. "Religion on the West End," Commonweal, 59# 19: 477-478 (Feb 12, 1954).

Sainer, Arthur. *The Sleepwalker and the Assassin,* 50-51.

Scott, Nathan A. (ed). *The Climate of Faith,* 192-193.

POTTING SHED, THE

Clurman, H. *Lies Like Truth,* 176-177.

Cottrell, Beekman W. "Second Time Charm: The Theatre of Graham Greene," *Modern Fiction Studies,* 3#3: 251-255 (Aut, 1957).

H., T. *"The Plotting Shed:* Figmentum Fi dei," *Dublin Review,* 232#475: 71-73 (Spring, 1958).

Hortmann, Wilhelm. "Graham Greene: The Burnt-Out Catholic," *Twentieth Century Literature,* 10#2: 75-76 (July, 1964).

Killinger, John. *The Failure of Theology in Modern Literature,* 183-185.

McCarthy, Mary. *Theater Chronicle,* 179-185.

Murphy, John P. *"The Potting Shed,"* *Renascence,* 12#1: 43-49 (Autumn, 1959).

Rewak, William J. *"The Potting Shed,"* *Catholic World,* 186: 210-213 (Dec, 1957).

Scott, Nathan A. (ed). *The Climate of Faith,* 193-194.

Wassmer, Thomas A. "The Problem and the Mystery of Sin in the Works of Graham Greene," *Christian Scholar,* 43#4: 309-315 (Winter, 1960).

——————————. "The Sinners of Graham Greene," *Dalhousie Review*, 39#3: 328-329; 332 (Aut, 1959).

GREENE, ROBERT

ALPHONSUS KING OF ARAGON

Clemen, Wolfgang. *English Tragedy Before Shakespeare*, 179-180.

Harrison, George. *Elizabethan Plays and Players*, 82-86.

McDonnell, R. F. *The Aspiring Mind*, 152-153.

Ribner, Irving. "Greene's Attack on Marlowe," *Studies in Philology*, 52#2: 162-171 (April, 1955).

Sanders, Norman. "The Comedy of Greene and Shakespeare," *Stratford-Upon-Avon-Studies*, 3:37-39 (1961).

FRIAR BACON AND FRIAR BUNGAY

Clemen, Wolfgang. *English Tragedy Before Shakespeare*, 182-185.

Harrison, George. *Elizabethan Plays and Players*, 91-93.

Hart, Jeffrey P. "Prospero and Faustus," *Boston University Studies in English*, 2#4: 197-206 (Winter, 1956).

Maclaine, Allan H. "Greene's Borrowings From his own Prose Fiction in *Bacon and Bungay* and *James the Fourth*," *Philological Quarterly*, 30#1: 22-26 (Jan, 1951).

McNeir, Waldo F. "Traditional Elements in the Character of Greene's Friar Bacon," *Studies in Philology*, 45#2: 172-179 (April, 1948).

——————————. "Robert Greene and *John of Bordeux*," *PMLA*, 64#4: 781-801 (Sept, 1949).

Muir, Kenneth. "Robert Greene as Dramatist," in Richard Hosley (ed), *Essays on Shakespeare and Elizabethan Drama in Honor of Hardin Craig*, 47-50.

Price, Hereward T. "Shakespeare and his Young Contemporaries," *Philological Quarterly*, 41#1: 45-46 (Jan, 1962).

Sanders, Norman. "The Comedy of Greene and Shakespeare," *Stratford-Upon-Avon-Studies*, 3: 40-50 (1961).

JAMES IV

Clemen, Wolfgang. *English Tragedy Before Shakespeare*, 186-191.

Maclaine, Allan H. "Greene's Borrowings From his own Prose Fiction in *Bacon and Bungay* and *James the Fourth*," *Philological Quarterly*, 30#1: 22-24; 26-27 (Jan, 1951).

Muir, Kenneth. "Robert Greene as Dramatist," in Richard
  Hosley (ed), *Essays on Shakespeare and Elizabethan
  Drama in Honor of Hardin Craig,* 50-54.
Sanders, Norman. "The Comedy of Greene and Shakespeare,"
  Stratford-Upon-Avon-Studies, 3: 40-44; 51-53 (1961).
Talbert, Ernest W. *Elizabethan Drama and Shakespeare's
  Early Plays,* 92-95.

JOHN OF BORDEUX
See: Anon

LOCRINE
See: Anon

ORLANDO FURIOSO
Clemen, Wolfgang. *English Tragedy Before Shakespeare,*
  180-182.
Houk, Raymond A. "Shakespeare's *Shrew* and Greene's *Or-
  lando,*" *PMLA,* 62#3: 657-671 (Sept, 1947).
McDonnell, R. F. *The Aspiring Mind,* 153-156.
McNeir, Waldo F. "Greene's Medievalization of Aristo,"
  Revue de Litterature Comparee, 29#3: 351-360 (July-
  Sept, 1955).
Sanders, Norman. "The Comedy of Greene and Shakespeare,"
  Stratford-Upon-Avon-Studies, 3: 39-41 (1961).
Soellner, Rolf. "The Madness of Hercules and the Eliza-
  bethans," *Comparative Literature* (Ore.) 10#4: 317-318
  (Fall, 1958).

SELIMUS
Clemen, Wolfgang. *English Tragedy Before Shakespeare,* 130-
  134.
McDiarmid, Matthew P. "The Influence of Robert Garnier on
  Some Elizabethan Tragedies," *Etudes Anglaises,* 11#4:
  296-298 (Oct-Dec, 1958).
McDonnell, R. F. *The Aspiring Mind,* 158-161.
Ribner, Irving. "Greene's Attack on Marlowe: Some Light on
  Alphonsus and *Selimus,*" *Studies in Philology,* 52#1:
  167-171 (Jan, 1955).

GREGORY, LADY AUGUSTA

GRANIA
Ellis-Fermor, Una. *The Irish Dramatic Movement,* 152-161.
SPREADING OF THE NEWS, THE
Ellis-Fermor, Una. *The Irish Dramatic Movement,* 141-145.

GREVILLE, FULKE
  ALAHAM
    Morris, Ivor. "The Tragic Vision of Fulke Greville," *Shakes-
      peare Survey,* 14: 66-75 (1961).
    Ure, Peter. "Fulke Greville's Dramatic Characters," *Review
      of English Studies,* N.S. 1#4: 313-318; 320-323 (Oct,
      1950).

  MUSTAPHA
    Morris, Ivor. "The Tragic Vision of Fulke Greville," *Shakes-
      peare Survey,* 14: 66-75 (1961).
    Ure, Peter. "Fulke Greville's Dramatic Characters," *Review
      of English Studies,* N.S. 1#4: 318-323 (Oct, 1950).

HAINES, WILLIAM WISTER

  COMMAND DECISION
    Brown, J. Mason. *Seeing More Things,* 273-281.
    Dusenbury, Winfred L. *The Theme of Lonliness in Modern
      American Drama,* 190-196.

HANSBERRY, LORRAINE

  A RAISIN IN THE SUN
    Lewis, Theophilus. "Social Protest in *A Raisin in the Sun,"
      Catholic World,* 190: 31-35 (Oct, 1959).
    Weales, Gerald. 'Thoughts on *A Raisin in the Sun,"* Commen-
      tary, 27: 527-530 (June, 1959).

HARBURG, EDGAR Y.
—AND FRED SAIDY

  FINIAN'S RAINBOW
    Brown, J. Mason. *Seeing More Things,* 121-128.

HARDING, SAMUEL

  SICILY AND NAPLES
    Bowers, Fredson T. *Elizabethan Revenge Tragedy,* 188-189.

HART, MOSS
  (See Also: Kaufman, George S. & Moss Hart)

  CLIMATE OF EDEN, THE
    Sievers, W. D. *Freud on Broadway,* 296-298.

LADY IN THE DARK
>Fagin, N. Bryllon. " 'Freud' on Broadway," *Educational Theatre Journal*, 2#4: 298-299 (Dec, 1950).
>Sievers, W. D. *Freud on Broadway*, 291-294.

HAUSTED, PETER

THE RIVAL FRIENDS
>Mills, Laurens J. "Peter Hausted: Playwright, Poet, and Preacher," *Indiana University Publications: Humanities Series*, 12: 17-37 (1944).

SENILE ODIUM
>Mills, Laurens J. "Peter Hausted's *Senile Odium,*" *Indiana University Publications. Humanities Series,* 19: 196-201 (1949).

HECHT, BEN

FRONT PAGE
>Sievers, W. D. *Freud on Broadway*, 303-305.

TO QUITO AND BACK
>McCarthy, Mary. *Theater Chronicle*, 3-6.

HEGGEN, THOMAS
—AND JOSHUA LOGAN

MISTER ROBERTS
>Brown, J. Mason. *Seeing More Things*, 282-288.

HELLMAN, LILLIAN

ANOTHER PART OF THE FOREST
>Dusenbury, Winifred L. *The Theme of Loneliness in Modern American Drama*, 143-145.
>Sievers, W. D. *Freud on Broadway*, 283-285.

AUTUMN GARDEN, THE
>Clurman, Harold. *Lies Like Truth,* 47-49.
>Felheim, Marvin. *"The Autumn Garden:* Mechanics and Dialectics," *Modern Drama*, 3#2: 191-195 (Dec, 1960).

CHILDREN'S HOUR, THE
>Lawson, John H. *Theory and Technique of Playwriting*, 263-266.
>Sievers, W. D. *Freud on Broadway*, 279-281.

LITTLE FOXES, THE
>   Dusenbury, Winifred L. *The Theme of Loneliness in Modern American Drama*, 143-149.
>   Sievers, W. D. *Freud on Broadway*, 282-283.

MONTSERRAT**
>   Clurman, H. *Lies Like Truth*, 260-266.

SEARCHING WIND, THE
>   Sievers, W. D. *Freud on Broadway*, 285-287.

TOYS IN THE ATTIC
>   Kerr, Walter. *The Theater in Spite of Itself*, 235-238.

HEMINGE, WILLIAM

FATAL CONTRACT, THE
>   Bowers, Fredson T. *Elizabethan Revenge Tragedy*, 236-242.

JEWES TRAGEDY, THE
>   Bowers, Fredson T. *Elizabethan Revenge Tragedy*, 235-236.

HERNE, JAMES A.

DRIFTING APART
>   Edwards, Herbert. "Howells and Herne," *American Literature,* 22 : 432-433 (June, 1951).

MARGARET FLEMING
>   Bucks, Dorothy S. and Arthur H. Nethercot. "Ibsen and Herne's *Margaret Fleming:* A Study of the Early Ibsen Movement in America" *American Literature,* 17 :311-333 (Jan, 1946).
>   ———————. "A Reply to Professor Quinn," *American Literature,* 19: 177-180 (May, 1947).
>   Edwards, Herbert. "Howells and Herne" *American Literature,* 22: 435-438 (Jan, 1951).
>   Edwards, Herbert J. (and Julie A. Herne). "James A. Herne —Rise of Realism in the American Drama," *University of Maine Bulletin, 67#8:* 57-73 (Nov, 1964).
>   Pizer, Donald. "An 1890 Account of *Margaret Fleming,*" *American Literature, 27#2:* 264-267 (May, 1955).
>   Quinn, Arthur. "Ibsen to Herne : Theory and Facts" *American Literature,* 19: 171-177 (May, 1947).

**Hellman's version of Robles' play.

REVEREND GRIFFITH DAVENPORT, THE

Edwards, Herbert J. (and Julie A. Herne). "James A. Herne
—Rise of Realism in the American Drama," *University
of Maine Bulletin,* 67#8: 114-134 (Nov, 1964).

Herne, Julie A. and A. H. Quinn. "Act III of James A.
Herne's *Griffith Davenport,*" *American Literature,* 24:
330-351 (Nov, 1952).

SHORE ACRES

Edwards, Herbert. "Herne, Garland, and Henry George,"
American Literature, 28: 363-364 (Nov, 1956).

Edwards, Herbert J. (and Julie A. Herne). "James A. Herne
—Rise of Realism in the American Drama," *University
of Maine Bulletin,* 67#8: 85-111 (Nov, 1964).

HEYWOOD, DuBOSE

BRASS ANKLE

Egri, Lajos. *The Art of Dramatic Writing,* 287-289.

HEYWOOD, JOHN

THE FOUR PRENTICES OF LONDON

Bevington, David M. *From Mankind to Marlowe,* 38-39.

Miller, Edwin S. "Guilt and Penalty in Heywood's Pardoner's
Lie," *Modern Language Quarterly,* 10: 58-60 (1949).

HEYWOD, THOMAS

THE "AGE" PLAYS**

Holaday, Allan. "Heywood's *Trioa Brittanica* and the *Ages,*"
Journal of English and Germanic Philology, 45#4: 430-
439 (Oct, 1946).

APPIUS AND VIRGINIA

See: John Webster

CAPTIVES, THE

Townsend, Freda L. "The Artistry of Thomas Heywood's
Double Plots," *Philological Quarterly,* 25#2: 110-114
(April, 1946).

CHALLENGE FOR BEAUTIE, A

Townsend, Freda L. "The Artistry of Thomas Heywood's
Double Plots," *Philological Quarterly,* 25#2: 104-108
(April, 1946).

**The Brazen Age, The Golden Age, The Iron Age, The Silver Age, etc.*

ENGLISH TRAVELLER, THE
>   Adams, Henry H. *English Domestic or Homiletic Tragedies, 1575-1642,* 169-173.
>   Eliot, T. S. *Essays on Elizabethan Drama,* 110-114.
>   Grivelet, Michel. "The Simplicity of Thomas Heywood," *Shakespeare Survey,* 14 : 56-65 (1961).
>   Rabkin, Norman. "Dramatic Deception in Heywood's *The English Traveller,*" *Studies in English Literature 1500-1900,* 1#2 : 1-16 (Spring, 1961).
>   Townsend, Freda L. "The Artistry of Thomas Heywood's Double Plots," *Philological Quarterly,* 25#2: 110-112; 114-116 (April, 1946).

HENRY IV
>   Adams, Henry H. *English Domestic or Homiletic Tragedies 1575-1642,* 88-98.
>   Bethell, S. L. "The Comic Element in Shakespeare's Histories," *Anglia,* 71#1 : 89-92 (1952).
>   Knights, L. C. *Drama and Society in the Age of Jonson,* 249-255.

JOHAN JOHAN
>   Craik, J. W. "The True Source of John Heywood's *Johan Johan,*" *Modern Language Review,* 45#3: 289-295 (July, 1950).
>   Sultan, Stanley. "The Audience Participation Episode in *Johan Johan,*" *Journal of English and Germanic Philology,* 52#4: 491 (Oct, 1953).
>   —————. *"Johan Johan* and its Debt to French Farce," *Journal of English and Germanic Philology,* 53#1: 23-37 (Jan, 1954).

- - - AND RICHARD BROME

LATE LANCASHIRE WITCHES, THE
>   Adams, Henry H. *English Domestic or Homiletic Tragedy 1575-1642,* 204-205.

LOVE'S MISTRESS
>   Halstead, W. L. "Dekker's *Cupid and Psyche* and Thomas Heywood," *ELH,* 11#3: 182-191 (Sept, 1944).

PLAY OF LOVE
>   Schoeck, R. J. "A Common Tudor Expletive and Legal Parody in Heywood's *Play of Love,*" *Notes and Queries,* 201: 375-376 (Sept, 1956).

————————. "Satire of Wolsey in Heywood's *Play of Love*," *Notes and Queries*, 196: 112-114 (March, 1951).

Withington, Robert. "Paronomasia in John Heywood's Plays," *Smith College Studies in Modern Languages*, 21#1-4: 230-235 (Oct, 1939-July, 1940).

PLAY OF THE WETHER

Withington, Robert. "Paronomasia in John Heywood's Plays," *Smith College Studies in Modern Languages*, 21#1-4: 228-230 (Oct, 1939-July, 1940).

RAPE OF LUCRECE, THE

Cunningham, James. *Woe or Wonder*, 57-58; 116-117.

Holaday, Alan. "Robert Browne and the Date of Heywood's *Lucrece*," *Journal of English and Germanic Philology*, 44#2: 171-180 (April, 1945).

————————. "Thomas Heywood's *The Rape of Lucrece*," *University of Illinois Studies in Language and iLterature*, 34#3: 1-44 (1950).

Ribner, Irving. *Jacobean Tragedy*, 59-71.

WISE WOMAN OF HOGSDOM, THE

Wells, Henry W. *Elizabethan and Jacobean Playwrights*, 221-223.

WIT AND WITLESS

Withington, Robert. "Parosomasia in John Heywood's Plays," *Smith College Studies in Modern Languages*, 21#1-4: 235-239 (Oct, 1939-July, 1940).

WOMAN KILLED WITH KINDNESS, A

Adams, Henry H. *English Domestic or Homiletic Tragedy 1575-1642*, 144-159.

Berry, Llyod E. "A Note on Heywood's *A Woman Killed With Kindness*," *Modern Language Review*, 58#1: 64-65 (Jan, 1963).

Cook, D. J. "*A Woman Killed With Kindness:* An Unshakespearian Tragedy," *English Studies*, 45#5: 353-372 (Oct, 1964).

Coursen, Herbert R. "The Subplot of *A Woman Killed With Kindness*," *English Language Notes*, 2#3: 180-185 (Mar, 1965).

Eliot, T. S. *Essays on Elizabethan Drama*, 107-110.

Hooper, A. G. "Heywood's *A Woman Killed With Kindness*," *English Studies in Africa*, 4#1: 54-57 (March, 1961).

McNeir, Waldo. "Heywood's Sources for the Main Plot of *A Woman Killed With Kindness,*" in *Studies in the English Renaissance Drama in Memory of Karl J. Holzknecht,* 189-211.

Prior, Moody E. *The Language of Tragedy,* 94-99.

Ribner, Irving. *Jacobean Tragedy,* 8-9; 51-58.

Spacks, Patricia Meyer. "Honor and Perception in *A Woman Killed With Kindness,*" *Modern Language Quarterly,* 20#4: 321-332 (Dec, 1959).

Townsend, Freda L. "The Artistry of Thomas Heywood's Double Plots," *Philological Quarterly,* 25#2: 99-102 (1946).

Ure, Peter. "Marriage and the Domestic Drama of Heywood and Ford," *English Studies,* 32#5: 203-207 (Oct, 1951).

HILL, AARON

KING HENRY THE FIFTH; OR THE CONQUEST OF FRANCE

Burns, Landon C. "Three Views of King Henry V," *Drama Survey,* 1#3: 291-300 (Feb, 1962).

ZARA

Bergman, Fred L. "Garrick's *Zara,*" *PMLA,* 74#3: 225-232 (June, 1959).

HIVNOR, ROBERT

THE TICKLISH ACROBAT

Barbour, Thomas. "The Stuff of the Theater," *Hudson Review,* 15#1: 133-135 (Spring, 1957).

HOME, JOHN

ALFRED

Boas, F. S. *An Introduction to Eighteenth Century Drama,* 280-285.

ALONZO

Boas, F. S. *An Introduction to Eighteenth Century Drama,* 276-280.

DOUGLAS

Boas, F. S. *An Introduction to Eighteenth Century Drama,* 264-270.

FATAL DISCOVERY, THE
Boas, F. S. *An Introduction to Eighteenth Century Drama,* 274-276.

HOOD, THOMAS
LAMIA
Whitley, Alvin. "Thomas Hood as Dramatist," *Studies in English,* 30: 185-187 (1951).

HORNE, R. H.
COSMO DE MEDICI
Boas, F. S. "R. H Horne: His Plays and 'Farthing Epic'," *Essays by Divers Hands,* 21: 30-31 (1944).

DEATH OF MARLOWE, THE
Boas, F. S. "R. H Horne: His Plays and 'Farthing Epic'," *Essays by Divers Hands,* 21: 31-34 (1944).

HILDEBRAND
Boas, F. S. "R. H Horne: His Plays and 'Farthing Epic'," *Essays by Divers Hands,* 21: 35-37 (1944).

JUDAS ISCARIOT
Boas, F. S. "R. H Horne: His Plays and 'Farthing Epic'," *Essays by Divers Hands,* 21:37-38 (1944).

SPIRIT OF PEERS AND PEOPLE:
A NATIONAL TRAGI-COMEDY
Boas, F. S. "R. H Horne: His Plays and 'Farthing Epic'," *Essays by Divers Hands,* 21: 28-29 (1944).

HOWARD, BRONSON
THE AMATEUR BENEFIT
Halline, A. G. "Bronson Howard's *The Amateur Benefit,*" *American Literature,* 14: 74-76 (March, 1942).

HOWARD, EDWARD
SIX DAYS ADVENTURE, THE
Gagen, Jean E. *The New Woman,* 175-177.

WOMAN'S CONQUEST, THE
Gagen, Jean E. *The New Woman,* 173-175.

HOWARD, SIR ROBERT
GREAT FAVOURITE, THE; OR THE DUKE OF LERMA
See: John Ford

HOWARD, SIDNEY

MADAM, WILL YOU WALK
Sievers, W. D. *Freud on Broadway,* 170-171.

SILVER CORD, THE
Brooks, Cleanth and R. Heilman. *Understanding Drama,* pp.
9-10 (Appendix—1961 ed.) ; 461-462 (1945 ed.).
Dusenbury, Winifred L. *The Theme of Lonliness in Modern
American Drama,* 67-74.
Fagin, N. Bryllon. " 'Freud' on Broadway," *Educational The-
atre Journal,* 2#4 : 301-302 (Dec, 1950).
Sievers, W. D. *Freud on Broadway,* 166-168.
Young, Stark. *Immortal Shadows,* 76-79.

YELLOW JACK
Clurman, H. *The Fervent Years,* 101-103.

HOWELLS, WILLIAM DEAN

A SEA CHANGE; OR LOVE'S STOWAWAY
Baatz, Wilmer H. "William Dean Howells' Opera," *The University of Rochester Library Bulletin,* 10#2: 34-36 (Winter, 1955).

HUGHES, THOMAS

MISFORTUNES OF ARTHUR, THE
Armstrong, William A. "The Topicality of *The Misfortunes of
Arthur,*" *Notes and Queries,* 200: 371-373 (Sept, 1955).
————————. "Elizabethan Themes in *The Misfortunes of
Arthur,*" *The Review of English Studies,* N.S. 7#27 : 238-
249 (July, 1956).
Clemen, Wolfgang. *English Tragedy Before Shakespeare,*
85-91.
McDonnel, R. F. *The Aspiring Mind,* 86-90.
Reese, Gertrude. "Political Import of *The Misfortunes of
Arthur,*" *Review of English Studies,* 21#82: 81-91 (April,
1945).
————————. "The Succession Question in Elizabethan
Drama," *Studies in English,* pp. 68-69 (1942).
Ribner, Irving. *The English History Play in the Age of
Shakespeare,* 229-236.

HUNTER, ROBERT

ANDROBOROS

Leder, Lawrence H. "Robert Hunter's *Androboros*," *Bulletin of New York Public Library*, 68#3: 153-160 (March, 1964).

McNamara, Brooks. "Robert Hunter and *Androboros*," *The Southern Speech Journal*, 30#2: 106-116 (Winter, 1964).

HUXLEY, ALDOUS

THE WORLD OF LIGHT

MacCarthy, Desmond. *Humanities*, 99-104.

INGE, WILLIAM

BUS STOP

Hogan, Robert G. *Drama*, 634-640.

Wolfson, Lester M. "Inge, O'Neill, and the Human Condition," *The Southern Speech Journal*, 22#4: 226-227 (Summer, 1957).

COME BACK, LITTLE SHEBA

Dusenbury, Winifred L. *The Theme of Loneliness in Modern American Drama*, 8-16.

Sievers, W. D. *Freud on Broadway*, 352-354.

Wolfson, Lester M. "Inge, O'Neill, and the Human Condition," *The Southern Speech Journal*, 22#4: 224-225 (Summer, 1957).

DARK AT THE TOP OF THE STAIRS, THE

Driver, Tom F. " 'Psychologism': Roadblock to Religious Drama," *Religion in Life*, 29#1: 59-60 (Winter, 1959/60).

Scott, Nathan A. (ed). *The Climate of Faith*, 38.

LOSS OF ROSES, A

Kerr, Walter. *The Theater in Spite of Itself*, 238-242.

PICNIC

Clurman, H. *Lies Like Truth*, 60-62.

Sievers, W. D. *Freud on Broadway*, 354-356.

Wolfson, Lester M. "Inge, O'Neill, and the Human Condition, *The Southern Speech Journal*, 22#4: 225-226 (Summer, 1957).

JAMES, HENRY

GUY DOMVILLE

Greene, Graham. *The Lost Childhood,* 46-48..

Shaw, G. B. *Plays and Players,* 1-5.

Staub, August W. "The Well-Made Failures of Henry James," *Southern Speech Journal, 27#2*: 91-92 (Winter, 1961).

HIGH BID, THE

Levy, B. M. *"The High Bid* and the Forbes-Robertsons," *College English,* 8#6: 284-292 (March, 1947).

OTHER HOUSE, THE

McElderry, B. R. Jr. "Henry James' Neglected Thriller: *The Other House," Arizona Quarterly,* 8#4: 328-322 (Winter, 1952).

OUTCRY, THE

Edel, Leon. "Henry James and *The Outcry," University of Toronto Quarterly,* 18#4: 340-346 (July, 1949).

Evans, R. D. "Henry James on *The Outcry," Modern Language Notes,* 70#2: 105-106 (Feb, 1955).

REPROBATE, THE

Barzun, Jacques. *The Energies of Art,* 236-237.

JEFFERS, ROBINSON

MEDEA

Brown, J. Mason. *Seeing More Things,* 234-236.

Fitts, Dudley. "The Hellenism of Robinson Jeffers," *Kenyon Review,* 8#4: 678-683 (Autumn, 1946).

Weingarten, Samuel. "Jeffers' *Medea:* A General Semantics Reading," *Etc,* 9#4: 258-262 (Summer, 1952).

TOWER BEYOND TRAGEDY, THE

Sievers, W. D. *Freud on Broadway,* 123-124.

JELLICOE, ANN

KNACK, THE

Taylor, John R. *Anger and After,* 69-71.

SPORT OF MY MAD MOTHER, THE

Taylor, John R. *Anger and After,* 65-68.

JEPHSON, ROBERT

THE LAW OF LOMBARDY

Parrott, T. M. "Two Late Dramatic Versions of the Slandered

Bride Theme," in James G. McManaway (ed), *Joseph Q. Adams Memorial Studies,* 548-551.

JERROLD, DOUGLAS WILLIAM

BLACK EY'ED SUSAN; OR ALL IN THE DOWNS
McElderry, B. R. "Three Earlier Treatments of the *Billy Budd* Theme," *American Literature, 27*: 251-254 (May, 1955).

MUTINY AT THE NORE
McElderry, B. R. Jr. "Three Eearlier Versions of the *Billy Budd* Theme," *American Literature, 27*: 254-255 (May, 1955).

JOHNSON, CHARLES

GENEROUS HUSBAND, THE
Gagen, Jean E. *The New Woman,* 61-63; 132-133.

VILLAGE OPERA, THE
Boas, F. S. *An Introduction to Eighteenth Century Drama,* 208-212.

JONES, A. H.

MASQUERADERS, THE
Nethercot, Arthur H. "The Quintessence of Idealism: Or, The Slaves of Duty," *PMLA,* 62#3: 849-851 (Sept, 1947).

JONES, HENRY A.

MICHAEL AND HIS LOST ANGEL
Shaw, G. B. *Plays and Players,* 66-75.

PHYSICIAN, THE
Shaw, G. B. *Plays and Players,* 204-214.

JONES, JOSEPH S.

PEOPLE'S LAWYER, THE
See: *Solon Shingle*

SOLON SHINGLE
Curvin, Jonathan W. "The Stage Yankee," in *Studies in Speech and Drama in Honor of Alexander M. Drummond,* 145-146.

JONSON, BEN

ALCHEMIST, THE
Bacon, Wallace A. "The Magnetic Field: The Structure of Jonson's Comedies," *Huntington Library Quarterly,* 19#2: 142-145 (Feb, 1956).

Curry, John V. *Deception in Elizabethan Comedy,* 142-143.

Duncan, Edgar Hill. "Jonson's *Alchemist* and the Literature of Alchemy," *PMLA* 61#3: 699-710 (Sept, 1946).

————————. "Jonson's Use of Arnald of Villa Nova's *Rosarium,*" *Philological Quarterly,* 21#4: 435-438 (Oct, 1942).

Goldberg, S. L. "Folly Into Crime: The Catastrophe of *Volpone,*" *Modern Language Quarterly,* 20: 238; 241 (Sept, 1959).

Goodman, Paul. *The Structure of Literature,* 82-103.

Hoy, Cyrus H. *The Hyacinth Room,* 119-127.

————————. "The Pretended Piety of Jonson's Alchemist," *Renaissance Papers, pp.* 15-19 (1957).

Hussey, Maurice. "Ananias the Deacon: A Study of Religion in Jonson's *The Alchemist,*" *English,* 9#54: 207-212 (Aut, 1953).

Knoll, Robert E. "How to Read *The Alchemist,*" *College English,* 21#8: 456-460 (May, 1960).

Kronenberger, Louis. *The Thread of Laughter,* 18-24.

Leech, Clifford. "Caroline Echoes of *The Alchemist,*" *Review of English Studies,* 16#64: 432-438 (Oct, 1940).

McCullen, Joseph T. Jr. "Conference With the Queen of Fairies: A Study of Jonson's Workmanship in *The Alchemist,*" *Studia Neophilologica,* 23#2-3: 87-95 (1951).

Parr, Johnstone. "Non-Alchemical Pseudosciences in *The Alchemist,*" *Philological Quarterly,* 24#1: 85-89 (Jan, 1945).

Rankin, Dave. "Ben Jonson: Semanticist," *Etc,* 19#3: 289-297 (Oct, 1962).

Shaaber, M. A. "The 'Uncleane Birds' in *The Alchemist,*" *Modern Language Notes,* 65#2: 106-109 (Feb, 1950).

Sission, C. J. "A Topical Reference in *The Alchemist,*" in James G. McManaway (ed), *Joseph Q. Adams Memorial Studies,* 739-741.

Stoll, E. E. *Shakespeare and Other Masters,* 104-106.

Targan, Barry. "The Dramatic Structure of *The Alchemist,*" *Discourse: A Review of Liberal Arts,* 6#4: 315-324 (Aut, 1963).

Thayer, C. G. "Theme and Structure in *The Alchemist*," *ELH*, 26#1: 23-35 (March, 1959).

Wells, Henry W. *Elizabethan and Jacobean Playwrights*, 200-203.

BARTHOLOMEW FAIR

Bacon, Wallace A. "The Magnetic Field: The Structure of Jonson's Comedies," *Huntington Library Quarterly*, 19#2: 145-148 (Feb, 1956).

Barish, Jonas A. "*Bartholomew Fair* and its Puppets," *Modern Language Quarterly*, 20: 3-17 (March, 1959).

Enright, D. J. "Crime and Punishment in Ben Jonson," *Scrutiny*, 9#3: 231-234 (Dec, 1940).

Hays, H. R. "Satire and Identification: An Introduction to Ben Jonson," *Kenyon Review*, 19#2: 276-283 (Spring, 1957).

Heffner, Ray L. "Unifying Symbols in the Comedy of Ben Jonson," *English Institute Essays*, pp. 89-97 (1954).

Kronenberger, Louis. *The Thread of Laughter*, 30-34.

Olive, W. J. "A Chaucer Allusion in Johnson's *Bartholomew Fair*," *Modern Language Quarterly*, 13: 21-22 (1952).

Robinson, James E. "*Bartholomew Fair*: Comedy of Vapors," *Studies in English Literature 1500-1900*, 1#2: 65-80 (Spring, 1961).

Sackton, Alexander H. "The Paradoxical Encomium in Elizabethan Drama," *Studies in English*, 28: 100-101 (1949).

Symons, Julian. "Ben Jonson as Social Realist: *Bartholomew Fair*," *Southern Review* (Louisiana), 6#2: 375-386 (Aut, 1940).

Waith, Eugene M. "A Misrprint in *Bartholomew Fair*," *Notes and Queries*, 208#3: 103-104 (March, 1963).

——————. "The Staging of *Bartholomew Fair*," *Studies in English Literature 1500-1900*, 2#2: 181-196 (Spring, 1962).

Wells, Henry W. *Elizabethan and Jacobean Playwrights*, 204-206.

CASE IS ALTERED, THE

Enck, John J. "*The Case is Altered*: Initial Comedy of Humours," *Studies in Philology*, 50#2: 195-214 (Apr, 1953).

Nosworthy, J. M. "*The Case is Altered*," *Journal of English and Germanic Philology*, 51#1: 61-70 (Jan, 1952).

Schrickx, W. "Onion, A Sobriquet Relevant to Thomas

Nashe?" *Revue des Langues Vivantes,* 27: 322-324
(1961).

CATALINE

Bryant, Joseph A. *"Cataline* and the Nature of Jonson's Tragic
Fable," *PMLA,* 69#1: 265-277 (Mar, 1954).

Burton, K. M. "The Political Tragedies of Chapman and
Jonson,' *Essays in Criticism,* 2#4: 401-404; 411-412 (Oct,
1952).

Duffy, Ellen M. "Ben Jonson's Debt to Renaissance Scholarship in *Sejanus* and *Cataline," Modern Language Review,*
42#1: 24-30 (Jan, 1947).

Eliot, T. S. *Essays on Elizabethan Drama,* 68-73.

Enright, D. J. "Crime and Punishment in Ben Jonson," *Scrutiny,* 9#3: 244-248 (Dec, 1940).

Hill, Geoffrey. "The World's Proportion: Jonson's Dramatic
Poetry in *Sejanus and Cataline," Stratford-Upon-Avon
Studies,* 1: 113-132 (1960).

Kirschbaum, Leo. "Jonson, Seneca, and Mortimer," in A.
Dayle Wallace (ed), *Studies in Honor of John Wilcox,*
16-18.

Nash, Ralph. "Ben Jonson's Tragic Poems," *Studies in Philology,* 55: 164-186 (April, 1958).

Ornstein, Robert. *The Moral Vision of Jacobean Tragedy,*
97-103.

Ransome, J. C. *The New Critics,* 160-163.

Sackton, Alexander H. "The Rhymed Couplet in Ben Jonson's
Plays," *Studies in English,* 30: 101-103 (1951).

Schlosser, Anselm. "Ben Jonson's Roman Plays," *Kwartalnik
Neofilologiczny,* 8#2: 144-159 (1961).

Villiers, J. I. de. "Ben Jonson's Tragedies," *English Studies,*
45#6: 440-442 (Dec, 1964).

Wells, Henry W. *Elizabethan and Jacobean Playwrights,* 53-
57.

Williams, Weldon M. "The Influence of Ben Jonson's *Cataline* upon John Oldham's *Satyrs Upon the Jesuits," ELH,*
11#1: 38-62 (March, 1944).

CHLORIDA

Graziani, R. I. C. "Ben Jonson's *Chlorida:* Fame and Her At-
tendants," *The Review of English Studies,* N. S. 7#25:
56-58 (Jan, 1956).

CYNTHIA'S REVELS

Bacon, Wallace A. "The Magnetic Field: The Structure of

Jonson's Comedies," *Huntington Library Quarterly*, 19#2: 132-133 (Feb, 1956).

Berringer, Ralph. "Johnson's *Cynthia's Revels* and the War of the Theatre," *Philological Quarterly*, 22#1: 1-22 (Jan, 1943).

Boyce, B. *Theophrastan Character in England to 1642*, 102-107.

Gilbert, Allan H. "The Function of the Masques in *Cynthia's Revels*," *Philological Quarterly*, 22#3: 211-230 (July, 1943).

Harrison, George. *Elizabethan Plays and Players*, 233-236.

Kallich, Martin. "Unity of Time in *Every Man in His Humour* and *Cynthia's Revels*," *Modern Language Notes*, 57#6: 447-449 (June, 1942).

McEuen, Kathryn A. "Jonson and Juvenal," *Review of English Studies*, 21#82: 102-104 (April, 1945).

McPeek, James A. S. "The Thief 'Deformed' and Much Ado About 'Noting,' " *Boston University Studies in English*, 4#2: 77-84 (Summer, 1960).

Potts, Abbie Findlay. *"Cynthia's Revels, Poetaster* and *Troilus and Cressida,"* *Shakespeare Quarterly*, 5#3: 297-299 (Summer, 1954).

Sackton, Alexander H. "The Paradoxical Encomium in Elizabethan Drama," *Studies in English*, 28: 95-96 (1949).

Savage, James E. "Ben Jonson in Ben Jonson's Plays," *University of Mississippi Studies in English*, 3#1: 8-13; 16-17 (1962).

Talbot, Ernest W. "The Classical Mythology and the Structure of *Cynthia's Revels,"* *Philological Quarterly*, 22#3: 193-210 (July, 1943).

DEVIL IS AN ASS, THE
Gagen, Jean E. *The New Woman*, 102-104.

EASTWARD HOE
See: George Chapman

EPICENE (or EPICOENE)
See: *The Silent Wowan*

EVERY MAN IN HIS HUMOUR
Bryant, J. A., Jr. "Jonson's Revision of *Every Man in His Humour*," *Studies in Philology*, 59#4: 641-650 (Oct, 1962).

Harrison, George. *Elizabethan Plays and Players*, 184-188.

Johnson, Francis R. "Did Shakespeare, Actor, Improvise in

Every Man in His Humour," in James G. McManaway (ed), *Joseph Q. Adams Memorial Studies,* 21-32.

Kallich, Martin. "Unity of Time in *Every Man in His Humour* and *Cynthia's Revels,"* *Modern Language Notes,* 57#6: 445-446 (June, 1942).

McEuen, Kathryn A. "Jonson and Juvenal," *Review of English Studies,* 21#82: 93-94 (April, 1945).

Marx, Milton. *The Enjoyment of Drama,* 147-149.

Maxwell, J. C. "Comic Mispunctuation in *Every Man in His Humour,"* *English Studies,* 33#5: 218-219 (Oct, 1952).

Rankin, Dave. "Ben Jonson: Semanticist," *Etc.,* 19#3: 289-297 (Oct, 1962).

Sackton, Alexander H. "The Rhymed Couplet in Ben Jonson's Plays," *Studies in English,* 30: 89-90 (1951).

Savage, James E. "Ben Jonson in Ben Jonson's Plays," *University of Mississippi Studies in English,* 3#1: 1-5; 16-17 (1962.)

Snuggs, Henry L. "The Comic Humours: A New Interpretation," *PMLA,* 62#1: 114-122 (March, 1947).

Stoll, E. E. *Shakespeare and Other Masters,* 98-104.

EVERY MAN OUT OF HIS HUMOUR

Bacon, Wallace A. "The Magnetic Field: The Structure of Jonson's Comedies," *Huntington Library Quarterly,* 19#2: 129-132 (Feb, 1956).

Boyce, B. *Theophrastan Character in England to 1642,* 99-101.

Eliot, Samuel A. Jr. "The Lord Chamberlain's Company as Portrayed in *Every Man Out of His Humor,"* *Smith College Studies in Modern Languages,* 21#1-4: 64-80 (Oct, 1939-July, 1940).

Gilbert, Allan H. "The Italian Names in *Every Man Out of His Humour,"* *Studies in Philology,* 44#2: 195-208 (April, 1947).

Harrison, George. *Elizabethan Plays and Players,* 198-201.

McEuen, Kathryn A. "Jonson and Juvenal," *Review of English Studies,* 21#82: 94-99 (April, 1945).

Main, W. W. " 'Insula Fortunata' in Jonson's *Every Man Out of His Humour,"* *Notes and Queries,* 199: 197-198 (May, 1954).

Sackton, Alexander H. "The Paradoxical Encomium in Elizabethan Drama," *Studies in English,* 28: 96-97 (1949).

Savage, James E. "Ben Jonson in Ben Jonson's Plays," *Uni-*

versity of Mississippi Studies in English, 3#1: 5-8; 16-17
(1962).

Snuggs, Henry L. The Comic Humours, 114-119.

—————————. "The Comic Humours: A New Interpretation," PMLA, 62#1: 114-122 (March, 1947).

Talbert, Ernest W. Elizabethan Drama and Shakespeare's
Early Plays, 55-57.

Wells, Henry W. Elizabethan and Jacobean Playwrights, 196-
198.

GYPSIES METAMORPHOSED, THE

Taylor, Dick Jr. "Claredon and Ben Jonson as Witnesses for
the Earl of Pembroke's Character," in Studies in the English Renaissance in Memory of Karl J. Holzknecht, 326-
331.

HADDINGTON MASQUE

Gordon, D. J. "Ben Jonson's Haddington Masque: The Story
and the Fable," Modern Language Review, 42#2: 180-187
(April, 1947).

HYMENAEI

Gordon, D. J. "Hymenaei: Ben Jonson's Masque of Union,"
Journal of the Warburg and Courtauld Institutes, 8: 107-
145 (1945).

MASQUE OF AUGURS

Talbert, Ernest W. "Current Scholarly Work and the 'Erudi-
tion' of Jonson's Masque of Augurs," Studies in Philology, 44#4: 605-624 (Oct, 1947).

MASQUE OF BEAUTIE, THE

Gordon, D. J. "The Imagery of Ben Jonson's The Masque of
Blacknesse and The Masque of Beautie," Journal of the
Warburg and Courtauld Institutes, 6: 122-141 (1943).

MASQUE OF BLACKNESSE, THE

Gordon, D. J. "The Imagery of Ben Jonson's The Masque of
Blacknesse and The Masque of Beautie," Journal of the
Warburg and Courtauld Institutes, 6: 122-141 (1943).

MASQUE OF QUEENES

Furness, W. Todd. "The Annotation of Ben Jonson's Masqque
of Queenes," Review of English Studies, N.S. 5#20: 344-
360 (Oct, 1954).

MORTIMER HIS FALL

Kirschbaum, Leo. "Jonson, Seneca, and *Mortimer*," in A. Dayle Wallace (ed), *Studies in Honor of John Wilcox*, 9-13; 18-21.

NEW INNE, THE

Champion, L. S. "The Comic Intent of Jonson's *The New Inn*," *Western Humanities Review*, 18#1: 66-74 (Winter, 1964).

Moore, Rayburn S. "Some Notes on the 'Courtly Love' System in Jonson's *The New Inn*," *Vanderbilt Studies in Humanities*, 2: 133-142 (1954).

Partridge, E. B. "A Crux in Jonson's The *New Inne*," *Modern Language Notes*, 71#3: 168-169 (March, 1956).

—————————. "The Symbolism of Clothes in Jonson's Last Plays," *Journal of English and Germanic Philology*, 56#3: 401-406 (July, 1957).

MERCURY VINDICATED

Duncan, Edgar Hill. "The Alchemy of Jonson's *Mercury Vindicated*," *Studies in Philology*, 39#4: 625-637 (Oct, 1942).

POETASTER

Bacon, Wallace A. "The Magnetic Field: The Structure of Jonson's Comedies," *Huntington Library Quarterly*, 19#2: 133-134 (Feb, 1956).

Gray, Henry D. *"The Chamberlain's Men* and *The Poetaster*," *Modern Language Review*, 42#2: 173-179 (April, 1947).

Harrison, George. *Elizabethan Plays and Players*, 261-271.

McEven, Kathryn A. "Jonson and Juvenal," *Review of English Studies*, 21#82: 99-102 (April, 1945).

Nash, Ralph. "The Parting Scene in Jonson's *Poetaster*, (IV, ix)" *Philological Quarterly*, 31#1: 54-62 (Jan, 1952).

Potts, Abbie Findlay. *"Cynthia's Revels, Poetaster* and *Troilus and Cressida*," *Shakespeare Quarterly*, 5#3: 300-302 (Summer, 1954).

Sackton, Alexander H. "The Rhymed Couplet in Ben Jonson's Plays," *Studies in English*, 30: 91-94 (1951).

Savage, James E. "Ben Jonson in Ben Jonson's Plays," *University of Mississippi Studies in English*, 3#1: 11-17 (1962).

Talbert, William E. "The Purpose and Technique of Jonson's *Poetaster*," *Studies in Philology*, 42#2: 225-252 (April, 1945).

Wait, Eugene M. "The Poet's Morals in Jonson's Poetaster,"
  Modern Language Quarterly, 12: 13-19 (1951).
SAD SHEPHERD, THE
  Harrison, T. P. "Jonson's *The Sad Shepherd* and Spenser,"
    Modern Language Notes, 58#4: 257-262 (April, 1943).

SEJANUS
  Boughner, Daniel C. "Sejanus and Machiavelli," *Studies in
    English Literature 1500-1900,* 1#2: 81-100 (Spring,
    1961).
  —————————. "Jonson's Use of Lipsius in *Sejanus,*" *Mod-
    ern Language Notes,* 73#4: 247-255 (April, 1958).
  —————————. "Juvenal, Horace and *Sejanus,*" *Modern
    Language Notes,* 75#7: 545-550 (Nov, 1960).
  Bryant, Joseph Allen Jr. "The Nature of the Conflict in Jon-
    son's *Sejanus,*" *Vanderbilt Studies in Humanities,* 1: 197-
    219 (1951).
  Burton, K. M. "The Political Tragedies of Chapman and Jon-
    son," *Essays in Criticism,* 2#4: 401-404; 409-411 (Oct,
    1952).
  Duffy, Ellen M. T. "Ben Jonson's Debt to Renaissance Schol-
    arship in *Sejanus* and *Cataline,*" *Modern Language Re-
    view,* 42#1: 24-30 (Jan, 1947).
  Enright, D. J. "Crime and Punishment in Ben Jonson," *Scrut-
    iny,* 9#3: 239-244 (Dec, 1940).
  Gilbert, Allan. "The Eavesdroppers in Jonson's *Sejanus,*"
    Modern Language Notes, 69#3: 164-166 (March, 1954).
  Hill, Geoffrey. "The World's Proportion: Jonson's Dramatic
    Poetry in *Sejanus* and *Cataline,*" *Stratford-Upon-Avon-
    Studies,* 1: 113-132 (1960).
  Honig, Edwin. "*Sejanus* and *Coriolanus:* A Study in Aliena-
    tion," *Modern Language Quarterly,* 12: 408-421 (1951).
  Kirschbaum, Leo. "Jonson, Seneca, and *Mortimer,*" in A.
    Dayle Wallace (ed), *Studies in Honor of John Wilcox,*
    14-16.
  Nash, Ralph. "Ben Jonson's Tragic Poems," *Studies in Phil-
    ology,* 55: 164-186 (April, 1958).
  Ornstein, Robert. *The Moral Vision of Jacobean Tragedy,*
    86-97.
  Prior, Moody E. *The Language of Tragedy,* 113-119.
  Ricks, Christopher, "*Sejanus* and Dismemberment," *Modern
    Language Notes,* 76#4: 301-308 (April, 1961).
  Sackton, Alexander H. "The Rhymed Couplet in Ben Jon-
    son's Plays," *Studies in English,* 30: 94-100 (1951).

Schlosser, Anselm. "Ben Jonson's Roman Plays," *Kwartalnik Neofilologiczny,* 8#2: 125-144 (1961).

Villiers, J. I. de. "Ben Jonson's Tragedies," *English Studies,* 45#6: 433-440 (Dec, 1964).

Wells, H. *Elizabethan and Jacobean Playwrights,* 53-57.

SILENT WOMAN, THE

Bacon, Wallace A. "The Magnetic Field: The Structure of Jonson's Comedies," *Huntington Library Quarterly,* 19#2: 139-142 (Feb, 1956).

Barish, Jonas A. "Ovid, Juvenal and *The Silent Woman,*" *PMLA,* 71#1: 213-224 (March, 1956).

Bradbrook, M. C. "Dramatic Role as Social Image: A Study of the *Taming of the Shrew,*" *Shakespeare Jahrbuck,* 94: 148-150 (1958).

Dryden, John. "Essays on Dramatic Poesy," in H. H. Adams & Baxter Hathaway (eds), *Dramatic Essays of the Neoclassic Age,* 83-88.

Heffner, Ray L. "Unifying Symbols in the Comedy of Ben Jonson," *English Institute Essays,* pp. 74-89 (1954).

Hogan, Robert G. *Drama,* 211-212; 261-271.

Kronenberger, Louis. *The Thread of Laughter,* 34-38.

Partridge, Edward B. "The Allusiveness of *Epicoene,*" *ELH,* 22#2: 93-107 (June, 1955).

STAPLE OF NEWES, THE

Parr, Johnstone. "A Note on Jonson's *The Staple of News,*" *Modern Language Notes,* 60#2: 117 (Feb, 1945).

Partridge, Edward B. "The Symbolism of Clothes in Jonson's Last Plays," *Journal of English and Germanic Philology,* 56#3: 396-400 (July, 1957).

TALE OF A TUB, A

Bryant, J. A. Jr. "*A Tale of a Tub:* Jonson's Comedy of the Human Condition," *Renaissance Papers,* pp. 95-105 (1963).

Sackton, Alexander H. "The Rhymed Couplet in Ben Jonson's Plays," *Studies in English,* 30: 88-89 (1951).

VOLPONE

Bacon, Wallace A. "The Magnetic Field: The Structure of Jonson's Comedies," *Huntington Library Quarterly,* 19#2: 134-139 (Feb, 1956).

Barish, Jones A. "The Double Plot in *Volpone,*" *Modern Philology,* 51: 83-92 (1953).

Cope, Jackson I. *"Volpone* and the Authorship of *Eastward Ho,"* *Modern Language Notes,* 72#4: 253-256 (April, 1957).

✗Davison, P. H. *"Volpone* and the Old Comedy," *Modern Language Quarterly,* 24: 151-157 (1963).

✗Dessen, A. C. *"Volpone* and the Late Morality Tradition," *Modern Language Quarterly,* 25: 383-399 (Dec, 1964).

✗ Enright, Dennis J. *The Apothecary's Shop,* 54-64.

————————. "Crime and Punishment in Ben Jonson," *Scrutiny,,* 9#3: 235-239 (Dec, 1940).

————————. "Poetic Satire·and Satire in Verse: A Consideration of Jonson and Massinger," *Scrutiny,* 18#4: 211-217 (Winter, 1952).

✗Goldberg, S. L. "Folly Into Crime: The Catastrophe of *Volpone,"* *Modern Language Quarterly,* 20: 233-242 (Sept, 1959).

Hays, H. R. "Satire and Identification: An Introduction to Ben Jonson," *Kenyon Review,* 19#2: 267-272, (Spring, 1957).

Hoy, Cyrus H. *The Hyacinth Room,* 127-141; 172-174.

Kronenberger, Louis. *The Thread of Laughter,* 24-30.

MacCarthy, Desmond. *Humanities,* 54-59.

Musgrove, S. "Shakespeare and Jonson," *University of Aukland English Series,* 9: 21-39 (1957).

Nash, Ralph. "The Comic Intent of *Volpone,"* *Studies in Phililogy,* 44#1: 26-40 (Jan, 1947).

Newton, Gloria E. "Dramatic Imagery in *Volpone,"* *The Manitoba Arts Review,* 8#1: 9-17 (Winter, 1952).

Ornstein, Robert. *The Moral Vision of Jacobean Tragedy,* 112-113; 124-125.

Pineas, Rainer. "The Morality of Vice in *Volpone,"* *Discourse: A Review of Liberal Arts,* 5#4: 451-459 (Autumn, 1962).

————————. *"Volpone* and Renaissance Psychology," *Notes and Queries,* 201#11: 471-472 (Nov, 1956).

Perkinson, Richard H. *"Volpone* and the Reputation of Venetian Justice," *Modern Language Review,* 35#1: 11-18 (Jan, 1940).

Praz, Mario. *The Flaming Heart,* 170-185.

Putney, Rufus. "Jonson's Poetic Comedy," *Philological Quar terly,* 41#1: 188-204 (Jan, 1962).

Ransome, J. C. *The New Critics,* 165-169.

Sackton, Alexander H. "The Paradoxical Encomium in Elizabethan Drama," *Studies in English,* 28: 97-100 (1949).

Scheve, D. A. "Jonson's *Volpone* and Traditional Fox Lore," *Review of English Studies,* N.S. 1#3: 242-244 (July, 1950).

South, Malcolm H. "Animal Imagery in Volpone," *Tennessee Studies in Literature,* 10: 141-150 (1965).

— Sternfeld, Frederick W. "Song in Jonson's Comedy: A Gloss on *Volpone,*" in *Studies in the English Renaissance Drama in Memory of Karl J. Holzknecht,* 310-321.

Stoll, E. E. *Shakespeare and Other Masters,* 106-110.

Talbert, Ernest W. *Elizagethan Drama and Shakespeare's Early Plays,* 46-47.

Weld, John S. "Christian Comedy: *Volpone,*" *Studies in Philology,* 51#2: 172-193 (April, 1954).

Wells, Henry W. *Elizabethan and Jacobean Playwrights,* 198-200.

JOYCE, JAMES

EXILES

Aitken, D. J. F. "Dramatic Archetypes in Joyce's *Exiles*" *Modern Fiction Studies,* 4#1: 42-52 (Spring, 1958).

Douglas, James W. "James Joyce's *Exiles:* A Portrait of the Artist," *Renascence,* 15#2: 82-87 (Winter, 1963).

Fergusson, Francis. *The Human Image in Dramatic Literature,* 72-84.

Iyengar, S. *The Adventure of Criticism,* 539-541.

Joyce, Stanislaus. "James Joyce: A Memoir," *Hudson Review,* 2#4: 510-511 (Winter, 1950).

Kenner, Hugh. "Joyce's *Exiles,*" *Hudson Review,* 5#3: 389-403 (Autumn, 1952).

MacCarthy, Desmond. *Humanities,* 88-93.

Moseley, Virginia Douglas. "Joyce's *Exiles* and the Prodigal Son," *Modern Drama,* 1#4: 218-227 (Feb, 1959).

Tysdahl, Bjorn. "Joyce's *Exiles* and Ibsen," *Orbis Litterarum,* 19#4: 177-186 (1964).

von Weber, Roland. "On and About Joyce's *Exiles,*" *A James Joyce Yearbook,* pp. 47-67 (1949).

Williams, Raymond. "The *Exiles* of James Joyce," *Politics and Letters,* 1#4: 13-21 (Summer, 1948).

Worsley, T. C. *The Fugitive Art,* 140-143.

KAHN, ARTHUR LEE

BABY OF THE FAMILY

Nolan, Paul T. "A Southern Playwright: Arthur Lee Kahn,"

    Southern Speech Journal, 27#3: 208-209 (Spring, 1962).

BURGLARY A LA MODE
    Nolan, Paul T. "A Southern Playwright: Arthur Lee Kahn,"
    Southern Speech Journal, 27#3: 209-212 (Spring, 1962).

FOX, THE
    Nolan, Paul T. "A Southern Playwright: Arthur Lee Kahn,"
    Southern Speech Journal, 27#3: 207-208 (Spring, 1962).

LAST OF THE HARGROVES, THE
    Nolan, Paul T. "A Southern Playwright: Arthur Lee Kahn,"
    Southern Speech Journal, 27#3: 209-211 (Spring, 1962).

PUTTING IT OVER
    Nolan, Paul T. "A Southern Playwright: Arthur Lee Kahn,"
    Southern Speech Journal, 27#3: 208 (Spring, 1962).

WE-UNS OF TENNESSEE
    Nolan, Paul T. "A Southern Playwright: Arthur Lee Kahn,"
    Southern Speech Journal, 27#3: 206-207 (Spring, 1962).

KAUFMAN, GEORGE S.
- - - AND EDNA FERBER

DINNER AT EIGHT
    Egri, Lajos. *The Art of Dramatic Writing,* 291-292.
    MacCarthy, Desmond. *Humanities,* 113-117.

- - - AND MOSS HART

MERRILY WE ROLL ALONG
    Lawson, John H. *Theory and Technique of Playwriting,* 257-
    260.

- - - AND M. RYSKIND

OF THEE I SING
    Jackson, Stoney. *This Is Love?,* 47-52.

- - - AND MOSS HART

YOU CAN'T TAKE IT WITH YOU
    Kaplan, Charles. "Two Depression Plays and Broadway's Pop-
    ular Idealism," *American Quarterly,* 15#4: 579-585
    (Winter, 1963).
    Sievers, W. D. *Freud on Broadway,* 289-291.

KELLY, GEORGE EDWARD

CRAIG'S WIFE
Dusenbury, Winifred L. *The Theme of Lonliness in Modern American Drama,* 164-171.

TORCH-BEARERS, THE
Young, Stark. *Immortal Shadows,* 5-7.

KELLY, HUGH

FALSE DELICACY
Boas, F. S. *An Introduction to Eighteenth Century Drama,* 292-295.
Rawson, C. J. "Some Remarks on Eighteenth Century 'Delicacy,' With a Note on Hugh Kelly's *False Delicacy* (1768)" *Journal of English and Germanic Philology,* 61#1: 1-13 (Jan, 1962).

WORD FOR THE WISE, A
Boas, F. S. *An Introduction to Eighteenth Century Drama,* 295-299.

KILLIGREW, HENRY

CONSPIRACY, THE
See: *Pallantas and Eudora*

PALLANTAS AND EUDORA
Bowers, Fredson T. *Elizabethan Revenge Tragedy,* 218-219.

KILLIGREW, THOMAS

THE PARSON'S WEDDING
Gagen, Jean E. *The New Woman,* 104-106.

KINGSLEY, SIDNEY

DETECTIVE STORY
Taylor, N. H. "Theatre," *Frontier,* 2: 20-21 (Aug., 1951).

MEN IN WHITE
Dusenbury, Winifred L. *The Theme of Loneliness in Modern American Drama,* 185-190.

PATRIOTS, THE
Shirk, S. *Characterization of George Washington in American Drama Since 1875,* 77-81.

WORLD WE MAKE, THE
Sievers, W. D. *Freud on Broadway,* 300-301.

KOPIT, ARTHUR

OH DAD, POOR DAD, MAMMA'S HUNG YOU IN THE
CLOSET AND I'M FEELING SO BAD
Mottram, Eric. "The New American Wave," *Encore,* 11#1:
30-32 (Jan-Feb, 1964).
Wellwarth, George E. "Hope Deferred—The New American
Drama," *The Literary Review, 7#1:* 21-23 (Autumn,
1963).

KOPS, BERNARD

THE HAMLET OF STEPNEY GREEN
Taylor, John R. *Anger and After,* 123-125.

KYD, THOMAS

SPANISH TRAGEDY, THE
Bowers, Fredson T. *Elizabethan Revenge Tragedy,* 66-85; 95-
100.
Cannon, Charles K. "The Relation of the Additions of *The
Spanish Tragedy* to the Original Play," *Studies in Eng-
lish Literature 1500-1900, 2#2:* 229-240 (Spring, 1962).
Chickera, Ernest de. "Divine Justice and Private Revenge
in *The Spanish Tragedy," Modern Language Review,*
57#2: 228-232 (April, 1962).
Clemen, Wolfgang. *English Tragedy Before Shakespeare,*
100-112; 267-277.
Empson, William. *"The Spanish Tragedy," Nimbus, 3#3:*
16-29 (Summer, 1956).
Harrison, George. *Elizabethan Plays and Players,* 64-68.
Johnson, S. F. *"The Spanish Tragedy,"* in Richard Hosley
(ed), *Essays on Shakespeare and Elizabethan Drama in
Honor of Hardin Craig,* 23-38.
Johnston, R. C. "Divine Justice and Private Revenge in *The
Spanish Tragedy," Modern Language Review, 57#2:* 228-
235 (April, 1962).
Levin, Harry. "An Echo From *The Spanish Tragedy," Mod-
ern Language Notes,* 64#5: 297-302 (May, 1949).
Levin, Michael Henry. 'Vindicta mihi!': Meaning, Morality,
and Motivation in *The Spanish Tragedy," Studies in Eng-
lish Literature 1500-1900,* 4#2: 307-324 (Spring, 1964).

Prior, Moody E. *The Language of Tragedy,* 46-58.

Simpson, Percy. *Studies in Elizabethan Drama,* 145-150.

Stoll, E. E. *"Hamlet* and *The Spanish Tragedy,"* *Modern Philology,* 37#2: 173-186 (Nov, 1939).

Talbert, Ernest W. *Elizabethan Drama and Shakespeare's Early Plays,* 62-64; 72-79; 138-140.

Wells, Henry W. *Elizabethan and Jacobean Playwrights,* 21-24.

Wiatt, William H. "The Dramatic Function of the Alexandre-Villuppo Episode in *The Spanish Tragedy," Notes and Queries,* 203: 327-329 (August, 1958).

UR-HAMLET, THE

Bowers, Fredson T. *Elizabethan Revenge Tragedy,* 85-98.

Cleeve, B. T. "The Lost *Hamlet," Studies,* 46: 447-456 (Winter, 1957).

LACY, ERNEST

RINALDO, THE DOCTOR OF FLORENCE

Feldman, Abraham. "Earnest Lacy: Forgotton Immortal," *Poet Lore,* 47#1: 87-88; 90-91 (Spring, 1941).

LACY, JOHN

THE DUMB LADY

Wilcox, John. *The Relation of Moliere to Restoration Comedy,* 48-53.

LARSON, CLINTON F.

THE MANTLE OF THE PROPHET

Woodbury, Lael J. "Director's Foreward to *The Mantle of the Prophet," Brigham Young University Studies,* 2#2: 189-192 (Spring-Summer, 1960).

LAURENT, ARTHUR

CLEARING IN THE WOODS, A

Cerf, Walter. "Psychoanalysis and the Realistic Drama," *Journal of Aesthetics and Art Criticism,* 16#3: 330-336 (March, 1958).

HOME OF THE BRAVE

Sievers, W. D. *Freud on Broadway,* 347-349.

TIME OF THE CUCKOO, THE
Sievers, W. D. *Freud on Broadway*, 351-352.

LAWLER, RAY

THE SUMMER OF THE SEVENTEENTH DOLL
Cherry, Wal. *"Summer of the Seventeenth Doll," Meanjin
Papers*, 15#1: 82-84 (Autumn, 1956).
Davison, P. H. "Three Australian Plays: National Myths
Under Criticism," *Southerly*, 23#2: 110-118 (1963).
Grant, Bruce. "English Critics and *The Doll*," *Meanjin Quar-
terly*, No. 70 (16#3): 295-298 (Spring, 1957).
Macartney, Keith. *"The Shifting Heart," Meanjin Papers*,
17#2: 188-190 (Winter, 1958).

LAWRENCE, DAVID H.

DAVID
Panichas, George A. "D. H. Lawrence's Biblical Play *David*,"
Modern Drama, 6#2: 164-176 (Sept., 1963).

LAWSON, JOHN HOWARD

MARCHING SONG
Rabkin, Gerald. *Drama and Commitment*, 157-160.

PROCESSIONAL
Rabkin, Gerald. *Drama and Commitment*, 134-137.

ROGER BLOOMER
Fulton, A. R. *Drama and Theatre*, 200-209.
Rabkin, Gerald. *Drama and Commitment*, 130-134.
Sievers, W. D. *Freud on Broadway*, 140-142.

SUCCESS STORY
Rabkin, Gerald. *Drama and Commitment*, 143-146.

LEACOCK, JOHN

THE FALL OF BRITISH TYRANNY; OR AMERICAN
LIBERTY TRIUMPHANT
Glenn, Stanley. "The Development of the Negro Character
in American Comedy Before the Civil War., *Southern
Speech Journal*, 26#2: 135-137 (Winter, 1960).

LEE, NATHANIEL

CONSTANTINE THE GREAT

Cooke, A. L. and Thomas B. Stroup. "The Political Implications in Lee's *Constantine the Great*," *Journal of English and Germanic Philology,* 49#4: 560-515 (Oct., 1950).

GLORIANA

Barbour, Francis. "The Unconventional Heroic Plays of Nathaniel Lee," *Studies in English (University of Texas),* 4026: 109-116 (July 8, 1940).

MITHRADATES

Barbour, Francis. "The Unconventional Heroic Plays of Nathaniel Lee," *Studies in English (University of Texas),* 4026: 109-116 (July 8, 1940).

NERO

Barbour, Francis. "The Unconventional Heroic Plays of Nathaniel Lee," *Studies in English (University of Texas),* 4026: 109-116 (July 8, 1940).

RIVAL QUEENS, THE; OR THE DEATH OF ALEXANDER THE GREAT

Bailey, Robert. *Sunk Without a Trace,* 40-75.

Barbour, Francis. "The Unconventional Heroic Plays of Nathaniel Lee," *Studies in English (University of Texas),* 4026: 109-116 (July 8, 1940).

SOPHONISBA

Barbour, Francis. "The Unconventional Heroic Plays of Nathaniel Lee," *Studies in English (University of Texas),* 4026: 109-116 (July 8, 1940).

LEGGE, THOMAS

RICHARDUS TERTIUS

Lordi, Robert S. "The Relationship of *Richard Tertius* to the Main Richard III Plays," *Boston University Studies in English,* 5#3: 139-153 (Autumn, 1961).

McDonnell, R. F. *The Aspiring Mind,* 90-94.

Ribner, Irving. *The English History Play in the Age of Shakespeare,* 68-70.

LEVY, BENN W.

RETURN TO TYASSI

Hobson, Harold. *The Theatre Now,* 49-52.

Worsley, T. C. *The Fugitive Art,* 180-182.

LEWES, GEORGE HENRY

CAPTAIN BLAND

Hirshberg, Edgar W. "Captain Bland on the New York Stage." *Bulletin of the New York Public Library,* 57#8: 382-388 (August, 1953).

LEWIS, M. G.

THE TWINS

Guthke, Karl S. "M. G. Lewis's *The Twins,*" *Huntington Library Quarterly,* 25#3: 189-194 (May, 1962).

LILLO, GEORGE

ARDEN OF FAVERSHAM
See: Anon

CHRISTIAN HERO, THE

Boas, F. S. *An Introduction to Eighteenth Century Drama,* 244-248.

ELMERICK, THE

Boas, F. S. *An Introduction to Eighteenth Century Drama,* 251-254.

FATAL CURIOSITY, THE

Boas, F. S. *An Introduction to Eighteenth Century Drama,* 248-251.

Virtanen, Reino. "Camus Malentendu," *Comparative Literature (Oregon),* 10#3: 232-240 (Summer, 1958).

LONDON MERCHANT, THE

Adams, Henry H. and Baxter Hathaway (eds). *Dramatic Essays of the Neoclassic Age,* 270-273.

Boas, F. S. *An Introduction to Eighteenth Century Drama,* 239-244.

Brooks, Cleanth and Robert Heilman. *Understanding Drama,* 180-189.

Daunicht, R. "The First German Translation of George Lillo's *Merchant of London* and the First Performances of the Play in Germany," *Symposium,* 9#2: 324-330 (Fall, 1955).

Havens, Raymond D. "The Sentimentalism of *The London Merchant,*" *ELH,* 12#3: 183-187 (Sept, 1945).

Loftis, John. "The Eighteenth Century Beginnings of Modern

Drama," *Emory University Quarterly,* 7#4: 230-234 (Dec, 1951).

Rodman, George B. "Sentimentalism in Lillo's *The London Merchant,*" *ELH,* 12#1: 45-61 (March, 1945).

LINDSAY, SIR DAVID

THE SATIRE OF THE THREE ESTATES
Kinsley, James. "Lindsay's *Satyre* and the Modern Theatre," *Saltire Review,* 4#12: 37-40 (Autumn, 1957).

Miller, E. S. "The Christening in *Satire of the Three Estates,*" *Modern Language Notes,* 60#1: 42-45 (Jan, 1945).

LODGE, GEORGE CABOT

CAIN
Riggs, Thomas Jr. "Prometheus 1900," *American Literature,* 22: 417-418; 421-422 (Jan, 1951).

HERAKLES
Riggs, Thomas Jr. "Prometheus 1900," *American Literature,* 22: 417-423 (Jan, 1951).

WOUNDS OF CIVIL WAR, THE
Clemen, Wolfgang. *English Tragedy Before Shakespeare,* 134-140.

McDonnell, R. F. *The Aspiring Mind,* 144-148.

LOVELL, GEORGE W.

THE WIFE'S SECRET
Dunkel, Wilbur D. "Ellen Kean's Appraisal of American Playgoers," *American Literature,* 22: 163-166 (May, 1950).

LUCE, CLARE BOOTHE

See: Clare Boothe

LUPTON, THOMAS

ALL FOR MONEY
Bevington, David M. *From Mankind to Marlowe,* 165-169.

LYLY, JOHN

ALEXANDER AND CAMPASPE
Price, Hereward T. "Shakespeare and His Young Contem-

poraries," *Philological Quarterly,* 41#1: 40-41 (January, 1962).

ENDYMION

Bryant, J. A. Jr. "The Nature of the Allegory in Lyly's *Endymion," Renaissance Papers,* pp. 4-11 (1956).

Gamal, Sand M. "The Function of Song in Shakespeare's Comedies," *Cairo Studies in English,* pp. 112-113 (1961-1962).

Stevenson, David Lloyd. "The Love-Game Comedy," *Columbia University Studies in English and Comparative Literature,* 164: 159-162 (1946).

LOVE'S METAMORPHOSIS

Parnell, Paul E. "Moral Allegory in Lyly's *Love's Metamorphosis," Studies in Philology,* 52#1: 1-16 (Jan, 1955).

Stevenson, David Lloyd. "The Love-Game Comedy," *Columbia University Studies in English and Comparaive Literature,* 164: 168-171 (1946).

LYTTON, EDWARD GEORGE EARLE LYTTON BULWER

THE LADY OF LYONS

Faverty, Frederic E. "The Source of the Jules-Phene Episode in *Pippa Passes," Studies in Philology,* 38#1: 97-105 (Jan, 1941).

MABLEY, EDWARD
---AND LEONARD MIMS

TEMPER THE WIND

Brown, J. Mason. *Seeing More Things,* 92-98.

MACKAYE, PERCY

WAKEFIELD

Shirk, S. *Characterization of George Washington in American Drama Since 1875,* 92-94.

WASHINGTON, THE MAN WHO MADE US

Shirk, S. *Characterization of George Washington in American Drama Since 1875,* 108-115.

MACKENZIE, HENRY
FORCE OF FASHION, THE

Quaintance, Richard E. Jr. "Henry Mackenzie's Sole Comedy,"

Huntington Library Quarterly, 25#3: 249-251 (May, 1962).

MACKLIN, CHARLES

CONVENT GARDEN THEATRE

Smith, Dane Farnsworth. "The Critics in the Audience," *University of New Mexico Publications in Language and Literature,* 12: 87-96 (1953).

MACLEISH, ARCHIBALD

FALL OF THE CITY, THE

Gurko, Leo. *The Angry Decade,* 247-250.

J B

Abel, Lionel. "Bad by North and South," *Partisan Review,* 25#3: 461-466 (Summer, 1958).

Bond, Charles M. "J. B. is not Job," *Bucknell University Studies,* 9#4: 272-280 (March, 1961).

Broussard, Louis. *American Drama,* 122-126.

Campbell, Colin C. "The Transformation of Biblical Myth: MacLeish's Use of the Adam and Job Stories," in Bernice Slote (ed), *Myth and Symbol,* 79-88.

Christensen, Parley A. *"J. B.,* the Critics, and Me," *Western Humanities Review,* 15#2: 111-126 (Spring, 1961).

Ciardi, John. "The Birth of a Classic," in Ralph E. Hone, (ed), *The Voice Out of the Whirlwird,* 276-281.
ALSO IN: *Saturday Review of Literature,* pp. 11-12; 48 (March 8, 1958).

D'Arcy, Martin C. "J. B., Wrong Answer to the Problem of Evil," *Catholic World,* 190: 81-85 (Nov., 1959).

Davis, Thurston. "Arid Repudiation of Religion," in Ralph E. Hone (ed), *The Voice Out of the Whirlwind,* 308-310.
ALSO IN: *Life Magazine,* pp. 135 & 138 (May 18, 1959).

Donoghue, Denis. *The Third Voice,* 207-212.

Driver, Tom F. "Notable, Regrettable," in Ralph E. Hone (ed), *The Voice Out of the Whirlwind,* 282-285.
ALSO IN: *The Christian Century,* pp. 21-22 (Jan. 7, 1959).

Finkelstein, Louis. "Insight Into Our Deep Need," in Ralph E. Hone (ed), *The Voice Out of the Whirlwind,* 305-307.
ALSO IN: *Life Magazine,* pp. 135, 137; 138 (May 18, 1959).

Fitch, Robert E. "The Sickness of an Affluent Society," *Religion in Life*, 29#4: 611-614 (Aut, 1960).

Gledhill, Preston R. *"JB:* Successful Theatre Versus 'Godless' Theology," *Brigham Young University Studies*, 3#2: 9-14 (Winter, 1961).

Gray, Paul. "The Theater of the Marvellous," *Tulane Drama Review*, 7#4: 146-150 (Summer, 1963).

Grebstein, Sheldon. *"J. B.* and the Problem of Evil," *University of Kansas City Review*, 29#4: 253-261 (Summer, 1963).

Hamilton, K. "The Patience of J. B.," *Dalhousie Review*, 41#1: 32-39 (Spring, 1961).

Life Magazine (The Editors). "A Fine Play Reveals a Need," in Ralph E. Hone (ed), *The Voice Out of the Whirlwind*, 298-301.
ALSO IN: *Life Magazine*, pg. 42 (May 18, 1959).

MacLeish, Andrew. "The Poet's Three Comforters: *J. B.* and the Critics," *Modern Drama*, 2#3: 224-230 (Dec, 1959).

Montgomery, Marion. "On First Looking into Archibald MacLeish's Play in Verse, *J. B." Modern Drama*, 2#3: 231-242 (Dec, 1959).

Niebuhr, Reinhold. "Modern Answers to an Enigma," in Ralph E. Hone (ed), *The Voice Out of the Whirlwind*, 302-304.
ALSO IN: *Life Magazine*, pp. 135 & 137 (May 18, 1959).

Sickels, Eleanor M. "MacLeish and the Fortunate Fall," *American Literature*, 63#2: 205-217 (May, 1963).

Stock, Ely. *"A Masque of Reason* and *J.B.:* Two Treatments of the Book of Job," *Modern Drama*, 3#4: 378-386 (Feb, 1961).

Terrien, Samuel. "J. B. and Job," in Ralph E. Hone (ed), *The Voice Out of the Whirlwind*, 286-292.
ALSO IN: *The Christian Century, pp.* 9-11 (Jan 7, 1959).

Van Dusen, Henry P. "Third Thoughts on *J.B." in Ralph E. Hone (ed), *The Voice Out of the Whirlwind*, 293-297.
ALSO IN: *The Christian Century*, pp. 106-107 (Jan 28, 1959).

MUSIC CREPT BY ME ON THE WATER, THE
Donoghue, Denis. *The Third Voice*, 195-207.

NOBODADDY
Campbell, Colin C. "The Transformation of Biblical Myth:

MacLeish's Use of the Adam and Job Stories," in Bernice
Slote (ed), *Myth and Symbol,* 79-81.
Sickels, Eleanor M. "MacLeish and the Fortunate Fall,"
American Literature, 35: 205-209 (May, 1963).

MACNEICE, LOUIS

CHRISTOPHER COLUMBUS
Malone, W. F. "Louis MacNeice as a Radio Writer" *Irish
Writing,* 17 : 54-58.

DARK TOWER, THE
Bentley, Eric. *From the Modern Repertoire, Series Two,* 500-
507.
Malone, W. F. "Louis MacNeice as a Radio Writer," *Irish
Writing,* 17 : 58-63.

MALTZ, ALBERT

THE BLACK PIT
Egri, Lajos. *The Art of Dramatic Writing,* 293-294.

MANSON, HARLEY

GREEN KNIGHT, THE
Van Heynigen, Christina. "Harley Manson—Playwright,"
Contrast, 1#4 : 73-76 (Dec, 1961).

NOOSE-KNOT BALLAD, THE
Van Heynigen, Christina. "Harley Manson — Playwright,"
Contrast, 1#4: 76-80 (Dec, 1961).
Whittock, Trevor. "The Crippled Tree : A Study of The *Noose-
Knot Ballad* by H. W. D. Manson," *Makerere Journal,*
7: 61-75 (1963).

MARLOWE, CHRISTOPHER

DIDO, QUEEN OF CARTHAGE
Allen, Don Cameron. "Marlowe's *Dido* and the Tradition," in
Richard Hosley (ed), *Essays on Shakespeare and Eliza-
bethan Drama in Honor of Hardin Craig,* 64-68.
Clemen, Wolfgang. *English Tragedy Before Shakespeare,* 161-
162.
Harrison, Thomas P. "Shakespeare and Marlowe's *Dido,
Queen of Carthage,*" *Studies in English,* 35:57-63 (1956).
Leech, Clifford. "Marlowe's Humor" in Richard Hosley (ed),
*Essays on Shakespeare and Elizabethan Drama in Honor
of Hardin Craig,* 71-75.

Pearce, T. M. "Evidence for Dating Marlowe's *Tragedy of Dido*," in *Studies in the English Renaissance Drama in Memory of Karl J. Holzknecht*, 231-247.

Powell, Jocelyn. "Marlowe's Spectacle," *Tulane Drama Review*, 8#2: 199-203 (Summer, 1964).

Ribner, Irving. "Marlowe's 'Tragicke Glassé'," in Richard Hosley (ed), *Essays on Shakespeare and Elizabethan Drama in Honor of Hardin Craig*, 96-99.

DOCTOR FAUSTUS

Barber, C. L. "The Form of Faustus' Fortunes Good or Bad," *Tulane Drama Review*, 8#4: 92-119 (Summer, 1964).

Battenhouse, Roy W. "Marlowe Reconsidered—Some Reflections on Levin's *Overreacher*," *Journal of English and Germanic Philology*, 52#4: 537-542 (Oct, 1953).

Beall, Charles N. "Definition of Theme by Unconsecutive Event: Structure as Induction in Marlowe's *Dr. Faustus*," *Renaissance Papers*, pp. 53-62 (1962).

Blau, Herbert. "Language and Structure in Poetic Drama," *Modern Language Quarterly*, 18: 29-32 (1957).

Bradbrook, Muriel C. "Marlowe's *Dr. Faustus* and the Eldritch Tradition," in Richard Hosley (ed), *Essays on Shakespeare and Elizabethan Drama in Honor of Hardin Craig*, 83-90.

Brooke, Nicholas. "The Moral Tragedy of *Dr. Faustus*," *The Cambridge Journal*, 5#11: 662-687 (Aug, 1952).

Brooks, Cleanth & Robert Heilman. *Understanding Drama*, 503; 529-542.

Cameron, Kenneth W. "Transcendental Hell in Emerson and Marlowe," *Emerson Society Quarterly*, 6: 9-10 (First Quarter, 1957).

Campbell, Lily B. *"Doctor Faustus:* A Case of Conscience," *PMLA*, 67#2: 219-239 (March, 1952).

Carpenter, Nan Cooke. "Miles' Versus 'Clericus' in Marlowe's *Faustus*," *Notes and Queries*, 197: 91-93 (March, 1952).

Clemen, Wolfgang. *English Tragedy Before Shakespeare*, 147-154.

Crabtree, John H. Jr. "The Comedy in Marlowe's *Dr. Faustus*," *Furman Studies*, N.S. 9#1: 1-9 (Nov, 1961).

Davidson, C. "Dr. Faustus of Wittenberg," *Studies in Philology*, 59#3: 514-523 (July, 1962).

Edith, Sister Mary. "The Devil in Literature," *Catholic World*, 158: 358-359 (Jan, 1944).

Ellis-Fermor, Una. *The Frontiers of Drama*, 22-24; 139-143.

Fabian, Bernhard. "Marlowe's *Dr. Faustus,*" *Notes and Queries,* 201: 56-57 (Feb, 1956).

——————. "A Note on Marlowe's *Faustus,*" *English Studies,* 41#6: 365-368 (Dec, 1960).

Faverty, Frederic E. *Your Literary Heritage,* 64-66.

Friedman, Maurice. *Problematic Rebel,* 37-41.

Frye, Roland M. "Marlowe's *Doctor Faustus:* The Repudiation of Humanity," *South Atlantic Quarterly,* 55#3: 322-328 (July, 1956).

Gardner, Helen. "Milton's 'Satan' and the Theme of Damnation in Elizabethan Tragedy," *Essays and Studies* (English Association), 1: 48-53 (1948).

Green, Clarence. *"Dr. Faustus:* Tragedy of Individualism," *Science and Society,* 10#3: 275-283 (Summer, 1946).

Greg. W. W. "The Damnation of Faustus," *Modern Language Review,* 41#2: 97-107 (April, 1946).

Grotowski, Jerzy. *"Doctor Faustus* in Poland," *Tulane Drama Review,* 8#4: 120-133 (Summer, 1964).

Hankins, John E. "Biblical Echoes in the Final Scene of *Doctor Faustus,*" *University of Kansas Publications. Humanistic Studies,* 6#4: 3-7 (1940).

Harrison, George. *Elizabethan Plays and Players,* 114-116.

Hart, Jeffrey P. "Prospero and Faustus," *Boston University Studies in English,* 2#4: 197-206 (Winter, 1956).

Hatfiield, Harry. "Can One Sell One's Soul?" in R. M. McIver (ed), *Great Moral Dilemmas,* 83-88.

Heilman, Robert B. "The Tragedy of Knowledge: Marlowe's Treatment of Faustus," *Quarterly Review of Literature,* 2#4: 316-332 (April, 1946).

——————. "A Critical Method for Poetic Drama," *Perspective,* 1#2: 106-107 (Winter, 1948).

——————. "The Cult of Personality: Hell's Spells," *College English,* 23#2: 97-98 (Nov, 1961).

Heller, Erich. "Faust's Damnation: The Morality of Knowledge," *Chicago Review,* 15#4: 1-10 (Summer-Autumn, 1962).

Houk, Raymond A. *"Doctor Faustus* and *A Shrew,*" PMLA, 62#4Pt.1: 950-957 (Dec, 1947).

Hoy, Cyrus H. *The Hyacinth Room,* 226-230.

——————. "Ignorance in Knowledge: Marlowe's Faustus and Ford's Giovanni," *Modern Philology,* 57#3: 145-154 (Feb, 1960).

Hunter, G. K. "Five-Act Structure in *Doctor Faustus,*" *Tulane Drama Review,* 8#4: 77-91 (Summer, 1964).

film   Jarret, Hobart S. "Verbal Ambiguities in Marlowe's *Dr. Faustus*," *College English*, 5#6: 339-340 (March, 1964).

Johnson, Francis R. "Marlowe's 'Imperiall Heaven'" *ELH*, 12#1: 35-44 (March, 1945).

———. "'Ignorance in Knowledge': Marlowe's Faustus and Ford's Giovanni," *Modern Philology*, 57#3: 145-154 (Feb, 1960).

———. "Marlowe's Astronomy and Renaissance Skepticism," *ELH*, 13#4: 241-254 (Dec, 1946).

Jones, Harford. "*Dr. Faustus*," *The Use of English*, 13#1: 25-29 (Aut, 1961).

Kaula, David. "Time in *Everyman* and *Dr. Faustus*," *College English*, 22#1: 9-14 (Oct, 1960).

Kirschbaum, Leo. "Mephistopheles and the Lost 'Dragon'," *Review of English Studies*, 18#71: 312-315 (July, 1942).

Kocher, Paul H. "The Witchcraft Basis in Marlowe's *Faustus*," *Modern Philology*, 38#1: 9-36 (August, 1940).

"Nashe's Authorship of the Prose Scenes in *Faustus*," *Modern Language Quarterly*, 3: 17-40 (1942).

→ Leaska, Mitchell. *The Voice of Tragedy*, 87-90.

Leech, Clifford. "The Action of Marlowe & Shakespeare," *Colorado Quarterly*, 13#1: 29-30 (Summer, 1964).

Lerner, Laurence. "Tragedy: Religious and Humanist," *Review of English Literature*, 2#4: 30-33 (Oct, 1961).

McCloskey, John C. "The Theme of Despair in Marlowe's *Faustus*," *College English*, 4#2: 110-113 (Nov, 1942).

✗ McCullen, J. T. "Dr. Faustus and Renaissance Learning," *Modern Language Review*, 51#1: 6-16 (Jan, 1956).

McDonnell, R. F. *The Aspiring Mind*, 123-128.

Mahood, M. M. *Poetry and Symbolism*, 64-74.

⌐ Maxwell, J. C. "Notes on *Dr. Faustus*," *Notes and Queries*, 209#7:262 (July, 1964).

———. "The Plays of Christopher Marlowe," *Guide to English Literature*, 2: 160-167.

———. "The Sins of Faustus," *Wind and the Rain*, 4: 49-52 (1947).

✗ Mizener, Arthur. "The Tragedy of Marlowe's *Dr. Faustus*," *College English*, 5#2: 70-74 (Nov, 1943).

Morris, Harry. "Marlowe's Poetry," *Tulane Drama Review*, 8#4: 149-154 (Summer, 1964).

Nosworthy, J. M. "Coleridge on a Distant Prospect of Faust," *Essays and Studies*, 10: 73-90 (1957).

Ornstein, Robert. "The Comic Synthesis in *Doctor Faustus*," *ELH*, 22#3 : 165-172 (Sept, 1955).
————————. *The Moral Vision of Jacobean Tragedy*, 121-125.
Osato, Kazuo. "*Doctor Faustus*," *The Humanities* (Yokohama), Sect. 11 #7 : 1 (Sept., 1958).
Palmer, D. J. "Magic and Poetry in *Dr. Faustus*," *The Critical Quarterly*, 6#1 : 56-67 (Spring, 1964).
Parrott, T. M. & R. H. Bale. *A Short View of Elizabethan Tragedy*, 83-5 ; 88-9.
Patrides, C. A. "Renaissance and Modern Views of Hell," *Harvard Theological Review*, 57#3: 224-226 (July, 1964).
Pitcher, Seymour M. "Some Observations on the 1663 Edition of *Faustus*," *Modern Language Notes*, 56#8: 588-594 (Dec, 1941).
Putney, Rufus. "What 'Praise to Give?' Jonson vs. Stoll," *Philological Quarterly*, 23#4: 309-310 (Oct, 1944).
Ransom, Mariann, et. al. "German Valdes and Cornelius in Marlowe's *The Tragicall History of Dr Faustus*," *Notes and Queries*, 207: 329-331 (Sept, 1962).
Read, Herbert. *A Coat of Many Colors*, 166-177.
Ribner, Irving. "Marlowe's 'Tragicke Glassé'," in Richard Hosley (ed), *Essays on Shakespeare and Elizabethan Drama in Honor of Hardin Craig*, 108-113.
————————. "Marlowe and Shakespeare," *Shakespeare Quarterly*, 15#2: 49-51 (Spring, 1964).
ALSO IN: James G. McManaway (ed), *Shakespeare 400*, 49-53.
Sachs, Arieh. "The Religious Despair of Doctor Faustus," *Journal of English and Germanic Philology*, 63#4: 625-647 (Oct, 1964).
Schwartz, Elias. "The Possibilities of Christian Tragedy," *College English*, 21#4: 210 (Jan, 1960).
Sewall, Richard B. *The Vision of Tragedy*, 57-67.
Shaw, G. B. *Plays and Players*, 105-112.
Simpson, Percy. *Studies in Elizabethan Drama*, 95-111.
Steiner, George. *The Death of Tragedy*, 133-135.
Sternlicht, Sanford. "Imagery in Elizabethan Drama," *English Record*, 14#4: 4-6 (April, 1964).
Styan, J. L. *The Elements of Drama*, 48-49 ; 65.
Versfeld, M. "Some Remarks on Marlowe's *Faustus*," *English Studies in Africa*, 1#2: 134-143 (Sept, 1958).
Westlund, Joseph. "The Orthodox Christian Framework of

Marlowe's *Faustus,*" *Studies in English Literature 1500-1900,* 3#2: 191-206 (Spring, 1963).

White, W. *"Faust* and *Dr. Faustus,*" *Aberdeen University Review,* 33#2: 113-117 (Autumn, 1949).

Wolthuis, G. W. "Marlowe's *Dr. Faustus* II, ii, 172," *English Studies,* 30#1: 14-15 (Feb, 1949).

Young, Stark. *Immortal Shadows,* 174-177.

Zimansky, Curt A. "Marlowe's *Faustus:* The Date Again," *Philological Quarterly,* 41#1: 181-187 (Jan, 1962).

EDWARD II

Bent, Sunesen. "Marlowe and the Dumb Show," *English Studies,* 35#6: 241-253 (Dec, 1954).

Brodwin, Leonora Leet. *"Edward II:* Marlowe's Culminating Treatment of Love," *ELH,* 31#2: 139-155 (June, 1964).

Clemen, Wolfgang. *English Tragedy Before Shakespeare,* 154-161; 283-284.

Fricker, Robert. "The Dramatic Structure of *Edward II,*" *English Studies,* 34#5: 204-217 (Oct, 1953).

Johnson, S. F. "Marlowe's *Edward II,*" *The Explicator,* 10#8: 53 (June, 1952).

Kustow, Michael. *"Asking New Questions,"* *Encore,* 8#3: 25-30 (May-June, 1961).

Laboulle, Louise J. "A Note on Bertolt Brecht's Adaptation of Marlowe's *Edward II,*" *Modern Language Review,* 54#2: 214-220 (April, 1959).

Leech, Clifford. "Marlowe's *Edward II:* Power and Suffering," *The Critical Quarterly,* 1#3: 181-196 (Autumn, 1959).

Leech, Clifford. "The Acting of Marlowe and Shakespeare," *Colorado Quarterly,* 13#1: 30-32 (Summer, 1964).

McDonnell, R. F. *The Aspiring Mind,* 128-139.

Mahood, M. M. *Poetry and Symbolism,* 81-86.

Maxwell, J. C. "The Plays of Christopher Marlowe," *Guide to English Literature,* 2: 167-169.

Price, Hereward T. "Shakespeare and His Young Contemporaries," *Philological Quarterly,* 41#1: 44-45 (Jan, 1962).

Ribner, Irving. *The English History Play in the Age of Shakespeare,* 127-136.

——————. "Marlowe's *Edward II* and the Tudor History Play," *ELH,* 22#4: 243-253 (Dec, 1955).

——————. "Marlowe's 'Tragicke Glassé'," in Richard

Hosley (ed), *Essays on Shakespeare and Elizabethan Drama in Honor of Hardin Craig,* 106-108.

Robertson, Toby. "Directing *Edward II,*" *Tulane Drama Review,* 8#4: 174-183 (Summer, 1964).

Talbert, Ernest W. *Elizabethan Drama and Shakespeare's Early Plays,* 95-110.

Waith, Eugene. "*Edward II:* The Shadow of Action," Tulane Drama Review, 8#4: 59-76 (Summer, 1964).

Wells, Henry W. *Elizabethan and Jacobean Playwrights,* 98-103.

JEW OF MALTA, THE

Babb, Howard S. "Policy in Marlowe's *The Jew of Malta,*" *ELH,* 24#2: 85-94 (June, 1957).

Bowers, Fredson T. *Elizabethan Revenge Tragedy,* 104-109; 179-180.

Clemen, Wolfgang. *English Tragedy Before Shakespeare,* 141-147.

Cooke, Nan. "Infinite Riches: A Note on Marlovian Unity," *Notes and Queries,* pp. 50-52 (Feb. 3, 1951).

Fisch, Harold. *The Dual Image,* 25-30.

Gross, Harvey. "From Barabas to Bloom: Notes on the Figures of the Jew," *Western Humanities Review,* 11#2: 150-156 (Spring, 1957).

Harbage, Alfred. "Innocent Barabas," *Tulane Drama Review,* 8#4: 47-58 (Summer, 1964).

Harrison, Thomas P. "Further Background for *The Jew of Malta* and *The Massacre At Paris,*" *Philological Quarterly,* 27#1: 52-56 (Jan, 1948).

Hulsopple, Bill G. "Barabas and Shylock Against a Background of Jewish History in England," *Central States Speech Journal,* 12#1: 38-50 (Autumn, 1960).

Hunter, G. K. "The Theology of Marlowe's *The Jew of Malta,*" *Journal of the Warburg and Courtauld Institutes,* 27: 211-240 (1964).

Kirschbaum, Leo. "Some Light on *The Jew of Malta,*" *Modern Language Quarterly,* 7:53-56 (1946).

Kocher, Paul H. "English Legal History in Marlowe's *Jew of Malta,*" *Huntington Library Quarterly,* 26#2: 147-154 (Feb, 1963).

Landa, M. J. *The Jew in Drama,* 56-69.

Leech, Clifford. "Marlowe's Humor," in Richard Hosley (ed), *Essays on Shakespeare and Elizabethan Drama in Honor of Hardin Craig,* 39-40.

Mahood, M. M. *Poetry and Symbolism,* 74-81.

Maxwell, J. C. "The Assignment of Speeches in *The Jew of Malta,*" *Modern Language Review,* 43#4: 510-512 (Oct, 1948).

——————. "The Plays of Christopher Marlowe," *Guide to English Literature,* 2: 158-160.

Pearce, T. M. "Marlowe's *The Jew of Malta,* IV [vi], 7-10," *The Explicator,* 9#6: 40 (April, 1951).

Peavy, Charles E. *"The Jew of Malta*—Antisemitic or Anti-Catholic?" *McNeese Review,* 11: 57-60 (Winter, 1959/60).

Ribner, Irving. "Marlowe and Shakespeare," *Shakespeare Quarterly,* 15#2: 44-49 (Spring, 1964).
ALSO IN: James G. McManaway, (ed), *Shakespeare 400,* 45-49.

Talbert, Ernest W. *Elizabethan Drama and Shakespeare's Early Plays,* 79-87 ; 225-226.

MASSACRE AT PARIS, THE

Gallaway, David. "The Ramus Scene in Marlowe's *The Massacre at Paris,*" *Notes and Queries,* 198: 146-147 (April, 1953).

Harrison, Thomas P. "Further Background for *The Jew of Malta* and *The Massacre At Paris,*" *Philological Quarterly,* 27#1: 52-56 (Jan, 1948).

Kocher, Paul H. "Contemporary Pamphlet Backgrounds for Marlowe's *Massacre At Paris,*" *Modern Language Quarterly,* 8: 151-173 (1947).

——————. "Contemporary Pamphlet Backgrounds for Marlowe's *Massacre At Paris—Part II,*" *Modern Language Quarterly,* 8: 309-318 (1947).

——————. "Francois Hotman and Marlowe's *Massacre at Paris,*" *PMLA,* 56#2: 349-368 (June, 1941).

Leech, Clifford. "The Acting of Marlowe and Shakespeare," *Colorado Quartely,* 13#1: 34-35 (Summer, 1964).

McDonnell, R. F. *The Aspiring Mind,* 139-140.

Ribner, Irving. "Marlowe's 'Tragicke Glasse,' " in Richard Hosley (ed), *Essays on Shakespeare and Elizabethan Drama in Honor of Hardin Craig,* 101-104 ; 104-106.

Talbert, Ernest W. *Elizabethan Drama and Shakespeare's Early Plays,* 87-90.

TAMBURLAINE, PART I

Cunningham, James. *Woe or Wonder,* 93-95.

Lever, Katherine. "The Image of Man in *Tamburlaine I*," *Philological Quarterly,* 35#4 : 421-426 (Oct, 1956).

Lin, J. Y. "The Interpretation of Three Lines in Marlowe's *Tamburlaine Part I*," *Notes and Queries,* 195 : 137-138 (April, 1950).

Maxwell, J. C. "*Tawburlaine, Part I,* IV, iv. 77-79," *Notes and Queries,* 197 : 444 (11 Oct, 1952).

Parr, Johnstone. "The Horoscope of Mycetes in Marlowe's *Tamburlaine I*," *Philological Quarterly,* 25#4: 371-377 (Oct, 1946).

Talbert, Ernest W. *Elizabethan Drama and Shakespeare's Early Plays,* 110-121 ; 370-371.

Thomson, J. Oliver. "Marlowe's 'River Araris'," *Modern Language Review,* 48#3: 323-324 (July, 1953).

TAMBURLAINE, PART II

Gardner, Helen L. "The Second Part of *Tamburlaine The Great,*" *Modern Language Review,* 37#1: 18-24 (Jan, 1942).

Pearce, T. M. "Tamburlaine's 'Discipline to Three Sonnes': An Interpretation of *Tamburlaine, Part II,*" *Modern Language Quarterly,* 15#1: 18-27 (March, 1954).

TAMBURLAINE (PARTS I & II)

Allen, Don Cameron. "Renaissance Remedies for Fortune: Marlowe and the *Fortunati,*" *Studies in Philology,* 38#2: 188-197 (April, 1941).

Battenhouse, Roy W. "Marlowe Reconsidered: Some Reflections on Levin's *Overreacher,*" *Journal of English and Germanic Philology,* 52#4: 536-537 (Oct, 1953).

——————. "Tamburlaine, The 'Scourge of God'," *PMLA,* 56#2: 337-348 (June, 1941).

Blau, Herbert. "Language and Structure in Poetic Drama," *Modern Language Quarterly,* 18: 31 (1957).

Boas, Guy. "Tamburlaine and the Horrific," *English,* 8#48: 275-277 (Autumn, 1951).

Brooks, Charles. "*Tamburlaine* and Attitudes Toward Women," *ELH,* 24#1 : 1-11 (March, 1957).

Clemen, Wolfgang. *English Tragedy Before Shakespeare,* 113-143 ; 238-240; 247-249 ; 278-283.

Clurman, H. *Lies Like Truth,* 146-148.

Dick, Hugh C. "*Tamburlaine* Sources Once More," *Studies in Philology,* 46#2: 154-166 (April, 1949).

Duthie, G. I. "The Dramatic Structure of Marlowe's *Tam-*

burlaine The Great, Parts I & II," Essays and Studies *(English Association)*, 1: 101-126 (1948).

Feasey, Lynette and Eveline Feasey. "Marlowe and the Homilies," *Notes and Queries*, 195: 7-10 (Jan, 1950).

Harrison, George. *Elizabethan Plays and Players*, 71-73.

Hunter, G. K. *"Henry IV* and the Elizabethan Two-Part Play," *Review of English Studies*, N.S. 5#19: 239-241 (July, 1954).

Izard, T. C. "The Principal Source for Marlowe's *Tamburlaine,"* *Modern Language Notes*, 58#6: 411-417 (June, 1943).

Johnson, Francis R. "Marlowe's 'Imperiall Heaven,' " *ELH*, 12#1: 35-44 (March, 1945).

Jones, Eldred. *Othello's Countrymen*, 38-40.

Kocher, Paul H. "Marlowe's Art of War," *Studies in Philology*, 39#2: 207-225 (April, 1942).

Leech, Clifford. "The Structure of *Tamburlaine,"* *Tulane Drama Review*, 8#4: 32-46 (Summer, 1964).

——————. "The Acting of Marlowe and Shakespeare," *Colorado Quarterly*, 13#1: 32-34 (Summer, 1964).

McDiarmid, Matthew P. "The Influence of Robert Garnier on Some Elizabethan Tragedies," *Etudes Anglaises*, 11#4: 291-293 (Oct-Dec, 1958).

McDonnell, R. F. *The Aspiring Mind*, 98-99; 101-122.

Mahood, M. M. *Poetry and Symbolism*, 54-64.

Maxwell, J. C. "The Plays of Christopher Marlowe," *Guide to English Literature*, 2: 154-158.

Merchant, W. M. "Marlowe and Machiavelli," *Comparative Literature Studies* (Cardiff), 13: 1-7 (1944).

Oras, Ants. "Lyrical Instrumentation in Marlowe: A Step Towards Shakespeare," *University of Miami Publications in English and American Literature*, 1: 74-87 (March, 1953).

Parr, Jonstone. "Tamburlaine's Malady," *PMLA*, 59#3: 696-714 (Sept, 1944).

Pearce, T. M. "Marlowe and Castiglione," *Modern Language Quarterly*, 12: 3-12 (1951).

Peet, Donald. "The Rhetoric of *Tamburlaine,"* *ELH*, 26#2: 137-155 (June, 1959).

Powell, Jocelyn. "Marlowe's Spectacle," *Tulane Drama Review*, 8#2: 204-210 (Summer, 1964).

Price, Hereward T. "Shakespeare and His Young Contemporaries," *Philological Quarterly,* 41#1: 41-44 (Jan, 1962).

Prior, Moody E. *The Language of Tragedy,* 33-46.

Quinn, Michael. "The Freedom of Tamburlaine," *Modern Language Quarterly,* 21: 315-320 (1960).

Ribner, Irving. *The English History Play in the Age of Shakespeare,* 63-67; 89-91; 129-132; 134-136.

——————. "Greene's Attack on Marlowe," *Studies in Philology,* 52#2: 162-171 (April, 1955).

——————. "The Idea of History in Marlowe's *Tamburlaine,*" *ELH,* 20#4: 251-266 (Dec, 1953).

——————. "Shakespeare and Marlowe," in James G. McManaway (ed), *Shakespeare 400,* 41-43.

——————. "*Tamburlaine* and *The Wars of Cyprus,*" *Journal of English and Germanic Philology,* 53#4: 569-573 (Oct, 1954).

Rickey, Mary Ellen. "Astronomical Imagery in *Tamburlaine,*" *Renaissance Papers,* pp. 63-70 (1954).

Sewall, Richard B. *The Vision of Tragedy,* 69-70.

Taylor, Robert T. "Maximinus and Tamburlaine," *Notes and Queries,* 202#10: 417-418 (Oct, 1957).

Thompson, J. O. "Marlowe's 'River Araris'," *Modern Language Review,* 48#3: 323-324 (July, 1953).

Wehling, Mary M. "Marlowe's Mnemonic Nominology With Especial Reference to Tamburlaine," *Modern Language Notes,* 73#4: 243-247 (April, 1958).

Wells, Henry W. *Elizabethan and Jacobean Playwrights,* 80-83.

MARSTON, JOHN

ANTONIO AND MELLIDA

Foakes, R. A. "John Marston's Fantastical Plays: *Antonio and Mellida* and *Antonio's Revenge,*" *Philological Quarterly,* 41#1: 229-235 (Jan, 1962).

Harrison, George. *Elizabethan Plays and Players,* 208-213.

Higgins, Michael. "The Convention of the Stoic Hero as Handled by Marston," *Modern Language Review,* 39#4: 339-346 (Oct, 1944).

Hunter, G. K. "English Folly and Italian Vice: The Moral Landscape of John Marston," *Stratford-Upon-Avon-Studies,* 1: 85-91; 98-100 (1960).

——————. "*Henry IV* and the Elizabethan Two-Part

Play," *Review of English Studies,* N.S.5#19: 241-243 (July, 1954).

Schoenbaum, Samuel. "The Precious Balance of John Marston," *PMLA,* 67#6: 1070-1071 (Dec, 1952).

Soellner, Rolf. "The Madness of Hercules and the Elizabethans," *Comparative Literature* (Ore.) 10#4: 319-320 (Fall, 1958).

Wells, Henry W. *Elizabethan and Jacobean Playwrights,* 26-29.

ANTONIO'S REVENGE

Bowers, Fredson T. *Elizabethan Revenge Tragedy,* 118-125.

Cross, Gustav. "The Retrograde Genius of John Marston," *Review of English Literature,* 2#4: 21-23 (Oct, 1961).

Foakes, R. A. "John Marston's Fantastical Plays: *Antonio and Mellida* and *Antonio's Revenge,*" *Philological Quarterly,* 41#1: 232-239 (Jan, 1962).

Harrison, George. *Elizabethan Plays and Players,* 214-221.

Leech, Clifford. *Shakespeare's Tragedies and Other Studies in Seventeenth Century Drama,* 29-31.

Maxwell, J. C. "The Ghost From the Grave: A Note on Shakespeare's Apparitions," *Durham University Journal,* 48#2: 58-59 (March, 1956).

O'Donnell, Norbert F. "Shakespeare, Marston, and the University: The Sources of Thomas Goffe's *Orestes,*" *Studies in Philology,* 50#3: 483-484 (July, 1953).

Ornstein, Robert. *The Moral Vision of Jacobean Tragedy,* 155-158.

Schoenbaum, Samuel. "The Precious Balance of John Marston," *PMLA,* 67#6: 1071-1074 (Dec, 1952).

Simpson, Percy. *Studies in Elizabethan Drama,* 154-158.

DUTCH COURTESAN, THE

Cross, Gustav. "Marston, Montaigne, and Morality: *The Dutch Courtezan* Reconsidered," *ELH,* 27#1: 30-43 (March,
————————. "The Retrograde Genius of John Marston," *Review of English Literature,* 2#4: 24-25 (Oct, 1961).

Hoy, Cyrus H. *The Hyacinth Room,* 192-198.

Lacy, M. *The Jacobean Problem Play,* 84-104.

O'Connor, John J. "The Chief Sources of Marston's *Dutch Courtezan,*" *Studies in Philology,* 54#4: 509-515 (Oct, 1957).

Ornstein, Robert. *The Moral Vision of Tragedy,* 159-163.

Presson, Robert K. "Marston's *Dutch Courtezan:* The Study of an Attitude in Adaptation," *Journal of English and Germanic Philology,* 55#3: 406-413 (July, 1956).

Sackton, Alexander H. "The Paradoxical Encomium in Elizabethan Drama," *Studies in English,* 28: 91-92 (1949).

Schoenbaum, Samuel. "The Precious Balance of John Marston," *PMLA, 67#6*: 1077-1078 (Dec, 1952).

FAWN, THE

Curry, John V. *Deception in Elizabethan Comedy,* 78-81.

Lacy, Margaret. *The Jacobean Problem Play,* 104-114.

EASTWARD HOE

See: George Chapman

HISTRIOMASTIX

Kernan, Alvin. "John Marston's Play *Histriomastix,*" *Modern Language Quarterly,* 25: 134-140 (June, 1958).

LUST'S DOMINION

See: Anon

MALCONTENT, THE

Bowers, Fredson T. *Elizabethan Revenge Tragedy,* 130-132.

Cross, Gustav. "The Retrograde Genius of John Marston," *Review of English Literature,* 2#4: 23-24 (Oct, 1961).

Curry, John V. *Deception in Elizabethan Comedy,* 115-118.

Eliot, T. S. *Essays on Elizabethan Drama,* 186-189.

Hunter, G. K. "English Folly and Italian Vice: The Moral Landscape of John Marston," *Stratford-Upon-Avon-Studies,* 1: 100-102 (1960).

Kiefer, Christian. "Music and Marston's *The Malcontent,*" *Studies in Philology,* 51#2: 163-171 (April, 1954).

Schoenbaum, Samuel. "The Precious Balance of John Marston," *PMLA, 67#6*: 1069-1070 (Dec, 1952).

PARASITASTER

See—The Fawn

SOPHONISBA

Cross, Gustav. "The Retrograde Genius of John Marston," *Review of English Literature,* 2#4: 26-27 (Oct, 1961).

Eliot, T. S. *Essays on Elizabethan Drama,* 191-194.

Jones, Eldred. *Othello's Countrymen,* 72-78.

Ribner, Irving. *Jacobean Tragedy,* 13-14.

WHAT YOU WILL

Harrison, George. *Elizabethan Plays and Players,* 241-244; 259-261.

MARTYN, EDWARD

HEATHER FIELD, THE
Setterquist, Jan. *"The Heather Field," Edda,* 61#1: 82-96 (1961).

REGINA EYRE
Ryan, Stephen P. "Edward Martyn's Last Play," *Studies,* 47: 192-199 (Summer, 1958).

MASEFIELD, JOHN

THE COMING OF CHRIST
Eastman, Fred. *Christ in the Drama,* 73-77.

MASON, JOHN

TURKE, THE
Bowers, Fredson T. *Elizabethan Revenge Tragedy,* 161-162.
Wadsworth, Frank W. "The Relation of *Lust's Dominion* and John Mason's *The Turke,"* ELH, 20#3: 194-199 (Sept, 1953).

MASSINGER, PHILIP

BEGGAR'S BUSH, THE
See: John Fletcher

BELIEVE AS YOU LIST
Wells, H. *Elizabethan and Jacobean Playwrights,* 106-110.

BONDSMAN, THE
Edwards, Philip. "The Sources of Massinger's *The Bondsman,"* *Review of English Studies,* N.S.15#57: 21-26 (Feb, 1964).

CITY MADAME, THE
Knights, L. C. *Drama and Society in the Age of Jonson,* 280-292.

CUSTOM OF THE COUNTRY, THE
See: Beaumont and Fletcher

DOUBLE MARRIAGE, THE
See: Beaumont and Fletcher

DUKE OF MILAN, THE
Bowers, Fredson T. *Elizabethan Revenge Tragedy,* 193-195.

Wells, Henry W. *Elizabethan and Jacobean Playwrights,* 65-67.

EMPEROUR OF THE EAST, THE
Gray, J. E. "The Source of *The Emperour of the East,*" *Review of English Studies,* 1#2: 126-135 (April, 1950).
Phialas, Peter G. "The Sources of Massinger's *Emperour of the East,*" *PMLA,* 65#4: 473-482 (June, 1950).

FATAL DOWRY, THE
Bowers, Fredson T. *Elizabethan Revenge Tragedy,* 189-192.
Waith, Eugene M. "Controversia in the English Drama: Medwall and Massinger," *PMLA,* 68: 286-303 (1953).

GREAT DUKE OF MILAN, THE
Wells, Henry W. *Elizabethan and Jacobean Playwrights,* 178-182.

KNIGHT OF MALTA, THE
See: Beaumont and Fletcher

NEW WAY TO PAY OLD DEBTS, A
Bowers, R. H. "A Note on Massinger's *New Way,*" *Modern Language Review,* 53#2: 214-215 (April, 1958).
Enright, D. J. "Poetic Satire and Satire in Verse: A Consideration of Jonson and Massinger," *Scrutiny,* 18#4: 219-223 (Winter, 1952).
Knights, L. C. *Drama and Society in the Age of Jonson,* 273-280.
Thomson, Patricia. "The Old Way and the New Way in Dekker and Massinger," *Modern Language Review,* 51#2: 168-178 (April, 1956).

ROMAN ACTOR, THE
Crabtree, John H., Jr. "Philip Massinger's Use of Rhetoric in *The Roman Actor,*" *Furman Studies,* N.S.7#3: 40-58 (May, 1960).
Davison, Peter H. "The Theme and Structure of *The Roman Actor,*" *AUMLA,* 19: 39-56 (May, 1963).

THIERRY AND THEODORENT
See: John Fletcher and Philip Massinger, *Thierry and Theodorent*

UNNATURAL COMBAT, THE
Bowers, Fredson T. *Elizabethan Revenge Tragedy,* 195-199.

MAUGHAM, WILLIAM SOMERSET

BREADWINNERS, THE
MacCarthy, Desmond. *Humanities,* 97-98.

CIRCLE, THE
Brooks, Cleanth and Robert Heilman. *Understanding Drama,* 12-15 (Appendix—1961 ed.) ; 464-467 (1945 ed.).
Fielden, John S. "Mrs. Beamish and *The Circle,*" *Boston University Studies in English,* 2#2: 113-123 (Summer, 1956).
Kronenberger, Louis. *The Thread of Laughter,* 294-298.
Thompson, A. R. *Dry Mock,* 40-42.

NOBLE SPANIARD, THE
Sainer, Arthur. *The Sleepwalker and the Assassin,* 91-92.

OUR BETTERS
Kronenberger, Louis. *The Thread of Laughter,* 290-294.

MAVOR, O. H.
See : Bridie, James

MAYHEW, HENRY

THE WANDERING MINSTREL
Bradley, John L. "Henry Mayhew: Farce Writer of the 1830's," *Victorian Newsletter,* 23: 21-23 (Spring, 1963).

MEDBOURNE, MATTHEW

TARTUFFE; OR THE FRENCH PURITAN
Wilcox, John. *The Relation of Moliere to Restoration Comedy,* 59-64.

MEREDITH, GEORGE

THE SATIRIST
Beer, Gillian. "George Meredith and *The Satirist,*" *The Review of English Studies,* N. S. 15#59: 285-295 (August, 1964).

MERRILL, JAMES

THE IMMORTAL HUSBAND
Barbour, Thomas. "The Stuff of the Theater," *Hudson Review,* 10#1: 135-137 (Spring, 1957).

MIDDLETON, THOMAS
—AND WILLIAM ROWLEY
   CHANGELING, THE
      Bowers, Fredson T. *Elizabethan Revenge Tragedy,* 204-206.
      Dennis, Nigel F. *Dramatic Essays,* 133-140.
      Eliot, T. S. *Essays on Elizabethan Drama,* 89-95.
      Engleberg, E. "Tragic Blindness in *The Changeling* and
         Women Beware Women," Modern Language Quarterly,
         23#2: 20-28 (March, 1962).
      Helton, Tinsley. "Middleton and Rowley's *The Changeling,* V,
         iii, 175-177," *The Explicator,* 21#9: 74 (May, 1963).
      Hibbard, G. R. "The Tragedies of Thomas Middleton and
         the Decadence of the Drama," *Renaissance and Modern
         Studies,* 1: 54-64 (1957).
      Holzknecht, Karl L. "The Dramatic Structure of *The Change-
         ling," Renaissance Papers,* pp. 77-87 (1954).
      Jump, John D. "Middleton's Tragedies," *Guide to English
         Literature,* 2: 353-360.
      Matthews, Ernst G. "The Murdered Substitute Tale," *Modern
         Language Quarterly,* 6: 187-195 (1945).
      Ornstein, Robert. *The Moral Vision of Jacobean Tragedy,*
         179-190.
      Reed, Robert R. Jr. "A Factual Interpretation of *The Change-
         ling's* Madhouse Scenes," *Notes and Queries,* 195: 247-
         248 (June 10, 1950).
      Ribner, Irving. *Jacobean Tragedy,* 126-137.
      Ricks, Christopher. "The Moral and Poetic Structure of *The
         Changeling," Essays in Criticism,* 10#3: 290-306 (July,
         1960).
      Schoenbaum, Samuel. "Middleton's Tragedies—a Critical
         Study," *Columbia University Studies in English and
         Comparative Literature,* 168: 132-150 (1955).
      Stoll, E. E. *From Shakespeare to Joyce,* 309-312.
      Tomlinson, T. B. "Poetic Naturalism—*The Changeling,"
         Journal of English and Germanic Philology,* 63#4: 648-
         659 (Oct, 1964).
      Wells, Henry W. *Elizabethan and Jacobean Playwrights,* 39-
         41.
   CHASTE MAID IN CHEAPSIDE, A
      Parker, R. B. "Middleton's Experiments with Comedy and
         Judgement," *Stratford-Upon-Avon Studies,* #1: 188-192
         (1960).
      Schoenbaum, Samuel. *"A Chaste Maid in Cheapside* and Mid-

dleton's City Comedy," in *Studies in the English Renaissance Drama in Memory of Karl J. Holzknecht*, 287-309.

FAIR QUARREL, A

Bowers, Fredson T. *Elizabethan Revenge Tragedy*, 187-188.

Levin, Richard. "The Three Quarrels of *A Fair Quarrel*," *Studies in Philology*, 61#2 Pt. 1: 219-231 (April, 1964).

Schoenbaum, Samuel. "Middleton's Tragi-Comedies," *Modern Philology*, 54#1: 16-19 (Aug, 1956).

FAMILY OF LOVE, THE

Eberle, Gerald J. "Dekker's Part in *The Familie of Love*," in James G. McManaway (ed), *Joseph Q. Adams Memorial Studies*, 723-738.

Maxwell, Baldwin. " 'Twenty Good Nights'—*The Knight of the Burning Pestle* and Middleton's *Family of Love*," *Modern Language Notes*, 63#4: 233-237 (April, 1948).

Olive, W. J. "Imitation of Shakespeare in Middleton's *The Family of Love*," *Philological Quarterly*, 29#1: 75-78 (Jan, 1950).

——————. " 'Twenty Good Knights'—*The Knight of The Burning Pestle, The Family of Love*, and *Romeo and Juliet*," *Studies in Philology*, 47#2: 182-189 (April, 1950).

GAME OF CHESS, A

Bald, R. C. "An Early Version of Middleton's *Game of Chesse*," *Modern Language Review*, 38#3: 177-180 (July, 1943).

Bullough, Geoffrey. *"The Game of Chesse:* How it Struck a Contemporary," *Modern Language Review*, 49#2: 156-163 (April, 1954).

Price, George R. "The Latin Oration in *A Game of Chesse*," *Huntington Library Quarterly*, 23#4: 389-393 (Aug, 1960).

Wells, H. *Elizabethan and Jacobean Playwrights*, 209-211.

Wilson, Edward M. "The Spanish Protest Against *A Game of Chesse*," *Modern Language Review*, 44#4: 476-482 (Oct, 1949).

HENGIST, KING OF KENT

See under *Mayor of Queensborough*

HONEST WHORE (I & II)

See: Thomas Dekker

MAYOR OF QUEENSGOROUGH, THE

Schoenbaum, Samuel. *"Hengist, King of Kent* and Sexual

Preoccupation in Jacobean Drama," *Philological Quarterly*, 29#2 : 182-198 (April, 1950).

—————————. "Middleton's Tragedies—A Critical Study," *Columbia University Studies in English and Comparative Literature*, 168: 69-101 (1955).

MICHAELMAS TERM

Curry, John V. *Deception in Elizabethan Comedy*, 46-52.

Knight, L. C. *Drama and Society in the Age of Jonson*, 263-265.

Maxwell, Baldwin. "Middleton's *Michaelmas Term*," *Philological Quarterly*, 22#1: 29-35 (Jan, 1943).

Teagarten, Lucetta J. "The Dekker-Middleton Problem in *Michaelmas Term*," *Studies in English*, pp. 49-58 (1947).

MORE DISSEMBLERS BESIDES WOMEN

Schoenbaum, Samuel. "Middleton's Tragi-Comedies," *Modern Philology*, 54#1 : 13-16 (Aug, 1956).

NO WIT [NO HELP] LIKE A WOMAN'S

Gordon, D. J. "Middleton's *No Wit, No Help Like a Woman's* and Della Porta's *La Sorella*," *Review of English Studies*, 17#68: 400-414 (Oct, 1941).

Wells, Henry W. *Elizabethan and Jacobean Playwrights*, 227-229.

OLD LAW

See: Anon

PHOENIX, THE

Bawcutt, N. W. "Middleton's *The Phoenix* as a Royal Play," *Notes and Queries*, 201#7: 287-288 (July, 1956).

Maxwell, Baldwin. "Middleton's *The Phoenix*," in James G. McManaway, *Joseph Q. Adams Memorial Studies*, 743-753.

Parker, R. B. "Middleton's Experiments with Comedy and Judement," *Stratford-Upon-Avon-Studies*, 1: 179-185 (1960).

REVENGER'S TRAGEDY, THE

See: Cyril Tourneur

—AND THOMAS DEKKER

ROARING GIRL, THE

Price, George R. "The Shares of Middleton and Dekker in a

Collaborated Play," *Michigan Academy of Science, Arts, and Letters. Papers,* 30: 601-615 (1944).

SECOND MAIDEN'S TRAGEDY, THE
See: Anon

TRICK TO CATCH THE OLD ONE, A
Falk, Signi. "Plautus, Persa and Middleton's *A Trick to Catch an Old One,*" *Modern Language Notes,* 66#1: 19-21 (Jan, 1951).
George, J. "Millipood," *Notes and Queries,* 193: 149-150 (April, 1948).
Knight, L. C. *Drama and Society in the Age of Jonson,* 262-263.
Levin, Richard. "The Dampit Scenes in *A Trick to Catch The Old One,*" *Modern Language Quarterly,* 25#2: 140-152 (June, 1964).
Parker, R. B. "Middleton's Experiments with Comedy and Judgement," *Stratford-Upon-Avon Studies,* 1: 185-188 (1960).

WITCH, THE
Flatter, Richard. "Who Wrote the Hecate-Scene?" *Shakespeare Quarterly,* 94: 204-210 (1958).
Schoenbaum, Samuel. "Middleton's Tragicomedies," *Modern Philology,* 54#1: 8-10 (Aug, 1956).

WOMEN BEWARE WOMEN
Bowers, Fredson T. *Elizabethan Revenge Tragedy,* 163-165.
Cope, Jackson I. "The Date of Middleton's *Women Beware Women,*" *Modern Language Notes,* 76#4: 295-300 (April, 1961).
Dodson, Daniel. "Middleton's Livia," *Philological Quarterly,* 27#4: 376-381 (Oct, 1948).
Engleberg, E. "Tragic Blindness in *The Changeling* and *Women Beware Women,*" *Modern Language Quarterly,* 23#2: 20-28 (March, 1962).
Feldman, A Bronson. "The Yellow Malady: Short Studies of Five Tragedies of Jealousy," *Literature and Psychology,* 5#2: 44-46; 51-52 (May, 1956).
Hibbard, G. R. "The Tragedies of Thomas Middleton and the Drama," *Renaissance and Modern Studies,* 1: 42-54 (1957).
Jump, John D. "Middleton's Tragedies," *Guide to English Literature,* 2:347-353.

Ornstein, Robert. *The Moral Vision of Tragedy,* 190-199.

Parker, R. B. "Middleton's Experiments With Comedy and Judgement," *Stratford-Upon-Avon-Studies,* 1: 192-199 (1960).

Ribner, Irving. *Jacobean Tragedy,* 9-10; 137-152.

——————. "Middleton's *Women Beware Women:* Poetic Imagery and the Moral Visions," *Tulane Studies in English,* 9: 19-34 (1959).

Ricks, Christopher. "Word-Play in *Women Beware Women" The Review of English Studies,* 12 N.S. #47: 238-250 (Aug, 1961).

Schoenbaum, Samuel. "Middleton's Tragedies—A Critical Study," *Columbia University Studies in English and Comparative Literature,* 168: 104-132 (1955).

——————. "Middleton's Tragicomedies," *Modern Philology,* 54#1: 19 (Aug, 1956).

Ure, Peter. "Marriage and the Domestic Drama of Heywood and Ford," *English Studies,* 32#5: 210-211 (Oct, 1951).

Wells, Henry W. *Elizabethan and Jacobean Playwrights,* 41-44.

YOUR FIVE GALLANTS

Maxwell, Baldwin. "Thomas Middleton's *Your Five Gallants,*" *Philological Quarterly,* 30#1: 30-39 (Jan, 1951).

MILLAY, EDNA ST. VINCENT

THE KING'S HENCHMEN

Kies, Paul P. "Notes on Millay's *The King's Henchmen,*" *Washington State College Research Studies,* 14#3: 247-248 (Sept, 1946).

ARTHUR MILLER

AFTER THE FALL

Baxandall, Lee. "Arthur Miller: Still the Innocent," *Encore,* 11#3: 16-19 (May-June, 1964).

Ganz, Arthur. "Arthur Miller: After the Silence," *Drama Survey,* 3#4: 520-530 (Spring-Fall, 1964).

Mann, Paul (interviewed by Richard Schechner). "Theory and Practice: An Interview with Paul Mann," *Tulane Drama Review,* 9#2: 90-96 (Winter, 1964).

Steene, Birgitta. "Arthur Miller's *After the Fall:* A Strindbergian Failure," *Moderna Sprak,* 58#4: 446-452 (1964).

ALL MY SONS

Boggs, W. Arthur. *"Oedipus* and *All My Sons," The Personalist,* 42#4: 555-560 (Autumn, 1961).

Beardsley, Munroe. *Aesthetics,* 417-418.

Broussard, Louis. *American Drama,* 116-121.

Cassell, Richard A. "Arthur Miller's 'Rage of Conscience'," *Ball State Teachers College Forum,* 1#2: 31-33 (Winteer, 1960-1961).

Clurman, Harold. *Lies Like Truth,* 66-68.

Dillingham, William B. "Arthur Miller and the Loss of Conscience," *Emory University Quarterly,* 16#1: 40-43 (Spring, 1960).

Farnsworth, T. A. "Arthur Miller, Moralist and Crusader," *Contrast,* 1#3: 85-86 (Winter, 1961).

Fruchter, Norm. "On the Frontier: The Development of Arthur Miller," *Encore,* 9#1: 19-20; 23 (Jan-Feb, 1962).

Gassner, John. "Realism and Poetry in New American Playwriting," *World Theatre,* 2#4: 17 (Spring, 1953).

——————————. *The Theatre in Our Times,* 344-346.

Gorelik, Mordecai. "The Factor of Design," *Tulane Drama Review,* 5#3: 92-94 (March, 1961).

Hayes, Joseph A. "Arthur Miller and the Impasse of Naturalism," *South Atlantic Quarterly,* 62#3: 327-334 (Summer, 1963).

Hunt, Albert. "Realism and Intelligence: Some Notes on Arthur Miller," *Encore,* 7#3: 13-14 (May-June, 1960).

Loughlin, Richard L. "Tradition and Tragedy in *All My Sons," English Record,* 14#3: 23-27 (Feb, 1964).

Sievers, W. D. *Freud on Broadway,* 389-391.

Steinberg, M. W. "Arthur Miller and the Idea of Modern Tragedy," Dalhousie Review, 40#3: 333 (Fall, 1960).

Weales, Gerald. "Arthur Miller: Man and His Image," *Tulane Drama Review,* 7#1: 165-169 (Fall, 1962).

Wells, Arvin R. "The Living and the Dead in *All My Sons," Modern Drama,* 7#1: 46-51 (May, 1964).

Williams, Raymond. "From Hero to Victim: Ibsen, Miller and the Development of the Liberal Tragedy," *Studies on the Left,* 4#2: 95 (Spring, 1964).

——————————. "The Realism of Arthur Miller," *Critical Quarterly,* 1#2: 141-144 (Summer, 1959).

CRUCIBLE, THE

Dillingham, William B. "Arthur Miller and the Loss of Conscience," *Emory University Quarterly*, 16#1: 46-48 (Spring, 1960).

Farnsworth, T. A. "Arthur Miller, Moralist and Crusader," *Contrast*, 1#3: 85 (Winter, 1961).

Fruchter, Norm. "On the Frontier: The Development of Arthur Miller," *Encore*, 9#1: 22-24 (Jan-Feb, 1962).

Hunt, Albert. "Realism and Intelligence: Some Notes on Arthur Miller," *Encore*, 7#3: 15-17 (May-June, 1960).

Miller, Raymond. "The Realism of Arthur Miller," *Critical Quarterly*, 1#2: 146-147 (Summer, 1959).

Popkin, Henry. "Arthur Miller's *The Crucible*," *College English*, 26#2: 139-146 (Nov, 1964).

Raphael, D. D. *Paradox of Tragedy*, 103-105.

Steinberg, M. W. "Arthur Miller and the Idea of Modern Tragedy," *Dalhousie Review*, 40#3: 335-337 (Fall, 1960).

Walker, Phillip. "Arthur Miller's *The Crucible*: Tragedy, or Allegory?" *Western Speech*, 20#4: 222-224 (Fall, 1956).

Warshow, Robert. *The Immediate Experience*, 189-206.

—————————. "The Liberal Conscience in *The Crucible*," *Commentary*, 15: 265-271 (March, 1953).

Weales, Gerald. "Arthur Miller: Man and His Image," *Tulane Drama Review*, 7#1: 172-174 (Fall, 1962).

West, Paul. "Arthur Miller and the Human Mice," *The Hibbert Journal*, 61#241: 84-85 (Jan, 1963).

Wiegand, William. "Arthur Miller and the Man Who Knows," *Rocky Mountain Review*, 21#2: 93; 95-96 (Winter, 1957).

DEATH OF A SALESMAN

Barrington, Maeve. "The Salesman was Human," *Irish Monthly*, 80#12: 398-402 (Dec, 1952).

Beaufort, John. "A Matter of Hopelessness in *Death of Salesman*," *Tulane Drama Review*, 2#3: 63-70 (May, 1958).

Bentley, Eric. *The Play*, 729-747.

Bettina, Sister M. "Willy Loman's Brother Ben: Tragic Insight in *Death of a Salesman*," *Modern Drama*, 4#4: 409-412 (Feb, 1962).

Boas, George. "The Evolution of the Tragic Hero," *The Carleton Drama Review*, 1#1: 18-21 (1955-1956).

Brooks, Charles. "The Multiple Set in American Drama," *Tulane Drama Review*, 3#2: 37-41 (Dec, 1958).

Brown, John M. *Dramatis Personae*, 94-100.

Carson, Herbert L. "A Modern *Everyman*," *Central States Speech Journal*, 12#2: 111-113 (Winter, 1961).

—————————. "The Tragic Quest," *The Personalist,* 44#3: 318-320 (Summer, 1963).

Cassell, Richard A. "Arthur Miller's 'Rage of Conscience,'" *Ball State Teachers College Forum,* 1#2: 33-36 (Winter, 1960-1961).

Clurman, Harold. *Lies Like Truth,* 68-72.

Couchman, Gordon W. "Arthur Miller's Tragedy of Babbitt," *Educational Theatre Journal,* 7#3: 206-211 (Oct, 1955).

Dillingham, William B. "Arthur Miller and the Loss of Conscience," *Emory University Quarterly,* 16#1: 43-46 (Spring, 1960).

Driver, Tom F. "Strength and Weakness in Arthur Miller," *Tulane Drama Review,* 4#4: 45-52 (May, 1960).

Dusenbury, Winifred L. *The Theme of Lonliness in Modern American Drama,* 16-26.

Farnsworth, T. A. "Arthur Miller Moralist and Crusader," *Contrast,* 1#3: 86 (Winter, 1961).

Foster, Richard J. "Confusion and Tragedy: The Failure of Miller's *Salesman,*" in John D. Hurrell (ed), *Two Modern American Tragedies,* 82-88.

Fruchter, Norm. "On the Frontier: The Development of Arthur Miller," *Encore,* 9#1: 20-24 (Jan-Feb, 1962).

Ganz, Arthur. "The Silence of Arthur Miller," *Drama Survey,* 3#2: 224-237 (Oct, 1963).

Gassner, John. "The Possibilities and Perils of Modern Drama," *The Tulane Drama Review,* 1#3: 3-14 (June, 1957).

—————————. "Realism and Poetry in New American Playwriting," *World Theatre,* 2#4: 17-19; 21 (Spring, 1953).

—————————. *The Theatre in Our Times,* 346-348; 364-373.

Groff, Edward. "Point of View in Modern Drama," *Modern Drama,* 2#3: 274-277 (Dec, 1959).

Hagopian, John V. "Arthur Miller: The *Salesman's* Two Cases," *Modern Drama,* 6#2: 117-125 (Sept, 1963).

Hallman, Rolph J. *Psychology of Literature,* 114-122.

Hayes, Joseph A. "Arthur Miller and the Impasse of Naturalism," *South Atlantic Quarterly,* 62#3: 327-334 (Summer, 1963).

Hobson, Harold. *The Theatre Now,* 121-123.

Hunt, Albert. "Realism and Intelligence: Some Notes on Arthur Miller," *Encore,* 7#3: 14 (May-June, 1960).

Hynes, Joseph A. "Attention Must be Paid," *College English,* 23: 574-578 (April, 1962).

Jackson, Esther Merle. *"Death of a Salesman:* Tragic Myth in the Modern Theatre," *CLA Journal,* 7#1 : 63-76 (Sept, 1963).

Kennedy, Sighe. "Who Killed the Salesman?" *Catholic World,* 171 : 110-116 (May, 1950).

Kernodle, George R. "The Death of the Little Man," *The Carleton Drama Review,* 1#2: 47-60 (1955-1960).

Krutch, J. W. *Modernism in Modern Drama,* 123-126.

Lawrence, Stephen A. "The Right Dream in Miller's *Death of a Salesman,"* *College English,* 25#7 : 547-549 (April, 1964).

Leaska, Mitchell. *The Voice of Tragedy,* 273-278.

Levich, Marvin. *Aesthetics and the Philosophy of Criticism,* 204-209.

Lewis, Allan. *The Contemporary Theatre,* 295-300.

McAnny, Emile G. "The Tragic Commitment: Some Notes on Arthur Miller," *Modern Drama,* 5#1 : 11-20 (May, 1962).

McElroy, Davis D. *Existentialism and Modern Literature,* 54-58.

Mander, John. *The Writer and Commitment,* 138-152.

Miller, Arthur *et. al.* (Philip Gelb, moderator). *Death of a Salesman:* a Symposium With Arthur Miller, Gore Vidal, Richard Watts, and Others," *The Tulane Drama Review,* 2#3 : 63-69 (May, 1958).

Popkin, Henry. "Arthur Miller : The Strange Encounter," *Sewanee Review,* 68#1 : 48-60 (Winter, 1960).

Robson, John M. "Tragedy and Society," *Queen's Quarterly,* 71#3: 432-433 (Aut, 1964).

Ross, George. *"Death of a Salesman* in the Original: The Yiddish Version Reveals the Real Willy Loman," *Commentary,* 11: 184-186 (Feb, 1951).

Sastre, Alfonso. "Drama and Society," *Tulane Drama Review,* 5#2: 105-108 (Dec, 1960).

Schneider, D. E. "Play of Dreams," *Theater Arts,* 33: 18-21 (Oct, 1949).

Schweinitz, George de. *"Death of a Salesman:* A Note on Epic and Tragedy," *Western Humanities Review,* 14#1: 91-96 (Winter, 1960).

Sharpe, Robert B. "Nine Steps to the Tragic Triumph," *University of North Carolina Extension Bulletin,* 36#3: 28-31 (March, 1957).

Siegel, Paul N. "Willy Loman and King Lear," *College English,* 17#6: 341-345 (March, 1956).

Sievers, W. D. *Freud on Broadway,* 391-394.

Stallknecht, Newton P. *"Death of a Salesman:* Symposium," *Folio (Indiana),* 17#2: 3-26 (March, 1952).

Steinberg, M. W. "Arthur Miller and the Idea of Modern Tragedy," *Dalhousie Review,* 40#3: 333-335 (Fall, 1960).

Weales, Gerald. "Arthur Miller: Man and His Image," *Tulane Drama Review,* 7#1: 165-172; 176-178 (Fall, 1962).

Wiegand, William. "Arthur Miller and the Man who Knows," *Rocky Mountain Review,* 21#2: 85-93 (Winter, 1957).

Williams, Raymond. "From Hero to Villain: Ibsen, Miller and the Development of Liberal Tragedy," *Studies on the Left,* 4#2: 95-96 (Spring, 1964).

————————. "The Realism of Arthur Miller," *Critical Quarterly,* 1#2: 144-146 (Summer, 1959).

Worsley, T. C. *The Fugitive Art,* 93-96.

ENEMY OF THE PEOPLE, AN**
Divorkin, Martin S. "Miller and Ibsen," *The Humanist,* 11#3: 110-115 (June, 1951).

Wiegand, William. "Arthur Miller and the Man who Knows," *Rocky Mountain Review,* 21#2: 93-96 (Winter, 1957).

MAN WHO HAD ALL THE LUCK, THE
Sievers, W. D. *Freud on Broadway,* 388-389.

MISFITS, THE
Popkin, Henry. "Arthur Miller Out West," *Commentary,* 31: 432-436 (May, 1961).

VIEW FROM THE BRIDGE, A
Cubeta, Paul M. *Molern Drama for Analysis—Third Edition* (1963), 382-390.

Dillingham, William B. "Arthur Miller and the Loss of Conscience," *Emory University Quarterly,* 16#1: 48-10 (Spring, 1960).

Hayes, Joseph A. "Arthur Miller and the Impasse of Naturalism," *South Atlantic Quarterly,* 62#3: 327-334 (Summer, 1963).

Hunt, Albert. "Realism and Intelligence: Some Notes on Arthur Miller," *Encore,* 7#3: 14-15 *(May-June,* 1960).

Steinberg, M. W. "Arthur Miller and the Idea of Modern Tragedy," *Dalhousie Review,* 40#3: 337-338 (Fall, 1960).

Weales, Gerald. "Arthur Miller: Man and His Image," *Tulane Drama Review,* 7#1: 174-176 (Fall, 1962).

Williams, Raymond. "From Hero to Victim: Ibsen, Miller

**Loose translation of Ibsen play

and the Development of Liberal Tragedy," *Studies on the Left,* 4#2: 96-97 (Spring, 1964).

——————. "The Realism of Arthur Miller," *Critical Quarterly,* 1#2: 147-149 (Summer, 1959).

MILTON, JOHN

COMUS

Allen, Don C. "Milton's *Comus* as a Failure in Artistic Compromise," *ELH,* 16#2: 104-119 (June, 1949).

——————. "A Note on Comus," Modern Language Notes, 64#3: 179-180 (1949).

Arthos, John. "Milton, Ficino, and the Charmides," *Studies in Renaissance,* 6: 261-274 (1959).

——————. "The Realms of Being in the Epilogue of *Comus,*" *Modern Language Notes,* 76#4: 321-324 (April, 1961).

Barber, C. L. "*A Mask Presented at Ludlow Castle:* The Masque as a Masque," *English Institute Essays,* 11: 35-64 (1964).

Bruser, Fredelle. "*Comus* and the Rose Song," *Studies in Philology,* 44#4: 625-644 (Oct, 1947).

Diekhoff, John S. "A Note on *Comus,* lines 75-77," *Philological Quarterly,* 20#4: 603-604 (Oct, 1941).

— Dyson, A. E. "The Interpretation of *Comus,*" *Essays and Studies,* N.S.#8: 89-114 (1955).

Finney, Gretchen Ludke. "*Comus, Dramma per Musica,*" *Studies in Philology,* 37#3: 482-500 (July, 1940).

Grossman, Ann and George W. Whiting. "*Comus,* Once More," *Review of English Studies,* 11N.S.#41: 56-60 (Feb, 1960).

Harrison, Thomas P. "The 'Haemony' Passage in *Comus* Again," *Philological Quarterly,* 22#3: 251-254 (July, 1943).

Haun, Eugenee. "An Inquiry Into the Genre of *Comus,*" *Vanderbilt Studies in the Humanities,* 2: 221-239 (1954).

Jane, Sears. "The Subject of Milton's *Ludlow Mask,*" *PMLA,* 74#5: 533-543 (Dec, 1959).

Leahy, William. "Pollution and *Comus,*" *Essays in Criticism,* 11#1: 111 (Jan, 1961).

LeCompte, Edward S. "New Light on the 'Haemony' Passage in *Comus,*" *Philological Quarterly,* 21#3: 283-298 (July, 1942).

Madsen, William G. "The Idea of Nature in Milton's Poetry," *Yale Studies in English,* 138: 185-218 (1958).

Major, John M. *"Comus* and *The Tempest," Shakespeare Quarterly,* 10#2: 177-184 (Spring, 1959).

Rans, Geoffrey. "Mr. Wilkinson on *Comus," Essays in Criticism,* 10#3: 364-369 (July, 1960).

Robins, Harry F. "The Key to a Problem in Milton's *Comus," Modern Language Quarterly,* 12:422-428 (1951).

Ross, Malcolm M. "Milton and the Protestant Aesthetic," *University of Toronto Quarterly,* 17#4: 354-359 (July, 1948).

Schaus, Hermann. "The Relationship of *Comus* to *Hero and Leander* and *Venus and Adonis," Studies in English,* pp. 129-141 (1945/46).

Scott-Craig, T. S. K. "Miltonic Tragedy and Christian Vision," in Nathan A. Scott, Jr. (ed), *The Tragic Vision and the Christian Faith,* 99-104.

Sensabaugh, G. F. "The Milieu of *Comus," Studies in Philology,* 41#2: 238-249 (April, 1944).

Shattuck, Charles H. "Macready's *Comus:* A Prompt Book Study," *Journal of English and Germanic Philology,* 60#4: 731-748 (Oct, 1961).

Singleton, R. H. "Milton's *Comus* and the *Comus* of Erycius Puteanus," *PMLA,* 58#4: 949-957 (Dec, 1943).

Stroup, T. B. *"The Cestus:* Manuscript of an Anonymous 18th Century *Comus," Studies in English Literature 1500-1900,* 2#1: 47-55 (Winter, 1962).

Wells, Henry W. *Elizabethan and Jacobean Playwrights,* 173-175.

Wilkinson, David. "The Escape From Pollution: A Comment on *Comus," Essays in Criticism,* 10#1: 32-43 (Jan, 1960).

Woodhouse, A. S. P. "The Argument in Milton's *Comus," University of Toronto Quarterly,* 11#1: 47-71 (Oct, 1941).

——————. *"Comus* Once More," *University of Toronto* Quarterly, 19#3: 218-223 (April, 1950).

SAMSON AGONISTES

Battenhouse, Henry W. *Poets of Christian Thought,* 59-60.

Baumgartner, Paul R. "Milton and Patience," *Studies in Philology,* 60#2Pt. 1: 203-204; 208-210 (April, 1963).

Beum, Robert. "The Rhyme in *Samson Agonistes," Texas Studies in Literature and Language,* 4#2: 177-182 (Summer, 1962).

Chambers, A. B. "Wisdom and Fortitude in *Samson Agonistes," PMLA,* 78#4: 315-320 (Sept, 1963).

Cook, Albert. "Milton's Abstract Music," *University of Toronto Quarterly*, 29#3: 381-385 (April, 1960).

Cox, Lee S. "The 'Evening Dragon' in *Samson Agonistes:* A Reappraisal," *Modern Language Notes*, 76#7: 577-584 (Nov, 1961).

Dawson, S. W. "Two Points of View: *Samson Agonistes,*" *The Anglo-Welsh Review*, 14#34: 92-95 (Winter, 1964-1965).

Ebbs, John D. "Milton's Treatment of Poetic Justice in *Samson Agonistes,*" *Modern Language Quarterly*, 22: 377-389 (Dec, 1961).

Ellis-Fermor, Una. *Frontiers of Drama,* 17-34; 148-153.

Fell, Kenneth. "From Myth to Martyrdom: Towards a View of Milton's *Samson Agonistes,*" *English Studies*, 34#4: 144-155 (Aug, 1953).

Faverty, Frederic E. *Your Literary Heritage,* 69-71.

Finney, Gretchen L. "Chorus in *Samson Agonistes,*" *PMLA*, 58#3: 649-664 (Sept, 1943).

Fisch, Harold. *The Dual Image,* 40-41.

Ghosh, P. C. "On *Samson Agonistes,*" *University of Calcutta Bulletin of the Department of English*, 5#16-17: 39-42 (1963).

Gilbert, Allan H. "Is *Samson Agonistes* Finished?" *Philological Quarterly*, 28#1: 98-106 (Jan, 1949).

Gilles, Christopher. *"Samson Agonistes,"* *The Use of English*, 5#4: 223-230 (Summer, 1954).

Gohn, Ernest S. "The Christian Epic of *Paradise Lost* and *Samson Agonistes,*" *Studia Neophilolgica* 34#2: 243-252; 261-268 (1962).

Grenander, M. E. "Samson's Middle: Aristotle and Dr. Johnson," *University of Toronto Quarterly*, 24#4: 377-389 (July, 1955).

Griffin, Earnest G. "Hardy and the Growing Consciousness of the Immanent Will: A Study of the Relationship of Philosophy to Literary Form," *Cairo Studies in English*, pp. 127-128 (1961-1962).

Grossman, A. "Samson, Job, and the Exercise of Saints," *English Studies*, 45#3: 212-234 (June, 1964).

Hanford, James H. *"Samson Agonistes* and Milton in his Old Age," *University of Michigan Studies in Shakespeare*, pp. 165-190 (1964).

Harris, William O. "Despair and 'Patience' as the Truest Fortitude' in *Samson Agonistes,*" *ELH*, 30#2: 107-120 (June, 1963).

Henn, Thomas R. *The Harvest of Tragedy,* 263-265.

Kermode, Frank. "Milton's Hero," *Review of English Studies,* N.S.4#16: 320-321 (Oct, 1953).

——————. *"Samson Agonistes* and Hebrew Prosody," *Durham University Journal,* 45#2: 49-63 (March, 1953).

Kirkconnell, Watson. "Six Sixteenth Century Forerunners of Milton's *Samson Agonistes," Royal Society of Canada Proceedings and Transactions,* 43 Sect. 2: 73-81 (June, 1949).

Le Compte, Edward S. *"Samson Agonistes* and *Aureng-Zebe," Etudes Anglaises,* 11#1: 18-22 (Jan, 1958).

Lerner, Laurence. "Tragedy: Religious and Humanist," *Review of English Literature,* 2#4: 34-35 (Oct, 1961).

McDavid, Raven I. *"Samson Agonistes* 1096: A Re-examination," *Philological Quarterly,* 33#1: 86-89 (Jan, 1954).

Madsen, William G. "From Shadowy Types to Truth," *English Institute Essays,* pp. 95-114 (1964).

Mahood, M. M. *Poetry and Symbolism,* 237-239.

Marilla, E. L. *"Samson Agonistes:* Interpretation," *Studia Neophilologica,* 29#1: 67-76 (1957).

Maxwell, J. C. "Milton's Samson and Sophocles' Heracles," *Philological Quarterly,* 33#1: 90-91 (Jan, 1954).

Miller, Martin E. "Pathos' and 'Katharsis' in *Samson Agonistes," ELH,* 31#2: 156-174 (June, 1964).

Nash, Ralph. "Chivalric Themes in *Samson Agonistes,"* in A. Dayle Wallace & Woodburn O. Ross (eds), *Studies in Honor of John Wilcox,* 23-38.

Parker, William R. "The Date of *Samson Agonistes," Philological Quarterly,* 28#1: 149-155; 160-166 (Jan, 1949).

Raphael, D. D. *Paradox of Tragedy,* 57-59.

Ridley, Maurice R. *Studies in Three Literatures,* 125-128.

Samuels, Charles T. "Milton's *Samson Agonistes* and Rational Christianity," *Dalhousie Review,* 43#4: 495-506 (Winter 1963/64).

Scott-Craig, T. S. K. "Miltonic Tragedy and Christian Vision," in Nathan A. Scott, Jr. (ed), *The Tragic Vision and the Christian Faith,* 104-109.

Sellin, Paul R. "Milton's Epithet," *Studies in English Literature 1500-1900,* 4#1: 137-162 (Winter, 1964).

Smith, A. J. "Two Points of View: *Samson Agonistes," The Anglo-Welsh Review,* 14#34: 95-101 (Winter, 1964-1965).

Steadman, John M. " 'Faithful Champion!' The Theological

Basis of Milton's Hero of Faith," *Anglia,* 56#2: 214-226 (April, 1959).

Steiner, George. *The Death of Tragedy,* 31-33.

Tillyard, E. M. W. "Milton and the Classics," *Essays By Divers Hands,* 26:70-72 (1953).

Tinker, Chauncey B. *"Samson Agonistes,"* in Cleanth Brooks (ed), *Tragic Themes in Western Literature,* 59-76.

Waggoner, George R. "The Challenge to Single Combat in *Samson Agonistes,"* *Philological Quarterly,* 39#1: 82-91 (Jan, 1960).

Wilkes, G. A. "The Interpretation of *Samson Agonistes,"* *Huntington Library Quarterly,* 26#4: 363-380 (Oct, 1963).

Williams, Arnold. "A Note on *Samson Agonistes,* LL 90-94," *Modern Language Notes,* 63#8: 537 (Dec, 1948).

Woodhouse, A. S. P. *"Samson Agonistes* and Milton's Experience," *Royal Society of Canada Proceedings and Transactions,* 43 Sect. 2: 157-175 (June, 1949).

——————. "Tragic Effects in *Samson Agonistes,"* *University of Toronto Quarterly,* 28#3: 205-222 (April, 1959).

MONSEY, DEREK

LESS THAN KIND

Monsey, Derek. "Quite an Experience," *Encore,* 4#1: 8 unnumbered pp. (Sept-Oct, 1957).

MOODY, WILLIAM VAUGHN

FIRE BRINGER, THE

Riggs, Thomas, Jr. "Prometheus 1900," *American Literature,* 22: 412-416 (Jan, 1951).

MASQUE OF JUDGEMENT, THE

Jones, Howard M. The Bright Medusa, 57-64.

MOORE, EDWARD

THE GAMESTER

Boas, F. S. *An Introduction to Eighteenth Century Drama,* 257-260.

MOORE, GEORGE A.

THE BENDING OF THE BOUGH

Ellis-Fermor, Una. *The Irish Dramatic Movement,* 124-132.

MORTON, THOMAS

SPEED THE PLOUGH

Brooks, Cleanth and Robert Heilman. *Understanding Drama,*
15-16 (Appendix, 1961 ed.) ; 467-468 (1945 ed.).

MUNFORD, ROBERT

THE CANDIDATES

Glenn, Stanley. "The Development of the Negro Character in
American Comedy Before the Civil War," *Southern
Speech Journal,* 26#2: 133-135 (Winter, 1960).

MURDOCK, FRANK

DAVY CROCKETT

Kernodle, Portia. "Yankee Types on the London Stage, 1824-
1880," *Speech Monographs,* 14: 143-144 (1947).

MURDOCK, JOHN

THE TRIUMPH OF LOVE

Glenn, Stanley. "The Development of the Negro Character in
American Comedy Before the Civil War," *Southern
Speech Journal,* 26#2: 138-141 (Winter, 1960).

MURPHY, ARTHUR

ALL IN THE WRONG

Boas, F. S. *An Introduction to Eighteenth Century Drama,*
314-317.

WAY TO KEEP HIM, THE

Boas, F. S. *An Introduction to Eighteenth Century Drama,*
309-324.

MURRAY, T. C.

AUTUMN FIRE

Conlin, Matthew T. "The Tragic Effect in *Autumn Fire* and
Desire Under the Elms," *Modern Drama,* 1#4: 288-235
(Feb, 1959).

NASH, N. R.

THE RAINMAKER

Weales, Gerald. "The Video Boys on Broadway," *Antioch Review,* 22: 219-221 (Summer, 1962).

NORTON, THOMAS
—AND THOMAS SACKVILLE

GORBODUC, OR FERREX AND PORREX
Clemen, Wolfgang. *English Tragedy Before Shakespeare,*
56-74; 253-257.
Herrick, Marvin T. "Senecan Influence in *Gorboduc,*" in
*Studies in Speech and Drama in Honor of Alexander M.
Drummond,* 78-104.
Johnson, S. F. "The Tragic Hero in Early Elizabethan Drama,"
in *Studies in the English Renaissance Drama in Memory
of Karl J. Holzknecht,* 164-171.
McDonnell, R. F. *The Aspiring Mind,* 70-86.
Mendonca, Barbara Heliodora Carneiro de. "The Influence of
Gorboduc on *King Lear,*" *Shakespeare Survey,* 13: 41-48
(1960).
Prior, Moody E. *The Language of Tragedy,* 31-33.
Reese, Gertrude C. "The Succession Question in Elizabethan
Drama," *Studies in English,* pp. 61-66 (1942).
Ribner, Irving. *The English History Play in the Age of Shakes-
speare,* 41-52.
Turner, Robert Y. "Pathos and the *Gorboduc* Tradition, 1560-
1590," *Huntington Library Quarterly,* 25#2: 97-120
(Feb, 1962).
Watson, Sarah Ruth. "*Gorboduc* and the Theory of Tyranni-
cide," *Modern Language Review,* 34#3: 355-366 (July,
1939).

O'CASEY, SEAN

COCK-A-DOODLE DANDY
Rollins, Ronald G. "O'Casey's *Cock-A-Doodle Dandy,*" *The
Explicator,* 23#1: #8 (Sept, 1964).

DRUMS OF FATHER NED, THE
Knight, G. Wilson. *The Christian Rennaissance,* 341-347.
JUNO AND THE PAYCOCK
Cubeta, Paul. *Modern Drama for Analysis, First Edition,*
617-621.
Fox, R. M. "Sean O'Casey and the Soul of Man," *Aryan Path,*
34#8: 367-368 (Aug, 1963).
Krause, David. "Realism in the Drama of Charles Reade,"
English, 12: 99 (Aut, 1958).
Knight, G. W. *The Christian Renaissance,* 341-347.
Krutch, J. W. *Modernism in Modern Drama,* 97-99.

Robinson, Eric. *"Juno and the Paycock,"* The Use of English, 11#2: 111-118 (Winter, 1959).

Styan, J. L. *The Elements of Drama,* 190-191.

KATHLEEN LISTENS IN

Hethmon, Robert. "Great Hatred, Little Room," *Tulane Drama Review,* 5#4: 51-55 (June, 1961).

NANNIE'S NIGHT OUT

Ayling, Ronald. "Nannie's Night Out" Modern Drama, 5#2: 154-163 (Sept, 1962).

OAK LEAVES AND LAVENDER

Boas, Guy. "The Drama of Sean O'Casey," *College English,* 10#2: 85-86 (Nov, 1948).

PLOUGH AND THE STARS, THE

Armstrong, W. A. "The Sources and Themes of *The Plough and The Stars,"* Modern Drama, 4#3: 234-242 (Dec, 1961).

DeBoun, Vincent C. "Sean O'Casey and the Road to Expressionism," *Modern Drama,* 4#3 254-259 (Dec, 1961).

Styan, J. L. *The Elements of Drama,* 190-195.

PURPLE DUST

Boas, Guy. "The Drama of Sean O'Casey," *College English,* 10#2: 84-85 (Nov, 1948).

Daniel, Walter C. "Patterns of Greek Comedy in O'Casey's *Purple Dust,"* Bulletin of the New York Public Library, 66#11 : 603-612 (Nov, 1962).

RED ROSES FOR ME

Boas, Guy. "The Drama of Sean O'Casey," *College English,* 10#2: 85 (Nov, 1948).

Clurman, Harold. *Lies Like Truth,* 122-124.

Esslinger, Pat M. "Sean O'Casey and the Lockout of 1913: *Materia Poetica* of the Two Red Plays," *Modern Drama,* 6#1 : 53-56 (May, 1963).

Lewis, Allan. *The Contemporary Theatre,* 175-191.

SHADOW OF A GUNMAN, THE

Armstrong, William A. "History, Autobiography and *The Shadow of a Gunman,"* Modern Drama, 2#3: 417-424 (Dec, 1959).

Freedman, Morris. "The Modern Tragicomedy of O'Casey and Wilde," *College English,* 25#7: 521-522 (April, 1964).

SHIFTING HEART, THE

  Davison, P. H. "Three Australian Plays: National Myths
    Under Criticism," *Southerly,* 23#2: 118-120 (1963).

SILVER TASSIE, THE

  Boas, Guy. "The Drama of Sean O'Casey," *College English,*
    10#2: 82-83 (Nov, 1948).

  Bromage, Mary C. "The Yeat-O'Casey Quarrel," *The Mich-
    igan Alumnus,* 64#14: 135-143 (Mar, 1, 1958).

  Krause, David. "The Playwright not for Burning," *University
    Quarterly Review,* 34#1: 68-76 (Winter, 1958).

  Rollins, Ronald G. "O'Casey's *The Silver Tassie,*" *Explicator,*
    20#8: 62 (April, 1962).

  Smith, Winifred. "The Dying God in Modern Theatre," *Re-
    view of Religion,* 5#3: 269-273 (March, 1941).

  Styan, J. L. *The Dark Comedy,* 149-152.

STAR TURNED RED, THE

  Esslinger, Pat M. "Sean O'Casey and the Lockout of 1913:
    Materia Poetica of the Two Red Plays," *Modern Drama,*
    6#1: 53-63 (May, 1963).

  Rollins, Ronald G. "Sean O'Casey's The Star Turns Red: A
    Political Prophecy," *Mississippi Quarterly,* 16#2: 67-75
    (Spring, 1963).

WITHIN THE GATES

  Boas, Guy. "The Drama of Sean O'Casey," *College English,*
    10#2: 83-84 (Nov, 1948).

  Ellis-Fermor, Una. *The Frontiers of Drama,* 122-125.

  Rollins, Ronald G. "O'Casey, O'Neill and Expressionism in
    Within the Gates," *University of West Virginia Bulletin.
    Philological Papers,* 13: 76-81 (1961).

ODETS, CLIFFORD

  AWAKE AND SING

    Clurman, H. *The Fervent Years,* 135-136; 139-141.

    Gassner, John. *The Theatre in our Times,* 303-307.

    Kaplan, Charles. "Two Depression Plays and Broadway's Pop-
      ular Idealism," *American Quarterly,* 15#4: 579-582
      (Winter, 1963).

    Meister, Charles W. "Comparative Drama: Chekhov, Shaw,
      Odets," *Poet Lore,* 55#3: 255-257 (Autumn, 1950).

    Rabkin, Gerald. *Drama and Commitment,* 182-187.

    Sargeant, E. N. "*Awake and Sing,*" *New Directions in Prose
      and Poetry,* 16: 54-59 (1957).

WAITING FOR LEFTY
    Clurman, H. *The Fervent Yeears*, 138-139; 140-143.
    Hunt, Albert. "Only Soft Centered Left: Odets and Social
        Theatre," *Encore*, 8#3: 5-11 (May-June, 1961).
    Mendelsohn, Michael J. "Clifford Odets: The Artist's Com-
        mitment," in Bernice Slote (ed), *Literature and Society*,
        145-148.
    Rabkin, Gerald. *Drama and Commitment*, 172-176.
    Shuman, R. Baird. *"Waiting For Lefty:* A Problem of Struc-
        ture," *Revue des Langues Vivantes*, 28#6: 521-526
        (1962).
    Sievers, W. D. *Freud on Broadway*, 261.

O'HARA, JOHN

    PAL JOEY
        Borneman, Ernest. "A Difference of Taste," *Twentieth Cen-
            tury*, 155#928: 555-563 (June, 1954).

O'NEILL, EUGENE

    AH, WILDERNESS
        Adler, Jacob H. "The Worth of *Ah, Wilderness*," *Modern
            Drama*, 3#3: 280-288 (Winter, 1960).
        App, Austin J. "Presenting Sin and Temptation in Litera-
            ture," *Catholic World*, 158: 247; 251 (Dec, 1943).
        Brustein, Robert. *The Theater of Revolt*, 336-339.
        Shawcross, John T. "The Road to Ruin: The Beginning of
            O'Neill's *Long Day's Journey*," *Modern Drama*, 3#3:
            289-296 (Winter, 1960).

    ALL GOD'S CHILLUN GOT WINGS
        Black, Eugene. "Catharsis and Eugene O'Neill," *Mandrake*,
            1#6: 37-39 (1949).
        Daniel, Anne. "The Frozen Countenance," *The Southern
            Speech Journal*, 25#3: 190-191 (Spring, 1960).
        Frenz, Horst. "Eugene O'Neill in Russia," *Poet Lore*, 49#3:
            246-247 (Autumn, 1943).
        Smeets, Marcel. "Four Aspects of Eugene O'Neill's Plays,"
            Revue des Langues Vivantes, 16: 48; 57 (1950).
        Waith, Eugene M. "Eugene O'Neill: An Exercise in Un-
            Masking," *Educational Theatre Journal*, 13#3: 186-187
            (Oct, 1961).

ANNA CHRISTIE

Dusenbury, Winifred L. *The Theme of Loneliness in Modern American Drama*, 50-56.

Fleisher, Frederic. "Swedes in the Published Plays of Eugene O'Neill," *Orbis Litterarcm*, 12#2: 101-103 (1957).

Krause, David. "Realism in the Drama of Charles Reade," *English*, 12: 99 (Aut, 1958).

Leech, Clifford. "Eugene O'Neill and his Plays," *Critical Quarterly*, 3#3: 246-248 (Aut, 1961).

McAleere, John J. "Christ Symbolism in *Anna Christie*," *Modern Drama*, 4#4: 389-396 (Feb, 1962).

Smeets, Marcel. "Four Aspects of Eugene O'Neill's Plays," *Revue des Langues Vivantes*, 16: 52 (1950).

BEYOND THE HORIZON

Carson, Herbert L. "The Tragic Quest," *Personalist*, 44#3: 313-315 (Summer, 1963).

Fiskin, A. M. I. "The Basic Unity of Eugene O'Neill," *University of Denver Publications. Studies in Humanities*, #1: 106-107 (1950).

Fulton, A. R. *Drama and Theatre*, 108-122.

Millet, Fred B. *Reading Drama*, 15-16; 21-22; 27-29; 226-230.

DAYS WITHOUT END

Alexander, Doris M. "Eugene O'Neill, 'The Hound of Heaven,' and the 'Hell Hole'," *Modern Language Quarterly*, 20: 307-314 (Dec, 1959).

Brustein, Robert. *The Theater of Revolt*, 331-332; 336-337.

Daniel, Anne. "The Frozen Countenance," *The Southern Speech Journal*, 25#3: 195-198 (Spring, 1960).

Eastman, Fred. *Christ in the Drama*, 97-103.

Geier, W. "O'Neill's Miracle Plays," *Religion in Life*, 16#4: 515-526 (Aut, 1947).

Miller, Jordan Y. "The Georgia Plays of Eugene O'Neill," *Georgia Review*, 12#3: 280-284 (Fall, 1958).

Sievers, W. D. *Freud on Broadway*, 125-127.

Smeets, Marcel. "Four Aspects of Eugene O'Neill's Plays," *Revue des Langues Vivantes*, 16: 49-50; 57 (1950).

Stamm, R. "Dramatic Experiments of Eugene O'Neill," *English Studies*, 28#1: 14-15 (Feb, 1947).

Waith, Eugene M. "Eugene O'Neill: An Exercise in Unmasking," *Educational Theatre Journal*, 13#3: 185-186 (Oct, 1961).

DESIRE UNDER THE ELMS

Brooks, Charles. "The Multiple Set in American Drama,'
Tulane Drama Review, 3#2: 32-34 (Dec, 1958).

Conlin, Matthew T. "The Tragic Effect in *Autumn Fire* and
Desire Under the Elms," Modern Drama 1#4: 228-23!
(Feb, 1959).

Cubeta, Paul M. *Modern Drama for Analysis, Third Edition*
143-150.

Downer, Alan S. *Fifty Years of American Drama*, 68-70.

Engel, Edwin A. "Ideas in the Plays of Eugene O'Neill," in
John Gassner (ed), *Ideas in the Drama*, 107-109.

Fiskin, A. M. I. "The Basic Unity of Eugene O'Neill," *Uni
versity of Denver Publications. Studies in Humanities*
#1: 111-113 (1950).

Hartman, Murray. *"Desire Under The Elms* in the Light of
Strindberg's Influence," *American Literature*, 33: 360
369 (Nov, 1961).

Leaska, Mitchell. *The Voice of Tragedy*, 264-268.

Racey, Edgar Jr. "Myth as Tragic Structure in *Desire Under
The Elms," Modern Drama*, 5#1: 42-46 (May, 1962).

Sievers, W. D. *Freud on Broadway*, 68-69; 112-115.

Walley, Harold R. *The Book of the Play*, 486-488; 672-674.

Weissman, Philip. "Conscious and Unconscious Autobiograph
ical Dramas of Eugene O'Neill" *Journal of the Psycho
analytic Association*, 5: 432-460 (1957).

Winther, Sophus Keith. *"Desire Under The Elms*, A Modern
Tragedy," *Modern Drama*, 3#3: 326-332 (Winter, 1960)

DIFF'RENT

Sievers, W. D. *Freud on Broadway*, 101-102.

DYNAMO

Dahlstrom, Carl E. W. L. *"Dynamo* and *Lazarus Laughed—*
Some Limitations," *Modern Drama*, 3#3: 224-230 (Win
ter, 1960).

Sievers, W. D. *Freud on Broadway*, 119-121.

Smeets, Marcel. "Four Aspects of Eugene O'Neill's Plays,'
Revue des Langues Vivantes, 16: 47; 49 (1950).

Young, Stark. *Immortal Shadows*, 91-95.

EMPEROR JONES

(n.a.). "American Dramatist: O'Neill," *Times Literary Sup
plement*, pp. lxxviii-lxxx (Sept 17, 1954).

Blackburn, Clara. "Continental Influences on Eugene O'Neill'

Expressionistic Dramas," *American Literature,* 13#2: 109-116 (May, 1941).

Dace, Wallace. "The Dramatic Structure in Schonberg's *Erwartung,*" *Educational Theatre Journal,* 5: 423-326 (Dec, 1953).

Mierow, Herbert E. "The Greeks Started It," *Catholic World,* 166: 65-66 (Oct, 1947).

Sievers, W. D. *Freud on Broadway,* 105-106.

Smeets, Marcel. "Four Aspects of Eugene O'Neill's Plays," *Revue des Langues Vivantes,* 16: 53-54 (1950).

Stamm, R. "Dramatic Experiments of Eugene O'Neill," *English Studies,* 28#1: 11-12 (Feb, 1947).

Waith, Eugene M.: "Eugene O'Neill: An Exercise in Unmasking," *Educational Theatre Journal,* 13#3: 186 (Oct, 1961).

FOUNTAIN, THE

Fisken, A. M. I. "The Basic Unity of Eugene O'Neill," *University of Denver Publications. Studies in Humanities,* #1: 107-108 (1950).

Smeets, Marcel. "Four Aspects of Eugene O'Neill's Plays," *Revue des Langues Vivantes,* 16: 51 (1950).

Waith, Eugene M. "Eugene O'Neill: An Exercise in Unmasking," *Educational Theatre Journal,* 13#3: 187 (Oct, 1961).

GREAT GOD BROWN, THE

Berkelman, Robert. "O'Neill's Everyman," *South Atlantic Quarterly,* 58#4: 609-616 (Autumn, 1959).

Blackburn, Clara. "Continental Influences on Eugene O'Neill's Expressionistic Dramas," *American Literature,* 13#2: 122-125 (May, 1941).

Daniel, Anne. "The Frozen Countenance," *The Southern Speech Journal,* 25#3: 190-193 (Spring, 1960).

Day, Cyrus. "*Amor Fati:* O'Neill's Lazarus as Superman and Savior," *Modern Drama,* 3#3: 297-305 (Winter, 1960).

Dusenbury, Winifred L. *The Theme of Loneliness in Modern American Drama,* 171-178.

Fagin, N. Bryllon. " 'Freud' on Broadway," *Educational Theatre Journal,* 2#4: 300-301 (Dec, 1950).

Fiskin, A. M. I. "The Basic Unity of Eugene O'Neill," *University of Denver Publications. Studies in Humanities,* #1: 108-109 (1950).

Sievers, W. D. *Freud on Broadway,* 108-112.

Skene, Reg. "The *Bacchae* of Euripides and *The Great God Brown,*" *Manitoba Arts Review,* 10#3: 55-65 (Winter, 1956).
Smeets, Marcel. "Four Aspects of Eugene O'Neill's Plays," *Revue des Langues Vivantes,* 16: 55 (1950).
Stamm, R. "Dramatic Experiments of Eugene O'Neill," *English Studies,* 28#1: 13-14 (Feb, 1947).
Waith, Eugene M. "Eugene O'Neill: An Exercise in Unmasking," *Educational Theatre Journal,* 13#3: 187-189 (Oct, 1961).
Young, Stark. *Immortal Shadows,* 61-66.

HAIRY APE, THE
Alexander, Doris M. "Eugene O'Neill as Social Critic," *American Quarterly,* 6#4: 349-356 (Winter, 1954).
Bacon, Wallace A. and Robert S. Breen. *Literature as Experience,* 297-298.
Baum, Bernard. "*Tempest* and *The Hairy Ape*—The Literary Incarnation of Mythos," *Modern Language Quarterly,* 14#3: 258-273 (Sept, 1953).
Blackburn, Clara. "Continental Influences on Eugene O'Neill's Expressionistic Dramas," *American Literature,* 13#2: 116-122 (May, 1941).
Dusenbury, Winifred L. *The Theme of Loneliness in Modern American Drama,* 125-134.
Engel, Edwin A. "Ideas in the Plays of Eugene O'Neill," in John Gassner (ed), *Ideas in the Drama,* 101-107.
Fiskin, A. M. I. "The Basic Unity of Eugene O'Neill," *University of Denver Publications. Studies in Humanities,* #1: 105-106 (1950).
Gump, Margaret. "From Ape to Man and From Man to Ape," Kentucky Foreign Language Quarterly, 14#4: 181-183 (1957).
Leech, Clifford. "Eugene O'Neill and his Plays," *Critical Quarterly,* 3#3: 248-250 (Aut, 1961).
Main, William W. "The Meaning of Meaningless," *Western Humanities Review,* 12#3: 247 (Summer, 1958).
Rollins, Ronald G. "O'Casey, O'Neill and Expressionism in *Within the Gates,*" *University of West Virginia Bulletin: Philological Papers,* 13: 76-81 (1961).
Ross, J. L. *Philosophy in Literature,* 218-222.
Smeets, Marcel. "Four Aspects of Eugene O'Neill's Plays," *Revue des Langues Vivantes,* 16: 54-55 (1950).
Styan, J. L. The Elements of Drama, 245-248.
Walton, Ivan H. "Eugene O'Neill and the Folklore and Folkways of the Sea," *Western Folklore,* 14#3: 157, 160-162 (July, 1955).

ICEMAN COMETH, THE

Alexander, Doris. "Hugo of *The Iceman Cometh:* Realism and O'Neill," *American Quarterly,* 5#4: 357-366 (Winter, 1953).

Arestad, Sverre. *"The Iceman Cometh and The Wild Duck,"* *Scandinavian Studies,* 20#1: 1-11 (Feb, 1948).

Bentley, Eric. "The Return of Eugene O'Neill," *Atlantic Monthly,* 178: 64-66 (Nov, 1946).

—————————. "Trying to Like O'Neill," *Kenyon Review,* 14#3: 476-488 (Summer, 1952).

Black, Eugene. "Catharsis and Eugene O'Neill," *Mandrake,* 1#6: 40-41 (1949).

Brashear, William R. "The Wisdom of Silenus in O'Neill's *Iceman,"* *American Literature,* 36#2: 180-188 (May, 1964).

Brown, J. Mason. *Seeing More Things,* 257-265.

Brustein, Robert. *The Theater of Revolt,* 338-348.

Carson, Herbert L. "The Tragic Quest," *Personalist,* 44#3: 317 (Summer, 1963).

Chabrowe, Leonard. "Dionysus in *The Iceman Cometh,"* *Modern Drama,* 4#4: 377-388 (Feb, 1962).

Council of Learned Societies. *Soviet Interpretations of Contemporary Literature,* 21-22.

Day, Cyrus. "The Iceman and the Bridegroom," *Modern Drama,* 1#1: 3-9 (May, 1958).

Dobree, Bonamy. "Mr. O'Neill's Latest Play," *Sewanee Review,* 56#1: 118-126 (Winter, 1948).

Driver, Tom F. "On the Late Plays of Eugene O'Neill," *Tulane Drama Review,* 3#2: 8-10; 12-15; 17-20 (Dec, 1958).

Dusenbury, Winifred L. *The Theme of Loneliness in Modern American Drama,* 26-37.

Engel, Edwin A. "Eugene O'Neill's Long Day's Journey Into Light," *The Michigan Alumnus,* 63#21: 348-351 (Aug 10, 1957).

Fiskin, A. M. I. "The Basic Unity of Eugene O'Neill," *University of Denver Publications. Studies in Humanities,* #1: 116-117 (1950).

Gagey, Edmond M. *Revolution in American Drama,* 64-68.

Glicksberg, Charles I. "The Modern Playwright and the Absolute," *Queen's Quarterly,* 45#3: 466-467 (Aut, 1958).

Granger, Bruce I. "Illusion and Reality in Eugene O'Neill," *Modern Language Notes,* 73#3: 185-186 (March, 1958).

Hopkins, Vivian C. *"The Iceman* as Seen Through *The Lower Depths,"* *College English,* 11: 81-87 (Nov, 1949).

Hudson, Lynton. *Life and the Theatre,* 167-171.

Iyengar, K. R. Srinivasa. "O'Neill: The Last Phase," *The Literary Criterion*, 5#1: 44-50 (Winter, 1961).

Larson, Gerald. "From Ten Nights to Harvey: Drinking on the American Stage," *Western Humanities Review*, 10#4: 389-390 (Aut, 1956).

Leaska, Mitchell. *The Voice of Tragedy*, 269-271.

Leech, Clifford. "Eugene O'Neill and his Plays," *Critical Quarterly*, 3#4: 340-348 (Winter, 1961).

McCarthy, Mary. *Theater Chronicle*, 81-88.

——————. *Sights and Spectacles*, 81-88.

Mendelsohn, Moris O. *Soviet Intrepretations of Contemporary American Literature*, 21-22.

Muchnir, Helen. "Circe's Swine: Plays by Gorky and O'Neill," *Comparative Literature*, 3#2: 119-128 (Spring, 1951).

Myers, Henry A. *Tragedy*, 100-102.

Sievers, W. D. *Freud on Broadway*, 127-129.

Stamm, R. "A New Play by Eugene O'Neill," *English Studies*, 29#5: 138-145 (Oct, 1948).

Times Literary Supplement. "Counsels of Despair," *Times Literary Supplement*, pp. 197-199 (April 10, 1948).

Waith, Eugene M. "Eugene O'Neill: An Exercise in Unmasking," *Educational Theatre Journal*, 13#3: 189 (Oct, 1961).

Winther, Sophus. "*The Iceman Cometh*: A Study in Techniques," *Arizona Quarterly*, 3#4: 293-300 (Winter, 1947).

Wolfson, Lester M. "Inge, O'Neill and the Human Condition," *The Southern Speech Journal*, 22#4: 227-229 (Summer, 1957).

Young, Stark. *Immortal Shadows*, 271-274.

ILE

Knickerbocker, K. L. and H. Willard Reninger (eds), *Interpreting Literature*, 474-483.

IN THE ZONE

Goldhurst, William. "A Literary Source for O'Neill's *In The Zone*," *American Literature*, 35#4: 530-534 (Jan, 1964).

MacGowan, K .*Primer on Playwrighting*, 173-176.

LAZARUS LAUGHED

Alexander, Doris M. "*Lazarus Laughed* and Buddha," *Modern Language Quarterly*, 17#4: 357-365 (Dec, 1956).

Black, Eugene. "Catharsis and Eugene O'Neill," *Mandrake*, 1#6: 34-35 (1949).

EUGENE O'NEILL, CON'T. 165

Blackburn, Clara. "Continental Influences on Eugene O'Neill's Expressionistic Dramas," *American Literature*, 13#2: 125-126 (May, 1941).

Carpenter, Frederic I. *American Literature and the Dream*, 138-140.

Dahlstrom, Carl E. W. L. "*Dynamo* and *Lazarus Laughed*— Some Limitations," *Modern Drama*, 3#3: 224-230 (Winter, 1960).

Daniel, Anne. "The Frozen Countenance," *The Southern Speech Journal*, 25#3: 193-194 (Spring, 1960).

Day, Cyrus. "*Amor Fati:* O'Neill's Lazarus as Superman and Savior," *Modern Drama*, 3#3: 297-305 (Winter, 1960).

Fiskin, A. M. I. "The Basic Unity of Eugene O'Neill," *University of Denver Publications. Studies in Humanities*, #1: 109-111 (1950).

Killinger, John. *The Failure of Theology in Modern Literature*, 181-183.

Smeets, Marcel. "Four Aspects of Eugene O'Neill's Plays," *Revue des Langues Vivantes*, 16: 48-49 (1950).

LONG DAY'S JOURNEY INTO NIGHT, A

Brustein, Robert. *The Theater of Revolt*, 28-31; 348-358.

Cerf, Walter. "Psychoanalysis and the Realistic Drama," *Journal of Aesthetics and Art Criticism*, 16#3: 328-330; 333-336 (March, 1958).

Chiaromonte, Nicola. "Eugene O'Neill (1958)" *Sewanee Review*, 68#3: 494-497 (Summer, 1960).

Clurman, Harold. *Lies Like Truth*, 28-33.

Driver, Tom F. "On the Late Plays of Eugene O'Neill," *Tulane Drama Review*, 3#2: 8-12; 17-20 (Dec, 1958).

Engel, Edwin A. "Eugene O'Neill's Long Day's Journey Into Light," *The Michigan Alumnus*, 63#21: 348-354 (Aug, 10, 1957).

Iyengar, K. R. Srinivasa. "O'Neill: The Last Phase," *The Literary Criterion*, 5#1: 50-52 (Winter, 1961).

Langford, Richard. "Eugene O'Neill: The Mask of Illusion," in Richard E. Langford (ed), *Essays in Modern American Literature*, 71-75.

Leech, Clifford. "Eugene O'Neill and his Plays," *Critical Quarterly*, 3#4: 348-353 (Winter, 1961).

McDonnell, Thomas P. "O'Neill's Drama of the Psyche," *Catholic World*, 197: 120-125 (May, 1963).

Raleigh, John H. "O'Neill's *Long Day's Journey Into Night* and New England Irish Catholicism," *Partisan Review*, 26#4: 573-592 (Aut, 1959).

Redford, Grant H. "Dramatic Art vs. Autobiography. A Look

at *Long Day's Journey Into Night,*" *College English,* 25#7: 527-535 (April, 1964).

Stamm, Rudolf. " 'Faithful Realism': Eugene O'Neill and the Problem of Style," *English Studies,* 40#4: 242-250 (Aug, 1959).

Waith, Eugene M. "Eugene O'Neill: An Exercise in Unmasking," *Educational Theatre Journal,* 13#3: 189-191 (Oct, 1961).

Weissman, Philip. "Conscious and Unconscious Autobiographical Dramas of Eugene O'Neill" *Journal of the Psychoanalytic Association,* 5: 432-460 (1957).

Winther, Sophus Keith. "O'Neill's Tragic Themes: *Long Day's Journey Into Night,*" *Arizona Quarterly,* 13#4: 295-307 (Winter, 1957).

Wolfson, Lester M. "Inge, O'Neill, and the Human Condition," *The Southern Speech Journal,* 22#4: 230-232 (Summer, 1957).

MARCO MILLIONS
Sievers, W. D. *Freud on Broadway,* 115.
Smeets, Marcel. "Four Aspects of Eugene O'Neill's Plays," *Revue des Langues Vivantes,* 16: 51-52; 58-59 (1950).

MOON FOR THE MISBEGOTTEN, A
Chiaromonte, Nicola. "Eugene O'Neill (1958)" *Sewanee Review,* 68#3: 498-501 (Summer, 1960).
Clurman, Harold. *Lies Like Truth,* 26-28.
Iyengar, K. R. Srinivasa. "O'Neill: The Last Phase," *The Literary Criterion,* 5#1: 52-54 (Winter, 1961).
Langford, Richard E. "Eugene O'Neill: The Mask of Illusion," in Richard E. Langford (ed), *Essays in Modern American Literature,* 69-71.
Sievers, W. D. *Freud on Broadway,* 129-132.
Wolfson, Lester M. "Inge, O'Neill, and the Human Condition," *The Southern Speech Journal,* 22#4: 229 (Summer, 1957).

MOON OF THE CARIBBEES
MacGowan, K. *Primer on Playwrighting,* 176-178.

MOURNING BECOMES ELECTRA
Alexander, Doris M. "Captain Brant and Captain Brassbound: The Origin of an O'Neill Character," *Modern Language Notes,* 74#4: 306-310 (April, 1959).

Asselineau, Roger. *"Mourning Becomes Electra,"* *Modern Drama,* 1#3: 143-150 (Dec, 1958).

Battenhouse, Roy W. *"Mourning Becomes Electra,"* *Christendom,* 7#3: 332-345 (Summer, 1942).

Bentley, Eric. "Trying to Like O'Neill," *Kenyon Review,* 14#3: 488-492 (Summer, 1952).

Brooks, Cleanth and Robert Heilman. *Understanding Drama,* 454-457.

Burke, Kenneth. *A Grammar of Motives,* 5-6; 9-10.

Dusenbury, Winifred L. *The Theme of Loneliness in Modern American Drama,* 74-85.

Eastman, Fred. *Christ in the Drama,* 93-97.

Egri, Lajos. *The Art of Dramatic Writing,* 289-291.

Feldman, Abraham. "The American Aeschylus?" *Poet Lore,* 52#2: 149-155 (Summer, 1946).

Fiskin, A. M. I. "The Basic Unity of Eugene O'Neill," *University of Denver Publications. Studies in Humanities,* #1: 115-116 (1950).

Gagey, Edmond M. *Revolution in American Drama,* 59-61.

Gassner, John. "The Electras of Giradoux and O'Neill" in *The Theatre in Our Times,* 257-266.

Granger, Bruce I. "Illusion and Reality in Eugene O'Neill," *Modern Language Notes,* 73#3: 184-185 (March, 1958).

Hanzelli, Victor E. "The Progeny of Artreus," *Modern Drama,* 3#1: 75-81 (May, 1960).

Jones, C. Meredith. "From Aeschylus to Existentialism," *Manitoba Arts Review,* 6#1: 23 (Spring, 1948).

Lawson, John H. *Theory and Technique of Playwrighting,* 139-141.

Lecky, Eleazer. *"Ghosts* and *Mourning Becomes Electra:* Two Versions of Fate," *Arizona Quarterly,* 13#4: 320-338 (Winter, 1957).

Leech, Clifford. "Eugene O'Neill and his Plays," *Critical Quarterly,* 3#3: 252-256 (Autumn, 1961).

Mitchell, Francis M. "O'Neill's *Mourning Becomes Electra,"* *Folio (Indiana),* 8#2: 21-26 (Dec, 1942).

Muller, Herbert J. *The Spirit of Tragedy,* 313-315.

Nagarajan, S. "Eugene O'Neill's *Mourning Becomes Electra:* The Classical Aspect," *The Literary Criterion,* 5#3: 148-154 (Winter, 1962).

Olson, Elder. *Tragedy and the Theory of Drama,* 237-243.

O'Neill, Eugene. "Working Notes and Extracts From a Fragmentary Work Diary," in John Gassner (ed), *Theatre and Drama in the Making*, 830-839.

O'Neill, Joseph P. "The Tragic Theory of Eugene O'Neill," *Texas Studies in Literature and Language*, 4#4: 482-498 (Winter, 1963).

Pratt, Norman T., Jr. "Aeschylus and O'Neill: Two Worlds," *Classical Journal*, 51#4: 163-167 (Jan, 1956).

Ramsey, Warren. "The Oresteia Since Hofmannsthal: Images and Emphasis," *Revue de Litterature Comparee*, 38#3: 359-361 (July-Sept, 1964).

Sievers, W. D. *Freud on Broadway*, 121-124.

Stafford, John. "Mourning Becomes America," *Texas Studies in Literature and Language*, 3#4: 549-556 (Winter, 1962).

Stamm, R. "The Orestes Theme in Three Plays by Eugene O'Neill, T. S. Eliot, and Jean Paul Sartre," *English Studies*, 30#5: 244-247 (Oct, 1949).

Vincent, W. Ernest. "Five Electras—Aeschylus to Sartre," *The Southern Speech Journal*, 24#4: 224-226; 231-234 (Summer, 1959).

Walton, Ivan H. "Eugene O'Neill and the Folklore and Folkways of the Sea," *Western Folklore*, 14#3: 157-158 (July, 1955).

Weissman, Philip. *"Mourning Becomes Electra* and The Prodigal Electra and Orestes," *Modern Drama*, 3#3: 257-259 (Winter, 1960).

Young, Stark. *Immortal Shadows*, 132-139.

STRANGE INTERLUDE

Alexander, Doris M. *"Strange Interlude* and Schopenhauer," *American Literature,* 25#2: 213-228 (May, 1953).

Battenhouse, Roy. *"Strange Interlude* Restudied," *Religion in Life,* 15#2: 202-213 (Spring, 1946).

Black, Eugene. "Catharsis and Eugene O'Neill," *Mandrake,* 1#6: 39-40 (1949).

Blackburn, Clara. "Continental Influences on Eugene O'Neill's Expressionistic Dramas," *American Literature,* 13#2: 126-131 (Hay, 1941).

Brashear, William R. "O'Neill's Schopenhauer Interlude," *Criticism,* 6#3: 256-265.

Carpenter, Frederic I. *American Literature and the Dream,* 140-141.

Dusenbury, Winifred L. *The Theme of Loneliness in Modern American Drama,* 101-112.

Fiskin, A. M. I. "The Basic Unity of Eugene O'Neill," *University of Denver Publications. Studies in Humanities,* #1: 113-114 (1950).

Geier, Woodrow A. "Exile and Salvation in Modern Drama," *Religion in Life,* 30#4: 596 (Aut, 1961).

Glicksberg, Charles I. "Eros and the Death of God," *Western Humanities Review,* 13#4: 366-367 (Aut, 1959).

Granger, Bruce I. "Illusion and Reality in Eugene O'Neill," *Modern Language Notes,* 73#3: 179-180; 183-184 (Mar, 1958).

Leech, Clifford. "Eugene O'Neill and his Plays," *Critical Quarterly,* 3#3: 250-252 (Autumn, 1961).

McCoy, Elizabeth C. "Amorality and Dramatic Tragedy," *Asides,* 2: 17-22 (1941).

Sievers, W. D. *Freud on Broadway,* 115-119.

Smeets, Marcel. "Four Aspects of Eugene O'Neill's Plays," *Revue des Langes Vivantes,* 16: 55-57 (1950).

TOUCH OF THE POET, A

Alexander, Doris. "Eugene O'Neill and Charles Lever," *Modern Drama,* 5#4: 415-420 (Feb, 1963).

Driver, Tom F. "On the Late Plays of Eugene O'Neill," *Tulane Drama Review,* 3#2: 8-10; 16-20 (Dec, 1958).

Iyengar, K. R. Srinivasa. "O'Neill: The Last Phase," *The Literary Criterion,* 5#1: 54-57 (Winter, 1961).

McCarthy, Mary. *Theater Chronicle,* 199-208.

Marcus, Mordecai. "Eugene O'Neill's Debt to Thoreau in *A Touch of The Poet,*" *Journal of English and Germanic Philology,* 62#2: 270-279 (April, 1963).

Pallette, Drew B. "O'Neill's *A Touch of The Poet* and His Other Last Plays," *Arizona Quarterly,* 13#4: 308-320 (Winter, 1957).

Winther, S. K. "O'Neill's Posthumous Play: A Touch of the Poet," *Prairie Schooner,* 32#1: 7-12 (Spring, 1958).

WELDED

Alexander, Doris M. "Eugene O'Neill, 'The Hound of Heaven,' and the 'Hell Hole'," *Modern Language Quarterly,* 20: 307-314 (Dec, 1959).

Sievers, W. D. *Freud on Broadway,* 104-105.

OSBORNE, JOHN

ENTERTAINER, THE

Deming, Barbara. "John Osborne's War Against the Phili-

stines," *Hudson Review,* 11#3 : 415-419 (Autumn, 1958).
Hastings, Michael. *"The Entertainer,"* *Encore,* 4#2 : 2 pp. (Nov-Dec, 1957).
Taylor, John R. *Anger and After,* 47-50.
West, Alick. "John Osborne," *Filologiai Kozlony,* 9: 26-27 (Supplement 1963).

EPITAPH FOR GEORGE DILLON
MacCarthy, Mary. *Theater Chronicle,* 199-208.
Taylor, John R. *Anger and After,* 45-47.
Watt, David. "Early Osborne," *Encore,* 5#1 : 41-42 (May-June, 1958).

INADMISSIBLE EVIDENCE
Taylor, John Russell. *"Inadmissible Evidence,"* *Encore,* 11#6: 43-46 (Nov-Dec, 1964).

LOOK BACK IN ANGER
Deming, Barbara. "John Osborne's War Against the Philistines," *Hudson Review,* 11#3 : 411-415 (Autumn, 1958).
Huss, Roy. "John Osborne's Backward Half-Way Look," *Modern Drama,* 6#1 : 20-25 (May, 1963).
Kerr, Walter. *The Decline of Pleasure,* 96.
————————. *The Theater in Spite of Itself,* 129-131.
Langman, F. H. "The Generation That Got Lost Staying Home," *Theoria,* 11 : 29-30 (1958).
MacCarthy, Mary. *Theater Chronicle,* 186-198.
Mander, John. *The Writer and Commitment,* 182-187.
Weiss, Samuel A. "Osborne's Angry Young Play," *Educational Theatre Journal,* 12#4: 285-288 (Dec, 1960).
West, Alick. "John Osborne," *Filologiai Kozlony,* 9: 25-26 (Supplement—1963).

LUTHER
Marowitz, Charles. "The Ascension of John Osborne," *Tulane Drama Review,* 7#2 : 175-179 (Winter, 1962).
Milne, Tom. *"Luther* and *The Devils,"* *New Left Review,* 12: 55-57 (Nov-Dec, 1961).
Taylor, John R. *Anger and After,* 54-57.
West, Alick. "John Osborne," *Filologiai Kozlony,* 9: 27-28 (Supplement—1963).

SUBJECT OF SCANDAL AND CONCERN, A
Taylor, John A. *Anger and After,* 52-54.

WORLD OF PAUL SLICKEY, THE
Findlater, Richard. "The Case of P. Slickey," *Twentieth Century*, 167#995: 29-38 (Jan, 1960).
Taylor, John A. *Anger and After*, 50-52.

OTWAY, THOMAS

CAIUS MARIUS
Hook, Lucyle. "Shakespeare Improv'd, or a Case for the Affirmative," *Shakespeare Quarterly*, 4#3: 295-298 (July, 1953).

VENICE PRESERVED
Fellheimer, J. "Michele Leoni's *Venezia Salvata*, The First Italian Translation of Otway's Tragedy," *Italica*, 22#1: 1-13 (March, 1945).
Hauser, David R. "Otway Preserved: Theme and Form in *Venice Preserved*," *Studies in Philology*, 55#3: 481-493 (July, 1958).
Hughes, R. E. "Comic Relief in Otway's *Venice Preserv'd*," *Notes and Queries*, 203: 65-66 (Feb, 1958).
McBurney, William H. "Otway's Tragic Muse Debauched: Sensuality in *Venice Preserv'd*," *Journal of English and Germanic Philology*, 58#3: 380-399 (July, 1959).
Mackenzie, Aline. "*Venice Preserv'd*," *Tulane Studies in English*, 1: 81-118 (1949).
Meyerstein, E. H. "The Dagger in *Venice Preserv'd*," *Times Literary Supplement*, pg. 565 (Sept 7, 1951).
Prior, Moody E. *The Language of Tragedy*, 186-192.
Voris, W. Van. "Tragedy Through Restoration Eyes: *Venice Preserv'd* in it Own Theatre," *Hermathena*, 99: 55-65 (Autumn, 1964).

OWEN, ALUN

PROGRESS TO THE PARK
Taylor, John R. Anger and After, 188-192.

ROUGH AND READY LOT, THE
Taylor, John R. *Anger and After*, 185-188.

WAYS OF LOVE, THE
Taylor, John R. *Anger and After*, 199-201.

PEELE, GEORGE

ARRAIGNMENT OF PARIS, THE
Clemen, Wolfgang. *English Tragedy Before Shakespeare,*
163-167.

BATTLE OF ALCAZAR
Bevington, David M. *From Mankind to Marlowe,* 104-107;
110-113.
Clemen, Wolfgang. *English Tragedy Before Shakespeare,*
171-173.
McDonnell, R. F. *The Aspiring Mind,* 150-152.
Reese, Gertrude C. "The Succession Question in Elizabethan
Drama," *Studies in English,* pp. 67-68 (1942).
Rice, Warner G. "A Principal Source of *The Battle of Alca-
zar,*" *Modern Language Notes,* 58#6: 428-431 (June,
1943).

DAVID AND BETHSABE
Clemen, Wolfgang. *English Tragedy Before Shakespeare,*
173-176; 262-267.
Ekeblad, I. S."*The Love of King David and Fair Bethsabe:*
A Note on George Peele's Biblical Drama," *English
Studies,* 39#2: 57-62 (April, 1958).
McDonnell, R. F. *The Aspiring Mind,* 148-150.

EDWARD I
Clemen, Wolfgang. *English Tragedy Before Shakespeare,*
167-173.
Norgaard, Holgar. "Peele's *Edward I* and Two Queen Elinor
Ballads," *English Studies Supplement,* 45: 165-168
(1964).
Reeves, John D. "Two Perplexities in Peele's *King Edward
the First,*" *Notes and Queries,* 201: 328-329 (Aug, 1956).
——————. "Persus and the Flying Horse in Peele and
Heywood," *Review of English Studies,* N.S.6#24: 397
(Nov, 1955).
Ribner, Irving. *The English History Play in the Age of Shakes-
peare,* 89-94.

HUNTING OF CUPID, THE
Cutts, John P. "Peele's *Hunting of Cupid,*" *Studies in the
Renaissance,* 5: 121-129 (1958).

LIFE AND DEATH OF JACK STRAWE, THE
See: Anon

OLD WIVES TALE

Bradbrook, M. C. "Peele's *Old Wives Tale:* A Play of Enchantment," *English Studies,* 43#5: 323-330 (Oct, 1962).

Clemen, Wolfgang. *English Tragedy Before Shakespeare,* 176-177.

Goldstone, Herbert. "Interplay in Peele's *The Old Wives' Tale,*" *Boston University Studies in English,* 4#4: 202-222 (Winter, 1960).

Lyons-Render, Sylvia. "Folk Motifs in George Peele's *The Old Wives Tale,*" *Tennessee Folklore Society Bulletin,* 26#3: 62-71 (Sept, 1960).

Talbert, Ernest W. *Elizabethan Drama and Shakespeare's Early Drama,* 28-30.

PERCY, WILLIAM

FOREST TRAGAEDYE IN VACUNIUM, A

Dodds, Madeline H. *"A Forest Tragaedye in Vacunium,"* *Modern Language Review,* 40#4: 246-258 (Oct, 1945).

PHARIS, GWEN

Brodersen, G. L. "Gwen Pharis—Canadian Dramatist," *Manitoba Arts Review,* 4#1: 12-14 (Spring, 1944).

COURTING OF MARIE JENVRIN, THE

Brodersen, G. L. "Gwen Pharis—Canadian Dramatist," *Maniitoba Arts Review,* 4#1: 14-16 (Spring, 1944).

ONE MAN'S HOUSE

Brodersen, G. L. "Gwen Pharis—Canadian Dramatist," *Manitoba Arts Review,* 4#1: 17 (Spring, 1944).

PASQUE FLOWERS

Brodersen, G. L. "Gwen Pharis—Canadian Dramatist," *Manitoba Arts Review,* 4#1: 7-12 (Spring, 1944).

STILL STANDS THE HOUSE

Brodersen, G. L. "Gwen Pharis—Canadian Dramatist," *Manitoba Arts Review,* 4#1: 4-6 (Spring, 1944).

PHILIPS, AMBROSE

DISTRESSED MOTHER, THE

Boas, F. S. *An Introduction to Eighteenth Century Drama,* 126-130.

Parnell, Paul E. *"The Distrest Mother,* Ambrose Philips' Morality Play," *Comparative Literature,* 11#12: 111-123 (Spring, 1959).

Wheatley, Katherine E. "Andromaque as the 'Distrest Mother,'" *Romanic Review,* 39#1: 3-21 (Feb, 1948).

HUMFREY, DUKE OF GLOUCESTER
Boas, F. S. *An Introduction to Eighteenth Century Drama,* 133-136.
Bryan, Adolphus J. "Ambrose Philips' *Humfrey, Duke of Gloucester:* A Study in Eighteenth-Century Adaptation," in N. M. Caffee and T. A. Kirby (eds), *Studies for William A. Read,* 221-236.

PHILIPS, WATTS

THE DEAD HEART
Dolmetsch, Carl R. "Dickens and *The Dead Heart,*" *Dickensian,* 55#3: 179-185 (Autumn, 1959).

PICKERZNG, JOHN

HORESTES
Phillips, James E. "A Revaluation of *Horestes* (1567)," *Huntington Library Quarterly,* 18#3: 227-244 (May, 1955).

PINERO, SIR ARTHUR WING

IRIS
Burns, Winifred. "Certain Women Characters of Pinero's Serious Drama," *Poet Lore,* 54#3: 195-197; 203-207; 217-219 (Autumn, 1948).

MAGISTRATE, THE
Takeuchi, H. "The First Two Farces of Sir Arthur W. Pinero's Court Series," *The Humanities* (Yokohama), 2: 1-13; 17-27 (March, 1953).

MID-CHANNEL
Burns, Winifred. "Certain Women Characters of Pinero's Serious Drama," *Poet Lore,* 54#3: 195-197; 212-219 (Autumn, 1948).

NOTORIOUS MRS. EBBSMITH
Burns, Winifred. "Certain Women Characters of Pinero's Serious Drama," *Poet Lore,* 54#3: 195-197; 207-212; 217-219 (Autumn, 1948).
Shaw, G. B.*Plays and Players,* 25-32.

PRINCESS AND THE BUTTERFLY, THE;
OR THE FANTASTICS
>Shaw, G. B. *Plays and Players,* 204-214.

PROFLIGATE, THE
>Wellwarth, George E. "The Career of Sir Arthur Wing Pinero: A Study in Theatrical Taste," *Southern Speech Journal,* 26#1: 48-50 (Fall, 1960).

SCHOOLMISTRESS, THE
>Takeuchi, H. "The First Two Farces of Sir Arthur W. Pinero's Court Series," *The Humantiies* (Yokohama), 2: 1-11; 14-27 (March, 1953).

SECOND MRS. TANQUERAY, THE
>Burns, Winifred. "Certain Women Characters of Pinero's Serious Drama," *Poet Lore,* 54#3: 195-203; 217-219 (Autumn, 1948).
>Fulton, A. R. *Drama and Theatre,* 1-11.
>Kornbluth, Martin L. "Two Fallen Women," *Shavian,* 14: 14-15 (Feb, 1959).
>Nethercot, Arthur H. "The Quintessence of Idealism: Or, the Slaves of Duty," *PMLA,* 62#3: 852 (Sept, 1947).
>Shaw, G. B. *Plays and Players,* 21-25.
>Snell, Joseph. *"The Second Mrs. Tanqueray,"* *World Review,* pp. 23-28 (Oct, 1950).
>Wellwarth, George E. "The Career of Sir Arthur Wing Pinero: A Study in Theatrical Taste," *Southern Speech Journal,* 26#1: 51-53; 57-58 (Fall, 1960).
>Worsley, T. C. *The Fugitive Art,* 168-171.

TRELAWNY OF THE WELLS
>Shaw, G. B. *Plays and Players,* 299-306.

PINTER, HAROLD

BIRTHDAY PARTY, THE
>Cohn, Ruby. "The World of Harold Pinter," *Tulane Drama Review,* 6#3: 58-59; 63-65 (March, 1962).
>Dukore, Bernard. "The Theater of Harold Pinter," *Tulane Drama Review,* 6#3: 43-54 (March, 1962).
>Esslin, Martin. "Pinter and the Absurd," *Twentieth Century,* 169#1008: 179-182 (Feb, 1961).
>—————————. *Theatre of the Absurd,* 202-207.

Hoefer, Jacqueline. "Pinter and Whiting: Two Attitudes Towards the Alienated Artist," *Modern Drama*, 4#4: 402-
408 (Feb, 1962).

Leech, Clifford. "Two Romantics: Arnold Wesker and Harold
Pinter," *Stratford-Upon-Avon-Studies*, 4: 23-26 (1962).

Milne, Tom. "The Hidden Face of Violence," *Encore*, 7#1:
16-20 (Jan-Feb, 1960).

Taylor, John R. *Anger and After*, 236-239.

Wardle, Irving. "*The Birthday Party*," *Encore*, 5#2: 39-40
(July-August, 1958).

CARETAKER, THE

Chabrowe, L. E. "The Pains of Being Diversified," *Kenyon
Review*, 25#1: 142-145 (Winter, 1963).

Cohn, Ruby. "The World of Harold Pinter," *Tulane Drama
Review*, 6#3: 65-68 (March, 1962).

Dukore, Bernard. "The Theater of Harold Pinter," *Tulane
Drama Review*, 6#3: 43-54 (March, 1962).

Esslin, Martin. "Pinter and the Absurd," *Twentieth Century*,
169#1008: 182-185 (Feb, 1961).

——————. *Theatre of the Absurd*, 210-214.

Goodman, F. J. "Pinter's *The Caretaker:* The Lower Depths
Descended," *Modern Drama*, 5: 117-126 (Winter, 1964)

Kerr, Walter. *The Theater in Spite of Itself*, 116-119.

Leech, Clifford. "Two Romantics: Arnold Wesker and Harold
Pinter," *Stratford-Upon-Avon Studies*, 4: 23-26 (1962)

Minogue, Valerie. "Taking Care of the Caretaker," *Twentieth
Century*, 168#1003: 243-248 (Sept, 1960).

Taylor, John R. *Anger and After*, 246-250.

COLLECTION, THE

Cohn, Ruby. "Latter Day Pinter," *Drama Survey*, 3#3: 372-
374 (Feb, 1964).

DUMB WAITER, THE

Cohn, Ruby. "The World of Harold Pinter," *Tulane Drama
Review*, 6#3: 61-63 (March, 1962).

Dukore, Bernard. "The Theater of Harold Pinter," *Tulane
Drama Review*, 6#3: 43-54 (March, 1962).

Esslin, Martin. "Pinter and the Absurd," *Twentieth Century*,
169#1008: 179 (Feb, 1961).

Taylor, John R. *Anger and After*, 238-240.

DWARFS, THE

Cohn, Ruby. "Latter Day Pinter," *Drama Survey*, 3#3: 367-
370 (Feb, 1964).

Taylor, John R. *Anger and After,* 255-258.

NIGHT OUT, A
Taylor, John R. *Anger and After,* 250-252.

ROOM, THE
Cohn, Ruby. "The World of Harold Pinter," *Tulane Drama Review,* 6#3: 59-61 (March, 1962).
Dukore, Bernard. "The Theater of Harold Pinter," *Tulane Drama Review,* 6#3: 43-54 (March, 1962).
Esslin, Martin. "Pinter and the Absurd," *Twentieth Century,* 169#1008: 176-179 (Feb, 1961).
—————————. *Theatre of the Absurd,* 199-201.
Taylor, John R. *Anger and After,* 234-236.

SILENT ACHE, A
Cohn, Ruby. "Latter Day Pinter," *Drama Survey,* 3#3: 370-372 (Feb, 1964).
Sainer, Arthur. *The Sleepwalker and the Assassin,* 99-102.

PORTER, HENRY
TWO ANGRY WOMEN OF ABINGTON, THE
Bowers, R. H. "Notes on *The Two Angry Women of Abington,*" *Notes and Queries,* 193: 311-314 (24 July, 1948).
Maxwell, Baldwin. *"The Two Angry Women of Abington* and *Wily Beguiled,"* in B. Maxwell (ed), *Renaissance Studies in Honor of Hardin Craig,* 142-147.
ALSO IN: *Philological Quarterly,* 20#3: 334-339 (July, 1941).
Nosworthy, J. M. "The Two Angry Families of Verona," *Shakespeare Quarterly,* 3#3: 219-226 (July, 1952).
—————————. "Henry Porter," *English,* 6#32: 65-69 (Summer, 1946).

POUND, EZRA
WOMEN OF TRACHIS
Donoghue, Denis. *The Third Voice,* 213-222.
Mason, H. A. *"The Women of Trachis,"* *Arion,* 2#1: 59-81 (Spring, 1963).
—————————. *"The Women of Trachis,"* *Arion,* 2#2: 105-121 (Summer, 1963).
Sutherland, Donald. "Ezra Pound on Sophocles," *Colorado Quarterly,* 8#2: 182-191 (Aut, 1959).

PRESTON, THOMAS
CAMBISES, KING OF PERSIA
Bevington, David M. *From Mankind to Marlowe,* 81-89; 183-189; 211-216.

Clemen, Wolfgang. *English Tragedy Before Shakespeare,*
193-194.

Harrison, George. *Elizabethan Plays and Players,* 5-9.

McDonnell, R. F. *The Aspiring Mind,* 99-100.

Ribner, Irving. *The English History Play in the Age of*
Shakespeare, 53-60.

PRIESTLY, JOHN BOYNTON

DANGEROUS CORNER, THE
Dutt, Aruna. "The Time Plays of J B. Priestly," *The Visua-*
bharati Quarterly, 20#4: 307-309; 316-320 (Spring,
1955).

DEATH HIGHWAY
Dutt, Aruna. "The Time Plays of J. B. Priestley," *The Visua-*
bharati Quarterly, 20#4: 315-320 (Spring, 1955).

EVER SINCE PARADISE
Gibbs, Patrick. "Mr. Priestley's New Play," *The World Re-*
view, pp. 56-60 (March, 1947).

I HAVE BEEN HERE BEFORE
Dutt, Aruna. "The Time Plays of J. B. Priestley," *The Visua-*
bharati Quarterly, 20#4: 310-312; 316-320 (Spring,
1955).

INSPECTOR CALLS, AN
Styan, J. L *The Elements of Drama,* 197-198.

LINDEN TREE, THE
Schlosser, Anselm. "A Crtical Survey of Some of Priestley's
Plays," *Zeitschrift fur Anglistik und Amerikanistik,* 10:
139-142 (1962).

LONG MIRROR, THE
Dutt, Aruna. "The Time Plays of J. B. Priestley," *The Visua-*
bharati Quarterly, 20#4: 314-320 (Spring, 1955).
Smith, Grover, Jr. "Time Alive: J. W. Dunne and J. B.
Priestly," *South Atlantic Quarterly,* 58#2: 230-231
(April, 1959).

MUSIC AT NIGHT
Dutt, Aruna. "The Time Plays of J. B. Priestley," *The Visua-*
bharati Quarterly, 20#4: 313-314; 316-320 (Spring,
1955).

TIME AND THE CONWAYS

Dutt, Aruna. "The Time Plays of J. B. Priestley," *The Visua-bharati Quarterly,* 20#4: 309-310; 316-320 (Spring, 1955).

Schlosser, Anselm "A Critical Survey of Some of Priestley's Plays," *Zeitschrift fur Anglistik und Amerikanistik,* 10: 135-137 (1962).

Smith, Grover Jr. "Time Alive: J. W. Dunne and J. B. Priestly," *South Atlantic Quarterly,* 58#2: 228-229 (April, 1959).

—AND JACQUETTA HAWKES
THE WHITE COUNTESS

Findlater, Richard. *"The Two Countesses,"* Twentieth Century, 156#930: 175-179 (August, 1954).

RANDOLPH, THOMAS

PRAELUDIUM

Bentley, Gerald E. "Randolph's *Praeludium* and the Salisbury Court Theatre," in James G. McManaway, (ed), *Joseph Q. Adams Memorial Studies,* 775-783.

RASTELL, JOHN

NATURE OF THE FOUR ELEMENTS, THE
See: Anon

OF GENTLENESS AND NOBILITY
Bevington, David M. *From Mankind to Marlowe,* 42-43.

RATTIGAN, TERENCE

ADVENTURE STORY
Worsley, T. C. *The Fugitive Art,* 66-69.

SEPARATE TABLES
Styan, J. L. *The Elements of Drama,* 270-271

WINSLOW BOY, THE
Brown, J. Mason. *Seeing More Things,* 38-42.

RAWLINS, THOMAS

THE REBELLION
Bowers, Fredson T. *Elizabethan Revenge Tragedy,* 221-223

READE, CHARLES

    IT IS NEVER TOO LATE
        Krause, David. "Realism in the Drama of Charles Reade,"
           English, 12: 94-100 (Aut, 1958).

REANEY, JAMES

    EASTER EGG, THE
        Tait, Michael. "The Limits of Innocence," *Canadian Litera-*
           ture, 19: 46-48 (Winter, 1964).

    KILLDEER, THE
        Tait, Michael. "The Limits of Innocence," *Canadian Litera-*
           ture, 19: 43-46 (Winter, 1964).

RELLA, ETTORE

    SIGN OF DEATH
        Humboldt, Charles. "No Hard Feelings," *Mainstream,* 11#10:
           35-42 (Oct, 1958).

REDFORD, JOHN

    WIT AND SCIENCE
        Brown, Arthur. "The Play of *Wit and Science,*" *Philological*
           Quarterly, 48#4: 429-442 (Oct, 1949).
        Broussard, Louis. *American Drama,* 41-43.

RICE, ELMER

    ADDING MACHINE, THE
        Marx, Milton. *The Enjoyment of Drama,* 207-209.
        Popkin, Henry. "Elmer Rice: The Triumph of 'Mr. Zero',"
           Commentary, 11: 283-285 (March, 1951).
        Rabkin, Gerald. *Drama and Commitment,* 243-245.
        Sievers, W. D. *Freud on Broadway,* 147-149.

    LEFT BANK, THE
        Sievers, W. D. *Freud on Broadway,* 150-152.

    NOT FOR CHILDREN
        Rabkin, Gerald. *Drama and Commitment,* 239-241.
        Sievers, W. D. *Freud on Broadway,* 154-155.

    STREET SCENE
        Brooks, Cleanth and Robert Heilman. *Understanding Drama,*
           19-20 (Appendix—1961 ed.) ; 471-472 (1945 ed).

Dusenbury, Winifred L. *The Theme of Loneliness in Modern American Drama*, 113-119.

Fulton, A. R. *Drama and Theatre*, 296-303.

Rabkin, Gerald. *Drama and Commitment*, 246-247.

Watts, Harold. "Maxwell Anderson: The Tragedy of Attrition," *College English*, 4#4: 220-221 (Jan, 1943).

Young, Stark. *Immortal Shadows*, 106-109.

SUBWAY, THE
Rabkin, Gerald. *Drama and Commitment*, 245-247.
Sievers, W. D. *Freud on Broadway*, 149-150.

RICHARDSON, HOWARD

—AND WILLIAM BERNEY
DARK OF THE MOON
Baxter, Beverley and Craddock Munro. *"Dark of the Moon,"* *World Review*, pp. 17-21 (May, 1949).

RICHARDSON, JACK

GALLOW'S HUMOR
Mottram, Eric. "The New American Wave," *Encore*, 11#1: 38-40 (Jan-Feb, 1964).
Wellwarth, George E. "Hope Deferred—The New American Drama," *The Literary Review*, 7#1: 18-20 (Autumn, 1963).

LORENZO
Wellwarth, George E. "Hope Deferred—The New American Drama," *The Literary Review*, 7#1: 20-21 (Autumn, 1963).

PRODIGAL, THE
Mottram, Eric. "The New American Wave," *Encore*, 11#1: 35-38 (Jan-Feb, 1964).
Wellwarth, George E. "Hope Deferred—The New American Drama," *The Literary Review*, 7#1: 16-18 (Autumn, 1963).

RODMAN, HOWARD

THE EXPLORER
Borgers, Edward W. "Meaning in Broadcasts," *Western Speech*, 26#4: 201-204 (Fall, 1964).

ROGERS, RICHARD & OSCAR HAMMERSTEIN

ALLEGRO
Brown, John Mason. *Seeing More Things,* 134-141.

OKLAHOMA
Bentley, Eric. *The Playwright as Thinker,* 6-7; 281-285; 363-364.

SOUTH PACIFIC
Jackson, Stoney. *This Is Love?,* 41-46.

ROWE, NICHOLAS

AMBITIOUS STEPMOTHER, THE
Boas, F. S. *An Introduction to Eighteenth Century Drama,* 2-8.
Magill, Lewis M. "Poetic Justice: The Dilemma of the Early Creators of Sentimental Tragedy," *Washington State College Research Studies,* 25#1: 27-29 (March, 1957).
Singh, Amrik. "The Argument on Poetic Justice (Addison vs. Dennis)" *Indian Journal of English Studies,* 3#1: 62-63 (1962).

FAIR PENITENT, THE
Boas, F. S. *An Introduction to Eighteenth Century Drama,* 13-17.
Clark, Donald B. "An Eighteenth Century Adaptation of Massinger," *Modern Language Quarterly,* 13: 239-252 (1952).
Wyman, Lindley A. "The Tradition of the Formal Meditation in Rowe's *The Fair Penitent,*" *Philological Quarterly,* 42#3: 412-416 (July, 1963).

JANE SHORE
Schwarz, Alfred. "An Example of Eighteenth Century Pathetic Tragedy: Rowe's *Jane Shore,*" *Modern Language Quarterly,* 22: 236-247 (1961).

LADY JANE GRAY
Boas, F. S. *An Introduction to Eighteenth Century Drama,* 27-31.

ROYAL CONVERT, THE
Boas, F. S. *An Introduction to Eighteenth Century Drama,* 21-24.

TAMERLANE
    Boas, F. S. *An Introduction to Eighteenth Century Drama,*
       8-12.
    Clark, Donald B. "The Source and Characterization of Nich-
       olas Rowe's *Tamerlaine,*" *Modern Language Notes,* 65#3:
       145-152 (March, 1950).
    Thorp, Willard. "A Key to Rowe's *Tamerlane,*" *Journal of
       English and Germanic Philology,* 39#1: 124-127 (Jan,
       1940).

ULYSSES
    Boas, F. S. *An Introduction to Eighteenth Century Drama,*
       18-21.

ROWLEY, SAMUEL

WHEN YOU SEE ME YOU KNOW ME
    Ribner, Irving. *The English History Play in the Age of
       Shakespeare,* 278-284.

ROWLEY, WILLIAM

ALL'S LOST BY LUST
    Bowers, Fredson T. *Elizabethan Revenge Tragedy,* 200-202.

BIRTH OF MERLIN, THE
    Daube, David. "The Date of *The Birth of Merlin,*" *Aberdeen
       University Review,* 35#1: 49-50 (Spring, 1953).

WITCH OF EDMONTON, THE
    See: John Ford

RUDKIN, DAVID

AFORE NIGHT CAME
    Milne, Tom. *"Afore Night Came,"* *Encore,* 9#4: 50-54 (July-
       Aug, 1962).

RUSSELL, GEORGE WILLIAM
    See: A E

S., J.

ANDROMANA
    Bowers, Fredson T. *Elizabethan Revenge Tragedy,* 249-252.

S., W.

LOCRINE
See: Anon

SACKVILLE, THOMAS

GORBODUC
See: Thomas Norton

SAMPSON, WILLIAM

THE VOW BREAKER; OR THE FAIR MAIDEN
OF CLIFTON
Adams, Henry. *English Domestic or Homiletic Tragedies,* 173-
177.

SANTAYANA, GEORGE

LUCIFER; OR THE HEAVENLY TRUCE
Jones, Howard M. *The Bright Medusa,* 54-56.

SARGESON, FRANK

A TIME FOR SHOWING
Chapman, Robert. *"A Time For Showing,"* Comment, 9: 6-7
(Spring, 1961).

SAROYAN, WILLIAM

BEAUTIFUL PEOPLE, THE
Sievers, W. D. *Freud on Broadway,* 248.

GET AWAY OLD MAN
Sievers, W. D. *Freud on Broadway,* 248-249.

HELLO, OUT THERE
Bacon, Wallace A. and Robert S. Breen. *Literature as Experience,* 266-271.

JIM DANDY
Dolman, John. *"Jim Dandy, Pioneer,"* Quarterly Journal of
Speech, 30#1: 72-75 (Feb, 1944).
Sievers, W. D. *Freud on Broadway,* 249-250.

LOVE'S OLD SWEET SONG
Sievers, W. D. *Freud on Broadway,* 248.
Young, Stark. *Immortal Shadows,* 215-217.

MY HEART'S IN THE HIGHLANDS
Clurman, H. *The Fervent Years,* 232-236.
Sievers, W. D. *Freud on Broadway,* 246-247.

TIME OF YOUR LIFE, THE
Carpenter, Frederic I. *American Literature and the Dream,* 179-180.
Clurman, H. *Lies Like Truth,* 57-59.
Dusenbury, Winifred L. *The Theme of Loneliness in Modern American Drama,* 157-164.
Gassner, John. *The Theatre in our Time,* 297-302; 573-576.
Healy, Robert C. "Anderson, Saroyan, Sherwood: New Directions," *Catholic World,* 151: 176-178 (Nov, 1940).
McCarthy, Mary. *Theater Chronicle,* 46-52.

SAUNDERS, JAMES

A SCENT OF FLOWERS
Fenwick, J. H. *"A Scent of Flowers," Encore,* 11#6: 49-51 (Nov-Dec, 1964).

SEYMOUR, ALAN

FIRST DAY OF THE YEAR, THE
Davison, P. H. "Three Australian Plays: National Myths Under Criticism," *Southerly,* 23#2: 120-127 (1963).

SHADWELL, THOMAS
BURY FAIR
Mignon, Elizabeth. *Crabbed Age and Youth,* 29-30; 77-79.

EPSOM-WELLS
Mignon, Elizabeth. *Crabbed Age and Youth,* 27-28; 79-80.

MISER, THE
Mignon, Elizabeth. *Crabbed Age and Youth,* 74-77.
Wilcox, John. *The Relation of Moliere to Restoration Comedy,* 65-67.

SQUIRE OF ALSATIA, THE
Kronenberger, Louis. *The Thread of Laughter,* 94-98.
Wilcox, John. *The Relation of Moliere to Restoration Comedy,* 21-23.

TIMON OF ATHENS
Vernon, T. F. "Social Satire in Shadwell's *Timon,*" *Studia Neophilologica,* 35#2: 221-226 (1963).

VIRTUOSO, THE
Evans, C. Blakemore. "The Source of Shadwell's Character of Sir Formal Trifle in *The Virtuoso*," *Modern Language Review*, 35#2: 211-214 (April, 1940).

TRUE WIDOW, A
Kronenberger, Louis. *The Thread of Laughter*, 98-101.

SHAFFER, PETER

FIVE FINGER EXERCISE
Taylor, John R. *Anger and After*, 227-229.

SHAKESPEARE, WILLIAM

See Shakespeare Section of this Checklist beginning on Page 236.

SHAPIRO, KARL

TELESCOPE FOR THE EMPEROR, A
Fukuda, Rikutaro. "Japanese Elements in Western Literature," *Yearbook of Comparative and General Literature*, 11: 206-208 (1962 Supplement).

SHAW, GEORGE BERNARD

ANDROCLES AND THE LION
Brown, John M. *Seeing More Things*, 181-187.
Eastman, Fred. *Christ in the Drama*, 44-54.
Ross, Julian. *Philosophy in Literature*, 124-126.

APPLE CART, THE
Clurman, H. *Lies Like Truth*, 142-144.
McDowell, Frederick P. W. "The External Against the Expedient: Structure and Theme in Shaw's *The Apple Cart*," *Modern Drama*, 2#2: 99-113 (Sept, 1959).
Styan, J. L. *The Elements of Drama*, 101-103.

ARMS AND THE MAN
Clurman, Harold. *Lies Like Truth*, 136-137.
Elliott, R. C. "Shaw's Captain Bluntschli: A Latter-Day Falstaff," *Modern Language Notes*, 67#7: 461-465 (Nov, 1952).
Perrine, Laurence. "Shaw's *Arms and the Man*," *The Explicator*, 15#9: 54 (June, 1957).
Styan, J. L. *The Elements of Drama*, 100-101; 170-175.

ALSO IN: "Manipulation of the Characters," in Robert
W. Corrigan and James L. Rosenberg (eds), *The Context and Craft of Drama,* 105-109.

West, E. J. " 'Arma Virumque' Shaw did not Sing," *Colorado
Quarterly,* 1#3: 267-280 (Winter, 1953).
————————. "Hollywood and Mr. Shaw: Some Reflections on Shavian Drama-Into-Cinema," *Educational Theatre Journal,* 5: 223-232 (Oct, 1953).

BACK TO METHUSELAH

Barnet, Sylvan. "Bernard Shaw on Tragedy," *PMLA,* 71#5:
896-897 (Dec, 1956).

Brustein, Robert. *The Theater of Revolt,* 18-21; 195-204.

Geduld, H. M. "Place and Treatment of Persons in *Back to
Methuselah,*" *The California Shavian,* 5#6: 1-11 (Nov-
Dec, 1964).
————————. "Shaw's Philosophy and Cosmology," *The
California Shavian,* 1#4 (May, 1960).
————————. "Shaw's Philosophy as Expounded in *Back to
Methuselah,*" *The California Shavian,* 5#5: 11-19 (Sept-
Oct, 1964).
————————. "Sources and Influences of Shaw's Penta-
teuch," *The California Shavian,* 5#3: 1-10 (May-June,
1964).

Glicksberg, Charles I. "Shaw versus Science," *Dalhousie
Review,* 28#3: 277-280 (Oct, 1948).

Gupta, P. C. *The Art of Galsworthy and Other Essays,* 89-91.

Hopper, Stanley R. (ed). *Spiritual Problems in Contemporary
Literature,* 195-196.

Jones, William. *The Priest and the Siren,* 72-78.

Krutch, J. W. *Modernism in Modern Drama,* 61-62.

Leary, Daniel and Richard Foster. "Adam and Eve: Evolving
Archetypes in *Back to Methuselah,*" *The Shaw Review,*
4#2: 12-24 (May, 1961).

Morgan, Margery M. "*Back to Methuselah:* The Poet and the
City," *Essays and Studies (English Association),* 13: 82-
98 (1960).

Pettet, Edwin B. "Shaw's Socialist Life," *Educational Theatre Journal,* 3#2: 109-114 (May, 1951).

Ross, J. L. *Philosophy in Literature,* 208-209.

Thornton, Duesbery. "The Electric Hedge," *Notes and Queries,* 204: 388 (Sept, 1959).

Walker, Kenneth. "The Philosophy of Bernard Shaw," *World
Review,* N.S. 29: 18-20 (July, 1951).

Williams, Ray. *Drama From Ibsen to Eliot,* 147-149.

BUOYANT BILLIONS
McDowell, Frederick P. W. "The World, God, and World
Bettering: Shaw's *Buoyant Billions," Boston University
Studies in English,* 3#3: 167-176 (Autumn, 1957).
Shaw, George Bernard and Stephen Winsten. *"Buoyant Bil-
lions," World Review,* pp. 17-22 (Sept, 1949).

CAESAR AND CLEOPATRA
Austin, Don. "Dramatic Structure in *Caesar and Cleopatra,"
The California Shavian,* 3#5: (Sept-Oct, 1962).
Clurman, H. *Lies Like Truth,* 267-269.
Couchman, Gordon W. "Comic Catharsis in *Caesar and Cleo-
patra," The Shaw Review,* 3#1: 11-14 (Jan, 1960).
————————. "Shaw, Caesar, and the Critics," *Speech
Monographs,* 23#4: 262-271 (Nov, 1956).
————————. "Here was a Caesar: Shaw's Comedy To-
day," *PMLA,* 72#1: 272-285 (March, 1957).
Hobson, Harold. *The Theatre Now,* 150-152.
Kronenberger, Louis. *The Thread of Laughter,* 235-239.
Leary, Daniel J. "The Moral Dialectic in *Caesar and Cleo-
patra," The Shaw Review,* 5#2: 42-54 (May, 1962).
Ludeke, H. "Some Remarks on Shaw's History Plays," *Eng-
lish Studies,* 36#5: 241-243 (Oct, 1955).
Reinert, Otto. "Old History and New: Anachronism in *Caesar
and Cleopatra," Modern Drama,* 3#1: 37-41 (May, 1960).
Scott, Charles. "Genius, Superman; Species, Multiform,"
Educational Theatre Journal, 12#4: 292-293 (Dec, 1960).
Weintraub, Stanley. "Shaw's Mommsenite Caesar," in Philip
A. Shelley (ed), *Crosscurrents,* Volume II, 257-272.
Young, Stark. *Immortal Shadows,* 57-60.

CANDIDA
Alder, Jacob H. "Ibsen, Shaw, and *Candida," Journal of Eng-
lish and Germanic Philology,* 59#1: 50-58 (Jan, 1960).
Bentley, Eric. *The Playwright as Thinker,* 165-168; 348-350.
Deming, Barbara. "The Playwright as Playwright," *Chimera,*
5#1: 26-27 (Aut, 1946).
King, Walter N. "The Rhetoric of *Candida," Modern Drama,*
2#2: 71-83 (Sept, 1959).
Lewis, Allan. *The Contemporary Theatre,* 84-87.
Nethercot, Arthur H. "The Truth About *Candida," PMLA,*
64#4: 639-647 (Sept, 1949).

Stanton, Stephens S. "Shaw's Debt to Scribe," *PMLA, 76#5*:
578-582 (Dec, 1961).

Williams, Ray. *Drama From Ibsen to Eliot,* 144-147.

Young, Stark. *Immortal Shadows,* 193-195.

CAPTAIN BRASSBOUND'S CONVERSION
Alexander, Doris M. "Captain Brant and Captain Brassbound:
The Origin of an O'Neill Character," *Modern Language
Notes,* 74#4: 306-310 (April, 1959).

Bentley, Eric. "The Theory and Practice of Shavian Drama,"
Accent, 5#1: 12-14 (Autumn, 1944). ALSO IN: *The
Playwright as Thinker,* 168-172.

DARK LADY OF THE SONNETS, THE
Wilshire, Lewis. "Shaw's Last Play," *English,* 8#46: 193-
195 (Spring, 1951).

DEVIL'S DECIPLE
Cubeta, Paul M. *Modern Drama for Analysis, Third Edition*
(1963), 74-81.

Dickson, Ronald J. "Diabolonian Character in Shaw's Plays,"
University of Kansas City Review, 26#2: 145-148 (Winter, 1959).

Kronenberger, Louis. *The Thread of Laughter,* 233-235.

Ludeke, H. "Some Remarks on Shaw's History Plays," *English Studies,* 36#5: 240 (Oct, 1955).

Stanton, Stephen S. "Shaw's Debt to Scribe," *PMLA, 76#5*:
582-584 (Dec, 1961).

DOCTOR'S DILEMMA, THE
Barnet, Sylvan. "Bernard Shaw on Tragedy," *PMLA, 71#5*:
894-895 (Dec, 1956).

Glicksberg, Charles I. "Shaw Versus Science," *Dalhousie Review,* 28#3: 273-275 (Oct, 1948).

Henn, Thomas R. *The Harvest of Tragedy,* 190-192.

McCarthy, Mary. *Theater Chronicle,* 151-162.

——————. *Sights and Spectacles,* 151-162.

Smith, J. Percy. "A Shavian Tragedy: *The Doctor's Dilem-
ma,*" in B. H. Lehman, *The Image of the Work,* 189-210.
ALSO IN: *University of California Publications. English
Studies,* 11: 189-207 (1955).

Walker, Kenneth. "The Philosophy of Bernard Shaw," *The
World Review,* N.S. 29: 20-21 (July, 1951).

GENEVA, ANOTHER POLITICAL EXTRAVAGANZA
Sharp, Sister M. Corona. "The Theme of Masks in *Geneva,*"
The Shaw Review, 5#3: 82-91 (Sept, 1962).

GETTING MARRIED

Kronenberger, Louis. *The Thread of Laughter,* 256-260.

Sharp, William. "New Dramaturgy in Comedy," *Educational Theatre Journal,* 11#2: 103-109 (May, 1959).

Solomon, Stanley J. "Theme and Structure in *Getting Married," The Shaw Review,* 5#3: 92-96 (Sept, 1962).

HEARTBREAK HOUSE

Barnet, Sylvan. "Bernard Shaw on Tragedy," *PMLA,* 71#5: 895-896 (Dec, 1956).

Brewster, Dorothy. *East-West Passage,* 202-204.

Brustein, Robert. *The Theater of Revolt,* 220-227.

Clurman, Harold. "Notes for a Production of *Heartbreak House," Tulane Drama Review,* 3#3: 58-67 (Mar, 1961).

Corrigan, Robert W. *"Heartbreak House:* Shaw's Elegy for Europe," *The Shaw Review,* 2#9: 2-6 (Sept, 1959).

Fergusson, Francis. *The Idea of a Theater,* 181-185

Gassner, John (ed). "From Myth to Ideas and Back," in *Ideas in the Drama,* 65-70.

Gatch, Katherine H. " 'The Real Sorrow of Great Men': Mr. Bernard Shaw's Sense of Tragedy," *College English,* 8#5: 235-236 (Feb, 1947).

Glicksberg, Charles I. "The Modern Playwright and the Absolute," *Queen's Quarterly,* 45#3: 465-466 (Aut, 1958).

——————. "Shaw Versus Science," *Dalhousie Review,* 28#3: 276-277 (Oct, 1948).

Jordan, John. "Shaw's *Heartbreak House," Threshold,* 1#1: 50-56 (Feb, 1957).

Kronenberger, Louis. *The Thread of Laughter,* 266-272.

Krutch, J. W. *Modernism in Modern Drama,* 58-64.

Lewis, Allan. *The Contemporary Theatre,* 93-101; 106-108.

McDowell, Frederick P. W. "Technique, Symbol, and Theme in *Heartbreak House," PMLA,* 68#3: 335-356 (June, 1953).

Meister, Charles W. "Comparative Drama: Chekhov, Shaw, Odets," *Poet Lore,* 55#3: 251-255 (Autumn, 1950).

Mizener, Arthur. "Poetic Drama and the Well-Made Play," *English Institute Essays,* pp. 49-54 (1949).

Reed, Robert R. Jr. "Boss Mangan, *Peer Gynt,* and *Heartbreak House," The Shaw Review,* 2#7: 6-12 (Jan, 1959).

Styan, J. L. *The Dark Comedy,* 144-146.

Worsley, T. C. *The Fugitive Art,* 150-151.

Young, Stark. *Immortal Shadows,* 206-210.

IN GOOD KING CHARLES' GOLDEN DAYS
O'Donnell, Norbert F. "Harmony and Discord in *Good King Charles*," *The Shaw Review*, 2#4: 5-8 (Jan, 1958).

JOHN BULL'S OTHER ISLAND
Kronenberger, Louis. *The Thread of Laughter*, 247-250.
Smith, Warren S. "*John Bull's Other Island*," *Educational Theatre Journal*, 3: 237-241 (Oct, 1951).
Veilleux, Jere. "Shavian Drama: A Dialectical Convention for the Modern Theater," *Twentieth Century Literature*, 3#4: 172-174 (Jan, 1958).

MAJOR BARBARA
Bentley, Eric. "Bernard Shaw, Caesar, and Stalin," *The Antioch Review*, 3#1: 117-124 (March, 1943).
Brooks, Cleanth and Robert Heilman. *Understanding Drama*, 24-26 (Appendix—1961 ed.) ; 476-478 (1954 ed.).
Caudwell, Christopher. "George Bernard Shaw: A Study of the Bourgeois Superman," in Wilbur S. Scott, *Five Approaches of Literary Criticism*, 151-152.
Clurman, H. *Lies Like Truth*, 144-146.
Crompton, Louis. "Shaw's Challenge to Liberalism," *Prairie Schooner*, 37#3: 229-244 (Fall, 1963).
Dickson, Ronald J. "Diabolian Character in Shaw's Plays," *University of Kansas City Review*, 26#2: 149-151 (Winter, 1959).
Dukore, Bernard F. "Toward an Interpretation of *Major Barbara*," *The Shaw Review*, 6#2: 62-70 (May, 1963).
Fergusson, Francis. *The Idea of a Theater*, 179-181.
Frank, Joseph. "*Major Barbara*—Shaw's Divine Comedy," *PMLA*, 71#1: 61-74 (March, 1956).
Frankel, Charles. "Efficient Power and Inefficient Virture," in R. M. McIver (ed), *Great Moral Dilemmas*, 15-24.
Frunk, Joesph. "*Major Barbara*—Shaw's *Divine Comedy*," *PMLA*, 71#1: 61-74 (March, 1956).
Irvine, William. "*Major Barbara*," *Shavian*, 7: 43-47 (1956).
Kronenberger, Louis. *The Thread of Laughter*, 250-256.
Krutch, J. W. *Modernism in Modern Drama*, 55-59; 63-64.
Lewis, Allan. *The Contemporary Theatre*, 88-91.
Ozy. "The Dramatist's Dilemma: An Interpretation of *Major Barbara*," *The Shaw Review*, 2#4: 18-24 (Jan, 1958).
Scott, Charles. "Genius, Superman; Species, Multiform," *Educational Theatre Journal*, 12#4: 291-292 (Dec, 1960).
Slote, Bernice (ed). "*Major Barbara*: Shaw's Challenge to Liberalism," in *Literature and Society*, 112-120.

ꞰSmoker, Barbara. "Andrew Undershaft, Economic Rogue,"
Shavian, 7: 57-59 (1956).
Whittmore, Reed. "Shaw's Abstract Clarity," *Tulane Drama
Review,* 2#1: 46-57 (Nov, 1957).

MAN AND SUPERMAN

Albert, Sidney P. "Bernard Shaw: The Artist as Philosopher,"
Journal of Aesthetics and Art Criticism, 14#4: 419-420;
428-430 (June, 1956).
Beardsley, Munroe. *Aesthetics,* 424-425.
Bentley, Eric. "The Making of a Dramatist," *Tulane Drama
Review,* 5#1: 9-12; 19-20 (Sept, 1960).
Brown, John Mason. *Dramatis Personae,* 121-129.
ALSO IN: *Seeing More Things,* 90-91; 188-199.
Brustein, Robert. *The Theater of Revolt,* 213-220.
Cohn, Ruby. "Hell on the Twentieth Century Stage," Wis-
consin Studies in Contemporary Literature, 5#1: 49-51
(Winter-Spring, 1964).
Gassner, John. "The Puritan in Hell," *Shaw Society Bulletin,*
46: 7-14 (Sept, 1952).
ALSO IN: *The Theatre in our Times,* 156-162.
Irvine, William. *"Man and Superman,* a Step in Shavian Dis-
illusionment," *Huntington Library Quarterly,* 10#2: 209-
224 (Feb, 1947).
Kronenberger, Louis. *The Thread of Laughter,* 239-247.
Leary, Daniel J. "Shaw's Use of Stylized Characters and
Speech in *Man and Superman,"* *Modern Drama,* 5#4:
477-490 (Feb, 1963).
ALSO IN: *The California Shavian,* 4#3: (May-June,
1963).
McDowell, Frederick P. W. "Reflections Upon Shaw's *Man
and Superman,"* *Drama Survey,* 2#3: 245-268 (Feb,
1963).
Mandel, Oscar. *The Theatre of Don Juan,* 547-551.
Nethercot, Arthur H. "The Schizophrenia of Bernard Shaw,"
The American Scholar, 21#4: 461-463 (Autumn, 1952).
Pettet, Edwin B. "Shaw's Socialist Life Force," *Educational
Theatre Journal,* 3: 109-114 (May, 1951).
Scott, Charles. "Genius, Superman; Species, Multiform," *Edu-
cational Theatre Journal,* 12#4: 289-291 (Dec, 1960).
Stanton, Stephen S. "Shaw's Debt to Scribe," *PMLA,* 76#5:
584-585 (Dec, 1961).
Walker, Kenneth. "The Philosophy of Bernard Shaw," *World
Review,* N.S. 29: 18-20 (July, 1951).

MISALLIANCE

Sharp, William L. *"Misalliance:* An Evaluation," *Educational Theatre Journal,* 8#1: 9-16 (March, 1956).

MRS. WARREN'S PROFESSION

Bullough, Geoofrey. "Literary Relations of Shaw's Mrs. Warren," *Philological Quarterly,* 41#1: 339-349 (Jan, 1962).

Kornbluth, Martin L. "Two Fallen Women," *Shavian,* 14: 14-15 (Feb, 1959).

Nethercot, Arthur H. "The Quintessence of Idealism: Or, the Slaves of Duty," *PMLA,* 62#3: 848-849 (Sept, 1947).

——————. "The Vivie-Frank Relationship in *Mrs. Warren's Professsion,"* Shavian, 15: 7-9 (June, 1959).

ON THE ROCKS

McDowell, Frederick P. W. "Crisis and Unreason: Shaw's *On the Rocks,"* Educational Theatre Journal, 13#3: 192-200 (Oct, 1961).

PHILANDERER

Nethercot, Arthur H. "The Quintessence of Idealism: Or, The Slaves of Duty," *PMLA,* 62#3: 847-848 (Sept, 1947).

Williams, Ray. *Drama From Ibsen to Eliot,* 142-144.

PYGMALION

Burke, Kenneth. *The Philosophy of Literary Form,* 96-97.

Faverty, Frederic E. *Your Literary Heritage,* 178-181.

Kronenberger, Louis. *The Thread of Laughter,* 263-266.

Lerner, Alan J. *"Pygmalion* and *My Fair Lady,"* Shaw Bulletin, 1#10: 4-7 (Nov, 1956).

Matlaw, Myron. "The Denouement of *Pygmalion,"* Modern Drama, 1#1: 29-34 (May, 1958).

——————. "Will Higgins Marry Eliza?" *The Shavian.* 12: 14-19 (May, 1958).

Solomon, Stanley J. "The Ending of *Pygmalion:* A Structural View," *Educational Theatre Journal,* 16#1: 59-63 (March, 1964).

Styan, J. L. *The Elements of Drama,* 87-9: 89-92.

SAINT JOAN

Barnet, Sylvan. "Bernard Shaw on Tragedy," *PMLA,* 71#5: 897-899 (Dec, 1956).

Becker, William. "Joan and Margaret," *Hudson Review,* 4#4: 597-602 (Winter, 1952).

194 DRAMA CRITICISM

Boas, Frederick S. "Joan of Arc in Shakespeare, Schiller and Shaw," *Shakespeare Quarterly*, 2#1: 42-45 (Jan, 1951).
Connolly, Thomas E. "Shaw's *St. Joan*," *Explicator*, 14#3: 19 (Dec, 1955).
Davidson, Arthur. *The Solace of Literature*, 79-82.
Eastman, Fred. *Christ in the Drama*, 54-60.
Erwitt, Elliott. "The Historic Place," *Show*, 2#1: 76-81 (Jan, 1962).
Fielden, John. "Shaw's *Saint Joan* as Tragedy," *Twentieth Century Literature*, 3#2: 59-67 (July, 1957).
Gassner, John. *The Theatre in our Times*, 144-147; 151-152.
Gatch, Katherine H. " 'The Real Sorrow of Great Men': Mr. Bernard Shaw's Sense of Tragedy," *College English*, 8#5: 237-240 (Feb, 1947).
Henn, Thomas R. *The Harvest of Tragedy*, 107-108; 193-195.
Kronenberger, Louis. *The Thread of Laughter*, 272-277.
Lane, Clarinda. "Saint Joan Through the Eyes of Saint Bernard," *Western Speech*, 22#2: 81-87 (Spring, 1958).
Ludeke, H. "Some Remarks on Shaw's History Plays," *English Studies*, 36#5: 244-246 (Oct, 1955).
Martz, L. L. "The Saint as Tragic Hero. *Saint Joan* and *Murder in the Cathedral*" in Cleanth Brooks (ed), *Tragic Themes in Western Literature*, 156-159; 164-177.
Mierow, Herbert E. "The Greeks Started It," *Catholic World*, 166: 67-68 (Oct, 1964).
Mizener, Arthur. "Poetic Drama and the Well Made Play," *English Institute Essays*, pp. 45-48 (1949).
Olson, Elder. *Tragedy and the Theory of Drama*, 51-53.
Rosselli, John. "The Right Joan and the Wrong One," *Twentieth Century*, 157#938: 374-383 (April, 1955).
Solomon, Stanley J. "*Saint Joan* as Epic Tragedy," *Modern Drama*, 6#4: 437-449 (Feb, 1964).
Stoppel, Hans. "Shaw and Saint Hood," *English Studies*, 36#2: 50-63 (April, 1955).
Styan, J. L. *The Elements of Drama*, 146-148.
Takeuchi, H. "*Saint Joan*," The Humanities (Yokohama), 2#5: 1-8 (Sept, 1956).
Vancura, Zd. "The Dramatic Structure of G. B. Shaw's *Saint Joan*," *Casopis Pro Moderni Filologii*, 40: 17-18 (1958).
W. W. "Shaw and Shakespeare on Saint Joan," *The Independent Shavian*, 2#1: 6 (Fall, 1963).
Williams, Raymond. *Drama From Ibsen to Eliot*, 149-152.
Worsley, T. C. *The Fugitive Art*, 19-20.

SHEWING UP OF BLANCO POSNET, THE
  Mason, Ellsworth. "James Joyce's Shrill Note: The *Piccolo Della Sera* Articles," *Twentieth Century Literature, 2#3*: 129-130 (Oct, 1956).

SIMPLETON OF THE UNEXPECTED ISLES, THE
  McDowell, Frederick P. W. "Spiritual and Political Reality: Shaw's *The Simpleton of the Unexpected Isles,*" *Modern Drama, 3#2*: 196-210 (Sept, 1960).

TOO TRUE TO BE GOOD
  McDowell, Frederick P. W. "The 'Pentecostal Flame' and the 'Lower Centers': *Too True to be Good,*" *The Shaw Review, 2#9*: 27-38 (Sept, 1959).

WIDOWERS' HOUSES
  Bentley, Eric. "The Making of a Dramatist," *Tulane Drama Review, 5#1*: 3-8 (Sept, 1960).
  Lewis, Allan. *The Contemporary Theatre,* 81-83.

YOU NEVER CAN TELL
  Behrman, S. N. "The Paddy Vien," *Prairie Schooner, 35#1*: 10-13 (Spring, 1961).
  Brodersen, G. L. "Parody and Farce in the Early Shaw," *Manitoba Arts Review,* pp. 40-46 (1956/1957).
  Coxe, Louis O. *"You Never Can Tell: G. B. Shaw Reviewed,"* *Western Humanities Review, 9#4*: 323-325 (Aut, 1955).

SHAW, IRWIN

GENTLE PEOPLE, THE
  Clurman, H. *The Fervent Years,* 223-224.

RETREAT TO PLEASURE
  Clurman, H. *The Fervent Years,* 253-259.

SHAW, SAMUEL

WORDS MADE VISIBLE
  Bowers, R. H. "Samuel Shaw's *Words Made Visible* (1678-1679)" *Southern Speech Journal, 22#3*: 135-143 (Spring,

SHELDON, EDWARD

SALVATION NELL
  Cohn, Albert. "Salvation Nell: An Overlooked Milestone in the American Theater," *Educational Theatre Journal,*

9#1: 11-22 (Mar, 1957).

SHELLEY, PERCY

CENCI, THE

Hicks, Arthur C. "An American Performance of *The Cenci*," in *Stanford Studies in Language and Literature*, 287-311.

Jamison, William A. "Arnold and the Romantics," *Anglistica*, 10: 125-128 (1958).

Prior, Moody E. *The Language of Tragedy*, 228-243; 244.

Rees, Joan. "Shelley's Orsino: Evil in *The Cenci*," *Keats-Shelley Memorial Bulletin*, 12: 3-6 (1961).

—————————. "The Preface to *The Cenci*," *Review of English Studies*, NS8#30: 172-173 (May, 1957).

Shaw, G. B. "Shaw on Shelley," *The Independent Shavian*, 1#2: 3-5 (Dec, 1962).

Smith, Paul. "Restless Casuistry: Shelley's Composition of *The Cenci*," *Keats-Shelley Journal*, 13: 77-85 (Winter, 1964).

States, Bert O. "Addendum: The Stage History of *The Cenci*," *PMLA*, 72#4Pt 1: 633-644 (Sept, 1957).

Watson, Sarah R. "A Comparison of *Othello* and *The Cenci*," *PMLA*, 55#2: 611-614 (June, 1940).

Whitman, Robert F. "Beatrice's 'Pernicious Mistake' in *The Cenci*," *PMLA*, 74#3: 249-253 (June, 1959).

CHARLES I

Cameron, Kenneth N. "Shelley's use of Source Material in *Charles I*," *Modern Language Quarterly*, 6: 197-210 (1945).

PROMETHEUS UNBOUND

Bodkin, Maud. *Archetypal Patterns in Poetry*, 255-261; 268.

Bowra, C. M. *The Romantic Imagination*, 103-125.

Cameron, Kenneth N. "The Political Symbolism in *Prometheus Unbound*," *PMLA*, 58#3: 728-753 (Sept, 1943).

Drew, P. "Shelley's Use of 'Recall', *Times Literary Supplement*, pg. 761 (Dec 16, 1955).

Hughes, D. J. "Potentiality in *Prometheus Unbound*," *Studies in Romanticism*, 2#2: 107-126 (Winter, 1963).

Mabbott, T. O. "Shelley's *Prometheus Unbound*, III, iv," *The Explicator*, 2#3: 24 (Dec, 1943).

Marshall, William H. "The Father-Child Symbolism in *Prometheus Unbound*," *Modern Language Quarterly*, 22#1: 41-45 (March, 1961).

Marshall, William H. "Plato's Myth of Aristophanes and Shelley's *Panthea*," *Classical Journal*, 55: 121-123 (1959).

Matthews, G. M. "A Volcano's Voice in Shelley," *ELH*, 24#3: 203-228 (Sept, 1957).

Nitchie, Elizabeth. "Shelley's *Prometheus Unbound* II, v, 109-110," *Explicator*, 19#9: 69 (June, 1961).

Oras, Ants. "The Multitudinous Orb—Some Miltonic Elements in Shelley," *Modern Language Quarterly*, 16: 247-257 (1955).

Potter, Frederick A. "Shelley's Use of 'Recall'," *Times Literary Supplement*, pg. 97 (Feb 15, 1957).

Prins, A. A. "The Religious Background of Shelley's *Prometheus Unbound*," *English Studies*, 45 (Supplement) : 223-234 (1964).

Raben, Joseph. "Shelley's *Prometheus Unbound:* Why the Indian Caucasus?" *Keats-Shelley Journal*, 12: 95-106 (Winter, 1963).

Ragan, B. "The Motivation of Shelley's *Prometheus Unbound*," *Review of English Studies*, 45#75: 229-304 (July, 1943).

Smith, Wiltrude L. "An Overlooked Source for *Prometheus Unbound*," *Studies in Philology*, 48#4: 783-792 (Oct, 1951).

Thomson, James S. "The Unbinding of Prometheus," *University of Toronto Quarterly*, 15#1: 1-16 (Oct, 1945).

Tilyard, Eustace M. *Some Mythical Elements in English Literature*, 136-138.

Wasserman, E. R. "Myth-Making in *Prometheus Unbound*," *Modern Language Notes*, 70#3: 182-184 (March, 1955).

Weaver, Bennett. *"Prometheus Bound* and *Prometheus Unbound*," *PMLA*, 64#1 Pt. 1: 115-133 (March, 1949).

Wormhoudt, A. *A Demon Lover*, 88-112.

SHERIDAN, RICHARD

CRITIC, THE

Smith, Dane Farnsworth. "The Critics in The Audience," *University of New Mexico Publications in Language and Literature*, 12: 115-154 (1953).

RIVALS, THE

Boas, F. S. *An Introduction to Eighteenth Century Drama*, 345-349.

Davies, A. *"The Rivals," The Use of English*, 14#2: 91-94 (Winter, 1962).

Kronenberger, Louis. *The Thread of Laughter*, 193-195.

Murdick, Marvin. "Restoration Comedy and Later," *English Institute Essays*, pp. 115-120 (1954).

SCHOOL FOR SCANDAL

Boas, F. S. *An Introduction to Eighteenth Century Drama*, 354-357.

Brooks, Cleanth and Robert Heilman. *Understanding Drama*, 194; 243-255.

Deelman, Christian. "The Original Cast for *The School for Scandal*," *Review of English Studies*, NS13#51: 257-266 (Aug, 1962).

Hubay, Miklos. "On Staging Sheridan," *New Hungarian Quarterly*, 1#1: 220-226 (Sept, 1960).

Jackson, J. R. "The Importance of Witty Dialogue in *The School for Scandal*," *Modern Language Notes*, 76 (Pt. 2)#7: 601-607 (Nov, 1961).

James, Henry. *The Scenic Art*, 13-21.

Kronenberger, Louis. *The Thread of Laughter*, 195-202.

Moore, John Robert. "Sheridan's Little Bronze Pliny," *Modern Language Notes*, 59#3: 164-165 (March, 1944).

Schiller, Andrew. *"The School for Scandal:* The Restoration Unrestored," *PMLA*, 71#4: 694-704 (Sept, 1956).

Shaw, G. B. *Plays and Players*, 95-104.

Sinko, Grzegorz. "Sheriden and Kotzebue," *Prace Wroclawskiego Towarzystwa Naukowego, Ser* A#27: 23-27 (1949).

Sprague, Arthur C. "In Defence of a Masterpiece: *The School for Scandal* Re-Examined," in G. I. Duthie (ed), *English Studies Today*—Third Series (1964), 125-136.

Styan, J. L. *The Elements of Drama*, 133-4; 154-157.

TRIP TO SCARBOROUGH, A
Mignon, Elizabeth. *Crabbed Age and Youth*, 138-141.

SHERWOOD, ROBERT

ABE LINCOLN IN ILLINOIS
Dusenbury, Winifred L. *The Theme of Loneliness in Modern American Drama*, 180-185.

IDIOT'S DELIGHT
Egri, Lajos. *The Art of Dramatic Writing*, 292-293.

PETRIFIED FOREST, THE
Sievers, W. D. *Freud on Broadway*, 182-184

THERE SHALL BE NO NIGHT
>Healy, Robert C. "Anderson, Saroyan, Sherwood: New Directions," *Catholic World*, 151: 178-180 (Nov, 1950).
>Sievers, W. D. *Freud on Broadway*, 184-185.

SHIRLEY, JAMES

CARDINAL, THE
>Bland, D. S. "A Word in Shirley's *The Cardinal*," *Review of English Studies*, 4N.S.#16: 358-359 (Oct, 1953).
>Bowers, Fredson T. *Elizabethan Revenge Tragedy*, 228-234.
>Forker, Charles R. "Archbishop Laud and Shirley's *The Cardinal*," *Wisconsin Academy of Sciences, Arts, and Letters*, v. 47: 241-251 (1958).

CHANGES, OR LOVE IN A MAZE
>Reed, Robert R. Jr. "James Shirley, and the Sentimental Comedy," *Anglia*, 73#2: 149-170 (1955).

EXAMPLE, THE
>Reed, Robert R. Jr. "James Shirley, and The Sentimental Comedy," *Anglia*, 73#2: 149-170 149-170 (1955).

GAMESTER, THE
>Reed, Robert R. Jr. "James Shirley, and the Sentimental Comedy," *Anglia*, 73-2: 149-170 (1955).

HYDE PARK
>Reed, Robert R. Jr. "James Shirley, and the Sentimental Comedy," *Anglia*, 73#2: 149-170 (1955).
>Wells, Henry W. *Elizabethan and Jacobean Playwrights*, 183-186.

MAID'S REVENGE, THE
>Bowers, Fredson T. *Elizabethan Revenge Tragedy*, 223-225.

SAINT PATRICK OF IRELAND
>Flood, J. M. "An Elizabethan Dramatist on St. Patrick," *Irish Monthly*, 60: 421-426 (Sept, 1948).

TRAITOR, THE
>Bowers, Fredson T. *Elizabethan Revenge Tragedy*, 226-227.
>Riemer, A. P. "A Source for Shirley's *The Traitor*," *Review of English Studies*, NS14#56: 380-383 (Nov, 1963).

WITTY FAIR ONE, THE
>Leech, Clifford. *Shakespearian Tragedies and Other Studies in Seventeenth Century Drama*, 190-194.
>Reed, Robert R. Jr. "James Shirley, and the Sentimental Comedy," *Anglia*, 73#2: 149-170 (1955).

SIFTON, CLAIRE
—AND PAUL SIFTON
  1931 (OR SON OF GOD)
    Clurman, H. *The Fervent Years,* 64-70.

SIMPSON, NORMAN F.
  ONE WAY PENDULUM
    Esslin, M. *Theatre of the Absurd,* 221-224.
    Swanson, Michele A. *"One Way Pendulum:* A New Dimen-
      sion in Farce," *Drama Survey,* 2#7: 322-332 (Feb, 1963).
    Taylor, John R. *Anger and After,* 62-64.
  RESOUNDING TINKLE, THE
    Esslin, Martin. *Theatre of the Absurd,* 218-220.
    Taylor, John R. *Anger and After,* 60-62.

SKELTON, JOHN
  MAGNIFICENCE
    Bevington, David M. *From Mankind to Marlowe,* 132-137;
      144-145.
    Harris, William O. "The Thematic Importance of Skelton's
      Allusion to Horace in *Magnyfycence," Studies in English
      Literature 1500-1900,* 3#1: 1-8 (Winter, 1963).
      ALSO IN: *Studies in Philology,* 57#2: 99-122 (Apr,
      1960).

SMITH, EDMUND
  PHAEDRA AND HIPPOLYTUS
    Wheatley, Katherine. "The Relationship of Edmund Smith's
      Phaedra and Hippolitus to Racine's *Phedre* and Racine's
      Bajazet," Romanic Review, 37#4: 307-328 (Dec, 1946).

SOTHEBY, WILLIAM
  ORESTES
    Cohen, Ralph. "St. Coleride and William Sotheby's *Orestes,"
      Modern Language Review,* 52#1: 19-27 (Jan, 1957).

STEELE, RICHARD
  CONSCIOUS LOVERS, THE
    Boas, F. S. *An Introduction to Eighteenth Century Drama,*
      78-82.
    Loftis, John. "The Eighteenth Century Beginnings of Modern
      Drama," *Emory University Quarterly,* 7#4: 229-230
      (Dec, 1951).
    —————————. "The Genesis of Steele's *The Conscious Lov-*

ers," in *Essays Critical and Historical Dedicated to Lily
B. Campbell,* 173-184.

Mignon, Elizageth. *Crabbed Age and Youth,* 179-183.

FUNERAL, THE
Boas, F. S. *An Introduction to Eighteenth Century Drama,*
66-69.

LYING LOVERS, THE
Boas, F. S. *An Introduction to Eighteenth Century Drama,*
70-74.

SCHOOL FOR ACTION
Boas, F. S. *An Introduction to Eighteenth Century Drama,*
83-85.

TENDER HUSBAND, THE
Boas, F. S. *An Introduction to Eighteenth Century Drama,*
74-78.

STEIN, GERTRUDE

COUNTING HER DRESSES
Russell, Francis. *Three Studies in Twentieth Century Obscurity,* 97-98.

FOUR SAINTS IN THREE ACTS
Garvin, Harry R. "Sound and Sense in *Four Saints in Three
Acts,*" *Bucknell University Studies,* 5#1: 1-11 (1954).
Russell, Francis. *Three Studies in Twentieth Century Ob-
scurity,* 98-103.
Sievers, W. D. *Freud on Broadway,* 243-244.
Young, Stark. *Immortal Shadows,* 150-152.

WHAT HAPPENED
Russell, Francis. *Three Studies in Twentieth Century Obscurity,* 97-98.

STEWART, DOUGLAS

FIRE ON THE SNOW, THE
Burrows, J. F. "An Approach to the Plays of Douglas Stew-
art," *Southerly,* 23#2: 94-108 (1963).
Oliver, Harold J. "Douglas Stewart and the Art of the Radio
Play," *Texas Quarterly,* 5#2: 193-203 (Summer, 1962).

GOLDEN LOVER, THE
Burrows, J. F. "An Approach to the Plays of Douglas Stewart," *Southerly,* 23#2: 94-108 (1963).

Oliver, Harold J. "Douglas Stewart and the Art of the Radio Play," *Texas Quarterly*, 5#2: 193-203 (Summer, 1962).

NED KELLY

Burrows, J. F. "An Approach to the Plays of Douglas Stewart," *Southerly*, 23#2: 94-108 (1963).

SHIPWRECK

Burrows, J. F. "An Approach to the Plays of Douglas Stewart," *Southerly*, 23#2: 94-108 (1963).

STONE, JOHN AUGUSTUS

METAMORA; OR THE LAST OF THE WAMPANOAGS

Moody, Richard. "Lost and Found: The Fourth Act of *Metamora*," *American Literature*, 34: 353-364 (Nov, 1962).

Peavy, Charles D. "The American Indian in the Drama of the United States," *McNeese Review*, 10: 72-76 (Winter, 1958).

STRICKNEY, TRUMBELL

PROMETHEUS PYRPHOROS

Riggs, Thomas Jr. "Prometheus 1900," *American Literature*, 22: 399-423 (Jan, 1951).

SUCKLING, JOHN

AGLAURA

Bowers, Fredson T. *Elizabethan Revenge Tragedy*, 242-244.

SWINBURNE, ALGERNON

ATALANTA IN CALYDON

Bowra, C. M. *The Romantic Imagination*, 221-244.

SYNGE, JOHN

ARAN ISLANDS, THE

Ellis-Fermor, Una. *The Irish Dramatic Movement*, 179-180; 182-183.

Price, Alan. *Synge and Anglo-Irish Drama*, 78-89.

DEIRDRE OF THE SORROWS

Brown, Alan. "John Millington Synge," *London Quarterly and Holborn Review*, 175#1: 47-48 (Jan, 1950).

Ellis-Fermor, Una. *The Irish Dramatic Movement,* 171-172; 179-184.

Greene, David H. "Synge's Unfinished *Diedre,*" *PMLA,* 63#4: 1314-1321 (Dec, 1948).

McHugh, Roger. "The Deidre Legend," *Threshold,* 1#1: 45-46 (Feb, 1957).

O'Connor, Anthony. "Synge and National Drama," *Unitas* (Manila), 27#3: 430-444 (1954).

Peacock, R. *Poet in the Theater,* 108-109.

Price, Alan. *Synge and Anglo-Irish Drama,* 39-41; 191-215.

Setterquist, Jan. "Ibsen and Synge," *Studia Neophilologica,* 24#1-2: 131-135 (1952).

Styan, J. L. *The Elements of Drama,* 126-128.

Williams, Raymond. *Drama From Ibsen to Eliot,* 156-157; 164-168.

IN THE SHADOW OF THE GLEN

Ellis-Fermor, Una. *The Irish Dramatic Movement,* 168-169.

O'Connor, Anthony C. "Synge and National Drama," *Unitas* (Manila), 27#2: 318-321 (1954).

Price, Alan F. "A Consideration of Synge's *The Shadow of The Glen,*" *The Dublin Magazine,* 26#4 (N.S.): 15-24 (Oct-Dec, 1951).

Setterquist, Jan. "Ibsen and Synge," *Studia Neophilologica,* 24#1-2: 76-86 (1952).

PLAYBOY OF THE WESTERN WORLD

Blissett, William. "Synge's *Playboy,*" *Adam International Review,* #239-240: 17-20 (1954).

Collins, Arthur S. *English Literature of The Twentieth Century,* 292-293.

Ellis-Fermor, Una. *The Irish Dramatic Movement,* 49-51; 55-57; 170-171; 175-179.

Greene, David H. "The *Playboy* and Irish Nationalism," *Journal of English and Germanic Philology,* 46#2: 199-204 (April, 1947).

Henn, Thomas R. *The Harvest of Tragedy,* 204-205.

Kronenberger, Louis. *The Thread of Laughter,* 284-288.

Krutch, J. W. *Modernism in Modern Drama,* 96-98.

MacLean, Hugh H. "The Hero as Playboy," *University of Kansas City Review,* 21#1: 9-19 (Autumn, 1954).

Murphy, Daniel J. "The Reception of Synge's *Playboy* in Ireland and America: 1907-1912," *Bulletin of the New York Public Library,* 64#10: 515-533 (Oct, 1960).

O'Connor, Anthony C. "Synge and National Drama," *Uuitas* (Manila), 27#2: 322-324 (1954).

Peacock, Ronald. *The Poet in the Theater,* 112-114.

Podhoretz, Norman. "Synge's *Playboy:* Morality and the Hero," *Essays in Criticism,* 3#3: 337-344 (July, 1953).

Price, Allan. *Synge and Anglo-Irish Drama,* 24-28; 45-49; 161-180.

Setterquist, Jan. "Ibsen and Synge," *Studia Neophilologica,* 24#1-2: 112-130 (1952).

Spacks, Patricia Meyer. "The Making of the *Playboy*," *Modern Drama,* 4#3: 314-323 (Dec, 1961).

Styan, J. L. *The Elements of Drama,* 57-63.

Suss, Irving D. "The *Playboy* Riots," *Irish Writing,* 18: 39-42.

Walley, Harold R. *The Book of the Play,* 445-447; 671-672.

Williams, Raymond. *Drama From Ibsen to Eliot,* 162-164.

RIDERS TO THE SEA

Brooks, Cleanth and Robert Heilman. *Understanding Drama,* 26-27 (Appendix—1961 ed.) ; 478-479 (1945 ed.).

Brown, Alan. "John Millington Synge," *London Quarterly and Holborn Review,* 175#1: 46-47 (Jan, 1950).

Collins, Arthur S. *English Literature and the Twentieth Century,* 291-292.

Collins, R. L. "The Distinction of *Riders to the Sea*," *University of Kansas City Review,* 8#4: 278-284 (Summer, 1947).

Ellis-Fermor, Una. *The Irish Dramatic Movement,* 169-170.

Henn, Thomas R. *The Harvest of Tragedy,* 202-203.

Laan, Thomas F. Van. "Form as Agent in Synge's *Riders to The Sea*," *Drama Survey,* 3#3: 352-366 (Feb, 1964).

Millet, Fred B. *Reading Drama,* 22-23; 36-37; 103-104.

O'Connor, Anthony C. "Synge and National Drama," *Unitas* (Manila), 27#2: 319-320; 327-337 (1954).

Peacock, Ronald. *The Poet in the Theater,* 109-110.

Price, Alan. *Synge and Anglo-Irish Drama,* 181-191.

Setterquist, Jan. "Ibsen and Synge," *Studia Neophilologica,* 24#1-2: 87-99 (1952).

Williams, Raymond. *Drama From Ibsen to Eliot,* 159-160.

SHADOW OF THE GLEN, THE

Williams, Raymond. *Drama From Ibsen to Eliot,* 157-159.

TINKER'S WEDDING, THE
Donoghue, Denis. "Too Immortal for Dublin: Synge's *The Tinker's Wedding,*" *Irish Writing,* 30: 56-62.
Greene, David H. "*The Tinker's Wedding,* A Revaluation," *PMLA,* 62#3: 824-827 (Sept, 1947).
O'Connor, Anthony C. "Synge and National Drama," *Unitas* (Manila), 27#2: 339-345 (1954).
Price, Alan. *Synge and Anglo-Irish Drama,* 127-137.
Setterquist, Jan. "Ibsen and Synge," *Studia Neophilologica,* 24#1-2: 100-102 (1952).

WELL OF THE SAINTS, THE
Brown, Alan. "John Millington Synge," *London Quarterly and Holborn Review,* 175#1: 47-48 (Jan, 1950).
Price, Alan. *Synge and the Anglo-Irish Drama,* 138-162.
Setterquist, Jan. "Ibsen and Synge," *Studia Neophilologica,* 24#1-2: 103-111 (1952).
Williams, Raymond. *Drama From Ibsen to Eliot,* 160-162.

TALFOURD, SIR THOMAS

ION
Miller, Betty. "'This Happy Evening': The Story of *Ion,*" *Twentieth Century,* 154#917: 53-61 (July, 1953).

TATE, NAHUM

DUKE AND NO DUKE, A
Golden, Samuel A. "An Early Defense of Farce," in A. Dayle Wallace (ed), *Studies in Honor of John Wilcox,* 62-69.

KING LEAR
Prior, Moody E. *The Language of Tragedy,* 180-185.

TATHAM, JOHN

DISTRACTED STATE, THE
Wallace, John M. "The Date of John Tatham's *The Distracted State,*" *Bulletin of the New York Public Library,* 64#1: 29-40 (Jan, 1960).

RUMP, THE
Scott, Virgil Joseph. "A Reinterpretation of John Tatham's *The Rump; or The Mirrour of the Late Times,*" *Philological Quarterly,* 24#2: 114-118 (April, 1945).

TAYLOR, GEORGE E.

—AND GEORGE M. SAVAGE
   THE PHOENIX AND THE DWARFS
      Michael, Franz. *"The Phoenix and the Dwarfs,"* Interim, 1#2:
      34-36 (Fall, 1944).

TAYLOR, PETER

   DEATH OF A KINSMAN, THE
      Cheney, Brainard. "Peter Taylor's Plays," *Sewanee Review,*
      70#4: 579-587 (Autumn, 1962).

   TENNESSEE DAYS IN ST. LOUIS
      Cheney, Brainard. "Peter Taylor's Plays," *Sewanee Review,*
      70#4: 579-487 (Aut, 1962).
      Lytle, Andrew. "The Displaced Family," *Sewanee Review,*
      66#1: 115-120 (Winter, 1958).

TENNYSON, ALFRED LORD

   BECKET
      Decleyre, J. "Thomas A. Becket in West-European Litera-
      ture," *Revue des Langues Vivantes,* 19: 411 (1953).
      Prior, Moody E. *The Language of Tragedy,* 265-271.

   QUEEN MARY
      Eidson, John O. "Tennyson's First Play on the American
      Stage," *American Literature,* 35#4: 519-528 (Jan, 1964).

THOMAS, DYLAN

   UNDER MILK WOOD
      Baro, Gene. "The Orator of Llareggub," *Poetry Magazine,*
      87#2: 119-122 (Nov, 1955).
      Daiches, David. "The Poetry of Dylan Thomas," *College Eng-
      lish,* 16#1: 7-8 (Oct, 1954).
      Davies, M. Bryn. "A Few Thoughts About *Milk Wood,"*
      Literary Half-Yearly, 5#1: 41-44 (Jan, 1964).
      Manley, Frank. "The Text of Dylan Thomas' *Under Milk
      Wood,"* *Emory University Quarterly,* 20#2: 131-144
      (Summer, 1964).
      Noel, J. "Dylan Thomas and the State of Modern Poetry,"
      Revue des Langues Vivantes, 29#6: 532-533 (1963).
      Pike, Stephan and Stuart Itolroyd. *"Under Milk Wood* Yes

and No," *Poetry Review,* 45#3: 164-167 (July-Sept, 1954).

Rea, J. "Topographical Guide to *Under Milk Wood," College English,* 25#7: 535-542 (April, 1964).

Taylor, Geoffrey. "Studied Wood-notes" *Time and Tide* 35: 550 (Apr. 24, 1954).

Wells, Henry W. "Voice and Verse in Dylan Thomas' Play," *College English,* 15#8: 438-44 (May, 1954).

THOMSON, JAMES

AGAMEMNON

Boas, F. S. *An Introduction to Eighteenth Century Drama,* 155-157.

EDWARD AND ELEANORA

Boas, F. S. *An Introduction to Eighteenth Century Drama,* 158-162.

SOPHONISBA

Boas, F. S. *An Introduction to Eighteenth Century Drama,* 150-155.

TANCRED AND SIGISMUNDA

Boas, F. S. *An Introduction to Eighteenth Century Drama,* 162-166.

THURBER, JAMES

—AND ELLIOTT NUGENT
THE MALE ANIMAL

Elias, Robert H. "James Thurber: The Primitive, the Innocent, and the Individual," *American Scholar,* 27#3: 360 (Summer, 1958).

Sievers, W. D. *Freud on Broadway,* 225-226.

TOMKINS, THOMAS

See: Tomkis, Thomas

TOMKIS, THOMAS

ALBUMAZAR

Dick, Hugh G. *"Albumazar:* A Comedy (1615)" *University of California Publications in English,* 13: 155-200 (1944).

TOURNEUR, CYRIL

ATHEIST'S TRAGEDY, THE

Adams, Henry H. "Cyril Tourneur on Revenge," *Journal of English and Germanic Philology,* 48#1: 79-87 (Jan, 1949).

Bowers, Fredson T. *Elizabethan Revenge Tragedy,* 139-144.

Cope, Jackson I. "Tourner's *Atheist Tragedy* and the Jig of 'Singing Simkin'," *Modern Language Notes,* 70: 571-573 (Dec, 1955).

Ekeblad, Inga-Stina. "An Approach to Tourneur's Imagery,' *Modern Language Review,* 54#4: 489-498 (Oct, 1959)

Eliot, T. S. *Essays on Elizabethan Drama,* 121-129.

Jenkins, Harold. "Cyril Tourneur," *Review of English Studies,* 17#65: 21-35 (Jan, 1941).

Leech, Clifford. *"The Atheist's Tragedy* as a Dramatic Comment on Chapman's *Bussy* Plays," *Journal of English and Germanic Philology,* 52#1: 525-530 (Oct, 1953).

——————. "Catholic and Protestant Drama," *Durham University Journal,* 33#3: 175-176 (June, 1941).

Love, Glen A. "Morality and Style in *The Atheist's Tragedy," The Humanities Association Bulletin,* 5#1: 38-45 (Spring 1964).

Ornstein, Robert. *"The Atheist's Tragedy* and Renaissance Naturalism," *Studies in Philology,* 51#2: 194-207 (April 1954).

——————. *The Moral Vision of Jacobean Tragedy,* 118-127; 203-205.

Parrott, T. M. and R. H. Ball. *A Short View of Elizabethan Drama,* 218-222.

Ribner, Irving. *Jacobean Tragedy,* 86-96.

Simpson, Percy. *Studies in Elizabethan Drama,* 172-176.

Smith, Grover. "Tourneur and Little Gidding," *Modern Language Notes,* 65#6: 418-420 (June, 1950).

Wells, Henry W. *Elizabethan and Jacobean Playwrights,* 31-34.

REVENGER'S TRAGEDY, THE

Adams, Henry H. "Cyril Tourneur on Revenge," *Journal of English and Germanic Philology,* 48#1: 72-87 (Jan, 1949).

Berry, Francis. *Poet's Grammar,* 80-86.

Bowers, Fredson T. *Elizabethan Revenge Tragedy,* 132-138

Craik, T. W. *"The Revenger's Tragedy,"* Essays in Criticism, 6#4: 482-485 (Oct, 1956).

Ekeblad, Inga-Stina. "An Approach to Tourneur's Imagery," *Modern Language Review,* 54#4: 489-498 (Oct, 1959).

——————————. "On the Authorship of *The Revenger's Tragedy,"* English Studies, 41#4: 226-240 (Aug, 1960).

Eliot, T. S. *Essays on Elizabethan Drama,* 121-125; 129-133.

Foakes, K. J. "On the Authorship of *The Revenger's Tragedy,"* Modern Language Review, 48#2: 129-138 (April, 1953).

Hunter, G. K. "A Source for *The Revenger's Tragedy,"* Review of English Studies, 10#38: 181-182 (May, 1959).

Jenkins, Harold. "Cyril Tourneur," *Review of English Studies,* 17#65: 21-35 (Jan, 1941).

Leech, Clifford. "A Speech Heading in *The Revenger's Tragedy,"* Review of English Studies, 17#67: 335-336 (July, 1941).

Lisca, Peter. *"The Revenger's Tragedy:* A Study in Irony," *Philological Quarterly,* 38#2: 242-251 (April 1959).

Maxwell, J. C. "Two Notes on *The Revenger's Tragedy,"* Modern Language Review, 44#4: 545 (Oct, 1949).

Nicoll, Allardyce. *"The Revenger's Tragedy* and the Virtue of Anonymity," in Richard Hosley (ed), *Essays on Shakespeare and Elizabethan Drama in Honor of Hardin Craig,* 309-316.

Oates, J. C. "The Comedy of Metamorphosis in *The Revenger's Tragedy,"* Bucknell University Studies, 11#1: 38-52 (Dec, 1962).

Ornstein, Robert. "The Ethical Design of *The Revenger's Tragedy,"* ELH, 21#2: 81-93 (June, 1954).

——————————. *The Moral Vision of Jacobean Tragedy,* 105-121.

Parrott, T. M. and R. H. Ball. *A Short View of Elizabethan Tragedy,* 215-218.

Peter, John. *"The Revenger's Tragedy* Reconsidered," *Essays in Criticism,* 6#2: 131-143 (April, 1956).

——————————. *"The Revenger's Tragedy,"* Essays in Criticism, 6#4: 485-486 (Oct, 1956).

Prior, Moody E. *The Language of Tragedy,* 136-144.

Ribner, Irving. *Jacobean Tragedy,* 75-86; 95-96.

Salingar, L. G. "Tourneur and the Tragedy of Revenge," *Guide to English Literature,* 2: 334-340.

Schoenbaum, Samuel. "Middleton's Tragedies — A Critical

Study," *Columbia University Studies in English and Comparative Literature*, 168: 157-182 (1955).

————————. *"The Revenger's Tragedy:* Jacobean Dance of Death," *Modern Language Quarterly*, 15: 201-207 (1954).

Simpson, Percy. *Studies in Elizabethan Drama*, 168-172.

Tomlinson, T. B. "The Morality of Revenge: Tourneur's Critics," *Essays in Criticism*, 10#2: 134-147 (April, 1960).

Wadsworth, Frank W. *"The Revenger's Tragedy," Modern Language Review*, 50#3: 307 (July, 1955).

Waith, Eugene M. "The Ascription of Speeches in *The Revenger's Tragedy," Modern Language Notes*, 57#2: 119-121 (Feb, 1942).

Wells, Henry W. *Elizabethan and Jacobean Playwrights*, 34-38.

TOWNELEY

HARROWING OF HELL

Frampton, Mendel G. "The Towneley *Harrowing of Hell," PMLA*, 56#1: 105-119 (March, 1941).

NOAH

Nelson, Alan H. " 'Sacred' and 'Secular' Currents in *The Towneley Play of Noah," Drama Survey*, 3#3: 393-401 (Feb, 1964).

PEREGRINI

Clark, Edward Murray. *"The Towneley Peregrini,* an Unnoticed Step Toward the Vernacular," *Modern Language Notes*, 61#4: 236-241 (April, 1946).

PRIMA PASTORUM

Cawley, A. C. "The 'Grotesque' Feast in the *Prima Pastorum," Speculum*, 30#2: 213-217 (April, 1955).

————————. "Iak Garcio of the *Prima Pastorum," Modern Language Notes*, 68#3: 169-173 (March, 1953).

Morgan, Margery M. " 'High Fraud': Paradox and Double-Plot in the English *Shepherds'* Plays," *Speculum*, 39#4: 676-689 (Oct, 1964).

SECUNDA PASTORUM

Carpenter, Nan Cooke. "Music in the *Secunda Pastorum," Speculum*, 26#4: 696-700 (Oct, 1951).

Manly, William M. "Shepherds and Prophets: Religious Unity in the Towneley *Secunda Pastorum,*" *PMLA,* 78#3: 151-162 (June, 1963).

Morgan, Margery M. "'High Fraud': Paradox and Double-Plot in the English *Shepherds' Plays,*" *Speculum,* 39#4: 676-689 (Oct, 1964).

Peel, Donald F. "The Allegory in *Secunda Pastorum,*" *Northwest Missouri State College Studies,* 24#4: 3-11 (Nov, 1960).

Ross, Lawrence J. "Art and the Study of Early English Drama," *Renaissance Drama,* 6: 38-39 (1963).

Williams, Raymond. *Drama in Performance,* 45-46.

TURNER, W. J.

MAN WHO ATE THE POPMACK, THE

Hausermann, W. "W. J. Turner and Bernard Shaw: A Disagreement," *English Miscellany,* 10: 312-317 (1959).

SMARAGDA'S LOVER

Hausermann, W. "W. J. Turner and Bernard Shaw: A Disagreement," *English Miscellany,* 10: 317-322 (1959).

TYLER, ROYALL

THE CONTRAST

Curvin, Jonathan W. "The Stage Yankee," in *Studies in Speech and Drama in Honor of Alexander M. Drummond,* 139-142.

Lauber, John. *"The Contrast:* A Study in the Concept of Innocence," *English Language Notes,* 1#1: 33-37 (Sept, 1963).

Nethercot, Arthur H. "The Dramatic Background of Royall Tyler's *The Contrast,*" *American Literature,* 12#4: 435-446 (Jan, 1941).

UDALL, NICHOLAS

RALPH ROISTER DOISTER

Miller, Edwin S. "Roister Doister's 'Funeralls'," *Studies in Philology,* 43#1: 42-58 (Jan, 1946).

Perry, William. "The Prayer for the Queen in *Roister Doister,*" *Studies in English (University of Texas),* 27#1: 222-233 (June, 1948).

Plunestlad, A. W. "Satirical Parody in *Roister Doister:* A

Reinterpretation," *Studies in Philology,* 60#2: 141-154 (April, 1963).

Towne, Frank. *"Roister Doister's* Assault on *The Castle of Perserverance," Washington State College Research Studies,* 18#4: 175-180 (Dec, 1950).

USTINOV, PETER

THE MOMENT OF TRUTH
Hobson, Harold. *The Theatre Now,* 93-98.

VANBRUGH, JOHN
Mignon, Elizabeth. *Crabbed Age and Youth,* 153-159.

MISTAKE, THE
Wilcox, John. *The Relation of Moliere to Restoration Comedy,* 169-174.

PROVOKED HUSBAND, THE
Boas, F. S. *An Interpretation to Eighteenth Century Drama,* 96-99.

PROVOKED WIFE, THE
Gagen, Jean E. *The New Woman,* 154-156.
Kronenberger, Louis. *The Thread of Laughter,* 159-162.
Mignon, Elizabeth. *Crabbed Age and Youth,* 141-144.
Wilcox, John. *The Relation of Moliere to Restoration Comedy,* 167-169.

RELAPSE, THE
Kronenberger, Louis. *The Thread of Laughter,* 151-159.
Styan, J. L. *The Elements of Drama,* 260-262.
Mignon, Elizabeth. *Crabged Age and Youth,* 133-140.

VANE, SUTTON

OUTWARD BOUND
Marx, Milton. *The Enjoyment of Drama,* 175-177.

VILLIERS, GEORGE

THE REHEARSAL
Smith, Dane. "The Critics in the Audience," *University of New Mexico Publications in Language and Literature,* 12: 18-25 (1953).

WAGER, LEWIS

  LIFE AND REPENTANCE OF MARY MAGDALENE
    Bevington, David M. *From Mankind to Marlowe,* 94-99;
    171-175.

WAGER, WILLIAM

  ENOUGH IS AS GOOD AS A FEAST
    Adams, Henry H. *English Domestic or Homiletic Tragedies
    1575-1642,* 59-63.
    Bevington, David M. *From Mankind to Marlowe,* 158-161.
    Creeth, Edmund H. "Moral and Tragic Recognition: The
      Uniqueness of *Othello, Macbeth,* and *King Lear," Mich-
      igan Academy of Science, Arts, and Letters. Papers,* 45:
      381-384; 388-389 (1960).

  LONGER THOU LIVEST THE MORE FOOL
  THOU ART, THE
    Bevington, David M. *From Mankind to Marlowe,* 91-99; 163-
    165.

  TRIAL OF TREASURE, THE
    Olives, Leslie M. "William Wager and *The Trial of Treas-
      ure," Huntington Library Quarterly,* 9#4: 419-430 (Aug,
      1946).

WAKEFIELD MASTER, THE

  CRUCIFIXTION
    Samuels, Charles T. "The Dramatic Rhythm of the Wakefield
      Crucifixtion," College English, 22#5: 343-344 (Feb,
      1961).

WAPULL, GEORGE

  THE TIDE TARRIETH FOR NO MAN
    Bevington, David M. *From Mankind to Marlowe,* 149-151.

WATLING, PETER

  INDIAN SUMMER
    Hobson, Harold. *The Theatre Now,* 112-117.

WATSON, THOMAS

ABSALOM

Smith, John Hazel. "A Humanist's 'Trew Imitation': Thomas Watson's *Absalom,*" *Illinois Studies in Language and Literature,* 52: 1-293 (1964).

WEBSTER, JOHN

APPIUS AND VIRGINIA

Adams, Henry H. *English Domestic or Homiletic Tragedy* 1575-1642, 75-78.

Haworth, Peter. *English Hymns and Ballads,* 137-148.

Irgat, Mina. "Disease Imagery in the Plays of J. Webster," *Litera,* 2: 22-24 (1955).

Seiden, Melvin. "Two Notes on Webster's *Appius and Virginia,*" *Philological Quarterly,* 35#4: 408-417 (Oct, 1956).

CURE FOR A CUCKOLD, A

Ekeblad, Inga-Stina. "Webster's Constructional Rhythm," *ELH* 24#3: 165-176 (Sept, 1957).

Irgat, Mina. "Disease Imagery in the Plays of J. Webster," *Litera,* 2: 22 (1955).

DEVIL'S LAW CASE, THE

Haworth, Peter. *English Hymns and Ballads,* 117-136.

Irgat, Mina. "Disease Imagery in the Plays of J. Webster," *Litera,* 2: 19-22 (1955).

Merchant, W. M. "Lawyer and Actor: Process of Law in Elizabethan Drama," in G. I. Duthie (ed), *English Studies Today—Third Series* (1964), 107-124.

DUCHESS OF MALFI, THE

Akrigg, D. P. V. "A Phase in Webster," *Notes and Queries,* 193: 454 (16 Oct, 1948).

Allison, Alexander W. "Ethical Themes in *Duchess of Malfi,*" *Studies in English Literature 1500-1900,* 4#2: 263-273 (Spring, 1964).

Bowers, Fredson T. *Elizabethan Revenge Tragedy,* 177-179.

Bradbrook, M. C. "Two Notes Upon Webster," *The Modern Language Review,* 42#3: 281-291 (July, 1947).

Brennan, Elizabeth. "The Relationship Between Brother and Sister in the Plays of John Webster," *Modern Language Review,* 58#4: 488-494 (Oct, 1963).

Calderwood, James L. *"The Duchess of Malfi:* Styles of Ceremony," *Essays in Criticism,* 12#2: 133-147 (April, 1962).

Cecil, David. *Poets and Story Tellers,* 34-43.

Davies, Cecil W. "The Structure of *The Duchess of Malfi:* An Approach," *English,* 12#69: 89-93 (Autumn, 1958).

Ekeblad, Inga-Stina. "The 'Impure Art' of John Webster," *Review of English Studies,* 9N.S.#35: 253-267 (August, 1958).

——————. "A Webster's Villain: A Study of Character Imagery in *The Duchess of Malfi," Orpheus,* 3#3: 126-133 (Sept, 1956).

Empson, William. "Mine Eyes Dazzle," *Essays in Criticism,* 14#1: 80-86 (Jan, 1964).

Emslie, M. "Motives in *Malfi," Essays in Criticism,* 9#4: 391-405 (Oct, 1959).

Haworth, Peter. *English Hymns and Ballads,* 98-116.

Henn, Thomas R. *The Harvest of Tragedy,* 109-110; 128-129.

Irgat, Mina. "Disease Imagery in the Plays of J. Webster," *Litera,* 2: 10-19 (1955).

Jenkins, Harold. "The Tragedy of Revenge in Shakespeare and Webster," *Shakespeare Survey,* 14: 53-55 (1961).

Leech, Clifford. "An Addendum on Webster's *Duchess," Philological Quarterly,* 37#2: 253-256 (April, 1958).

——————. "John Webster—A Critical Study," *Hogarth Lectures on Literature,* 16: 58-89 (1951).

——————. *Shakespeare's Tragedies and Other Studies in Seventeenth Century Drama,* 23-26.

Lewis, George L. "Eelements of Medieval Horror Tragedy in *The Duchess of Malfi," Central States Speech Journal,* 12#2: 106-111 (Winter, 1961).

Luecke, Jane Marie. *"The Duchess of Malfi:* Comic and Satiric Confusion in a Tragedy," *Studies in English Literature 1500-1900,* 4#2: 275-290 (Spring, 1964).

Mill, Adair. "John Webster as Moralist," *Litera,* 3: 27-34 (1956).

Mulrvne, J. R. *"The White Devil* and *The Duchess of Malfi," Stratford-Upon-Avon Studies,* 1: 214-226 (1960).

Ornstein, Robert. *The Moral Vision of Jacobean Tragedy,* 140-148.

Parrott, T. M. and R. H. Ball. *A Short View of Elizabethan Tragedy,* 228-232.

Praz, M. "John Webster and *The Maid's Tragedy," English Studies,* 37#6: 255-258 (Dec, 1956).

Prior, Moody E. *The Language of Tragedy*, 121-135.

Ribner, Irving. *Jacobean Tragedy*, 108-122; 124-125.

—————. "Webster's Italian Tragedies," *Tulane Drama Review*, 5#3: 106-118 (March, 1961).

Riewald, J. G. "Shakespeare Burlesque in John Webster's *The Duchess of Malfi*," *English Studies*, 45 (Supplement): 177-189 (1964).

Salingar, L. G. "Tourneur and the Tragedy of Revenge," *Guide to English Literature*, 2: 341-345.

Sastri, J. S. "The Latent Motive for Ferdinand's Conduct in *The Duchess of Malfi*," *Osmania Journal of English Studies*, 2: 13-28 (1962).

—————. "Webster's Masque of Madmen: An Examination," *The Indian Journal of English Studies*, 3#1: 33-43 (1962).

Sharpe, Robert B. "Nine Steps to the Tragic Triumph," *University of North Carolina Extension Bulletin*, 36#3: 29; 36-37 (Mar, 1957).

Thayer, C. G. "The Ambiguity of Bosola," *Studies in Philology*, 54#2: 162-171 (April, 1957).

Todd, F. M. "Webster and Cervantes," *Modern Language Review*, 51#3: 321-323 (July, 1956).

Vernon, P. F. "The Duchess of Malfi's Guilt," *Notes and Queries*, 208: 335-338 (Sept, 1963).

Wadsworth, Frank W. "Webster's *The Duchess of Malfi* in the Light of Some Contemporary Ideas on Marriage and Remarriage," *Philological Quarterly*, 35#4: 394-407 (Oct, 1956).

Wells, Henry W. *Elizabethan and Jacobean Playwrights*, 45-49.

SIR THOMAS WYATT
See: Thomas Dekker

WHITE DEVIL, THE

Akrigg, G. P. V. "John Webster's Devil in Crystal," *Notes and Queries*, 199: 52 (Feb, 1954).

Blau, Herbert. "Language and Structure in Poetic Drama," *Modern Language Quarterly*, 18: 29-31 (1957).

Boklund, G. "The Sources of *The White Devil*," *University of Upsala. Essays and Studies on English Language and Literature*, 17: 1-26 (1956).

Bowers, Fredson T. *Elizabethan Revenge Tragedy*, 179-183.

Brown, John R. "The Papal Election in John Webster's *The*

White Devil (1612)," *Notes and Queries,* 202#11: 490-494 (Nov, 1957).

Cecil, David. *Poets and Story Tellers,* 27-37; 41-43.

Clark, John E. *"The White Devil:* A Critique," *Manitoba Arts Review,* 8#2: 22-28 (Winter, 1953).

Coombs, H. *Literature and Criticism,* 57-58.

Feldman, A Bronson. "The Yellow Malady: *Short Studies of Five Tragedies of Jealousy,"* *Literature and Psychology,* 6#2: 41-43; 51-52 (May, 1956).

Franklin, H. Bruce. "The Trial Scene in Webster's *The White Devil* Examined in Terms of Renaissance Rhetoric" *Studies in English Literature 1500-1900,* 1#2: 35-52 (Spring, 1961).

Freeman, Arthur. "A Note on *The White Devil,"* *Notes and Queries,* 205: 421 (Nov, 1960).

——————. *"The White Devil,* I. 11. 295: An Emendation," *Notes and Queries,* 208: 101-102 (March, 1963).

Gill, Roma. " 'Quaintly Done': A Reading of *The White Devil,"* *Essays and Studies (English Association),* 19: 41-59 (1966).

Haworth, Peter. *English Hymns and Ballads,* 80-97.

Hurt, James R. "Inverted Ritual in Webster's *The White Devil,"* *Journal of English and Germanic Philology,* 61#1: 42-47 (Jan, 1962).

Irgat, Mina. "Disease Imagery in the Plays of J. Webster," *Litera,* 2: 2-10 (1955).

Jenkins, Harold. "The Tragedy of Revenge in Shakespeare and Webster," *Shakespeare Survey,* 14: 48-53 (1961).

Jones, Eldred. *Othello's Countrymen,* 24-25; 78-80.

Layman, B. J. "The Equilibrium of Opposites in *The White Devil:* A Reinterpretation," *PMLA,* 74 Pt. 1: 336-347 (Sept, 1959).

Leech, Clifford. "John Webster—A Critical Study," *Hogarth Lectures on Literature,* 16: 29-57 (1951).

McCollom, William G. *Tragedy,* 115-117.

Mill, Adair. "John Webster as Moralist," *Litera,* 3: 12-27 (1956).

Mulryne, J. R. *"The White Devil* and *The Duchess of Malfi,"* *Stratford-Upon-Avon Studies,* 1: 201-214 (1960).

Ornstein, Robert. *The Moral Vision of Tragedy,* 129-140.

Parrott, T. M. and R. H. Ball. *A Short View of Elizabethan Tragedy,* 225-228.

Ribner, Irving. *Jacobean Tragedy,* 97-98; 100-108.

——————————. "Webster's Italian Comedies," *Tulane Drama
    Review,* 5#3: 106-118.
Roth, Robert. "Another World of Shakespeare," *Modern Phil-
    ology,* 49#1: 49-51 (Aug, 1951).
Salingar, L. G. "Tourneur and the Tragedy of Revenge,"
    Guide to English Literature, 2: 341-345.
Stroup, Thomas B. "Flamineo and the Comfortable Words,"
    Renaissance Papers, pp. 12-16 (1964).
Wadsworth, Frank W. "Webster's *The White Devil,* III, ii,
    75-80," *The Explicator,* 11#4: #28 (Feb, 1953).
Wells, Henry W. *Elizabethan and Jacobean Playwrights,* 45-
    49.

WESKER, ARNOLD

CHICKEN SOUP WITH BARLEY

Findler, Richard. "Plays and Politics," *Twentieth Century,*
    168#1003: 235-240 (Sept, 1960).
Goodman, Henry. "Arnold Wesker," *Drama Survey,* 1#2:
    218-219 (Oct, 1961).
Leech, Clifford. "Two Romantics: Arnold Wesker and Harold
    Pinter," *Stratford-Upon-Avon Studies,* 4: 11-23 (1962).
Spencer, Charles S. "Arnold Wesker as a Playwright," *Jewish
    Quarterly,* 7#1: 40-41 (Winter, 1959-1960).
Taylor, John R. Anger and After, 144-148.

CHIPS WITH EVERYTHING

Hewitt, Ben. *"Chips With Everything," Encore,* 9#4: 49-50
    (July-Aug, 1962).

I'M TALKING ABOUT JERUSALEM

Findler, Richard. "Plays and Politics," *Twentieth Century,*
    168#1003: 241-242 (Sept, 1960).
Goodman, Henry. "Arnold Wesker," *Drama Survey,* 1#2:
    220-222 (Oct, 1961).
Leech, Clifford. "Two Romantics: Arnold Wesker and Harold
    Pinter," *Stratford-Upon-Avon Studies,* 4: 11-23 (1962).
Taylor, John R. *Anger and After,* 152-154.

KITCHEN, THE

Goodman, Henry. "Arnold Wesker," *Drama Survey,* 1#2:
    217-218 (Oct, 1961).
Leech, Clifford. "Two Romantics: Arnold Wesker and Harold
    Pinter," *Stratford-Upon-Avon Studies,* 4: 11-23 (1962).
Taylor, John R. *Anger and After,* 155-157.

Woodroofe, K. S. "Mr. Wesker's *Kitchen,*" *Hibbert Journal,*
62#246: 148-151 (April, 1964).

Findler, Richard. "Plays and Politics," *Twentieth Century,*
168#1003: 240-241 (Sept, 1960).

Goodman, Henry. "Arnold Wesker," *Drama Survey,* 1#2:
219-220 (Oct, 1961).

Leech, Clifford. "Two Romantics: Arnold Wesker and Harold
Pinter," *Stratford-Upon-Avon Studies,* 4: 11-23 (1962).

Mander, John. *The Writer and Commitment,* 194-211.

Taylor, John R. *Anger and After,* 148-152.

WEVER, R.

LUSTY JUVENTUS
Bevington, David M. *From Mankind to Marlowe,* 143-146.

WHETSTONE, GEORGE

PROMOS AND CASSANDRA
Prouty, Charles T. "George Whetstone and the Sources of
Measure for Measure," *Shakespeare Quarterly,* 15#2:
131-145 (Spring, 1964).

WHITE, PATRICK

CHEERY SOUL, A
Brissenden, R. F. "The Plays of Patrick White," *Meanjin
Quarterly,* 23#3: 212 (1964).

Macartney, Keith. "Patrick White's *A Cheery Soul,*" *Meanjin
Quarterly,* 23#1: 93-95 (1964).

HAM FUNERAL, THE
Brissenden, R. F. "The Plays of Patrick White," *Meanjin
Quarterly,* 23#3: 243-250 (1964).

Loder, Elizabeth. "*The Ham Funeral:* Its Place in the Drama
of Patrick White," *Southerly,* 23#2: 78-91 (1963).

Tasker, John. "Notes on *The Ham Funeral,*" *Meanjin Quarterly,* 23#3: 299-302 (1964).

NIGHT ON BALD MOUNTAIN
Brissenden, R. F. "The Plays of Patrick White," *Meanjin
Quarterly,* 23#3: 255-256 (1964).

SEASON OF SARSAPARILLA, THE
Brissenden, R. F. "The Plays of Patrick White," *Meanjin
Quarterly,* 23#3: 250-252 (1964).

WHITING, JOHN

> DEVILS, THE
>> Milne, Tom. *"Luther* and *The Devils," New Left Review,* 12: 57-58 (Nov-Dec, 1961).
>> O'Connor, Garry. "The Obsession of John Whiting," *Encore,* 11#4: 26-27; 33-36 (July-Aug, 1964).

> MARCHING SONG
>> Cairns, Adrian. "The Significance of John Whiting's Plays," *International Theatre Annual,* 1: 150-152 (1956).
>> Hayman, Ronald. "John Whiting and *Marching Song," Nimbus,* 2#3: 50-58 (Autumn, 1954).
>> O'Connor, Garry. "The Obsession of John Whiting," *Encore,* 11#4: 26-27; 29-33 (July-Aug, 1964).

> PENNY FOR A SONG, A
>> Cairns, Adrian. "The Significance of John Whiting's Plays," *International Theatre Annual,* 1: 150 (1956).
>> O'Connor, Garry. "The Obsession of John Whiting," *Encore,* 11#4: 29-30 (July-Aug, 1964).

> SAINT'S DAY
>> Cairns, Adrian. "The Significance of John Whiting's Plays," *International Theatre Annual,* 1: 148-149 (1956).
>> Hoefer, Jacqueline. "Pinter and Whiting: Two Attitudes Towards the Alienated Artist," *Modern Drama,* 4#4: 402-408 (Feb, 1962).
>> Milne, Tom. "The Hidden Face of Violence," *Encore, 7#1:* 16-20 (Jan-Feb, 1960).
>> O'Connor, Garry. "The Obsession of John Whiting," *Encore,* 11#4: 26-29 (July-Aug, 1964).

WILDE, OSCAR

> IDEAL HUSBAND, AN
>> Ganz, Arthur. "The Divided Self in the Society Comedies of Oscar Wilde," *Modern Drama,* 3#1: 16-23 (May, 1960).
>> Kronenberger, Louis. *The Thread of Laughter,* 216-220.
>> Nethercot, Arthur H. "The Quintessence of Idealism: Or, the Slaves of Duty,*"PMLA,* 62#3: 853-854 (Sept, 1947).
>> Shaw, G. B. *Plays and Players,* 5-9.

> IMPORTANCE OF BEING EARNEST, THE
>> Bentley, Eric. *The Play,* 140; 210-213.
>> —————————. *The Playwright as Thinker,* 172-176.

E., D. V. "The Importance of Publishing *'Ernest'*," *Bulletin of the New York Public Library*, 60#7: 368-372 (July, 1956).

Faverty, Frederic E. *Your Literary Heritage*, 180-182.

Foster, Richard. "Wilde as Parodist: A Second Look at *The Importance of Being Earnest*," *College English*, 18#1: 18-23 (Oct, 1956).

Ganz, Arthur. "The Meaning of *The Importance of Being Earnest*," *Modern Drama*, 6#1: 42-52 (May, 1963).

Kronenberger, Louis. *The Thread of Laughter*, 222-225.

Morgan, Charles. "Dialogue in Novels and Plays," *Etudes Anglaises*, 6#2: 97; 101-103 (May, 1953).
    ALSO IN: Wedgwood, C. V. *Mightier Than the Sword*, 7-10.

Murdick, Marvin. "Restoration Comedy and Later," *English Institute Essays*, pp. 120-125 (1954).

Nethercot, Arthur H. "Prunes and Miss Prism," *Modern Drama*, 6#2: 112-116 (Sept, 1963).

———————. "The Quintessence of Idealism: Or, the Slaves of Duty," *PMLA*, 62#3: 852-853 (Sept, 1947).

Partridge, E. B. "The Importance of Not Being Earnest," *Bucknell University Studies*, 9#2: 143-158 (May, 1960).

Reinert, Otto. "The Courtishy Dance in *The Importance of Being Earnest*," *Modern Drama*, 1#4: 256-257 (Feb, 1959).

———————. "Satiric Strategy in *The Importance of Being Earnest*," *College English*, 18#1: 14-18 (Oct, 1956).

Shaw, G. B. *Plays and Players*, 17-20.

Stanford, Derek. "The Importance of Not Being Earnest," *The Norseman*, 10#5: 329-332 (Sept-Oct, 1952).

Styan, J. L. *The Elements of Drama*, 20-24, 53-54; 143-146.

Toliver, Harold E. "Wilde and The Importance of 'Sincere and Studied Triviality,'" *Modern Drama*, 5#4: 389-399 (Feb, 1963).

Vordtriede, Werner. "A Dramatic Device in *Faust* and *The Importance of Being Earnest*," *Modern Language Notes*, 70#8: 584-585 (Dec, 1955).

LADY WINDEMERE'S FAN

Brooks, Cleanth and Robert Heilman. *Understanding Drama*, 34; 43-45; 54-56; 63-66; 73-82.

Freedman, Morris. "The Modern Tragicomedy of O'Casey and Wilde," *College English*, 25#7: 518-522 (April, 1964).

Ganz, Arthur. "The Divided Self in the Society Comedies of Oscar Wilde," *Modern Drama,* 3#1 : 16-23 (May, 1960).

Harris, Alan. "Oscar Wilde as Playwright: A Centenary Review," *Adelphi,* 30#3 : 222-225 ; 230 (Second Quarter, 1954).

Kronenberger, Louis. *The Thread of Laughter,* 213-216.

Nethercot, Arthur H. "The Quintessence of Idealism: Or, the Slaves of Duty," *PMLA,* 62#3 : 854-855 (Sept, 1947).

Peckham, Morse. "What Did Lady Windermere Learn?" *College English,* 18#1 : 11-14 (Oct, 1956).

SALOME

Bergler, Edmund. *"Salome,* the Turning Point in the Life of Oscar Wilde," *Psychoanalytic Review,* 43#1 : 97-103 (Jan, 1956).

Harris, Alan. "Oscar Wilde as Playwright: A Centenary Review," *Adelphi,* 30#3 : 226-229 (Second Quarter, 1954).

Jasper, G. R. *Adventure in the Theater,* 206-213.

VERA, OR THE NIHILISTS

Harris, Alan. "Oscar Wilde as Playwright: A Centenary Review," *Adelphi,* 30#3 : 217-219 (Second Quarter, 1954).

WOMAN OF NO IMPORTANCE, A

Ganz, Arthur. "The Divided Self in the Society Comedies of Oscar Wilde," *Modern Drama,* 3#1 : 16-23 (May, 1960).

Kronenberger, Louis. *The Thread of Laughter,* 220-222.

WILDER, THORNTON

HAPPY JOURNEY FROM TRENTON TO CAMDEN, A

Fabian, Sister Mary. "The Contributions of Thornton Wilder to American Drama," *Horizontes,* 7#4 : 76-77 (April, 1964).

LONG CHRISTMAS DINNER, THE

Millet, Fred B. *Reading Drama,* 17-18; 37-38; 136-138.

MATCHMAKER, THE

Fabian, Sister Mary. "The Contributions of Thornton Wilder to American Drama," *Horizontes,* 7#4 : 84-86 (April, 1964).

Hewitt, Bernard. "Thornton Wilder Says 'Yes,' " *Tulane Drama Review,* 4#2 : 110-114 (Dec, 1959).

OUR TOWN

Adler, Henry. "Thornton Wilder's Theatre," *Horizon,* 12#68: 89-95 (Aug, 1945).

Broussard, Louis. *American Drama,* 95-99; 101-129.

Duerrenmatt, Friedrich. "Problems of the Theater," *Tulane Dram Review,* 3#1: 10-14 (Oct, 1958).

Eastman, Fred. *Christ in the Drama,* 113-119.

Engler, Walter J. "A Project on *Our Town* for Communication Classes," *College English,* 14#3: 150-156 (Dec, 1952).

Fabian, Sister Mary. "The Contributions of Thornton Wilder to American Drama," *Horizontes,* 7#4: 77-81 (April, **1964**).

Fergusson, Francis. "Three Allegories: Brecht, Wilder, and Eliot," *Sewanee Review,* 66#4: 554-559. (Fall, 1956).

Fulton, A. R. *Drama and Theatre,* 390-396.

Gardner, Martin. "Thornton Wilder and the Problem of Providence," *University Review,* 7#2: 88-91 (Dec, 1940).

Hewitt, Bernard. "Thornton Wilder Says 'Yes,'" *Tulane Drama Review,* 4#2: 114-117 (Dec, 1959).

McCarthy, Mary. *Theater Chronicle,* 26-29.

Nelson, Robert J. *Play Within a Play,* 1-3.

Scott, Winfield T. "*Our Town* and the Golden Veil," *Virginia Quarterly Review,* 29#1: 103-117 (Winter, 1953).

Sievers, W. D. *Freud on Broadway,* 255-258.

Stevens, George D. "*Our Town*—Great American Tragedy?" *Modern Drama,* 1#4: 258-264 (Feb, 1959).

SKIN OF OUR TEETH, THE

Adler, Henry. "Thornton Wilder's Theatre," *Horizon,* 12#68: 95-99 (Aug, 1945).

Broussard, Louis. *American Drama,* 99-101.

Cubeta, Paul M. *Modern Drama for Analysis, Third Edition* (1963), 577-586.

Fabian, Sister Mary. "The Contributions of Thornton Wilder to American Drama," *Horizontes,* 7#4: 81-84 (April, 1964).

Fergusson, Francis. "Three Allegorists: Brecht, Wilder, and Eliot." *Sewanee Review,* 64#4: 549-562 (Aut, 1956).

Hewitt, Bernard. "Thornton Wilder Says 'Yes,'" *Tulane Drama Review,* 4#2: 117-120 (Dec, 1959).

McCarthy, Mary. *Theater Chronicle,* 53-56.

Modic, John. "The Eclectic Mr. Wilder," *Ball State Teachers College Forum,* 1#2: 55-61 (Winter, 1960-1961).

Sievers, W. D. *Freud on Broadway,* 258-261.

WILKINS, GEORGE

THE MISERIES OF ENFORCED MARRIAGE
Adams, Henry H. *English Domestic or Homiletic, Tragedies 1575-1642,* 160-163.
Blayney, Glenn A. "Wilkin's Revisions in *The Miseries of Inforst Mariage,"* Journal of English and Germanic Philology, 56#1: 23-41 (Jan, 1957).

WILLIAMS, CHARLES

JUDGEMENT AT CHELMSFORD
Spanos, William V. "Charles Williams' *Judgement at Chelmsford:* A Study in the Aesthetic of Sacramental Time," *Christian Scholar,* 45#2: 107-117 (Summer, 1962).

WILLIAMS, EMLYN

ACOLADE
Hobson, Harold. *The Theatre Now,* 2-5.

CORN IS GREEN, THE
Eastman, Fred. Christ in the Drama, 78-86.

WILLIAMS, ESPY

DANTE AND BEATRICE
Nolan, Paul T. "Williams' *Dante:* The Death of the Nineteenth Century Heroic Drama," *Southern Speech Journal,* 25#4: 255-256; 262 (Summer, 1960).

PARRHASIUS
Nolan, Paul T. "Classical Tragedy in the Province Theater," *American Quarterly,* 13#3: 410-413 (Fall, 1961).

WILLIAMS, J. ELLIS

THE AFTERMATH
Richards, Tom. "A New Direction for Welsh Playwrights," *Welsh Review,* 4#4: 275-279 (Dec, 1945).

WILLIAMS, TENNESSEE

BATTLE OF ANGELS
Iyengar, Srinivasa K. *The Adventure of Criticism,* 489-491.

Sharp, William. "An Unfashionable View of Tennessee Williams," *Tulane Drama Review,* 6#3: 163-167 (March, 1962).

CAMINO REAL
Clurman, H. *Lies Like Truth,* 83-86.

Glicksberg, Charles I. "The Modern Playwright and the Absolute," *Queen's Quarterly,* 45#3: 468-470 (Aut, 1958).

Sievers, W. D. *Freud on Broadway,* 385-388.

CAT ON A HOT TIN ROOF
Becker, William. "Reflections on Three New Plays," *Hudson Review,* 9#2: 268-272 (Summer, 1955).

Brooks, Charles. "The Comic Tennessee Williams," *Quarterly Journal of Speech,* 44#3: 278-279 (Oct, 1958).

DaPonte, Durant. "Tennessee's Tennessee Williams," *Tennessee Studies in Literature,* 1: 12-13 (1956).

Dukore, Bernard F. "The Cat Has Nine Lives," *Tulane Drama Review,* 8#1: 95-100 (Fall, 1963).

Finkelstein, Sidney. "The Critics Havve Problems," *Mainstream,* 13#9: 31-37 (Sept, 1960).

Gellert, Roger. "A Survey of the Treatment of the Homosexual in Some Plays," *Encore,* 8#1: 34-35 (Jan-Feb, 1961).

Kotake, Kazyo. "Elia Kazan and Tennessee Williams," in *English Studies in Japan,* 299-304.

Lolli, Giorgio. "Alcoholism and Homosexuality in Tennessee Williams' *Cat on a Hot Tin Roof,*" *Quarterly Journal of Studies on Alcohol* (Yale), 17: 543-553 (1956).

Magid, Marion. "The Innocence of Tennessee Williams," *Commentary,* 35: 40-42 (Jan, 1963).

Mitchell, John D. "Applied Psychoanalysis in the Drama," *American Imago,* 14#3: 272-273 (Fall, 1953).

Vowles, Richard B. "Tennessee Williams: The World of His Imagery," *Tulane Drama Review,* 3#2: 54-56 (Dec, 1958).

GLASS MENAGERIE, THE
Bluefarb, Sam. "*The Glass Menagerie,*" *College English,* 24#7: 513-517 (April, 1963).

Brooks, Charles. "The Multiple Set in American Drama," *Tulane Drama Review,* 3#2: 35-37 (Dec, 1958).

Brown, J. Mason. *Seeing More Things,* 266-268.

Cubeta, Paul M. *Modern Drama For Analysis, Third Edition* (1963), 202-209.

DaPonte, Durant. "Tennessee's Tennessee Williams," *Tennessee Studies in Literature*, 1: 13-14 (1956).

Dusenbury, Winifred L. *The Theme of Loneliness in Modern American Drama*, 136-140.

Ellis, Brobury P. "The True Originall Copies," *Tulane Drama Review*, 5#1 : 113-116 (Sept, 1960).

Gassner, John. "Realism and Poetry in New American Playwrighting," *World Theatre*, 2#4 : 19-20 (Spring, 1953).

Popkin, Henry. "The Plays of Tennessee Williams," *Tulane Drama Review*, 4#7 : 45-64 (March, 1960).

Sievers, W. D. *Freud on Broadway*, 372-374.

Stavrou, C. N. "The Neurotic Heroines in Tennessee Williams," *Literature and Psychology*, 5#2: 26-29 (May, 1955).

Young, Stark. *Immortal Shadows*, 249-253.

LADY OF LARKSPUR LOTION, THE

Weissman, Philip. "Psychopathological Characters in Current Drama: A Study of a Trio of Heroines," *American Imago*, 17#3: 274-275 ; 277-280 (Fall, 1960).

NIGHT OF THE IGUANA

Adler, Jacob H. *"Night of the Iguana:* A New Tennessee Williams?" *Ramparts*, 1#3 : 59-68 (Nov, 1962).

Kerr, Walter. *The Theater in Spite of Itself*, 252-255.

Magid, Marion. "The Innocence of Tennessee Williams," *Commentary*, 35: 38-39 (Jan, 1963).

ORPHEUS DESCENDING

Sagar, K. M. "What Mr. Williams Has Made of D. H. Lawrence," *Twentieth Century*, 168#1002: 142-148 (August, 1960).

Sharp, William. "An Unfashionable View of Tennessee Williams," *Tulane Drama Review*, 6#3: 163-167 (March, 1962).

PERIOD OF ADJUSTMENT

Magid, Marion. "The Innocence of Tennessee Williams," *Commentary*, 35: 42-43 (Jan, 1963).

Simon, John. "Theater Chronicle," *Hudson Review*, 14#1: 83-84 (Spring, 1961).

ROSE TATTOO, THE

Brooks, Charles. "The Comic Tennessee Williams," *Quarterly Journal of Speech*, 44#3: 275-277 (Oct, 1958).

Sievers, W. D. *Freud on Broadway*, 383-385.

Simpson, Alan. *Beckett and Behan*, 138-167.
Stavrou, C. N. "The Neurotic Heroine in Tennessee Williams," *Literature and Psychology*, 5#2: 26-27; 32-33 (May, 1955).
Styan, J. L. *The Dark Comedy*, 53-57.

STREETCAR NAMED DESIRE, A
Bernard, Kenneth. "The Mercantile Mr. Kowalski," *Discourse*, 7#2: 337-340 (Spring, 1964).
Brooks, Charles. "The Comic Tennessee Williams," *Quarterly Journal of Speech*, 44#3: 275-277 (Oct, 1958).
Brown, J. Mason. *Seeing More Things*, 266-272.
Capon, Eric and Harold Hobson. *"A Streetcar Named Desire,"* *World Review*, pp. 18-22 (Oct, 1949).
Clurman, H. *Lies Like Truth*, 72-80.
Dusenbury, Winifred L. *The Theme of Loneliness in Modern American Drama*, 140-143.
Ganz, Arthur. "The Desperate Morality of the Plays of Tennessee Williams," *American Scholar*, 31#2: 284-286 (Spring, 1962).
Gassner, John. *"A Streetcar Named Desire:* A Study in Ambiguity," in *The Theatre in our Times*, 355-363.
Goodman, Randolf. *Drama on Stage*, 274-315.
Gray, Paul. "The Theater of the Marvelous," *Tulane Drama Review*, 7#4: 143-145 (Summer, 1963).
Iyengar, Srinivasa K. *The Adventure of Criticism*, 495-500.
Kernan, Alvin B. "Truth and Dramatic Mode in the Modern Theatre: Checkhov, Pirandello and Williams," *Modern Drama*, 1#2: 111-114 (Sept, 1958).
Krutch, J. W. *Modernism in Modern Drama*, 123-130.
Law, Richard A. *"A Streetcar Named Desire* as Melodrama," *The English Record*, 14#3: 2-8 (Feb, 1964).
Leaska, Mitchell. *The Voice of Tragedy*, 279-285.
Lewis, Allan. *The Contemporary Theatre*, 290-291.
Lewis, Theophilus. "Freud and Split-Level Drama," *Catholic World*, 187: 102-103 (May, 1958).
McCarthy, Mary. *Theater Chronicle*, 131-135.
—————. *Sights and Spectacles*, 131-135.
Magid, Marion. "The Innocence of Tennessee Williams," *Commentary*, 35: 35-38 (Jan, 1963).
Popkin, Henry. "The Plays of Tennessee Williams," *Tulane Drama Review*, 4#3: 45-64 (March, 1960).
Riddel, Joseph N. *"A Streetcar Named Desire*—Nietzsche Descending," *Modern Drama*, 5#4: 421-430 (Feb, 1963).

Sagar, K. M. "What Mr. Williams has Made of D. H. Lawrence," *Twentieth Century*, 168#1002: 149-152 (Aug, 1960).

Sievers, W. D. *Freud on Broadway*, 376-380.

Stavrou, C. N. "The Neurotic Heroine in Tennessee Williams," *Literature and Psychology*, 5#2: 26-27; 31-32 (May, 1955).

Styan, J. L. *The Dark Comedy*, 219-220; 224-226.

——————. *The Elements of Drama*, 271-272.

Taylor, Harry. "The Dilemma of Tennessee Williams," *Masses and Mainstream*, 1: 53-55 (April, 1948).

Weissman, Philip. "Psychopathological Characters in Current Drama: A Study of a Trio of Heroines," *American Imago*, 17#3: 275-287 (Fall, 1960).

SUDDENLY LAST SUMMER

Hurt, James R. *"Suddenly Last Summer:* Williams and Melville," *Modern Drama* 3#4: 396-400 (Feb, 1961).

Johnson, Mary Lynn. "Williams' *Suddenly Last Summer,* Scene One," *The Explicator*, 21#8: #66 (April, 1963).

Taylor, William E. "Tennessee Williams: Academia on Broadway," in Richard E. Langford (ed), *Essays in Modern American Literature*, 90-96.

SUMMER AND SMOKE

Brooking, Jack. "Directing *Summer and Smoke:* An Existential Approach," *Modern Drama*, 2#3: 377-385 (Dec, 1959).

Clurman, Harold. *Lies Like Truth*, 80-83.

Sievers, W. D. *Freud on Broadway*, 380-382.

Stavrou, C. N. "The Neurotic Heroine in Tennessee Williams," *Literature and Psychology*, 5#2: 26-27; 29-30 (May, 1955).

SWEET BIRD OF YOUTH

Brustein, Robert. "Williams' Nebulous Nightmare," *Hudson Review*, 12#2: 255-260 (Summer, 1959).

Duprey, Richard A. "Tennessee Williams' Search for Innocence," *Catholic World*, 189: 191-194 (June, 1959).

Kerr, Walter. *The Theater in Spite of Itself*, 246-252.

THIS PROPERTY IS CONDEMNED

Weissman, Philip. "Psychopathological Characters in Current Drama: A Study of a Trio of Heroines," *American Imago*, 17#3: 273-275 (Fall, 1960).

YOU TOUCHED ME
>   Clayton, John S. "The Sister Figure in the Works of Tennes-
>   see Williams," *Carolina Quarterly,* 11#3: 53-57 (Sum-
>   mer, 1960).
>   Sievers, W. D. *Freud on Broadway,* 375-376.

WILMOT, JOHN

SODOM; OR THE QUINTESSENCE OF DEBAUCHERY
>   Graves, Wallace. "The Uses of Rhetoric in the Nadir of Eng-
>   lish Morals," *Western Speech,* 28#2: 98-105 (Spring,
>   1964).

WILMOT, ROBERT

GISMOND OF SALERNE
>   Clemen, Wolfgang. *English Tragedy Before Shakespeare,*
>   75-76.
>   Griffin, Ernest G. "Gismond of Salerne: A Critical Apprecia-
>   tion," *Review of English Literature,* 4#2: 94-107 (April,
>   1963).
>   Rottenberg, Annette T. "The Early Love Drama," *College
>   English,* 23#7: 582-583 (April, 1962).

TANCRED AND GISMUND
>   See: *Gismond of Salerne*

WILSON, EDMUND

THE LITTLE BLUE LIGHT
>   Sievers, W. D. *Freud on Broadway,* 241-242.

WILSON, ROBERT

COBBLER'S PROPHECY, THE
>   Talbert, Ernest W. *Elizabethan Drama and Shakespeare's
>   Early Drama,* 18-21; 23-24.

THREE LADIES OF LONDON, THE
>   Fisch, Harold. *The Dual Image,* 24-25.

WINTER, JOHN KEITH

THE SHINING HOUR
>   Lawson, John H. *Theory and Technique of Playwriting,* 192-
>   196.

WOLFE, THOMAS

MANNERHOUSE
Carpenter, Frederic I. *American Literature and the Dream*, 155-158.
——————————. "The Autobiography of an Idea," *University of Kansas City Review*, 12#3: 179-187 (Spring, 1946).

WOODE, NATHANIEL

THE CONFLICT OF CONSCIENCE
Bevington, David M. *From Mankind to Marlowe*, 245-251.

WORDSWORTH, WILLIAM

THE BORDERERS
Fry, Christopher. "Poetry and the Theater," *Adam International Review*, 214-215: 4-6 (1951).
Hartman, G. H. "Wordsworth's *The Borderers* and Intellectual Murder," *Journal of English and Germanic Philology*, 62#4: 761-768 (Oct, 1963).
Hayden, Donald. "Toward an Understanding of Wordsworth's *The Borderers*," *Modern Language Notes*, 66#1: 1-6 (1951).
Smith, Charles J. "The Effect of Shakespeare's Influence on *The Borderers*," *Studies in Philology*, 50#4: 625-639 (Oct, 1953).

WYCHERLEY, WILLIAM

COUNTRY WIFE, THE
Avery, Emmett L. *"The Country Wife* in the Eighteenth Century," *Washington State College Research Studies*, 10#2: 141-172 (June, 1942).
Bateson, F. W. "Second Thoughts II: L. C. Knights and Restoration Comedy," *Essays in Criticism*, 7#1: 63-67 (Jan, 1957).
Blakeslee, Richard C. "Wycherley's Use of the Aside," *Western Speech*, 28#4: 212-217 (Fall, 1964).
Bowman, John S. "Dance, Chant and Mask in the Plays of Wycherley," *Drama Survey*, 3#2: 181-205 (Fall, 1963).
Cecil, C. D. "Libertine and Precieux Elements in Restoration Comedy," *Essays in Criticism*, 9#3: 249-253 (July, 1959).
Craik, T. W. "Some Aspects of Satire in Wycherley's Plays," *English Studies*, 41#3: 177-179 (June, 1960).

Fujimura, Thomas H. *The Restoration Comedy of Wit*, 139-146.

Holland, Norman. *The First Modern Comedies*, 73-85.

Kronenberger, Louis. *The Thread of Laughter*, 61-70.

Mignon, Elizabeth. *Crabbed Age and Youth*, 53-54.

Murdick, Marvin. "Restoration Comedy and Later," *English Institute Essays*, pp. 106-111 (1954).

Vernon, P. F. "Marriage of Convenience and the Moral Code of Restoration Comedy," *Essays in Criticism*, 12#4: 370-387 (Oct, 1962).

Wilcox, John. *The Relation of Moliere to Restoration Comedy*, 87-94.

Wooton, Carl. "*The Country Wife* and Contemporary Comedy: A World Apart," *Drama Survey*, 2#3: 333-343 (Feb, 1963).

Young, Stark. *Immortal Shadows*, 181-184.

GENTLEMAN DANCING MASTER, THE

Bowman, John S. "Dance, Chant and Mask in the Plays of Wycherley," *Drama Survey*, 3#2: 181-205 (Fall, 1963).

Craik, T. W. "Some Aspects of Satire in Wycherley's Plays," *English Studies*, 41#3: 172-174 (June, 1960).

Fujimura, Thomas H. *The Restoration Comedy of Wit*, 133-139.

Holland, Norman. *The First Modern Comedies*, 64-72.

Kronenberger, Louis. *The Thread of Laughter*, 59-61.

Mignon, Elizabeth. *Crabbed Age and Youth*, 50-53.

Wilcox, John. *The Relation of Moliere to Restoration Comedy*, 83-87.

LOVE IN A WOOD

Bowman, John S. "Dance, Chant and Mask in the Plays of Wychereley," *Drama Survey*, 3#2: 181-205 (Fall, 1963).

Craik, T. W. "Some Aspects of Satire in Wycherley's Plays," *English Studies*, 41#3: 168-172 (June, 1960).

Fujimura, Thomas H. *The Restoration Comedy of Wit*, 127-133.

Holland, Norman. *The First Modern Comedies*, 38-44.

Kronenberger, Louis. *The Thread of Laughter*, 56-59.

Mignon, Elizabeth. *Crabbed Age and Youth*, 48-50.

Rundle, James U. "Wycherley and Calderon: A Source for *Love in a Wood*," *PMLA*, 64#4: 701-707 (Sept, 1949).

MAN OF MODE, THE
See: George Etherege

PLAIN DEALER, THE

Avery, Emett L. *"The Plain Dealer* in the Eighteenth Century," *Washington State College Research Studies,* 11#3: 234-256 (Sept, 1943).

Bowman, John S. "Dance, Chant and Mask in the Plays of Wycherley," *Drama Survey,* 3#2: 181-205 (Fall, 1963).

Chorney, Alexander H. "Wycherley's Manly Reinterpreted," in *Essays Critical and Historical Dedicated to Lily B. Campbell,* 161-169.

Craik, T. W. "Some Aspects of Satire in Wycherley's Plays," *English Studies,* 41#3: 174-177 (June, 1960).

Fujimura, Thomas H. *The Restoration Comedy of Wit,* 146-153.

Gagen, Jean E. *The New Woman,* 106-108.

Holland, Norman. *The First Modern Comedies,* 96-113.

Kronenberger, Louis. *The Thread of Laughter,* 70-76.

Mignon, Elizabeth. *Crabbed Age and Youth,* 54-59.

O'Regan, M. J. "Furetiere and Wycherley," *Modern Language Review,* 53#1: 77-81 (Jan, 1958).

Rogers, K. M. "Fatal Inconsistency: Wycherley and *The Plain Dealer,*" *ELH,* 28#2: 148-162 (June, 1961).

Wilcox, John. *The Relation of Moliere to Restoration Comedy,* 94-102.

Zimbardo, Rose A. "Structural Design in *The Plain Dealer,*" *Studies in English Literature 1500-1900,* 1#3: 1-18 (Summer, 1961).

YARINGTON, ROBERT

TWO LAMENTABLE TRAGEDIES

Adams, Henry. *English Domestic or Homiletic Tragedies 1575-1642,* 108-114.

YEATS, WILLIAM BUTLER

AT THE HAWK'S WELL

Donoghue, Denis. *The Third Voice,* 50-54.

Iremonger, Valentin. "Yeats as a Playwright," *Irish Writing,* 31: 53-56.

Sandberg, Anna. "The Anti-Theatre of William Butler Yeats," *Modern Drama,* 4#2: 131-137 (Sept, 1961).

Sharp, William L. "W. B. Yeats: A Poet Not in the Theater," *Tulane Drama Review,* 4#2: 67-79 (Dec, 1959).

Thwaite, Anthony. "Yeats and the Noh," *Twentieth Century,* 162#967: 235-242 (Sept, 1957).

CALVARY

Gose, Elliott B. Jr. "The Lyric and the Philosophic in Yeats' *Calvary,*" *Modern Drama,* 2#3: 370-376 (Dec, 1959).

Times Literary Supplement. "Ideas Into Drama," *Times Literary Supplement,* p. 529 (Aug. 19, 1960).

Ure, Peter. "Yeats' Christian Mystery Plays," *Review of English Studies,* NS11#42: 171-182 (May, 1960).

CATHLEEN NI HOULIHAN

Millet, Fred B. *Reading Drama,* 16-17; 115-117; 245-246.

COUNTESS CATHLEEN, THE

Gilkes, Martin. *"Countess Cathleen* by the Avon," *English,* 3#16: 159-164 (Spring, 1941).

Orel, Harold. "Dramatic Values, Yeats, and *The Countess Cathleen,*" *Modern Drama,* 2#1: 8-16 (May, 1959).

Ure, Peter. "The Evolution of Yeats' *The Countess Cathleen,*" *Modern Language Review,* 57#1: 12-24 (Jan, 1962).

Williams, Raymond. *Drama From Ibsen to Eliot,* 211-213.

DEATH OF CUCHULAIN, THE

Moore, John R. "Cuchulain, Christ, and the Queen of Love: Aspects of Yeatsian Drama," *Tulane Drama Review,* 6#3: 150-154 (March, 1962).

Pearce, Donald R. "Yeats' Last Plays: An Interpretation," *ELH,* 18#1: 67; 75-76 (March, 1951).

DIERDRE

Clark, David Ridgley. "The Rigour of Logic," *The Dublin Magazine,* 33#1 (N.S.): 13-21 (Jan-Mar, 1958).

Ellis-Fermor, Una. *The Irish Dramatic Movement,* 113-115.

McHugh, Roger. "The Deirdre Legend," *Threshold,* 1#1: 42-45 (Feb, 1957).

Ure, Peter. "Yeats' *Deirdre,*" *English Studies,* 42#4: 218-230 (Aug, 1961).

Williams, Raymond. *Drama From Ibsen to Eliot,* 215-216.

DREAMING OF THE BONES, THE

Iremonger, Valentin. "Yeats as a Playwright," *Irish Writing,* 31: 53-56.

Warschausky, Sidney. "Yeats' Purgatorical Plays," *Modern Drama,* 7#3: 280-282 (Dec, 1964).

HERNE'S EGG, THE
   Moore, John R. "Cold Passion: A Study of *The Herne's Egg*,"
      Modern Drama, 7#3: 287-298 (Dec, 1964).
   Pearce, Donald R. "Yeats' Last Plays: An Interpretation,"
      ELH, 18#1: 67-71 (March, 1951).
   Ure, Peter. "Yeats' Hero Fool in *The Herne's Egg*," *Hunting-*
      ton Library Quarterly, 24#2: 125-136 (Feb, 1961).

HOUR GLASS, THE
   Donoghue, Denis. *The Third Voice*, 46-50.
   Ellis-Fermor, Una. *The Irish Dramatic Movement*, 107-109.

KING'S THRESHOLD, THE
   Block, Haskell M. "Yeats' *The King's Threshold*: The Poet
      and Society," *Philological Quarterly, 34#2*: 206-218
      (April, 1955).

ON BAILE'S STRAND
   Williams, Raymond. *Drama From Ibsen to Eliot*, 216-217.

ONLY JEALOUSY OF EMER, THE
   Iremonger, Valentin. "Yeats as a Playwright," *Irish Writing,*
      31: 53-56.
   Scanlon, Aloyse. "The Sustained Metaphor in *The Only Jeal-*
      ousy," *Modern Drama, 7#3*: 273-277 (Dec, 1964).
   Wilson, T. A. C. "Yeats and Gerhart Hauptmann," *Southern*
      Review (South Australia), 1#1: 69-73 (1963).

PLAYER QUEEN, THE
   Becker, William. "The Mask Mocked; Or, Farce and The
      Dialectic of Self (Notes on Yeats' *The Player Queen)*,"
      Sewanee Review, 61#1: 82-108 (Winter, 1953).
   Newton, Norman. "Yeats as Dramatist: *The Player Queen*,"
      Essays in Criticism, 8: 269-284 (1958).

PURGATORY
   Gaskell, Ronald. "*Purgatory*," *Modern Drama, 4#4*: 397-401
      (Dec, 1961).
   Henn, Thomas R. *The Harvest of Tragedy*, 209-211.
   Lightfoot, Marjorie J. "*Purgatory* and *The Family Reunion*:
      In Pursuit of Prosodic Description," *Modern Drama,*
      7#3: 256-266 (Dec, 1964).
   Moore, John Rees. "An Old Man's Tragedy— Yeats' *Purga-*
      tory," *Modern Drama, 5#4*: 440-450 (Feb, 1963).
   Pearce, Donald R. "Yeats' Last Plays: An Interpretation,"
      ELH, 18#1: 67; 71-75 (March, 1951).

Warschausky, Sidney. "Yeats' Purgatorical Plays," *Modern Drama,* 7#3: 283-286 (Dec, 1964).

RESURRECTION, THE
Alt, Peter. "Yeats, Religion, and History," *Sewanee Review,* 60#4: 651-658 (Autumn, 1952).
Times Literary Supplement. "Ideas Into Drama," *Times Literary Supplement,* pg. 529 (Aug 19, 1960).
Ure, Peter. "Yeats' Christian Mystery Plays," *Review of English Studies,* NS11#42: 171-182 (May, 1960).

SHADOWY WATERS, THE
Donoghue, Denis. *The Third Voice,* 33-46.
——————————. "Yeats and the Clean Outline," *Sewanee Review,* 65#2: 202-213 (Spring, 1957).

UNICORN FROM THE STARS, THE
Ellis-Fermor, Una. *The Irish Dramatic Movement,* 104-107.

WORDS UPON THE WINDOW PANE, THE
Clarke, David R. "Yeats and the Modern Theatre," *Threshold,* 4#2: 47-55 (Aut/Winter, 1960).
Miner, Earl R. "A Poem by Swift and W. B. Yeats' *Words Upon the Window Pane,*" *Modern Language Notes,* 72#4: 273-275 (April, 1957).
Warschausky, Sidney. "Yeats' Purgatorical Plays," *Modern Drama,* 7#3: 282-283 (Dec, 1964).

YOUNG, STARK

THE SAINT
Sommers, John J. "The Critic as Playwright: A Study of Stark Young's *The Saint,*" *Modern Drama,* 7#4: 446-453 (Feb, 1965).

THE PLAYS OF WILLIAM SHAKESPEARE

ALLS WELL THAT ENDS WELL

Adams, John F. *"All's Well That Ends Well:* The Paradox of Procreation," *Shakespeare Quarterly,* 12#3: 261-270 (Summer, 1961).

Arthos, John. "The Comedy of Generation," *Essays in Criticism,* 5#2: 97-117 (April, 1955).

Blistein, E. M. "The Object of Scorn: An Aspect of the Comic Antagonist," *Western Humanities Review,* 14#2: 210-212 (Spring, 1960).

Bradbrook, M. C. "Virtue is the True Nobility: A Study of the Structure of *All's Well That Ends Well,"* *Review of English Studies,* N.S. 1#4: 289-301 (Oct, 1950).

Calderwood, James L. "The Mingled Yarn of *All's Well,"* *Journal of English and Germanic Philology,* 62#1: 61-76 (Jan, 1963).

——————. "Styles of Knowing in *All's Well,"* *Modern Language Quarterly,* 25#3: 272-294 (Sept, 1964).

Carter, Albert Howard. "In Defense of Bertram," *Shakespeare Quarterly,* 7#1: 21-32 (Winter, 1956).

Draper, John W. "Shakespeare and Florence and the Florentines," *Italica,* 23#4: 288-289; 292-293 (Dec, 1946).

Gassner, John. "Shaw on Shakespeare," *Independent Shavian,* 2#1: 4-5 (Fall, 1963).

Halio, Jay L. *"All's Well That Ends Well,"* *Shakespeare Quarterly,* 15#1: 33-44 (Winter, 1964).

——————."Traitor in *All's Well* and *Troilus and Cressida,"* *Modern Language Notes,* 72#6: 408-409 (June, 1957).

Hapgood, Robert (and Robert Y. Turner). "Dramatic Conventions in *All's Well That Ends Well,"* *PMLA,* 79#1: 177-182 (March, 1963).

Hart, Edward L. "A Mixed Consort: Leontes, Angelo, Helena," *Shakespeare Quarterly,* 15#1: 80-83 (Winter, 1964).

Hethmon, Robert H. "The Case for *All's Well;* What's Wrong With the King?" *Drama Critique,* 7#1: 26-31 (Winter, 1964).

Hunter, G. K. "Atavism and Anticipation in Shakespeare's Style," *Essays in Criticism,* 7#4: 451-453 (Oct, 1957).

Jones, H. W. *"All's Well,* IV, ii, 38 Again," *Modern Language Review,* 55#2: 241-242 (April, 1960).

King, Walter N. "Shakespeare's 'Mingled Yarn'," *Modern Language Quarterly,* 21: 33-44 (1960).

Knight, G. W. *The Sovereign Flower,* 95-160.

La Guardia, Eric. "Chastity, Regeneration, and World Order in *All's Well That Ends Well,"* in Bernice Slote (ed), *Myth and Symbol,* 119-132.

Leech, Clifford. "The Theme of Ambition in *All's Well That Ends Well,"* ELH, 21#1: 17-29 (March, 1954).

McKenzie, Jame. "A Shakespearean Emendation," *Notes and Queries,* 197: 160 (Apr 12, 1952).

Melander, Rudolf. *"All's Well That Ends Well:* Shakespeare's Most Personal Play," *The Swan of Avon,* 1#3: 6-25 (Sept, 1948).

Nagarajan, S. "The Structure of *All's Well That Ends Well,"* *Essays in Criticism,* 10#1: 24-31 (Jan, 1960).

Pettigrew, Helen P. "The Young Count Rousillon," *University of West Virginia Bulletin: Philological Studies,* 4: 22-30 (1943).

Price, Joseph G. "From Farce to Romance: *All's Well That Ends Well,"* *Shakespeare Jahrbuck,* 99: 57-71 (1963).

Ranald, Margaret L. "The Bethrothals in *All's Well That Ends Well,"* *Huntington Library Quarterly,* 26#2: 179-192 (Feb, 1963).

Schanzer, Ernest. "Atavism and Anticipation in Shakespeare's Style," *Essays in Criticism,* 7#3: 252-255 (July, 1957).

Schoff, Francis G. "Claudio, Bertram, and a Note on Interpretation," *Shakespeare Quarterly,* 10#1: 11-23 (Winter, 1959).

Shaw, G. B. *Play and Players,* 9-16.

Siegel, Paul N. "Shakespeare and the Neo-Chivalric Cult of Honor," *Centenniel Review,* 8#1: 56-60 (Winter, 1964).

Sisson, C. J. "Shakespeare, Helena and Dr. William Harvey," *Essays and Studies (English Association),* 13: 1;5; 13-20 (1960).

Tannenbaum, Samuel A. "Removing a Scar From *All's Well,"* *Shakespeare Association Bulletin,* 18#3: 133-136 (July, 1943).

Turner, Robert Y. "Dramatic Conventions in *All's Well That Ends Well,"* PMLA, 75#5: 497-502 (Dec, 1960).

Wilson, Harold S. "Dramatic Emphasis in *All's Well That Ends Well*," *Huntington Library Quarterly*, 13#3: 217-240 (May, 1950).

ANTONY AND CLEOPATRA

Aldus, Paul J. "Analogical Probability in Shakespeare's Plays," *Shakespeare Quarterly*, 6#4: 409-414 (Autumn, 1955).

Aronson, Alex. "A Note on Shakespeare's Dream Imagery," *Visuabharati Quarterly*, 18#2: 181-182 (Aug-Oct, 1952).

Bacon, Wallace A. "The Suicide of Antony," *Shakespeare Association Bulletin*, 24#3: 193-202 (July, 1949).

Baker, Donald C. "The Purging of Cleopatra," *Shakespeare Newsletter*, 10#1: 9 (Feb, 1960).

Bamborough, J. *The Little World of Man*, 48-49; 95.

Barnet, Sylvan. "Recognition and Reversal in *Antony and Cleopatra*," *Shakespeare Quarterly*, 8#3: 331-334 (Summer, 1957).

Barroll, J. Leeds. "Antony and Pleasure," *Journal of English and Germanic Philology*, 57#4: 708-720 (Oct, 1958).

————. "Scarrus and the Scarred Soldier," *Huntington Library Quarterly*, 22#1: 31-40 (Oct, 1958).

————. "Shakespeare and Roman History," *Modern Language Review*, 53#3: 327-343 (July, 1958).

Battenhouse, Roy W. "Shakespearean Tragedy as Christian: Some Confusions in the Debate," *Centenniel Review*, 8#1: 94-98 (Winter, 1964).

Behrens, Ralph. "Cleopatra Exonerated," *Shakespeare Newsletter*, 9#5: 36 (Nov, 1959).

Berkeley, David S. "Antony, Cleopatra, and Proculeius," *Notes and Queries*, 195: 534-535 (9 Dec, 1950).

————. "The Crux of *Antony and Cleopatra*," *Oklahoma A&M College Arts and Science Studies: Humanities Series*, 4: 1-13 (1953).

————. "On Desentimentalizing Antony," *Notes and Queries*, 209: 138-142 (Apr, 1964).

Bonjour, Adrien. "From Shakespeare's Venus to Cleopatra's Cupids," *Shakespeare Survey*, 15: 73-80 (1962).

Bowers, Fredson. "Shakespeare's Art: The Point of View," in Carroll Camden (ed.), *Literary Views*, 46-48; 50-53.

————. "Shakespeare's Dramatic Vagueness," *Virginia Quarterly Review*, 39#3: 477-479 (Summer, 1963).

Bowling, Lawrence Edward. "Antony's Internal Disunity,"

Studies in English Literature 1500-1900, 4#2: 239-246 (Spring, 1964).

—————————. "Duality in the Minor Characters in *Antony and Cleopatra," College English,* 18#5: 251-255 (Feb, 1957).

Bowman, Thomas D. "Antony and the 'lass unparalled'd'," *Shakespeare Newsletter, 7#6:* 47 (Dec, 1957).

Bradley, A. C. *Oxford Lectures on Poetry,* 279-310.

Brooks, Cleanth and R. Heilman. *Understanding Drama,* 673-674.

Brown, John M. *Dramatis Personae,* 227-235.
    ALSO IN: *Seeing More Things,* 238-248.

Burke, Kenneth. "Shakespearean Persuasion," *Antioch Review,* 24#1: 19-36 (Spring, 1964).

Cairns, Huntington et. al. *Invitation to Learning,* 198-212.

Cecil, David. *Poets and Story Tellers,* 3-24.

Charney, Maurice. "Shakespeare's Antony: A Study of Image Themes," *Studies in Philology,* 54#2: 149-161 (April, 1957).

—————————. "Shakespeare's Style in *Julius Caesar* and *Antony and Cleopatra," ELH,* 26#3: 355-367 (Sept, 1959).

Cook, Albert. "Shakespeare's *Antony and Cleopatra,* V, ii, 338-341," *The Explicator,* 6#2: 9 (Nov, 1947).

Coombe, H. *Literature and Criticism,* 97-99; 129-131.

Couchman, Gordon W. *"Antony and Cleopatra* and the Subjective Convention," *PMLA, 76#4:* 420-425 (Sept. 1961).

Cunningham, Delora G. "The Characterization of Shakespeare's Cleopatra," *Shakespeare Quarterly,* 6#1: 9-17 (Winter, 1955).

Daiches, David. "Imagery and Meaning in *Anthony and Cleopatra," English Studies,* 43#5: 343-358 (Oct, 1962).

—————————. *Critical Approaches to Literature,* 204-205.

Danby, John F. "The Shakespearean Dialectic: An Aspect of *Antony and Cleopatra" Scruitiny,* 16#3: 196-212 (Sept, 1949).
    ALSO IN: *Poets on Fortune's Hill,* 128-151.

Davidson, Arthur. *The Solaces of Literature,* 57-61.

Deming, Barbara. "The Playwright as Playwright," *Chimera,* 5#1: 24-25; 27-28 (Aut, 1946).

Donno, Elizabeth Story. "Cleopatra Again," *Shakespeare Quarterly, 7#2:* 227-233 (Spring, 1956).

Draper, John W. "Subjective Conflct in Shakespearean Tragedy," *Neuphilologische Mitteilungen,* 2#61: 219 (1960).

Galloway, David. " 'I am Dying, Egypt Dying': Folio Repititions and the Editors," *Notes and Queries,* 203: 330-335 (Aug, 1958).

Grill, Cynthia. "Antony, Cleopatra, and Proculeius," *Notes and Queries,* 205: 191 (May, 1960).

Harrier, Richard C. "Cleopatra's End," *Shakespeare Quarterly,* 13#1: 63-65 (Winter, 1962).

Harrison, Thomas P. "Shakespeare and Marlowe's *Dido, Queen of Carthage,*" *Studies in English (University of Texas),* 35: 58-63 (1956).

Hawkes, Terence. "Two Points of View on *Antony and Cleopatra,*" *Anglo-Welsh Review,* 13#32: 7-11 (Winter, 1963).

Haywood, Richard M. "Shakespeare and the Old Roman," *College English,* 16#2: 101 (Nov, 1954).

Heilman, Robert B. "From Mine Own Knowledge: A Theme in the Late Tragedies," *Centenniel Review,* 8#1: 17-29 (Winter, 1964).

Henn, Thomas R. *The Harvest of Tragedy,* 47-48; 147-148.

Herbert, T. Walker. "Shakespeare and the Craft of Fiction," *Emory University Quarterly,* 20#2: 87-88 (Summer, 1964).

Hewett, R. P. *Reading and Response,* 115-120.

Holloway, John. *The Story of the Night,* 99-120.

Jenkin, Bernard. "Some Suggestions on the Monument Scenes," *Review of English Studies,* 21#81: 1-14 (Jan, 1945).

Jepsen, Laura. *Ethical Aspects of Tragedy,* 95-101.

Kaula, David. "The Time Sense of *Antony and Cleopatra,*" *Shakespeare Quarterly,* 15#3: 211-223 (Summer, 1964).

Kirschbaum, Leo. "Shakespeare' Cleopatra," *Shakespeare Association Bulletin,* 19#4: 161-171 (Oct, 1944).

Knight, George W. *The Golden Labyrinth,* 81-82; 236-237.

——————. *The Imperial Theme,* 199-350.

Knights, L. C. "On the Tragedy of *Antony and Cleopatra,*" *Scrutiny,* 16#4: 318-322 (Winter, 1949).

——————. "*King Lear* and the Great Tragedies," *Guide to English Literature,* 2: 237-241.

Lerner, Lawrence. "Tragedy: Religious and Humanist," *Review of English Literature,* 2#4: 35-37 (Oct, 1961).

Lever, J. W. "Venus and the Second Chance," *Shakespeare Survey*, 15: 87-88 (1962).

Lloyd, Michael. "Antony and the Game of Chance," *Journal of English and Germanic Philology*, 61#3: 548-554 (July, 1962).

——————. "Cleopatra as Isis," *Shakespeare Survey*, 12: 88-94 (1959).

——————. "The Roman Tongue," *Shakespeare Quarterly*, 10#4: 461-468 (Autumn, 1959).

Long, John H. *"Antony and Cleopatra:* A Double Critical Reversal," *Renaissance Papers*, pp. 28-34 (1964).

Lord, John B. "Comic Scenes in Shakepearean Tragedy," *Washington State College Research* Studies, 32#3: 238-239 (Sept, 1964).

McCollom, William G. *Tragedy*, 200-203.

McFarland, Thomas. "Antony and Octavius," *Yale Review*, 48#2: 204-228 (Dec, 1958).

McGinn, Donald J. "Cleopatra's Immolation Scene," in Kirk, Rudolph (ed), *Essays in Literary History*, 57-80.

MacLure, Millar. "Shakespeare and the Lonely Dragon," *University of Toronto Quarterly*, 24#2: 118-120 (Jan, 1955).

McManaway, James G. "Notes on Act V of *Antony and Cleopatra,*" *Shakespeare Studies*, 1: 1-6 (1962).

MacMullan, Katherine V. "Death Imagery in *Antony and Cleopatra,*" *Shakespeare Quarterly*, 14#4: 399-410 (Autumn, 1963).

Mahnken, Harry E. and Janine S. Mahnken. "Harley Granville-Barker's Shakespearean Criticism," *Southern Speech Journal*, 27#1: 28-29 (Fall, 1961).

Marsh, D. R. C. "The Conflict of Love and Responsibility in *Antony and Cleopatra,*" *Theoria*, 15: 1-27 (1960).

Mendel, Sydney. "Hamletian Man," *Arizona Quarterly*, 16#3: 233-236 (Autumn, 1960).

Michel, Laurence (& Cecil C. Seronsy). "Shakespeare's History Plays and Daniel: An Assessment," *Studies in Philology*, 52#4: 569-577 (Oct, 1955).

Mills, L. J. "Cleopatra's Tragedy," *Shakespeare Quarterly*, 11#2: 147-162 (Spring, 1960).

Muir, Kenneth. *"Antony and Cleopatra,* III, xiii. 73-8," *Notes and Queries*, 206: 142 (Apr, 1961).

——————. "The Imagery of *Antony and Cleopatra,*" *Kwartalnik Neofilologiczny*, 8#3: 249-264 (1961).

Nathan, Norman. *"Antony and Cleopatra:* IV, vii, 6-10," *Notes and Queries,* 200: 293-294 (July, 1955).

Norman, Arthur M. Z. "Daniel's *The Tragedie of Cleopatra* and *Antony and Cleopatra,"* *Shakespeare Quarterly,* 9#1: 11-18 (Winter, 1958).
ALSO IN: *Modern Language Review,* 54#1: 1-9 (Jan, 1959).

Nosworthy, J. M. "Symbol and Character in *Antony and Cleopatra,"* *Shakespeare Newsletter,* 6#1: 4 (Feb, 1956).

Nyland, Waino S. "Pompey as the Mythical Lover of Cleopatra," *Modern Language Notes,* 64#8: 515-516 (Dec, 1949).

Pearce, T. M. "Shakespeare's *Antony and Cleopatra,* V, ii, 243-359," *The Explicator,* 12#3: 17 (Dec, 1953).

Pearson, N. H. "Shakespeare's *Antony and Cleopatra,"* *The Literary Criterion,* 4: 53-73 (Summer, 1959).

Phillips, James Emerson Jr. "The State in Shakespeare's Greek and Roman Plays," *Columbia University Studies in English and Comparative Literature,* 149: 188-205 (1940).

Pogson, Beryl. *In the East My Pleasure Lies,* 107-116.

Purcell, J. M. *"A & C,* I, ii, 42-43," *Notes and Queries,* 203: 187-188 (May, 1958).

Quinn, Michael. "Two Points of View on *Antony and Cleopatra,"* *Anglo-Welsh Review,* 13#32: 12-17 (Winter, 1963).

Rees, Joan. "Shakespeare's use of *Daniel,"* *Modern Language Review,* 55#1: 81-82 (Jan, 1960).

Roddman, Philip. "Andre Gide on Shakespeare," *The City College Papers,* 1: 80 (1964).

Roth, Robert. "Another World of Shakespeare," *Modern Philology,* 49#1: 58-59 (Aug, 1951).

Salerno, Nicholas A. "Shakespeare and Arnold's 'Dover Beach," *Shakepeare Quarterly,* 11#4: 495-49 6(Autumn, 1960).

Sanford, Charles L. *The Quest for Paradise,* 69-70.

Schwalb, Harry M. "Shakespeare's *Antony and Cleopatra,* I, ii, 1-5," *The Explicator,* 8#7: 53 (May, 1950).

Schwartz, Elias. *"Antony and Cleopatra,"* *College English,* 23#7: 550-558 (April, 1962).

Seaton, Ethel. *"Antony and Cleopatra* and the *Book of Revelation,"* *Review of English Studies,* 22#87: 219-224 (July, 1946).

Shaw, G. B. *Plays and Players,* 187-195.

Siegel, Paul N. "Foreshadowings of Cleopatra's Death," *Notes and Queries,* 203: 386-387 (Sept, 1958).

Smith, J. Oates. "The Alchemy of *Antony and Cleopatra,*" *Bucknell University Studies,* 12#1: 37-50 (March, 1964).

Smith, S. M. "This Great Solemnity': A Study of the Presentation of Death in *Antony and Cleopatra,*" *English Studies,* 45#2: 163-176 (April, 1964).

Spencer, Benjamin T. *"Antony and Cleopatra* and the Paradoxial Metaphor," *Shakespeare Quarterly,* 9#3: 373-378 (Summer, 1958).

Stauffer, Donald A. *The Nature of Poetry,* 253-259.

Stein, Arnold. "The Image of Antony's Lyric and Tragic Imagination," *Kenyon Review,* 21#4. 586-606 (Autumn, 1959).

Stempel, Daniel. "The Transmigration of the Crocodile," *Shakespeare Quarterly,* 7#1: 59-72 (Winter, 1956).

Stirling, Brents. "Cleopatra's Scene with Seleucus: Plutarch, Daniel, and Shakespeare," *Shakespeare Quarterly,* 15#2: 299-311 (Spring, 1964).

Stroup, Thomas B. "The Structure of *Antony and Cleopatra,*" *Shakespeare Quarterly,* 15#2: 289-298 (Spring, 1964).

Stull, Joseph S. "Cleopatra's Magnanimity: The Dismissal of the Messenger," *Shakespeare Quarterly,* 7#1: 73-78 (Winter, 1956).

Styan, J. L. *The Elements of Drama,* 214-217.

Thomas, Mary Olive. "Cleopatra and the 'Mortal Wretch'," *Shakespeare Jahrbuck,* 99: 174-183 (1963).

——————. "The Repetitions in Antony's Death Scene," *Shakepeare Quarterly,* 9#2: 153-157 (Spring, 1958).

Torbarina, Josip. "The Nakedness of the Shakespearean Tragic Hero," *Studia Romanica et Anglica Zagrabiensia,* 12: 5 (Dec, 1961).

Waith, Eugene M. "Manhood and Valor in Two Shakespearean Tragedies," *ELH,* 17#4: 268-273 (Dec, 1950).

Walker, Roy. "The Northern Star: An Essay on the Roman Plays," *Shakespeare Quarterly,* 2#4: 290-291 (Oct, 1951).

Warner, Alan. "A Note on *Antony and Cleopatra,*" *English,* 11#64: 139-144 (Spring, 1957).

Watkins, W. B. C. "Shakepeare's Banquet of Sense," *Southern Review (Louisiana),* 7#4: 727-734 (Spring, 1942).

Westbrook, Perry D. "Horace's Influence on *Antony and Cleopatra,*" *PMLA,* 72#2: 392-398 (June, 1957).

Williams, George W. "Shakespeare's *Antony and Cleopatra,* III, xiii, 26," *The Explicator,* 20#9 : 79 (May, 1962).

Williams, Raymond. *Drama in Performance,* 54-74.

Wilson, Elkin C. "Shakespeare's Enobarbus," in James G. McManaway (ed), *Joseph Q. Adams, Memorial Studies,* 391-408.

Wright, Austin. *Carnegie Series in English,* 4: 37-52 (1958).

AS YOU LIKE IT

Babb, Lawrence. *The Elizabethan Malady,* 92-93; 170-172.

Baird, Ruth C. "*As You Like It* and Its Source," *Vanderbilt Studies in Humanities,* 2: 143-160 (1954).

Barber, C. L. "The Use of Comedy in *As You Like It,*" *Philological Quarterly,* 21#4 : 353-367 (Oct, 1942).

Brooks, Charles. "*Shakepeare's Heroine-Actresses,*" *Shakespeare Jahrbuck,* 96: 139-141 (1960).

Brown, John M. *Dramatis Personae,* 235-239.

Carson, William G. "*As You Like it* and the Stars," *Quarterly Journal of Speech,* 43#2: 117-127 (April, 1957).

Conn, Naomi. "The Promise of Arcadia: Nature and the Natural Man in Shakespeare's Comedies," *The City College Papers,* 1: 115-119 (1964).

Cunningham, James. *Woe or Wonder,* 13.

Doran, Madelein. "'Yet Am I Inland Bred,'" *Shakespeare Quarterly,* 15#2: 99-100; 104; 112-114 (Spring, 1964).

Draper, John W. "Shakespeare's Orlando Innamorato," *Modern Language Quarterly,* 2#2: 179-184 (June, 1941).

Draper, R. P. "Shakespeare's Pastoral Comedy," *Etudes Anglaise,* 11#1: 1-17 (Jan, 1958).

Emslie, Macdonald. "*As You Like it,*" *The Use of English,* 6#2: 99-104 (Winter, 1954).

Gamal, Sand M. "The Function of Song in Shakespeare's Comedies," *Cairo Studies in English,* pp. 117-118 (1961/ 1962).

Gilbert, Allan H. "Jacques, 'Seven Ages' and Censorinus," *Modern Language Notes,* 55#2: 103-105 (Feb, 1940).

Goldsmith, Robert H. "'Touchstone' Critic in Motley," *PMLA,* 68#4Pt.1: 884-895 (Sept, 1953).

Halio, Jay L. "'No Clock in the Forest': Time in *As You Like It*" *Studies in English Literature 1500-1900,* 2#2: 197-208 (Spring, 1962).

Jenkins, Harold. "*As You Like It,*" *Shakespeare Survey,* 8: 40-51 (1955).

Jones, Buford. "Spenser and Shakespeare in *The Encantadas:*

Sketch VI," *Emerson Society Quarterly,* 35: 69; 71-72 (Second Quarter, 1964).

Jones, J. T. "What's That 'Ducdame'," *Modern Language Notes,* 62#8: 563-564 (Dec, 1947).

Jones, William M. "William Shakespeare as William in *As You Like It,"* *Shakespeare Quarterly,* 11#2: 228-231 (Spring, 1960).

Knight, George W. *The Golden Labyrinth,* 68-70.

Kokeritz, Helge. "Touchstone in Arden: *As You Like It,* 11, iv, 16," *Modern Language Quarterly,* 7#1: 61-65 (March, 1946).

McCollom, William. "Form and Attitude in Comedy," *Drama Survey,* 3#1: 60-68 (May, 1963).

McIntosh, Angus. *"As You Like It:* A Grammatical Clue to Character," *Review of English Literature,* 4#2: 68-81 (April, 1963).

McQueen, John. *"As You Like It* and Medieval Literary Tradition," *Forum for Modern Language Studies,* 1#3: 216-229 (July, 1965).

Major, John M. "Eliot's *Gerontion* and *As You Like it,"* *Modern Language Notes,* 74#1: 28-31 (Jan, 1959).

Marx, Milton. *The Enjoyment of Drama,* 141-144.

Maxwell, J. C. "Shakespeare: The Middle Plays," *Guide to English Literature,* 2: 194-197.

Miller, William E. "All the World's a Stage," *Notes and Queries,* 208: 99-101 (March, 1963).

Mincoff, Marco. "What Shakespeare Did to Rosalynde," *Shakespeare Jahrbuck,* 96: 78-89 (1960).

Rickey, Mary Ellen. "Rosalind's Gentle Jupiter," *Shakespeare Quarterly,* 13#3: 365-366 (Summer, 1962).

Schrickx, W. *Shakespeare's Early Contemporaries,* 71-72.

Seng, Peter J. "The Foresters' Song in *As You Like It,"* *Shakespeare Quarterly,* 10#2: 246-249 (Spring, 1959).

Seronsy, Cecil C. "The Seven Ages of Man Again," *Shakespeare Quarterly,* 4: 364-365 (1953).

Shaw, John. "Fortune and Nature in *As You Like It,"* *Shakespeare Quarterly,* 6#1: 45-50 (Winter, 1955).

Singh, Sarup. "A Note on *As You Like It,"* *Indian Journal of English Studies,* 4#1: 162-168 (1963).

Smith, James. *"As You Like It,"* *Scrutiny,* 9#1: 9-32 (June, 1940).
ALSO IN: Eric Bentley (ed), *The Importance of Scrutiny,* 99-119.

Staebler, Warren. "Shakespeare's Play of Atonement," *Shakespeare Association Bulletin*, 24#2: 91-105 (April, 1949).

Stevenson, David Lloyd. "The Love-Game Comedy," *Columbia University Studies in English and Comparative Literature*, 164: 198-207 (1946).

Styan, J. L. *The Elements of Drama*, 153-154.

Tannenbaum, Samuel A. "The Names in *As You Like It*," *Shakespeare Association Bulletin*, 15#4: 255-256 (Oct, 1940).

Thompson, Karl F. "Shakespeare's Romantic Comedies," *PMLA*, 67: 1079-1081; 1090-1093 (Dec, 1952).

Tucker, William John. "Irish Aspects of Shakespeare," *Catholic World*, 156: 700-702 (March, 1943).

Wilcox, John. "Putting Jacques into *As You Like it*," *Modern Language Review*, 36#3: 388-394 (July, 1941).

COMEDY OF ERRORS, THE

Barber, C. L. "Shakespearian Comedy," *College English*, 25#7: 493-497 (April, 1964).

Brooks, Charles. "Shakespeare's Romantic Shrews," *Shakespeare Quarterly*, 11#3: 351-356 (Summer, 1960).

Brooks, Cleanth and Robert Heilman. *Understanding Drama*, 22-24 (Appendix—1961 ed.); 474-476 (1945 ed.).

Brooks, Harold. "Themes and Structure in *The Comedy of Errors*," *Stratford-Upon-Avon Studies*, 3: 55-72 (1961).

Elliott, G. R. "Weirdness in *The Comedy of Errors*," *University of Toronto Quarterly*, 9#1: 95-106 (Oct, 1939).

Feldman, A. Bronson. "Portals of Discovery," *American Imago*, 16#1: 77-107 (Spring, 1959).

——————. "Shakespeare's Early Errors," *International Journal of Psychoanalysis*, 36#2: 114-133 (March-April, 1955).

Fergusson, Francis. *"The Comedy of Errors* and *Much Ado About Nothing*," *Sewanee Review*, 62#1: 24-37 (Winter, 1954).

ALSO IN: *The Human Image in Dramatic Literature*, 144-160.

Kery, Laszlo. "Shakespearean Comedy," *Acta Litteraria Academiae Scientiarum Hungarica*, 6#3-4: 245-252 (1964).

Leech, Clifford. "Shakespeare's Comic Dukes," *Review of English Literature*, 5#2: 102 (April, 1964).

Maxwell, J. C. " 'Fat and Scant of Breath' Again—*Comedy of Errors*, III, i, 64-65," *English Studies*, 32#1: 29-30 (Feb, 1951).

Parks, George B. "Shakespeare's Map for *The Comedy of Errors*," *Journal of English and Germanic Philology*, 39#1: 93-97 (Jan, 1940).

Purcell, J. M. *"Comedy of Errors*, II ii, 57," *Notes and Queries*, 203: 180 (April, 1958).

Ravich, Robert A. "A Psychoanalytic Study of Shakespeare's Early Plays," *Psychoanalytic Quarterly*, 33#3: 396-399 (July, 1964).

——————. "Shakespeare and Psychiatry," *Literature and Psychology*, 14#3-4: 99-101 (Summer-Fall, 1964).

Shaw, G. B. *Plays and Players*, 50-57.

Simpson, Percy. *Studies in Elizabethan Drama*, 13-17.

Thomas, Sidney. "The Date of *The Comedy of Errors*," *Shakespeare Quarterly*, 7#4: 337-384 (Autumn, 1956).

Weld, John S. "Old Adam New Apparelled," *Shakespeare Quarterly*, 7#4: 453-456 (Autumn, 1956).

Williams, Gwyn. *"The Comedy of Errors* Rescued from Tragedy," *Review of English Literature*, 5#4: 63-71 (Oct, 1964).

CORIOLANUS

Barron, David B. *"Coriolanus:* Portrait of the Artist as Infant," *American Imago*, 19#2: 171-193 (Summer, 1962).

Bowden, William R. "The 'Unco Guid' and Shakespeare's *Coriolanus*," *Shakespeare Quarterly*, 13#1: 41-48 (Winter, 1962).

Britten, Norman A. *"Coriolanus, Alceste,* and Dramatic Genres," *PMLA*, 71#4Pt.1: 799-807 (Sept, 1956).

Brown, David. "My Gracious Silence!" *Shakespeare Association Bulletin*, 15#1: 57-58 (Jan, 1940).

Browning, I. R. "Coriolanus: Boy of Tears," *Essays in Criticism*, 5#1: 18-31 (Jan, 1955).

Burns, Winifred. "The Character of Marcius Coriolanus," *Poet Lore*, 52#1: 31-48 (Spring, 1946).

Charney, Maurice. "The Dramatic Use of Imagery in Shakespeare's *Coriolanus*," *ELH*, 23#3: 183-193 (Sept, 1956).

——————. "The Imagery of Food and Eating in *Coriolanus*," in Rudolph Kirk (ed), *Essays in Literary History*, 37-56.

Combes, H. *Literature and Criticism*, 28-30.

Dean, Leonard F. "Voice and Deed in *Coriolanus*," *University of Kansas City Review*, 21#3: 177-183 (March, 1955).

Draper, John W. "Shakespeare's *Coriolanus:* A Study in

Renaissance Psychology," *University of West Virginia Bulletin: Philological Studies,* 3: 22-36 (1939).

——————————. "Subjective Conflict in Shakespearean Tragedy," *Neuphilologische Mitteilungen,* 2#61: 220-221 (1960).

Ellis-Fermor, Una. *Frontiers of Drama,* 51-52.

——————————. "Some Functions of Verbal Music in Drama," *Shakespeare Jahrbuck,* 90.: 43-48 (1954).

Enright, Dennis J. *"Coriolanus:* Tragedy or Debate?" *Essays in Criticism,* 4#1: 1-19 (Jan, 1954).
ALSO IN: *The Apothecary Shop,* 32-53.

Frye, Northrop. "The Tragedies of Nature and Fortune," *Stratford Papers on Shakespeare,* 2: 42-56 (1961).

Granville-Barker, Harley. "Verse and Speech in *Coriolanus,"* *Review of English Studies,* 23#89: 1-15 (Jan, 1947).

Harrison, G. B. "A Note on *Coriolanus,"* in James G. McManaway (ed), *Joseph Q. Adams Memorial Studies,* 239-252.

Heilman, Robert B. "From Mine Own Knowledge: A Theme in the Late Tragedies," *Centenniel Review,* 8#1: 28-36 (Winter, 1964).

Henn, Thomas R. *The Harvest of Tragedy,* 99-100.

Heuer, Hermann. "From Plutarch to Shakespeare: A Study of *Coriolanus,"* *Shakespeare Survey,* 10: 50-59 (1957).

Hill, R. F. *"Coriolanus:* Violentest Contrariety," *Essays and Studies (English Association),* 17: 12-23 (1964).

Hofling, Charles K. "An Interpretation of Shakespeare's *Coriolanus,"* *American Imago,* 14#4: 407-435 (Winter, 1957).

Holland, Norman N. "Realism and the Psychological Critic," *Literature and Psychology,* 10#1: 5-10 (Winter, 1960).

Holloway, John. *The Story of the Night,* 121-130.

Honig, Edwin. *Dark Conceit,* 10-12; 186-187.

——————————. *"Sejanus* and *Coriolanus:* A Study in Alienation," *Modern Language Quarterly,* 12: 407-421 (Dec, 1951).

Honigmann, E. A. J. "Shakespeare's Plutarch," *Shakespeare Quarterly,* 10#1: 25-29 (Winter, 1959).

Hunter, G. K. "Shakespeare's Hydra," *Notes and Queries,* 198: 100-101 (March, 1953).

Jorgensen, Paul A. "Shakespeare's Coriolanus: Elizabethan Soldier," *PMLA,* 64#1Pt. 1: 221-235 (March, 1949).

——————————. "Divided Command in Shakespeare," *PMLA,* 70: 750-761 (Sept, 1955).

Kirschbaum, Leo. "Shakespeare's Stage Blood and its Critical Significance," *PMLA*, 64#3: 525-528 (June, 1949).

Knight, George W. *The Golden Labyrinth*, 145-146.

——————. *The Imperial Theme*, 154-198.

Knights, L. C. "Shakespeare and Political Wisdom: A Note on the Personalism of *Julius Caesar* and *Coriolanus*," *Sewanee Review*, 61#1 :43-55 (Winter, 1953).

——————. "Shakespeare's Politics: With Some Reflections on the Nature of Tradition," *Annual Shakespeare Lecture of the British Academy*, pp. 121-122 (1957).

——————. "*King Lear* and the Great Tragedies," *Guide to English Literature*, 2: 243-246.

Knox, George. *Critical Moments*, 20-21.

Lees, F. N. "*Coriolanus*, Aristotle, and Bacon," *Review of English Studies*, NS1#2: 114-125 (April, 1950).

MacLure, Millar. "Shakespeare and the Lonely Dragon," *University of Toronto Quarterly*, 24#2: 114-118 (Jan, 1955).

Maxwell, J. C. "Animal Imagery in *Coriolanus*," *Modern Language Review*, 42#4: 417-421 (Oct, 1947).

——————. "Menenius's Fable," *Notes and Queries*, 198: 329 (Aug, 1953).

McCollom, William G. *Tragedy*, 1-2; 47-48; 126-129; 145-146.

Muir, Kenneth. "The Background of *Coriolanus*," *Shakespeare Quarterly*, 10#2: 137-145 (Spring, 1959).

Neumeyer, Peter F. "*Coriolanus*: Ingratitude Is Monstrous," *College English*, 26#3: 192-197 (Dec, 1964).

Noel, J. "Shakespeare Criticism Today," *Revue des Langues Vivantes*, 26: 465-466 (1960).

Oliver, H. J. "Coriolanus as Tragic Hero," *Shakespeare Quarterly*, 10#1: 53-60 (Winter, 1959).

Pettet, E. C. "*Coriolanus* and the Midlands Insurrection of 1607," *Shakespeare Survey*, 3: 34-42 (1950).

Phillips, James Emerson Jr. "The State in Shakespeare's Greek and Roman Plays," *Columbia University Studies in English and Comparative Literature*, 149: 147-171 (1940).

Prior, Moody E. "Coriolanus as a Tragic Hero," *Northwestern University Tri-Quarterly*, 2#3: 43-44 (Spring, 1960).

Proser, Matthew. "Coriolanus: The Constant Warrior and the State," *College English*, 24#7: 507-512 (April, 1963).

Purcell, J. M. "Shakepeare's *Coriolanus*, III, i, 101," *The Explicator*, 15#6: 36 (March, 1957).

250 DRAMA CRITICISM

Putney, Rufus. "Coriolanus and His Mother," *Psychoanalytic Quarterly*, 31#3: 364-381 (1962).

Ribner, Irving. "The Tragedy of *Coriolanus*," *English Studies*, 34#1: 1-9 (Feb, 1953).

Rogers, Carmen. "Heavenly Justice in the Tragedies of Shakespeare," *University of Miami Publications in English and American Literature*, 1: 116-128 (March, 1953).

Ronda, F. H. *"Coriolanus—A Tragedy of Youth,"* *Shakespeare Quarterly*, 12#2: 103-106 (Spring, 1961).

Roth, Robert. "Another World of Shakespeare," *Modern Philology*, 49#1: 59-60 (Aug, 1951).

Schlosser, Anselm. "Reflections in Shakespeare's *Coriolanus*," *Philologica Pragensia*, 1: 11-21 (1963).

Sen, Sailendra Kumar. "What Happens in *Coriolanus*" *Shakespeare Quarterly*, 9#3: 331-345 (Summer, 1958).

Sheldon, Esther K. "Sheriden's *Coriolanus*," *Shakespeare Quarterly*, 14#2: 153-161 (Spring, 1963).

Siegel, Paul N. "Shakespeare and the Neo-Chivalric Cult of Honor," *Centenniel Review*, 8#1: 60-65 (Winter, 1964).

Smith, Gordon Ross. "Authoritarian Patterns in Shakespeare's *Coriolanus*," *Literature and Psychology*, 9#3-4: 45-51 (Summer-Fall, 1959).

Speaight, Robert. "A Memory of William Poel," *Drama Survey*, 3#4: 500-506 (Spring-Fall, 1964).

Spencer, Theodore. "The Isolation of the Shakespearean Hero," *Sewanee Review*, 52#3: 328-330 (July/Sept, 1944).

Starnes, D. T. "Imitation of Shakespeare in Dryden's *All For Love*," *Texas Studies in Literature and Language*, 6#1: 44-46 (Spring, 1964).

Stirling, Brents. "Shakespeare's Mob Scenes," *Huntington Library Quarterly*, 8#3: 221-225 (May, 1945).

Tanselle, G. Thomas and Florence W. Dunbar. "Legal Language in *Coriolanus*," *Shakespeare Quarterly*, 13#2: 231-238 (Spring, 1962).

Theall, Donald F. "Traditional Satire in Eliot's *Coriolan*," *Accent*, 11#4: 194-202 (Autumn, 1951).

Traversi, D. A. *"Coriolanus"* in R. W. Stallman (ed), *Critiques and Essays in Criticism*, 141-153.

Walker, Roy. "The Northern Star: An Essay on the Roman Plays," *Shakespeare Quarterly*, 2#4: 291-292 (Oct, 1951).

Watson, Robert I. *"Coriolanus:* An Exercise in Psychoanalysis," *Northwestern University Tri-Quarterly,* 2#3: 41-43 (Spring, 1960).

Williams, Gwyn. "The Oedipus Complex in *Coriolanus,*" *Bulletin of the Faculty of Arts (Alexandria University),* 4: 61-66 (1948).

Zeevald, Gordon W. *"Coriolanus* and Jacobean Politics," *Modern Language Review,* 57#3: 321-334 (July, 1962).

CYMBELINE

Behrens, Ralph. "On Possible Inconsistencies in Two Character Portrayals in *Cymbeline,*" *Notes and Queries,* 201: 379-380 (Sept, 1956).

Brockbank, J. P. "History and Histrionics in *Cymbeline,*" *Shakespeare Survey,* 11: 42-49 (1958).

Brooks, Charles. "Shakespeare's Heroine-Actresses," *Shakespeare Jahrbuck,* 96: 143-144 (1960).

Camden, Carroll. "The Elizabethan Imogen," *Rice Institute Pamphlet,* 38#1: 1-17 (April, 1951).

Corin, F. "A Note on the Dirge in *Cymbeline,*" *English Studies,* 40#3: 173-179 (June, 1959).

Danby, J. F. *Poets on Fortune's Hill,* 103-105.

Duncan-Jones, E. E. " 'Forlorn' in *Cymbeline* and *I Henry IV,*" *Notes and Queries,* 202: 64 (Feb, 1957).

Gesner, Carol. *"Cymbeline* and the Greek Romance: A Study in Genre," in Waldo F. McNeir (ed), *Studies in English Renaissance Literature,* 105-131.

Harrison, Thomas P., Jr. "Aspects of Primitivism in Shakespeare and Spenser," *Studies in English (University of Texas),* 4026: 61-64 (July 8, 1940).

Hoeniger, F. D. "Irony and Romance in *Cymbeline,*" *Studies in English Literature 1500-1900,* 2#2: 219-228 (Spring, 1962).

——————. "Two Notes on *Cymbeline,*" *Shakespeare Quarterly,* 8#1: 132-133 (Winter, 1957).

Hunter, G. K. "The Spoken Dirge in Kyd, Marston and Shakespeare: A Background to *Cymbeline,*" *Notes and Queries,* 209: 146-147 (April, 1964).

Iyengar, K. R. Srinivasa. "Imogen," *Visuabharati Quarterly,* 12#3: 213-227 (Nov-Jan, 1946/47).

Jones, E. "Stuart *Cymbeline,*" *Essays in Criticism,* 11#1: 84-99 (Jan, 1961).

Kane, Robert J. " 'Richard du Champ' in *Cymbeline,*" *Shakespeare Quarterly,* 4#2: 206 (April, 1953).

Kermode, Frank. "The Mature Comedies," *Stratford-Upon-Avon Studies,* 3: 211-213 (1961).

Knight, G. Wilson. *The Crown of Life,* 129-202.

——————. *The Golden Labyrinth,* 83-84.

——————. *The Sovereign Flower,* 73-80.

Kokeritz, Helge. "Five Shakespeare Notes," *Review of English Studies,* 23#92: 313-314 (Oct, 1947).

Leavis, Frank R. *The Common Pursuit,* 173-179.

Mahnken, Harry E. and Janine S. Mahnken. "Harley Granville-Barker's Shakespearean Criticism," *Southern Speech Journal,* 27#1: 29-30 (Fall, 1961).

Main, W. W. "Shakespeare's 'Fear no More the Heat O' Th' Sun," *The Explicator,* 9#5: 36 (March, 1951).

Melchiori, Barbara. " 'Still Harping on my Daughter'," *English Miscellany,* 11: 64-65 (1960).

Moffet, Robin. *"Cymbeline* and the Nativity," *Shakespeare Quarterly,* 13#2: 207-218 (Spring, 1962).

Nolan, Edward F. "Shakespeare's 'Fear no More The Heat O' Th' Sun'," *The Explicator,* 11#1: 4 (Oct, 1952).

Nosworthy, J. M. "The Integrity of Shakespeare: Illustrated from *Cymbeline," Shakespeare Survey,* 8: 52-56 (1955).

Phillip, George L. "Shakespeare's 'Fear no More The Heat O' Th' Sun," *The Explicator,* 12#1: 2 (Oct, 1953).

Pogson, Beryl "Esoteric Significance of *Cymbeline," Baconiana,* 32#129: 192-198; 228 (Autumn, 1948).

——————. *In the East My Pleasure Lies,* 47-57.

Ribner, Irving. "Shakespeare and Legendary History: *Lear* and *Cymbeline," Shakespeare Quarterly,* 7#1: 47-52 (Winter, 1956).

Rogers, H. L. "The Prophetic Label in *Cymbeline," Review of English Studies,* 11#43 (n.s.): 296-299 (Aug, 1960).

Sevander, Homer. *"Cymbeline* and the 'Blameless Hero,' " *ELH,* 31#3: 259-270 (Sept, 1964).

Shaw, G. B. *Plays and Players,* 114-124.

Smith, Warren D. "Cloten With Caius Lucius," *Studies in Philology,* 49#2: 185-194 (April, 1952).

Stephenson, A. A. "The Significance of *Cymbeline," Scrutiny,* 10#4: 329-338 (April, 1942).

Swander, Homer. *"Cymbeline* and the Blameless Hero," *ELH,* 31#3: 259-270 (Sept, 1964).

——————. *"Cymbeline* and the Woman Falsely Accused," *Shakespeare Newsletter,* 4#6: 50 (Dec, 1954).

Traversi, D. A. "The Last Plays of Shakespeare," *Guide to English Literature,* 2: 255-259.

Wilson, Harold S. *"Philaster* and *Cymbeline,"* *English Institute Essays,* pp. 146-147 (1951).

Woodruff, Neal Jr. *"Cymbeline,"* *Carnegie Series in English,* 4: 53-70 (1958).

HAMLET

Aaron, Stephen. "An Old Play for a Modern Audience," *Harvard Advocate,* 140#1: 6-7; 24-26 (Sept, 1956).

Abel, Lionel. *Metatheatre,* 41-58.

Adler, Jacob H. "Shakespeare in *Winterset,"* *Educational Theatre Journal,* 6#3: 241-244 (Oct, 1954).

Allen, Glen O. " 'The Dram of Eale' Again," *Notes and Queries,* 200: 292-293 (July, 1955).

Allen, N. B. "A Note on Wilson's *Hamlet,"* *Shakespeare Association Bulletin,* 16#3: 154-165 (July, 1941).

——————. "Polonius's Advice to Laertes," *Shakespeare Association Bulletin,* 18#4: 187-190 (Oct, 1943).

Alticke, Richard D. *"Hamlet* and the Odor of Morality," *Shakespeare Quarterly,* 5#2: 167-176 (Spring, 1954).

Altman, George. "Good Advice From the 'Bad' *Hamlet* Quarto," *Educational Theatre Journal,* 2: 308-318 (Dec, 1950).

Armstrong, William A. "Bernard Shaw and Forbes-Robertson's *Hamlet,"* *Shakespeare Quarterly,* 15#1: 27-32 (Winter, 1964).

Aronson, Alex. "A Note on Shakespeare's Dream Imagery," *Visuabharati Quarterly,* 18#2: 180-181 (Aug-Oct, 1952).

Arriola, Paul M. "Two Baroque Heroes: Segismundo and Hamlet," *Hispania,* 43#4: 537-540 (Dec, 1960).

Ashe, Geoffrey. "Hamlet and Pyrrhus," *Notes and Queries,* 192: 214-215 (May 17, 1947).

Babb, Lawrence. "Hamlet, Melancholy, and the Devil," *Modern Language Notes,* 59#2: 120-122 (Feb, 1944).

——————. *The Elizabethan Malady,* 106-110.

Bacon, Wallace A. "A Footnote to Mr. Harbage's *Hamlet, II,* ii, 306-24," *Notes and Queries,* 200: 475-477 (Nov, 1955).

Bailey, Margery. "Shakespeare in Action," *College English,* 15#6: 311-314 (March, 1954).

Bamborough, J. *The Little World of Man,* 34-35; 91-92; 112-114.

Barrett, David. "Take Him for all in all," *Neuphilologische Mitteilungen,* 3#62: 164-168 (1961).

Battenhouse, Henry W. *Poets of Christian Thought,* 34-39.

Battenhouse, Roy W. "The Ghost in *Hamlet:* A Catholic 'Linchpin?' " *Studies in Philology,* 48#2: 161-192 (April, 1951).

——————. "Hamlet's Apostrophe on Man: Clue to the Tragedy," *PMLA,* 66#6: 1073-1113 (Dec, 1951).

——————. "Shakespearean Tragedy as Christian: Some Confusions in the Debate," *Centenniel Review,* 8#1: 84-93 (Winter, 1964).

Baughan, Denver E. "The Very Cause of Hamlet's Lunacy," *Shakespeare Newsletter,* 9#4: 30 (Sept, 1959).

Beardsley, Munroe. *Aesthetics,* 245-246.

Bennett, Josephine Waters. "Characterization in Polonius' Advice to Laertes," *Shakespeare Quarterly,* 4#1: 3-9 (Jan, 1953).

——————. "These Few Precepts," *Shakespeare Quarterly,* 7#2: 275-276 (Spring, 1956).

Bergler, Edmund. "The Seven Paradoxes in Shakespeare's *Hamlet,*" *American Imago,* 16#4: 379-405 (Winter, 1959).

Berry, E. G. "*Hamlet* and Suetonius," *The Phoenix* (Toronto), 2#3: 73-81 (Autumn, 1948).

Berry, Francis. "Young Fortinbras," *Life and Letters Today,* 52#114: 94-103 (Feb, 1947).

Bickersteth, G. L. "The Philosophy of Shakespeare," *Aberdeen University Review,* 28#3: 175-179 (Summer, 1941).

Birin, Julia. "Sir Laurence Olivier's Film Representation of *Hamlet,*" *Baconiana,* 32#128: 166-168 (Summer, 1948).

Blau, Herbert. "Language and Structure in Poetic Drama," *Modern Language Quarterly,* 18:30; 32-33 (1957).

Boberg, Inger M. "Saxo's *Hamlet*" *American-Scandinavian Review,* 44#1: 50-56 (Spring, 1956).

Bodkin, Maud. *Archetypal Patterns in Poetry,* 9-13; 59-60.

Bogholm, N. "The *Hamlet* Drama," *Orbis Litterarum,* 4: 157-228 (1946).

Bonjour, Adrien. "*Hamlet* and the Phantom Clue," *English Studies,* 35#6: 253-259 (Dec, 1954).

——————. "The Question of Hamlet's Grief," *English Studies,* 43#5: 336-343 (Oct, 1962).

——————. "The Test of Poetry," *Shakespeare Jahrbuck,* 100: 149-158 (1964).

Bowden, William R. '.Teaching Structure in Shakespeare," *College English,* 23#7: 530-531 (April, 1962).

The sad and intellectual side of Hamlet

Bowers, Fredson. "The Death of Hamlet: A Study in Plot and Character," in *Studies in the English Renaissance Drama in Memory of Karl J. Holzknecht,* 28-42.

——————. "Dramatic Structure and Criticism: Plot in *Hamlet*," *Shakespeare Quarterly,* 15#2: 207-218 (Spring, 1964).

——————. "Hamlet as Minister and Scourge," *PMLA,* 55#4: 741-749 (Sept, 1955).

——————. "A Note on *Hamlet* I. v. 33 and II. ii 181," *Shakespeare Quarterly,* 4#1: 51-56 (Jan, 1953).

——————. "Shakespeare's Art: The Point of View," in Carroll Camden (ed.), *Literary Views,* 48-50.

——————. "Hamlet's 'Sallied Flesh': A Bibliographical Case History," *Shakespeare Newsletter,* 6#2: 11 (April, 1956).

——————. "Shakespeare's Dramatic Vagueness," *Virginia Review,* 39#3: 447; 480-484 (Summer, 1963).

Bowers, R. H. "Polonius: Another Postscript," *Shakespeare Quarterly,* 4: 362-364 (1953).

Boyce, Benjamin. "Shakespeare's *Hamlet,* II, ii, 198-208," *The Explicator,* 7#1: 2 (Oct, 1948).

Braddy, Haldeen. "I Know a Hawk From a Handsaw," *Shakespeare Association Bulletin,* 16#1: 29-32 (Jan, 1941).

Bridgewater, Howard. "The Character of Hamlet," *Baconiana,* 36#144: 143-145 (Nov, 1952).

Bronson, Bertrand H. "Costly Thy Habit," *Shakespeare Quarterly,* 7: 280-281 (1956).

Brown, A. D. Fitton. "Two Points of Interpretation," *Notes and Queries,* 202: 51 (Feb, 1957).

Brown, John M. *Dramatis Personae,* 219-226.

Brown, John R. "The Setting for *Hamlet,*" *Stratford-Upon-Avon Studies,* 5: 163-184 (1963).

Brown, John. "Shakespeare's Subtext: II," *Tulane Drama Review,* 8#2: 86-95; 99-101 (Winter, 1963).

Bullough, Geoffrey. *Mirror of Minds,* 80-83.

Burge, Barbara. "Hamlet: The Search for Identity," *Review of English Literature,* 5#2: 58-71 (April, 1964).

Burris, Quincy Guy. " 'Soft! Here Follows Prose'—*Twelfth Night* II. v. 154," *Shakespeare Quarterly,* 2#3: 233-236 (July, 1951).

Bush, Douglas. "Tennyson's *Ulysses* and *Hamlet,*" *Modern Language Review,* 38#1: 38 (Jan, 1943).

Cairncross, Andrew S. "Two Notes on *Hamlet,*" *Shakespeare Quarterly,* 9#4: 586-588 (Autumn, 1958).

Camden, Carroll. "On Ophelia's Madness," *Shakespeare Quarterly,* 15#2: 247-255 (Spring, 1964).

Campbell, Lily B. "Polonius: The Tyrant's Ears," in James G. McManaway (ed), *Joseph Q. Adams Memorial Studies,* 295-313.

Candlin, E. Frank. "Hamlet's Successor," *The Norseman,* 7#5: 348-355 (Sept/Oct, 1949).

Chandrasekhara, B. "The Plays of K. V. Puttapa," *Literary Half Yearly (Mysore),* 1#2: 38-41 (July, 1960).

Chiari, Joseph. *The Contemporary French Theatre,* 5-7; 91-93; 105-106; 158-159; 206-207.

Childs, Herbert E. "On Elizabethan Staging of *Hamlet,*" *Shakespeare Quarterly,* 13#4: 463-474 (Autumn, 1962).

Clair, John A. "Shakespeare's *Hamlet,* III, i, 92," *The Explicator,* 14#1: 5 (Oct, 1955).

Clarke, C. C. "A Note on 'To be or not to be,'" *Essays in Criticism,* 10#1: 18-23 (Jan, 1960).

Clarke, George Herbert. "*Hamlet* in the 20th Century," *Royal Society of Canada Proceedings and Transactions,* 34#2: 1-13 (May, 1940).

Cline, Ruth H. "A Note on *Hamlet,*" *Modern Language Notes,* 66#1: 40 (Jan, 1951).

Clurman, Harold. "All the Hamlets," in Lester Markel (ed), *Background and Foreground,* 306-313.

Coe, C. N. "As Kill a King," *CEA Critic,* 27: 5; 10 (Nov, 1964).

Confrey, Burton. *The Moral Mission of Literature,* 175-200.

Connolly, Thomas F. "Shakespeare and the Double Man," *Shakespeare Quarterly,* 1#1: 30-33 (Jan, 1950).

Copley, J. "They say the Owle was a Baker's Daughter," *Notes and Queries,* 200: 512-513 (Dec, 1955).

Coursen, Herbert R. Jr. "That Within: Hamlet and Revenge," *Bucknell University Studies,* 11#3: 19-34 (May, 1963).

Craig, Hardin. "Shakespeare and the Normal World: The Range of Action," *Rice Institute Pamphlets,* 31#1: 15-32 (Jan, 1944).

—————. *The Written Word,* 32-48.

—————. "Hamlet as a Man of Action," *Huntington Library Quarterly,* 27#3: 222-238 (May, 1964).

—————. "Renaissance Ideal: A Lecture on Shakespeare," *University of North Carolina Extension Bulletin,* 24#4: 25-30 (Nov, 1944).

Crocker, Lester G. *"Hamlet, Don Quixote,* and *La Vida es Suena,"* *PMLA,* 69#1: 278-313 (March, 1954).

Cruttwell, Patrick. "The Morality of Hamlet—'Sweet Prince' or 'Arrant Knight'?" *Stratford-Upon-Avon Studies,* 5: 110-128 (1963).

Cunningham, James. *Woe or Wonder,* 11-13; 17-21; 21-23; 28-30; 32-37; 34-36; 43-44; 62; 109-111.

Daiches, David. *Critical Approaches to Literature,* 195-196; 236-237.

Daniels, R. Balfour. "Ophelia Reconsidered," *North Dakota University Quarterly,* 28#1: 30-32 (Winter, 1960).

Danks, K. B. "Hamlet's Love-Letter," *Notes and Queries,* 193: 266-268 (June 29, 1948).

Datta, A. "Hamlet: A Study and an Interpretation," *Journal of the University of Saugar,* 7#7Pt.1: 34-54 (1958).

Davidson, Arthur. *The Solace of Literature,* 75-78.

Davis, Joe Lee. "Something of What Happens in *Hamlet,"* *University of Toronto Quarterly,* 12#4: 426-434 (July, 1943).

Davis, O. B. "A Note on the Function of Polonius' Advice," *Shakespeare Quarterly,* 9#1: 85-86 (Winter, 1958).

Davison, Charles A. "Hamlet the Actor," *South Atlantic Quarterly,* 47#4: 522-533 (Oct, 1948).

Dawson, Charles A. "Hamlet the Actor," *South Atlantic Quarterly,* 47#4: 522-533 (Oct, 1948).

Dean, Leonard F. "Shakespeare's Treatment of Conventional Ideas," *Sewanee Review,* 52#3: 418-419 (Summer, 1944).

Deming, Barbara. "The World of *Hamlet,"* *Tulane Drama Review,* 4#2: 36-44 (Dec, 1959).

Detmold, George. "Hamlet's 'All But Blunted Purpose,'" *Shakespeare Association Bulletin,* 24#1: 23-36 (Jan, 1949).

Dickinson, Donald Hugh. "The Two Queens in *Hamlet,"* *Drama Critique,* 2#3: 106-119 (Nov, 1959).

Doggett, Frank. "Shakespeare's *Hamlet,* II, ii, 116-119," *The Explicator,* 16#4: 25 (Jan, 1958).

Donaghy, J. Lyle. "Hamlet and Ophelia," *Dublin Magazine,* 24#1 (N.S.): 23-28 (Jan-Mar, 1949).

Donoghue, Denis. "Shakespeare's Rhetoric," *Studies,* 47: 431-436 (Winter, 1958).

Donovan, James L. "A Note on Hamlet's 'Not Shriving Time Allow'd,'" *Notes and Queries,* 201: 467-469 (Nov, 1956).

Doran, Madeleine. "That Undiscovered Country," in B. Maxwell (ed), *Renaissance Studies in Honor of Hardin Craig*, 221-230.

——————. "The Language of *Hamlet*," *Huntington Library Quarterly*, 27#3: 259-278 (May, 1964).

Draper, John W. "Subjective Conflict in Shakespearean Tragedy," *Neuphilolgische Mitteilungen*, 2#61: 214-216 (1960).

——————. "The Tempo of Hamlet's Role," *Revista di Letterature Moderne*," 2#3-4 (O.S.): 193-203 (Sept/Dec, 1947).

Durrell, Lawrence and Henry Miller. *A Private Correspondence*, 20-21; 25-33; 49-55.

Eberhart, Richard. "Tragedy as Limitations: Comedy as Control and Resolution," *Tulane Drama Review*, 6#4: 3-9 (June, 1962).

Eckert, Charles W. "The Festival Structure of the *Orestes-Hamlet Tradition*," *Comparative Literature (Oregon)*, 15#4: 321-337 (Fall, 1963).

Eissler, K. R. "On *Hamlet*," *Samiksa*, 7:85-132 (1953).

Eliot, T. S. "The Aims of Poetic Drama," *Adam International Review*, 200: 13-14 (Nov, 1949).

——————. *Essays on Elizabethan Drama*, 55-63.

——————. "Hamlet and His Problems," in Mark Schorer, et. al. (eds), *Criticism*, 266-268.

ALSO IN: R. W. Stallman (ed), *Critiques and Essays in Criticism*, 384-388.

Ellis-Fermor, Una. *The Frontiers of Drama*, 88-93.

——————. "Shakespeare and the Dramatic Mode," *Neophilologus*, 37#2: 104-112 (April, 1953).

Emery, John P. "The Dumb Show in *Hamlet*," *Notes and Queries*, 205: 77-78 (Feb, 1960).

Empson, William. "*Hamlet* When New," *Sewanee Review*, 61#1: 15-42 (Winter, 1953).

——————. "*Hamlet* When New (Part II)," *Sewanee Review*, 61#2: 185-205 (Spring, 1953).

Ekwitt, Elliott. "The Historic Place," *Show*, 2#1: 76-81 (Jan, 1962).

Estraellas, Juan. "*Don Quixote* and *Hamlet* as Symbols of Contrasting Cultural and Educational Patterns," *Topic*, 3: 15-23 (Spring, 1962).

Euwema, Ben. "The Universal in *Hamlet*," *Journal of General Education*, 16#1: 1-3 (April, 1964).

Evans, G. Blakemore. "My Tables, Meet it is I Set it Down," *Modern Language Review,* 42#2: 235-236 (April, 1947).

Faber, M. D. "The Conscience of the King," *Literature and Psychology,* 14#3-4: 80-85 (Summer-Fall, 1964).

Fairchild, Arthur H. R. "*Hamlet* as a Tragedy of Transition," *University of Missouri Studies,* 19#2: 11-27 (1944).

Farrison, W. Edward. "Ophelia's Reply Concerning Her Father," *CLA Journal,* 1#2: 53-57 (March, 1958).

——————. "Horatio's Report to Hamlet," *Modern Language Notes,* 72#6: 406-408 (June, 1957).

Feibleman, James. "The Theory of *Hamlet,*" *Journal of the History of Ideas,* 7#2: 131-150 (April, 1946).
ALSO IN: *American Thought,* 311-323.

Feinstein, George W. (& Demetrius Tarlton). "On Understanding *Hamlet,*" *College English,* 13#3: 163 (Dec, 1951).

Feldman, A. Bronson. "The March of Hamlet," *Shakespeare Newsletter,* 13#6: 55 (Dec, 1963).

Fergusson, Francis. "*Hamlet:* The Analogy of Action," *Hudson Review,* 2#2: 165-210 (Summer, 1949).
ALSO IN: *The Idea of a Theatre,* 98-142.

Fiedler, Leslie A. "The Defense of the Illusion and the Creation of Myth," *English Institute Essays,* pp. 85-94 (1948).

Fisher, H. K. "Dance of Death," *Life and Letters Today,* 36#65: 27-34 (Jan, 1943).

Flatter, Richard. "The Climax of the Play—Scene in *Hamlet,*" *Shakespeare Jahrbuck,* 87: 26-42 (1951).

Flint, Robert W. "The Tragedy of *Hamlet,*" *Union Seminary Quarterly Review,* 2#3: 20-25 (March, 1947).

Foakes, R. A. "Character and Speech in *Hamlet,*" *Stratford-Upon-Avon Studies,* 5: 148-162 (1963).

——————. "Hamlet and the Court of Elsinore," *Shakespeare Survey,* 9: 35-43 (1956).

Forker, Charles R. "Shakespeare's Theatrical Symbolism and Its Function in *Hamlet,*" *Shakespeare Quarterly,* 14#3: 215-229 (Summer, 1963).

Foster, Richard. "Hamlet and the Word," *University of Toronto Quarterly,* 30#3: 229-245 (April, 1961).

Foulds, Elizabeth. "Enter Ophelia, Distracted," *Life and Letters Today,* 36#65: 36-41 (Jan, 1943).

Fraiberg, Louis. *Psychoanalysis and American Literary Criticism,* 47-63; 208-212.

Freud, Sigmund. "Psychopathic Characters on the Stage," *Psychoanalytic Quarterly,* 11#4: 463-464 (Oct, 1942).

Freidman, Neil. "On the Mutability of the Oedipus Complex: Note on the Hamlet Case," *American Imago,* 20#2: 107-131 (Summer, 1963).

Frye, Prosser H. *Romance and Tragedy,* 292-293.

Fryxell, Donald R. "The Significance of Hamlet's Delay," *Discourse,* 6#4: 270-284 (Autumn, 1963).

Fust, Milán. "On Staging Shakespeare," *New Hungarian Quarterly,* 5#13: 61-68 (Spring, 1964).

Gabor, Miklos. "An Actor's Thoughts," *New Hungarian Quarterly,* 5#13: 73; 75 (Spring, 1964).

Gardner, Helen L. "Lawful Espials," *Modern Language Review,* 33#3: 345-355 (July, 1938).

Garner, Ross. "Three Steps Through a Glass Darkly," *Prairie Schooner,* 32#1: 62 (Spring, 1958).

Gassner, John. *Producing a Play,* 452-460.

Gertrude, M. Teresa. "Hamlet, Prince of Denmark: Allusions to Music," *Horizontes,* 7#14: 48-51 (April, 1964).

Gierasch, Walter. "Hamlet's Polonius, and Shakespeare's," *College English,* 2#7: 699-701 (April, 1941).

Gilbert, Allan H. "The Fencing Match in *Hamlet,*" *Shakespeare Association Bulletin,* 16#2: 124-125 (April, 1941).

—————————. *The Principles and Practice of Criticism,* 95-147.

Glaz, A. Andre. "*Hamlet,* or the Tragedy of Shakespeare," *American Imago,* 18#2: 129-158 (Summer, 1961).

Goddard, Harold C. "Hamlet to Ophelia," *College English,* 16#7: 403-415 (April, 1955).

—————————. "In Ophelia's Closet," *Yale Review,* 34#3: 462-474 (March, 1946).

Godfrey, D. R. "The Player's Speech in *Hamlet:* A New Approach," *Neophilologus,* pp. 162-169 (July, 1950).

Goodman, Paul. *The Structure of Literature,* 162-172.

Goodwin, Rosemary. "Backgrounds of Shakespeare: Was Claudius a Malcontent?" *Asides,* 4: 8-10 (Supplement 1943/4).

Gordon, R. K. "Scott and Shakespeare's Tragedies," *Royal Society of Canada Proceedings and Transactions,* 39#2: 115-116 (1945).

Gray, Henry David. "Some Methods of Approach to the Study of *Hamlet,*" *Studies in Philology,* 45#2: 203-215 (April, 1948).

Green, Andrew J. "The Cunning of the Scene," *Shakespeare Quarterly,* 4#4: 395-404 (Oct, 1953).

—————————. "Exit Horatio," *Philological Quarterly,* 30#2: 220-221 (April, 1951).

Greene, Thomas. "The Postures of Hamlet," *Shakespeare Quarterly,* 11#3: 357-366 (Summer, 1960).

Greg, W. W. "The Mouse Trap—A Postscript," *Modern Language Review,* 35#1: 8-10 (Jan, 1940).

Guthrie, Tyrone. "*Hamlet* in Modern Dress," *Drama Survey,* 3#1: 73-77 (May, 1963).

Gutteling, J. F. C. "Modern *Hamlet* Criticism," *Neophilologus,* pp. 276-286 (July, 1940).

Gwynn, Frederick L. "*Hamlet* and Hardy," *Shakespeare Quarterly,* 4#2: 207-208 (April, 1953).

Haines, C. "Hamlet and Ophelia," *Biblioteca dell' Archivum Romanicum,* 74: 321-334 (1965).

Hallman, Ralph J. *Psychology of Literature,* 140-143; 150-151.

Hamilton, William. "*Hamlet* and Providence," *Christian Scholar,* 47#3: 193-207 (Fall, 1964).

Hankins, John E. "Hamlet's 'God-Kissing Carrion': A Theory of the Generation of Life," *PMLA,* 64#3Pt. 1: 507-516 (June, 1949).

—————————. "*Hamlet* and *Oedipus* Reconsidered," *Shakespeare Newsletter,* 6#2: 11 (April, 1956).

Hankiss, Elemer. "The *Hamlet* Experience," *New Hungarian Quarterly,* 5#13: 100-111 (Spring, 1964).

ALSO IN: *Zagadienia Rodzajow Literackich,* 4#1: 49-70 (1961).

Hardison, O. B., Jr. "The Dramatic Triad in *Hamlet,*" *Studies in Philology,* 57#2: 144-164 (April, 1960).

Hart, A. "Once More the Mouse Trap," *Review of English Studies,* 17#65: 11-20 (Jan, 1941).

Hart, Walter Morris. "Shakespeare's Use of Verse and Prose," in L. B. Bennion and G. R. Potter, *Five Gayley Lectures 1947-1954,* 2-6.

ALSO IN: *University of California Publications. English Studies,* 10: 2-6 (1954).

Hawkes, Terence. "Hamlet's Apprehension," *Modern Language Review,* 55#2: 238-241 (April, 1960).

Hawthorn, Richard Y. *Tragedy, Myth, and Mystery,* 143-173.

Heilbrum, Carolyn. "The Character of Hamlet's Mother," *Shakespeare Quarterly,* 8#2: 201-206 (Spring, 1957).

Heilman, Robert B. "Twere Best not Know Myself: Othello, Lear, Hamlet," *Shakespeare Quarterly,* 15#2: 89-98 (Spring, 1964).

——————. "To Know Himself: An Aspect of Tragic Structure," *Review of English Literature,* 5#2: 43-57 (April, 1964).

Heller, Agnes. "Shakespeare and Human Nature," *New Hungarian Quarterly,* 5#13: 16-20 (Spring, 1964).

Heller, Lora and Abraham Heller. "Hamlet's Parents: The Dynamic Formulation of a Tragedy," *American Imago,* 17#4: 413-421 (Winter, 1960).

Henn, Thomas R. *The Harvest of Tragedy,* 98-99; 157-158.

Herbert, T. Walker. "Shakespeare Announces a Ghost," *Shakespeare Quarterly,* 1#4: 247; 251-254 (Oct, 1950).

——————. "Dramatic Characters Viewed by Others in the Same Play," *Shakespeare Newsletter, 7#2:* 12 (April, 1957).

Hethmon, Robert. "The Annotated *Hamlet,* an interview with Mordecai Gorelik," *Drama Survey,* 2#1: 80-94 (June, 1962).

Hewitt, Bernard (ed). "Four Hamlets of the Nineteenth Century American Stage, Part I," *Tulane Drama Review,* 6#3: 193-207 (March, 1962).

——————. "Four Hamlets of the Nineteenth Century American Stage, Part II," *Tulane Drama Review,* 6#4: 156-167 (June, 1962).

Highet, Gilbert. *A Clerk of Oxenford,* 142-148.

——————. *The Powers of Poetry,* 286-292; 306-307.

Himelick, Raymond. "Hamlet and the Contempt of the World," *South Atlantic Quarterly,* 58#2: 167-175 (Spring, 1949).

Hodgart, M. J. C. "Shakespeare and *Finnegan's Wake,*" *Cambridge Journal,* 6#12: 738-743 (Sept, 1953).

Hogrefe, Pearl. "Artistic Unity in *Hamlet,*" *Studies in Philology,* 46#2: 184-195 (April, 1949).

Holland, Norman N. "The Dumb Show Revisited," *Notes and Queries,* 203: 191 (May, 1958).

——————. "Freud on Shakespeare," *PMLA,* 75#3: 163-167 (July, 1960).

Holloway, John. "Dramatic Irony in Shakespeare," *Northern Miscellany of Literary Criticism,* 1: 10-13 (Autumn, 1953).

——————. *The Story of the Night,* 21-36.

Honigmann, E. A. J. "The Politics in *Hamlet,* and The World of the Play," *Stratford-Upon-Avon Studies*, 5: 129-147 (1963).

Horvath, Istvan Karoly. "A Few Words on the Riddle of *Hamlet*," *Filologiai Kozlony*, 7—Supplement: 15-16 (1961).

Houston, Percy H. "There's Nothing Either Good or Bad But Thinking Makes it so," *Shakespeare Association Bulletin*, 24#1: 48-53 (Jan, 1949).

Howard, D. R. "*Hamlet* and the Contempt of the World," *South Atlantic Quarterly*, 58#2: 167-175 (Spring, 1959).

Hoy, Cyrus. "Comedy, Tragedy, Tragicomedy," *Virginia Quarterly Review*, 36#1: 108-110 (Winter, 1960).

Hudson, Arthur P. "Romantic Apologiae for Hamlet's Treatment of Ophelia," *ELH*, 9#1: 59-70 (March, 1942).

Huhner, Max. "Polonius's Advice to Laertes," *Shakespeare Association Bulletin*, 19#1: 29-35 (Jan, 1944).

Humphreys, Arthur. "The Poetry of *Hamlet*," *The Literary Half-Yearly*, 5#2: 37-48 (July, 1964).

Hunter, G. K. "*Hamlet Criticism*," *The Critical Quarterly*, 1#1: 27-32 (Spring, 1959).

——————. "The Heroism of Hamlet," *Stratford-Upon-Avon Studies*, 5: 90-109 (1963).

——————. "Socrates' Precepts and Polonius' Character," *Shakespeare uarterly*, 8#4: 501-506 (Autumn, 1957).

Hutcheson, Harold R. "Hamlet's Delay," *Shakespeare Newsletter*, 1#5: 19 (Oct, 1951).

Ingram, R. W. "*Hamlet, Othello*, and *King Lear*: Music and Tragedy," *Shakespeare Jahrbuck*, 100: 159-167 (1964).

James, D. G. *The Dream of Learning*, 33-68.

Janaro, Richard Paul. "Dramatic Significance in *Hamlet*," *University of Miami Publications in English and American Literature*, 1: 107-115 (March, 1953).

Jenkins, Harold. "How Many Grave-Diggers has *Hamlet?*" *Modern Language Review*, 51#4: 562-565 (Oct, 1956).

——————. "The Tragedy of Revenge in Shakespeare and Webster," *Shakespeare Survey*, 14: 45-48 (1961).

——————. "Two Readings in *Hamlet*," *Modern Language Review*, 50#3: 393-395 (July, 1959).

——————. "Hamlet and Ophelia," *Proceedings of the British Academy*, 49: 135-152 (1963).

Jepsen, Laura. *Ethical Aspects of Tragedy*, 68-74.

Jofen, Jean . "Two Mad Heroines," *Literature and Psychology,*
    11#3: 70-77 (Summer, 1961).
Johnson, Edgar. "The Dilemma of Hamlet," in R. M. McIver
    (ed), *Great Moral Dilemmas,* 99-112.
Johnson, S. F. "The Regeneration of Hamlet," *Shakespeare*
    Quarterly, 3#3: 187-207 (July, 1952).
Johnston, Arthur. "The Player's Speech in *Hamlet," Shake-*
    speare Quarterly, 13#1: 21-30 (Winter, 1962).
Jones, Ernest. "The Death of Hamlet's Father," *International*
    Journal of Psychoanalysis, 29: 174-176 (1950).
    ALSO IN: *Yearbook of Psychoanalysis,* 6: 276-280
    (1950).
    ALSO IN: *Essays in Applied Psychoanalysis,* 323-328.
    ALSO IN: Hendrik M. Ruitenbeek, *Psychoanalysis and*
    Literature, 14-18.
Jones, H. W. *"Hamlet,* I, i. 60-63," *Notes and Queries,* 194:
    535 (10 Dec, 1949).
Jordan, Hoover H. "Shakespeare's *Hamlet,* III, i, 56-87," *The*
    Explicator, 8#3: 28 (Dec, 1949).
Jorgensen, Paul A. "Hamlet's Therapy," *Huntington Library*
    Quarterly, 27#3: 239-258 (May, 1964).
——————————. "Hamlet's World of Words," *Shakespeare*
    Newsletter, 12#1: 3 (Feb, 1962).
Joseph, B. L. "Correspondence," *English,* 8#43: 47-48
    (Spring, 1950).
Joseph, Fortinian. "A Caveat Against Realism," *Four Quar-*
    ters, 8#4: 24-29 (May, 1959).
Joesph, Miriam. "Discerning the Ghost in *Hamlet," PMLA,*
    76#5: 493-502 (Dec, 1961).
——————————. *"Hamlet:* A Christian Tragedy," *Studies in*
    Philology, 59#2Pt. 1: 119-140 (April, 1962).
Kaufman, Walter. "Goethe Versus Shakespeare: Some
    Changes in Dramatic Sensibility," *Partisan Review,* 19#6:
    629-632 (Nov/Dec, 1952).
Kelvin, Norman. "Fortinbras' Links With Hamlet," *Bulletin*
    of the New York Public Library, 66#12: 657-660 (Dec,
    1962).
Kemp, Lysander. "Understanding *Hamlet," College English,*
    13#1: 9-13 (Oct, 1951).
Kenner, Hugh. "Joyce's *Ulysses:* Homer and *Hamlet," Es-*
    says in Criticism, 2#1: 100-104 (Jan, 1952).
Kettle, Arnold. *"Hamlet," Zeitschrift fur Anglistik und Ameri-*
    kanistick, 10: 117-127 (1962).

Kirschbaum, Leo. "Hamlet and Ophelia," *Philological Quarterly,* 35#4: 376-393 (Oct, 1956).

——————. "The Sequence of Scenes in *Hamlet,*" *Modern Language Notes,* 55#5: 382-387 (May, 1940).

Kishimoto, G. S. "An Observation on the Modern Production
of the Play Scene in *Hamlet,*" *Studies in English Literature (Tokyo),* 20#4: 457-465 (Oct, 1940).

Kitto, H. D. *Form and Meaning in Drama,* 246-338.

Knight, G. Wilson. "Byron and *Hamlet,*" *John Rylands Library Bulletin,* 45#1: 115-147 (Sept, 1962).

——————. *Explorations,* 82-93; 101-107.

——————. *The Golden Labyrinth,* 7-8; 75-79; 81-84;
222-224; 256-257.

——————. *The Imperial Theme,* 96-124.

——————. *The Olive and the Sword,* 41-44.

——————. *The Sovereign Flower,* 47-51.

——————. "The Embassy of Death: An Essay on *Hamlet,* "in *The Wheel of Fire,* 17-46 (1962 ed.).

——————."*Hamlet* Reconsidered," in *The Wheel of
Fire,* 298-325 (1962 ed.).

——————. "Two Notes on the Text of *Hamlet* (1947),"
in *The Wheel of Fire,* 326-343 (1962 ed.).

Knights, L. C. "Prince Hamlet," *Scrutiny,* 9#2: 148-160
(Sept, 1940).

Kocher, P. H. "The Exchange of Weapons in *Hamlet,*" *Modern Language Notes,* 57#1: 50-55 (Jan, 1942).

Kott, Jan. "*Hamlet* of the Mid-Century," *Encounter,* 23#2:
33-39 (Aug, 1964).

Krabbe, Henning. "Bernard Shaw on Shakespeare," *Acta Jutlanda,* 27#41: 39-47.

Krinkin, Alexandra V. "The Romantic Revolution of the Ego:
Ego as Hamlet," *Hopkins Review,* 1#3: 13-24 (Summer,
1948).

Krutch, J. W. *Modernism in Modern Drama,* 110-112; 114-
115.

Lamont, Rosette. "The Hamlet Myth," *Yale French Studies,*
33: 80-91 (Dec, 1964).

Langenfelt, Gosta. "Shakespeare's Danskers *(Hamlet* II, i, 7)"
Zeitschrift fur Anglistik und Amerikanistik, 12#3: 266-
277 (1964).

Latham, Jacqueline E. M. "The Imagery in *Hamlet*—Acting,"
Educational Theatre Journal, 14#3: 197-202 (Oct, 1962).

Law, Robert Adger. "Belleforst, Shakespeare and Kyd," in James G. McManaway (ed), *Joseph Q. Adams Memorial Studies,* 279-282; 286-294.

Lawlor, J. J. "The Tragic Conflict in *Hamlet,*" *Review of English Studies,* 1NS#2: 97-113 (April, 1950).

Lawrence, W. W. "Ophelia's Heritage," *Modern Language Review,* 42#4: 409-416 (Oct, 1947).

——————. "Ophelia's Heritage: A Correction," *Modern Language Review,* 44#2: 236 (April, 1949).

——————. "Hamlet and Fortinbras," *PMLA,* 61#3: 673-698 (Sept, 1946).

——————. "Hamlet's Sea Voyage," *PMLA,* 59#1: 45-70 (March, 1944).

Leaska, Mitchell. *The Voice of Tragedy,* 96-108; 216-217.

Le Comte, Edward S. "The Ending of *Hamlet* as a Farewell to Essex," *ELH,* 17#2: 87-114 (June, 1950).

Lennan, T. "The Happy Hunting Ground," *University of Toronto Quarterly,* 29#3: 388-397 (April, 1960).

Lesser, Simon O. *Fiction and the Unconscious,* 73-75; 107-110; 199-200.

——————. "Freud and Hamlet Again," *American Imago,* 12: 207-220 (1955).

Lever, J. W. "Three Notes on Shakespeare's Plants," *Review of English Studies,* NS3#10: 123-129 (1952).

Levi, Albert William. *Literature, Philosophy and the Imagination,* 274-282.

Levich, Marvin. *Aesthetics and the Philosophy of Criticism,* 221-222; 225-226.

Levin, Harry. "The Antic Disposition," *Shakespeare Jahrbuck,* 94: 175-190 (1958).

——————. "An Explication of the Player's Speech," *Kenyon Review,* 12#2: 273-296 (Spring, 1950).

Levine, Richard A. "The Tragedy of Hamlet's World View," *College English,* 23#7: 539-546 (April, 1962).

Lewis, C. S. "Hamlet, the Prince or the Poem?" *Annual Shakespeare Lecture of the British Academy,* 28: 147-152 (1942).
    ALSO IN: *They Asked for a Paper,* 51-71.

Lord, John B. "Comic Scenes in Shakespearean Tragedy," *Washington State College Research Studies,* 32#3: 235-236 (Sept, 1964).

Lucas, Frank L. *Literature and Psychology,* 27-61.

McCanse, Ralph A. "Hamlet's Lack of Balance," *College English,* 10#8: 476-478 (May, 1949).

McCloskey, John C. "Hamlet's Quest of Certainty," *College English,* 2#5: 445-450 (Feb, 1941).

McElroy, D. "Rhetorical Patterns in *Hamlet,* III. i. 56-60," *Notes and Queries,* 206: 136-138 (April, 1961).

——————. " 'To Be, or Not to Be'—Is That the Question?" *College English,* 25#7: 543-545 (April, 1964).

Mack, Maynard. "The Jacobean Shakespeare: Some Observations on the Construction of the Tragedies," *Stratford-Upon-Avon Studies,* 1: 11-42 (1960).

——————. "The World of *Hamlet,*" in Cleanth Brooks (ed), *Tragic Themes in Western Literature,* 30-58. ALSO IN: *The Yale Review,* 41#4: 502-523 (June, 1952).

McKenzie, James. "Hamlet: A 'Youth,' " *Notes and Queries,* 197: 76 (Feb 16, 1952).

——————. "A Shakespearean Interpretation," *Notes and Queries,* 197: 160 (April 12, 1952).

——————. "Hamlet's Age Again," *Notes and Queries,* 201: 151-152 (1956).

McLaughlin, John. "Burton's *Hamlet,*" *Catholic World,* 199: 308-312 (Aug, 1964).

McLaughlin, Peter. "The Elements of Tragedy," *Queen's Quarterly,* 71#1: 104-107 (Spring, 1964).

McManaway, James G. "The Two Earliest Prompt Books of *Hamlet,*" *Papers of the Bibliographical Society of America,* 43: 288-320 (Third Quarter, 1949).

Mahnken, Harry E. and Janine S. Mahnken. "Harley Granville-Barker's Shakespearean Criticism," *Southern Speech Journal,* 27#1: 30-33 (Fall, 1961).

Major, John M. "The 'Letters Seal'd' in *Hamlet* and the Character of Claudius," *Journal of English and Germanic Philology,* 57#3: 512-521 (July, 1958).

Manfull, Lowell L. "The Histrionic Hamlet," *Educational Theatre Journal,* 16#2: 103-113 (May, 1964).

Marsh, Louis. "Jean-Louis Barrault's *Hamlet,*" *Quarterly Journal of Speech,* 36#3: 360-364 (Oct, 1950).

Maurer, K. W. "Tonio Kroger and Hamlet," *Modern Language Review,* 43#3: 519-521 (Oct, 1948).

Maxwell, Baldwin. "Hamlet's Mother," *Shakespeare Quarterly,* 15#2: 235-246 (Spring, 1964).

Maxwell, J. C. "Claudius and the Curse of Cain," *Notes and Queries*, 194: 142 (2 April, 1949).

――――――. " 'Fat and Scant of Breath' Again," *English Studies*, 32#1: 29-30 (Feb, 1951).

――――――. "The Ghost From the Grave: A Note on Shakespeare's Apparitions," *Durham University Journal*, 48#2: 57-58 (March, 1956).

――――――. "Shakespeare: The Middle Plays," *Guide to English Literature*, 2: 201-205.

Mayo, Thomas F. "A World Fit for Hamlet," *Southwest Review*, 34#4: 350-355 (Autumn, 1949).

Melander, Rudolf. "The Real Pajock," *The Swan of Avon*, 1#3: 3-5 (Sept, 1948).

Mendel, Sydney. "Hamletian Man," *Arizona Quarterly*, 16#3: 223-236 (Autumn, 1960).

――――――. "The Revolt Against the Father: The Adolescent Hero in *Hamlet* and *The Wild Duck*," *Essays in Criticism*, 14#2: 171-178 (April, 1964).

Menninger, C. F. "The Insanity of Hamlet," *Menninger Quarterly* 6#1: 1-8 (1952).

Merchant, W. M. "Lawyer and Actor: Process of Law in Elizabethan Drama," in G. I. Duthie (ed), *English Studies Today—Third Series* (1964), 118-120.

――――――. "Shakespeare's Theology," *Review of English Literature*, 5#4: 81-84 (Oct, 1964).

Meyers, Walter L. "Shakespeare's *Hamlet*," *The Explicator*, 9#2: 10 (Nov, 1950).

Michel, Laurence. "Hamlet: Superman, Subchristian," *Centenniel Review*, 6#2: 230-244 (Spring, 1962).

――――――. "Shakespearean Tragedy: Critique of Humanism From the Inside," *Massachusetts Review*, 2#4: 644-645 (Summer, 1961).

Miles, L. Wardlaw. "Shakespeare's Old Men," *ELH*, 7#4: 293-294 (Dec, 1940).

Millet, Joseph. *Reading Drama*, 29-30.

Milne, Evander. "On the Death of Cordelia," *English*, 6#35: 244-248 (Summer, 1947).

Mincoff, M. "Shakespeare and Hamartia," *English Studies*, 45#2: 130-136 (April, 1964).

――――――. "The Structural Pattern of Shakespeare's Tragedies," *Shakespeare Survey*, 3: 58-65 (1950).

Moloney, J. M. and L. Rockelin. "A New Interpretation of *Hamlet*," *International Journal of Psycholanalysis*, 30Pt. 2: 92-107 (1949).

Montgomerie, William. "Sporting Kid," *Life and Letters To-day*, 36#65 : 18-24 (Jan, 1943).

———————. "Lucianus, Nephew to the King," *Notes and Queries*, 201: 149-151 (1956).

Moore, John R. "A Spanish *Hamlet*," *Modern Language Review*, 45#4: 512 (Oct, 1950).

Morgan, Roberta. "The Philosophic Basis of Coleridge's *Hamlet* Criticism," *ELH*, 6#4 : 256-270 (Dec, 1949).

———————. "Some Stoic Lines in *Hamlet* and the Problem of Interpretation," *Philological Quarterly*, 20#4: 549-558 (Oct, 1941).

Morley, F. V. "The Impersonal Hamlet," *University of Arizona Bulletin*, pp. 7-22 (July, 1959).

Morozov, Mikhail M. "The Individualization of Shakespeare's Characters Through Imagery," *Shakespeare Survey*, 2: 83-84 ; 93-106 (1949).

Morris, Harry. "Ophelia's 'Bonny Sweet Robin,' " *PMLA*, 73#5Pt.1 : 601-603 (Dec, 1958).

Muir, K. "Imagery and Symbol in *Hamlet*," *Etudes Anglaises*, 17#4: 352-363 (Oct-Dec, 1964).

———————. "Some Freudian Interpretations of Shakespeare," *Proceedings of the Leeds Philosophical and Literary Society*, 7Pt.1 : 43-46 (July, 1952).

Muller, Herbert J. *The Spirit of Tragedy*, 171-181.

Murphy, George H. "Reflections on the Tragedies of Shakespeare," *Dalhousie Review*, 36#3: 269-271 (Aut, 1956).

Murphy, Mallie John. "Hamlet's Sledded Polack," *Notes and Queries*, 201: 509 (Dec, 1956).

Murray, Gilbert. "Hamlet and Orestes," in Wilbur S. Scott, *Five Approaches of Literary Criticism*, 254-257 ; 260-261 ; 279-281.

Murry, John M. "The Doctrine of Will in Shakespeare," *Aryan Path*, 35: 339-342 (Aug, 1964).

Myrick, Kenneth. "Kittredge on *Hamlet*," *Shakespeare Quarterly*, 15#2: 219-234 (Spring, 1964).

———————. "The Theme of Damnation in Shakespearean Tragedy," *Studies in Philology*, 38#2: 221-230 (April, 1941).

Nahm, Milton C. *Aesthetic Experience and its Presuppositions*, 373-386; 413-417.

Nathan, Norman. "Horatio's 'You Might Have Rhymed,' " *Notes and Queries*, 198: 282-283 (July, 1953).

———————. " 'Sallied' May Mean 'Sallied,' " *Notes and Queries*, 202: 279-280 (July, 1957).

——————. "Shakespeare's Initial *Hamlet*," *The Person-alist,* 43#4: 493-496 (Aut, 1962).

Nelson, C. E. "Power and Politics in *Hamlet*," *Washington State College Research Studies,* 32#3: 217-227 (Sept, 1964).

Nelson, Robert J. *Play Within a Play,* 17-30.

Newby, P. H. "Supper With Polonius," *The Mint,* 2: 112-115; 119.

Newell, Alex. "The Dramatic Context and Meaning of Hamlet's 'To Be or not to be' Soliloquy," *PMLA,* 80#1: 38-50 (March, 1965).

Noel, J. "Shakespeare Criticism Today," *Revue des Langues Vivantes,* 26: 462-464 (1960).

Nosworthy, J. M. "The Death of Ophelia," *Shakespeare Quarterly,* 15#4: 345-348 (Autumn, 1964).

——————. *"Hamlet* and the Player Who Could not Keep Counsel," *Shakespeare Survey,* 3: 74-82 (1950).

——————. "A Reading of the Play Scene in *Hamlet*," *English Studies,* 22#5: 161-170 (Oct, 1940).

——————. "The Structural Experiment in *Hamlet*," *Review of English Studies,* 22#88: 282-288 (Aug, 1946).

Nowottny, Winifred. "The Application of Textual Theory to Hamlet's Dying Words," *Modern Language Review,* 52: 161-167 (1957).

O'Brien, Gordon W. *"Hamlet* IV. v. 156-157," *Shakespeare Quarterly,* 10#2: 249-251 (Spring, 1959).

O'Donnell, Norbert F. "Shakespeare, Marston, and the University: The Sources of Thomas Goffe's *Orestes*," *Studies in Philology,* 50#3: 481-482 (July, 1953).

Okhlopkov, Nikolai. "The Producer's Treatment of *Hamlet*," *Shakespeare Newsletter,* 5#5-6: 41 (Nov/Dec, 1955).

Olley, Francis R. "Claudius at Prayer: The Problem of Motivation in *Hamlet*," *Drama Critique,* 7#1: 22-25 (Winter, 1964).

Olson, Elder. *"Hamlet* and the Hermeneutics of Drama," *Modern Philology,* 61#3: 225-237 (Feb, 1964).

Orange, L. E. "Hamlet's Mad Soliloquy," *South Atlantic Quarterly,* 64#1: 60-71 (Winter, 1965).

Ornstein, Robert. *The Moral Vision of Jacobean Tragedy,* 234-240.

——————. "The Mystery of *Hamlet:* Notes Toward an Archetypal Solution," *College English,* 21#1: 30-36 (Oct, 1959).

—————————. "Teaching *Hamlet*," *College English*, 25#7: 502-508 (April, 1964).

Oyama, Toshikazu. "The Cloud Theme in *Hamlet*," *Shakespeare Studies*, 1: 47-60 (1962).

Paolucci, Andre. *Hegel on Tragedy*, xxviii; 294-296.

Paris, Jean. "The Three Sons in *Hamlet*," *Atlantic Monthly*, 203: 68-76 (June, 1959).

Parrott, T. M. "Fullness of Bread," *Shakespeare Quarterly*, 3#4: 379-380 (Oct, 1952).

—————————. "Hamlet's Sea-Voyage—Bandits or Pirates?" *Shakespeare Association Bulletin*, 19#2: 51-59 (April, 1944).

Parsons, Howard. "The Dram of Eale," *Notes and Queries*, 200: 409 (Sept, 1955).

Paterson, John. "The Word in *Hamlet*," *Shakespeare Quarterly*, 2#1: 47-55 (Jan, 1951).

Patrick, J. Max. "The Problem of Ophelia," *University of Miami Publications in English and American Literature*, 1: 139-144 (March, 1953).

Paul, David. "The Immortal Gods," *Twentieth Century*, 153# 911: 62-64 (Jan, 1953).

Pearson, Lu Emily. "Elizabethan Widows," in *Stanford Studies in Language and Literature*, 129.

Peery, William. "The *Hamlet* of Stephan Dedalus," *Studies in English*, 31: 109-119 (1952).

Phialas, Peter G. "Hamlet and the Grave-Maker," *Journal of English and Germanic Philology*, 63#2: 226-234 (April, 1964).

Pitcher, Seymour M. "Two Notes on Shakespeare," *Philological Quarterly*, 21#2: 239-240 (April, 1942).

Plant, Richard. "Report on Shakespeare's Germany," *The City College Papers*, 1: 90-97 (1964).

Pogson, Beryl. *In the East My Pleasure Lies*, 92-106.

Polanyi, Karl. "*Hamlet*," *Yale Review*, 43#3: 336-350 (March, 1954).

Potts, Abbie Findlay. "Hamlet and Gloriana's Knights," *Shakespeare Quarterly*, 6#1: 31-43 (Winter, 1954).

Prior, Moody E. "The Play Scene in *Hamlet*," *ELH*, 9#3: 188-197 (Sept, 1942).

—————————. "The Thought of *Hamlet* and the Modern Temper," *ELH*, 15#4: 261-285 (Dec, 1948).

Purdie, Edna. "Hamann, Herder, and Hamlet," *German Life and Letters*, 10#3: 198-209 (April, 1957).

Putney, Rufus. "What 'Praise to Give'?" *Philological Quarterly,* 23#4: 312-313 (Oct, 1944).

Putzel, Rosamond. "Queen Gertrude's Crime," *Renaissance Papers,* pp. 37-46 (1961).

Pyles, Thomas. "Ophelia's 'Nothing,'" *Modern Language Notes,* 64#5: 322-323 (May, 1949).

Quinlan, Maurice T. "Shakespeare and the Catholic Burial Services," *Shakespeare Quarterly,* 5#3: 303-306 (Summer, 1954).

Ray, Sibnarayan. "A Note on *Hamlet,*" *The Humanist Way,* 5#1: 40-51 (Spring, 1952).

Reed, Robert R. Jr. "Hamlet, the Pseudo-Procrastinator," *Shakespeare Quarterly,* 9#2: 177-186 (Spring, 1958).

Reid, B. L. "The Last Act and the Action of *Hamlet,*" *Yale Review,* 54#1: 59-80 (Oct, 1964).

Reik, Theodor. "In My Mind's Eye, Horatio," *Complex,* 7: 15-30 (Winter, 1952).
    ALSO IN: Theodor Reik, *The Secret Self,* 17-32.

Rein, David M. "Hamlet's Self Knowledge," *CEA Critic,* 22: 8-9 (March, 1960).

Renfrow, Jack N. "Hamlet and the Psychologists," *Shakespeare Newsletter,* 13#2: 20 (April, 1963).

Reno, Raymond H. "Hamlet's Quintessence of Dust," *Shakespeare Quarterly,* 12#2: 107-113 (Spring, 1961).

Richmond, Hugh M. " 'To be or not to be' and the Hynne de la Morte," *Shakespeare Quarterly,* 13#3: 317-320 (Summer, 1962).

Robbins, William. *"Hamlet* as Allegory," *University of Toronto Quarterly,* 21#3: 217-223 (April, 1952).

Robson, John M. "Tragedy and Society," *Queen's Quarterly,* 71#3: 424-425 (Aut, 1964).

Roddman, Philip. "Andre Gide on Shakespeare," *The City College Papers,* 1: 72-79; 81-88 (1964).

Roppolo, Joseph Patrick. *"Hamlet* in New Orleans," *Tulane Studies in English,* 6: 71-86 (1956).

Rosenberg, Harold. "Character Change and the Drama," in Robert W. Corrigan and James L. Roenberg (eds), *The Context and Craft of Drama,* 92-95.

Ross, J. L. *Philosophy in Literature,* 104-105; 233-234; 255-263.

Sampley, Arthur M. "Hamlet Among the Mechanists," *Shakespeare Association Bulletin,* 17#3: 134-149 (July, 1942).

Sanders, London A. "Horatio—Friend to the Dane," *Madison Quarterly,* 2#2: 77-88 (March, 1942).

Sanford, Charles L. *The Quest for Paradise,* 66-69.

Saunders, Hade. " 'Who Would Fardels Bear?': *Hamlet,* III, i, 76" *Centenniel Review,* 8#1 : 71-76 (Winter, 1964).

Savage, D. S. "An Alchemical Metaphor in *Hamlet,*" *Notes and Queries,* 197 : 157-160 (April 12, 1952).

——————. "Heraldry and Alchemy in Shakespeare's *Hamlet,*" *University of Kansas City Review,* 17#3 : 231-240 (Spring, 1951).

Schoff, Francis G. "Hamlet and His Critics: A Series I. The Problem and One Approach," *Discourse,* 4#2 : 125-138 (Spring, 1961).

——————. "Hamlet and His Critics: A Series II. Elizabethan Psychology," *Discourse,* 4#4 : 248-260 (Autumn, 1961).

——————. "Hamlet and His Critics: A Series III. The 'New Critics,'" *Discourse,* 5#2 : 156-168 (Spring, 1962).

——————. "Hamlet and His Critics: A Series IV," *Discourse,* 5#3 : 297-307 (Summer, 1962).

——————. "Hamlet and His Critics: A Series V. Conclusion." *Discourse,* 5#4 : 373-381 (Autumn, 1962).

——————. "Horatio: A Shakespearian Confidant," *Shakespeare Quarterly,* 7#1 : 53-57 (Winter, 1956).

Schwartz, Delmore. *Vaudeville for a Princess,* 15-19.

Schwartz, Elias. "The Possibilities of Christian Tragedy," *College English,* 21#4 : 210-212 (Jan, 1960).

Schrero, Elliot M. "A Misinterpretation of Freud," *College English,* 10#8 : 476 (May, 1949).

Semper, I. J. "The Ghost in *Hamlet:* Pagan or Christian?" *The Month,* 9#4 : 222-234 (1953).

Sen, Taraknath. "Hamlet's Treatment of Ophelia in the Nunnery Scene," *Modern Language Review,* 35#2 : 145-152 (April, 1940).

Sharpe, Rogert B. "Nine Steps to the Tragic Triumph," *University of North Carolina Extension Bulletin,* 36#3 : 27-31 (March, 1957).

Shaw, G. B. *"Hamlet*—2 October 1897," in Robert W. Corrigan and James L. Rosenberg (eds), *The Context and Craft of Drama,* 409-417.

——————. *"Hamlet* Revisited—18 December 1897," in Robert W. Corrigan and James L. Rosenberg (eds), *The Context and Craft of Drama,* 417-421.

——————. *Plays and Players,* 265-274; 285-290.

Shepard, Warren. "Hoisting the Enginer With His Own Petar," *Shakespeare Quarterly*, 7#2: 281-285 (Spring, 1956).

Shoben, Edward J. Jr. "A Clinical View of Tragedy," *The Colorado Quarterly*, 11#4: 352-363 (Spring, 1963). ALSO IN: *Literature and Psychology*, 14#1: 23-34 (Winter, 1964).

Shoemaker, Francis. *Aesthetic Experience and the Humanities*, 192-227.

Siegel, Paul N. "Discerning the Ghost in *Hamlet*," *PMLA*, 78#1: 148-149 (March, 1963).

Simpson, Percy. *Studies in Elizabethan Drama*, 150-154.

Sisson, C. J. "The Mouse Trap Again," *Review of English Studies*, 16#62: 129-136 (April, 1940).

Sjogren, Gunnar. "How Old is 'Young Hamlet'?" *Edda*, 62#4: 319-325 (1962).

Slochower, Harry. "Shakespeare's *Hamlet*: The Myth of Modern Sensibility," *American Imago*, 7#3: 197-238 (Nov, 1950).

Smidt, Kristian. "Notes on *Hamlet*," *English Studies*, 31#4: 136-141 (Aug, 1950).

Smith, J. Percy. "Shaw on *Hamlet*," *Shavian*, 8: 14-17 (Feb, 1957).

Smith, James. "The Funeral of Ophelia," *Irish Monthly*, 79#2: 60-66 (Feb, 1951).

Smith, John H., et. al. *"Hamlet, Antonio's Revenge and the Ur-Hamlet,"* *Shakespeare Quarterly*, 9#4: 493-498 (Autumn, 1958).

Smith, Roland M. "Hamlet said 'Pajock,'" *Journal of English and Germanic Philology*, 44#3: 392-395 (July, 1945).

Soule, George. "Hamlet's Quietus," *College English*, 26#3: 231 (Dec, 1964).

Spaeth, J. Duncan. "Horatio's Hamlet," *Shakespeare Association Bulletin*, 24#1: 37-47 (Jan, 1949).

Spencer, Theodore. "The Decline of Hamlet," *Stratford-Upon-Avon Studies*, 5: 185-199 (1963).

——————. *"Hamlet* and the Nature of Reality," *ELH*, 5#4: 253-277 (Dec, 1938).

——————. "The Isolation of the Shakespearean Hero," *Sewanee Review*, 52#3: 317-321; 323-325 (Summer, 1944).

Spender, Stephen. *The Making of a Poem*, 119-123.

Spenser, Benjamin. "This Elizabethan Shakespeare," *Sewanee Review*, 49#4: 536-548 (Oct-Dec, 1941).

Sperber, Hans. "The Conundrums in Saxo's Hamlet Episode," *PMLA*, 64#4: 864-870 (Sept, 1949).

Sprinchorn, Evert. "The Odds on Hamlet," *Columbia University Forum*, 7#4: 41-45 (Fall, 1964).

Stabler, Arthur P. "The Sources of *Hamlet:* Some Corrections of the Record," *Washington State College Research Studies*, 32#3: 207-216 (Sept, 1964).

Stamm, R. "*Hamlet* in Richard Flatter's Translation," *English Studies*, 36#5: 228-238 (Oct, 1955).

—————————. "Hamlet in Richard Flatter's Translation," *English Studies*, 36#6: 299-308 (Dec, 1955).

Stauffer, Donald A. "Poetry and the Easy Life," in *Annie Talbot Cole Lectures—Wheaton College*, 1948: 4-16.

Stavrou, Constantine N. P. "Hamlet as Existentialist," *Shakespeare Newsletter*, 7: 13 (1957).

Stearns, Marshall W. "Hamlet and Freud," *College English*, 10#5: 265-272 (Feb, 1949).

Sterling, Brents. "Theme and Character in *Hamlet*," *Modern Language Quarterly*, 13: 323-332 (Dec, 1952).

Stevenson, David L. "An Objective Correlative for T. S. Eliot's *Hamlet*," *Journal of Aesthetics and Art Criticism*, 13#1: 69-79 (Sept, 1954).

Stevenson, G. H. "Social Pychiatry and *Hamlet*," *Royal Society of Canada. Proceedings and Transactions*, 43Sect.2: 143-151 (June, 1949).

Stewart, Charles D. "Four Shakespearean Cruxes," *College English*, 9#4: 187-188 (Jan, 1948).

Stoll, E. E. "A German Producer's *Hamlet*," *Shakespeare Quarterly*, 1#1: 36-43 (Jan, 1950).

—————————. "Not Fat or Thirty," *Shakespeare Quarterly*, 2#4: 295-301 (Oct, 1951).

—————————. "*Hamlet* and *The Spanish Tragedy* Again," *Modern Philology*, 37#2: 173-186 (Nov, 1939).

—————————. "Mainly Controversy: *Hamlet; Othello*," *Philological Quarterly* 24#4: 289-312 (Oct, 1945).

—————————. "A Spanish *Hamlet*," *Modern Philology*, 47#1: 12-23 (Aug, 1949).

Strathmann, Ernest A. "The Devil Can Cite Scripture," *Shakespeare Quarterly*, 15#2: 20-22 (Spring, 1964).

Strindberg, August. "*Hamlet*," *Adam International Review*, 190-191: 21-22 (1949).

Strough, L. A. G. *The Sacred River*, 62-63; 67-68.

Stroud, T. A. "*Hamlet* and *The Seagull*," *Shakespeare Quarterly*, 9#3: 367-372 (Summer, 1958).

Styan, J. L. *The Elements of Drama,* 28-29; 95-96; 174-175; 271-272.

Sutherland, W. O. S. Jr. "Polonius, Hamlet, and Lear in Aaron Hill's Prompter," *Studies in Philology,* 49#4: 605-613; 616-619 (Oct, 1952).

Swart, J. "I Know not 'Seems': A Study of *Hamlet,*" *Review of English Literature,* 2#4: 60-76 (Oct, 1961).

Taine, H. A. "The Brink of an Abyss," *Yale French Studies,* 33: 33-36 (Dec, 1964).

Tannenbaum, Samuel A. "Claudius Not a Patchock," *Shakespeare Association Bulletin,* 20#4: 156-159 (Oct, 1945).

——————. Hamlet and the Gonzago Murders," *Shakespeare Association Bulletin,* 16#3: 169-174 (July, 1941).

——————. "The Hamlet-Laertes Bout," *Shakespeare Association Bulletin,* 16#1: 60 (Jan, 1941).

——————. "Hamlet, Sr.—Merchant or Knight?" *Shakespeare Association Bulletin,* 15#1: 61-62 (Jan, 1940).

——————. "Hamlet's 'Sect and Force,'" *Shakespeare Association Bulletin,* 15#2: 125-126 (April, 1940).

——————. "Meddling With Shakepeare's Text," *Shakespeare Association Bulletin,* 15#1: 62-64 (Jan, 1940).

——————. "Ophelia's Lies," *Shakespeare Association Bulletin,* 16#4: 215-219 (Oct, 1941).

Tarlton, Demetrius. "On 'Understanding *Hamlet,*'" *College English,* 13#3: 163 (Dec, 1951).

Taupin, Rene. "The Myth of Hamlet in France in Mallarme's Generation," *Modern Language Quarterly,* 14: 432-447 (1953).

Taylor, Marion A. "A Note on the Sources of *Hamlet:* The Vilification of Gertrude," *Shakespeare Newsletter,* 14#5: 74 (Nov, 1964).

——————. "Ophelia Exonerated," *Shakespeare Newsletter,* 10#3: 27 (May, 1960).

Thaler, Alwin. "In My Mind's Eye, Horatio," *Shakespeare Quarterly,* 7#4: 351-354 (Autumn, 1956).

Thayer, C. G. "*Hamlet:* Drama as Discovery and as Metaphor," *Studia Neophilologica,* 28#2: 118-129 (1956).

Torbarina, J. "A Minor Crux in *Hamlet,*" *Studia Romanica et Anglica Zagrabiensia,* 6: 3-13 (Dec, 1958).

——————. "The Nakedness of the Shakespearean Tragic Hero," *Studia Romanica et Anglica Zagrabiensia,* 12: 5-7 (Dec, 1961).

Traschen, Isadore. "The Elements of Tragedy," *Centenniel Review,* 6#2: 215-229 (Spring, 1962).

——————————. "Tragic Hamlet and Comic Engineers and Scientists," *Western Humanities Review*, 14#1: 13-17 (Winter, 1960).

Trehern, E. M. " 'Dear, They Durst Not,' " *English*, 10#56: 59-60 (Summer, 1954).

——————————. "Notes on *Hamlet*," *Modern Language Review*, 40#3: 213-216 (July, 1945).

Trienens, Roger J. "The Symbolic Cloud in *Hamlet*," *Shakespeare Quarterly*, 5#2: 211-213 (Spring, 1954).

Trilling, Lionel. "Freud and Literature," *Horizon*, 16#92: 191-196 (Sept, 1943).
ALSO IN: *The Liberal Imagination*, 44-49.

Tucker, William John. "Irish Aspect of Shakespeare," *Catholic World*, 156: 700 (March, 1943).

Turgenev, Ivan. "*Hamlet* and *Don Quixote*," *Chicago Review*, 17#4: 92-109 (1965).

Turner, Paul. "True Madness (A Note on *Hamlet*)," *Notes and Queries*, 202: 194-196 (1957).

Tyler, Parker. "Hamlet as the Murdered Poet," *Quarterly Review of Literature*, 3#2: 156-166 (Fall, 1946).

Tynan, Kenneth. "*Hamlet—Stratford-on-Avon*, 1958," in Robert W. Corrigan and James L. Rosenberg (eds), *The Context and Craft of Drama*, 430-432.

Uhr, Leonard. "Hamlet's 'Coold Mother,' " *Notes and Queries*, 203: 189-190 (May, 1958).

Ure, Peter. "Character and Role from *Richard III to Hamlet*," *Stratford-Upon-Avon Studies*, 5: 19-28 (1963).

Van Doren, Mark (ed). *The New Invitation to Learning*, 44-58.

Utter, Robert Palfrey Jr. "In Defense of Hamlet," *College English*, 12#3: 138-143 (Dec, 1950).

Virtue, John. "Shakespeare's *Hamlet*, 1, iii, 78-80," *The Explicator*, 16#9: 55 (June, 1958).

Wadsworth, Frank W. "*Hamlet* and the Methods of Litererary Analysis: A Note," *American Imago*, 19#1: 85-90 (Spring, 1962).

——————————. "Shakespeare in Action—A Report," *College English*, 16#8: 489-491 (May, 1955).

Wagenknecht, Edward. "The Perfect Revenge—Hamlet's Delay," *College English*, 10#4: 188-195 (Jan, 1949).

Wagner, Linda W. "Ophelia: Shakespeare's Pathetic Plot Device," *Shakespeare Quarterly*, 14#1: 94-97 (Winter, 1963).

Waith, Eugene M. "Manhood and Valor in Two Shakespearean Tragedies," *ELH*, 17#4: 264 (Dec, 1950).

Waldron, John. " 'Machine': *Hamlet*, II. ii. 124," *Notes and Queries*, 199: 515-516 (Dec, 1954).

Wales, Julia Grace. "Horatio's Commentary," *Shakespeare Association Bulletin*, 17#1: 40-56 (Jan, 1942).

Walker, Roy. *The Time is Out of Joint*, 1-153.

Walley, Harold R. *The Book of the Play*, 103-104; 655-658.

Walter, J. W. "The Dumb Show and the 'Mouse Trap,'" *Modern Language Review*, 39#3: 286-287 (July, 1944).

Walton, J. K. "The Structure of *Hamlet*," *Stratford-Upon-Avon Studies*, 5: 44-89 (1963).

← Warhaft, Sidney. "Hamlet's Solid Flesh Resolved," *ELH*, 28#1: 21-30 (March, 1961).

————. "The Mystery of *Hamlet*," *ELH*, 30#3: 193-208 (Sept, 1963).

Watson, Sara Ruth. "The 'Mousetrap' Play in *Hamlet*," *Notes and Queries*, 200: 477-478 (Nov, 1955).

Webster, Peter Dow. "Arrested Individuation or the Problem of Joseph K. and Hamlet," *American Imago*, 5#3: 225-245 (Nov, 1948).

Weightman, J. G. "Edinburgh, Elsinor and Chelsea," *Twentieth Century*, 154#920: 302-306; 308-310 (Oct, 1953).

Weiner, Albert B. "Evidence of a Stray Sheet in the Q1 *Hamlet* MS," *AUMLA*, 19: 88-92 (May, 1963).

————. "Two *Hamlet* Emendations," *Notes and Queries*, 207: 143-145 (April, 1962).

Weisinger, Herbert. *The Agony and the Triumph*, 104-106; 108-109.

————. "A Shakespeare all too Modern," *Arizona Quarterly*, 20#4: 297-301 (Winter, 1964).

Weiss, Daniel. "Freudian Criticism: Frank O'Connor as Paradign," *Northwest Review*, 2#2: 7-8 (Spring, 1959).

Weitz, Morris. *Philosophy in Literature*, 41-68.

Wertham, Frederic. *Dark Legend*, 237-254.

West, Rebecca. *The Court and the Castle*, 6-32; 72-84.

West, Robert H. "King Hamlet's Ambiguous Ghost," *PMLA* 55#5: 1107-1117 (Dec, 1955).

Westfall, Alfred. "Why Did Shakespeare Send Hamlet to Wittengberg?" *Western Humanities Review*, 6#3: 229-233 (Summer, 1952).

White, Beatrice. "Two Notes on *Hamlet*," *Neuphilologische Mitteilungen*, 65: 92-96 (1964).

Willey, Norman L. "Oehlenschlager's *Amleth," Scandinavian Studies,* 17#1: 1-19 (Feb, 1942).

William, David. *"Hamlet in the Theatre," Stratford-Upon-Avon Studies,* 5: 29-43 (1963).

Williams, George W. "Hamlet's Reason, Jangled Out of Time, III i 166," *Notes and Queries,* 205: 329-331 (Sept, 1960).

——————. "Sleep in *Hamlet," Renaissance Papers,* pp. 17-20 (1964).

Williams, Gwyn. "The Pale Cast of Thought," *Modern Language Review,* 45#2: 216-218 (April, 1950).

Williams, Raymond. *Drama in Performance,* 75-79.

Wilson, Elkin C. "Polonius in the Round," *Shakespeare Quarterly,* 9#1: 83-85 (Winter, 1958).

Windolph, F. Lyman. *Reflections of the Law in Literature,* 44-46.

Winner, Thomas G. "Chekov's *Seagull* and Shakespeare's *Hamlet:* A Study of a Dramatic Device," *American Slavic and East European Review,* 15#1: 103-111 (Feb, 1956).

Wiseman, Nicholas C. "William Shakespeare," *Wiseman Review,* 500: 107-111 (Summer, 1964).

Whithey, J. A. "Action in Life and in Drama," *Educational Theatre Journal,* 10#3: 233-236 (Oct, 1960).

Withington, Robert. "Shakespeare, Hamlet and Us," *South Atlantic Quarterly,* 53#3: 379-383 (July, 1954).

——————. "Why Put Freud Into *Hamlet?" College English,* 10#8: 475-476 (May, 1949).

Wray, William R. *"Hamlet and the Detective Story," Shakespeare Newsletter,* 10#4-5: 38 (Sept/Nov, 1960).

Yaggy, Elinor. "Shakespeare and Melville's *Pierre," Boston Public Library Quarterly,* 6: 49-51 (Jan, 1954).

Yoklavich, J. *"Hamlet in Shammy Shoes," Shakespeare Quarterly,* 3#3: 209-218 (July, 1952).

Young, Stark. *"Hamlet*—Sam Harris Theatre, November 20, 1922," in Robert W. Corrigan and Jame L. Rosenberg (eds), *The Context and Craft of Drama,* 422-429.

——————. *Immortal Shadows,* 8-14; 211-214.

I HENRY IV

Adams, Henry Hitch. "Falstaff's Instinct," *Shakespeare Quarterly,* 5#2: 208-209 (Spring, 1954).

——————. "Two Notes on *I Henry IV," Shakespeare Quarterly,* 3#3: 282-283 (July, 1952).

Aldus, Paul J. "Analogical Probability in Shakespeare's Plays," *Shakespeare Quarterly,* 6#4: 402-409 (Autumn, 1955).

Aronson, Alex. "A Note on Shakespeare's Dream Imagery," *Visuabharati Quarterly*, 18#2: 174-175 (Aug-Oct, 1952).

Auden, W. H. "Notes on the Comic," *Thought*, 27#104: 63-64; 69-71 (Spring, 1952).

Barber, C. L. "From Ritual to Comedy: An Examination of *Henry IV*," *English Institute Essays*, pp. 22-51 (1954).

Bass, Eben. "Falstaff and the Succession," *College English*, 24#7: 502-506 (April, 1963).

Berry, Francis. *Poet's Grammar*, 62-64.

Bethel, S. L. "The Comic Element in Shakespeare's Histories," *Anglia*, 71#1: 92-101 (1952).

Bluestone, Max. "Shakespeare Supine, or the Bard in T-Shirts," *Drama Survey*, 1#1: 66-76 (Spring, 1961).

Bogard, Samuel. "*1 King Henry the Fourth*, II, iv, 315ff," *Shakespeare Quarterly* 1#2: 76-77 (Apr, 1950).

Bowden, William R. "Teaching Structure in Shakespeare," *College English*, 23#7: 525-528 (April, 1962).

Bowers, Fredson. "Shakespeare's Art: The Point of View," in Carroll Camden (ed.), *Literary Views*, 54-58.

Bowman, Thomas D. "A Further Note on the Mother Reference in *Henry IV, Part I*," *Shakespeare Quarterly*, 1#4: 295 (Oct, 1950).

—————————. "Two Addenda to Hotspur's Tragic Behavior," *Journal of General Education*, 16#1: 68-71 (April, 1964).

Bradley, A. C. *Oxford Lectures on Poetry*, 247-275.

Brooks, Cleanth and Robert Heilman. *Uunderstanding Drama*, 317-318; 376-388.

Bryant, J. A. Jr. "Prince Hal and the Epesians," *Sewanee Review*, 67#2: 204-219 (Spring, 1959).

—————————. "Shakespeare's Falstaff and the Mantle of Dick Tarlton," *Studies in Philology*, 51#2: 149-162 (April, 1954).

Bullough, Geoffrey. *Mirror of Minds*, 69-71.

Cain, H. Edward. "Further Light on the Relation of *1 and 2 Henry IV*," *Shakespeare Quarterly*, 3#1: 21-38 (Jan, 1952).

Camden, Carroll. "Three Notes on Shakespeare," *Modern Language Notes*, 72: 253 (1957).

Chapman, Frank. "*Henry IV, Part I*," *The Use of English*, 5#1: 12-15 (Aut, 1953).

Chapman, Raymond. "The Wheel of Fortune in Shakespeare's Historical Plays," *Review of English Studies*, NS1#1: 1-3; 6-7 (Jan, 1950).

Claeyssens, Astere E. *"Henry IV, Part One," Carnegie Series in English*, 1:19-34 (1953).

Connor, Seymour B. "The Role of Douglas in *Henry IV, Part One," Studies in English*, 27#1: 215-221 (June, 1948).

Daniel, Neva. "Looking at Shakespeare With an 'Existential' Eye," *Journal of Communication*, 7#4: 176-178 (Winter, 1957).

Dean, Leonard F. "Shakespeare's Treatment of Conventional Ideas," *Sewanee Review*, 52#3: 414-423 (Summer, 1944).

Dickinson, Hugh. "The Reformation of Prince Hal," *Shakespeare Quarterly*, 12#1: 33-46 (Winter, 1961).

Doran, Madeleine. "Imagery in *Richard II* and in *Henry IV*," *Modern Language Review*, 37#2: 113-122 (Apr, 1942).

Draper, John W. "Falstaff, 'A Fool and Jester'," *Modern Language Quarterly*, 17: 453-462 (1946).

Duncan-Jones, E. E. " 'Forlorn' in *Cymbeline* and *I Henry IV*," *Notes and Queries*, 202: 64 (Feb, 1957).

Eagle, Roderick L. "Who Wrote *The Life and Reign of King Henry IV*?" *Baconiana*, 35#138: 17-21 (Jan, 1951).

Empson, William. "Falstaff and Mr. Dover Wilson," *Kenyon Review*, 15#2: 213-262 (Spring, 1953).

Evans, G. Blakemore. "The 'Dering MS' of Shakespeare's *Henry IV*, and Sir Edward Dering" *Journal of English and Germanic Philology*, 54#4: 498-503 (Oct, 1955).

Evans, G. Blakemore (ed). "Supplement to *Henry IV Part 1*," *Shakespeare Quarterly*, 7#3: 56-104 (Summer, 1956).

Evans, Gareth Lloyd. "The Comical-Tragical-Historical Method: *Henry IV*," *Stratford-Upon-Avon Studies*, 3: 145-164 (1961).

Farnham, Willard. "The Medieval Comic Spirit in the English Renaissance," in James G. McManaway (ed), *Joesph Q. Adams Memorial Studies*, 435-437.

Fish, Charles. "Henry IV: Shakespeare and Holinshed," *Studies in Philology*, 61#2: 205-218 (April, 1964).

Freeman, Lesie. "Shakespeare's Kings and Machiavelli's Prince," *The City College Papers*, 1: 25-42 (1964).

Goodman, Paul. *The Structure of Literature*, 103-116.

Greer, C. A. "Falstaff a Coward?" *Notes and Queries*, 200: 176-177 (April, 1955).

——————. "Shakespeare and Prince Hal," *Notes and Queries*, 198: 424-426 (1953).

Griffith, G. Stewart. "Professor Dover Wilson's Falstaff," *English*, 5#26: 51-53 (Summer, 1944).

Heilman, R. B. "Falstaff and Smollett's Mickelwhimmer," *Review of English Studies,* 22#87: 226-228 (July, 1946).

Hemingway, Samuel B. "On Behalf of Falstaff," *Shakespeare Quarterly,* 3#4: 307-311 (Oct, 1952).

Hemlin, William B. "Falstaff," *South Atlantic Quarterly,* 50#1: 86-92 (Jan, 1951).

Humphreys, Arthur. "Shakespeare's Political Justice in *Richard II and Henry IV,*" *Stratford Papers on Shakespeare,* 5: 30-50 (1964).

Hunter, G. K. *"Henry IV* and the Elizabethan Two-Part Play," *Review of English Studies,* NS5#19: 243-248 (July, 1954).

Hunter, William B. "Falstaff," *South Atlantic Quarterly,* 50#1: 86-95 (Jan, 1951).

Jorgensen, Paul A. " 'Redeeming Time' in Shakespeare's *Henry IV,*" *Tennessee Studies in Literature,* 5: 101-110 (1960).

————————. "Divided Command in Shakespeare," *PMLA,* 70: 750-761 (Sept, 1955).

————————. "My Name is Pistol Call'd," *Shakespeare Quarterly,* 1: 73-75 (April, 1950).

Kaiser, Walter J. *Praisers of Folly,* 14-16; 195-275.

Khan, Razia. "The Hero in Shakespeare's *Henry IV,*" *Dacca University Studies,* 12Pt.A: 35-40 (June, 1964).

King, Arthur H. "Some Notes on Ambiguity in *Henry IV Part I,*" *Studia Neophilologica,* 14: 161-183 (1941/1942).

Kirschbaum, Leo. "The Demotion of Falstaff," *Philological Quarterly,* 41#1: 58-60 (Jan, 1962).

Kleinstuck, J. "The Problem of Order in Shakespeare's Histories," *Neophilologus, pp.* 273-277 (Oct, 1954).

Knight, George W. *The Golden Labyrinth,* 71-74; 77-78; 82-84; 236-237.

————————. *The Olive and the Sword,* 25-29.

————————. *The Sovereign Flower,* 33-37.

Knights, L. C. "Notes on Comedy," in Eric Bentley, *The Importance of Scrutiny,* 232-237.

Knoepflmacher, U. C. "The Humors in *Henry IV, Part 1,*" *College English,* 24#7: 497-501 (April, 1963).

Kris, E. "Prince Hal's Conflict" *Psychoanalytic Quarterly,* 17#4: 487-506 (Oct, 1948).
ALSO IN: *Psychoanalytic Explorations in Art,* 273-288.
ALSO IN: Gerald Goldberg and Nancy Goldberg (eds), *The Modern Critical Spectrum,* 262-275.

Lascelles, Mary. "Shakespeare's Comic Insight," *Proceedings of the British Academy,* 48: 180-185 (1962).

Levin, Harry. "Falstaff Uncolted," *Modern Language Notes,* 61#4: 305-310 (April, 1946).

McCollom, William G. "Formalism and Illusion in Shakespeare's Drama," *Quarterly Journal of Speech,* 31#4: 450-452 (Dec, 1945).

McLuhan, Herbert Marshall. *"Henry IV,* A Mirror for Magistrates," *University of Toronto Quarterly,* 17#2: 152-160 (Jan, 1948).

McNamara, Anne Marie. "Henry IV: The King as Protagonist," Shakespeare Quarterly, 10#3: 423-431 (Summer, 1959).

McNeir, Waldo F. "Shakespeare, *Henry IV, Part I,* II, i, 76-85," *The Explicator,* 10#6: 37 (April, 1952).

Marder, Louis. "Shakespeare's' Lincolnshire Bagpipe,'" *Notes and Queries,* 195: 383-385 (2 Sept, 1950).

Marvin, John Trumbull. "The Nature of Causation in the History Plays" in Margery Bailey (ed), *Ashland Studies for Shakespeare 1962,* 67-77.

Michel, Laurence (& Cecil C. Seronsy). "Shakespeare's History Plays and Daniel: An Assessment," *Studies in Philology,* 52#4: 563-568 (Oct, 1955).

Miles, L. Wardlaw. "Shakespeare's Old Men," *ELH,* 7#4: 291-293 (Dec, 1940).

Muir, Edwin. *Essay on Literature and Society,* 166-181.

Musgrove, S. "The Birth of Pistol," *Review of English Studies,* 10#37: 56-58 (Feb, 1959).

Olive, W. J. "Shakespeare Parody in Davenport's *A New Tricke to Cheat the Devil,"* *Modern Language Notes,* 66#7: 478-480 (Nov, 1951).

Pearce, T. M. "Shakespeare's 'Mother Reference', *1 Henry IV* (II, iv, 265f)" *Notes and Queries,* 197: 25-26 (Jan 19, 1952).

Perot, Ruth S. "Shakespeare's *I Henry IV,* III, iii, 91-97," *The Explicator,* 20#4: 36 (Dec, 1961).

Putney, Rufus. "Sir John Falstaff, Comic Hero: Or the Rejection of Bradley," *Shakespeare Newsletter,* 9#1: 5 (Feb, 1959).

Reno, Raymond H. "Hotspur: The Integration of Character and Theme," *Renaissance Papers,* pp. 17-26 (1962).

Ribner, Irving. *The English History Play in the Age of Shakespeare,* 169-182.

——————. "Bolingbroke, A True Machiavellian," *Modern Language Quarterly*, 9: 177-184 (1948).

——————. "The Political Problem in Shakespeare's Lancatrian Tetralogy," *Studies in Philology*, 49#2: 182-184 (April, 1952).

Roddier, Henri. "A Freudian Detective's Shakespeare," *Modern Philology*, 48#2: 130-131 (Nov, 1950).

Ross, Julian. *Philosophy in Literature*, 32-38.

Schevill, James. "Towards a Rhythm of Comic Action," *Western Speech*, 20#1: 5-8 (Winter, 1956).

Shaaber, M. A. "The Unity of *Henry IV*," in James G. McManaway (ed), *Joseph Q. Adams Memorial Studies*, 217-227.

Shaw, G. B. *Plays and Players*, 85-95.

Shorter, Robert N. "Footnotes to Shakespeare," *Union College Symposium*, pp. 28-30 (Summer, 1964).

Siegel, Paul N. "Shakespeare and the Neo-Chivalric Cult of Honor," *Centenniel Review*, 8#1: 47-51 (Winter, 1964).

Small, Samuel A. "Hotspur and Falstaff," *Shakespeare Association Bulletin*, 16#4: 243-248 (Oct, 1941).

Sprague, Arthur Colby. "Gadshill Revisited," *Shakespeare Quarterly*, 4#2: 125-137 (April, 1953).

Steele, Oliver L. Jr. "Shakespeare's *1 Henry IV*, II, iii, 64," *The Explicator*, 14#9: 59 (June, 1956).

Steiner, George. *The Death of Tragedy*, 253-255.

Stoll, E. E. "A Falstaff for the 'Bright'," *Modern Philology*, 51#3: 145-159 (Feb, 1954).

Tave, Stuart M. "Notes on the Influence of Morgann's Essay on Falstaff," *Review of English Studies*, NS3#12: 371-375 (Oct, 1952).

Tillyard, E. M. W. "Shakespeare's Historical Cycle: Organism or Compilation," *Studies in Philology*, 51#1: 37-38 (Jan, 1954).

Traversi, D. A. "*Henry IV—Part I*," *Scrutiny*, 15#1: 24-35 (Dec, 1947).

——————. "Shakespeare: The Young Dramatist," *Guide to English Literature*, 2: 186-192.

Tucker, William John. "Irish Aspects of Shakespeare," *Catholic World*, 156: 702-704 (March, 1943).

Waldock, A. J. "The Men in Buckram," *Review of English Studies*, 23#89: 16-23 (Jan, 1947).

Walker, Saxon. "Mime and Heraldry in *Henry IV, Part 1*," *English*, 11#63: 91-96 (Autumn, 1956).

Webb, Henry J. "Falstaff's Clothes," *Modern Language Notes*, 59#3: 162-164 (March, 1944).

———————. "Falstaff's Tardy Tricks," *Modern Language Notes*, 58#5: 377-379 (May, 1943).

Weisinger, Herbert. "A Shakespeare all too Modern," *Arizona Quarterly*, 20#4: 295-297 (Winter, 1964).

Whitcombe, V. *"Henry IV, Part I,"* The Use of English, 13#3: 178-183 (Spring, 1962).

Whittemore, Reed. "Shakespeare Yet," *Poetry Magazine*, 92: 189-195 (June, 1958).

Williams, Charles. *The Image of the City*, 40-42.

Wilson, Elkin C. "Falstaff—Clown and Man," in *Studies in the English Renaissance in Memory of Karl J. Holzknecht*, 345-356.

Zeeveld, W. Gordon. "'Food for Powder' — 'Food for Worms'," *Shakespeare Quarterly*, 3#3: 249-253 (July, 1952).

II HENRY IV

Aldus, Paul J. "Analogical Probability in Shakespeare's Plays," *Shakespeare Quarterly*, 6#4: 402-409 (Autumn, 1955).

Aronson, Alex. "A Note on Shakespeare's Dream Imagery," *Visuabharati Quarterly*, 18#2: 174-175 (Aug-Oct, 1952).

Atthill, Robin. *"Henry IV, Part II,"* The Use of English, 9#4: 253-258 (Summer, 1958).

Auden, W. H. "Notes on the Comic," *Thought*, 27#104: 63-64; 69-71 (Spring, 1952).

Bamborough, J. *The Little World of Man*, 146-147.

Barber, C. L. "From Ritual to Comedy: An Examination of *Henry IV*," *English Institute Essays*, pp. 22-51 (1954).

Bass, Eben. "Falstaff and the Succession," *College English*, 24#7: 502-506 (April, 1963).

Berry, Francis. *Poet's Grammar*, 62-64.

Bluestone, Max. "Shakespeare Supine, or the Bard in T-Shirts," *Drama Survey*, 1#1: 66-76 (Spring, 1961).

Bradley, A. C. *Oxford Lectures on Poetry*, 247-275.

Brennecke, Ernest. "Shakespeare's 'Singing Man of Windsor'," *PMLA*, 66#6: 1188-1192 (Dec, 1951).

Bryant, J. A. Jr. "Prince Hal and the Ephesians," *Sewanee Review*, 67#2: 204-219 (Spring, 1959).

———————. "Shakespeare's Falstaff and the Mantle of Dick Tarlton," *Studies in Philology*, 51#2: 149-162 (April, 1954).

Cain, H. Edward. "Further Light on the Relation of *1 and 2*

Henry IV," *Shakespeare Quarterly,* 3#1: 21-38 (Jan, 1952).

Chapman, Raymond. "The Wheel of Fortune in Shakespeare's Historical Plays," *Review of English Studies,* NS1#1: 1-3; 6-7 (Jan, 1950).

Cutts, John P. "The Original Music of a Song in *2 Henry IV,"* *Shakespeare Quarterly,* 7: 385-393 (1956).

Daniel, Neva. "Looking at Shakespeare With an 'Existential' Eye," *Journal of Communications,* 7#4: 178-180 (Winter, 1957).

Doran, Madeleine. "Imagery in *Richard II* and in *Henry IV,"* *Modern Language Review,* 37#2: 113-122 (April, 1942).

Dorius, R. J. "A Little More Than a Little," *Shakespeare Quarterly,* 11#1: 22-26 (Winter, 1960).

Draper, John W. "Falstaff, 'A Fool and Jester'," *Modern Language Quarterly,* 17: 453-462 (1946).

Empson, William. "Falstaff and Mr. Dover Wilson," *Kenyon Review,* 15#2: 213-262 (Spring, 1953).

Evans, G. Blakemore. "The 'Dering MS' of Shakespeare's *Henry IV* and Sir Edward Dering," *Journal of English and Germanic Philology,* 54#4: 498-503 (Oct, 1955).

Evans, Gareth Lloyd. "The Comical-Tragical-Historical Method: *Henry IV,"* *Stratford-Upon-Avon Studies,* 3: 145-164 (1961).

Fallon, Gabriel. "The Falstaff Affair," *Irish Monthly,* 73: 471-478 (Nov, 1945).

Fish, Charles. "Henry IV: Shakespeare and Holinshed," *Studies in Philology,* 61#2: 205-218 (April, 1964).

Fox, C. Overbury. "The 'Haunch of Winter,' " *Notes and Queries,* 199: 21 (Jan, 1954).

Freeman, Leslie. "Shakespeare's Kings and Machiavelli's Prince," *The City College Papers,* 1: 25-42 (1964).

Goodman, Paul. *The Structure of Literature,* 103-116.

Greer, C. A. "Falstaff a Coward?" *Notes and Queries,* 200: 176-177 (April, 1955).

——————————. "Falstaff's Diminuation of Wit," *Notes and Queries,* 199: 468 (Nov, 1954).

——————————. "Shakespeare and Prince Hal," *Notes and Queries,* 198: 424-426 (1953).

Griffith, G. Stewart. "Professor Dover Wilson's Falstaff," *English,* 5#26: 51-53 (Summer, 1944).

Hemingway, Samuel B. "On Behalf of Falstaff," *Shakespeare Quarterly,* 3#4: 307-311 (Oct, 1952).

Hemlin, William B. "Falstaff, *South Atlantic Quarterly,* 50#1: 92-95 (Jan, 1951).

Hewett, R. P. *Reading and Response,* 106-110.

Humphreys, A. R. "A Note on *2 Henry IV,* II, iv. 362-3," *Notes and Queries,* 208: 98 (March, 1963).

——————————. "Two Notes on *2 Henry IV,*" *Modern Language Review,* 59#2: 171-172 (April, 1964).

——————————. "Shakespeare's Political Justice in *Richard II and Henry IV,*" *Stratford Papers on Shakespeare,* 5: 30-50 (1964).

Hunter, G. K. *"Henry IV* and the Elizabethan Two-Part Play," *Review of English Studies,* NS5#19: 243-248 (July, 1954).

Hunter, William B. "Falstaff," *South Atlantic Quarterly,* 50#1: 86-95 (Jan, 1951).

Jorgensen, Paul A. "The 'Dastardly Treachery' of Prince John of Lancaster," *PMLA,* 76#5: 488-492 (Dec, 1961).

——————————. "My Name is Pistol Call'd," *Shakespeare Quarterly,* 1#2: 73-75 (April, 1950).

——————————. " 'Redeeming Time' in Shakespeare's *Henry IV,*" *Tenessee Studies in Literature,* 5: 101-110 (1960).

——————————. "Divided Command in Shakespeare," *PMLA,* 70: 750-761 (Sept, 1955).

Kaiser, Walter J. *Praises of Folly,* 14-16; 195-275.

Khan, Razia. "The Hero in Shakespeare's *Henry IV,*" *Dacca University Studies,* 12Pt.A: 35-40 (June, 1964).

Kirschbaum, Leo. "The Demotion of Falstaff," *Philological Quarterly,* 41#1: 58-60 (Jan, 1962).

Kleinstuck, J. "The Problem of Order in Shakespeare's Histories," *Neophilologus,* pp. 273-277 (Oct, 1954).

Knight, George W. *The Golden Labyrinth,* 71-74; 77-78; 82-84; 236-237.

——————————. *The Olive and the Sword,* 25-29.

——————————. *The Sovereign Flower,* 33-37; 280-286.

Knights, L. C. "Notes on Comedy," in Eric Bentley, *The Importance of Scrutiny,* 232-237.

Kris, Ernst. "Prince Hal's Conflict," *Psychoanalytical Quarterly,* 17#4: 487-506 (Oct, 1948).
    ALSO IN: Gerald J. Goldberg and Nancy M. Goldberg (eds), *The Modern Critical Spectrum,* 262-275.

Leech, Clifford. "The Unity of *2 Henry IV,*" *Shakespeare Survey,* 6: 16-24 (1953).

Lever, J. W. "Three Notes on Shakespeare's Plants," *Review of English Studies,* NS3#10: 120-123 (1952).

Levin, Harry. "Falstaff Uncolted," *Modern Language Notes,* 61#4: 305-310 (April, 1946).

McCollom, William G. "Formalism and Illusion in Shakespeare's Drama," *Quarterly Journal of Speech,* 31#4: 446-447; 450-452 (Dec, 1945).

McLuhan, Herbert Marshall. *"Henry IV,* a Mirror for Magistrates," *University of Toronto Quarterly,* 17#2: 152-160 (Jan, 1948).

McManaway, James G. "The Cancel in the Quarto of 2 Henry IV," *University of Missouri Studies,* 21#1: 67-80 (1946).

Martin, Burns. "Falstaff," *Dalhousie Review,* 19#4: 439-448 (Jan, 1940).

Marvin, John T. "The Nature of Causation in the History Plays," in Margery Bailey, *Ashland Studies for Shakespeare 1962,* 67-77.

Maxwell, J. C. *"2 Henry IV,* II. iv. 91ff," *Modern Language Review,* 42#4: 485 (Oct, 1947).

Michel, Laurence (& Cecil C. Seronsy). "Shakespeare's History Plays and *Daniel:* An Assessment," *Studies in Philology,* 52#4: 563-568 (Oct, 1955).

Miles, L. Wardlaw. "Shakespeare's Old Men," *ELH,* 7#4: 291-293 (Dec, 1940).

Muir, Edwin. *Essays on Literature and Society,* 166-181.

Musgrove, S. "The Birth of Pistol," *Review of English Studies,* 10#37: 56-58 (Feb, 1959).

Prosser, Eleanor. "Colley Cibber at San Diego," *Shakespeare Quarterly,* 14#3: 253-261 (Summer, 1963).

Putney, Rufus. "Sir John Falstaff, Comic Hero: Or the Rejection of Bradley," *Shakespeare Newsletter,* 9#1: 5 (Feb, 1959).

Ribner, Irving. *The English History Play in the Age of Shakespeare,* 169-182.

——————. "Bolingbroke, A True Machiavellian," *Modern Language Quarterly,* 9: 177-184 (1948).

——————. "The Political Problem in Shakespeare's Lancastrian Tetralogy," *Studies in Philology,* 49#2: 182-184 (April, 1952).

Schevill, James. "Towards a Rhythm of Comic Action," *Western Speech,* 20#1: 5-8 (Winter, 1956).

Schutte, William M. *"Henry IV, Part 2,"* *Carnegie Series in English,* 1: 35-52 (1953).

Seng, Peter J. "Songs, Time and the Rejection of Falstaff," *Shakespeare Survey,* 15: 31-40 (1962).

Shaaber, M. A. "The Unity of *Henry IV,"* in James McManaway (ed), *Joseph Q. Adams Memorial Studies,* 217-227

Siegel, Paul N. "Shakespeare's *King Henry IV, Part II,*" *The Explicator,* 9#2: 9 (Nov, 1950).

Small, Samuel A. "Hotspur and Falstaff," *Shakespeare Association Bulletin,* 16#4: 243-248 (Oct, 1941).

Spencer, Benjamin T. "The Stasis of *Henry IV, Part II,*" *Tennessee Studies in Literature,* 6: 61-70 (1961).

——————. "*2 Henry IV* and the Theme of Time," *University of Toronto Quarterly,* 13#4: 394-399 (July, 1944).

Sprague, Arthur Colby. "Gadshill Revisited," *Shakespeare Quarterly,* 4#2: 125-137 (April, 1953).

Steiner, George. *The Death of Tragedy,* 253-255.

Tillyard, E. M. W. "Shakespeare's Historical Cycle: Organism or Compilation," *Studies in Philology,* 51#1: 37-38 (Jan, 1954).

Traversi, D. A. "*Henry IV—Part II,*" *Scrutiny,* 15#2: 117-127 (Spring, 1948).

——————. "Shakespeare: The Young Dramatist," *Guide to English Literature,* 2: 186-192.

Tucker, William J. "Irish Aspects of Shakespeare," *Catholic World,* 156: 702-704 (March, 1943).

Webb, Henry J. "Falstaff's Clothes," *Modern Language Notes,* 59#3: 162-164 (March, 1964).

——————. "Falstaff's Tardy Tricks," *Modern Language Notes,* 58#5: 377-379 (May, 1943).

Williams, Charles. *The Image of the City,* 40-42.

HENRY V

Bamborough, J. *The Little World of Man,* 83-84.

Barrell, Charles W. "Shakespeare's 'Fluellen' Identified," *Shakespeare Fellowship Newsletter,* 2#5: 59-62 (Aug, 1941).

——————. "Shakespeare's *Henry V,*" *Shakespeare Fellowship Quarterly,* 7#4: 49-54 (Oct, 1946).

Bateson, F. W. "A Table of Green Fields," *Essays in Criticism,* 7#2: 222-226 (April, 1957).

Berkelman, Robert. "Teaching *Henry V,*" *College English,* 13#2: 94-99 (Nov, 1951).

Berman, Ronald S. "Shakespeare's Alexander: *Henry V,*" *College English,* 23#7: 532-539 (April, 1962).

Blumert, Edythe. "Antechamber to Agincourt (A Study of Tempo in *Henry V),*" *University of West Virginia Bulletin: Philological Papers,* 6: 22-30 (1949).

Braddy, Haldeen. "The Flying Horse in *Henry V,*" *Shakespeare Quarterly,* 5#2: 205-207 (Spring, 1954).

————————. "Shakespeare's Henry V and the French Nobility," *Texas Studies in Literature and Language,* 3#2:
189-196 (Summer, 1961).

Burns, Landon C. "Three Views of King Henry V," *Drama*
Survey, 1#3: 278-284; 298-300 (Feb, 1962).

Chapman, Raymond. "The Wheel of Fortune in Shakespeare's
Historical Plays," *Review of English Studies,* NS1#1:
1-3: 5-6 (Jan, 1950).

Davidson, Arthur. *The Solace of Literature,* 102-105.

Draper, Charles L. "Falstaff's Bardolf," *Neophilolgus,* pp. 222-
226 (Oct, 1949).

Draper, John W. "Falstaff, 'A Fool and Jester," *Modern Lan-*
guage Quarterly, 17: 453-462 (1946).

————————. "Falstaff's Death," *Baconiana,* 50#155: 91-
93 (Nov, 1956).

Eagle, Roderick L. "Falstaff's Death," *Baconiana,* 50#155:
91-93 (Nov, 1956).

Ellis-Fermor, Una. *The Frontiers of Drama,* 42-47.

Empson, William. "Falstaff and Mr. Dover Wilson," *Kenyon*
Review, 15#2: 213-262 (Spring, 1953).

Erwitt, Elliott. "The Historic Place," *Show,* 2#1: 76-81 (Jan,
1962).

Fallon, Gabriel. "The Falstaff Affair," *Irish Monthly,* 73: 471-
478 (Nov, 1945).

Fleissner, Robert F. "Falstaff's Green Sickness Unto Death,"
Shakespeare Quarterly, 12#1: 47-55 (Winter, 1961).

Fogel, Ephim G. "'A Table of Green Fields': A Defense of
the Folio Reading," *Shakespeare Quarterly,* 9#4: 485-
492 (Autumn, 1958).

Freeman, Leslie. "Shakespeare's Kings and Machiavelli's
Prince," *The City College Papers,* 1: 25-42 (1964).

Gilbert, Allan. "Patriotism and Satire in *Henry V,*" *Univer-*
sity of Miami Publications in English and American Lit-
erature, 1: 40-64 (Mar, 1953).

Highet, Gilbert. *The Powers of Poetry,* 13-14.

Holmes, Martin. "A Heraldic Allusion in *Henry V,*" *Notes*
and Queries, 195: 333 (5 Aug, 1950).

Hotson, Leslie. "Falstaff's Death and Green Fields," *Times*
Literary Supplement, pg. 212 (April 6, 1956).

————————. "Ancient Pistol," *Yale Review,* pp. 51-66
(Sept, 1948).

Hulme, Hilda M. "Falstaff's Death: Shakespeare or Theo-
bald?" *Notes and Queries,* 201: 283-287 (July, 1956).

Hulme, Hilda M. *et. al.* "'A Table of Green Fields'," *Essays in Criticism, 7#2:* 222-226 (April, 1957).

Hulme, Hilda M. (& Earnest Schanzer). "'The Table of Green Fields'," *Essays in Criticism, 7:* 117-119 (1957).

Hunter, William B. "Falstaff," *South Atlantic Quarterly,* 50#1: 86-95 (Jan, 1951).

Jorgensen, Paul A. "Accidental Judgements, Casual Slaughters, and Purposes Mistook: Critical Reactions to Shakespeare's *Henry The Fifth,*" *Shakespeare Association Bulletin, 22#2:* 51-61 (April, 1947).

——————. "The Courtship Scene in *Henry V,*" *Modern Language Quarterly,* 11: 180-188 (1950).

——————. "Divided Command in Shakespeare," *PMLA,* 70: 750-761 (Sept, 1955).

——————. "My Name is Pistol Call'd," *Shakespeare Quarterly,* 1: 73-75 (April, 1950).

Keirce, William F. "*Henry V,*" *Carnegie Series in English,* 1: 53-69 (1953).

Kleinstuck, J. "The Problem of Order in Shakespeare's Histories," *Neophilologus,* pp. 268-273 (Oct, 1954).

Knight, G. Wilson. *The Olive and the Sword,* 29-40.

Koller, Katherine. "Falstaff and the Art of Dying," *Modern Language Notes,* 60#6: 383-386 (June, 1945).

Krempel, Daniel. "Oliver's *Henry V:* Design in Motion Picture," *Educational Theatre Journal, 2#4:* 322-328 (Dec, 1950).

Kris, Ernst. "Prince Hal's Conflict," *Psychoanalytic Quarterly,* 17#4: 487-506 (Oct, 1948).
  ALSO IN: Psychoanalytic Explorations in Art, 273-288.
  ALSO IN: Gerald Goldberg and Nancy Goldberg (eds), The Modern Critical Spectrum, 262-275.

Laird, John. *Philosophical Incursions Into English Literature,* 4-5; 8; 12; 18; 19; 20.

Law, Robert Adger. "The Choruses in *Henry The Fifth,*" *Studies in English,* 35: 11-21 (1956).

——————. "An Echo of Homer in *Henry V,*" *Studies in English (University of Texas),* pp. 105-109 (1942).

McCloskey, John C. "The Mirror of All Christian Kings," *Shakespeare Association Bulletin,* 19#1: 36-40 (Jan, 1944).

McCollom, William G. "Formalism and Illusion in Shakespeare's Drama," *Quarterly Journal of Speech,* 31#4: 446-447; 450-453 (Dec, 1945).

McLuhan, Hergert Marshall. "*Henry IV,* A Mirror for Magistrates," *University of Toronto Quarterly,* 17#2: 152-160 (Jan, 1948).

Marvin, John Trumbull. "The Nature of Causation in the History Plays," in Margery Bailey (ed.), *Ashland Studies for Shakespeare 1962, 77*.

Maxwell, J. C. *"Henry V,* II, ii, 17-29," *Notes and Queries,* 199: 195 (May, 1954).

Mendilow, A. A. "Falstaff's Death of a Sweat," *Shakespeare Quarterly,* 9#4: 479-483 (Autumn, 1958).

Moore, John Robert. "Shakespeare's *Henry V," The Explicator,* 1#8: 61 (June, 1943).

Muir, Edwin. *Essays on Literature and Society,* 166-181.

Nathan, Norman. "A Table of Green Fields," *Notes and Queries,* 204: 92-94 (March, 1959).

Parrott, T. M. "Fullness of Bread," *Shakespeare Quarterly,* 3#4: 379-381 (Oct, 1952).

Price, George R. "Henry V and Germanicus," *Shakespeare Quarterly,* 12#1: 57-60 (Winter, 1961).

Ribner, Irving. *The English History Play in the Age of Shakespeare,* 181-191.

Schevill, James. "Towards a Rhythm of Comic Action," *Western Speech,* 20#1: 5-8 (Winter, 1956).

Shaw, John. "The Minor Plot and *Henry V," Shakespeare Newsletter,* 8#1: 2 (Feb, 1958).

Smith, Warren D. "The 'Henry V' Choruses in the First Folio," *Journal of English and Germanic Philology,* 53#1: 38-57 (Jan, 1954).

Smith, William G. "Thomas Dekker's Welshmen," *Dock Leaves,* 4#11: 47-52 (Summer, 1953).

Spaeight, Robert. "Shakepeare and Politics," *Essays by Divers Hands,* 24: 14-16 (1948).

Stearns, Monroe M. "Shakespeare's *Henry V," The Explicator,* 2#3: 19 (Dec, 1943).

Stedman, John M. "Falstaff's 'Facies Hippocratica': A Note on Shakespeare and Renaissance Medical Theory," *Studia Neophilologica,* 29#2: 130-135 (1957).

Traversi, D. A. *"Henry The Fifth," Scrutiny,* 9#4: 352-373 (March, 1941).
   ALSO IN: Eric Bentley, *The Importance of Scrutiny,* 120-140.

Tuckey, John S. " 'Table of Greene Fields' Explained," *Essays in Criticism,* 6: 486-491 (1956).

Ure, Peter. "A Table of Green Fields," *Essays in Criticism,* 7#2: 223-224 (April, 1957).

Walter, J. H. "With Sir John in it," *Modern Language Review,* 41#3: 237-245 (July, 1946).

West, Rebecca. *The Court and the Castle,* 38-41.

Wilkinson, Allan. "A Note on *Henry V* Act IV," *Review of English Studies,* 1N.S.#4: 345-346 (Oct, 1950).

Williams, Charles. *The Image of the City,* 40-42.

Williams, Philip. "The Birth and Death of Falstaff Reconsidered," *Shakespeare Quarterly,* 8#3: 359-365 (Summer, 1957).

Wilson, E. C. "Falstaff—Clown and Man," in *Studies in the English Renaissance Drama in Memory of Karl J. Holzknecht,* 345-356.

Zimbardo, Rose A. "The Formalism of *Henry V,*" *The City College Papers,* 1: 16-24 (1964).

I HENRY VI

Berman, Ronald S. "Fathers and Sons in the *Henry VI* Plays," *Shakespeare Quarterly,* 13#4: 487-490 (Autumn, 1962).
———————. "Shakespeare's Conscious Histories," *Dalhousie Review,* 41#4: 485-495 (Winter, 1961/62).

Boas, Frederick S. "Joan of Arc in Shakespeare, Schiller, and Shaw," *Shakespeare Quarterly,* 2#1: 35-39 (Jan, 1951).

Brockbank, J. C. "The Frame of Disorder: *Henry VI,*" *Stratford-Upon-Avon Studies,* 3: 73-100 (1961).

Clemens, Wolfgang H. "Anticipation and Foreboding in Shakespeare's Early Histories," *Shakespeare Survey,* 6: 25-26 (1953).

Cunningham, James. *Woe or Wonder,* 54-55.

Draper, John W. "The 'Turk' in *Henry VI, Part 1,*" *University of West Virginia Bulletin: Philological Papers,* 10: 37-39 (1956).

Geer, C. A. "Revision and Adaptation in *1 Henry VI,*" *Studies in English (University of Texas),* 4226: 110-120 (July 8, 1942).

Kirschbaum, Leo. "The Authorship of *1 Henry VI,*" *PMLA,* 67#5: 809-822 (Sept, 1952).

Knight, G. Wilson. *The Olive and the Sword,* 4-11.
———————. *The Sovereign Flower,* 14-23.

Knights, L. C. *"King Lear* and the Great Tragedies,' *Guide to English Literature,* 2: 241-243.

Law, Robert A. *"The Chronicles* and the *Three Parts of Henry VI,*" *Studies in English (University of Texas),* 33: 13-32 (1954).

McDonnell, R. F. *The Aspiring Mind,* 176-179.

McNeal, Thomas H. "Margaret of Anjou: Romantic Princess and Troubled Queen," *Shakespeare Quarterly,* 9#1: 1-10 (Winter, 1958).

Marvin, John T. "The Nature of Causation in the History

Plays," in Margery Bailey (ed), *Ashland Studies for Shakespeare 1962,* 43-50.

Michel, Laurence (& Cecil C. Seronsy). "Shakespeare's History Plays and *Daniel:* An Assessment," *Studies in Philology,* 52#4: 568-569 (Oct, 1955).

Nilsson, P. G. "The Upstart Crow and *Henry VI,*" *Moderna Sprak,* 58#3: 293-303 (1964).

Okada, M. "Was 'Joan La Pucelle' Written by Shakespeare?" in *English Studies in Japan,* 133-142.

Ravich, Robert A. "A Psychoanalytic Study of Shakespeare's Early Plays," *Psychoanalytic Quarterly,* 33#3: 393-395 (July, 1964).

Ribner, Irving. *The English History Play in the Age of Shakespeare,* 96-116.

Steene, Brigitta. "Shakespearean Elements in History Plays of Strindberg," *Comparative Literature (Oregon),* 11#3: 213-216 (Summer, 1959).

Swayne, Mattie. "Shakespeare's King Henry VI as a Pacifist," *College English,* 3#2: 143-148 (Nov, 1941).

Tillyard, E. M. W. *Essays Literary and Educational,* 39-46.

——————. "Shakespeare's Historical Cycle: Organism or Compilation?" *Studies in Philology,* 51#1: 34-39 (Jan, 1954).

W., W. "Shaw and Shakespeare on Saint Joan," *The Independent Shavian,* 2#1: 6 (Fall, 1963).

II HENRY VI

Berman, Ronald S. "Fathers and Sons in the *Henry VI* Plays," *Shakespeare Quarterly,* 13#4: 490-494 (Autumn, 1962).

——————. "Shakespeare's Conscious Histories," *Dalhousie Review,* 41#4: 485-495 (Winter, 1961/62).

Brockbank, J. P. "The Frame of Disorder: *Henry VI,*" *Stratford-Upon-Avon Studies,* 3: 73-100 (1961).

Clemen, Wolfgang H. "Anticipation and Foreboding in Shakespeare's Early Histories," *Shakespeare Survey,* 6: 25-26 (1953).

Cunningham, James. *Woe or Wonder,* 55.

Jordan, John E. "The Reporter of *Henry VI, Part 2,*" *PMLA,* 64#5: 1089-1113 (Dec, 1949).

Knight, G. Wilson. *The Olive and the Sword,* 4-11.

——————. *The Sovereign Flower,* 14-23.

Knights, L. C. "*King Lear* and the Great Tragedies," *Guide to English Literature,* 2: 241-243.

Law, Robert A. "The Chronicles and the Three Parts of

Henry VI," Studies in English (University of Texas), 33: 13-32 (1954).

McDonnell, R. F. *The Aspiring Mind*, 179-183.

McManaway, James G. *"The Contention and 2 Henry VI*, in Siegried Korniger (ed), *Studies in English Presented to Karl Brunner*, 143-154.

McNeal, Thomas H. "Margaret of Anjou: Romantic Princess and Trouble Queen," *Shakespeare Quarterly*, 9#1 : 1-10 (Winter, 1958).

Marvin, John T. "The Nature of Causation in the History Plays," in Margery Bailey (ed), *Ashland Studies for Shakespeare 1962*, 43-50.

Michel, Laurence (& Cecil C. Seronsy). "Shakespeare's History Plays and *Daniel:* An Assessment," *Studies in Philology*, 52#4: 568-569 (Oct, 1955).

Nemeth, Lazlo. "A Translator's Report," *New Hungarian Quarterly*, 5#13 : 24-32 (Spring, 1964).

Nilsson, P. G. "The Upstart Crow and *Henry VI," Moderna Sprak*, 58#3: 293-303 (1964).

Okada, Minoru. "Was 'Joan La Pucelle' Written by Shakespeare?" in *English Studies in Japan*, 133-142.

Quinn, Michael. "Providence in Shakespeare's Yorkist Plays," *Shakespeare Quarterly*, 10#1 : 45-48 (Winter, 1959).

Ravich, Robert A. "A Psychoanalytic Study of Shakespeare's Early Plays," *Psychoanalytic Quarterly*, 33#3: 393-395 (July, 1964).

Ribner, Irving. *The English History Play in the Age of Shakespeare*, 96-116.

Steene, Brigitta. "Shakespearean Elements in History Plays of Strindberg," *Comparative Literature (Oregon)*, 11#3: 213-216 (Summer, 1959).

Swayne, Mattie. "Shakespeare's King Henry VI as a Pacifist," *College English*, 3#2 : 143-148 (Nov, 1941).

Tillyard, E. M. W. "Shakespeare's Historical Cycle: Organism or Compilation?" *Studies in Philology*, 51#1: 34-39 (Jan, 1954).

W., W. "Shaw and Shakespeare on Saint Joan," *The Independent Shavian*, 2#1 : 6 (Fall, 1963).

III HENRY VI

Berman, Ronald S. "Fathers and Sons in the *Henry VI* Plays," Shakespeare Quarterly, 13#4: 494-497 (Autumn, 1962).
————————. "Power and Humility in Shakespeare," *South Atlantic Quarterly*, 60#4: 412-415 (Fall, 1961).

Brockbank, J. P. "The Frame of Disorder: *Henry VI,*" *Stratford-Upon-Avon Studies,* 3: 73-100 (1961).

Bullough, Geoffrey. *Mirror of Minds,* 51-53.

Cairncross, Andrew S. "An Inconsistency in *3 Henry VI,*" *Modern Language Review,* 50#4: 492-494 (Oct, 1955).

Clemen, Wolfgang H. "Anticipation and Foreboding in Shakespeare's Early Histories," *Shakespeare Survey,* 6: 25-26 (1953).

Kernan, Alvin B. "A Companion of the Imagery in *Henry VI* and the *True Tragedie of Richard Duke of York,*" *Studies in Philology,* 51#3: 431-442 (July, 1954).

Knight, G. Wilson. *The Olive and the Sword,* 4-11.

——————. *The Sovereign Flower,* 14-23.

Knights, L. C. "*King Lear* and the Great Tragedies," *Guide to English Literature,* 2: 241-243.

Krieger, Murray. "The Dark Generations of *Richard III,*" *Crticism,* 1#1: 32-48 (Winter, 1959).

Law, Robert A. "The Chronicles and the Three Parts of *Henry VI,*" *Studies in English (University of Texas),* 33: 13-32 (1954).

McDonnell, R. F. *The Aspiring Mind,* 183-187.

McNeal, Thomas H. "Margaret of Anjou: Romantic Princess and Troubled Queen," *Shakespeare Quarterly,* 9#1: 1-10 (Winter, 1958).

Marvin, John T. "The Nature of Causation in the History Plays," in Margery Bailey (ed.), *Ashland Studies for Shakespeare 1962,* 43-50.

Michel, Laurence (& Cecil C. Seronsy). "Shakespeare's History Plays and *Daniel:* An Assessment," *Studies in Philology,* 52#4: 568-569 (Oct, 1955).

Mincoff, M. "*Henry VI, Part Three* and *The True Tragedy,*" *English Studies,* 42#5: 273-288 (Oct, 1961).

Nemeth, Lazlo. "A Translator's Report," *New Hungarian Quarterly,* 5#13: 24-32 (Spring, 1964).

Nilsson, P. G. "The Upstart Crow and *Henry VI,*" *Moderna Sprak,* 58#3: 293-303 (1964).

Okada, Minoru. "Was 'Joan La Pucelle' Written by Shakespeare?" in *English Studies in Japan,* 133-142.

Ravich, Robert A. "A Psychoanalytic Study of Shakespeare's Early Plays," *Psychoanalytic Quarterly,* 33#3: 393-395 (July, 1964).

Ribner, Irving. *The English History Play in the Age of Shakespeare,* 96-116.

Steene, Birgitta. "Shakespearean Elements in History Plays of Strindberg," *Comparative Literature (Oregon)*, 11#3: 213-216 (Summer, 1959).

Swayne, Mattie. "Shakespeare's King Henry VI as a Pacifist," *College English*, 3#2: 143-148 (Nov, 1941).

Tillyard, E. M. W. "Shakespeare's Historical Cycle: Organism or Compilation?" *Studies in Philology*, 51#1: 34-39 (Jan, 1954).

W., W. "Shaw and Shakespeare on Saint Joan," *The Independent Shavian*, 2#1: 6 (Fall, 1963).

- - - AND JOHN FLETCHER
KING HENRY VIII

Bertram, Paul. "Henry VIII: The Conscience of the King," in Reuben A. Bower (ed), *In Defense of Reading*, 153-173.

Byrne, Muriel St. Clare. "A Stratford Production: *Henry VIII*," *Shakespeare Survey*, 3: 120-129 (1950).

Cunningham, James. *Woe or Wonder*, 52-54.

Cutts, John P. "Shakespeare's Song and Masque Hand in *Henry VIII*," *Shakespeare Jahrbuck*, 99: 184-195 (1963).

Duncan-Jones, E. E. "Queen Katherine's Vision and Queen Margaret's Dream," *Notes and Queries*, 206: 142-143 (April, 1961).

Howarth, Herbert. "An Old Man Looking at Life: *Henry VIII* and the Late Plays," *Stratford Papers on Shakespeare*, 2: 177-194 (1961).

Kermode, Frank. "What is Shakespeare's *Henry VIII* all About?" *Durham University Journal*, 40#2: 48-55 (March, 1948).

Knight, G. Wilson. *The Crown of Life*, 256-336.

————.*The Olive and the Sword*, 76-85.

————. *The Sovereign Flower*, 80-87.

Law, Robert A. "The Double Authorship of *Henry VIII*," *Studies in Philology*, 56#3: 471-488 (July, 1959).

————. "Holinshed and *Henry the Eighth*," *Studies in English (University of Texas)*, 36: 3-11 (1957).

Oras, Ants. " 'Extra Monosyllables' in *Henry VIII* and the Problem of Authorship," *Journal of English and Germanic Philology*, 52#2: 198-213 (April, 1953).

Parker, Alexander A. "Henry VIII in Shakespeare and Calderone," *Modern Language Review*, 43: 327-352 (July, 1948).

Richey, Dorothy. "The Dance in *Henry VIII*: A Production Problem," *Furman Studies*, 35#3: 1-11 (Spring, 1952).

Tillyard, E. M. W. *Essays Literary and Educational,* 47-54.
───────. "Why Did Shakespeare Write *Henry VIII?*"
Critical Quarterly, 3#1: 22-27 (Spring, 1961).
Wasson, John. "In Defense of Henry VIII," *Washington
State College Research Studies,* 32#3: 261-276 (Sept,
1964).

JULIUS CAESAR
Aldus, Paul J. "Analogical Probability in Shakespeare's Plays,"
Shakespeare Quarterly, 6#4: 401-402 (Autumn, 1955).
Allen, John. "A Note on Dr. Nyerere's Translation of *Julius
Caesar,*" *Makerere Journal,* 9: 53-61 (March, 1964).
Barnes, T. R. *"Julius Caesar,"* *The Use of English,* 8#4: 233-
236 (Summer, 1957).
Barroll, J. Leeds. "Shakespeare and Roman History," *Mod-
ern Language Review,* 53#3: 327-343 (July, 1958).
Blau, Herbert. "Language and Structure in Poetic Drama,"
Modern Language Quarterly, 18: 34 (1957).
Bloom, Allan. "Political Philosophy and Poetry," *American
Political Science Review,* 54#2: 462-463 (June, 1960).
Brewer, D. S. "Brutus' Crime: A Footnote to *Julius Caesar,*"
Review of English Studies, NS3#9: 51-54 (1952).
Breyer, Bernard R. "A New Look at *Julius Caesar,*" *Vander-
bilt Studies in Humanities,* 2: 161-180 (1954).
Brown, John Russell. "Shakespeare's Subtext: I," *Tulane
Drama Review,* 8#1: 78-94 (Fall, 1963).
Burke, Kenneth. *Perspectives by Incongruity,* 64-75.
───────. "Antony in Behalf of the Play," *The Phil-
osophy of Literary Form,* 279-290.
ALSO IN: Mark Schorer (ed) et. al., *Criticism,* 533-538.
Carson, David L. "The Dramatic Importance of Prodigies in
Julius Caesar, Act II, Scene 1," *English Language Notes,*
2#3: 177-180 (March, 1965).
Charney, Maurice. "Shakespeare's Style in *Julius Caesar* and
Antony and Cleopatra," *ELH,* 26#3: 355-367 (Sept,
1959).
Coursen, Herbert R. "The Fall and Decline of Julius Caesar,"
Texas Studies in Literature and Language, 4#2: 241-250
(Summer, 1962).
── Dean, L. F. *"Julius Caesar* and Modern Criticism," *English
Journal,* 50: 451-456 (Oct, 1961).
Draper, John W. "The Speech Tempo of Brutus and Cassius,"
Neophilologus, pp. 184-186 (Oct, 1946).
Ellis-Fermor, Una. *The Frontiers of Drama,* 48-50.

Evans, G. Blakemore. "Shakespeare's *Julius Caesar*—A 17th Century MS," *Journal of English and Germaanic Philology,* 41#4: 401-417 (Oct, 1942).

Feldman, Harold. "Unconscious Envy in Brutus," *American Imago,* 9#3-4: 307-335 (Fall-Winter, 1952).

Felheim, Marvin. "The Problem of Time in *Julius Caesar*," *Huntington Library Quarterly,* 13#4: 399-405 (Aug, 1950).

Finkelstein, Sidney. "On Updating Shakespeare: Part I," *Mainstream,* 14#7 : 23-32 (July, 1961).

Foakes, R. A. "An Approach to *Julius Caesar*," *Shakespeare Quarterly,* 5#3 : 259-270 (Summer, 1954).

Frye, Roland M. "Rhetoric and Poetry in *Julius Caesar*," *Quarterly Journal of Speech,* 37#1: 41-48 (Feb, 1951).

Gleckner, Robert F. "Eliot's 'The Hollow Men' and Shakespeare's *Julius Caesar*," *Modern Language Notes,* 75#1: 26-28 (Jan, 1960).

Goldstein, M. "Pope, Sheffield, and Shakespeare's *Julius Caesar*," *Modern Language Notes,* 71#1: 8-10 (Jan, 1956).

Guidi, Augusto. " 'Creature' in Shakespeare," *Notes and Queries,* 197 : 443-444 (11 Oct, 1952).

Hall, Vernon Jr. *"Julius Caesar:* A Play Without Political Bias," in *Studies in the English Renaissance Drama in Memory of Karl J. Holzknecht,* 106-124.

Haywood, Richard M. "Shakespeare and the Old Roman," *College English,* 16#2: 98-101 ; 151 (Nov, 1954).

Heilman, Robert B. "To Know Himself: An Aspect of Tragic Structure," *Review of English Literature,* 5#2: 39-43 (April, 1964).

Heller, Agnes. "Shakespeare and Human Nature," *New Hungarian Quarterly,* 5#13 : 22-23 (Spring, 1964).

Holland, Norman N. "The 'Anna' and 'Cynicke' Episodes in *Julius Caesar*," *Shakespeare Quarterly,* 11#4: 439-444 (Autumn, 1960).

Honigmann, E. A. J. "Shakespeare's Plutarch," *Shakespeare Quarterly,* 10#1 : 25-33 (Winter, 1959).

Hunt, F. C. "Shakespeare's Delineation of the Passion of Anger," *Baconiana,* 29#117 : 136-141 (Oct, 1945).

Jepsen, Laura. *Ethical Aspects of Tragedy,* 111-116.

Jones, R. T. "Shakespeare's *Julius Caesar*," *Theoria,* 12: 41-50 (1959).

Jorgensen, Paul A. "Divided Command in Shakespeare," *PMLA,* 70:750-761 (Sept, 1955).

Kararah, Azza. "Antony and Brutus," *Bulletin of the Faculty of Arts (Alexandria University)*, 14: 23-38 (1962).

Kirschbaum, Leo. "Shakespeare's Stage Blood and its Critical Significance," *PMLA*, 64#3Pt.1: 519-524 (June, 1949).

Knight, G. W. *The Imperial Theme*, 32-95.

——————. "Brutus and Macbeth," in *The Wheel of Fire*, 120-139 (1962 ed.).

Knights, L. C. "Shakespeare and Political Wisdom: A Note on the Personalism of *Julius Caesar* and *Coriolanus*," *Sewanee Review*, 61#1: 43-55 (Winter, 1953).

McDonnell, R. F. *The Aspiring Mind*, 232-246.

McDowell, John H. "Analyzing *Julius Caesar* for Modern Production," *Quarterly Journal of Speech*, 31#3: 303-314 (Oct, 1945).

McNamee, Lawrence F. "The First Production of *Julius Caesar* on the German Stage," *Shakespeare Quarterly*, 10#3: 409-421 (Summer, 1959).

Mahnken, Harry E. and Janine S. Mahnken. "Harley Granville-Barker's Shakesperean Criticism," *Southern Speech Journal*, 27#1: 24-26 (Fall, 1961).

Maxwell, J. C. "*Julius Caesar* and Elyot's *Governour*," *Notes and Queries*, 201: 147 (1956).

——————. "Shakespeare: The Middle Plays," *Guide to English Literature*, 2: 198-201.

Murry, John M. "The Doctrine of Will in Shakespeare," *Aryan Path*, 35: 338-339 (Aug, 1964).

Nathan, Norman. "Caius Ligarius and Julius Caesar," *Notes and Queries*, 205: 216-217 (Jan, 1960).

——————. "Flavius Leases his Audience," *Notes and Queries*, NS1: 149-150 (April, 1954).

——————. "*Julius Caesar* and *The Shoemaker's Holiday*," *Modern Language Review*, 48#2: 178-179 (April, 1952).

Noel, J. "Shakespeare Criticism Today," *Revue des Langues Vivantes*, 26: 461-462 (1960).

Ornstein, Robert. "Seneca and the Political Drama of *Julius Caesar*," *Journal of English and Germanic Philology*, 57#1: 51-56 (Jan, 1958).

Paolucci, Anne. "The Tragic Hero in *Julius Caesar*," *Shakespeare Quarterly*, 11#3: 329-333 (Summer, 1960).

Parsons, Howard. "Shakespeare's *Julius Caesar*," *Notes and Queries*, 199: 113 (March, 1954).

Pellegrini, Giuliano. "The Roman Plays of Shakespeare in Italy," *Italica*, 34#4: 228-233 (Dec, 1957).

Phillips, James Emerson Jr. "The State in Shakespeare's Greek and Roman Plays," *Columbia University Studies in English and Comparative Literature,* 149: 174-188 (1940).

Pogson, Beryl. *In the East My Pleasure Lies,* 119-120.

Rabkin, Norman. "Structure, Convention, and Meaning in *Julius Caesar,*" *Journal of English and Germanic Philology,* 63#2: 240-254 (April, 1964).

Rao, Kolar Surya Narayana. "A Note on Dr. Gordon R. Smith's Article, 'Brutus, Virtue, and Will'—" *Shakespeare Quarterly,* 12#4: 474-475 (Autumn, 1961).

Raubitschek, A. E. "Brutus in Athens," *The Phoenix,* (Toronto), 11#1: 1-11 (Spring, 1957).

Rees, Joan. *"Julius Caesar*—An Earlier Play, and and Interpretation," *Modern Language Review,* 50#2: 135-141 (April, 1955).

——————. "Shakespeare's Use of *Daniel,*" *Modern Language Review,* 55#1: 80-81 (Jan, 1960).

Ribner, Irving. "Political Issues in *Julius Caesar,*" *Journal of English and Germanic Philology,* 56#1: 10-22 (Jan, 1957).

Rogers, Carmen. "Heavenly Justice in the Tragedies of Shakespeare," *University of Miami Publication in English and American Literature,* 1: 116-128 (March, 1953).

Sanders, Norman. "The Shift of Power in *Julius Caesar,*" *Review of English Literature,* 5#2: 24-35 (April, 1964).

Schalla, Hans. "The Topical Interest of Shakespeare Today," *World Theatre,* 8#4: 269-272 (Winter, 1959-1960).

Schanzer, Ernest. "The Problem of *Julius Caesar,*" *Shakespeare Quarterly,* 6#3: 297-308 (Summer, 1955).

——————. "The Tragedy of Shakespeare's Brutus," *ELH,* 22#1: 1-15 (March, 1955).

Schwartz, Elias. "On the Quarrel Scene in *Julius Caesar,*" *College English,* 19#4: 168-170 (Jan, 1958).

Shaw, G. B. *Plays and Players,* 290-299.

Smith, Gordon Ross. "Brutus, Virtue, and Will," *Shakespeare Quarterly,* 10#3: 367-379 (Summer, 1959).

——————. "The Character of Brutus: An Answer to Mr. Rao," *Shakespeare Quarterly,* 12#4: 475-478 (Autumn, 1961).

Smith, Warren D. "The Duplicate Revelation of Portia's Death," *Shakespeare Quarterly,* 4#2: 153-161 (April, 1953).

Spaeight, Robert. "Shakespeare and Politics," *Essays by Divers Hands,* 24: 5-6 (1948).

Starnes, D. T. "Imitation of Shakespeare in Dryden's *All For Love*," *Texas Studies in Literature and Language,* 6#1: 41-42 (Spring, 1964).

Stewart, J. I. M. *"Julius Caesar* and *Macbeth.* Two Notes on Shakespearean Technique," *Modern Language Review,* 40#3: 166-171 (July, 1945).

Stirling, Brents. "Brutus and the Death of Portia," *Shakespeare Quarterly,* 10#2: 211-217 (Spring, 1959).

———————. *"Julius Caesar* in Revision," *Shakespeare Quarterly,* 13#2: 187-205 (Spring, 1962).

Styan, J. L. *The Elements of Drama,* 69-70.

Uhler, John Earle. *"Julius Caesar*—A Morality of Respublica," *University of Miami Publications in English and American Literature,* 1: 96-106 (March, 1953).

Ure, Peter. "Character and Role from *Richard III* to *Hamlet,"* *Stratford-Upon-Avon Studies,* 5: 9-13 (1963).

Walker, Roy. "The Northern Star: An Essay on the Roman Plays," *Shakespeare Quarterly,* 2#4: 287-290 (Oct, 1951).

Wilson, J. Dover. "Ben Jonson and *Julius Caesar,"* *Shakespeare Survey,* 2: 36-43 (1949).

Zandvoort, R. W. "Brutus' Forum Speech in *Julius Caesar,'* *Review of English Studies,* 16#61: 62-66 (Jan, 1940).

KING JOHN

Allen, Neal W. Jr. "Clio and the Bard," *Union College Symposium,* pp. 14-16 (Summer, 1964).

Bonjour, Adrien. "Bastinado for the Bastard?" *English Studies,* 45 (Supplement): 169-176 (1964).

———————. "The Road to Swinstead Abbey: A Study of the Sense and Structure of *King John,"* *ELH,* 18#4: 253-274 (Dec, 1951).

Calderwood, James L. "Commodity and Honour in *King John,"* *University of Toronto Quarterly,* 29#3: 341-356 (April, 1960).

Clemen, Wolfgang H. "Anticipation and Foreboding in Shakespeare's Early Histories," *Shakespeare Survey,* 6: 31-3: (1953).

Knight, G. Wilson. *The Olive and the Sword,* 12-16.

———————. *The Sovereign Flower,* 25-29.

Law, Robert A. "On the Date of *King John,"* *Studies in Philology,* 54#2: 119-127 (April, 1957).

McCollom, William G. "Formalism and Illusion in Shakes

peare's Drama," *Quarterly Journal of Speech,* 31#4: 446-450 (Dec, 1945).

Marvin, John Trumbell. "The Nature of Causation in the History Plays," in Margery Bailey (ed.), *Ashland Studies for Shakespeare 1962,* 56-61.

Matchett, William H. "Richard's Divided Heritage in *King John,*" *Essays in Criticism,* 12#3: 231-253 (July, 1962).

Maxwell, J. C. "*King John*—Textual Notes," *Notes and Queries,* 195: 473-474 (28 Oct, 1950).

Pettet, E. C. "Hot Irons and Fever: A Note on Some of the Imagery of *King John,*" *Essays in Criticism,* 4#2: 128-144 (April, 1954).

Salter, F. M. "The Problem of *King John,*" *Royal Society of Canada Proceedings and Transactions,* 43Sect.2: 115-136 (June, 1949).

Sisson, C. J. "*King John:* A History Play for Elizabethans," *Stratford Papers on Shakespeare,* 1: 1-20 (1960).

Stevick, Robert D. " 'Repentant Ashes': The Matrix of 'Shakespearian' Poetic Language," *Shakespeare Quarterly,* 13#3: 366-370 (Summer, 1962).

Takeuchi, Hideo. "What We Should Learn From Shakespeare's Historical Plays: The People's Voice Behind the Scenes: *King John* and *Richard II,*" *The Humanities* (Yokohama), Sect. II#3: 1-13 (June, 1954).

Van de Water, Julia C. "The Bastard in *King John,*" *Shakespeare Quarterly,* 11#2: 137-146 (Spring, 1960).

KING LEAR

Abenheimer, K. M. "On Narcissism—Including an Analysis of *King Lear,*" *British Journal of Medical Psychology* 20: 322-329 (1945).

Adams, John C. "The Original Staging of *King Lear,*" in James G. McManaway (ed), *Joseph Q. Adams Memorial Studies,* 315-335.

Adams, Robert P. "King Lear's Revenges," *Modern Language Quarterly,* 21: 223-227 (1960).

Adler, Jacob H. "Shakespeare in *Winterset,*" *Educational Theatre Journal,* 6#3: 245-248 (Oct, 1954).

Alpers, Paul J. "*King Lear* and the Theory of the 'Sight Pattern,' " in Reuben A. Bower (ed), *In Defense of Reading,* 133-152.

Anderson, D. M. "A Conjecture on *King Lear* IV, ii, 57," *Notes and Queries,* 199: 331 (Aug, 1954).

Anshutz, H. L. "Cordelia and the Fool," *Washington State College Research Studies,* 3: 240-260 (Sept, 1964).

Auden, W. H. "Balaam and the Ass—The Master-Servant Relationship in Literature," *Thought,* 29#113: 251-255 (Summer, 1954).

Baker, James V. "Existential Examaination of *King Lear,*" *College English,* 23#7: 546-550 (April, 1962).

Bald, R. C. " 'Thou, Nature, Art My Goddess': Edmund and Renaissance Free-Thought," in James G. McManaway (ed), *Joseph Q. Adams Memorial Studies,* 337-349.

Bamborough, J. *The Little World of Man,* 17-19; 77-78.

Barish, Jonas A. and Marshall Waingrow. " 'Service' in *King Lear,*" *Shakespeare Quarterly,* 9#3: 347-355 (Summer, 1958).

Barnet, Sylvan. *"King Lear* and *King Lear,*" *Prologue: The Tufts University Theatre,* 19#3: 4-5 (March, 1964).

Battenhouse, Roy W. "Shakespearean Tragedy as Christian: Some Confusions in the Debate," *Centenniel Review,* 8#1: 77-84 (Winter, 1964).

Beckensteth, G. L. "The Golden World of *King Lear,*" *Annual Shakespeare Lecture of the British Academy,* pp. 1-27 (1955).

Bennett, Josephine Waters. "The Storm Within: The Madness of Lear," *Shakespeare Quarterly,* 13#2: 137-155 (Spring, 1962).

Berman, Ronald S. "Power and Humility in Shakespeare," *South Atlantic Quarterly,* 60#4: 416-419 (Fall, 1961).

——————. "Sense and Substance in *King Lear,*" *Neuphilologische Mitteilungen,* 65: 96-103 (1964).

Bickersteth, Geoffrey L. "The Golden World of *King Lear,*" *Proceedings of the British Academy,* 32: 147-172 (1946).

Blau, Herbert. " A Subtext Based on Nothing," *Tulane Drama Review,* 8#2: 122-132 (Winter, 1963).

——————. "Language and Structure in Poetic Drama," *Modern Language Quarterly,* 18: 27-28 (1957).

Block, Edward A. *"King Lear:* A Study in Balanced and Shifting Sympathies," *Shakespeare Quarterly,* 10#4: 499-512 (Autumn, 1959).

Bloom, Allan D. "Political Philosophy and Poetry," *American Political Science Review,* 54#2: 458; 461 (June, 1960).

Bodkin, Maud. *Archetypal Patterns in Poetry,* 280-284.

Bradbrook, F. W. "Shylock and King Lear," *Notes and Queries,* 202: 142-143 (1957).

Brooks, Cleanth and Robert Heilman. *Understanding Drama,* 586; 650-661.

Brown, Huntington. "Lear's Fool: A Boy, Not a Man," *Essays in Criticism,* 13#2: 164-171 (April, 1963).

Brown, Jack R. "Shakespeare's *King Lear,* III, vi, 47," *The Explicator,* 23#4: 32 (Dec, 1964).

Bullough, Geoffrey. *Mirror of Minds,* 84-86.

Burckhardt, Sigurd. "*King Lear:* The Quality of Nothing," *The Minnesota Review,* 2#1: 33-50 (Oct, 1961).

——————. "On Reading Ordinary Prose," *American Political Science Review,* 54#2: 468-470 (June, 1960).

Burris, Quincy Guy. "'Soft! Here Follows Prose'—*Twelfth Night* II. v. 154," *Shakespeare Quarerly,* 2#3: 233-239 (July, 1951).

Camden, Carroll. "Three Notes on Shakespeare," *Modern Language Notes,* 72: 253 (1957).

Campbell, Oscar James. "The Salvation of Lear," *ELH,* 15#2: 93-109 (June, 1948).

Cauthen, I. B. Jr. "'The Foule Flibbertigibbet' *King Lear,* 111, iv. 113 IV. i. 60," *Notes and Queries,* 203: 98-99 (March, 1958).

Chiari, Joseph. *The Contemporary French Theatre,* 4-7; 105-106; 206-207.

Clay, James H. "A New Theory of Tragedy," *Educational Theatre Journal,* 8#4: 299-303 (Dec, 1956).

Confrey, Burton. *The Moral Mission of Literature,* 165-174.

Craik, T. W. "Cordelia as 'Last and Least' of Lear's Daughters," *Notes and Queries,* 201: 11 (1956).

Creeth, Edmund H. "Moral and Tragic Recognition: The Uniqueness of *Othello, Macbeth,* and *King Lear,*" *Michigan Academy of Science, Arts and Letters. Papers,* 45: 389-391 (1960).

Cunningham, James. *Woe or Wonder,* 9-14; 22; 40.

——————. "Plots and Errors: The Structure of *King Lear,*" *Shakespeare Newsletter,* 3#4: 29 (Sept, 1953).

Cutts, John P. "Lear's 'Learned Theban,'" *Shakespeare Quarterly,* 14#4: 477-481 (Autumn, 1963).

Danby, John F. "King Lear and Christian Patience," *Cambridge Journal,* 1#5: 305-320 (Feb, 1948).

ALSO IN: *Poets on Fortune's Hill,* 105-107; 118-127.

——————. "The Fool in *King Lear,*" *Durham University Journal,* 38#1: 17-24 (Dec, 1945).

Daniel, Neva. "Looking at Shakespeare With an 'Existential'

Eye," *Journal of Communication,* 7#4: 180-182 (Winter, 1957).

Davenport, A. "Notes on *King Lear,*" *Notes and Queries,* 198: 20-22 (Jan, 1953).

Donnelly, John. "Incest, Ingratitude and Insanity—Aspects of the Psychopathology of King Lear," *Psychoanalytic Review,* 40#2: 149-155 (April, 1953).

Draper, John W. "The Old Age of King Lear," *Journal of English and Germanic Philology,* 39#4: 527-540 (Oct, 1940).

————————. "Subject Conflict in Shakespearean Tragedy," *Neuphilologische Mitteilungen,* 2#61: 218-219 (1960).

Dunn, E. Catherine. "The Storm in *King Lear,*" *Shakespeare Quarterly,* 3#4: 329-333 (Oct, 1952).

Dutu, Al. "The Part of the Fool and That of Edgar in *King Lear:* The Significance of Some Repetitions," *Revista de Filologie Romanica si Germanica,* 5#2: 337 (1961).

Dye, Harriet. "Appearance-Reality Theme in *King Lear,*" *College Englsh,* 25#7: 514-517 (April, 1964).

Eastman, Arthur M. "King Lear's 'Poor Fool'," *Michigan Academy of Science, Arts and Letters. Papers,* 49: 531-540 (1964).

Eastman, Fred. *Christ in the Drama,* 28-35.

Echerou, M. J. C. "Dramatic Intensity and Shakespeare's *King Lear,*" *English Studies in Africa,* 6#1: 44-50 (March, 1963).

Elliott, G. R. "The Initial Contrast in *Lear,*" *Journal of English and Germanic Philology,* 58#2: 251-263 (April, 1959).

Ellis-Fermor, Una. *Frontiers of Drama,* 50-52; 57-58; 74-76; 81-82.

Elton, William. "Lear's 'Good Years,'" *Modern Language Review,* 59#2: 177-178 (April, 1964).

————————. " 'Our Means Secure Us' *(King Lear,* IV, i, 20)" *Neophilologus,* 47#3: 225-227 (1963).

Empson, William et. al. "Correspondence on *King Lear,*" *The Critical Quarterly,* 3#1: 67-75 (Spring, 1961).

————————. "Fool in *Lear,*" *Sewanee Review,* 57#2: 177-214 (Spring, 1949).

Everett, Barbara. "The New *King Lear,*" *The Critical Quarterly,* 2#4: 325-339 (Winter, 1960).

Explicator, The (The Editors). "Shakespeare's *King Lear,* V, iii," *The Explicator,* 3#3: 21 (Dec, 1944).

Fairchild, A. H. R. "Shakespeare and the Tragic Theme," *University of Missouri Studies,* 19#2: 44-57; 105-140 (1944).

Finklestein, Sidney. "*King Lear* and the Common People," *Mainstream,* 15#10: 7-19 (Oct, 1962).

Fleissner, Robert F. "The 'Nothing' Element in *King Lear,*" *Shakespeare Quarterly,* 13#1: 67-70 (Winter, 1962).

————————. "Lear's 'Poor Fool' and Dickens," *Essays in Criticism,* 14#4: 425 (Oct, 1964).

————————. "Lear's 'Poor Fool' as the Poor Fool," *Essays in Criticism,* 13#4: 425-427 (Oct, 1963).

Fraiberg, Louis. "Freud's Writings on Art," *Literature and Psychology,* 6#4: 124 (Nov, 1956).

French, Carolyn S. "Shakespeare's 'Folly': *King Lear,*" *Shakespeare Quarterly,* 10#4: 523-529 (Autumn, 1959).

Gabor, Miklos. "An Actor's Thoughts," *New Hungarian Quarterly,* 5#13: 73-74 (Spring, 1964).

Garson, Marjorie. "Imagery in *King Lear,*" *Manitoba Arts Review,* pp. 12-17 (1958/59).

Gild, David. "Antoine's Production of *King Lear,*" *The City College Papers,* 1: 135-150 (1964).

Gold, Charles H. "A Variant Reading in *King Lear,*" *Notes and Queries,* 206: 141-142 (Apr, 1961).

Goldsmith, Robert H. "Kent: Plain Blunt Englishman," *Shakespeare Newsletter,* 7#2: 12 (April, 1957).

Graham, Paul G. "Hebbel's Study of *King Lear,*" *Smith College Studies in Modern Languages,* 21#1-4: 81-90 (Oct, 1939-July, 1940).

Greenfield, Thelma Nelson. "The Clothing Motif in *King Lear,*" *Shakespeare Quarterly,* 5#3: 281-286 (Summer, 1954).

Greg, W. W. "Time, Place, and Politics in *King Lear,*" *Modern Language Review,* 35#4: 431-446 (Oct, 1940).

Hainsworth, J. D. "Shakespeare, Son of Beckett?" *Modern Language Quarterly,* 25: 348-355 (1964).

Hankins, John E. "Lear and the Psalmist," *Modern Language Notes,* 61#2: 88-90 (Feb, 1946).

————————. "Shakespeare's *King Lear,* V, iii," *The Explicator,* 3#6: 48 (April, 1945).

Harrier, Richard C. "The Lex Aeterna and *King Lear,*" *Journal of English and Germanic Philology,* 53#4: 574-584 (Oct, 1954).

Hart, Walter M. "Shakespeare's Use of Verse and Prose,"

University of California Publications. English Studies, 10: 7-8 (1954).

Hathorn, Richmond Y. "Lear's Equations," *Centenniel Review,* 4#1: 51-69 (Winter, 1960).

——————————. *Tragedy, Myth, and Mystery,* 174-194.

Hawkes, Terry. " 'Love' in *King Lear,*" *Review of English Studies,* 10N.S.#38: 178-181 (May, 1959).

Hazen, A. T. "Shakespeare's *King Lear,* IV, i," *The Explicator, 2#2:* 10 (Nov, 1943).

Heilman, Robert B. "The *Lear* World," *English Institute Essays,* pp. 29-57 (1948).

——————————. " 'Poor Naked Wretches and Proud Array': The Clothes Pattern," in Gerald J. Goldberg, *The Modern Critical Spectrum,* 18-31.
ALSO IN: *Rocky Mountain Review,* 12#1: 5-14 (Aut, 1947).

——————————. "Shakespeare's *King Lear,* IV, vi, 169," *The Explicator, 6#2:* 10 (Nov, 1947).

——————————. "Twere Best Not Know Myself: Othello, Lear, Macbeth," *Shakespeare Quarterly,* 15#2: 89-98 (Spring, 1964).

——————————. "The Two Natures in *King Lear,*" *Accent,* 8#1: 51-58 (Autumn, 1947).

——————————. "The Unity of *King Lear,*" *Sewanee Review,* 56#1: 58-68 (Winter, 1948).
ALSO IN: R. W. Stallman (ed.), *Critiques and Essays in Criticism,* 154-161.

——————————. "A Critical Method for Poetic Drama," *Perspective,* 1#2: 106-110 (Winter, 1948).

Heninger, S. K. Jr. "Shakespeare's *King Lear,* III, ii, 1-9," *The Explicator,* 15#1: 1 (Oct, 1956).

Henn, Thomas R. *The Harvest of Tragedy,* 154-155.

Hockey, Dorothy C. "The Trial Pattern in *King Lear,*" *Shakespeare Quarterly,* 10#3: 389-395 (Summer, 1959).

Hoepfner, Theodore C. "We That are Young," *Notes and Queries,* 199: 110 (March, 1954).

Hogan, Robert G. *Drama,* 152-156.

Holland, Norman N. "Freud on Shakespeare," *PMLA,* 75#3: 168-169 (July, 1960).

Holloway, John. *The Story of the Night,* 75-98.

Hulme, Hilda. "Three Shakespearean Glosses," *Notes and Queries,* 202: 237-238 (1957).

Hutchens, Eleanor N. "The Transfer of Power in *King Lear* and *The Tempest*," *Review of English Literature*, 4#2: 82-93 (April, 1963).

Ingram, Von R. W. "*Hamlet, Othello,* and *King Lear:* Music and Tragedy," *Shakespeare Jahrbuck*, 100: 159-161; 170-172 (1964).

Isenberg, Arnold. "Cordelia Absent," *Shakespeare Quarterly*, 2#3: 185-194 (July, 1951).

Jackson, MacD. P. " 'The Gods Deserve Your Kindness!': *King Lear*, III. vi. 5," *Notes and Queries*, 208: 101 (March, 1963).

Jaffa, Harry V. "The Limits of Politics: An Interpretation of *King Lear*, Act I, Scene I," *American Political Science Review*, 51#2: 405-427 (June, 1957).

James, D. G. "Keats and *King Lear*," *Shakespeare Survey*, 13: 58-68 (1960).

——————. *The Dream of Learning*, 69-126.

Jayne, Sears. "Charity in *King Lear*," *Shakespeare Quarterly*, 15#2: 277-288 (Spring, 1964).

Jenkins, Raymond. "The Socratic Imperative and *King Lear*," *Renaissance Papers*, pp. 85-94 (1963).

Jepsen, Laura. *Ethical Aspects of Tragedy*, 58-63.

Johnson, S. F. "Attitudes Towards Justice in *King Lear*," *Shakespeare Newsletter*, 4#1: 8 (Feb, 1954).

Jones, Graham. "The Goose in *Lear*," *Notes and Queries*, 195: 295 (8 July, 1950).

Jones, James Land. "*King Lear* and the Metaphysics of Thunder," *Xavier University Studies*, 3#2: 51-80 (June, 1964).

Joseph, Bertram L. "Character and Plot," *Drama Survey*, 4#4: 548-554 (Spring-Fall, 1964).

Kahn, Sholom J. " 'Enter Lear Mad,' " *Shakespeare Quarterly*, 8#3: 311-329 (Summer, 1957).

Keast, W. R. "The 'New Criticism' and *King Lear*," in Ronald S. Crane, *Critics of Criticism, Ancient and Modern*, 108-137.

ALSO IN: *Modern Philology*, 47#1: 45-64 (Aug, 1949).

Kernodle, George R. "The Symphonic Form of *King Lear*," in *Elizabethan Studies in Honor of George T. Reynolds*, 185-191.

Kirschbaum, Leo. "Albany," *Shakespeare Survey*, 13: 20-29 (1960).

——————. "A Detail in *King Lear*," *Review of English Studies*, 25#98: 153-154 (April, 1949).

—————. "The True Text of *King Lear*," *Shakespeare Association Bulletin*, 16#3: 140-153 (July, 1941).

—————. "Banquo and Edgar: Character or Function?" *Essays in Criticism*, 7#1: 8-21 (Jan, 1957).

Kitzhaber, A. R. *Drama: The Major Genres*, 151-161.

Knight, Carol. "Animal Imagery in *King Lear*," *Mantitoba Arts Review*, 8#3: 11-22 (Winter, 1954).

Knight, Eric A. "Shakespeare in the Theatre," *Central Literary Magazine*, pp. 135-138 (Aug, 1941).

Knight, George W. 'The Golden Labyrinth, 75-77.

—————. *The Olive and the Sword*, 51-54.

—————. "*King Lear* and the Comedy of the Grotesque," in *The Wheel of Fire*, 160-176 (1962 ed.).

—————. "The Lear Universe," in *The Wheel of Fire*, 177-206 (1962 ed.).

Knights, L. C. "*King Lear* as Metaphor," in Bernice Slote (ed.), *Myth and Symbol*, 21-38.

—————. "Shakespeare's Politics: With Some Reflections on the Nature of Tradition," *Annual Shakespeare Lecture of the British Academy*, pp. 119-121 (1957).

—————. "*King Lear* and the Great Tragedies," *Guide to English Literature*, 2: 223-232.

Kott, J. "*King Lear* or *Endgame*," *Evergreen Review*, 8#33: 53-65 (Aug/Sept, 1964).

Lash, Kenneth. "Captain Ahab and *King Lear*," *New Mexico Quarterly Review*, 19#4: 438-445 (Winter, 1949).

Leaska, Mitchell. *The Voice of Tragedy*, 117-131.

Loper, Robert. "*King Lear*," *Shakespeare Newsletter*, 8#4: 28 (Sept, 1958).

Lord, John B. "Comic Scenes in Shakespearean Tragedy," *Washington State College Research Studies*, 32#3: 236-238 (Sept, 1964).

Lucas, Frank L. *Literature and Psychology*, 62-71.

McCloskey, John C. "The Emotive Use of Animal Imagery in *King Lear*," *Shakespeare Quarterly*, 13#3: 321-325 (Summer, 1962).

McCollom, William G. *Tragedy*, 103-105; 144-145.

McDonnell, R. F. *The Aspiring Mind*, 246-264.

McIntosh, Angus and Colin Williamson. "*King Lear*, Act I, Scene 1. A Stylistic Approach," *Review of English Studies*, N.S. 14#53: 54-58 (Feb, 1963).

MacIntyre, Jean. "Shakespeare's *King Lear*, III, vi, 8," *The Explicator*, 21#3: 24 (Nov, 1962).

Mack, Maynard. "The Jacobean Shakespeare: Some Observations on the Construction of the Tragedies," *Stratford-Upon-Avon Studies,* 1: 11-42 (1960).

——————. " 'We Came Crying Hither': An Essay on Some Characteristics of *King Lear," The Yale Review,* 54#2: 161-186 (Dec, 1964).

McKenzie, James J. "Edgar's 'Persian Attire,' " *Notes and Queries,* 201: 98-99 (March, 1956).

Maclean, Hugh. "Disguise in *King Lear:* Kent and Edgar," *Shakespeare Quarterly,* 11#1: 49-54 (Winter, 1960).

Maclean, Norman. "Episode, Scene, Speech, and Word: The Madness of Lear," in Ronald S. Crane, *Critics of Criticism, Ancient and Modern,* 595-615.

McNeir, Waldo F. "The Staging of the Dover Cliff Scene in *King Lear,"* in Waldo F. McNeir, *Studies in English Renaissance Literature,* 87-104.

Maes-Jelinek, Hena. "Morality and World Order in Shakespeare's Plays," *Revue des Langues Vivantes,* 30#3: 277-279 (1964).

Mahnken, Harry E. and Janine S. Mahnken. "Harley Granville-Barker's Shakespearean Criticism," *Southern Speech Journal,* 27#1: 26-27 (Fall, 1961).

Major, John M. "Shakespeare's *King Lear,* IV, ii, 62," *The Explicator,* 17#2: 13 (Nov, 1958).

Markels, Julian. "Shakespeare's Confluence of Tragedy and Comedy: *Twelfth Night* and *King Lear," Shakespeare Quarterly,* 15#1: 75-88 (Winter, 1964).

Marowitz, Charles. *"Lear Log," Tulane Drama Review,* 8#2: 103-121 (Winter, 1963).

Martey, Herbert. "Shakespeare's *King Lear,* IV, vi, 1-80," *The Explicator,* 11#2: 10 (Nov, 1952).

Marx, Milton. *The Enjoyment of Drama,* 105-112.

Mavor, H. O. *Tedious and Brief,* 52-55.

Maxwell, J. C. "The Technique of Invocation in *King Lear," Modern Language Review,* 45#2: 142-147 (April, 1950).

Melchiori, Barbara. "Still Harping on my Daughter," *English Miscellany,* 11: 72-74 (1960).

Mendonca, Barbara Heliodora Carneiro de. "The Influence of *Gorboduc* on *King Lear," Shakespeare Survey,* 13: 41-48 (1960).

Merchant, W. M. "Costume in *King Lear" Shakespeare Survey,* 13: 72-80 (1960).

——————. "Lawyer and Actor: Process of Law in Elizabethan Drama," in G. I. Duthie (ed), *English Studies Today*—Third Series (1964). 116-117; 120-124.

——————————. "Shakespeare's Theology," *Review of English Literature,* 5#4: 75-78.

Michel, Laurence. "Shakespearean Tragedy: Critique of Humanism From the Inside," *Massachusetts Review,* 2#4: 645-646 (Summer, 1961).

Miles, L. Wardlaw. "Shakespeare's Old Men," *ELH,* 7#4: 295-297 (Dec, 1940).

Milne, Evander. "On the Death of Cordelia," *English,* 6#35: 244-248 (Summer, 1947).

Morris, Ivor. "Cordelia and Lear," *Shakespeare Quarterly,* 8#2: 141-158 (Spring, 1957).

Muir, Kenneth. *Essays on Literature and Society,* 33-49.

——————————. *"King Lear,* II, iv. 170," *Notes and Queries,* 196: 170 (14 April, 1951).

——————————. "Madness in *King Lear,*" *Shakespeare Survey,* 13: 30-40 (1960).

——————————. "Some Freudian Interpretations of Shakespeare," *Proceedings of the Leeds Philosophical and Literary Society,* 7Pt. 1: 47-49 (July, 1952).

——————————. "Three Shakespeare Adaptations," *Proceedings of the Leeds Philosophical and Literary Society,* 8Pt. 4: 238-239 (Jan, 1959).

——————————. "Samuel Harsnett and *King Lear,*" *Review of English Studies,* NS2#5: 11-21 (Jan, 1951).

Muller, Herbert J. *The Spirit of Tragedy,* 185-193.

Munro, John M. "The Problem of Choice in *King Lear,*" *South Atlantic Quarterly,* 63#2: 240-244 (Spring, 1964).

Musgrove, S. *"King Lear* I. i. 170," *Review of English Studies,* NS8#30: 170-171 (May, 1957).

——————————. "The Nomenclature of *King Lear,*" *Review of English Studies,* 7: 294-298 (1956).

——————————. "Shakespeare and Jonson," *University of Auckland English Series,* 9: 21-39 (1957).

Myrick, Kenneth. "On the Meaning of *King Lear,*" *Prologue,* 19#3: 9 (March, 1964).

Noel, J. "Shakespeare Criticism Today," *Revue des Langues Vivantes,* 26: 464-465 (1960).

Nowottny, Winifred M. T. "Lear's Questions," *Shakespeare Survey,* 10: 90-97 (1957).

——————————. "Some Aspects of the Style of *King Lear,*" *Shakespeare Survey,* 13: 49-57 (1960).

Olson, Elder. *Tragedy and the Theory of Drama,* 195-215.

Ornstein, Robert. *The Moral Vision of Tragedy,* 121-125; 260-273.

Oyama, Toshiko. "The World of Lear's Fool—The Dramatic Mode of His Speech," *Shakespeare Studies*, 2: 10-30 (1963).

Parnell, Paul. "Is There a Case for Goneril and Regan?" *Shakespeare Newsletter*, 2#5: 20 (May, 1952).

Parr, Johnstone. "Edmund's Nativity in *King Lear*," *Shakespeare Association Bulletin*, 21#4: 181-185 (Oct, 1946).

————————. "A Note on the 'Late Eclipses' in *King Lear*," *Shakespeare Association Bulletin*, 20#1: 46-48 (Jan, 1945).

Parrott, T. M. " 'Gods' or 'gods' in *King Lear*, V, iii, 17," *Shakespeare Quarterly*, 4#4: 427-432 (Oct, 1953).

Pauncz, Arpad. "The Lear Complex in World Literature," *American Imago*, 11#1: 58-62 (Spring, 1954).

————————. "Psychopathology of Shakespeare's *King Lear*," *American Imago*, 9#1: 57-78 (April, 1952).

Perkinson, Richard H. "Shakespeare's Revision of the Lear Story and the Structure of *King Lear*," *Philological Quarterly*, 22#4: 315-329 (Oct, 1943).

Pogson, Beryl. *In the East My Pleasure Lies*, 23-46.

Price, Alan. "The Blinding of Gloucester," *Notes and Queries*, 197: 313-314 (19 July, 1952).

Prior, Moody E. *The Language of Tragedy*, 180-185.

Pyle, Fitzroy. *"Twelfth Night, King Lear*, and *Arcadia,"* *Modern Language Review*, 43#4: 452-455 (Oct, 1948).

Raphael, D. D. *Paradox of Tragedy*, 52-57.

Ravich, Robert A. "Shakespeare and Psychiatry," *Literature and Psychology*, 14#3-4: 102-105 (Summer-Fall, 1964).

Reynolds, George F. "Two Conventions of the Open Stage (as illustrated in *King Lear),"* *Philological Quarterly*, 41#1: 82-95 (Jan, 1962).

Ribner, Irving. *The English History Play in the Age of Shakespeare*, 247-253.

————————. "The Gods are Just: A Reading of *King Lear*," *Tulane Drama Review*, 2#3: 34-54 (May, 1958).

————————. "Lear's Madness in the Nineteenth Century," *Shakespeare Association Bulletin*, 22#3: 117-129 (July, 1947).

————————. "Shakespeare and Legendary History: *Lear* and *Cymbeline*," *Shakespeare Quarterly*, 7#1: 47-52 (Winter, 1956).

————————. "Sidney's Arcadia and the Structure of *King Lear*," *Studia Neophilologica*, 24#1-2: 63-68 (1952).

Rinehart, Keath. "The Moral Background of *King Lear*,"

University of Kansas City Review, 20#4: 223-228 (Summer, 1954).

Ringler, William. "Exit Kent," *Shakespeare Quarterly,* 11#3: 311-317 (Summer, 1960).

Roddier, Henri. "A Freudian Detective's Shakespeare," *Modern Philology,* 48#2: 132 (Nov, 1950).

Rogers, Carmen. "Heavenly Justice in the Tragedies of Shakespeare," *University of Miami Publications in English and American Literature,* 1: 116-128 (March, 1953).

Rosier, James L. "The *Lex Aeterna* and *King Lear,*" *Journal of English and Germanic Philology,* 53#4: 574-580 (Oct, 1954).

Salter, K. W. "*King Lear* and the Morality Tradition," *Notes and Queries,* 199: 109-110 (March, 1954).

Sandford, Ernest. "Shakespeare's Comic Relief," *Central Literary Magazine,* pp. 171-172 (Nov, 1945).

Schanzer, Ernest. "*King John,* V. ii. 103-104," *Notes and Queries,* 200: 474-475 (Nov, 1955).

Schoff, Francis G. "King Lear: Moral Example or Tragic Protagonist," *Shakespeare Quarterly,* 13#2: 157-172 (Spring, 1962).

Schulz, Max F. "*King Lear,*" *Tulane Studies in English,* 7: 83-90 (1957).

Seronsy, Cecil C. "Shakespeare's *King Lear,* I, i, 159-163," *The Explicator,* 17#3: 21 (Dec, 1958).

Sewall, Richard B. *The Vision of Tragedy,* 68-79.

Siegel, Paul N. "Adversity and the Miracle of Love in *King Lear,*" *Shakespeare Quarterly,* 6#3: 325-336 (Summer, 1955).

——————. "Willy Loman and King Lear," *College English,* 17#6: 341-345 (March, 1956).

——————. "In Defense of Bradley," *College English,* 9#5: 254-255 (Feb, 1948).

Sitwell, Edith. "*King Lear,*" *Atlantic Monthly,* 185: 57-62 (May, 1950).

——————. "Some Notes on *King Lear,*" *New Writing and Daylight,* pp. 77-89 (1945).

Skriletz, Dorothy. "The Rhetoric: An Aid to the Study of Drama," *Southern Speech Journal,* 25#3: 217-222 (Spring, 1960).

Sledd, James. " 'Hause' and 'Slaves' in *King Lear,*" *Modern Language Notes,* 55#8: 594-595 (Dec, 1940).

Small, S. A. "The *King Lear* Quarto," *Shakespeare Association Bulletin,* 21#4: 177-180 (Oct, 1946).

Smidt, K. "The Quarto and the Folio *Lear*," *English Studies*, 45#2: 149-162 (April, 1964).

Smith, Gerald. "A Note on the Death of Lear," *Modern Language Notes*, 70#6: 403-404 (June, 1955).

Smith, Ronald M. *"King Lear* and the Merlin Tradition," *Modern Language Quarterly*, 17: 153-174 (1946).

Solomon, Emma B. *"King Lear* in France," *Prologue*, 19#3: 6-8 (March, 1964).

Speaight, Robert. "The Actability of *King Lear*," *Drama Survey*, 2#1: 49-55 (June, 1962).

Spencer, Benjamin T. *"King Lear:* A Propetic Tragedy," *College English*, 5#6: 302-307 (March, 1944).

Spencer, Christopher. "A Word for Tate's *King Lear*," *Studies in English Literature 1500-1900*, 3#2: 241-252 (Spring, 1963).

Spencer, Theodore. "The Isolation of the Shakespearean Hero," *Sewanee Review*, 52#3: 324-326 (July/Sept, 1944).

Spevack, Marvin. "Shakespeare's *King Lear,* IV, vi, 152," *Explicator*, 17#1: 4 (Oct, 1958).

Stampfer, J. "The Catharsis of King Lear," *Shakespeare Survey*, 13: 1-10 (1960).

Steiner, George. *The Death of Tragedy*, 256-259; 276-280.

Stewart, Charles D. "Four Shakespearean Cruxes," *College English*, 9#4: 188-191 (Jan, 1948).

Stolnitz, Jerome. "Notes on Comedy and Tragedy," *Philosophy and Phenomenological Research*, 16#1: 49-56 (Sept, 1955).

Stone, George W. "Garrick's Production of *King Lear:* A Study in the Temper of the Eighteenth Century Mind," *Studies in Philology*, 45#1: 89-103 (Jan, 1948).

Strachey, Lytton. *Spectatorial Essays*, 66-70.

Strathmann, Ernest A. "The Devil Can Quote Scripture," *Shakespeare Quarterly*, 15#2: 19-20 (Spring, 1964).

Strindberg, August. *"King Lear,"* *Adam International Review*, 190-191: 19-21 (1949).

Stroup, Thomas B. "Cordelia and the Fool," *Shakespeare Quarterly*, 12#2: 127-132 (Spring, 1961).

Styan, J. L. *The Elements of Drama*, 107-117; 121-122.

Sutherland, W. O. S. "Polonius, Hamlet, and Lear in Aaron Hill's Prompter," *Studies in Philology*, 49#4: 614-618 (Oct, 1952).

Tannenbaum, Samuel A. "An Emendation in *King Lear*,"

Shakespeare Association Bulletin, 16#1: 58-59 (Jan, 1941).

Taylor, E. M. M. "Lear's Philosopher," *Shakespeare Quarterly,* 6#3: 364-365 (Summer, 1955).

Taylor, Warren. "Lear and the Lost Self," *College English,* 25#7: 509-513 (April, 1964).

Thaler, Alwin. "The Gods and God in *King Lear*," *Renaissance Papers,* pp. 32-39 (1955).

Torbarina, Josip. "The Nakedness of the Shakespearean Tragic Hero," *Studia Romanica et Anglica Zagrabiensia,* 12: 4-5 (Dec, 1961).

Traschen, Isadore. "The Elements of Tragedy," *Centenniel Review,* 6#2: 215-229 (Spring, 1962).

Traversi, D. A. *"King Lear* (I)," *Scrutiny,* 19#1: 43-64 (Oct, 1952).

——————. *"King Lear* (II)," *Scrutiny,* 19#2: 126-141 (Winter, 1952-1953).

——————. *"King Lear* (III)," *Scrutiny,* 19#3: 206-230 (Spring, 1953).

——————. *"King Lear,"* Stratford Papers on Shakespeare,* 5: 183-200 (1964).

Turner, Darwin T. *"King Lear* Re-examined," *CLA Journal,* 3#1: 27-39 (Sept, 1959).

Tutt, Ralph M. "Dog Imagery in *The Two Gentlemen From Verona, King Lear,* and *Timon of Athens*," *The Serif,* 1#3: 15-16; 21-22 (Oct, 1964).

Viebrock, H. "Keats, *King Lear,* and Benjamin West's 'Death on a Pale Horse'," *English Studies,* 43#3: 174-180 (June, 1962).

Vivas, Eliseo. *The Artistic Transaction,* 127-129.

Walker, Roy. "Swinburne, Tolstoy, and *King Lear*," *English,* 7#42: 282-284 (Aut, 1949).

Walton, J. K. "Lear's Last Speech," *Shakespeare Survey,* 13: 11-19 (1960).

Warren, Phyllis. "Drama in the University," *Theoria,* 3: 27-30 (1950).

Watkins, W. B. C. "The Two Techniques in *King Lear*," *Review of English Studies,* 18#69: 1-26 (Jan, 1942).

Weidhorn, Manfred. "Lear's Schoolmasters," *Shakespeare Quarterly,* 13#3: 305-316 (Summer, 1962).

Weisinger, Herbert. *The Agony and the Triumph,* 109-110.

——————. "A Shakespeare all too Modern," *Arizona Quarterly,* 20#4: 304-308 (Winter, 1964).

West, Robert H. "Sex and Pessimism in *King Lear*," *Shakespeare Quarterly*, 11#1: 55-60 (Winter, 1960).

Williams, David. "On Producing *King Lear*," *Shakespeare Quarterly*, 2#3: 247-252 (July, 1951).

Williams, George W. "The Poetry of Storm in *King Lear*," *Shakespeare Quarterly*, 2#1: 57-71 (Jan, 1951).

Wolin, Sheldon J. "The Limits of Politics: An Interpretation of *King Lear*, Act I, Scene 1," *American Political Science Review*, 51#2: 405-427 (June, 1957).

Zandvoort, R. W. "*King Lear:* The Scholar and Critics," *Amsterdam Akademie van Wetenschappen Medelingen Afd. Letterkunde*, 19#7: 229-244 (1956).

LOVE'S LABOUR'S LOST

"Arden." "The 'Entrance' to Don Adriana's Letter Cryptograph," *Baconiana*, 35#138: 30-34 (Jan, 1951).

——————. "Don Adriana's Letter Cryptograph," *Baconiana*, 35#139: 92-97 (Apr, 1951).

——————. "Don Adriana's Letter Cryptograph, III," *Baconiana*, 35#141: 222-228 (Oct, 1951).

Arther, James. "Bacon's Cipher in *Love's Labour's Lost*," *Baconiana*, 31#122: 31-38 (Jan, 1947).

Ashe, Geoffrey. "Several Worthies," *Notes and Queries*, 195: 492-493 (Nov 11, 1950).

Auden, W. H. "Balaam and the Ass: The Master Servant Relationship in Literature," *Thought*, 29#113: 242-244 (Summer, 1954).

Babb, Lawrence. *The Elizabethan Malady*, 148-149.

Babcock, Weston. "Fools, Fowls, and Perttaunt-Like in *Love's Labour's Lost*," *Shakespeare Quarterly*, 2#3: 211-219 (July, 1951).

Baker, H. Kendra. "Facts that Fit," *Baconiana*, 27#106: 19-27 (Jan, 1943).

Berman, Ronald. "Shakespeare Comedy and the Uses of Reason," *South Atlantic Quarterly*, 63#1: 1-4 (Winter, 1964).

Berry, Francis. *Poetry and the Physical Voice*, 135-137; 144-145.

Blisset, William. " 'Strange Without Heresy' *(Love's Labour's Lost,* 5.1.6), *"English Studies*, 38#5: 209-211 (Oct, 1957).

Bronson, Bertrand H. "Daisies Pied and Icicles," *Modern Language Notes*, 63#1: 35-38 (Jan, 1948).

Bullough, Geoffrey. *Mirror of Minds*, 62-64.

Campbell, O. J. *"Love's Labour's Lost* Restudied," *University of Michigan Studies in Shakespeare*, pp. 1-46 (1964).

Clurman, Harold. *Lies Like Truth*, 156-158.

Draper, John W. "Tempo in *Love's Labour's Lost,"* *English Studies*, 29#5: 129-137 (Oct, 1948).

Eagle, R. L. *"Love's Labour's Lost* and Gray's Inn," *Baconiana*, 44#161: 99-102 (Feb, 1961).

Frye, Northrop. "Shakespeare's Experimental Comedy," *Stratford Papers on Shakespeare*, 2: 1-14 (1961).

Gamal, S. M. "The Function of Song in Shakespeare's Comedies," *Cairo Studies in English*, pp. 113-114 (1961-1962).

Gerard, Albert. "Searchlight on Literature," *Revue des Langues Vivantes*, 22: 573-577 (1956).

Gertrude, Sister M. Teresa. *"Love's Labour's Lost,"* *Horizontes*, 7#13: 47-52 (Oct, 1963).

Goodfellow, D. M. *"Love's Labour's Lost,"* *Carnegie Series in English*, 8: 1-16 (1964).

Greenfield, Stanley. "Moth's *L'Envoy* and the Courtiers in *Love's Labour's Lost,"* *Review of English Studies*, NS5#18: 167-168 (1954).

Harbage, Alfred. *"Love's Labor's Lost* and the Early Shakespeare," *Philological Quarterly*, 41#1: 18-36 (Jan, 1962).

Helton, Tinsley. "Shakespeare's *Love's Labour's Lost*, V, ii, 940-941," *The Explicator*, 22#4: 25 (Dec, 1963).

Heninger, S. K. "Chapman's *Hymnus in Noctem*, 376-377, and Shakespeare's *Love's Labour's Lost*, IV, iii, 346-347," *Explicator*, 16#8: 49 (May, 1958).

Hoy, Cyrus. *"Love's Labour's Lost* and the Nature of Comedy," *Shakespeare Quarterly*, 13#1: 31-40 (Winter, 1962).

ALSO IN: *The Hyacinth Room*, 22-38.

Jackson, M. "A Shakespeare Quibble," *Notes and Queries*, 207: 331-332 (Sept, 1962).

Low, J. T. *"Love's Labour's Lost,"* *The Use of English*, 12#4: 242-244 (Summer, 1961).

McCarthy, Mary. *Theater Chronicle*, 146-150.

Mahnken, Harry E. and J. S. Mahnken. "Harley Granville-Barker's Shakespearean Criticism," *Southern Speech Journal*, 27#1: 24 (Fall, 1961).

Matthews, William. "Language in *Love's Labour's Lost,"* *Essays and Studies (English Association)*, 17: 1-11 (1964).

Oakeshott, W. *The Queen and the Poet*, 100-130.

Pafford, J. H. "Schoole of Night *(L. L. L.* 4.3252)," *Notes and Queries,* 202: 143 (1957).

Parsons, Howard. "Cruxes in *Love's Labour's Lost,"* *Notes and Queries,* 200: 287-289 (July, 1955).

Parsons, Philip. "Shakespeare and the Mask," *Shakespeare Survey,* 16: 121-124 (1963).

Petti, Anthony G. "The Fox, the Ape, the Humble Bee and the Goose," *Neophilologus,* 44#3: 208-213 (July, 1960).

Phelps, John. "French Translations of a Passage in *Love's Labor's Lost,"* *Shakespeare Association Bulletin,* 22#2: 94 (April, 1947).

Ravich, Robert A. "A Psychoanalytic Study of Shakespeare's Early Plays," *Psychoanalytic Quarterly,* 33#3: 400-402 (July, 1964).

——————. "Shakespeare and Psychiatry," *Literature and Psychology,* 14#3-4: 101 (Summer, Fall, 1964).

Roesen, Bobbyann. *"Love's Labour's Lost,"* *Shakespeare Quarterly,* 4#4: 411-426 (Oct, 1953).

Schrickx, W. *Shakespeare's Early Contemporaries,* 235-238; 239-266.

Siler, H. D. "A French Pun in *Love's Labour Lost,"* *Modern Language Notes,* 60#2: 124-125 (Feb, 1945).

Stevenson, David Lloyd. "The Love-Game Comedy," *Columbia University Studies in English and Comparative Literature,* 164: 191-199 (1946).

Thompson, Karl F. "Shakespeare's Romantic Comedies," *PMLA,* 67#7: 1079-1085; 1091-1093 (Dec, 1952).

Ungerer, Gustav. "Two Items of Spanish Pronunciations in *Love's Labour's Lost,"* *Shakespeare Quarterly,* 14#3: 245-251 (Summer, 1963).

West, E. J. "On the Essential Theatricality of *Love's Labour's Lost,"* *College English,* 9#8: 427-429 (May, 1948).

MACBETH

Amneus, Daniel A. "The Cawdor Episode in *Macbeth,"* *Journal of English and Germanic Philology,* 63#2: 185-190 (April, 1964).

——————. "A Missing Scene in *Macbeth,"* *Journal of English and Germanic Philology,* 60#3: 435-440 (July, 1961).

Anderson, Ruth L. "The Foot of Motion," *Shakespeare Association Bulletin,* 22#2: 81-83 (April, 1957).

——————. "The Pattern of Behavior Culminating in

Macbeth," *Studies in English Literature 1500-1900,* 3#2. 151-174 (Spring, 1963).

Arnold, Aerol. "The Recapitulation Dream in *Richard III* and *Macbeth," Shakespeare Quarterly,* 6#1: 57-62 (Winter, 1955).

Aronson, Alex. "A Note on Shakespeare's Dream Imagery,' *Visuabharati Quarterly,* 18#2: 175-180 (Aug-Oct, 1952)

Arthos, John. "The Naive Imagination and the Destruction of Macbeth," *ELH,* 14#2: 114-126 (June, 1947).

Babock, Weston. "Macbeth's 'Cream-Fac'd Loone,' " *Shakespeare Quarterly,* 4#2: 199-202 (April, 1953).

Badawi, M. M. "Euphemism and Circumlocution in *Macbeth,'* *Cairo Studies in English,* pp. 25-46 (1960).

Bald, R. C. "Macbeth's 'Baby of a Girl' " *Shakespeare Association Bulletin,* 24#3: 220-222 (July, 1949).

Barrell, Charles W. "Dr. John Dover Wilson's 'New' *Macbeth," Shakespeare Fellowship Quarterly,* 8#4: 58-6 (Winter, 1947-1948).

Barron, David B. "The Babe That Milks: An Organic Study of *Macbeth," American Imago,* 17#2: 133-161 (Summer 1960).

Bateson, F. W. "Banquo and Edgar-Character or Function?" *Essays in Criticism,* 7#3: 324-325 (July, 1957).

Bernard, Miguel A. "The Five Tragedies in *Macbeth," Shakespeare Quarterly,* 13#1: 49-61 (Winter, 1962).

Berry, Francis. *Poet's Grammar,* 48-57.

—————. "*Macbeth:* Tense and Mood," *Orpheus (Revista di Umanita Classica e Christiana),* 6#1: 43-50 (1959).

Blau, Herbert. "Language and Structure in Poetic Drama," *Modern Lanuguage Quarterly,* 18: 33-34 (1957).

Blissett, William. "The Secret'st Man of Blood: A Study of Dramatic Irony in *Macbeth," Shakespeare Quarterly* 10#3: 379-408 (Summer, 1959).

Booth, Wayne C. "Macbeth as Tragic Hero," *Journal of General Education,* 6#1: 17-25 (Oct, 1951).

Bossler, Robert. "Was Macbeth a Victim of Battle Fatigue?" *College English,* 8#8: 436-438 (May, 1947).

Boyle Robert R. "The Imagery of *Macbeth,* I, vii, 21-28," *Modern Language Quarterly,* 16: 130-136 (1955).

Bradbrook, M. C. "The Sources of *Macbeth," Shakespeare Survey,* 4: 35-48 (1951).

Bradley, A. C. *Oxford Lectures on Poetry,* 87-90.

Brindley, D. J. "Reversal of Values in *Macbeth*," *English Studies in Africa*, 6#2: 137-143 (Sept, 1963).

Britton, John. "A. C. Bradley and Those Children of Lady Macbeth," *Shakespeare Quarterly*, 12#3: 349-351 (Summer, 1961).

Brooks, Cleanth. "The Naked Babe and the Cloak of Manliness," in *Well Wrought Urn*, 22-49.

Brooks, Cleanth and Robert Heilman. *Understanding Drama*, 668-673.

Burrell, Margaret D. "*Macbeth:* A Study in Paradox," *Shakespeare Jahrbuck*, 90: 167-190 (1954).

Burris, Quincy Guy. " 'Soft! Here Follows Prose'—*Twelfth Night*, II, v, 154," *Shakespeare Quarterly*, 2#3: 233-236 (July, 1951).

Campbell, Lily B. "Political Ideas in *Macbeth*, IV, iii," *Shakespeare Quarterly*, 2#4: 281-286 (Oct, 1951).

Campbell, Oscar James. "Shakespeare and the 'New' Critics," in James G. McManaway (ed), *Joseph Q. Adams Memorial Studies*, 85-91.

Carlisky, Mario. "Primal Scene, Procereation and The Number 13," *American Imago*, 19#1: 19-20 (Spring, 1962).

Clarke, C. C. "Darkened Reason in *Macbeth*," *Durham University Journal*, 53#1: 11-18 (Dec ,1960).

Clarkson, Paul S. *et. al.* "Copyhold Tenure and *Macbeth*, III, ii, 38," *Modern Language Notes*, 55#7: 483-493 (Nov, 1940).

Collmer, Robert G. "An Existentialist Approach to *Macbeth*," *The Personalist*, 41#4: 484-491 (Autumn, 1960).

Coombes, H. *Literature and Criticism*, 50-52.

Cossons, Judith. "*Macbeth*, I, vii," *Notes and Queries*, 196: 368 (18 Aug, 1951).

Craig, Hardin. *The Written Word*, 49-61.

Creeth, Edmund. "Moral and Tragic Recognition: The Uniqueness of *Othello, Macbeth,* and *King Lear*," *Michigan Academy of Science, Arts and Letters. Papers*, 45: 387-389 (1960).

Cunningham, Delora G. "*Macbeth:* The Tragedy of a Hardened Heart," *Shakespeare Quarterly*, 14#1: 39-48 (Winter, 1963).

Cunningham, James. *Woe or Wonder*, 20.

Dadawi, Muhammad M. "Euphemism and Circumlocution in *Macbeth*," *Bulletin of the Faculty of Arts (Alexandria University)*, 13: 101-122 (1959).

Daiches, David. *Critical Approaches to Literature*, 270-275.

Dasgupta, Arun Kumar. "A Note on *Macbeth* II, ii, 61-63," *Notes and Queries*, 205: 332-333 (Sept, 1960).

Davidson, Arthur. *The Solace of Literature*, 70-74.

Davies, Cecil W. "Action and Soliloquy in *Macbeth*," *Essays in Criticism*, 8#4: 451-453 (Oct, 1958).

De Quincey, Thomas. "On the Knicking at the Gate in *Macbeth*," in Mark Schorer (ed.), *Criticism*, 471-473.

Donner, H. W. "She Would Have Died Hereafter," *English Studies*, 40#5: 385-389 (Oct, 1959).

Donoghue, Denis. "Macklin's Shylock and Macbeth," *Studies*, 43: 425-430 (Winter, 1954).

Downer, Alan S. "The Life of Our Design," *Hudson Review*, 2#2: 252-254 (Summer, 1949).

Downer, Alan S. "Macready's Production in *Macbeth*," *Quarterly Journal of Speech*, 33#2: 172-181 (April, 1947).

Draper, John W. "Lady Macbeth," *Psychoanalytic Review*, 28#4: 479-486 (Oct, 1941).

——————. "Patterns of Humor and Tempo in *Macbeth*," *Neophilologus*, pp. 202-207 (Oct, 1947).

——————. "Subjective Conflict in Shakespearean Tragedy," *Neuphilolgische Mittleilungen*, 2#61: 216-217 (1960).

——————. "The 'Gracious Duncan'," *Modern Language Review*, 36#4: 495-499 (Oct, 1941).

Dyson, Peter. "The Structural Function of the Bouquet Scene in *Macbeth*," *Shakespeare Quarterly*, 14#4: 369-378 (Autumn, 1963).

Eastman, Fred. *Christ in the Drama*, 25-28; 31-35.

Elliott, G. R. "The Representatives of *Macbeth*," *Shakespeare Newsletter*, 4#3: 24 (May, 1954).

Ellis-Fermor, Una. *The Frontiers of Drama*, 50-52; 88-89.

——————. "The Nature of Character in Drama, With Special Reference to Tragedy," in C. L. Wrenn (ed.), *English Studies Today—First Series* (1950), 17-19.

——————. "The Nature of Plot in Drama," *Essays and Studies (English Association)*, 13: 77-80 (1960).

Empson, William. "Dover Wilson on *Macbeth*," *Kenyon Review*, 14#1: 84-102 (Winter, 1952).

Fairchild, A. H. R. "Shakespeare and the Tragic Theme," *University of Missouri Studies*, 19#2: 58-72; 105-140 (1944).

Fatout, Paul. "Shakespeare's *Macbeth*, II, ii, 40," The Explicator, 9#3: 22 (Dec, 1950).

Fergusson, Francis. *The Human Image in Dramatic Literature,* 115-125.

———. "Macbeth as the Imitation of an Action," *English Institute Essays,* pp. 31-43 (1951). ALSO IN: Robert W. Corrigan, *The Art of the Theatre,* 200-208.

Flatter, Richard. "Who Wrote the Hecate-Scene?" *Shakespeare Jahrbuck,* 94: 196-204 (1958).

———. "The Question of Free Will, and Other Observations on *Macbeth,*" *English Miscellany,* 10: 87-106 (1959).

Foakes, R. A. "Contrasts and Connections: Some Notes on Style in Shakespeare's Comedies and Tragedies," *Shakespeare Jahrbuck,* 90: 74-81 (1954).

———. "*Macbeth,*" *Stratford Papers on Shakespeare,* 3: 150-174 (1962).

Fraiberg, Louis. "Freud's Writings on Art," *Literature and Psychology,* 6#4: 122-123 (Nov, 1956).

Free, William J. "Shakespeare's *Macbeth,* III, iv, 122-126 and IV, i, 90-94," *The Explicator,* 19#7: 50 (April, 1961).

Frey, Leonard H. "The Shakespearian Symbolism in *The Sound and the Fury,*" *Faulkner Studies,* 2#3: 41-44 (Autumn, 1953).

Frye, Prosser H. *Romance and Tragedy,* 293-295.

Frye, Roland M. "Macbeth and the Powers of Darkness," *Emory University Quarterly,* 8#3: 164-174 (Oct, 1952).

———. "'Out, Out, Brief Candle' and the Jacobean Understanding," *Notes and Queries,* 200: 143-145 (April, 1955).

Fust, Milan. "On Staging Shakespeare," New *Hungarian Quarterly,* 5#13: 68-70 (Spring, 1964).

Gardner, Helen. "Milton's 'Satan' and the Theme of Damnation in Elizabethan Tragedy," *Essays and Studies (English Association),* 1: 53-55 (1948).

Gilbert, C. G. "*Macbeth,* V, iii, 22," *Notes and Queries,* 205: 33-34 (Sept, 1960).

Gillie, Christopher. "Banquo and Edgar—Character or Function?" *Essays in Criticism,* 7#3: 322-324 (July, 1957).

Glasson, T. Francis. "Did Shakespeare Read Aeschylus?" *London Quarterly and Holborn Review,* 173#1: 57-60 (Jan, 1948).

Glaz, A. Andre. "Iago or Moral Sadism," *American Imago,* 19#4: 323-348 (Winter, 1962).

Glencross, A. F. "Christian Tragedy," in A. Norton, *A Christian Approach to Western Literature,* 66-68.

Goode, Bill. "How the Lady Knew Her Lord: A Note on *Macbeth,*" *American Imago,* 20#4: 349-356 (Winter, 1963).

Goodman, Randolf. *Drama on Stage,* 116-142.

Gordon, R. K. "Scott and Shakespeare's Tragedies," *Royal Society of Canada Proceedings and Transactions,* 39 Sect. 2: 112-114; 117 (1945).

Grebanier, Bernard. "Lady Macbeth of London," *Shenandoah,* 13#4: 29-36 (Summer, 1962).

Halio, Jay L. "Bird Imagery in *Macbeth,*" *Shakespeare Newsletter,* 13#1: 7 (Feb, 1963).

Harcourt, John B. "I Pray You, Remember the Porter," *Shakespeare Quarterly,* 12#4: 393-402 (Autumn, 1961).

Hart, Walter M. "Shakespeare's Use of Verse and Prose," *University of California Publications. English Studies,* 10: 8-17 (1954).

Heilman, Robert B. "Twere Best not Know Myself: Othello, Lear, Macbeth," *Shakespeare Quarterly,* 15#2: 89-98 (Spring, 1964).

Henneberger, Olive. "Banquo, Loyal Subject," *College English,* 8#1: 18-22 (Oct, 1946).

Hewett, R. P. *Reading and Response,* 110-115.

Highet, G. *The Powers of Poetry,* 304-305.

Hodgart, M. J. C. "Shakespeare and *Finnegan's Wake,*" *Cambridge Journal,* 6#12: 743-746 (Sept, 1953).

Hoepfner, Theodore C. "Shakespeare's *Macbeth,* I, vii, 1-28," *The Explicator,* 7#5: 34 (March, 1949).

Holland, Norman N. "Macbeth as Hibernal Giant," *Literature and Psychology,* 10#2: 37-38 (Spring, 1960).

————————. "Freud on Shakespeare," *PMLA,* 75#3: 169-179 (July, 1960).

Holloway, John. "Dramatic Irony in Shakespeare," *Northern Miscellany of Literary Criticism,* 1: 3-10 (Autumn, 1953).

————————. *The Story of the Night,* 57-74.

Hunter, W. B. "Poe's 'The Sleeper' and *Macbeth,*" *American Literature,* 20: 55-57 (March, 1948).

Huntley, Frank L. "*Macbeth* and the Background of Jesuitical Equivocation," *PMLA,* 79#4: 390-400 (Sept, 1964).

Hyam, Lawrence W. "*Macbeth:* The Hand and the Eye," *Tennessee Studies in Literature,* 5: 97-100 (1960).

Hyde, Isabel. "*Macbeth:* A Problem," *English,* 13#75: 91-94 (Autumn, 1960).

Hyman, Laurence W. *"Macbeth:* The Hand and the Eye," *Tennessee Studies in Literature,* 5: 97-100 (1960).

Jack, Jane H. *"Macbeth,* King James, and the Bible," *ELH,* 22#3: 173-193 (Sept, 1955).

Jekels, Ludwig. "The Riddle of Shakespeare's *Macbeth,"* *Psychoanalytic Review,* 30#4: 361-385 (Oct, 1943).
ALSO IN: *Selected Papers,* 105-130.

Jepsen, Laura. *Ethical Aspects of Tragedy,* 27-31.

Johnson, Francis R. "Shakespearean Imagery and Senecan Imitation," in James G. McManaway (ed), *Joeseph Q. Adams Memorial Studies,* 43-53.

Joseph, Bertram L. "Character and Plot," *Drama Survey,* 4#4: 541-546 (Fall, 1964).

Kantak, V. Y. "An Approach to Shakespearian Tragedy: The 'Actor' Image in *Macbeth,"* *Shakespeare Survey,* 16: 42-52 (1963).

Kavanagh, Mary. "The Weird Sisters of *Macbeth,"* *Baconiana,* 32#127: 72-74 (Oct, 1948).

Kirschbaum, Leo. "Banquo and Edgar: Character or Function?" *Essays in Criticism,* 7#1: 1-8 (Jan, 1957).

Knight, G. Wilson. *The Christian Renaissance,* 45-47; 186-187.
————. *Explorations,* 31-54.
————. *The Golden Labyrinth,* 75-77; 231-233.
————. "The Milk of Concord: An Essay on the Life Themes in *Macbeth,"* in *The Imperial Theme,* 125-153; 327-342.
ALSO IN: Robert Stallman (ed), *Critiques and Essays in Criticism.* 119-140.
————. *The Olive and the Sword,* 54-58.
————. *The Sovereign Flower,* 58-64; 280-286.
————. "Brutus and *Macbeth,"* in *The Wheel of Fire,* 120-139 (1962 ed.).
————. *"Macbeth* and the Metaphysics of Evil," *The Wheel of Fire,* 140-159 (1962 ed.).

Knights, L. C. "On the Background of Shakespeare's Use of Nature in *Macbeth,"* *Sewanee Review,* 64#2: 207-217 (Spring, 1956).
————. "Shakespeare's Politics: With Some Reflections on the Nature of Tradition," *Annual Shakespeare Lecture of the British Academy,* p. 121 (1957).
————. *"King Lear* and the Great Tragedies," *Guide to English Literature,* 2: 233-237.

Knoepfle, John. *"Macbeth:* Despair in Seven Stages," *Shakespeare Newsletter,* 9#4: 26 (Sept, 1959).

Kocher, Paul H. "Lady Macbeth and the Doctor," *Shakespeare Quarterly,* 5#4: 341-350 (Autumn, 1954).

Law, Robert A. "The Composition of *Macbeth* With Reference to Holinshed," *Studies in English (University of Texas),* 31: 35-41 (1952).

Leaska, Mitchell. *The Voice of Tragedy,* 108-117.

Leavis, F. R. "Tragedy and the 'Medium'," *Scrutiny,* 12#4: 249-253 (Autumn, 1944).

ALSO IN: *The Common Pursuit,* 123-126.

ALSO IN: Eric Bentley. *The Importance of Scrutiny,* 214-218.

——————————. *Education and the University,* 78182; 121-125.

Lees, F. N. "A Biblical Connotation in *Macbeth,*" *Notes and Queries,* 195: 534 (9 Dec, 1950).

Lerner, Laurence. "Tragedy: Religious, Humanist," *Review of English Literature,* 2#4: 28-33 (Oct, 1961).

Levich, Marvin. *Aesthetics and the Philosophy of Criticism,* 228-229.

Loomis, E. A. "Master of the Tiger," *Shakespeare Quarterly,* 7: 457 (1956).

Lord, John B. "Comic Scenes in Shakespearean Tragedy," *Washington State College Research Studies,* 32#3: 238 (Sept, 1964).

Lucas, Frank L. *Literature and Psychology,* 76-77.

Lynch, James J. "Macduff, not Macbeth," *Modern Language Notes,* 56#8: 603-604 (Dec, 1941).

McCarthy, Mary. *Theater Chronicle,* 235-248.

McCollom, William G. *Tragedy,* 51-56.

McCutchan, J. Wilson. "He Has no Children," *McNeese Review,* 8: 41-52 (Spring, 1956).

McDonnell, R. F. *The Aspiring Mind,* 265-293.

Mack, Maynard. "The Jacobean Shakespear: Some Observations on the Construction of the Tragedies," *Stratford-Upon-Avon Studies,* 1: 11-42 (1960).

McNulty, J. H. "Bleak House and *Macbeth,*" *Dickensian,* 40: 188-190 (Autumn, 1944).

Makey, H. O. "In the Literature Class: Study of the Opening Scenes of *Macbeth,*" *English Journal,* 39: 360-366 (Sept, 1950).

Markels, Julian. "The Spectacle of Deterioration: *Macbeth* and the 'Manner' of Tragic Imitation," *Shakespeare Quarterly,* 12#3: 293-303 (Summer, 1961).

Mataraly, P. V. "The Hidden Cipher in the Porter's Soliloquy in *Macbeth,*" *Baconiana,* 32#129: 226-228.

Maxwell, B. (ed). "That Undiscovered Country," in *Renaissance Studies in Honor of Hardin Craig,* 230-235.

Maxwell, J. C. "The Ghost From the Grave: A Note on Shakespeare's Apparitions," *Durham University Journal,* 48#2: 58 (March, 1956).

——————. *"Macbeth,* 4, ii, 107," *Modern Language Review,* 51: 73 (1956).

——————. "Montaigne and *Macbeth,*" *Modern Language Review,* 43#1: 77-78 (Jan, 1948).

Mincoff, Marco. "The Structural Pattern of Shakespeare's Tragedies," *Shakespeare Survey,* 3: 63-65 (1950).

Mitchell, Lee. "Shakespeare's Legerdemain," *Speech Monographs,* 16#1: 144-152; 154-157; 160-161 (August, 1949).

Morozov, Mikhail M. "The Individualization of Shakespeare's Characters Through Imagery," *Shakespeare Survey,* 2: 83-84; 88-93 (1949).

Morris, Harry. *"Macbeth,* Dante, and the Greatest Evil," *Shakespeare Newsletter,* 12#1: 3 (Feb, 1962).

Muir, Kenneth. "Some Freudian Interpretations of Shakespeare," *Proceedings of the Leeds Philosophical and Literary Society,* 7Pt.1: 46 (July, 1952).

Murphy, George H. "Reflections on the Tragedies of Shakespeare," *Dalhousie Review,* 36#3: 271-273 (Aut, 1956).

Myers, Henry A. *Tragedy: A View of Life,* 13-15; 105-109.

Myrick, Kenneth O. "The Theme of Damnation in Shakespearean Tragedy," *Studies in Philology,* 38#2: 230-234 (April, 1941).

Nag, V. C. "Macbeth: A Character Study," in V. N. Bhushan (ed.), *The Moving Finger,* 194-212.

Nagarajan, S. "A Note on Banquo," *Shakespeare Quarterly,* 7#4: 371-376 (Autumn, 1956).

Nathan, Norman. "Duncan, Macbeth, and Jeremiah," *Notes and Queries,* 199: 243 (June, 1954).

Noel, J. "Shakespeare Criticism Today," *Revue des Langues Vivantes,* 26: 465 (1960).

Norgaard, Holger. "The Bleeding Captain Scene in *Macbeth* and Daniel's *Cleopatra,*" *Review of English Studies,* NS6#24: 395-396 (Oct, 1955).

Nosworthy, J. M. "The Bleeding Captain Scene in *Macbeth,*" *Review of English Studies,* 22#86: 126-130 (April, 1946).

Nosworthy, J. M. "The Hecate Scenes in *Macbeth,*" *Review of English Studies,* 24: 138-139 (April, 1948).

Olson, Elder. *Tragedy and the Theory of Drama,* 45-46; 113-125.

Ornstein, Robert. *The Moral Vision of Tragedy,* 230-234.

Pack, Robert. *"Macbeth:* The Anatomy of Loss," *Yale Review,* 45: 533-548 (1956).

Paolucci, Anne. *"Macbeth* and *Oedipus Rex,"* The City College *Papers,* 1: 44-70 (1964).

Parsons, Howard. *"Macbeth* Conjectures," *Notes and Queries,* 198: 464-466 (Nov, 1953).

——————. *"Macbeth:* Emendations," *Notes and Queries,* 199: 331-333 (Aug, 1954).

——————. *"Macbeth:* Some Emendations," *Notes and Queries,* 197: 403 (13 Sept, 1952).

——————. *"Macbeth:* Some Further Conjectures," *Notes and Queries,* 198: 54-55 (Feb, 1953).

——————. "Shakespeare's Emendations," *Notes and Queries,* 196: 27-29 (20 Jan, 1951).

Paul, Henry N. "The Imperial Theme in *Macbeth,"* in James G. McManaway (ed), *Joseph Q. Adams Memorial Studies,* 253-268.

Perma, B. S. "Lady Macbeth and Clytemnestra," *The Literary Criterion (Mysore),* pp. 15-19 (1952).

Pinto, V. de Sola. "Shakespeare and the Dictators," *Essays by Divers Hands,* 21: 96-99 (1944).

Pogson, Beryl. *In the East My Pleasure Lies,* 85-91.

. Purdie, Edna. "Observations on Some Eighteenth Century German Versions of the Witches Scene in *Macbeth,"* *Shakespeare Jahrbuck,* 92: 96-109 (1956).

Purdom, C. B. "Who was the Third Murderer in Macbeth?" *The Shakespeare Stage,* #6-7: 49-53 (Sept-Dec, 1954).

Quiller-Couch, Sir Arthur. *Cambridge Lectures,* 137-178.

. Reed, Robert R. Jr. "The Fatal Elizabethan Sisters in *Macbeth,"* *Notes and Queries,* 200: 425-427 (Oct, 1955).

Ribner, Irving. *"Macbeth:* The Pattern of Idea and Action," *Shakespeare Quarterly,* 10#2: 147-159 (Spring, 1959).

——————. "Marlowe and Shakespeare," *Shakespeare Quarterly,* 15#2: 49-51 (Spring, 1964).

——————. "Political Doctrine in *Macbeth,"* Shakespeare *Quarterly,* 4#2: 202-205 (April, 1953).
ALSO IN: Irving Ribner, *The English History Play in the Age of Shakespeare,* 254-259.

——————. "Shakespeare's Christianity and the Problem of Belief," *Centenniel Review,* 8#1: 103-106 (Winter, 1964).

Robb, Stewart. *"Macbeth and* James I," *Baconiana,* 35#141: 219-220 (Oct, 1951).

Roddier, Henri. "A Freudian Detective's Shakespeare," *Modern Philology,* 48#2: 122-125 (Nov, 1950).

Roth, Robert. "Another World of Shakespeare," *Modern Philology,* 49#1: 55-58 (Aug, 1951).

Ruggles, Henry I. "Bacon and *Macbeth,"* *Baconiana,* 25#97: 81-91 (Oct, 1940).

Sandoe, James. *"Macbeth,"* *Shakespeare Newsletter,* 8#4: 28 (Sept, 1958).

Sanford, Ernest. "Shakespeare's Comic Relief," *Central Literary Magazine,* pp. 170-171 (Nov, 1945).

Santayana, George. "Tragic Philosophy," in Eric Bentley, *The Importance of Scrutiny,* 203-205.

Schanzer, Ernest. "Four Notes on *Macbeth,"* *Modern Language Review,* 52#2: 223-227 (April, 1957).

Schoff, F. G. "Shakespeare's 'Fair is Foul'," *Notes and Queries,* 199: 241-243 (June, 1954).

Shanley, Lyndon. *"Macbeth:* The Tragedy of Evil," *College English,* 22#5: 305-311 (Feb, 1961).

Sherbo, Arthur. "Dr. Johnson on *Macbeth:* 1745 and 1746," *Review of English Studies,* NS2#5: 40-47 (Jan, 1951).

Siegel, Paul N. "Echoes of the Bible Story in *Macbeth,"* *Notes and Queries,* 200: 142-143 (April, 1955).

——————. "In Defense of Bradley," *College English,* 9#5: 250-252 (Feb, 1948).

Sitwell, Edith. *"Macbeth,"* *Atlantic Monthly,* 185: 43-48 (April, 1950).

Smith, Fred Manning. "The Relation of *Macbeth* to *Richard the Third,"* *PMLA,* 60#4: 1003-1020 (Dec, 1945).

Smith, Grover. "The Naked New-Born in *Macbeth:* Some Iconographical Evidence," *Renaissance Papers,* pp. 21-27 (1964).

Smith, R. M. "Macbeth's 'Cyme' Once More," *Modern Language Notes,* 60#1: 33-38 (Jan, 1945).

Spargo, John Webster. "The Knocking at the Gate in James G. McManaway (ed), *Joseph Q. Adams Memorial Studies,* 269-277.

Speaight, Robert. "Nature and Grace in *Macbeth,"* *Essays by Divers Hands,* 27: 89-108 (1955).

Spencer, Theodore. "The Isolation of the Shakespearean Hero," *Sewanee Review,* 52#3: 326-327 (July/Sept, 1944).

Spivack, Charlott. *"Macbeth* and Dante's *Inferno," North Dakota University Quarterly,* 28#2: 50-52 (Spring, 1960).

Stein, Arnold. "Macbeth and Word Magic," *Sewanee Review,* 59#2: 271-284 (Spring, 1951).

Stewart, J. I. M. *"Julius Caesar* and *Macbeth.* Two Notes on Shakespearean Technique," *Modern Language Review,* 40#3: 171-173 (July, 1945).

Stirling, Brents. "The Unity of *Macbeth," Shakespeare Quarterly,* 4#4: 385-394 (Oct, 1953).

Stone, George Winchester Jr. "Garrick's Handling of *Macbeth," Studies in Philology,* 38#4: 609-628 (Oct, 1941).

Strindberg, August. *"Macbeth," Adam International Review,* 190-191: 22-23 (1949).

Stunz, Arthur N. "The Date of *Macbeth," ELH,* 9#2: 95-105 (June, 1942).

Styan, J. L. *The Elements of Drama,* 130-132; 141-142; 273-274.

Syrkin, Marie. "Youth and Lady MacDuff," *A.A.U.P. Bulletin,* 40#2: 317-319 (Summer, 1954).
ALSO IN: *The Use of English,* 8#4: 257-258 (Summer, 1957).

Thurber, James. "The *Macbeth* Murder Mystery," in K. L. Knickerbocker and H. Willard Reninger (eds), *Interpreting Literature,* 805-807.

Tomlinson, T. B. "Action and Soliloquy in *Macbeth," Essays in Criticism,* 8#2: 147-155 (April, 1958).

Tucker, Susie I. "Johnson and the Lady Macbeth," *Notes and Queries,* 201: 210-211 (1956).

Tucker, William John. "Irish Aspects of Shakespeare," *Catholic World,* 156: 699-700 (March, 1943).

Waith, Eugene M. "Manhood and Valor in Two Shakespearean Tragedies," *ELH,* 17#4: 265-268 (Dec, 1950).

Weisinger, Herbert. *The Agony and the Triumph,* 110-112.

West, Robert H. "Night's Black Agents in *Macbeth," Renaissance Papers,* pp. 17-24 (1956).

Westbrook, Perry D. "A Note on *Macbeth,* Act II, Scene 1," *College English,* 7#4: 219-220 (Jan, 1946).

White, W. "Time in *Wallenstein* and *Macbeth," Abedreen University Review,* 34#3: 217-224 (Spring, 1952).

Wilson, Harold S. "Comentary," *Shakespeare Quarterly,* 9#3: 307-310 (Summer, 1958).

Wood, James O. "Hecate's 'Vap'rous' Drop, Profound," *Notes and Queries,* 209: 262-264 (July, 1964).

————. "Two Notes on *Macbeth*," *Notes and Queries,* 209: 137-138 (April, 1964).

Wrenn, C. L. and G. Bullough (eds). *English Studies Today* —First Series (1950), 17-19.

Young, Stark. *Immortal Shadows,* 96-100.

Zitner, Sheldon P. *"Macbeth* and the Moral Scale of Tragedy," *Journal of General Education,* 16#1 : 20-28 (April, 1964).

MEASURE FOR MEASURE

Babb, Lawrence. *The Elizabethan Malady,* 148-149.

Battenhouse, Henry W. *Poets of Christian Thought,* 39-42.

Battenhouse, Roy W. *"Measure for Measure* and Christian Doctrine of the Atonement," *PMLA,* 61#4: 1029-1059 (Dec, 1946).

Beardsley, Munroe. *Aesthetics,* 56-57.

Biggens, O. *"Measure for Measure* and *The Heart of Midlothian,"* *Etudes Anglaises,* 14#3 : 193-205 (July-Sept. 1961).

Bradbrook, M. C. "Authority, Truth and Justice in *Measure for Measure,"* *Review of English Studies,* 17#68 : 385-399 (Oct, 1941).

Brewer, D. S. *"Measure for Measure,* I. i, 3-9," *Notes and Queries,* 200: 425 (Oct, 1955).

Brown, John R. "Mr. Beckett's Shakespeare," *Critical Quarterly,* 5#4: 323-324 (Winter, 1963).

Campbell, Oscar James. "Shakespeare and the 'New' Critics," in James G. McManaway (ed), *Joseph Q. Adams Memmorial Studies,* 91-93.

Caputi, Anthony. "Scenic Design in *Measure for Measure,"* *Journal of English and Germanic Philology,* 60#3 : 423-434 (July, 1961).

Chambers, R. W. *Man's Unconquerable Mind,* 277-310.

Coghill, Nevill. "Comic Form in *Measure for Measure,"* *Shakespeare Survey,* 8: 14-27 (1955).

Cook, Albert. "Metaphysical Poetry and *Measure for Measure,"* *Accent,* 13#2: 122-127 (Spring, 1953).

Coombes, H. *Literature and Criticism,* 71-72.

Curry, John V. *Deception in Elizabethan Comedy,* 63-64; 152-154.

Cutts, John P. "Perfect Contrition: A Note on *Measure for Measure,"* *Notes and Queries,* 205: 416-419 (Nov, 1960).

Daiche, David. *Critical Approaches to Literature,* 349-355.

Dickinson, John W. "Renaissance Equity and *Measure for Measure,"* *Shakespeare Quarterly,* 13#3: 287-297 (Summer, 1962).

Dodds, W. M. T. "The Character of Angelo in *Measure for Measure,*" *Modern Language Review,* 41#3: 246-255 (July, 1946).

Draper, John W. "Patterns of Tempo in *Measure for Measure,*" *University of West Virginia Bulletin: Philological Papers,* 9: 11-19 (1953).

Dunkel, Wilbur. "Law and Equity in *Measure for Measure,*" *Shakespeare Quarterly,* 13#3: 275-285 (Summer, 1962).

Dutton, Geoffrey. "London Letter: A Measure for a Cocktail," *Meanjin Papers,* 42: 204-206 (Spring, 1950).

Empson, William. "Sense in *Measure for Measure,*" *Southern Review,* 4#2: 340-350 (Autumn, 1938).
ALSO IN: *The Structure of Complex Words,* 270-284.

Felver, Charles S. "A Proverb Turned Jest in *Measure for Measure,*" *Shakespeare Quarterly,* 11#3: 385-387 (Summer, 1960).

Fergusson, Francis. "Philosophy and Theatre in *Measure for Measure,*" *Kenyon Review,* 14#1: 103-120 (Winter, 1952).
ALSO IN: *The Human Image in Dramatic Literature,* 126-143.

Finkelstein, Sidney. "On Updating Shakespeare: Part II," *Mainstream,* 14#8: 35-40 (Aug, 1961).

Freedman, William A. "The Duke in *Measure for Measure,*" *Tennessee Studies in Literature,* 9: 31-38 (1964).

Gabor, Miklos. "An Actor's Thoughts," *New Hungarian Quarterly,* 5#13: 71 (Spring, 1964).

Gibian, George. "*Measure for Measure* and Puskin's *Angelo,*" *PMLA,* 66#4: 426-431 (June, 1951).

Hall, Lawrence S. "Isabella's Angry Ape," *Shakespeare Quarterly,* 15#3: 157-160 (Summer, 1964).

Hankins, John E. "Pains of the Afterworld in Milton and Shakespeare," *PMLA,* 71#3: 487-495 (June, 1956).

Hapgood, Robert. "The Provost and Equity in *Measure for Measure,*" *Shakespeare Quarterly,* 15#1: 114-115 (Winter, 1964).

Harbage, Alfred. "Shakespeare and the Myth of Perfection," *Shakespeare Quarterly,* 15#2: 7-10 (Spring, 1964).

Harding, Davis P. "Elizabethan Bethrothals and *Measure for Measure,*" *Journal of English and Germanic Philology,* 49#2: 139-148 (April, 1950).

Harrison, John L. "The Convention of Heart and Tongue and the Meaning of *Measure for Measure,*" *Shakespeare Quarterly,* 5#1: 1-10 (Jan, 1954).

Hart, Edward L. "A Mixed Consort: Leontes, Angelo, Helena," *Shakespeare Quarterly,* 15#1: 79-80 (Winter, 1964).

Hethmon, Robert H. "The Theatrical Design of *Measure for Measure,*" *Drama Survey,* 1#3: 261-277 (Feb, 1962).

Holland, Norman L. " 'Do' or 'Die' in *Measure for Measure,* I. iii. 43," *Notes and Queries,* 202: 52 (1957).

——————. "*Measure for Measure:* The Duke and the Prince," *Comparative Literature (Oregon),* 11#1: 16-20 (Winter, 1959).

Holloway, John. "Dramatic Irony in Shakespeare," *Northern Miscellany of Literary Criticism,* 1: 13-16 (Autumn, 1953).

Hoy, Cyrus H. *The Hyacinth Room,* 11-15.

——————. "Comedy, Tragedy, Tragicomedy," *Virginia Quarterly Review,* 36#1: 110-114 (Winter, 1960).

Hulme, Hilda. "Three Notes: *Troilus and Cressida,* V. vii. 11; *Midsummer Night's Dream,* II. i. 54; *Measure for Measure,* II. i. 39," *Journal of English and Germanic Philology,* 57#4: 724-725 (Oct, 1958).

Hunter, G. K. "Six Notes on *Measure for Measure,*" *Shakespeare Quarterly,* 15#3: 167-172 (Summer, 1964).

Hyman, Lawrence W. "Mariana in *Measure for Measure,*" *University Review,* 31#2: 123-127 (Dec, 1964).

Kaufman, Helen A. "Trappolin Supposed a Prince and *Measure for Measure,*" *Modern Language Quarterly,* 18: 113-124 (1957).

Knight, G. Wilson. *The Olive and the Sword,* 44-47.

——————. "*Measure for Measure* and the Gospels," in *The Wheel of Fire,* 73-96 (1962 ed.).

Knights, L. C. "The Ambiguity of *Measure for Measure,*" *Scrutiny,* 10#3: 222-232 (Jan, 1942).
ALSO IN: Eric Bentley, *The Importance of Scrutiny,* 141-149.

Krieger, Murray. "*Meascre for Measure* and Elizabethan Comedy," *PMLA,* 66#5: 75-784 (Sept, 1951).

Krumpelmann, John T. "Kleist's *Krug* and Shakespeare's *Measure for Measure,*" *Germanic Review,* 26#1: 13-21 (Feb, 1951).

Lacy, Margaret S. *The Jacobean Problem Play,* 1-6; 136-165.

Lascelles, Mary. " 'Glassie Essence', *Measure for Measure,* II. ii. 120," *Review of English Studies,* 2NS#6: 140-142 (April, 1951).

Lawrence, W. W. *"Measure for Measure* and Lucio," *Shakespeare Quarterly,* 9#4: 443-454 (Autumn, 1958).

Leavis, F. R. "The Greatness of *Measure for Measure,"* *Scrutiny,* 10#3: 234-246 (Jan, 1942).
      ALSO IN: *The Common Pursuit,* 160-172.
      ALSO IN: Eric Bentley, *The Importance of Scrutiny,* 150-162.

Leech, Clifford. "The 'Meaning' of *Measure for Measure,"* *Shakespeare Survey,* 3: 66-73 (1950).
      ――――――――――. "Shakespeare's Comic Dukes, *Review of English Literature,* 5#2: 110-113 (April, 1964).

Lever, J. W. "The Date of *Measure for Measure,"* *Shakespeare Quarterly,* 10#3: 381-388 (Summer, 1959).

McCollom, William G. *Tragedy,* 13-14; 105-106; 126-127; 197-199.

McGinn, Donald J. "The Precise Angelo," in James G. McManaway (ed), *Joseph Q. Adams Memorial Studies,* 129-139.

Mackay, Eleen. *"Measure for Measure,"* *Shakespeare Quarterly,* 14#2: 109-114 (Spring, 1963).

Marsh, D. R. C. "The Mood of *Measure for Measure,"* *Shakespeare Quarterly,* 14#1: 31-38 (Winter, 1963).

Maxwell, J. C. *"Measure for Measure:* A Footnote to Recent Criticism," *Downside Review,* 65#199: 45-59 (Jan, 1947).
      ――――――――――. "Creon and Angelo: A Parallel Study," *Greece and Rome,* 18#52: 32-36 (Jan, 1949).
      ――――――――――. "Shakespeare: The Middle Plays," *Guide to English Literature,* 2: 212-215.

Melsome, W. S. "Bacon and *Measure for Measure,"* *Baconiana,* 25#101: 264-279 (Oct, 1941).

Merchant, W. M. "Lawyer and Actor: Process of Law in Elizabethan Drama," in G. I. Duthie (ed), *English Studies Today—Third Series* (1964), 107-108.

Mikkelsen, Robert S. "To Catch a Saint: Angelo in *Measure for Measure,"* *Western Humanities Review,* 12#3: 261-275 (Summer, 1958).

Millet, Stanton. "The Structure of *Measure for Measure,"* *Boston University Studies in English,* 2#4: 207-217 (Winter, 1956).

Musgrave, S. "Some Composite Scenes in *Measure for Measure,"* *Shakespeare Quarterly,* 15#1: 67-74 (Winter, 1964).

Nagarajan, S. *"Measure for Measure* and Elizabethan Bethrothals," *Shakespeare Quarterly,* 14#2: 115-120 (Spring, 1963).

Nathan, Norman. "The Marriage of Duke Vincentio and Isabella," *Shakespeare Quarterly,* 7#1: 43-45 (Winter, 1956).

Ornstein, R. *The Moral Vision of Jacobean Tragedy,* 250-260. ALSO IN: *University of Kansas City Review,* 24#1: 15-22 (Aut, 1957).

Peterson, Doublas L. *"Measure for Measure* and the Anglican Doctrine of Contrition," *Notes and Queries,* 209#4: 135-137 (Apr, 1964).

Pogson, Beryl. "A Psychological Study of *Measure for Measure,*" *Baconiana,* 33#130: 35-42 (Jan, 1949).

—————————. *In the East My Pleasure Lies,* 58-69.

Pope, E. M. "The Renaissance Background of *Measure for Measure,*" *Shakespeare Survey,* 2: 66-82 (1949).

—————————. "Shakespeare on Hell," *Shakespeare Quarterly,* 1#3: 162-164 (July, 1950).

Prouty, C. T. "George Whetsone and the Sources of *Measure for Measure,*" *Shakespeare Quarterly,* 15#2: 131-145 (Spring, 1964).

Roscelli, William John. "Isabella, Sin and Civil Law," *University of Kansas City Review,* 28#3: 215-227 (Spring, 1962).

S., P. "Shakespeare's Ladies: Portia," *Baconiana,* 34:137: 230-233 (Oct, 1950).

Sachs, Hans. "The Measure in *Measure for Measure,*" *American Imago,* 1#1: 60-81 (Nov, 1939). ALSO IN: The Creative Unconscious, 63-99.

Schanzer, Ernest. "The Marriage Contracts in *Measure for Measure,*" *Shakespeare Survey,* 13: 81-89 (1960).

Sennett, M. "The Wisdom of Shakespeare," *Baconiana,* 34#134: 32-38 (Jan, 1950).

Siegel, Paul N. *"Measure for Measure:* The Significance of the Title," *Shakespeare Quarterly,* 317-320 (July, 1953).

—————————. "Angelo's Precise Guards," *Philological Quarterly,* 29#4: 442-443 (Oct, 1950).

Sjogren, G. "The Setting of *Measure for Measure,*" *Revue de Litterature Comparee,* 35#1: 25-39 (Jan, 1961).

Slack, Robert C. *"Measure for Measure,*" *Carnegie Series in English,* 4: 19-36 (1958).

Smith, Robert M. "Interpretations of *Measure for Measure,*" *Shakespeare Quarterly,* 1#4: 208-218 (Oct, 1950).

Smith, W. D. "More Light on *Measure for Measure,*" *Modern Language Quarterly,* 23: 309-322 (Dec, 1962).

Southall, Raymond. *"Measure for Measure* and the Protestant Ethic," *Essays in Criticism,* 11#1: 10-33 (Jan, 1961).

Stevenson, David L. "Design and Structure in *Measure for Measure:* A New Appraisal," *ELH,* 23#4: 256-278 (Dec, 1956).

———. "The Role of James I in Shakespeare's *Measure for Measure,"* *ELH,* 26#1&2: 188-208 (June, 1959).

Sypher, Wylie. "Shakespeare as Casuist: *Measure for Measure,"* *Sewanee Review,* 58#2: 262-280 (Spring, 1950).

Thaler, Alwin. "The 'Devil's Crest' in *Measure for Measure,"* *Studies in Philology,* 50#2: 188-194 (April, 1953).

Traversi, D. A. *"Measure for Measure,"* *Scrutiny,* 11#1: 40-58 (Summer, 1942).

Wasson, John. *"Measure for Measure:* A Play of Incontinence," *ELH,* 27#4: 262-275 (Dec, 1960).

Weisinger, Herbert. "Myth, Method, and Shakespeare," *Journal of General Education,* 16#1: 45-48 (April, 1964).

———. "A Shakespeare All Too Modern," *Arizona Quarterly,* 20#4: 308-313 (Winter, 1964).

West, Rebecca. *The Court and the Castle,* 44-48.

Whitaker, Virgil K. "Philosophy and Romance in Shakespeare's 'Problem' Comedies," in Richard F. Jones, *et. al., Seventeenth Century: Studies in the History of English Thought,* 351-354.

Wiles, R. M. *"Measure for Measure:* Failure in the Study, Triumph on the Stage," *Royal Society of Canada Proceeding and Transactions,* 2Sect.2: 181-193 (June, 1964).

Wilson, H. S. "Action and Symbol in *Measure for Measure* and *The Tempest,"* *Shakespeare Quarterly,* 4#4: 375-384 (Oct, 1953).

MERCHANT OF VENICE, THE

Arial, J. M. "In Defense of Bassanio," *Shakespeare Association Bulletin,* 16#1: 25-28 (Jan, 1941).

Bailey, Margery. "Shakespeare in Action," *College English,* 15#6: 310-311 (March, 1954).

Barrell, Charles W. "Historical Background of *The Merchant of Venice,"* *Shakespeare Fellowship Quarterly,* 8#3: 44-47 (Autumn, 1947).

Bishop, David H. "Shylock's Humor," *Shakespeare Association Bulletin,* 23#4: 174-180 (Oct, 1948).

Bloom, Allan. "Shakespeare on Jew and Christian: An Interpretation of *The Merchant of Venice," Social Research,* 30#1: 1-22 (Spring, 1963).

Bradbrook, F. W. "Shylock and *King Lear," Notes and Queries,* 202: 142-143 (1957).

Brooks, Charles. "Shakespeare's Heroine-Actresses," *Shakespeare Jahrbuck,* 96: 137-139 (1960).

Brown, John Russell. "The Realization of Shylock: A Theatrical Criticism," *Stratford-Upon-Avon Studies,* 3: 187-210 (1961).

Bullough, Geoffrey. *Mirror of Minds,* 65-68.

Burckhardt, Sigurd. *"The Merchant of Venice:* The Gentle Bond," *ELH,* 29#3: 239-262 (Sept, 1962).

Carnousky, Morris. "Mirror of Shylock," *Tulane Drama Review,* 3#1: 35-45 (Oct, 1958).

Chambers, R. W. *Man's Unconquerable Mind,* 407-408.

Clurman, H. *Lies Like Truth,* 151-153.

Cohen, Hening. "Shakespeare's *Merchant of Venice* II. vii. 8-79," *Shakespeare Quarterly,* 2#1: 79 (Jan, 1951).

Danks, K. B. "The Case of Antonio's Melancholy," *Notes and Queries,* 199: 111 (March, 1954).

Deshpande, M. G. "Loneliness in *The Merchant of Venice," Essays in Criticism,* 11#3: 368-369 (July, 1961).

Dillingham, William B. "Antonio and Black Bile," *Notes and Queries,* 202: 419 (Oct, 1957).

Donoghue, Denis. "Macklin's Shylock and Macbeth," *Studies,* 43: 420-425 (Winter, 1954).

Draper, John W. "Usury in *The Merchant of Venice," Modern Philology,* 33: 37-47 (1953).

Engle, Anita. "New Thesis on Origin of *The Merchant of Venice:* Was Shylock a Jew?" *Jewish Quarterly,* 1#2: 13-18 (Summer, 1953).

Finklestein, Sidney. "Shakespeare's Shylock," *Mainstream,* 15#6: 26-42 (June, 1962).

Fisch, Harold. *The Dual Image,* 24-25; 29-35.

Fodor, A. "Shakespeare's Portia," *American Imago,* 16#1: 49-64 (Spring, 1959).

Galloway, David. "Alcides and His 'Rage': A Note on *The Merchant of Venice," Notes and Queries,* 201: 330-331 (Aug, 1956).

Gamal, Sand M. "The Function of Song in Shakespeare's Comedies," *Cairo Studies in English,* pp. 115-117 (1961/62).

Garrett, John. *"The Merchant of Venice," Shakespeare Newsletter,* 6#4: 31 (Sept, 1956).

Gordon, Cyrus H. "A Daniel Come to Judgement," *Shakespeare Association Bulletin,* 15#4: 206-209 (Oct, 1940).

Gorelik, Mordecai. "This Side Idolatry," *Educational Theatre Journal,* 3: 189-191 (Oct, 1951).

Graham, Cary B. "Standards of Value in *The Merchant of Venice,*" *Shakespeare Quarterly,* 4#2: 145-151 (April, 1953).

Hannigan, John E. "Which Daniel," *Shakespeare Association Bulletin,* 16#1: 63-64 (Jan, 1941).

Hegedus, Geza. *"The Merchant of Venice* and Problems of Civil Law in the Renaissance," *New Hungarian Quarterly,* 5#13: 33-44 (Spring, 1964).

Heller, Arthur D. "Jewish Characters in World Theatre," *Jewish Quarterly,* 4#1: 21 (Summer, 1956).

Hulme, Hilde M. "Three Notes on *The Merchant of Venice,*" *Neophilologus,* pp. 46-50 (Jan, 1957).

Hurrell, J. D. "Love and Friendship in *The Merchant of Venice,*" *Texas Studies in Literature and Language,* 3#3: 328-341 (Autumn, 1961).

Jacob, Cary F. "Reality and *The Merchant of Venice,*" *Qcarterly Journal of Speech,* 28#3: 307-314 (Oct, 1942).

Jones, Eldred. *Othello's Countrymen,* 68-71.

Kenyon, John S. "Shakespeare's Pronunciation of Stephano: Te *Merchant of Venice,* V. i. 28, 51," *Philological Quarterly,* 37#1: 504-506.

Kermode, Frank. "The Mature Comedies," *Stratford-Upon-Avon Studies, 3:* 220-224 (1961).

Kirschbaum, Leo. "Shakespeare 'God' and 'Bad'," *Review of English Studies,* 47#82: 139-142 (April, 1945).

——————. "Shylock in the City of God," *Shakespeare Newsletter,* 4#4: 33 (Sept, 1954).

Knight, George W. *The Golden Labyrinth,* 69-71; 83-84.

Krapf, E. E. "A Psychoanalytic Study of Shakespeare and Antisemitism: Shylock and Antonio," *Psychoanalytic Review,* 42#2: 113-130 (April, 1955).

Landa, M. J. *The Jew in Drama,* 255-259.

——————. *The Shylock Myth,* 32-45.

Leech, Clifford. "Shakespeare's Comic Dukes," *Review of English Literature,* 5#2: 104-105 (April, 1964).

Levy, Milton A. "Did Shakespeare Join the Casket and Bond Plots in *The Merchant of Venice,*" *Shakespeare Quarterly,* 11#3: 388-391 (Summer, 1960).

Lewalski, Barbara K. "Biblical Allusion and Allegory in *The*

Merchant of Venice," *Shakespeare Quarterly,* 13#3: 327-343 (Summer, 1962).

McCollom, William G. "Formalism and Illusion in Shakespeare's Drama," *Quarterly Journal of Speech,* 31#4: 446-447; 450 (Dec, 1945).

MacCarthy, Desmond. *Humanities,* 49-53.

Mackay, Maxine. *"The Merchant of Venice:* A Reflection of the Early Conflict Between Courts of Law and Courts of Equity," *Shakespeare Quarterly,* 15#4: 371-376 (Autumn, 1964).

Mahnken, Harry E. and Janine S. Mahnken. "Harley Granville-Barker's Shakespearean Criticism," *Southern Speech Journal, 27#1:* 28 (Fall, 1961).

Merchant, W. M. "Lawyer and Actor: Process of Law in Elizabethan Drama," in G. I. Duthie (ed), *English Studies Today—Third Series* (1964), 123-124.

Midgley, Graham. *"Merchant of Venice:* A Reconsideration," *Essays in Criticism,* 10#2: 121-133 (April, 1960).

Millet, Joseph. *Reading Drama,* 20-21.

Mitchell, Charles. "The Conscience of Venice: Shakespeare's Merchant," *Journal of English and Germanic Philology,* 63#2: 214-225 (April, 1964).

Moore, John R. "Pantaloon as Shylock," *Boston Public Library Quarterly,* 1: 33-42 (July, 1949).

Nash, Ralph. "Shylock's Wolfish Spirit," *Shakespeare Quarterly,* 10#1: 125-128 (Winter, 1959).

Nathan, Norman. "Shylock, Jacob, and God's Judgement," *Shakespeare Quarterly,* 1#4: 255-259 (Oct, 1950).

——————. "Three Notes on *The Merchant of Venice,"* *Shakespeare Association Bulletin,* 23#4: 152-173 (Oct, 1948).

——————. "Balthaser, Daniel, Portia," *Notes and Queries,* 202: 334-335 (1957).

Parr, Johnstone. "A Note on Daniel," *Shakespeare Association Bulletin,* 23#4: 181-182 (Oct, 1948).

Pettet, E. C. *"Merchant of Venice* and the Problem of Usury, *Essays and Studies of the English Association,* 31: 19-33 (1946).

Pitcher, Seymour M. "Two Notes on Shakespeare," *Philological Quarterly,* 21#2: 239 (April, 1942).

Reik, Theodor. "Jessica, My Child," *American Imago,* 8#1: 3-27 (March, 1951).

DRAMA CRITICISM

ALSO IN: *The Secret Self*, 33-56.

Ribner, Irving. "Marlowe and Shakespeare," *Shakespeare Quarterly*, 15#2: 44-49 (Spring, 1964).

Schlauch, M. "Roman Controversiae and the Court Scene in *Merchant of Venice*," *Kwartalnik Neofilologiczny*, 7#1: 45-56 (1960).

Seng, Peter J. "The Riddle Song in *The Merchant of Venice*," *Notes and Queries*, 203: 191-193 (May, 1958).

Shackford, John B. "The Bond of Kindness: Shylock's Humanity," *University of Kansas City Review*, 21#2: 85-91 (Winter, 1954).

Shapiro, A. "Should *The Merchant of Venice* Offend Jewish Students?" *English Journal*, 41: 432-433 (Oct, 1952).

Siegel, Paul N. "Shylock and the Puritan," *Columbia University Forum*, 5#4: 14-19 (Fall, 1962).

——————. "Shylock and the Puritan Usurers," *University of Miami Publications in English and American Literature*, 1: 129-138 (March, 1953).

Smith, Fred Manning. "Shylock on the Right of Jews and Emilia on the Rights of Women," *University of West Virginia Bulletin: Philological Studies*, 5: 32-33 (1947).

Smith, John Hazel. "Shylock: 'Devil Incarnation' or 'Poor Man . . . Wronged'?" *Journal of English and Germanic Philology*, 60#1: 1-21 (Jan, 1961).

Smith, Lewis W. "Shakespeare and the Speaking Line," *Poet Lore*, 48#1: 69-70 (Spring, 1942).

Smith, Warren D. "Shakespeare's Shylock," *Shakespeare Quarterly*, 15#3: 193-199 (Summer, 1964).

Strathmann, Ernest A. "The Devil Can Quote Scripture," *Shakespeare Quarterly*, 15#2: 17 (Spring, 1964).

Strong, L. A. G. *The Sacred River*, 61-62.

Summers, Vivian. "*The Merchant of Venice*," *The Use of English*, 12#3: 161-166 (Spring, 1961).

Tillyard, E. M. W. "The Trial Scene in *The Merchant of Venice*," *Review of English Literature*, 2#4: 51-59 (Oct, 1961).

ALSO IN: E. M. W. Tillyard, *Essays Literary and Educational*, 30-38.

——————. "Loneliness in *The Merchant of Venice*," *Essays in Criticism*, 11#4: 487-488 (Oct, 1961).

Warhalft, Sidney. "Anti-Semitism in *The Merchant of Venice*," *Manitoba Arts Review*, 10#3: 3-15 (Winter, 1956).

West, E. J. "The Use of Contrast in *The Merchant of Venice*,"

Shakespeare Association Bulletin, 21#4: 172-176 (Oct, 1946).

Wilkins, Leah W. "Shylock's Pound of Flesh and Laban's Sheep," *Modern Language Notes,* 62#1: 28-30 (Jan, 1947).

Windolph, F. Lyman. *Revelations of the Law in Literature,* 44-58.

Withington, Robert. "A Second Daniel," *Shakespeare Association Bulletin,* 16#2: 123-124 (April, 1941).

——————. "Shakespeare and Race Prejudice," in *Elizabethan Studies in Honor of George T. Reynolds,* 177-184.

Young, Stark. *Immortal Shadows,* 41-44.

MERRY WIVES OF WINDSOR

Baker, H. Kendra. "*Facts that Fit, II,*" *Baconiana,* 26#105: 204-205 (Oct, 1942).

Blair, Frederick G. "Shakespeare's Bear 'Sackerson,,'" *Notes and Queries,* 198: 514-515 (Dec, 1953).

Bracy, William. "*The Merry Wives of Windsor:* The History and Transmission of Shakespeare's Text, *University of Missouri Studies,* 25#1: 113-120 (1952).

Bruce, Dorothy H. "*The Merry Wives* and Two Brethern," *Studies in Philology,* 39#2: 265-278 (April, 1942).

Cutts, John P. "Falstaff's 'Heavenlie Jewel': Incidental Music for *The Merry Wives of Windsor,*" *Shakespeare Quarterly,* 11#1: 89-92 (Winter, 1960).

Draper, Charles L. "Falstaff's Bardolf," *Neophilologus,* pp. 222-226 (Oct, 1949).

Draper, John W. "Falstaff, 'A Fool and Jester'," *Modern Language Quarterly,* 17: 453-462 (1946).

Gilbert, Allen H. *The Principles and Practice of Criticism,* 65-94.

Goldstein, Leonard. "Some Aspects of Marriage and Inheritance in Shakespeare's *The Merry Wives of Windsor* and Chapman's *All Fools,*" *Zeitschrift fur Anglistik und Amerikanistik,* 12#4: 375-386 (1964).

Greer, C. A. "Falstaff's Diminution of Wit," *Notes and Queries,* 199: 468 (Nov, 1954).

Hart, Dorothy B. "*The Merry Wives* and Two Brethren," *Studies in Philology,* 39#2: 261-278 (April, 1942).

Hunter, William B. "Falstaff," *South Atlantic Quarterly,* 50#1: 86-95 (Jan, 1951).

Kokeritz, Helge. "Five Shakespeare Notes," *Review of English Studies,* 23#92: 314-315 (Oct, 1947).

Montgomery, Roy F. "A Fair House Built on Another Man's

Ground," *Shakespeare Quarterly,* 5#2: 207-208 (Spring, 1954).

Muir, Edwin. *Essays on Literature and Society,* 166-181.

Niemeyer, Carl A. *"Shakespeare and Opera,"* Union College *Symposium,* pp. 22-23 (Summer, 1964).

Ogburn, Vincent H. *"The Merry Wives* Quarto, a Farce Interlude," *PMLA,* 37#3: 654-660 (Sept, 1942).

Reik, Theodor. "Comedy of Intrigue," in *The Secret Self,* 63-75.

Robb, Stewart. "Shakespeare and Cambridge University," *Baconiana,* 33#132: 149-151 (July, 1949).

Steadman, John M. "Falstaff as Actaeon: A Dramatic Emblem," *Shakespeare Quarterly,* 14#3: 231-244 (Summer, 1963).

Waiker, Alice. *"Merry Wives of Windsor,* III. iii. 176," *Review of English Studies,* NS9#34: 173 (May, 1958).

West, E. J. "On Master Slender," *College English,* 8#5: 228-230 (Feb, 1947).

White, David M. "An Explanation of the 'Brook-Broome' Question in Shakespeare's *The Merry Wives of Windsor," Philological Quarterly,* 25#3: 280-283 (July, 1946).

Williams, Charles. *The Image of the City,* 40-42.

MIDSUMMER NIGHT'S DREAM, A

Aronson, Alex. "A Note on Shakespeare's Dream Imagery," *Visuabharati Quarterly,* 18#2: 169-170 (Aug-Oct, 1952).

✳Bethurum, Dorothy. "Shakespeare's Comment on Mediaeval Romance in *A Midsummer Night's Dream," Modern Language Notes,* 60#2: 85-94 (Feb, 1945).

Bluestone, Max. "An Anti-Jewish Pun in *A Midsummer Night's Dream,* III. i, 97," *Notes and Queries,* 198: 325-329 (Aug, 1953).

Bonnard, George A. "Shakespeare's Purpose in *Midsummer Night's Dream," Shakespeare Jahrbuck,* 92: 268-279 (1956).

Braddy, Haldeen. "Shakespeare's Puck and Froissart's Orthon," *Shakespeare Quarterly,* 7#2: 276-280 (Spring, 1956).

Burridge, W. "An Idol of the Theatre," *Baconiana* 36#142: 35-36 (Jan, 1952).

Conn, Naomi. "The Promise of Arcadia: Nature and Natural Man in Shakespeare's Comedies," *The City College Papers,* 1: 120-122 (1964).

✳Cutts, John P. "The Fierce Vexations of a [Midsummer

Night's] Dreame," *Shakespeare Quarterly*, 14#2: 183-185 (Spring, 1963).

Dent, R. W. "Imagination in *A Midsummer Night's Dream*," *Shakespeare Quarterly*, 15#2: 115-129 (Spring, 1964).

Dillingham, William B. "Bottom: The Third Ingredient," *Emory University Quarterly*, 12#4: 230-237 (Deec, 1956).

Doran, Madelline. "*A Midsummer Night's Dream:* A Metamorphosis," *Rice Institute Pamphlets*, 46#4: 113-135 (Jan, 1960).

Fisher, Peter F. "The Argument of *A Midsummer Night's Dream*," *Shakespeare Quarterly*, 8#3: 307-310 (Summer, 1957).

Gamal, Sand M. "The Function of Song in Shakespeare's Comedies," *Cairo Studies in English*, pg. 115 (1961/62).

Generosa, Sister M. "Apuleius and *A Midsummer Night's Dream:* Analogue or Source, Which?" *Studies in Philology*, 42#2: 198-204 (April, 1945).

Gui, Weston A. "Bottom's Dream," *American Imago*, 9#3-4: 251-305 (Fall-Winter, 1952).

Harrison, Thomas P., Jr. "Flower Lore in Spenser and Shakespeare," *Modern Language Quarterly*, 7: 17-178 (1946).

——————. "Shakespeare and Marlowe's *Dido, Queen of Carthage*," *Studies in English (University of Texas)*, 35: 57-58 (1956).

Heninger, S. K. Jr. "'Wondrous Strange Snow'—*A Midsummer Night's Dream* V. i. 66," *Modern Language Notes*, 68#7: 481-483 (Nov, 1953).

Herbert, T. Walter. "Dislocation and the Modest Demand in *A Midsummer Night's Dream*," *Renaissance Papers*, pp. 31-36 (1961).

Hewett, R. P. *Reading and Response*, 102-106.

Hulme, Hilda. "Three Notes: *Troilus and Cressida*, V. vii. 11; *Midsummer Night's Dream*, II. i, 54; *Measure for Measure*, II. i. 39," *Journal of English and Germanic Philology*, 57#4: 722-724 (Oct, 1958).

——Jacobson, Gerald F. "A Note on Shakespeare's *Midsummer Night's Dream*," *American Imago*, 19#1: 21-26 (Spring, 1962).

Kermode, Frank. "The Mature Comedies," *Stratford-Upon-Avon Studies*, 3: 214-220 (1961).

Knight, George W. *The Golden Labyrinth*, 69-70.

Law, Robert A. "The 'Pre-Conceived Pattern' of *A Mid-*

summer Night's Dream," Studies in English (University of Texas), pp. 5-14 (1943).

Leech, Clifford. "Shakespeare's Comic Dukes," *Review of English Literature,* 5#2: 103-104 (April, 1964).

Liu, James. "Elizazbethan and Yuan: A Brief Comparison of Some Conventions in Poetic Drama," *China Society Occasional Papers,* 8: 5-6 (1955).

McKenzie, D. F. "Shakespeare's Dream of Knowledge," *Landfall,* 18#1: 41-48 (March, 1964).

Merchant, W. M. *"A Midsummer Night's Dream:* A Visual Recreation," *Stratford-Upon-Avon Studies,* 3: 165-186 (1961).

Muir, Kenneth. "Pyramus and Thisbe: A Study in Shakespeare's Method," *Shakespeare Quarterly,* 5#2: 141-153 (Spring, 1954).

Myers, H. A. *"Romeo and Juliet* and *A Midsummer Night's Dream:* Tragedy and Comedy," in Sylvan Barnet, *Aspects of the Drama,* 35-39; 43-49.
ALSO IN: *Tragedy: A View of Life,* 110-128.

Nelson, Robert J. *Play Within a Play,* 12-15.

Nemerov, Howard. "The Marriage of Theseus and Hippolyta," *Kenyon Review,* 18#4: 633-641 (Autumn, 1956)
ALSO IN: *Poetry and Fiction,* 17-24.

Nitze, William A. *"A Midsummer Night's Dream,* V, i ,4-17," *Modern Language Review,* 50#4: 495-497 (Oct, 1955).

Olson, Paul A. *"A Midsummer Night's Dream* and the Meaning of Court Marriage," *ELH,* 24#2: 95-119 (June, 1957).

Pearce, T. M. "Shakespeare's *A Midsummer Night's Dream,* IV, i, 214-215," *The Explicator,* 18#1: 8 (Oct, 1959).

Pogson, Beryl. *In the East My Pleasure Lies,* 70-77.

Poirier, Michel. "Sidney's Influence on *A Midsummer Night's Dream,*" *Studies in Philology,* 44#3: 483-489 (July, 1947).

Quiller-Couch, Arthur. *Cambridge Lectures,* 123-136.

Ravich, Robert A. "A Psychoanalytic Study of Shakespeare's Early Plays," *Psychoanalytic Quarterly,* 33#3: 405-407 (July, 1964).

————————. "Shakespeare and Psychiatry," *Literature and Psychology,* 14#3&4: 98 (Summer/Fall, 1964).

Reynolds, Lou Agnes and Paul Sawyer. "Folk Medicine and the Four Fairies of *A Midsummer Night's Dream,*" *Shakespeare Quarterly,* 10#4: 513-521 (Autumn, 1959).

Robinson, J. W. "Palpable Hot Ice: Dramatic Burlesque in *A*

Midsummer Night's Dream," Studies in Philology, 61#2: 192-204 (April, 1964).

— Savage, James E. "Notes on *A Midsummer Night's Dream," University of Mississippi Studies in English*, 2: 65-78 (1961).

↘ Schanzer, Ernest. "The Central Theme of *A Midsummer Night's Dream," University of Toronto Quarterly*, 20#3: 233-238 (Apr, 1951).

——————. "The Moon and the Fairies in *A Midsummer Night's Dream," University of Toronto Quarterly*, 24#3: 234-246 (Apr, 1955).

——————. "Atavism and Anticipation in Shakespeare's Style," *Essays in Criticism*, 7#3: 245-249 (July, 1957).

Siegel, Paul N. "*A Midsummer Night's Dream* and the Wedding Guests," *Shakespeare Quarterly*, 4#2: 139-144 (Apr, 1953).

Staton, Walter F., Jr. "Ovidian Elements in *A Midsummer Night's Dream," Huntington Library Quarterly*, 26#2: 165-178 (Feb, 1963).

Styan, J. L. *The Elements of Drama*, 178-180.
ALSO IN: Robert W. Corrigan and James L. Rosenberg (eds), *The Context and Craft of Drama*, 113-115.

Thomas, Sidney. "The Bad Weather in *A Midsummer Night's Dream," Modern Language Notes*, 64#5: 319-322 (May, 1949).

Tucker, William J. "Irish Aspects of Shakespeare," *Catholic World*, 156: 698-699 (March, 1943).

West, E. J. "Hypothesis Concerning *A Midsummer Night's Dream," College English*, 9#5: 247-249 (Feb, 1948).

↘ Zitner, Sheldon. "The Worlds of *A Midsummer Night's Dream," South Atlantic Quarterly*, 59#3: 397-403 (Summer, 1960).

MUCH ADO ABOUT NOTHING

Bastian, F. "George Vargis, Constable," *Notes and Queries*, 202: 11 (1957).

Bowers, Fredson T. "Shakespeare's Art: The Point of View," In Carroll Camden (ed), *Literary Views*, 55-54.

Cavalchini, Mariella. "A Reevaluation of the Italian Sources of *Much Ado About Nothing," English Miscellany*, 13: 45-56 (1962).

Conn, Naomi. "The Promise of Arcadia: Nature and the Natural Man in Shakespeare's Comedies," *The City College Papers*, 1: 119-120 (1964).

Craik, T. W. *"Much Ado About Nothing,"* Scrutiny, 19#4: 297-316 (Oct, 1953).

Dean, Leonard F. "Shakespeare's *Much Ado About Nothing,* IV, i, 291," *Explicator, 2#7:* 51 (May, 1944).

Draper, John F. "Dogberry's Due Process of Law," *Journal of English and Germanic Philology,* 42: 563-567 (1943).

——————. "Shakespeare and Florence and the Florentines," *Italica,* 23#4: 289-290 (Dec, 1946).

Everett, Barbara. *"Much Ado About Nothing,"* The Critical Quarterly, 3#4: 319-334 (Winter, 1961).

Felheim, Marvin. "Comic Realism in *Much Ado About Nothing,"* Philologica Pragensia, 3: 213-225 (1964).

Fergusson, Francis. *"The Comedy of Errors* and *Much Ado About Nothing,"* Sewannee Review, 62#1: 24-37 (Winter, 1954).

ALSO IN: *The Human Image in Dramatic Literature,* 144-160.

Gilbert, Allan. "Two Margarets: The Composition of *Much Ado About Nothing,"* Philological Quarterly, 41#1: 61-71 (Jan, 1962).

Gordon, D. J. *"Much Ado About Nothing:* A Possible Source for the Hero-Claudio Plot," *Studies in Philology,* 39#2: 279-290 (April, 1942).

Gulick, Sidney L. Jr. "More Ado About Ado," *Shakespeare Association Bulletin,* 23#2: 55-59 (April, 1948).

Harvey, P. *"Much Ado About Nothing,"* Theoria, 11: 32- 36 (1958).

Hawkes, Terry. "The Old and the New in *Much Ado About Nothing,"* Notes and Queries, 203: 524-525 (Dec, 1958).

Hockey, Dorothy C. "Notes, Notes, Forsooth . . ." *Shakespeare Quarterly,* 8#3: 353-358 (Summer, 1957).

King, W. N. "Much Ado About Something," *Shakespeare Quarterly,* 15#3: 143-156 (Summer, 1964).

Knight, George W. *The Golden Labyrinth,* 67-68.

Lacy, Margaret Swanson. *The Jacobean Problem Play,* 7-28.

Leonard, F. Dean. "Shakespeare's *Much Ado About Nothing,* IV, i, 291," *The Explicator,* 2#7: 51 (May, 1944).

Loper, Robert. *"Much Ado About Nothing,"* Shakespeare Newsletter. 8#4: 28 (Sept, 1958).

Macpherson, Margaret. "Claudio and the Conventions of Courtly Love," *Makerere Journal,* 6: 38-49 (1962).

McPeek, James A. S. "The Thief 'Deformed' and *Much Ado About 'Noting',"* Boston University Studies in English, 4#2: 65-75 (Summer, 1960).

Neill, Kerley. "Much Ado About Claudio: An Acquittal for the Slandered Groom," *Shakespeare Quarterly,* 3#2: 91-107 (April, 1952).

Owen, Charles A. "Comic Awareness, Style, and Dramatic Technique in *Much Ado About Nothing,*" *Boston University Studies in English,* 5#4: 193-207 (Winter, 1961).

Polk, Estus. "The Function of Dogberry and the Watch in *Much Ado About Nothing,*" *Descant,* 5#3: 33-35 (Spring, 1961).

Potts, Abbie Findlay. "Spenserian 'Courtesy' and 'Temperance' in Shakespeare's *Much Ado About Nothing,*" *Shakespeare Association Bulletin,* 17#2: 103-111 (April, 1942).

——————. "Spenserian 'Courtesy' and 'Temperance' in Shakespeare's *Much Ado About Nothing* (Concluded)" *Shakespeare Association Bulletin,* 17#3: 126-133 (July, 1942).

Prouty, C. T. "George Whetstone, Peter Beverly, and the Sources of *Much Ado About Nothing,*" *Studies in Philology,* 38#2: 211-220 (April, 1941).

——————. "A Lost Piece of Stage Business in *Much Ado About Nothing,*" *Modern Language Notes,* 65#3: 207-208 (March, 1950).

Shaw, G. B. *Plays and Players,* 312-319.

Smith, James. *"Much Ado About Nothing,"* *Scrutiny,* 13#4: 242-256 (Spring, 1946).

Snuggs, Henry L. "Act-Division of *Much Ado About Nothing,*" *Renaissance Papers,* pp. 65-74 (1955).

Sochatoff, A Fred. *"Much Ado About Nothing,"* Carnegie Series in English, 4: 3-18 (1958).

Stevenson, David Lloyd. "The Love-Game Comedy" *Columbia University Studies in English and Comparative Literature,* 164: 208-216 (1946).

Sypher, W. "Nietzsche and Socrates in Messina," *Partisan Review,* 16: 702-713 (1949).

Taylor, A. P. "The Sick Time," *Modern Language Notes,* 65#5: 344-345 (May, 1950).

Thaler, Alwin. "Spencer and *Much Ado About Nothing,*" *Studies in Philology,* 37#2: 225-235 (April, 1940).

Thompson, Karl F. "Shakespeare's Romantic Comedies," *PMLA,* 67#7: 1076-1081; 1088-1089; 1091-1093 (Dec, 1952).

West, E. J. "Much Ado About an Unpleasant Play," *Shakespeare Association Bulletin,* 22#1: 30-34 (Jan, 1947).

Wey, James J. " 'To Grace Haromy': Musical Design in *Much*

Ado About Nothing," *Boston University Studies in English,* 4#3: 181-188 (Autumn, 1960).

OTHELLO

Adams, Maurianne S. "'Ocular Proof' in *Othello* and its Source," *PMLA,* 79#3: 234-241 (June, 1964).

Alexander, Peter. "Under Which King, Bezonian?" in *Elizabethan and Jacobean Studies Presented to Frank Wilson,* 167-172.

Allen, Don C. "Three Notes on Donne's Poetry With a Side Glance at *Othello,*" *Modern Language Notes,* 65#2: 105-106 (Feb, 1950).

Allen Ned B. "The Source of *Othello,*" *Delaware Notes,* 21: 71-96 (1948).

Anderson, Viola H. "*Othello* and *Peregrina,* 'Richer Than all his Tribe'," *Modern Language Notes,* 64#6: 415-417 (June, 1949).

Arnold, Aerol. "The Function of Brabantio in *Othello,*" *Shakespeare Quarterly,* 8#1: 51-56 (Winter, 1957).

Arthos, John. "The Fall of Othello" *Shakespeare Quarterly,* 9#2: 93-104 (Spring, 1958).

Asides (Stanford University). "Historical Review of *Othello,*" *Asides,* 4: 12-15 (1943/44).

Acden, W. H. "The Alienated City: Reflections on *Othello,*" *Encounter, pp.* 3-14 (Aug, 1961).

Bayley, John. *The Characters of Love,* 125-202.

Bamborough, J. *The Little World of Man,* 18-19.

Bentley, Eric. *The Play,* 372-373; 484-488.

Berkeley, David S. "A Vulgarization of Desdemona," *Studies in English Literature* 1500-1900, 3#2: 233-239 (Spring, 1963).

Bethel, S. L. "Shakespeare's Imagery: The Diabolic Images in *Othello,*" *Shakespeare Survey,* 5: 62-80 (1952).

Bloom, Allan D. "Cosmopolitan Man and the Political Community: An Interpretation of *Othello,*" *American Political Science Review,* 54#1: 130-157 (March, 1960).

————. "Political Philosophy and Poetry," *American Political Science Review,* 54#2: 458-461 (June, 1960).

Bodkin, Maud. *Archetypal Patterns in Poetry,* 217-224; 227-229.

Bonnard, G. "Are Othello and Desdemona Innocent or Guilty?" *English Studies,* 30#5: 175-184 (Oct, 1949).

Bowman, Thomas D. "The Characterization and Motivation of Iago," *College English,* 4#8: 460-468 (May, 1943).

OTHELLO, CON'T.

————. "In Defense of Emilia," *Shakespeare Association Bulletin*, 22#3: 99-104 (July, 1947).

————. "Desdemona's Last Moments," *Philological Quarterly*, 39#1: 114-117 (Jan, 1960).

————. "An Honorable Murder, if you Will," *Shakespeare Newsletter*, 2#8: 43 (Dec, 1952).

Brenneckt, Ernest. "'Nay, That's Not Next!': The Significance of Desdemona's 'Willow Song'," *Shakespeare Quarterly*, 4#1: 35-38 (Jan, 1953).

Brooks, Cleanth and Robert Heilman. *Understanding Drama*, 661-668.

Brown, A. D. Fitton. "Two Points of Interpretation," *Notes and Queries*, 202: 51 (Feb, 1957).

Burke, Kenneth. *A Grammar of Motives*, 413-414.

————. "*Othello*: An Essay to Illustrate a Method," *Hudson Review*, 4#2: 165-203 (Summer, 1951).

ALSO IN: Stanley E. Hyman (ed.), *Perspectives by Incongruity*, 152-195.

————. *The Philosophy of Literary Form*, 64-65.

Burnim, Kalman A. "On *The Masks of Othello*," *Literarture and Psychology*, 13#1: 17-22 (Winter, 1963).

Burris, Quincy Guy. "'Soft! Here Follows Prose'—Twelfth Night II. v. 154," *Shakespeare Quarterly*, 2#3: 233-239 (July, 1951).

Butcher, Philip. "Othello's Racial Identity," *Shakespeare Quarterly*, 3#3: 243-247 (July, 1952).

Camden, Carroll. "Iago on Women," *Journal of English and Germanic Philology*, 48#1: 47-71 (Jan, 1949).

Chester, Allan G. "John Soowthern's *Pandora* and *Othello*, II. i. 184," *Modern Language Notes*, 66#7: 481-482 (Nov, 1951).

Clemen, Wolfgang. *English Tragedy Before Shakespeare*, 245-246.

Clurman, H. *Lies Like Truth*, 153-156.

Craig, Hardin. "Renaissance Ideal: A Lecture on Shakespeare, *University of North Carolina Extension Bulletin*, 24#4: 33-34 (Nov, 1944).

Creeth, Edmund H. "Moral and Tragic Recognition: The Uniqueness of *Othello, Macbeth*, and *King Lear*," *Michigan Academy of Science, Arts and Letters. Papers*, 45: 386-387 (1960).

Cunningham, James. *Woe or Wonder*, 24-27; 118.

Curry, Walter. "A Further Study in the Characterization and

Motivation of Iago," *College English*, 4#8: 460-469 (May, 1943).

Cutts, John P. "Notes on *Othello*," *Notes and Queries*, 204: 251-252 (July-Aug, 1959).

Datta, A. "*Othello*: A Study of the Poetic Approach to Tragic Problems," *Journal of the University of Saugar*, 6#6Pt 1: 1-18 (1957).

Donoghue, Denis. "Shakespeare's Rhetoric," *Studies*, 47: 436-440 (Winter, 1958),

Dorsch, T. S. "The Poor Trash of Venice," *Shakespeare Quarterly*, 6#3: 359-361 (Summer, 1955).

Draper, J. W. "Patterns of Tempo and Humor in *Othello*," *English Studies*, 28#3: 65-74 (June, 1947).

—————. "Shakespeare and Barbary," *Etudes Anglaises*, 14#3: 311-313 (July-Sept, 1961).

—————. "Shakespeare and Florence and the Florentines," *Italica*, 23-4: 290-293 (Dec, 1946).

—————. "Speech Tempo in Act I of *Othello*," *University of West Virginia Bulletin: Philological Papers*, **5**: 49-58 (1947).

—————. "Subjective Conflict in Shakespearean Tragedy," *Neuphilologische Mitteilungen*, 2#61: 217-218 (1960).

—————. "The Tempo of Shylock's Speech," *Journal of English and Germanic Philology*, 44#3: 281-285 (July, 1945).

—————. "Changes in the Tempo of Desdemona's Speech," *Anglica*, 1#4: 149-153 (Aug, 1946).

Eastman, Fred. *Christ in the Drama*, 11-12; 24-25; 31-35; 38.

Emery, John P. "Othello's Epilepsy," *Psychoanalysis and the Psychoanalytic Review*, 46#4: 30-32 (Winter, 1959).

Everett, Barbara. "Reflections on the Sentimentalist's *Othello*," *Critical Quarterly*, 3#2: 127-138 (Summer, 1961).

Faber, M. D. "Suicidal Patterns in *Othello*," *Literature and Psychology*, 14#3-4: 85-96 (Summer-Fall, 1964).

Fairchild, Arthur H. R. "Shakespeare and the Tragic Theme," *University of Missouri Studies*, 19#2: 28-43; 105-140 (1944).

Fallon, Gabriel. "Some Notes on *Othello*," *Irish Monthly*, 73: 204-210 (May, 1945).

Feldman, A. Bronson. "Othello in Reality," *American Imago*, 11#2: 147-179 (Summer, 1954).

—————. "Othello's Obsessions," *American Imago*, 9#2: 147-164 (June, 1952).

——————. "The Yellow Malady: Short Studies of Five Tragedies of Jealousy," *Literature and Psychology,* 6#2: 38-40; 51-52 (May, 1956).

Foakes, R. A. "Shakespeare's Imagery: The Diabolic Images in *Othello,*" *Shakespeare Survey,* 5: 62-80 (1952).

Gardner, Helen Louis. "The Noble Moor," *Annual Shakespeare Lecture of the British Academy,* pp. 189-205 (1955).

Gerard, Albert. "Alack, Poor Iago!: Intellect and Action in *Othello,*" *Shakespeare Jahrbuck,* 94: 218-232 (1958).

——————. "'Egregiously An Ass': The Dark Side of the Moor. A View of Othello's Mind," *Shakespeare Survey,* 10: 98-106 (1957).

Gerritsen, J. "More Paired Words in *Othello,*" *English Studies,* 39#5: 212-214 (Oct, 1958).

Gilbert, Allen H. *The Principles and Practice of Criticism,* 27-64.

Glaz, A. Andre. "Iago or Moral Sadism," *American Imago,* 19#4: 323-348 (Winter, 1962).

Gordon, R. K. "Scott and Shakespeare's Tragedies," *Royal Society of Canada Proceedings and Transactions,* 39#2: 114-115 (1945).

Hagopian, John V. "Psychology and the Coherent Form of Shakespeare's *Othello,*" *Michigan Academy of Science, Arts, and Letters. Papers,* 45: 373-380 (1960).

Hart, Walter M. "Shakespeare's Use of Verse and Prose," *University of California Publications. English Studies,* 10: 6 (1954).

Hastead, William L. "Artifice and Artistry in *Richard II* and *Othello,*" *University of Miami Publications in English and American Literature,* 7: 19-20; 33-35 (1964).

Hawkes, Terence. "Iago's Use of Reason," *Studies in Philology,* 58#2: 160-169 (April, 1961).

Hayes, Ann L. "*Othello,*" *Carnegie Series in English,* 8: 53-68 (1964).

Heilman, Robert. "Approach to *Othello,*" *Sewanee Review,* 64#1: 98-116 (Winter, 1956).

——————. "The Economics of Iago and Others," *PMLA,* 68#3: 555-571 (June, 1953).

——————. "More Fair Than Black: Light and Dark in *Othello,*" *Essays in Criticism,* 1#4: 315-335 (Oct, 1951).

——————. "'Twere Best Not Know Myself:' Othello, Lear, Macbeth," *Shakespeare Quarterly,* 15#2: 89-98 (Spring, 1964).

——————. "Wit and Witchcraft: Thematic Form in *Othello*," *Arizona Quarterly*, 12#1: 5-15 (Spring, 1956).

——————. "Dr. Iago and his Potions," *Virginia Quarterly Review*, 28#4: 568-584 (Aut, 1952).

Henn, Thomas R. *The Harvest of Tragedy,* 23-24; 96-98.

Herbert, Carolyn. "Comic Elements in *Othello*," *Renaissance Papers*, pp. 32-38 (1957).

Herbert, T. Walter. "Shakespeare and the Craft of Fiction," *Emory University Quarterly*, 20#: 85-86 (Summer, 1964).

Hoepfner, Theodore C. "Iago's Nationality," *Notes and Queries*, 200: 14-15 (Jan, 1955).

——————. "An *Othello* Gloss," *Notes and Queries*, 201: 470 (Nov, 1956).

Holloway, John. *The Story of the Night*, 37-56; 155-156.

Hubler, Edward. "The Damnation of Othello: Some Limitations on the Christian View of the Play," *Shakespeare Quarterly*, 9#3: 295-300 (Summer, 1958).

Hulsopple, Bill G. "Barabas and Shylock Against a Background of Jewish History in England," *Central States Speech Journal*, 12#1: 38-50 (Aut, 1960).

Hunter, Grace. "Notes on Othello's 'Base Indian'," *Shakespeare Association Bulletin*, 19#1: 26-28 (Jan, 1944).

Ingram, Von R. W. "*Hamlet,*" *Othello,* and *King Lear:* Music and Tragedy," *Shakespeare Jahrbuck*, 100: 159-161; 167-170 (1964).

Ivy, Geoffrey S. "Othello and the Rose-Lip'd Cherubin: An Old Reading Restored," *Shakespeare Quarterly*, 19#2: 208-212 (Spring, 1958).

Jepsen, Laura. *Ethical Aspects of Tragedy*, 46-55.

Jones, Eldred. *Othello's Countrymen*, 86-109.

Jones, Eldred D. "The Machiavel and the Moor," *Essays in Criticism*, 10#2: 234-238 (April, 1960).

Jordan, Hoover H. "Dramatic Illusion in *Othello*," *Shakespeare Quarterly*, 1#3: 146-152 (July, 1950).

Jorgensen, Paul A. "Honesty in *Othello*," *Studies in Philology*, 47#4: 557-567 (Oct, 1950).

——————. " 'Perplex'd in the Extreme': The Role of Thought in *Othello*," *Shakespeare Quarterly*, 15#2: 265-275 (Spring, 1964).

Kahin, Helen A. "A Note on Othello, II, i, 110-113," *Modern Language Quarterly*, 1: 475-479 (1940).

Kaufman, Walter. "Goethe Versus Shakespeare: Some Changes in Dramatic Sensibility," *Partisan Review*, 19#6: 623-627 (Nov/Dec, 1952).

Kerman, Joseph. "Verdi's *Otello*, or Shakespeare Explained," *Hudson Review*, 6#2: 266-277 (Summer, 1962).

Kirschbaum, Leo. "The Modern *Othello*," *ELH*, 11#4: 283-296 (Dec, 1944).

Kliger, Samuel. "Othello: The Man of Judgement," *Modern Philology*, 48#4: 221-224 (May, 1951).

Knight, Eric. "A Play by William Shakespeare," *Central Literary Magazine*, pp. 271-278 (Jan. 1948).

Knight, G. Wilson. "The *Othello* Music," in *The Wheel of Fire*, 97-119 (1962 ed.).

Knox, George. *Critical Moments*, 45; 47-48.

Krutch, J. W. *Modernism in Modern Drama*, 75-76.

Kurikoma, Masakazu. "An Essay on the Dialogues Between Othello and Iago," *Anglica*, 4#1: 83-93 (Oct, 1959).

Langbaum, Robert. "Character Versus Action in Shakespeare," *Shakespeare Quarterly*, 8#1: 60-62; 68 (Winter, 1957).

Leavis, Frank R. *The Common Pursuit*, 136-159.

Lerner, Laurence. "The Machival and the Moor," *Essays in Criticism*, 9#4: 339-360 (Oct, 1959).

Lesser, Simon O. *Fiction and the Unconscious*, 116-118.

Levich, Marvin. *Aesthetics and the Philosophy of Criticism*, 174-175.

Levin, Harry. "Othello and the Motive-Hunters," *Centenniel Review*, 8#1: 1-16 (Winter, 1964).

McCloskey, John C. "The Motivation of Iago," *College English*, 3#1: 25-30 (Oct, 1941).

McCollom, William G. *Tragedy*, 110-111.

McCullen, Joseph T. Jr. "Iago's Use of Proverbs for Persuasion," *Studies in English Literature 1500-1900*, 4#2: 247-262 (Spring, 1964).

McGee, Arthur. "Othello's Motive for Murder," *Shakespeare Quarterly*, 15#1: 45-54 (Winter, 1964).

Mack, Maynard. "The Jacobean Shakespeare: Some Observations on the Construction of the Tragedies," *Stratford-Upon-Avon Studies*, 1: 11-42 (1960).

McNamara, Leo F. "Dramatic Convention and the Psychological Study of Character in *Othello*," *Michigan Academy of Science, Arts and Letters. Papers*, 47: 649-658 (1962).

McPeek, James A. S. "The 'Arts Inhibited' and the Meaning of *Othello*," *Boston University Studies in English*, 1#3: 129-147 (Autumn, 1955).

Major, John M. "Desdemona and Dido," *Shakespeare Quarterly*, 10#1: 123-125 (Winter, 1959).

Marder, Louis. "In Defence of Shakespeare and Shylock,"
    Shakespeare Newsletter, 13#3: 28 (May, 1963).

Mason, Philip. "*Othello* and Race Prejudice," *Caribbean Quar-
    terly,* 8#3: 154-162 (Sept, 1962).

Maxwell, J. C. "Shakespeare: The Middle Plays," *Guide to
    English Literature,* 2: 215-218.

Michel, Laurence. "Shakespearean Tragedy: Critique of Hu-
    manism From the Inside," *Massachusetts Review,* 2#4:
    638-644 (Summer, 1961).

Miller, D. C. "Iago and the Problem of Time," *English Stud-
    ies,* 22#3: 97-115 (June, 1940).

Milward, Peter. "The Base Judean: Notes on the Interpreta-
    tion of *Othello,* V. ii. 346," *Shakespeare Studies* 1: 7-14
    (1962).

Mincoff, Marco. "The Structural Pattern of Shakespeare's
    Tragedies," *Shakespeare Survey,* 3: 62-63 (1950).

Mooney, John. "Othello's 'It is the cause . . .': An Analysis,"
    Shakespeare Survey, 6: 94-105 (1953).

Moore, John Robert. "The Character of Iago," *University of
    Missouri Studies,* 21#1: 37-46 (1946).

————. "Othello, Iago, and Cassio as Soldiers,"
    Philological Quarterly, 31#2: 189-194 (April, 1952).

Morozov, Mikhail M. "The Individualization of Shakespeare's
    Characters Through Imagery," *Shakespeare Survey,* 2:
    83-90 (1949).

Mueller, William R. "The Class of '50 Reads *Othello,*" *College
    English,* 10#2: 92-97 (Nov, 1948).

Muir, Kenneth. "Double Time in *Othello,*" *Notes and Queries,*
    197: 76-77 (Feb 16, 1952).

————. "Freedom and Slavery in *Othello,*" *Notes
    and Queries,* 199: 20-21 (Jan, 1954).

————. "The Jealousy of Iago," *English Miscellany,*
    2: 65-84 (1951).

Murphy, G. N. "A Note on Iago's Name," in Bernice Slote
    (ed.), *Literature and Society,* 38-43.

Murphy, George H. "Reflections on the Tragedies of Shakes-
    peare," *Dalhousie Review,* 36#3: 273-274 (Aut, 1956).

Murry, John M. "The Doctrine of Will in Shakespeare,"
    Aryan Path, 35: 338-342 (Aug, 1964).

————. "The Significance of Shylock," *The Adelphi,*
    22#1: 1-5 (Oct/Dec, 1945).

Myrick, Kenneth O. "The Theme of Damnation in Shake-
    spearean Tragedy," *Studies in Philology,* 38#2: 235-245
    (April, 1941).

Nash, W. "Paried Words in *Othello*: Shakespeare's Use of a Stylistic Device," *English Studies,* 39#2: 62-67 (April, 1958).

Nichols, Dorothy. "*Othello,* East and West," *Asides,* 4: 10-12 (1943/4).

Nieman, Fraser. "Shakespeare's *Othello,* IV, ii, 47-53," *The Explicator,* 6#8: 54 (June, 1948).

Niemeyer, Carl A. "Shakespeare and Opera," *Union College Symposium,* pp. 19-22 (Summer, 1964).

Nowottny, Winifred M. T. "Justice and Love in *Othello,*" *University of Toronto Quarterly,* 21#4: 330-344 (July, 1952).

Olson, Elder. *Tragedy and the Theory of Drama,* 104-107.

Olson, Robert C. "Shakespeare's *Othello,* I, i, 25-26," *The Explicator,* 22#7: 59 (March, 1964).

Onesta, P. A. "*Othello,*" *Theoria,* 15: 61-63 (1960).

Ornstein, Robert. *The Moral Vision of Jacobean Tragedy,* 227-230.

Oyama, Toshiko. "The Fate of a Shakespeare Machiavel: A Study of Language and Imagery in *Othello,*" *Anglica,* 3#3: 30-50 (June, 1958).

P., M. "*Othello,*" *Baconiana,* 47#164: 51-64 (Oct, 1964).

Pearce, Thomas W. "Wit and Wisdom in Mr. Heilman's *Othello,*" *Shakespeare Newsletter,* 8#6: 42 (Dec, 1958).

Pogson, Beryl. *In the East My Pleasure Lies,* 11-22.

Prager, Leonard. "The Clown in *Othello,*" *Shakespeare Quarterly,* 11#1: 94-96 (Winter, 1960).

Prior, Moody E. "Character in Relation to Action in *Othello,*" *Modern Philology,* 44#3: 225-237 (May, 1947).

——————. "A New Reading of *Othello,*" *Modern Philology,* 45#4: 270-272 (May, 1948).

Putney, Rufus. "What 'Praise to Give'?" *Philological Quarterly,* 23#4: 313-318 (Oct, 1944).

Ranald, Margaret L. "The Indiscretions of Desdemona," *Shakespeare Quarterly,* 14#2: 127-140 (Spring, 1963).

Rand, Frank P. "The Over Garrulous Iago," *Shakespeare Quarterly,* 1#3: 155-161 (July, 1950).

Raymond, William O. "Motivation and Character Portrayal in *Othello,*" *University of Toronto Quarterly,* 17#1: 80-96 (Oct, 1947).

Reik, Theodor. *The Secret Self,* 57-62.

Ribner, Irving. "*Othello* and the Pattern of Shakespearean Tragedy," *Tulane Studies in English,* 5: 69-82 (1955).

Ricks, Christopher. "The Machiaval and the Moor," *Essays in Criticism,* 10#1: 117 (Jan, 1960).

Robeson, Paul. "Some Reflections on *Othello* and the Nature of Our Time," *American Scholar,* 14#4: 391-392 (Autumn, 1945).

Robson, John M. "Tragedy and Society," *Queen's Quarterly,* 71#3: 432 (Aut, 1964).

Roddier, Henri. "A Freudian Detective's Shakespeare," *Modern Philology,* 48#2: 122-129 (Nov, 1950).

Rosenberg, Marvin. "In Defense of Iago," *Shakespeare Quarterly,* 6#2: 145-158 (Spring, 1955).

——————. "The 'Refinement' of *Othello* in the 18th Century British Theater," *Studies in Philology,* 51#1: 75-94 (Jan, 1954).

——————. "Reputation, Oft Lost Without Deserving . . ." *Shakespeare Quarterly,* 9#4: 502-506 (Autumn, 1958).

——————. "A Sceptical Look at Sceptical Criticism," *Philological Quarterly,* 33#1: 66-77 (Jan, 1954).

Ross, Lawrence J. "Marble, 'Crocodile,' and 'Turban'd Turk' in *Othello,*" *Philological Quarterly,* 40#4: 476-484 (Oct, 1961).

——————. *Philosophy in Literature,* 64-66; 255-263.

——————. "Three Reading in the Text of *Othello,*" *Shakespeare Quarterly,* 14#2: 121-126 (Spring, 1963).

——————. "The Use of a 'Fit-up' Booth in *Othello,*" *Shakespeare Quarterly,* 12#4: 359-370 (Autumn, 1961).

——————. "World and Chrysolite in *Othello,*" *Modern Language Notes,* 76Pt.2#8: 683-692 (Dec, 1961).

Rosetti, R. M. "A Crux and No Crux," *Shakespeare Quarterly,* 13#3: 299-303 (Summer, 1962).

Rueckert, William H. *Kenneth Burke,* 87-89; 212-219.

Rylands, George. "Shakespeare's Poetic Energy," *Annual Shakespeare Lecture of the British Academy,* pp. 114-118 (1951).

Rymer, Thomas. "A Short View of Tragedy," in H. H. Adams and Baxter Hathaway (eds), *Dramatic Essays of the Neoclassic Age,* 143-154.

Schueller, Hergert M. "*Othello* Transformed: Verdi's Interpretation of Shakespeare," in A. Dayle Wallce (ed), *Studies in Honor of John Wilcox,* 129-156.

Schwartz, Delmore. *Vaudeville for a Princess,* 42-46.

Sedgewick, G. G. *Of Irony,* 41-44; 85-116.

Shackford, John B. "The Motivation of Iago," *Shakespeare Newsletter,* 3#4: 30 (Sept, 1953).

Shapiro, Shephen A. "Othello's Desdemona," *Literature and Psychology,* 14#2: 56-61 (Spring, 1964).

Siegel, Paul N. "The Damnation of Othello: An Addendum," *PMLA,* 68: 1068-1078 (1953).

Sitwell, Edith. "Iago," *New Writing and Daylight,* pp. 141-151 (1946).

Smith, Fred Manning. "Shylock on the Rights of Jews and Emilia on the Rights of Women," *University of West Virginia Bulletin: Philological Papers,* 5: 32-33 (1947).

Smith, Gordon Ross. "Iago the Paranoiac," *American Imago,* 16#2: 155-167 (Summer, 1959).

————. "The Masks of Othello," *Literature and Psychology,* 12#3: 75-77 (Summer, 1962).

Smith, Philip A. "Othello's Diction," *Shakespeare Quarterly,* 9#3: 428-430 (Summer, 1958).

Spencer, Theodore. "The Isolation of the Shakespearean Hero," *Sewanee Review,* 52#3: 321-323 (July/Sept, 1944).

Sprinchorn, Evert. "The Handkerchief Trick *in Othello,*" *Columbia University Forum,* 7#1: 25-30 (Winter, 1964).

Sproule, Albert F. "A Time Scheme for *Othello,*" *Shakespeare Quarterly,* 7#2: 217-226 (Spring, 1956).

Stirling, Brents. "Psychology in *Othello,*" *Shakespeare Association Bulletin,* 19#3: 135-144 (July, 1944).

Stoll, E. E. "Another *Othello* Too Modern," in James G. McManaway (ed), *Joseph Q. Adams Memorial Studies,* 351-371.

————. "Iago not a 'Malcontent'," *Journal of English and Germanic Philology,* 51#2: 163-167 (April, 1952).

————. "Slander in Drama," *Shakespeare Quarterly,* 4#4: 433-450 (Oct, 1953).

————. "Mainly Controversy: *Hamlet, Othello,*" *Philological Quarterly,* 24#2: 312-316 (Oct, 1945).

————. "A 'New' Reading of *Othello,*" *Modern Philology,* 45#3: 208-210 (Feb, 1948).

————. "An *Othello* all-too-Modern," *ELH,* 13#1: 46-58 (Mar, 1946).

Strathmann, Earnest A. "The Devil Can Cite Scripture," *Shakespeare Quarterly,* 15#2: 17-19 (Spring, 1964).

Strong, L. A. G. *The Sacred River,* 58-60.

Styan, J. L. *The Elements of Drama,* 32-39; 54-55.

Sullivan, J. P. "The Machiaval and the Moor," *Essays in Criticism,* 10#2: 231-234 (April, 1960).

Thaler, Alwin. "Delayed Exposition in Shakespeare," *Shakespeare Quarterly,* 1#3: 140-143 (July, 1950).

Thompson, A. R. *Dry Mock,* 31-34.

Traversi, Derek. *"Othello," The Wind and the Rain,* 6#4: 248-269 (Spring, 1950).

Villiers, Jacob I. de. "The Tragedy of Othello," *Theoria,* 7: 71-78 (1955).

Walpole, V. "'And Cassio High in Oath' *(Othello,* II, iii, 227)" *Modern Language Review,* 40#1: 47-48 (Jan, 1945).

Walton, J. K. "'Strength's Abundance': A View of *Othello,*" *Review of English Studies,* 11#41 NS: 8-17 (Feb, 1960).

Wangh, Martin. *"Othello:* The Tragedy of Iago," *Psychoanalytic Quarterly,* 19: 202-212 (April, 1950).

Ware, M. "How was Desdemona Murdered?" *English Studies,* 45#2: 177-180 (April, 1964).

Warnken, Henry L. "Iago as a Projection of Othello," *The City College Papers,* 1: 1-15 (1964).

Watson, Sarah R. "A Comparison of *Othello* and *The Cenci,*" PMLA, 55#2: 611-614 (June, 1940).

Webb, Henry J. "The Military Background in *Othello,*" *Philological Quarterly,* 30#1: 40-52 (Jan, 1951).

——————. "Rude am I in my Speech," *English Studies,* 39#2: 67-72 (April, 1958).

Weisinger, Herbert. *The Agony and the Triumph,* 20-25; 106-109.

——————. "A Casebook on *Othello,*" *Literature and Psychology,* 12#3: 78-82 (Summer, 1962).

——————. "Iago's Iago," *University of Kansas City Review,* 20#2: 83-89 (Winter, 1953).

——————. "A Shakespeare All too Modern," *Arizona Quarterly,* 20#4: 301-304 (Winter, 1964).

Wells, Henry W. *Elizabethan and Jacobean Playwrights,* 61-63.

West, Robert H. "The Christianness of *Othello,*" *Shakespeare Quarterly,* 15#4: 333-344 (Autumn, 1964).

——————. "Iago and the Mystery of Inequity," *Renaissance Papers,* pp. 63-69 (1961).

Wilcox, John. "Othello's Crucial Moment," *Shakespeare Association Bulletin,* 24#3: 181-192 (July, 1949).

Williamson, Karina. "'Honest' and 'False' in *Othello,*" *Studia Neophilologica,* 35#2: 211-220 (1963).

Wilson, Arthur H. "Othello's Racial Identity," *Shakespeare Quarterly*, 4: 209 (1953).

Withington, Robert. "Shakespeare and Race Prejudice," in *Elizabethan Studies in Honor of George T. Reynolds*, 172-177; 183-184.

Young, Stark. *Immortal Shadows*, 230-235.

PERICLES

Arthos, John. "*Pericles, Prince of Tyre:* A Study in the Dramatic Use of Romantic Narrative," *Shakespeare Quarterly*, 4: 257-270 (1953).

Babb, Lawrence. *Elizazbethan Malady*, 105-106.

Barker, G. A. "Themes and Variations in Shakespeare's *Pericles*," *English Studies*, 44#6: 401-414 (Dec, 1963).

Craig, Hardin. "*Pericles* and *The Painfull Adventures*," *Studies in Philology*, 45#4: 600-605 (Oct, 1948).

Danby, J. F. *Poets on Fortune's Hill*, 87-103.

Edwards, Philip. "An Approach to the Problem of *Pericles*," *Shakespeare Survey*, 5: 25-49 (1952).

Elton, William. "*Pericles: A New Source or Analogue*," *Journal of English and Germanic Philology*, 48#1: 138-172 (Jan, 1949).

Evans, Bertrand. "The Poem of *Pericles*," *University of California Publications. English Studies*, 11: 35-56 (1955).

Goolden, P. "Antiochus' Riddle in Gower and Shakespeare," *Review of English Studies*, NS6#23: 245; 248-251 (Jcly, 1955).

Haight, Elizabeth. *More Essays on Greek Romances*, 171-189.

Hulme, Hilda M. "Two Notes on the Interpretation of Shakespeare's Text," *Notes and Queries*, 204: 354 (Oct, 1959).

Kane, Robert J. "A Passage in *Pericles*," *Modern Language Notes*, 68: 483-484 (1953).

King, S. K. "Eliot, Yeats, and Shakespeare," *Theoria*, 5: 113-115 (1953).

Knight, G. Wilson. *The Crown of Life*, 32-75.

————. The *Golden Labyrinth*, 82-84.

Long, John H. "Laying the Ghosts in *Pericles*," *Shakespeare Quarterly*, 7#1: 39-42 (Winter, 1956).

Melchiori, Bargara. "Still Harping on My Daughter," *English Miscellany*, 11: 60-63 (1960).

Muir, Kenneth. "*Pericles*, II, v," *Notes and Queries*, 194: 362 (21 Aug, 1948).

————. "The Problem of *Pericles*," *English Studies*, 30#3: 65-83 (June, 1949).

Nathan, Norman. *"Pericles* and Jonah," *Notes and Queries,* 201: 10-11 (1956).

Simpson, Percy. *Studies in Elizabethan Drama,* 17-22.

Tompkins, J. M. "Why Pericles?" *Review of English Studies,* NS3#12: 315-324 (Oct, 1952).

Traversi, D. A. "The Last Plays of Shakespeare," *Guide to English Literature, 2:* 251-255.

RICHARD II

Altick, R. H. " 'Conveyers' and Fortune's Buckets in *Richard II," Modern Language Notes,* 61#3: 179-180 (March, 1946).

Anderson, Donald K. Jr. *"Richard II* and *Perkin Warbeck," Shakespeare Quarterly,* 13#2: 260-263 (Spring, 1962).

Aronson, Alex. "A Note on Shakespeare's Dream Imagery," *Visuabharati Quarterly,* 18#2: 173 (Aug-Oct, 1952).

Attick, Richard D. "Symphonic Imagery in *Richard II," PMLA,* 62#2: 339-365 (June, 1947).

Bass, Eben. "Falstaff and the Succession," *College English,* 24#7: 502-506 (April, 1963).

Berman, Ronald. *"Richard II:* The Shapes of Love," *Moderna Sprak,* 58#1: 1-8 (1964).

Berry, Francis. *Poet's Grammar,* 61-62.

Black, Matthew W. "Problems in the Editing of Shakespeare: An Interpretation," *English Institute Essays,* pp. 117-136 (1947).

——————. "The Sources of Shakespeare's *Richard II,"* in James G. McManaway (ed), *Joseph Q. Adams Memorial Studies,* 199-216.

Bonnard, Georges A. "The Actor in *Richard II," Shakespeare Jahrbuck,* 87: 87-101 (1951).

Bryant, J. A. "The Linked Analogies of *Richard II," Sewanee Review,* 65#3: 420-433 (Summer, 1957).

Cauthen, I. B. Jr. *"Richard II* and the Image of the Betrayed Christ," *Renaissance Papers,* pp. 45-48 (1954).

Chapman, Raymond. "The Wheel of Fortune in Shakespeare's Historical Plays," *Review of English Studies* NS1#1: 1-5 (Jan, 1950).

Clemen, Wolfgang H. "Anticipation and Foreboding in Shakespeare's Early Histories," *Shakespeare Survey,* 6: 30-31 (1953).

Dean, Leonard F. *"Richard II:* The State and the Image of the Theater," *PMLA,* 67#2: 211-218 (March, 1952).

Doran, Madeleine. "Imagery in *Richard II* and in *Henry IV*," *Modern Language Review*, 37#2: 113-122 (April, 1942).

Dorius, R. J. "A Little More Than a Little," *Shakespeare Quarterly*, 11#1: 13-22 (Winter, 1960).

Downer, Alan S. "The Like of Our Design," *Hudson Review*, 2#2: 249-251; 255-258 (Summer, 1949).

Draper, John W. "The Character of Richard II," *Philological Quarterly*, 21#2: 228-236 (April, 1942).

Eastman, Arthur M. "Shakespeare's Negative Capability," *Michigan Academy of Science, Arts and Letters. Papers*, 42: 344-347 (1956).

Freeman, Leslie. "Shakespeare's Kings and Machiavelli's Prince," *The City College Papers*, 1: 25-42 (1964).

Goodman, Paul. *The Structure of Literature*, 59-66.

Gould, Anne. "Tragedy and the Heroism of Richard II," *Thoth*, 1#2: 1-13 (Fall, 1959).

Greenberg, Robert A. "Shakespeare's *Richard II*, IV, i, 244-250," *The Explicator*, 15#5: 29 (Feb, 1957).

Griffin, William J. "Conjectures on a Missing Line in *Richard II*," *Tennessee Studies in Literature*, 7: 105-112 (1962).

Hastead, William L. "Artilce and Artistry in *Richard II* and *Othello*," *University of Miami Publications in English and American Literature*, 7: 19-35 (1964).

Heninger, S. K., Jr. "The Sun King Analogy in *Richard II*," *Shakespeare Quarterly*, 11#3: 319-327 (Summer, 1960).

Hill, R. F. "Dramatic Techniques and Interpretation in *Richard II*," *Stratford-Upon-Avon Studies*, 3: 101-122 (1961).

Hockey, Dorothy C. "A World of Rhetoric in *Richard II*," *Shakespeare Quarterly*, 15#3: 179-191 (Summer, 1964).

Humphreys, Arthur. "Shakespeare's Political Justice in *Richard II* and *Henry IV*," *Stratford Papers on Shakespeare*, 5: 30-50 (1964).

Ionesco, Eugene. "Experience of the Theatre," in Robert W. Corrigan and James L. Rosenberg (eds.), *The Context and Craft of Drama*, 290-292.

Jorgensen, Paul A. "Vertical Patterns in *Richard II*," *Shakespeare Association Bulletin*, 23#3: 119-134 (July, 1948).

Kleinstuck, J. "The Character of Bolingbroke," *Neophilologus*, pp. 51-56 (Jan, 1957).

Kliger, Samuel. "The Sun Imagery in *Richard II*," *Studies in Philology*, 45#2: 196-202 (April, 1948).

Knight, George W. *The Golden Labyrinth*, 71-72.

——————. *The Imperial Theme*, 351-367.

——————. *The Olive and the Sword*, 20-24.

——————. *The Sovereign Flower,* 29-33.

Law, Robert A. "Deviations From Holinshed in *Richard II,*" *Studies in English (University of Texas),* 29: 91-101 (1950).

McAvoy, William C. "Form in *Richard II,* II, i, 40-66," *Journal of English and Germanic Philology,* 54#3: 355-361 (July, 1955).

McCollom, William G. *Tragedy,* 140-141 ; 193-196.

——————. "Formalism and Illusion in Shakespearian Drama," *Quarterly Journal of Speech,* 31#4: 446-448 (Dec, 1945).

McDonnell, R. F. *The Aspiring Mind,* 206-226.

McManaway, James G. "*Richard II* at Convent Garden," *Shakespeare Quarterly,* 15#2: 161-175 (Spring, 1964).

McPeek, James A. S. "Richard and His Shadow World," *American Imago,* 15#2: 195-212 (Summer, 1958).

Marvin, John Trumbull. "The Nature of Causation in the History Plays," in Margery Bailey (ed.), *Ashland Studies for Shakespeare,* 61-67.

Michel, Laurence (& Cecil C. Seronsy). "Shakespeare's History Plays and *Daniel:* An Assessment," *Studies in Philology,* 52#4: 551-563 (Oct, 1955).

Muir, Kenneth. "Three Shakespeare Adaptations," *Proceedings of the Leeds Philosophical and Literary Society,* 8Pt. 4: 239-240 (Jan, 1959).

Nearing, Homer Jr. "A Three-Way Pun in *Richard II,*" *Modern Language Notes,* 62#1: 31-33 (Jan, 1947).

Owen, Lewis J. "*Richard II,*" *Carnegie Series in English,* 1: 3-18 (1953).

Pearce, Josephine A. "Constituent Elements in Shakespeare's English History Plays," *University of Miami Publications in English and American Literature,* 1: 149-150 (March, 1953).

Phialas, Peter G. "The Medieval in *Richard II,*" *Shakespeare Quarterly,* 12#3: 305-310 (Summer, 1961).

Poisson, R. "*Richard II:* Tudor Orthodoxy or Political Heresy," *The Humanities Association Bulletin,* 14: 5-11 (Fall, 1963).

Provost, Forster. "The Sorrows of Shakespeare's Richard II," in Waldo McNeir (ed.), *Studies in English Renaissance,* 40-55.

Quinn, Michael. " 'The King is not Himself': The Personal Tragedy of Richard II," *Studies in Philology,* 56#2: 169-186 (April, 1959).

Reed, Robert R. Jr. "Richard II: Portrait of a Psychotic," *Journal of General Education,* 16#1: 55-67 (April, 1964).

Reiman, Donald H. "Appearance, Reality, and Moral Order in *Richard II,*" *Modern Language Quarterly,* 25#1: 34-45 (March, 1964).

Ribner, Irving. *The English History Play in the Age of Shakespeare,* 154-167.

——————————. "Bolingbroke, a True Machiavellian," *Modern Language Quarterly,* 9: 177-184 (1948).

——————————. "The Political Problem in Shakespeare's Lancastrian Tetralogy," *Studies in Philology,* 49#2: 174-182 (April, 1952).

Smith, Stella T. "Imagery of Downward Motion in Shakespeare's *King Richard The Second,*" *Shakespeare Newsletter,* 4#1: 8 (Feb, 1954).

Speaight, Robert. "Shakespeare and the Political Spectrum," *Stratford Papers on Shakespeare,* 5: 135-154 (1964).

Stirling, Brents. "Bolingbroke's 'Decision'," *Shakespeare Quarterly,* 2#1: 27-34 (Jan, 1951).

Suzman, Arthur. "Imagery and Symbolism in *Richard II,*" *Shakespeare Quarterly,* 7#4: 355-370 (Autumn, 1956).

Takeuchi, H. "What We Should Learn From Shakespeare's Historical Plays: The People's Voice Behind the Scenes: *King John* and *Richard II,*" *The Humanities (Yokahama),* 2#3: 1-13 (June, 1954).

Thompson, Karl F. "Richard II, Martyr," *Shakespeare Quarterly,* 8#2: 159-166 (Spring, 1957).

Traversi, Derek. *"Richard II,"* *Stratford Papers on Shakespeare,* 5: 11-29 (1964).

Tyler, Parker. "Phaeton: The Metaphysical Tension Between the Ego and the Universe in English Poetry," *Accent,* 16: 29-44 (1956).

Ure, Peter. "The Looking Glass of Richard II," *Philological Quarterly,* 34#2: 219-224 (April, 1955).

Yamamoto, Tadao. "The Verbal Structure of *Richard the Second,*" *Zeitschrift fur Anglistik und Amerikanistik,* 12#2: 163-172 (1964).

Young, Stark. *Immortal Shadows,* 196-199.

RICHARD III

Arnold, Aerol. "The Recapitulation Dream in *Richard III* and *Macbeth,*" *Shakespeare Quarterly,* 6#1: 51-56 (Winter, 1955).

Badawi, M. M. "The Paradox of *Richard III,*" *Bulletin of the*

Faculty of Arts (Alexandria University), 12: 49-68 (1958).

Bamborough, J. *The Little World of Man*, 131-132.

Bogard, Travis. "Shakespeare's Second Richard," *PMLA*, 70#1: 192-209 (March, 1955).

Brown, John R. "Mr. Beckett's Shakespeare," *Critical Quarterly*, 5#4: 319-323 (Winter, 1963).

Carnall, Geoffrey. "Shakespeare's Richard III and St. Paul," *Shakespeare Quarterly*, 14#2: 186-188 (Spring, 1963).

Clemen, Wolfgang H. "Anticipation and Foreboding in Shakespeare's Early Histories," *Shakespeare Survey*, 6: 26-30 (1953).

—————————. "Tradition and Originality in Shakespeare's *Richard III*," *Shakespeare Quarterly*, 5#3: 247-258 (Summer, 1954).

Cunningham, James. *Woe or Wonder*, 14; 56; 57.

Dollarhide, Louis E. "Two Unassimilated Movements of *Richard III*: An Interpretation," *Mississippi Quarterly*, 14#1: 40-46 (Winter, 1960-1961).

Draper, John W. "Patterns of Tempo in *Richard III*," *Neuphilologische Mitteilungen*, 50#1-2: 1-12 (1949).

Foote, Dorothy Norris. "Shakespeare's *Richard III*, IV, iv, 174-177," *The Explicator*, 23#3: 23 (Nov, 1964).

Gerber, R. "Elizabethan Convention and Psychological Realism in the Dream and Last Soliloquy of *Richard III*," *English Studies*, 40#4: 294-300 294-300 (Aug, 1959).

Hartsock, Mildred E. "Shakespeare's *Richard III*, IV, iv, 174-179," *The Explicator*, 20#9: 71 (May, 1962).

Heilman, Robert B. "Saiety and Conscience: Aspects of *Richard III*," *Antioch Review*, 24#1: 57-73 (Spring, 1964).

Hosley, Richard. "More About 'Tents on Bosworth Field'," *Shakespeare Quarterly*, 7: 458-459 (1956).

Knight, G. Wilson. *The Olive and the Sword*, 16-20.

—————————. *The Sovereign Flower*, 21-25.

Krieger, Murrary. "The Dark Generations of Richard III," *Criticism*, 1#1: 32-48 (Winter, 1959).

Lordi, Robert J. "The Relationship of *Richard Tertius* to the Main Richard III Plays," *Boston University Studies in English*, 5#3: 142-150 (Autumn, 1961).

McCollom, William G. *Tragedy*, 192-193.

McDonnell, R. F. *The Aspiring Mind*, 187-206.

Marvin, John T. "The Nature of Causation in the History Plays," in Margery Bailey (ed), *Ashland Studies for Shakespeare 1962*, 50-56.

Mellinkoff, Ruth and Marjorie Hexter. "Studies in *King Richard the Third,*" *Asides,* 4: 21-23 (1943/44).

Meyerstein, E. H. *"Richard III,* I.i.32," *Review of English Studies, 22#85:* 53 (Jan, 1946).

Morris, William C. "Consistency in *Richard III,*" *Drama Critique, 7#1:* 40-46 (Winter, 1964).

Nathan, Norman. "The Marriage of Richard and Anne," *Notes and Queries,* 200: 55-56 (Feb, 1955).

Parsons, Howard. *"Richard III,*" *Notes and Queries,* 200: 175-176 (April, 1955).

——————. "Shakespeare Emendations *Richard III,*" *Notes and Queries,* 200: 288-289 (July, 1955).

Petofi, Sandor. "Hungarian Poets on Shakespeare," *New Hungarian Quarterly,* 5#13: 48-51 (Spring, 1964).

Quinn, Michael. "Providence in Shakespeare's Yorkist Plays," *Shakespeare Quarterly,* 10#1: 45-46; 50-52 (Winter, 1959).

Ribner, Irving. *The English History Play in the Age of Shakespeare,* 116-124.

Shaw, G. B. *Plays and Players,* 142-151.

Smidt, Kristian. "Injurious Impostors and Richard III," *Norwegian Studies in English,* 12: 213 pages, (1964).

Tillyard, Eustace M. *Some Mythical Elements in English Literature,* 57-61.

Tucker, William John. "Irish Aspects of Shakespeare," *Catholic World,* 156: 702 (March, 1943).

Ure, Peter. "Character and Role From Richard III to Hamlet," *Stratford-Upon-Avon Studies,* 5: 13-19 (1963).

Williams, Philip. *"Richard The Third:* The Battle Orations," in *English Studies in Honor of James Southall Wilson,* 125-130.

Wilson, J. Dover. "Shakespeare's *Richard III* and the *True Tragedy of Richard The Third,* 1594," *Shakespeare Quarterly,* 3#4: 299-306 (Oct, 1952).

——————. "The Composition of the Clarence Scenes in *Richard III,*" *Modern Language Review,* 53#2: 211-214 (April, 1958).

——————. "A Note on *Richard III:* The Bishop of Ely's Strawberries," *Modern Language Review,* 52: 563-564 (1957).

Zuk, Gerald H. "A Note on Richard's Anxiety Dream," *American Imago,* 14#1: 37-39 (Spring, 1957).

ROMEO AND JULIET

Adams, J. C. "Shakespeare's Use of the Upper Stage in *Romeo and Juliet*," *Shakespeare Quarterly*, 7#2: 145-152 (Spring, 1956).

Adler, Jacob H. "Shakespeare in *Winterset*," *Educational Theatre Journal*, 6#3: 244-245 (Oct, 1954).

Allen, Ned B. "Shakespeare and Arthur Brooke," *Delaware Notes*, 17th Series: 91-110 (1944).

Aronson, Alex. "A Note on Shakespeare's Dream Imagery," *Visuabharati Quarterly*, 18#2: 171-172 (Aug-Oct, 1952).

Battenhouse, Roy A. "Shakespearean Tragedy: A Christian Interpretation," in Nathan A. Scott Jr. (ed.), *The Tragic Vision and the Christian Faith*, 89-93.

Bonnard, Georges A. "*Romeo and Juliet:* A Possible Significance?" *Review of English Studies*, 2NS#8: 319-327 (Oct, 1951).

Bowling, Lawrence Edward. "The Thematic Framework of *Romeo and Juliet*," *PMLA*, 64#1Pt.1: 208-220 (March, 1949).

Bulgin, Randolph M. "Drama Imagery in Shakespeare's *Romeo and Juliet*," *Shenandoah*, 11#2: 23-38 (Winter, 1960).

Cain, H. Edward. "An Emendation in *Romeo and Juliet*," *Shakespeare Association Bulletin*, 17#1: 57-60 (Jan, 1942).

——————. " 'Parting' and Justice in *Romeo and Juliet*," *Tennessee Studies in Literature*, 7: 99-104 (1962).

——————. "*Romeo and Juliet:* A Reinterpretation," *Shakespeare Association Bulletin*, 22#4: 163-192 (Oct, 1944).

——————. "A Technique of Motivation in *Romeo and Juliet*," *Shakespeare Association Bulletin*, 21#4: 186-190 (Oct, 1946).

Cairncross, A. S. "*The Impact*, 3, i, 15 and *Romeo*, 1, i, 121-128," *Shakespeare Quarterly*, 7: 448-450 (1956).

Chapman, Raymond. "Double Time in *Romeo and Juliet*," *Modern Language Review*, 44#3: 371-374 (July, 1949).

Cohen, Hennig. "Shakespeare's *Romeo and Juliet*, V, iii, 112-115," *The Explicator*, 8#3: 24 (Dec, 1949).

Coombes, H. *Literature and Criticism*, 127-129.

Culbert, Taylor. "A Note on *Romeo and Juliet*, I. iii. 89-90," *Shakespeare Quarterly*, 10#1: 129-132 (Winter, 1959).

Dean, Leonard F. "Shakespeare's *Romeo and Juliet*, II, i, 34-35," *The Explicator*, 3#6: 44 (April, 1945).

Draper, John W. "Contrast of Tempo in the Balcony Scene,"

Shakespeare Association Bulletin, 22#3: 130-135 (July, 1947).

Driver, Tom F. "The Shakespearean Clock: Time and the Vision of Reality in *Romeo and Juliet* and *The Tempest,*" *Shakespeare Quarterly,* 15#4: 363- 367 (Autumn, 1964).

Eardley-Wilmot, H. "Write me a Prologue," *English,* 8#48: 272-274 (Aut, 1951).

Evans, Bertrand. "The Brevity of Friar Laurence," *PMLA,* 65#5: 841-865 (Sept, 1950).

Evans, Robert O. "*Romeo and Juliet* II. i. 13: Further Commentary," *Neuphilologische Mitteilungen,* 64#4: 390-400 (1963).

Freeman, Arthur. "Shakespeare and *Solyman and Perseda,*" *Modern Language Review,* 58#4: 481-483 (Oct, 1963).

Frye, Prosser H. *Romance and Tragedy,* 290-291.

Gabor, Miklos. "An Actor's Thoughts," *New Hungarian Quarterly,* 5#13: 74-75 (Spring, 1964).

Gordon, R. K. "Scott and Shakespeare's Tragedies," *Royal Society of Canada Proceedings and Transactions,* 39#2: 116-117 (1945).

Harrison, Thomas P. Jr. "Hang Up Philosophy," *Shakespeare Association Bulletin,* 22#4: 203-209 (Oct, 1947).

Hart, John A. "*Romeo and Juliet,*" *Carnegie Series in English,* 8:17-32 (1964).

Heilman, Robert B. "To Know Himself: An Aspect of Tragic Structure," *Review of English Literature,* 5#2: 36-39 (April, 1964).

Henry, William A. "Theme and Image in *Romeo and Juliet,*" *Thoth,* 3#1: 13-17 (Winter, 1962).

Hepburn, James G. "A Dream That Hath no Bottom: Comment on Mr. Holland's Paper," *Literature and Psychology,* 14#1: 3-6 (Winter, 1964).

Holland, Norman. "Romeo's Dream and the Paradox of Literary Realism," *Literature and Psychology,* 13#4: 97-103 (Fall, 1963).

Hoppe, Harry R. "The Bad Quarto of *Romeo and Juliet:* A Bibliographical and Textual Study," *Cornell Studies in English,* 36: 230 pages (1948).

Hosley, Richard. "The 'Good Night, Good Night' Sequence in *Romeo and Juliet,*" *Shakepeare Quarterly,* 5#1: 96-98 (Jan, 1954).

————. "The Use of the Upper Stage in *Romeo and Juliet,*" *Shakespeare Quarterly,* 5#4: 371-379 (Autumn, 1954).

Jackson, Stoney. *This is Love?*, 15-20.

Jepsen, Laura. *Ethical Aspects of Tragedy*, 84-87.

Keil, Harry. "Scabies and the Queen Mab Passage in *Romeo and Juliet*," *Journal of the History of Ideas*, 18#3: 394-396; 407-410 (June, 1957).

Kildahl, Erling E. "*Romeo and Juliet:* Three Directing Problems," *Speech Teacher*, 1#3: 181-186 (Sept, 1952).

Krumpelmann, John T. "Lessing's *Faust* Fragment and *Romeo and Juliet*," *Modern Language Notes*, 64#6: 395-397 (June, 1949).

Laird, David. "The Generation of Style in *Romeo and Juliet*," *Journal of English and Germanic Philology*, 63#2: 204-213 (April, 1964).

Lawlor, John. "*Romeo and Juliet*," *Stratford-Upon-Avon Studies*, 3: 123-144 (1961).

Lawson, John H. *Theory and Technique of Playwriting*, 267-269.

Levin, Harry. "Form and Formality in *Romeo and Juliet*," *Shakespeare Quarterly*, 11#1: 3-11 (Winter, 1960).

Levin, Richard. "'Littera Canina' in *Romeo and Juliet* and 'Michaelmas Term'," *Notes and Queries*, 207: 333-334 (Sept, 1962).

Link, Frederick M. "*Romeo and Juliet:* Character and Tragedy," *Boston University Studies in English*, 1#1-2: 9-19 (Spring-Summer, 1955).

Lord, John B. "Comic Scenes in Shakespearean Tragedy," *Washington State College Research Studies*, 32#3: 235 (Sept, 1964).

McArthur, Herbert. "Romeo's Loquacious Friend," *Shakespeare Quarterly*, 10#1: 35-44 (Winter, 1959).

McNeir, Waldo F. "The Closing of the Capulet Tomb," *Studia Neophilologica*, 28#1: 3-8 (1956).

——————. "Shakespeare, *Romeo and Juliet*, III, i, 40-44," *The Explicator*, 11#7: #48 (May, 1953).

Mahnken, Harry E. and Janine S. Mahnken. "Harley Granville-Barker's Shakespearean Criticism," *Southern Speech Journal*, 27#1: 27-28 (Fall, 1961).

Mark, Milton. *The Enjoyment of Drama*, 103-105.

Myers, Henry A. "*Romeo and Juliet* and *A Midsummer Night's Dream:* Tragedy and Comedy," in Henry A. Myers, *Tragedy*, 110-128.

ALSO IN: Sylvan Barnet, *Aspects of the Drama*, 35-43.

Nolan, Paul T. "Congreve's Lovers: Art and the Critic," *Drama Survey*, 1#3: 335-339 (Feb, 1962).

Nosworthy, J. M. "The Two Angry Families of Verona," *Shakespeare Quarterly,* 3#3: 219-226 (July, 1952).

Olive, W. J. "Twenty Good Nights," *Studies in Philology,* 47#2: 182-189 (April, 1950).

Parsons, Philip. "Shakespeare and the Mask," *Shakespeare Survey,* 16: 124-131 (1963).

Pettet, E. C. "The Imagery of *Romeo and Juliet,*" *English,* 8#45: 121-126 (Autumn, 1950).

Praz, Mario. *The Flaming Heart,* 157-160.

Prior, Moody E. *The Language and Tragedy,* 61-73.

Rehder, Helmut. "Novalis and Shakespeare," *PMLA,* 63#2: 604-624 (June, 1948).

Ribner, Irving. " 'Then I Denie you Starres' :- A Reading of *Romeo and Juliet,*" in *Studies in the English Renaissance Drama in Memory of Karl J. Holzknecht,* 269-286.

Rosenheim, Edward W. Jr. *What Happens in Literature,* 97-108.

Ross, J. L. *Philosophy in Literature,* 255-263.

Rottenberg, Annette T. "The Early Love Drama," *College English,* 23#7: 579-582 (April, 1962).

Satin, Joseph. *"Romeo and Juliet* as Renaissance Vita Nuova," *Discourse: A Review of the Liberal Arts,* 3#2: 67-85 (April, 1960).

Schanzer, Ernest. "Atavism and Anticipation in Shakespeare's Style," *Essays in Criticism,* 7#3: 244-245 (July, 1957).

Shapiro, Stephen A. *"Romeo and Juliet:* Reversals, Contraries," *College English,* 25#7: 498-501 (April, 1964).

Shaw, G. B. *Plays and Players,* 41-49.

Siegel, Paul N. "Christianity and the Religion of Love in *Romeo and Juliet,*" *Shakespeare Quarterly,* 371-392 (Autumn, 1961).

Sjogren, Gunnar. " 'Sirrah, Go Hire Me Twenty Cunning Crooks'," *Shakespeare Quarterly,* 12#2: 161-163 (Spring, 1961).

Smith, Robert Metcalf. "Three Interpretations of *Romeo and Juliet,*" *Shakespeare Association Bulletin,* 23#2: 60-77 April, 1948).

Spencer, Theodore. "The Isolation of the Shakespearean Hero," *Sewanee Review,* 52#3: 315-316 (July/Sept, 1944).

Stone, George W. Jr. *"Romeo and Juliet:* The Source of its Modern Stage Career," *Shakespeare Quarterly,* 15#2: 191-206 (Spring, 1964).

Strong, L. A. G. *The Sacred River,* 56.

Styan, J. L. *The Dark Comedy,* 18-20.

—————. *The Elements of Drama,* 25-26; 66-67; 70-72; 129-130; 233-234.

Sultana, Donald E. "On Re-Reading Shakespeare's *Romeo and Juliet," Journal of the Faculty of Arts* (Royal University of Malta), 1#1: 75-81 (1957).

Tanselle, G. Thomas. "Time in *Romeo and Juliet," Shakespeare Quarterly,* 15#4: 349-362 (Autumn, 1964).

Thomas, Geoffrey. *The Theatre Alive,* 161-163.

Thomas, Sidney. "The Earthquake in *Romeo and Juliet," Modern Language Notes,* 64#6: 417-419 (June, 1949).

—————. "Henry Chettle and the First Quarto of *Romeo and Juliet," Review of English Studies,* NS1#1: 8-16 (Jan, 1950).

Vaughan, William A. "The Oldest Version of *Romeo and Juliet* Revived," *Baconiana,* 34#135: 111-112 (April, 1950).

Walley, Harold R. "Shakespeare's Debt to Marlowe in *Romeo and Juliet," Philological Quarterly,* 21#3: 262-266 (July, 1942).

Williams, George Walton. "A Note on *Romeo and Juliet," Notes and Queries,* 207: 332-333 (Sept, 1962).

Williams, Philip Jr. "*Romeo and Juliet:* Littera Canina," *Notes Queries,* 195: 181-182 (29 April, 1950).

—————. "The Rosemary Theme in *Romeo and Juliet," Modern Language Notes,* 68#6: 400-403 (June, 1953).

Yaggy, Elinor. "Shakespeare and Melville's *Pierre," Boston Public Library Quarterly,* 6: 43-49 (Jan, 1954).

Young, Stark. *Immortal Shadows,* 25-28.

TAMING OF A SHREW, THE
See: Anon

TAMING OF THE SHREW, THE

Bamborough, J. *The Little World of Man,* 68-69.

Berman, Ronald. "Shakespeare Comedy and the Uses of Reason," *South Atlantic Quarterly,* 63#1: 4-9 (Winter, 1964).

Bradbrook, M. C. "Dramatic Role as Social Image: A Study of *The Taming of the Shrew," Shakespeare Jahrbuck,* 94: 132-150 (1958).

Brooks, Charles. "Shakespeare's Romantic Shrews," *Shakespeare Quarterly,* 11#3: 351-356 (Summer, 1960).

Draper, John W. "Shakespeare and Florence and the Florentines," *Italica,* 23 #4: 287-288 (Dec, 1946).

Hosley, Richard. "Was There a 'Dramatic Epilogue' to *The Taming of the Shrew?*" *Studies in English Literature 1500-1900,* 1#2: 17-34 (Spring, 1961).

――――――. "Sources and Analogues of *The Taming of the Shrew,*" *Huntington Library Quarterly,* 27#3: 289-308 (May, 1964).

Houk, Raymond A. "The Integrity of Shakespeare: *The Taming of the Shrew,*" *Journal of English and Germanic Philology,* 39#1: 222-229 (April, 1940).

――――――. "Shakespeare's Heroic Shrew," *Shakespeare Asociation Bulletin,* 18#4: 175-186 (Oct, 1943).

――――――. "Strata in *The Taming of The Shrew,*" *Studies in Philology,* 39#2: 291-302 (April, 1942).

――――――. "The Evolution of *The Taming of the Shrew,*" *PMLA,* 57#4: 1009-1038 (Dec, 1942).

――――――. "Shakespeare's *Shrew* and Green's *Orlando,*" *PMLA,* 62#3: 657-671 (Sept, 1947).

Jackson, Stoney. *This is Love?,* 26-31.

King, Thomson. *"The Taming of The Shrew,"* *Shakespeare Association Bulletin,* 17#2: 73-79 (April, 1942).

Moore, William H. "An Allusion in 1593 to *The Taming of The Shrew,*" *Shakespeare Quarterly,* 15#1: 55-60 (Winter, 1964).

Ravich, Robert A. "A Psychoanalytic Study of Shakespeare's Early Plays," *Psychoanalytic Quarterly,* 33#3: 399-400 (July, 1964).

――――――. "Shakespeare and Psychiatry," *Literary and Psychology,* 14#3&4: 102 (Summer/Fall, 1964).

Sanders, Norman. "Themes and Imagery in *The Taming of The Shrew,*" *Renaissance Papers,* pp. 63-72 (1963).

Seronsy, C. C. " 'Supposes' as the Unifying Theme in *The Shrew,*" *Shakespeare Quarterly,* 14#1: 15-30 (Winter, 1963).

Shroeder, John W. *"The Taming of A Shrew and The Taming of The Shrew:* A Case Reopened," *Journal of English and Germanic Philology,* 57#3: 424-443 (July, 1958).

Simpson, Percy. *Studies in Elizabethan Drama,* 22-23.

Sisson, C. J. *"The Taming of The Shrew,"* *Drama—The Quarterly Theatre Review,* NS#38: 25-27 (Autumn, 1955).

Taylor, George C. "Two Notes on Shakespeare," in B. Maxwell (ed), *Renaissance Studies in Honor of Hardin Craig,* 181-184.

Thomas, Sidney. "Note on *The Taming of the Shrew,*" *Modern Language Notes,* 64#2: 94-96 (Feb, 1949).

Tillyard, E. M. W. "Some Consequences of a Lacuna in *The Taming of The Shrew*," *English Studies*, 43#5: 330-335 (Oct, 1962).

Wentersdorf, K. "The Authenticity of *The Taming of The Shrew*," *Shakespeare Quarterly*, 5#1: 11-32 (Jan, 1954).

TEMPEST, THE

Abenheimer, K. M. "Shakespeare's *Tempest*—A Psychological Analysis," *Psychoanalytic Review*, 33#4: 399-415 (Oct, 1946).

Allen, Don Cameron. *Image and Meaning*, 42-66.

Arnold, Paul. "From the Dream in Aeschylus to the Surrealist Theater," *Journal of Aesthetics and Art Criticism, 7#4*: 350-352 (June, 1949).

Aronson, Alex. "A Note on Shakespeare's Dream Imagery," *Visuabharati Quarterly*, 18#2: 168-169 (Aug-Oct, 1952).

Auden, W. H. "Balaam and the Ass: The Master-Servant Relationship in Literature," *Thought*, 29#113: 255-261 (Summer, 1954).

Babb, Lawrence. "The Bulgarian Origins of *The Tempest* of Shakespeare," *Studies in Philology, 37#2*: 236-256 (1940).

Bacon, Wallace A. "A Note on *The Tempest*, IV, i," *Notes and Queries*, 192: 343-344 (9 Aug, 1947).

Bate, Walter J. *From Classic to Romantic*, 124-125.

Baum, Bernard. *"The Tempest and The Hairy Ape:* The Literary Incarnation of Mythos," *Modern Language Quarterly*, 14: 258-273 (Sept, 1953).

Berry, Francis. *Poet's Grammar*, 76-78.

——————. "Shakespeare's Directive to the Player of Caliban," *Notes and Queries, 202*: 27 (1957).

Bickersteth, G. L. "The Philosophy of Shakespeare," *Aberdeen University Review*, 28#3: 179-183 (Summer, 1941).

Boas, Ralph P. "Shakespeare's *The Tempest*, V, i, 181-184," *The Explicator, 2#1*: 3 (Oct, 1943).

Bowen, H. E. " 'I'll Break My Staff . . . I'll Drown My Book'," *Renaissance Papers*, pp. 47-56 (1961).

Bower, Reuben A. "The Heresy of Plot," *English Institute Essays*, pp. 62-69 (1951).

Bowling, Lawrence E. "The Theme of Natural Order in *The Tempest*," *College English*, 12#4: 203-209 (Jan, 1951).

Brower, Reuben A. *The Fields of Light*, 13-14; 95-122; 210-215.

——————. "The Heresy of Plot," *English Institute Essays*, pp. 63-68 (1951).

Brown, J. R. "A Study of *The Tempest*," *Shakespeare News-letter*, 4#6: 49 (Dec, 1954).

Bullough, Geoffrey. *Mirror of Minds*, 87-89.

Bundy, Murray W. "The Allegory of *The Tempest*," *Washington State College Research Studies*, 32#3: 189-206 (Sept, 1964).

Cairncross, A. S. "*The Tempest*, 3, i, 15 and *Romeo and Juliet*, 1, i, 121-128," *Shakespeare Quarterly*, 7: 448-450 (1956).

Camden, Carroll. "Songs and Choruses in *The Tempest*," *Philological Quarterly*, 41#1: 114-122 (Jan, 1962).

Campbell, Oscar James. "Miss Webster and *The Tempest*," *American Scholar*, 14#3: 271-281 (Summer, 1945).

Craig, Hardin. "Propsero's Renunciation," *Shakespeare Newsletter*, 3#2: 13 (April, 1953).

—————————. "Introduction to the Tempest" (From his *An Introduction to Shakespeare*) in Robert W. Stallman and R. E. Walters (eds), *The Creative Reader*, 623-625.

Cutts, John P. "The Role of Music in *The Tempest*," *Shakespeare Newsletter*, 9#1: 4 (Feb, 1959).

Davidson, Frank. "*The Tempest*: An Interpretation," *Journal of English and Germanic Philology*, 62#3: 501-517 (July, 1963).

Dobree, Bonamy. "*The Tempest*," *Essays and Studies*, 5: 13-25 (1952).

Draper, J. W. "Humor and Tempo in *The Tempest*," *Neuphilologische Mitteilungen*, 52#7-8: 205-217 (1951).

—————————. " 'Indian' and 'Indies' in Shakespeare," *Neuphilologische Mitteilungen*, 56#3-4: 107-112 (1955).

Driver, Tom F. "The Shakespearean Clock: Time and the Vision of Reality in *Romeo and Juliet* and *The Tempest*," *Shakespeare Quarterly*, 15#4: 363-364; 367-370 (Autumn, 1964).

Fain, John T. "Ariel's Song," *Shakespeare Newsletter*, 4#6: 50 (Dec, 1954).

Flint, M. K. (& E. J. Dobson). "Weak Masters," *Review of English Studies*, 10#37: 58-60 (Feb, 1959).

Fox, Charles O. "A Crux in *The Tempest*," *Notes and Queries*, 202: 515-516 (Dec, 1957).

Gamal, Sand M. "The Function of Song in Shakespeare's Comedies," *Cairo Studies in English*, pg. 120 (1961/62).

Gesner, Carol. "*The Tempest* as Pastoral Romance," *Shakespeare Quarterly*, 10#4: 531-539 (Autumn, 1959).

Gillie, Christopher. "*The Tempest*," *The Use of English*, 7#1: 37-41 (Aut, 1955).

Goddard, Harold C. "The Meaning of the *Tempest*," in Robert W. Stallman and R. E. Walters (eds), *The Creative Reader*, 633-642.

Gohn, E. *"The Tempest:* Theme and Structure," *English Studies*, 45#2 : 116-125 (April, 1964).

Gregoire, Henri. "The Bulgarian Origins of *The Tempest*," *Studies in Philology*, 37#2: 236-256 (April, 1940).

Hankins, John E. "Caliban the Beastial Man," *PMLA*, 62#3: 793-801 (Sept, 1947).

Harris, R. G. "A Temperate in a Torrid Zone," *Makerere Journal*, 1 : 55-71 (1958).

Harrison, G. B. *"The Tempest,"* Stratford Papers on Shakespeare*, 3: 212-238 (1962).

Harrison, Thomas P. Sr. "The 'Broom-Groves' in *The Tempest*," *Shakespeare Association Bulletin*, 20#1 : 39-45 (Jan, 1945).

————————. "A Note on *The Tempest:* A Sequel," *Modern Language Notes*, 58#6 : 422-426 (June, 1943).

Harrison, Thomas P., Jr. "Aspects of Primitivism in Shakespeare and Spenser," *Studies in English (University of Texas)*, 4026: 49-61 (July 8, 1940).

Hart, Jeffrey P. "Prospero and Fautus," *Boston University Studies in English*, 2#4: 197-206 (Winter, 1956).

Hart, John A. *"The Tempest,"* Carnegie Series in English*, 4: 71-83 (1958).

Heller, Agnes. "Shakespeare and Human Nature," *New Hungarian Quarterly*, 5#13: 20-21 (Spring, 1964).

Hilberry, C. *"The Tempest,* Act IV," *College English*, 23#7: 586-588 (April, 1962).

Hoeniger, F. D. "Prospero's Storm and Miracle," *Shakespeare Quarterly*, 7#1 : 33-38 (Winter, 1956).

Honig, Edwin. *Dark Conceit*, 37-38.

Hoy, Cyrus H. *The Hyacinth Room*, 273-281.

Hutchens, Eleanor N. "The Transfer of Power in *King Lear* and *The Tempest*," *Review of English Literature*, 4#2: 82-93 (April, 1963).

James, Henry. *Selected Literary Criticism*, 296-310.

Jaroslav, Hornat. "Two Euphuistic Stories of Robert Greene: *The Carde of Fancie* and *Pandosto*," *Philologica Pragensia*, 1 : 34-35 (1963).

Johnson, W. Stacy. "The Genesis of Ariel," *Shakespeare Quarterly*, 2#3: 205-210 (July, 1951).

Jones, H. W. *"The Tempest,* III, i. 13-17," *Notes and Queries*, 195 : 293-294 (July, 1950).

King, A. H. "Some Notes on Shakespeare's *The Tempest*," *English Studies*, 22#2: 70-74 (April, 1940).

King, S. K. "Eliot, Yeats, and Shakespeare," *Theoria,* 5: 115-118 (1953).

Knight, G. Wilson. *The Crown of Life,* 203-255.

——————. *The Golden Labyrinth,* 83-85; 126-128; 348-349.

——————. *The Olive and the Sword,* 65-68.

——————. *The Sovereign Flower,* 69-73.

Knight, G. W. "On the Mystic Symolism of Shakespeare," *Aryan Path,* 35: 458 (Oct, 1964).

Knox, Bernard. "*The Tempest* and the Ancient Comic Tradition," *English Institute Essays,* pp. 52-73 (1954). ALSO IN: *Virginia Quarterly Review,* 31#1: 73-89 (Winter, 1955).

Kokeritz, Helge. "The Pole-Clipt Vineyard, *The Tempest,* IV, i, 68," *Modern Language Review,* 39#2: 178-179 (April, 1944).

Kuhl, E. P. "Shakespeare and the Founders of America: *The Tempest,*" *Philological Quarterly,* 41#1: 123-146 (Jan, 1962).

Laurent, Martha. "Shakespeare's *The Tempest,* V, i, 134-148," *The Explicator,* 22#8: 65 (April, 1964).

Leech, Clifford. "Shakespeare's Comic Dukes," *Review of English Literature,* 5#2: 113-114 (April, 1964).

Levin, Richard. "Anatomical Geography in *The Tempest,* IV. i. 235-238," *Notes and Queries,* 209: 142-146 (April, 1964).

Lodge, David. "Conrad's *Victory* and *The Tempest:* An Amplification," *Modern Language Review,* 59#2: 195-199 (April, 1964).

Long, John R. "The Dramatic Functions of the Music in *The Tempest,*" *Shakespeare Newsletter,* 2#3/4: 11 (March/April, 1952).

Lowenthal, Leo. *Literature and the Image of Man,* 57-97; 221-229.

McPeek, James A. "The Genesis of Caliban," *Philological Quarterly,* 25#4: 378-381 (Oct, 1946).

Madsen, William G. "The Destiny of Man in *The Tempest,*" *Emory University Quarterly,* 20#3: 175-182 (Fall, 1964).

Major, John M. "*Comus* and *The Tempest,*" *Shakespeare Quarterly,* 10#2: 177-184 (Spring, 1959).

Marx, Leo. "Shakespeare's American Fable," *Massachusetts Review,* 2#1: 40-71 (Aut, 1960).

Melchiori, Barbara. "Still Harping on my Daughter," *English Miscellany,* 11: 65-72 (1960).

Merton, Stephen. *"The Tempest* and *Troilus and Cressida,"* *College English,* 7#3 : 143-150 (Dec, 1945).

Miles, L. Wardlaw. "Shakespeare's Old Men," *ELH, 7#4:* 297-298 (Dec, 1940).

Mitchell, Lee. "Shakespeare's Legerdemain," *Speech Monographs,* 16#1 : 144-150; 152-153; 157-161 (Aug, 1949).

——————. "Two Notes on *The Tempest,"* *Educational Theatre Journal, 2#3 :* 228-234 (Oct, 1950).

Moore, John R. *"The Tempest* and *Robinson Crusoe,"* *Review of English Studies,* 21#81: 52-56 (Jan, 1945).

Munro, John. "Shakespeare's *Tempest,"* *New English Review,* 12#1 : 61-69 (Jan, 1946).

Nelson, Robert J. *Play Within a Play,* 30-34.

Nuzum, David G. "The London Company and *The Tempest,"* *University of West Virginia Bulletin: Philological Papers,* 12 : 12-23 (1959).

Orgel, Stephen K. "New Uses of Adversity: Tragic Experience in *The Tempest,"* in Reuben A. Bower (ed), *In Defense of Reading,* 110-132.

Parsons, Howard. "Further Emendations in *The Tempest,"* *Notes and Queries,* 195 : 74-75 (18 Feb, 1950).

——————. "Further Emendations in *The Tempest,"* *Notes and Queries,* 196: 54-55 (3 Feb, 1951).

——————. "Shakespeare's *Tempest:* A Further Emendation," *Notes and Queries,* 194: 424 (1 Oct, 1949).

——————. "Shakespeare's *Tempest:* An Emendation," *Notes and Queries,* 194: 121-122 (19 March, 1949).

——————. "Shakespeare's *Tempest:* An Emendation," *Notes and Queries,* 194: 303 (9 July, 1949).

——————. *"The Tempest:* Further Emendations," *Notes and Queries,* 195: 294-295 (8 July, 1950).

——————. "Shakespeare was Prospero," *Poetry Review,* 44#4: 468-470 (Oct/Dec, 1953).

Phillips, James E. *"The Tempest* and the Renaissance Idea of Man," *Shakespeare Quarterly,* 15#2: 147-159 (Spring, 1964).

Polak, A. Laurence. *"The Tempest* and The Magic Flute," *English,* 9#49: 2-7 (Spring, 1952).

Reed, Henry. "W. H. Auden in America," *New Writing and Daylight,* pp. 131-135 (1945).

Reed, Robert R., Jr. "The Probable Origin of Ariel," *Shakespeare Quarterly,* 11#1 : 61-65 (Winter, 1960).

Rickey, Mary Ellen. "Prospero's Living Drolleries," *Renaissance Papers,* pp. 35-42 (1964).

Robinson, James E. "Time and *The Tempest,*" *Journal of English and Germanic Philology,* 63#2: 255-267 (April, 1964).

Rose, B. W. *"The Tempest:* A Reconsideration of its Meaning," *English Studies in Africa,* 1#2: 205-217 (Sept, 1958).

Sachs, H. *The Creative Unconscious,* 243-323.

Semper, I. J. "Shakespeare's Religion Once More," *Catholic World,* 156: 595 (Feb, 1943).

Shaaber, M. A. "A Living Drollery (Tempest, III, iii. 21), *Modern Language Notes,* 60#6: 387-391 (June, 1945).

Shaw, G. B. *Plays and Players,* 275-279.

Shorter, Robert N. "Footnotes to Shakepeare," *Union College Symposium,* pp. 30-31 (Summer, 1964).

Simpson, Percy. "The Supposed Crux in *The Tempest,*" *Review of English Studies,* 22#87: 224-225 (July, 1946).

Sisson, C. J. "The Magic of Prospero," *Shakespeare Survey,* 11: 70-77 (1958).

Smith, Irwin. "Ariel as Ceres," *Shakespeare Quarterly,* 9#3: 430-432 (Summer, 1958).

Spaeight, Robert. "Shakespeare and Politics," *Essays by Divers Hands,* 24: 18-20 (1948).

Speaight, Robert. "Nature and Grace in *The Tempest,*" *Dublin Review,* 227#459: 28-51 (1953).

Spears, Monroe K. "Late Auden: The Satirist as Lunatic Clergyman," *Sewanee Review,* 59#1: 66-71 (Winter, 1951).

Spencer, Theodore. "The Isolation of the Shakespearean Hero," *Sewanee Review,* 52#3: 330-331 (July/Sept, 1944).

Subbotin, A. L. "Shakespeare and Bacon," *The Soviet Review,* 5#3: 10-13 (Fall, 1964).

Symons, Julian. "The Double Man," *Focus,* 2: 128-136 (1946).

Traversi, Derek. *"The Tempest,"* *Scrutiny,* 16#2: 127-157 (June, 1949).

———————. "The Last Plays of Shakespeare, *Guide to English Literature,* 2: 266-273.

Waterston, G. Chychele. "Shakespeare and Montaigne: A Footnote to *The Tempest,*" *Romanic Review,* 40#3: 161-164 (Oct, 1949).

West, Rebecca. *The Court and the Castle,* 49-58.

William, David. *"The Tempest* on Stage," *Stratford-Upon-Avon Studies,* 1: 133-158 (1960).

Williams, Joseph M. "Caliban and Ariel Meet Trager and Smith," *College English,* 24#2: 124-126 (Nov, 1962).

Wilson, H. S. "Action and Symbol in *Measure for Measure* and *The Tempest,*" *Shakespeare Quarterly,* 4#4: 381-384 (Oct, 1953).

Wincor, Richard. "Shakespeare's Festival Plays," *Shakespeare Quarterly,* 1#4: 219-223; 233-240 (Oct, 1950).

Young, Stark. *Immortal Shadow,* 246-248.

Zimbardo, Roe A. "Form and Disorder in *The Tempest,*" *Shakespeare Quarterly,* 14#1: 49-58 (Winter, 1963).

Zucker, David H. "Miranda's Nature and Her Education," *Thoth,* 5#2: 55-61 (Spring, 1964).

TIMON OF ATHENS

Babb, Lawrence. *Elizabethan Malady,* 94-95.

Bamborough, J. *The Little World of Man,* 18-19; 115-116.

Collins, A. S. "*Timon of Athens:* A Reconsideration," *Review of English Studies,* 22#86: 96-108 (April, 1946).

Cook, David. "*Timon of Athens,*" *Shakespeare Survey,* 16: 83-94 (1963).

——————————. "The Psychology of Shakespeare's *Timon,*" *Modern Language Review,* 35#4: 521-525 (Oct, 1940).

Draper, John W. "Patterns of Tempo in *Timon,*" *Shakespeare Association Bulletin,* 23#4: 188-194 (Oct, 1948).

——————————. "Subjective Conflict in Shakespearean Tragedy," *Neuphilologische Mitteilungen,* 61#2: 217 (1960).

Draper, R. P. "Timon of Athens," Shakespeare Quarterly, 8#2: 195-200 (Spring, 1957).

Elliott, Robert C. *The Power of Satire,* 141-167; 180-181.

Ellis-Fermor, Una. *Frontiers of Drama,* 74-75.

——————————. "*Timon of Athens:* An Unfinished Play," *Review of English Studies,* 18#71: 270-283 (July, 1942).

Farnham, Willard. "The Beast Theme in Shakespeare's *Timon,*" *University of California Publications in English,* 14: 49-56 (1943).

Gomme, Andor. "*Timon of Athens,*" *Essays in Criticism,* 9#2: 107-125 (April, 1959).

Harrison, Thomas P., Jr. "Aspects of Primitivism in Shakespeare and Spenser," *Studies in English (University of Texas)* 4026: 64-71 (July 8, 1940).

Heilman, Robert B. "From Mine Own Knowledge: A Theme in the Late Tragedies," *Centenniel Review,* 8#1: 36-39 (Winter, 1964).

Holloway, John. *The Story of the Night,* 121-123; 131-134.

Honigmann, E. A. J. *"Timon of Athens,"* Shakespeare Quarterly, 12#1: 3-20 (Winter, 1961).

Hulme, Hilda M. "Two Notes on the Interpretation of Shakespeare's Text," *Notes and Queries,* 204: 354-355 (Oct, 1959).

Johnson, Edward D. *"Timon of Athens,"* Baconiana, 30#121: 158 (Oct, 1946).

Knight, George W. *The Golden Labyrinth,* 78-81; 83-84; 242-246.

——————. *The Olive and the Sword,* 48-51.

——————. *The Sovereign Flower,* 53-57.

——————. *"Timon of Athens,"* Review of English Literature, 2#4: 9-18 (Oct, 1961).

——————. "The Pilgrimage of Hate: An Essay on *Timon of Athens,"* in *The Wheel of Fire,* 207-239 (1962 ed.).

Kokeritz, Helge. "Five Shakespeare Notes," *Review of English Studies,* 23#92: 312-313 (Oct, 1947).

Leech, Clifford. "Shakespeare's Greeks," *Stratford Papers on Shakespeare,* 4: 4-8; 15-18 (1963).

Maxwell, J. C. *"Timon of Athens,"* Scrutiny, 15#3: 195-208 (Summer, 1948).

Merchant, W. M. *"Timon* and the Conceit of Art," *Shakespeare Quarterly,* 6#3: 249-258 (Summer, 1954).

——————. "The Harmony of Disenchantment," *Stratford on Shakespeare,* 4: 111-125 (1963).

Nowottny, Winifred M. T. "Acts IV and V of *Timon of Athens,"* Shakespeare Quarterly, 10#4: 493-497 (Autumn, 1959).

Pettet, E. C. *"Timon of Athens:* The Disruption of Feudal Morality," *Review of English Studies,* 23#92: 321-336 (Oct, 1947).

Phillips, James Emerson Jr. "The State in Shakespeare's Greek and Roman Plays," *Columbia University Studies in English and Comparative Literature,* 149: 126-146 (1940).

Pogson, Beryl. *In the East My Pleasure Lies,* 78-84.

Pyle, Fitzroy. "Hostilius: *Timon of Athens,* III, ii. 70," *Notes and Queries,* 197: 48-49 (Feb 2, 1952).

Roth, Robert. "Another World of Shakespeare," *Modern Philology,* 49#1: 51-57 (Aug, 1951).

Siegel, Paul N. "Shakespeare and the Neochivalric Cult of Honor," *Centenniel Review,* 8#1: 65-70 (Winter, 1964).

Sorelius, Gunnar. "Shadwell Deviating into Sense: Timon of

Athens and the Duke of Buckingham," *Studia Neophilologica,* 36#2: 232-241 (1964).

Spencer, Terence. "Shakespeare Learns the Value of Money: The Dramatist at Work on *Timon of Athens,*" *Shakespeare Survey,* 6: 75-78 (1953).

Tidwell, James N. "Shakespeare's 'Wappen'd Widow,' " *Notes Notes and Queries,* 195: 139-140 (1 April, 1950).

Tutt, Ralph. "Dog Imagery in *The Two Gentlemen From Verona, King Lear* and *Timon of Athens,*" *The Serif,* 1#3: 15-16; 18-21 (Oct, 1964).

Wahr, F. B. "The Timon Mood and its Corrective in Gerhardt Hauptmann," *Germanic Review,* 16#2: 123-133 (April, 1941).

TITUS ANDRONICUS

Adams, John Crawford. "Shakespeare's Revisions in *Titus Andronicus,*" *Shakespeare Quarterly,* 15#2: 177-190 (Spring, 1964).

Bowers, Fredson T. *Elizabethan Revenge Tragedy,* 110-118.

Dasgupta, Arun Kumar. "A Note on *Titus Andronicus* II. i. I-II," *Shakespeare Quarterly,* 12#3: 340-341 (Summer, 1961).

Desmonde, William H. "The Ritual Origin of Shakespeare's *Titus Andronicus,*" *International Journal of Psychoanalysis,* 36Pt.1: 61-65 (1955).

Findlater, Richard. "Shakespearean Atrocities," *Twentieth Century,* 158#944: 364-372 (Oct, 1955).

Greg, W. W. "Alteration of Act I of *Titus Andronicus,*" *Modern Language Review,* 48#4: 439-440 (Oct, 1953).

Hamilton, A. C. *"Titus Andronicus:* The Form of Shakespearean Tragedy," *Shakespeare Quarterly,* 14#3: 201-213 (Summer, 1963).

Hastings, William T. "The Hardboiled Shakespeare," *Shakespeare Association Bulletin,* 17#3: 114-125 (July, 1942).

Hill, R. F. "The Composition of *Titus Andronicus,*" Shakespeare Survey, 10: 60-70 (1957).

Jepsen, Laura. "A Footnote on 'Hands' in Shakespeare's *Titus Andronicus,*" *Florida State University Studies,* 19: 7-10 (1955).

Jones, Eldred. *Othello's Countrymen,* 49-60.

————. "Aaron and Melancholy in *Titus Andronicus,*" *Shakespeare Quarterly,* 14#2: 178-179 (Spring, 1963).

Karr, Judith M. "The Pleas in *Titus Andronicus,*" *Shakespeare Quarterly,* 14#3: 278-279 (Summer, 1963).

Law, Robert A. "The Roman Background of *Titus Andronicus,*" *Studies in Philology,* 40#2: 145-153 (April, 1943).

McManaway, James G. "Writing in Sand in *Titus Andronicus* IV, i," *Review of English Studies,* NS9#34: 172-173 (May, 1958).

Parrott, D. E. "Further Observations on *Titus Andronicus,*" *Shakespeare Quarterly,* 1#1: 27-29 (Jan, 1950).

Price, Hereward T. " 'Do Good'," *Notes and Queries,* 207: 410 (Sept, 1962).

——————. "The Yew-Tree in *Titus Andronicus,*" *Notes and Queries,* 208: 98-99 (March, 1963).

Ravich, Robert A. "A Psychoanalytic Study of Shakespeare's Early Plays," *Psychoanalytic Quarterly,* 33#3: 396-397 (July, 1964).

Sargent, Ralph M. "The Source of *Titus Andronicus,*" *Studies in Philology,* 46#2: 167-183 (April, 1949).

Smith, Gordon Ross. "The Creditibility of Shakespeare's Aaron," *Literature and Psychology,* 10#1: 11-13 (Winter, 1960).

Sommers, Alan. *"Wilderness of Tigers:* Structure and Symbolism in *Titus Andronicus,*" *Essays in Criticism,* 10#3: 275-289 (July, 1960).

Sparks, W. H. M. "The Immortal Memory of William Shakespeare," *Central Literary Magazine,* pp. 118-121 (July, 1955).

Waith, Eugene M. "The Metamorphosis of Violence in *Titus Andronicus,*" *Shakespeare Survey,* 10: 39-49 (1957).

Weales, Gerald. "Titus Andronicus, Private Eye," *Southwest Review,* 44#3: 225-259 (Summer, 1959).

Williams, Gwyn. "Shakespeare and Black Beauty," in Robin Feddin, et. al., *Personal Landscape,* 52-55.

TROILUS AND CRESSIDA

Almeida, Barbara Heliodora C. de M.F. de. *"Troilus and Cressida:* Romantic Love Revisited," *Shakespeare Quarterly,* 15#4: 327-332 (Autumn, 1964).

Arnold, Aerol. "The Hector-Andromache Scene in Shakespeare's *Troilus and Cressida,*" *Modern Language Quarterly,* 14: 335-340 (Dec, 1953).

Bamborough, J. *The Little World of Man,* 126-127.

Battenhouse, Roy A. "Shakespearean Tragedy: A Christian

Interpretation," in Nathan A. Scott, Jr. (ed), *The Tragic Vision and the Christian Faith*, 78-81 ; 86-87.

Bayley, John. "Shakespeare's Only Play," *Stratford Papers on Shakespeare*, 4: 58-83 (1963).

Bejblik, Alois. "Shakespeare's *Troilus and Cressida*," *Casopis Pro Moderni Filologii*, 41 : 91-92 (1959).

Berry, Francis. *Poet's Grammar*, 65-67.

Boas, Guy. "*Troilus and Cressida* and the Time Scheme," *New English Review*, 13#11: 529-535 (Nov, 1946).

Bongiorno, Andrew. "*Troilus and Cressida* as One of a Kind," *Shakespeare Newsletter*, 2#6: 26 (Sept, 1952).

Bonjour, A. "Hector and the 'One in Sumptuous Armour'," *English Studies*, 45#2: 104-108 (April, 1964).

Bowden, William R. "The Human Shakespeare and *Troilus and Cressida*," *Shakespeare Quarterly*, 8#2: 167-177 (Spring, 1957).

Bradbrook, M. C. "What Shakespeare Did to Chaucer's *Troilus and Criseyde*," *Shakespeare Quarterly*, 9#3: 311-319 (Summer, 1958).

Bullough, G. "The Lost *Troilus and Cressida*," *Essays and Studies (English Association)*, 17: 24-40 (1964).

Carter, Thomas H. " 'An Universal Prey': A Footnote to The Lion and the Fox," *Shenandoah*, 9#2: 25-34 (Spring, 1958).

Daniels, F. Quinland. "Order and Confusion in *Troilus and Cressida* I. iii," *Shakespeare Quarterly*, 12#3: 285-291 (Summer, 1961).

Dunkel, Wilbur D. "Shakespeare's Troilus," *Shakespeare Quarterly*, 2#4: 331-334 (Oct, 1951).

Dyer, Frederick B. "The Destruction of Pandare," *The City College Papers*, 1: 123-133 (1964).

Ellis-Fermor, Una. *Frontiers of Drama*, 56-76; 92-93.

Evans, G. Blakemore. "Pandarus' House?: *Troilus and Cressida*, III. ii; IV. ii; IV. iv," *Modern Language Notes*, 62#1: 33-35 (Jan, 1947).

Farnham, Willard. "Troilus in Shapes of Infinite Desire," *Shakespeare Quarterly*, 15#2: 257-264 (Spring, 1964).

Foakes, R. A. "*Troilus and Cressida* Reconsidered," *University of Toronto Quarterly*, 32#2: 142-154 (Jan, 1962).

Gerard, A. "Meaning and Structure in *Troilus and Cressida*," *English Studies*, 40#3: 144-157 (June, 1959).

Halio, Jay Leon. "Traitor in *All's Well* and *Troilus and Cressida*," *Modern Language Notes*, 72#6: 408-409 (June, 1957).

Harrier, Richard C. "Troilus Divided," in *Studies in the English Renaissance Drama in Memory of Karl J. Holzknecht,* 142-156.

Hulme, Hilda. "Three Notes: *Troilus and Cressida* V. vii. 11; *Midsummer Night's Dream,* II. i. 54; *Measure for Measure* II. i. 39," *Journal of English and Germanic Philology,* 57#4: 921-922 (Oct, 1958).

James, D. G. *The Dream of Learning,* 55-57.

Jones, David E. " 'Mad Idolatry': Love in *Troilus and Cressida,*" *Drama Critique,* 7#1: 8-12 (Winter, 1964).

Jorgensen, Paul A. "Divided Command in Shakespeare," *PMLA,* 70: 750-761 (Sept, 1955).

Kaula, David. "Will and Reason in *Troilus and Cressida,*" *Shakespeare Quarterly,* 12#3: 271-283 (Summer, 1961).

Kendall, Paul M. "Inaction and Ambivalence in *Troilus and Cressida,*" in *English Studies in Honor of James Southall Wilson,* 131-146.

Kermode, Frank. "Opinion, Truth and Value," *Essays in Criticism,* 5#2: 181-187 (April, 1955).

Kimbraugh, Robert. "The *Troilus* Log: Shakespeare and 'Box-Office'," *Shakespeare Quarterly,* 15#3: 201-209 (Summer, 1964).

Kleinstuck, Johannes. "Ulysses' Speech on Degree as Related to the Play of *Troilus and Cressida,*" *Neophilologus,* pp. 58-63 (Jan, 1959).

Knight, G. Wilson. "The Philosophy of *Troilus and Cressida,*" in *The Wheel of Fire,* 47-72 (1962 ed.).

Knights, L. C. "*Troilus and Cressida* Again," *Scrutiny,* 18#2: 144-157 (Autumn, 1951).

——————. "Shakespeare's Politics: With Some Reflections on the Nature of Tradition," *Annual Shakespeare of the British Academy,* p. 119 (1957).

Knowland, A. S. "*Troilus and Cressida,*" *Shakespeare Quarterly,* 10#3: 353-365 (Summer, 1959).

Lacy, Margaret. *The Jacobean Problem Play,* 1-6; 165-198.

Lawrence, William W. "Troilus, Cressida and Thersites," *Modern Language Review,* 37#4: 422-437 (Oct, 1942).

Leech, Clifford. "Shakespeare's Greeks," *Stratford Papers on Shakespeare,* 4: 4-15; 18 (1963).

Levitchi, Leon. "An Attempt at Reestablishing the Thematic Unity of *Troilus and Cressida,*" *Revista de Filologie Romanica si Germanica,* 6#1: 55-56 (1962).

McCutchan, J. W. "Time's Wallet," *Notes and Queries,* 192: 430-431 (4 Oct, 1947).

MacLure, Miller. "Shakespeare and the Lonely Dragon," *University of Toronto Quarterly,* 24#2: 112-114 (Jan, 1955).

Main, William. "Character Amalgams in Shakespeare's *Troilus and Cressida,*" *Studies in Philology,* 58#2: 170-178 (April, 1961).

Maxwell, J. C. "Shakespeare: The Middle Plays," *Guide to English Literature,* 2: 205-212.

Meester, Johan de. "*Troilus and Cressida,*" *World Theatre,* 8#4: 273-279 (Winter, 1959-1960).

Megaw, Neil. "Shakespeare's *Troilus and Cressida,* I, iii, 354-356," *The Explicator,* 15#8: 52 (May, 1957).

——————. "The Sneaking Fellow: *Troilus and Cressida,*" *Notes and Queries,* 201: 469-470 (Nov, 1956).

Merchant, W. M. "The Harmony of Disenchantment," *Stratford Papers on Shakespeare,* 4: 111-125 (1963).

Merton, Stephen. "*The Tempest* and *Troilus and Cressida,*" *College English,* 7#3: 143-150 (Dec, 1945).

Meyer, George W. "Order Out of Chaos in Shakespeare's *Troilus and Cressida,*" *Tulane Studies in English,* 4: 45-56 (1954).

Morris, Brian. "The Tragic Structure of *Troilus and Cressida,*" *Shakespeare Quarterly,* 10#4: 481-491 (Autumn, 1959).

Muir, Kenneth. "Three Shakespeare Adaptations," *Proceedings of the Leeds Philosophical and Literary Society,* 8Pt. 4: 233-238 (Jan, 1959).

——————. "*Troilus and Cressida,*" *Shakespeare Survey,* 8: 28-39 (1955).

Muller, Herbert J. *The Spirit of Tragedy,* 180-185.

Munday, Mildred Brand. "Pejorative Patterns in Shakespeare's *Troilus and Cressida,*" *Bucknell University Studies,* 5#3: 39-49 (1955).

Nowottny, Winifred M. T. " 'Opinion' and 'Value" in *Troilus and Cressida,*" *Essays in Criticism,* 4#3: 282-296 (July, 1954).

Ornstein, Robert. *The Moral Vision of Jacobean Tragedy,* 240-249.

Pearce, T. M. " 'Another Knot, Five-Finger-Tied': Shakespeare's *Troilus and Cressida,* V. ii, 157," *Notes and Queries,* 205: 18-19 (Jan, 1960).

Petti, Anthony G. "The Fox, the Ape, the Humble Bee and the Goose," *Neophilologus,* 44#3: 208-211; 213-215 (July, 1960).

Pettigrew, Helen Puriton. "*Troilus and Cressida:* Shakespeare's Indictment of War," *University of West Virginia Bulletin: Philological Studies,* 5: 34-48 (1947).

Phillips, James Emerson Jr. "The State in Shakespeare's Greek and Roman Plays," *Columbia University Studies in English and Comparative Literature,* 149: 113-126 (1940).

Potts, Abbie Findlay. *"Cynthia's Revels, Poetaster* and *Troilus and Cressida,"* Shakespeare Quarterly, 5#3: 297-302 (Summer, 1954).

Presson, Robert K. "The Structural Use of a Traditional Theme in *Troilus and Cressida,"* Philological Quarterly, 31#2: 180-188 (April, 1952).

Reed, Victor B. *"Troilus and Cressida* IV. ii. 56," *Neuphilologische Mitteilungen,* 57#3-4: 128-132 (1956).

Reynolds, George F. *"Troilus and Cressida* on the Elizabethan Stage," in James G. McManaway (ed), *Joseph Q. Adams Memorial Studies,* 229-238.

Richards, I. A. *"Troilus and Cressida* and Plato," *Hudson Review,* 1#3: 362-376 (Autumn, 1948).

Rickey, Mary Ellen. " 'Twixt Dangerous Shores: *Troilus and Cressida* Again," *Shakespeare Quarterly,* 15#1: 3-14 (Winter, 1964).

Rossiter, A. P. *"Troilus and Cressida,"* Shakespeare Newsletter, 5#1: 3 (Feb, 1955).

Sandoe, James. *"Troilus and Cressida,"* Shakespeare Newsletter, 8#4: 28 (Sept, 1958).

Savage, James E. *"Troilus and Cressida* and Elizabethan Court Factions," *University of Mississippi Studies in English,* 5: 43-66 (1964).

Sherwood, John C. "Dryden and the Rules: The Preface to *Troilus and Cressida,"* Comparative Literature, 2#1: 73-83 (Winter, 1950).

Siegel, Paul N. "Shakespeare and the Neo-Chivalric Cult of Honor," *Centenniel Review,* 8#1: 51-56 (Winter, 1964).

Smith, R. J. "Personal Identity in *Troilus and Cressida,"* English Studies in Africa, 6#1: 7-26 (March, 1963).

Stamm, Rudolf. "The Glass of Pandar's Praise: The Word Scenery, Mirror Passages, and Reported Scenes in Shakespeare's *Troilus and Cressida,"* Essays and Studies (English Association), 17: 55-77 (1964).

Stanford, W. B. *The Ulysses Theme,* 164-171.

Sternfeld, Frederick W. *"Troilus and Cressida:* Music for the Play," *English Institute Essays,* pp. 107-137 (1952).

Stevenson, David Lloyd. "The Love-Game Comedy," *Colum-*

bia University Studies in English and Comparative Literature, 164: 215-222 (1946).

Swanston, Hamish F. G. "The Baroque Element in *Troilus and Cressida*," *Durham University Journal*, 50#1: 14-23 (Dec, 1957).

Thompson, Karl F. "The Feast of Pride in *Troilus and Cressida*," *Notes and Queries*, 203: 193-194 (May, 1958).

Thompson, Karl F. "Cressida's Diet," *Notes and Queries*, 201: 378-379 (1956).

Whitaker, Virgil K. "Philosophy and Romance in Shakespeare's 'Problem' Comedies," in Richard F. Jones, et. al., *Seventeenth Century: Studies in the History of English Thought*, 339-351.

TWELFTH NIGHT

Auden, W. H. "Notes on the Comic," *Thought*, 27#104: 61-62 (Spring, 1952).

Babb, Lawrence. *The Elizabethan Malady*, 170-171.

Barnet, Sylvan. "Charles Lamb's and the Tragic Malvolio," *Philological Quarterly*, 33#2: 178-188 (April, 1954).

Bentley, Eric. *The Play*, 285-289; 366-371.

Blistein, E. M. "The Object of Scorn: An Aspect of the Comic Antagonist," *Western Humanities Review*, 14#2: 217-222 (Spring, 1960).

Boas, Ralph P. "Shakespeare's *Twelfth Night*, II, iii, 25-27," *Explicator*, 3#4: 29 (Feb, 1945).

Bowden, William R. "Teaching Structure in Shakespeare," *College English*, 23#7: 528-259 (April, 1962).

Brittin, Norman A. "The *Twelfth Night* of Shakespeare and of Professor Draper," *Shakespeare Quarterly*, 7#2: 211-216 (Spring, 1956).

Brooks, Charles. "Shakespeare's Heroine-Actresses," *Shakespeare Jahrbuck*, 96; 141-143 (1960).

Brown, John R. "Directions for *Twelfth Night*, or What You Will," *Tulane Drama Review*, 5#4: 77-88 (June, 1961).

Burke, Kenneth. *The Philosophy of Literary Form*, 291-295.

Camden, Carroll. "Three Notes on Shakespeare," *Modern Language Notes*, 72: 251-252 (1957).

Cohen, Hennig. "Shakespeare's *Twelfth Night*, I, v, 128-130," *The Explicator*, 14#2: 12 (Nov, 1955).

Cox, Lee Sheriden. "The Riddle of *Twelfth Night*," *Shakespeare Quarterly*, 13#3: 360 (Summer, 1962).

Crane, Milton. "*Twelfth Night* and Shakespearean Comedy," *Shakespeare Quarterly*, 6#1: 1-8 (Winter, 1955).

Downer, Alan. "Feste's Night," *College English,* 13#5: 258-265 (Feb, 1952).

———————. "Feste's Night," *College English,* 22#2: 117-123 (Nov, 1960).

Forbes, Lydia. "What You Will?" *Shakespeare Quarterly,* 13#4: 475-385 (Autumn, 1962).

Gamal, Sand M. "The Function of Song in Shakespeare's Comedies," *Cairo Studies in English,* pp. 118-119 (1961/62).

Gerard, A. "Shipload of Fools: A Note on *Twelfth Night,*" *English Studies,* 45#2: 109-115 (April, 1964).

Gillie, Christopher. *"Twelfth Night,"* *The Use of English,* 4#3: 136-140 (Spring, 1953).

Greg, W. W. "Two Notes," in *Elizabethan and Jacobean Studies Presented to Frank Wilson,* 59-62.

Gundry, W. G. C. *"Twelfth Night,* or *What You Will* Performed in the Middle Temple Hall," *Baconiana,* 35#139: 98-99 (Apr, 1951).

Harrison, G. B. "A New Shakespeare Allusion," *Shakespeare Quarterly,* 8: 127 (1957).

Hoepfner, Theodore C. *"M.O.A.I.—Twelfth Night,"* *Notes and Queries,* 203: 193 (May, 1958).

Holland, Norman N. "Cuckhold or Counsellor in *Twelfth Night,* I v. 56," *Shakespeare Quarterly,* 8#1: 127-129 (Winter, 1957).

Hollander, John. *"Twelfth Night* and the Morality of Indulgence," *Sewanee Review,* 67#2: 220-238 (Spring, 1959).

———————*"Musica Mundana* and *Twelfth Night,"* *English Institute Essays,* pp. 55-82 (1956).

Jenkins, Harold. "Shakespeare's *Twelfth Night,"* *Rice Institute Pamphlets,* 45#4: 19-42 (Jan, 1959).

Johnson, Edward D. "Malvolio's Cryptic Word M.O.A.I." *Baconiana,* 30#118: 26-28 (Jan, 1946).

Kaufman, Helen Andrews. "Nicolo Secchi as a Source of *Twelfth Night,"* *Shakespeare Quarterly,* 5#3: 271-280 (Summer, 1954).

Kermode, Frank. "The Mature Comedies," *Stratford-Upon-Avon Studies,* 3: 224-227 (1961).

Knight, George W. *The Golden Labyrinth,* 67-69.

Leech, Clifford. "Shakespeare's Comic Dukes," *Review of English Literature,* 5#2: 108-110 (April, 1964).

Manheim, Leonard F. "The Mythical Joys of Shakespeare; or What You Will," *The City College Papers,* 1: 100-112 (1964).

Mare, F. H. "A Footnote to *Twelfth Night,* Act I, Scene 3," *Notes and Queries,* 204: 306-307 (Sept, 1959).

Markels, Julian. "Shakespeare's Confluence of Tragedy and Comedy: *Twelfth Night* and *King Lear,*" *Shakespeare Quarterly,* 15#2: 75-88 (Spring, 1964).

Maxwell, J. C. "Shakespeare: The Middle Plays," *Guide to English Literature,* 2: 197-198.

Merchant, W. M. "Shakespeare's Theology," *Review of English Literature,* 5#4: 84-85 (Oct, 1964).

Nagarajan, S. " 'What You Will': A Suggestion," *Shakespeare Quarterly,* 10#1: 61-67 (Winter, 1959).

Pearce, T. M. "Shakespeare's *Twelfth Night,* II, v, 5-7," *The Explicator, 7#3:* 19 (Dec, 1948).

Pogson, Beryl C. "The Esoteric Meaning of *Twelfth Night,*" *Baconiana, 32#127:* 65-71 (Spring, 1948).

Purcell, J. M. *"Twelfth Night,* II, ii, 27-28," *Notes and Queries,* 203: 375-376 (Sept, 1958).

Pyle, Fitzroy. *"Twelfth Night, King Lear* and *Arcadia,"* *Modern Laguage Review,* 43#4: 444-452 (Oct, 1948).

Salinger, L. G. "The Design of *Twelfth Night,*" *Shakespeare Quarterly, 9#2:* 117-139 (Spring, 1958).

Seiden, Melvin. "Malvolio Reconsidered," *University of Kansas City Review,* 28#2: 105-113 (Winter, 1961).

Sennett, M. "The Widom of Shakespeare," *Baconiana, 26#* 105: 189-195 (Oct, 1942).

Sochatoff, A Fred. *"Twelfth Night,"* *Carnegie Series in English,* 8: 33-52 (1964).

Solem, Delmar E. "An Experimental *Twelfth Night,*" *Southern Speech Journal,* 24#4: 197-200 (Summer, 1959).

Strong, L. A. G. *The Sacred River,* 60-61.

Summers, Joseph. "The Masks of *Twelfth Night,*" *University of Kansas City Review,* 22#1: 25-31 (Autumn, 1955).

Swander, Homer. *"Twelfth Night:* Critics, Players, and a Script," *Educational Theatre Journal,* 16#2: 114-121 (May, 1964).

Taylor, Marion A. " 'He That Did the Tiger Board'," *Shakespeare Quarterly,* 15#1: 110-113 (Winter, 1964).

Thompson, Karl F. "Shakespeare's Romantic Comedies," *PMLA, 67#7:* 1079-1081; 1090-1093 (Dec, 1952).

Walker, James. "Shakespeare Again in the Waterloo Bridge," *English,* 8#46: 190-192 (Spring, 1951).

Walley, Harold R. *The Book of the Play,* 172-175; 658-660.

West, E. J. "Bradleyan Reprise: On the Fool in *Twelfth*

Night," Shakespeare Association Bulletin, 24#4: 264-274 (Oct, 1949).

Williams, Charles. "The Use of the Second Person in *Twelfth Night,*" *English,* 9#52: 125-128 (Spring, 1953).

Williams, Porter Jr. "Mistakes in *Twelfth Night* and Their Resolution: A Study in Some Relationships of Plot and Theme," *PMLA,* 76#3: 193-199 (June, 1961).

Young, Stark. *Immortal Shadows,* 218-222.

TWO GENTLEMEN OF VERONA, THE

Atkinson, Dorothy F. "The Source of *Two Gentlemen of Verona,*" *Studies in Philology,* 41#2: 223-234 (April, 1944).

Brooks, Charles. "Shakespeare's Heroine-Actresses," *Shakespeare Jahrbuck,* 96: 134-137 (1960).

Brooks, H. F. "Two Clowns in a Comedy (to say Nothing of the dog): Speed, Launce (and Crab) in *The Two Gentlemen of Verona,*" *Essays and Studies,* 16: 91-111 (1963).

Campbell, O. J. *"The Two Gentlemen of Verona* and Italian Comedy," *University of Michigan Studies in Shakespeare,* pp. 47-64 (1964).

Danby, John F. "Shakespeare Criticism and *The Two Gentlemen of Verona,*" *The Critical Quarterly,* 2#4: 309-321 (Winter, 1960).

Gamal, Sand M. "The Function of Song in Shakespeare's Comedies," *Cario Studies in English,* pp. 114 & 117 (1961/62).

Guinn, John A. "The Letter Device in the First Act of *The Two Gentlemen of Verona,*" *Studies in English (University of Texas),* 4026: 72-81 (July 8, 1940).

Leech, Clifford. "Shakespear's Comic Dukes," *Review of English Literature,* 5#2: 105-108 (April, 1964).

Long, John H. "Music for the Replica Staging of Shakespeare," *University of Miami Publications in English and American Literature,* 1: 90-95 (March, 1953).

Nemerov, Howard. *Poetry and Fiction,* 25-33.

Perry, Thomas A. "Proteus, Wry-Transformed Traveller," *Shakespeare Quarterly,* 5#1: 33-40 (Jan, 1954).

Praz, Mario. *The Flaming Heart,* 152-156.

Ravich, Robert A. "A Psychoanalytic Study of Shakespeare's Early Plays," *Psychoanalytic Quarterly,* 33#3: 402-404 (July, 1964).

Sargent, Ralph M. "Sir Thomas Elyot and the Integrity of *The Two Gentlemen of Verona,*" *PMLA,* 65#6: 1166-1180 (Dec, 1950).

Thompson, Karl F. "Shakespeare's Romantic Comedies," *PMLA, 67#7*: 1079-1081; 1085-1088; 1091-1093 (Dec. 1952).

Tutt, Ralph M. "Dog Imagery in *The Two Gentlemen of Verona, King Lear,* and *Timon of Athens*," *The Serif,* 1#3: 15-18 (Oct, 1964).

Wells, Stanley. "The Failure of *The Two Gentlemen of Verona*," *Shakespeare Jahrbuck,* 99: 161-173 (1963).

TWO NOBLE KINSMEN, THE
See: John Fletcher

WINTER'S TALE, THE

Berry, Francis. *Poet's Grammar,* 69-74.

Biggins, Dennis. " 'Exit Pursued by a Beare': A Problem in *The Winter's Tale*," *Shakespeare Quarterly,* 13#1: 3-13 (Winter, 1962).

Bonjour, Adrien. "The Final Scene in *The Winter's Tale*," *English Studies,* 33#5: 193-208 (Oct, 1952).

Bryant, J. A. "Shakespeare's Allegory: *The Winter's Tale*," *Sewanee Review,* 63#2: 202-222 (Spring, 1955).

Bryant, J. H. "*The Winter's Tale* and the Pastoral Tradition," *Shakespeare Quarterly,* 387-398 (Autumn, 1963).

Bunnett, R. J. A. "*The Winter's Tale*," *Baconiana,* 33#131: 104-107 (Apr, 1949).

Coghill, Nevill. "Six Points of Stage Craft in *The Winter's Tale*," *Shakespeare Survey,* 11: 31-41 (1958).

Cottrell, Beekman, W. "*The Winter's Tale*," *Carnegie Series in English,* 8: 69-82 (1964).

Cunningham, James. *Woe or Wonder,* 34-36; 113-114.

Ellis, John. "Rooted Affection: The Genesis of Jealousy in *The Winter's Tale*," *College English,* 25#7: 545-547 (April, 1964).

Ewbank, Inga-Stina. "The Triumph of Time in *The Winter's Tale*," *Review of English Literature,* 5#2: 83-100 (April, 1964).

Fox, Charles O. "Clocks and Dials," *Shakespeare Newsletter,* 1#3: 10 (May, 1951).

Frye, Northrop. *Fables of Identity,* 107-118.

Gamal, Sand M. "The Function of Song in Shakespeare's Comedies," *Cario Studies in English,* pp. 119-120 (1961/62).

Harrison, Thomas P., Jr. "Aspects of Primitivism in Shakespeare and Spenser," *Studies in English (University of Texas),* 4026: 42-49 (July 8, 1940).

Hart, Edward L. "A Mixed Consort: Leontes, Angelo, Helena," *Shakespeare Quarterly,* 15#1: 75-79 (Winter, 1964).

Hewett, R. P. *Reading and Response,* 120-127.

Hoeniger, F. David. "The Meaning of *The Winter's Tale,*" *University of Toronto Quarterly,* 20#1: 11-26 (Oct, 1950).

Honigmann, E. A. J. "Secondary Sources of *The Winter's Tale,*" *Philological Quarterly,* 34#1: 27-38 (Jan, 1955).

Hughes, Merritt Y. "A Classical vs. a Social Approach to Shakespere's Autolycus," *Shakepeare Association Bulletin,* 15#4: 219-226 (Oct, 1940).

Irwin, Michael. *"The Winter's Tale* as an Experiment in Form," *Zagadienia Rodzajow Literackich,* 8#1: 5-16.

Joseph, Bertram L. "Character and Plot," *Drama Survey,* 4#4: 546-548 (Spring-Fall, 1964).

King, S. K. "Eliot, Yeats, and Shakespeare," *Theoria,* 5: 115 (1953).

Knight, G. Wilson. *The Crown of Life,* 76-128.
——————————. *The Golden Labyrinth,* 82-84.

Lawlor, John. "Pandosto and the Nature of Dramatic Romance," *Philological Quarterly,* 41#1: 96-113 (Jan, 1962).

Melchiori, Barbara. "Still Harping on my Daughter," *English Miscellany,* 11: 63-64 (1960).

Pafford, J. H. P. "Music, and the Songs in *The Winter's Tale,*" *Shakespeare Quarterly,* 10#2: 161-175 (Spring, 1959).

Parsons, Natalie. "Shakespeare's Ladies: Paulina in *Winter's Tale,*" *Baconiana,* 34#137: 228-230 (Oct, 1950).

Rashbrook, R. F. *"The Winter's Tale," Notes and Queries,* 192: 520-521 (29 Nov, 1947).

Roddier, Henri. "A Freudian Detective's Shakespeare," *Modern Philology,* 48#2: 129-130 (Nov, 1950).

Schanzer, Ernest. "The Structural Pattern of *The Winter's Tale," Review of English Literature* 5#2: 72-82 (April, 1964).

Scott, William O. "Seasons and Flowers in *The Winter's Tale," Shakespeare Quarterly,* 14#4: 411-417 (Autumn, 1963).

Siegel, Paul N. "Leontes a Jealous Tyrant," *Review of English Studies,* NS1#4: 302-307 (Oct, 1950).

Smith, Hallett. "Leontes' *Affectio," Shakespeare Quarterly,* 14#2: 163-166 (Spring, 1963).

Strong, L. A. G. *The Sacred River*, 58.

Tayler, Edward W. *Nature and Art in Renaissance Literature*, 121-141.

Traversi, D. A. "The Last Plays of Shakespeare," *Guide to English Literature*, 2: 259-266.

Trienens, Roger J. "The Inception of Leontes' Jealousy in *The Winter's Tale*," *Shakespeare Quarterly*, 4#3: 321-326 (July, 1953).

Wilson, Harold S. "Nature and Art in *The Winter's Tale*," *Shakespeare Association Bulletin*, 18#3: 114-120 (July, 1943).

Wincor, Richard. "Shakespeare's Festival Plays," *Shakespeare Quarterly*, 1#4: 219-223; 226-233 (Oct, 1950).

Wright, T. "Bohemia's Sea Coast in *The Winter's Tale*," *Baconiana*, 38#150: 117-124 (Dec, 1954).

BIBLIOGRAPHY

BOOKS—I

The following sources contained drama criticism
as defined by the authors in the introduction.

Abel, Lionel. *Metatheatre*. New York: Hill and Wang, 1963. PN/1623/A35

Adams, Henry Hitch (ed.). and Baxter Hathaway. *Dramatic Essays of* 809.2
the Neoclassic Age. New York: Columbia University Press, 1950. A213d

Adams, Henry Hitch. *English Domestic or Homilectic Tragedy 1575-
1642*. New York: Columbia University Press, 1943. 822.09/A213c

Adams, Robert M. *Strains of Discord: Studies in Literary Openness*.
Ithaca, New York: Cornell University Press, 1958. 809/A216n

Alleman, Gellert S. *Matrimonial Law and the Materials of Restoration
Comedy*. Philadelphia: University of Pennsylvania, 1942.

Allen, Don Cameron. *Image and Meaning*. Baltimore: The Johns Hop- 821.305
kins Press, 1960. A425c

American Thought. London: Kaye, 1947.

Anderson, Mary D. *Drama and Imagery in English Medieval Churches*. 822.0902
Cambridge: The University Press, 1963. A548d
1963.

Anderson, Quentin (ed.) and Joseph A. Mazzeo. *The Proper Study—* 809
Essays on Western Classics. New York: Saint Martin's Press, 1962. A548p

Arnott, Peter D. *An Introduction to Greek Theatre*. New York: Saint
Martin's Press, 1961. DF/77/A7/1967

Arrowsmith, William. *The Craft and Context of Translation*. Austin: 410.28
University of Texas Press, 1960. A779c

Artaud, Antonin. *The Theater and its Double*. (trans. Mary Caroline
Richards). New York: Grove Press, 1958.

Atkins, H. *German Literature Through Nazi Eyes*. London: Methuen,
1941.

Auerbach, Erich. *Mēmesis*. Princeton, New Jersey: Princeton Univer- PN
sity Press, 1953. 51
R3
A73

Babb, Lawrence. *The Elizabethan Malady*. East Lansing, Michigan:
Michigan State College Press, 1951. 820.9/B112c

Bacon, W. A. and R. S. Breen. *Literature as Experience*. New York: 801
McGraw-Hill, 1959. B129L

Bailey, A. E. (ed.). *The Arts and Religion*. New York: Macmillan, 701
1944. B154a

Bailey, Margery (ed.). *Ashland Studies for Shakespeare 1952*. Ashland,
Oregon: 1955.

Bailey, Robert. *Sunk Without Trace*. New York: Harcourt, Brace, 1962.

150.9
B199L Bamborough, J. *The Little World of Man.* New York/London: Longmans, Green, 1952.

PN
1621 Barnet, Sylvan (ed.). *Aspects of the Drama.* Boston: Little, Brown,
B3   1962.

PN
2635- Barrault, Jean L. *The Theatre of Jean-Louis Barrault.* London: Barrie
B273   and Rockliff, 1961.
1961 864 Barzun, Jacques. *The Energies of Art.* New York: Harper & Row, 1956.
     B296c Bate, Walter J. *From Classic to Romantic.* New York: Harper & Row,
      1946. 701/B328k

808.1 Battenhouse, Henry W. *Poets of Christian Thought.* New York: The
B335p   Ronald Press, 1947.

Battenhouse, R. W. *A Study of Renaissance Moral Philosophy.* Nash-
809.93 ville: Vanderbilt University Press, 1941.
B358c Bayley, John. *The Characters of Love—A Study in the Literature of
1960   Personality.* London: Constable & Co., 1960.

BH
201 Beardsley, Monroe C. *Aesthetics: Problems in the Philosophy of Crit-
B4   icism.* New York: Harcourt, Brace & Co., 1958. also UGC

Benniou, L. B. and G. R. Potter (eds.). *Five Gayley Lectures 1947-1954.*
    Berkeley: University of California Press, 1954.

Bentley, Eric. *From the Modern Repertoire, Series One.* Bloomington:
    Indiana University Press, 1949.

————————. *From the Modern Repertoire, Series Two.* Blooming-
    ton: Indiana University Press, 1952.
808.82 ————————. *From the Modern Repertoire, Series Three.* Bloom-
B477 ington: Indiana University Press, 1956.

PN
1851 ————————. *The Play.* New York: Prentice-Hall, 1962.
B4 ————————. *The Playwright as Thinker.* New York: Reynal &
1967   Hitchcock, 1946.

Bentley, Eric (ed.). *The Importance of Scrutiny.* New York: G. W.
    Stewart, 1948. 820.4/S435~/1964

Bergler, Edmund. *The Battle of the Conscience.* Washington, D.C.:
842.082 Washington Institute of Medicine, 1948.
B516g Bermel, Albert (ed.). *The Genius of the French Theater.* New York:
1961   Mentor Books, 1961.

821.09 Berry, Francis. *Poetry and the Physical Voice.* London: Routledge, 1962.
B534p/ 821.09/B534p ————. *Poet's Grammar.* London: Routledge, 1958.

Bevington, David M. *From Mankind to Marlowe.* Cambridge: Harvard
    University Press, 1962. 822.209/B571t

Bhushan, V. N. *The Moving Finger.* Bombay: Padma, 1945.

Bishop, Thomas. *Pirandello and the French Theatre.* New York: New
PN   York University Press, 1960. 858.91/P667Yb/1960
771 Block, Haskell M. and Herman Salinger (eds.). *The Creative Vision—
B58   Modern European Writers on Their Art.* New York: Grove Press,
      1960.

PR
703 Boas, F. S. *An Introduction to Eighteenth Century Drama.* Oxford:
B6   Clarendon Press, 1953. also UGC

PN
1031 Bodkin, Maud. *Archetypal Patterns in Poetry.* New York: Oxford Uni-
B63   versity Press, 1961.
1963

—————————. *The Quest for Salvation in an Ancient and a Modern Play.* London/New York: Oxford University Press, 1964.

—————————. *Studies of Type Images.* London: Oxford University Press, 1951.

Bonnard, G. A. (ed.). *English Studies Today—Second Series.* London: Oxford University Press, 1961.

Bower, Reuben A. and Richard Poirier (eds.). *In Defense of Reading—A Reader's Approach to Literary Criticism.* New York: Dutton, 1962.

Bowers, F. T. *Elizabethan Revenge Tragedy.* Princeton: Princeton University Press, 1940.

Bowra, C. M. *In General and Particular.* New York: World Publishing Co., 1964.

—————————. *The Romantic Imagination.* Cambridge: Harvard University Press, 1957.

Boyce, B. *Theophrastan Character in England to 1642.* Cambridge: Harvard University Press, 1947.

Boys, C. (ed.). *Studies in the Literature of the Augustan Age Honoring A. E. Case.* Ann Arbor: George Wahr, 1952.

Bradbrook, Muriel C. *The Growth and Structure of Elizabethan Comedy.* Berkeley: University of California Press, 1960.

Bradley, .A. C. *Oxford Lectures on Poetry.* New York: St. Martin's Press, 1963.

Brewster, Dorothy. *East-West Passage—A Study in Literary Relationships.* London: George Allen and Unwin, 1954.

Brooke, C. F. Tucker. *Essays on Shakespeare and Other Elizzabeethans.* New Haven: Yale University Press, 1948.

Brooks, Cleanth. *The Hidden God—Studies in Hemingway, Faulkner, Yeats, Eliot, and Warren.* New Haven/London: Yale University Press, 1963.

Brooks, Cleanth (ed.). *Tragic Themes in Western Literature—Seven Essays.* New Haven: Yale University Press, 1955.

Brooks, Cleanth and Robert Heilman. *Understanding Drama.* New York: Henry Holt, 1961.

Brooks, Cleanth. *Well-Wrought Urn.* New York: Harcourt, Brace, 1947.

Broussard, Louis. *American Drama—Contemporary Allegory From Eugene O'Neill to Tennessee Williams.* Norman: University of Oklahoma Press, 1962.

Brower, Reuben A. *The Fields of Light.* New York: Oxford University Press, 1951.

Brown, John M. *Dramatis Personae—A Retrospective Show.* New York: The Viking Press, 1963.

—————————. *Seeing More Things.* New York: Whittlesey House, 1948.

Brustein, Robert. *The Theater of Revolt.* Boston: Little, Brown, 1964.

Bullough, Geoffrey. *Mirror of Minds—Changing Psychological Beliefs in English Poetry.* London: University of London, 1962.

Burke, Kenneth. *A Grammar of Motives.* New York: Prentice-Hall, 1945.

——————————. *Perspectives by Incongruity.* (Edited by Stanley E. Hyman) Bloomington: Indiana University Press, 1964.

——————————. *The Philosophy of Literary Form.* New York: Vintage Books, 1957.

Burnshaw, Stanley (ed.). *Varieties of Literary Experience—Eighteen Essays in World Literature.* New York: New York University Press, 1962

Caffee, Nathaniel M. and Thomas A. Kirby (eds.). *Studies for William A. Read.* Baton Rouge: Louisiana State University Press, 1940.

Cairns, Huntington *et. al. Invitation to Learning.* New York: Random House, 1941.

Camden, Carroll (ed.). *Literary Views.* Chicago: University of Chicago Press, 1964.

Carpenter, Frederic I. *American Literature and the Dream.* New York: Philosophical Library, 1955.

Cary, Joyce. *Art and Society.* New York: Cambridge University Press, 1958.

Cecil, David. *Poets and Story Tellers.* New York: Macmillan, 1949.

Chambers, R. W. *Man's Unconquerable Mind.* London: J. Cape, 1939.

Cherpack, Clifton. *The Call of Blood in French Classical Tragedy.* Baltimore: Johns Hopkins Press, 1958.

Chews, Samuel C. *The Virtues Reconciled.* Toronto: University of Toronto Press, 1947.

Chiari, Joseph. *The Contemporary French Theatre, The Flight From Naturalism.* London: Rockliff, 1958.

Classical Studies in Honor of William Abbott Oldfather. Urbana; University of Illinois Press, 1943.

Clemen, Wolfgang. *English Tragedy Before Shakespeare.* London: Methuen, 1961.

Clurman, Harold. *The Fervent Years.* New York: Hill and Wang, 1961.

——————————. *Lies Like Truth.* New York: Macmillan, 1958.

Collins, Arthur S. *English Literature of the Twentieth Century.* London: University Tutorial Press, 1951.

Confrey, Burton. *The Moral Mission of Literature.* Manchester, New Hampshire: Magnificent Press, n.d.

Coombes, H. *Literature and Criticism.* London: Chatto and Windus, 1956.

Cooper, Lane (ed.). *The Greek Genius and its Influence.* Ithaca: Cornell University Press, 1952.

Cornwell, Ethel F. *The "Still Point".* New Brunswick, N.J.: Rutgers University Press, 1962.

Corrigan, Robert W. (ed.). *The Art of the Theatre—A Critical Anthology of Drama.* San Francisco: Chandler Publishing Co., 1964.

Corrigan, Robert W. and James L. Rosenberg (eds.). *The Context and Craft of Drama.* San Francisco: Chandler Publishing Co., 1964.

Craig, Hardin. *The Written Word*. Chapel Hill: University of North
  Carolina Press, 1953. *820.4/C88b w*
Crane, Ronald S. (ed.). *et. al. Critics and Criticism, Ancient and Mod-*
  ern. Chicago: University of Chicago Press, 1964. *801/C891c (1952 ed)*
Cubeta, Paul M. *Modern Drama For Analysis—Third Edition*. New
  York: Holt, Rinehart and Winston, 1963. *PN/b112/C6/1962*
Cunningham, James. *Woe or Wonder—The Emotional Effect of Shake-* *822.33*
  spearean Tragedy. Denver: University of Denver Press, 1951. *Dc 97w*
Curry, John Vincent. *Deception in Elizabethan Comedy*. Chicago: Loyola
  University Press, 1955. *822.09/C976d*
Daiches, David. *Critical Approaches to Literature*. Englewood Cliffs,
  New Jersey: Prentice-Hall, 1956. *801/D132c*
Danby, J. F. *Poets on Fortune's Hill*. London: Faber & Faber, 1952. *PR/535/56/D3*
  1966
Daniels, May. *The French Drama of the Unspoken*. Edinburgh: Edin-
  burgh University Publications, #3, 1953. *PQ/558/D3/1953*
Davidson, Arthur. *The Solace of Literature*. London: Mitre Press, 1948.
Davis, Herbert. *Elizabethan and Jacobean Studies Presented to F.P.*
  Wilson. London: Oxford, 1959.
Demorest, Jean J. (ed.). *Studies in Seventeenth Century French Litera-*
  ture Presented to Morris Bishop. Ithaca: Cornell University Press,
  1962.
Dennis, Nigel F. *Dramatic Essays*. London: Eeidenfeld & Nicholson,
  1962.
Donohue, Denis. *The Third Voice: Modern British and American Verse*
  Drama. Princeton: Princeton University Press, 1959.
Downer, Alan S. *Fifty Years of American Drama, 1900-1950*. Chicago:
  Henry Regnery Co., 1951.
Driver, Tom F. *The Sense of History in Greek and Shakespearean*
  Drama. New York: Columbia University Press, 1960. *882.09/D782 a*
Duprey, Richard A. *Just off the Aisle—The Ramblings of a Catholic*
  Critic. Westminster, Md.: Newman Press, 1962.
Durrell, Lawrence and Henry Miller. *A Private Correspondence*.
  (Edited by George Wickes) New York: E. P. Dutton, 1963.
Dusenbury, Winifred L. *The Theme of Lonliness in Modern American*
  Drama. Gainesville: University of Florida Press, 1960. *812.5093/D972 t*
Duthie, G. I. (ed.). *English Studies Today—Third Series*. Edinburgh:
  Edinburgh University Press, 1964.
Eastman, Fred. *Christ in the Drama*. New York: Macmillan, 1947. *822.09/E13c*
Egri, Lajos. *The Art of Dramatic Writing*. New York: Simon &
  Schuster, 1946. *808.2/E32a*
Eliot, T. S. *Essays on Elizabethan Drama*. New York: Haskell, 1964.
——————. *On Poets and Poetry*. New York: Farrar, Straus &
  Cudahy, 1957. *PN/511/E435*
Elizabethan and Jacobean Studies Presented to Frank Wilson in Honour *820.903*
  of His Seventieth Birthday. Oxford: The Clarendon Press, 1959. *E43*
Elliott, Robert C. *The Power of Satire: Magic, Ritual, Art*. Princeton:
  Princeton University Press, 1960. *808.7*
  E46p

Ellis-Fermor, Una. *The Frontiers of Drama*. London: Methuen, 1946.
——————. *The Irish Dramatic Movement*. London: Methuen,
    1954.
——————. *Shakespeare the Dramatist*. (Edited by Kenneth Muir)
    New York: Barnes & Noble, 1961.
Empson, William. *The Structure of Complex Words*. New York: New
    Directions, 1951.
English Studies in Honor of James Southall Wilson. Charlottesville, Va.:
    University of Virginia, 1951.
*English Studies in Japan. Essays & Studies Presented to Dr. Yasua
    Yamato*. Tokyo: English Literary Society of Nihon University,
    1958.
Enright, Dennis J. *The Apothecary's Shop—Essays on Literature*. Lon-
    don: Secker & Warburg, 1957.
Era of Goethe, The—Essays Presented to James Boyd. Oxford: Basil
    Blackwell, 1959.
Essays and Studies in Honor of Carleton Brown. New York: New York
    University Press, 1940.
Essays Critical and Historical Dedicated to Lily B. Campbell. Berkeley:
    University of California Press, 1950.
Esslin, Martin. *Theatre of the Absurd*. New York: Anchor Books, 1961.
Falk, Eugene H. *Renunciation as a Tragic Focus—A Study of Five
    Plays*. Minneapolis: University of Minnesota Press, 1954.
Faverty, Frederic E. *Your Literary Heritage*. Philadelphia: Lippincott,
    1959.
Fedden, Robin *et. al. Personal Landscape*. London: Cowell, Ltd., 1945.
Fergusson, Francis. *The Human Image in Dramatic Literature—Essays*.
    Garden City, New York: Doubleday, 1957.
——————. *The Idea of a Theatre, A Study of Ten Plays*. Prince-
    ton: Princeton University Press, 1949.
Fisch, Harold. *The Dual Image—A Study of the Figure of the Jew in
    English Literature*. London: Lincolns-Prager, 1959.
Fiskin, A. M. I. *Writers of Our Years*. Denver: University of Denver
    Press, 1950.
    SEE: UNIVERSITY OF DENVER PUBLICATIONS.
    STUDIES IN HUMANITNES (#1: 1950)
Ford, Boris (ed.). *The Pelican Guide to English Literature*. London:
    Cassel, 1957. (Listed in This Checklist as a Periodical)
Fowlie, Wallace. *The Clown's Grail*. Denver: Swallow, 1948.
Fraiberg, Louis B. *Psychoanalysis and American Literary Criticism*.
    Detroit: Wayne State University Press, 1960.
Fraser, George S. *The Modern Writer and his World*. London: Derek
    Verschoyle, Ltd., 1953.
Free, W. J. and Charles B. Lower. *History Into Drama*. New York:
    Odyssey Press, 1963.
Friedman, Maurice S. *Problematic Rebel—An Image of Modern Man*.
    New York: Random House, 1963.

Frye, Northrop. *Fables of Identity—Studies in Poetic Mythology.* New York: Harcourt, Brace & World, 1963.

Frye, Prosser H. *Romance and Tragedy.* Lincoln: University of Nebraska Press, 1961. PN/603/F7

Fujimura, Thomas H. *The Restoration Comedy of Wit.* Princeton: Princeton University Press, 1952. 822.09/F961r

Fulton, A. R. *Drama and Theater Illustrated by Seven Modern Plays.* New York: Henry Holt, 1946. PR/1272/F8

Gagen, Jean E. *The New Woman—Her Emergence in English Drama, 1600-1730.* New York: Twayne Publishers, 1954.

Gagey, Edmond M. *Revolution in American Drama.* New York: Columbia University Press, 1947.

Gassner, John. *Producing a Play.* New York: Dryden Press, 1941.

Gassner, John and Ralph G. Allen (eds.). *Theatre and Drama in the Making.* Boston: Houghton Mifflin, 1964. 792.04/G258t

Gassner, John. *The Theatre in Our Times.* New York: Crown Publishers, 1954. PN/1655/G3

Gilbert, Allan H. *The Principles and Practice of Criticism.* Detroit: Wayne State University, 1959.

Glicksberg, Charles I. *Literature and Religion—A Study in Conflict.* Dallas: Southern Methodist University Press, 1960.

_____. *The Self in Modern Literature.* University Park, Pennsylvania: Pennsylvania State University Press, 1963.

Goldberg, Gerald J. (ed.). *The Modern Critical Spectrum.* Englewood Cliffs, New Jersey: Prentice-Hall, 1962.

Goodman, Paul. *The Structure of Literature.* Chicago: University of Chicago Press, 1954.

Goodman, Randolf. *Drama on Stage.* New York: Holt, Rinehart and Winston, 1961. 792.082/G653d

Granville-Barker, Harley. *The Use of the Drama.* Princeton: Princeton University Press, 1945.

Green, Otis H. *Spain and the Western Tradition—The Castilian Mind in Literature From El Cid to Calderon, Volume II.* Madison/Milwaukee: University of Wisconsin Press, 1964.

Greene, Graham. *The Lost Childhood.* New York: Viking Press, 1952.

Greene, William C. *Moira,* Cambridge: Harvard University Press, 1944.

Grismer, Ronald L. *Influence of Plautus in Spain.* New York: Hispanic Institute, 1944.

Grossvogel, David I. *The Self-Conscious Stage in Modern French Drama.* New York: Columbia University Press, 1958.

Gupta, Prakash C. *The Art Galsworthy and Other Studies.* Allahabad: Granthagar, n.d.

Gurko, Leo. *Angry Decade.* New York: Dodd, Meade, 1947. 813.916/G979a

Haight, Elizabeth H. *More Essays on Greek Romances.*

_____. *The Symbolism of the House Door in Classical Poetry.* New York: Longmans, Green, 1950.

Hall, Robert A., Jr. *Cultural Symbolism in Literature.* Ithaca: Linguistica, 1963. 809.91/H118c

Hallman, Ralph J. *Psychology of Literature.* New York: Philosophical Library, 1961.

Hamburger, Michael. *Reason and Energy—Studies in German Literature.* New York: Grove Press, 1957.

Harrison, George. *Elizabethan Plays and Players.* Ann Arbor: University of Michigan Press, 1956.

Hatfield, Henry C. *Aesthetic Paganism in German Literature, From Winkelmann to the Death of Goethe.* Cambridge: Harvard University Press, 1964.

Hathorn, Richmond Y. *Tragedy, Myth, and Mystery.* Bloomington: Indiana University Press, 1962.

Haworth, Peter. *English Hymns and Ballads.* Oxford: Blackwell, 1947.

Hegel, Georg W. *Hegel on Tragedy.* (Edited by Anne & Henry Paolucci) New York: Doubleday, 1962.

Heitner, Robert R. *German Tragedy in the Age of Enlightenment.* Berkeley/Los Angeles: University of California Press, 1963.

Heller, Erich. *The Disinherited Mind.* New York: Farrar, Straus & Cudahy, 1952.

Henn, Thomas R. *The Harvest of Tragedy.* London: Methuen & Co. Ltd., 1956.

Heppenstall, Rayner. *The Fourfold Tradition.* London: Barrie & Rockliff, 1961.

Hewett, R. P. *Reading and Response—An Approach to the Criticism of Literature.* London: George G. Harrap & Co., 1960.

Highet, Gilbert. *A Clerk of Oxenford—Essays on Literature and Life.* New York: Oxford University Press, 1954.

————. *People, Places and Books.* New York: Oxford University Press, 1953.

————. *Powers of Poetry.* New York: Oxford University Press, 1960.

Hobson, Harold. *The Theatre Now.* New York: Longmans, Green, 1953.

Hofacker, Erich and Liselotte Dieckmann. *Studies in Germanic Languages and Literatures in Memory of Fred O. Nolte.* St. Louis: Washington University Press, 1963.

Hoffman, Frederick J. *The Mortal No: Death and the Modern Imagination.* Princeton, N.J.: Princeton University Press, 1964.

Hogan, Robert G. (ed.). *Drama: The Major Genres—An Introductory Critical Anthology.* New York/Toronto: Dodd, Mead, 1962.

Holland, Norman. *The First Modern Comedies.* Cambridge: Harvard University Press, 1959.

Holloway, John. *The Story of the Night.* Lincoln: University of Nebraska Press, 1961.

Hone, Ralph E. (ed.). *The Voice out of the Whirlwind.* San Francisco: Chandler, 1960.

Honig, Edwin. *Dark Conceit—The Making of Allegory.* Evanston: Northwestern University Press, 1959.

Hopper, Stanley R. (ed.). *Spiritual Problems in Contemporary Litera-*

ture. (Institute for Religious and Social Studies) New York: Harper & Brothers, 1952.

Hosley, Richard (ed.). *Essays on Shakespeare and Elizabethan Drama in Honor of Hardin Craig.* Columbia: University of Missouri Press, 1962.

Hoy, Cyrus H. *The Hyacinth Room.* New York: Alfred A. Knopf, 1964.

Hudson, Lynton. *Life and the Theatre.* London: George G. Harrap, 1949.

Hurrell, John D. *Two Modern American Tragedies.* New York: Scribner, 1961.

Hyman, Stanley E. *The Critical Performance.* New York: Vintage Books, 1956.

Ihrig, Grace P. *Heroines in French Drama of the Romantic Period.* Columbia University, New York: King's Crown Press, 1950.

Illinois, University. Department of English. *Studies by Members of the English Department in Memory of John Jay Parry.* Urbana: University of Illinois Press, 1955.

International Federation for Modern Languages and Literature. *Literature and Science* (Third Trienniel Proceedings). Oxford: Blackwell, 1955.

International Federation of the Societies of Classical Studies. *Acta Congressus Madvigiani.* Copenhagen: Munksgaard, 1958.

Ionesco, Eugene. *Notes and Counter Notes—Writings on the Theatre.* New York: Grove Press, Inc., 1964.

Isaacs, J. *An Assessment of Twentieth Century Literature.* London: Secker & Warburg, 1952.

Iyengar, Srinivasa K. *The Adventure of Criticism.* New York: Asia Publishing House, 1962.

Jackson, Stoney. *This is Love?* New York: Pageant Press, 1958.

Jaeger, Werner. *Phideia: The Ideals of Greek Culture.* New York: Oxford University Press, 1960.

James, D. G. *The Dream of Learning.* New York: Oxford University Press, 1951.

James, Henry. *The Scenic Art.* (Edited by A. Wade) New Brunswick: Rutgers University Press, 1948.

————————. *Selected Literary Criticism.* New York: Horizon Press, 1964.

Jasper, G. R. *Adventure in the Theater.* New Brunswick: Rutgers University Press, 1947.

Jekels, Ludwig. *Selected Papers.* London: Imago Publishing Co., 1952.

Jennings, Elizabeth. *Every Changing Shape.* Philadelphia: Dufaur, 1962.

Jepsen, Laura. *Ethical Aspects of Tragedy.* Gainsville: University of Florida Press, 1953.

Jones, Eldred. *Othello's Countrymen—The African in English Renaissance Drama.* London: Oxford University Press, 1965.

Jones, Ernest. *Essays in Applied Psychoanalysis.* London: Hogarth, 1951.

DRAMA CRITICISM

Jones, Henry J. *On Aristotle and Greek Tragedy.* London: Chatto & Windus, 1962.

Jones, Howard M. *The Bright Medusa.* Urbana: University of Illinois Press, 1952.

Jones, Richard F. et. al. *The Seventeenth Century.* Stanford: Stanford University Press, 1952.

Jones, William. *The Priest and the Siren.* London: Epworth Press, 1953.

Kaiser, Walter J. *Praisers of Folly.* Cambridge: Harvard University Press, 1963.

Kerenji, C. *Prometheus.* New York: Pantheon, 1963.

Kerr, Walter. *The Decline of Pleasure.* New York: Simon & Schuster, 1962.

——————. *The Theater in Spite of Itself.* New York: Simon & Schuster, 1963.

Killinger, John. *The Failure of Theology in Modern Literature.* New York/Nashville: Abingdon Press, 1963.

Kirk, Rudolph and C. F. Main (eds.). *Essays in Literary History.* New Brunswick: Rutgers University Press, 1960.

Kitto, H. D. *Form and Meaning in Drama—A Study of Six Greek Plays and of Hamlet.* London: Methuen, 1956.

Kitzhaber, A. R. *Drama: The Major Genres,* New York: Dodd, Mead & Co., 1962.

Knickerbocker, K. L. and H. Willard Reninger (eds.). *Interpreting Literature.* New York: Holt, Rinehart, & Winston, 1955.

Knight, G. Wilson. *The Christian Renaissance.* New York: W. W. Norton, 1962.

——————. *The Crown of Life.* New York: Oxford University Press, 1947.

——————. *Explorations.* New York: New York University Press, 1964.

——————. *The Golden Labyrinth—A Study of British Drama.* London: Phoenix House, 1962.

——————. *The Imperial Theme.* London: Methuen, 1961.

——————. *The Olive and the Sword.* London: Oxford University Press, 1943.

——————. *The Sovereign Flower.* London: Butler & Tanner, 1958.

——————. *The Wheel of Fire.* New York: World, 1962 Edition.

Knights, L. C. *Drama and Society in the Age of Jonson.* London: Chatto & Windus, 1947.

Knox, George. *Critical Moments.* Seattle: University of Washington Press, 1957.

Korninger, Siegfried (ed.). *Studies in English Presented to Karl Brunner.* Stuttgart, 1957.

Krailsheimer, A. J. *Studies in Self Interest—From Descartes to La Bruyere.* Oxford: Clarendon Press, 1962.

Kronenberger, Louis. *The Thread of Laughter,* New York: Alfred A. Knopf, 1952.

Kris, Ernst. *Psychoanalytic Explorations in Art.* New York: International Universities Press, 1952.

Krutch Joseph Wood. *"Modernism" in Modern Drama.* Ithaca: Cornell
     University Press, 1962. LiB HAS 1953 ಎ, 818.5/K94glm/1953
Kuehnemund, Richard. *Arminius and the Rise of a National Symbol in
     Literature.* Chapel Hill: University of North Carolina Press, 1953.
Lacy, M. S. *Jacobean Problem Play.* Ann Arbor: University of Michi-
     gan Press, 1956.
Laird, John. *Philosophical Incursions into English Literature.* New
     York: Russell & Russell, 1946.
Lamm, Martin. *Modern Drama.* New York: Philosophical Library, 1948.
Landa, M. J. *The Jew in Drama.* London: King, n.d.
_____. *The Shylock Myth.* London: Allen, 1942.
Langford, Richard E. (ed.). *Essays in Modern American Literature.*
     Deland, Fla.: Stetson University Press, 1963.
Lawson, John H. *Theory and Technique of Playwriting.* New York:
     Putnam, 1943.
Leaska, Mitchell. *The Voice of Tragedy.* New York: Speller, 1963.
Leavis, Frank R. *Education and the University.* London: Chatto and
     Windus, 1944. LiB. HAS 1965 ed. only
_____. *The Common Pursuit,* London: Chatto and Windus,
     1952. 820.9 L4752
Leech, Clifford. *Shakespeare's Tragedies, and Other Studies in Seven-
     teenth Century Drama.* London: Chatto & Windus, 1961. LiB Has 1950 ed
                                                                         2328.
Lehman, B. H. *et. al. The Image of the Work.* Berkeley: University of
     California Press, 1955.
Lesser, Simon O. *Fiction and the Unconscious.* Boston: Beacon Press,
     1957.
Lever, Katherine. *The Art of Greek Comedy.* London: Methuen, 1956.
Levi, Albert W. *Literature, Philosophy and the Imagination.* Blooming-
     ton: Indiana University Press, 1962.
Levich, Marvin (ed.). *Aesthetics and the Philosophy of Criticism.* New
     York: Random House, 1963.
Lewis, Allan. *The Contemporary Theatre.* New York: Crown Publish-
     ers, 1962.
Lewis, Clive S. *They Asked for a Paper: Papers and Addresses.* Lon-
     don: Geoffrey Bles, 1962.
Lewis, Naomi. *A Visit to Mrs. Wilcox.* London: Cresset, 1957.
Little, Alan M. G. *Myth and Society in Attic Drama.* New York: Co-
     lumbia University Press, 1942.
Lockert, Lacy. *Studies in French-Classical Tragedy.* Nashville: The Van-
     derbilt University Press, 1958.
Lowenthal, Leo. *Literature and the Image of Man—Sociological Studies
     of the European Drama and Novel.* Boston: Beacon Press, 1957.
Lucas, Donald W. *The Greek Tragic Poets: Their Contribution to
     Western Life and Thought.* (Second Edition) Aberdeen, England:
     Cohen & West, 1959.
Lucas, Frank L. *Literature and Psychology.* London: Cassell & Co.,
     1951.
MacCarthy, Desmond. *Humanities.* London: MacGibbon & Kee, 1953.

McCarthy, Mary. *Sights and Spectacles*. New York: Farrar, Strauss, and Cudahy, 1956.

————————. *Theater Chronicle*. New York: Noonday Press, 1963.

McCollom, William G. *Tragedy*. New York: Macmillan, 1957.

McDonnell, R. F. *The Aspiring Mind*. Ann Arbor: University of Michigan Press, 1958.

McElroy, Davis D. *Existentialism and Modern Literature*. New York: Philosophical Library, 1963.

MacGowan, K. *Primer on Playwritting*. New York: Random House, 1951.

McIver, R. M. (ed.). *Great Moral Dilemmas in Literature, Past and Present*. New York: Harper & Row, 1956.

McManaway, James G. et. al. (eds.). *Joseph Quincey Adams Memorial Studies*. Washington: Folger Shakespeare Library, 1948.

McManaway, James G. *Shakespeare 400*. New York: Holt, Rinehart & Winston, 1964.

McNeir, Waldo F. *Studies in Comparative Literature*. Baton Rouge: Louisiana State University Press, 1962.

————————. *Studies in English Renaissance Literature*. Baton Rouge: Louisiana State University Press, 1962.

Macurdy, G. M. *The Quality of Mercy*. New Haven: Yale University Press, 1940.

Mahood, M. M. *Poetry and Symbolism*. London: J. Cape, 1950.

Mandel, Oscar. *The Theatre of Don Juan*. Lincoln: University of Nebraska Press, 1963.

Mander, John. *The Writer and Commitment*. Philadelphia: Dufours Editions, 1962.

Markel, Lester (ed.). *Background and Foreground*. Great Neck: Channel Press, 1961.

Marx, Milton. *The Enjoyment of Drama*. New York: Appleton-Century-Crofts, 1947. 2nd ed. only, 1961 PN/1655/M17/1961

Mathewson, Rufus W. Jr. *The Positive Hero in Russian Literature*. New York: Columbia University Press, 1958.

Mavor, O. H. *Tedious and Brief*. London: Constable, 1945.

Maxwell, B. (ed.), et. al. *Renaissance Studies in Honor of Hardin Craig*. Stanford: Stanford University Press, 1941.

Melchiori, Giorgis. *The Tightrope Walkers—Studies of Mannerism in Modern English Literature*. London: Routledge & Kegan Paul, 1956.

Mendelsohn, Moris O. *Soviet Interpretation of Contemporary American Literature*. New York: Russian Translation Program of the American Council of Learned Societies, 1948.

Merkel, Gottfried F. (ed.). *On Romanticism and the Art of Translation —Studies in Honor of Edwin Hermann Zeydel*. Princeton: Princeton University Press, 1956.

Mignon, Elizabeth L. *Crabbed Age and Youth*. Durham: Duke University Press, 1947.

Miller, Henry. *Stand Still Like the Hummingbird.* New York: New Directions, 1962.

Millet, Fred B. *Reading Drama.* New York: Harper & Row, 1950.

Muir, Edwin. *Essays on Literature and Society.* London: Hogarth, 1965.

Muir, Kenneth. *Shakespeare as Collaborator.* London: Methuen, 1960.

Muller, Herbert J. *The Spirit of Tragedy.* New York: Alfred A. Knopf, 1956.

Murray, Gilbert C. *Greek Studies.* London: Oxford Univeristy Press, 1940.

Murry, John M. *John Clare and Other Studies.* London/New York: Peter Nevill, 1950.

——————. *Selected Criticism, 1916-1957.* London: Oxford University Press, 1960.

——————. *Unprofessional Essays.* London: J. Cape, 1956.

Myers, Henry A. *Tragedy: A View of Life.* Ithaca: Cornell University Press, 1956.

Myers, John. *The Structure of Stichomythia in Attic Tragedy.* Oxford: University Press, 1949.

Nahm, Milton C. *Aesthetic Experience and its Presuppositions.* New York: Harper & Brothers, 1946.

Nannes, Caspar H. *Politics in the American Drama.* Washington, D.C.: Catholic University of America Press, 1960.

Neff, Emery. *A Revolution in European Poetry: 1660-1900.* New York: Columbia University Press, 1940.

Nelson, Robert J. *Play Within a Play.* New Haven: Yale University Press, 1958.

Nemerov, Howard. *Poetry and Fiction: Essays.* New Brunswick, N.J.: Rutgers University Press, 1963.

Nicholson, Norman. *Man and Literature.* London: S.C.M. Press, 1944.

Norton, Aloysius (ed.). *A Christian Approach to Western Literature.* Westminster, Md.: Newman Press, 1961.

Nott, Kathleen. *The Emperor's Clothes.* London: William Heinemann, 1954.

Oakeshott, W. *The Queen and the Poet.* New York: Barnes and Noble, 1961.

O'Donnell, Donat. *Maria Cross.* New York: Oxford University Press, 1952.

Olson, Elder. *Tragedy and the Theory of Drama.* Detroit: Wayne State University Press, 1961.

Ornstein, Robert. *The Moral Vision of Jacobean Tragedy.* Madison: University of Wisconsin Press, 1960.

Oxford University. *Studies in Medieval French Presented to Alfred Evert.* Oxford: Oxford University Press, 1961.

Page, D. L. *A New Chapter in the History of Greek Tragedy.* Cambridge: Cambridge University Press, 1951.

Parr, Johnstone. *Tamburlaine's Malady, and Other Essays on Astrology in Elizabethan Drama.* University, Alabama: University of Alabama Press, 1953.

Parrott, T. M. and R. H. Ball. *A Short View of Elizabethan Drama.* New York: Scribner's, 1943.

Payne, Robert. *Hubris.* New York: Harper, 1960.

Peacock, R. *Poet in the Theater.* New York: Hill and Wang, 1960.

Perlman, L. *Jew in Retrospect.* New York: 1942.

Phillips, James E. *Images of a Queen—Mary Stuart in Sixteenth Century Literature.* Berkeley/Los Angeles: University of California Press, 1964.

Phillips, William (ed.). *Art and Psychoanalysis.* New York: Criterion Books, 1957.

Pierce, Francis W. *Hispanic Studies in Honour of I. Gonzalez Llubera.* Oxford: Dolphin Book Co., 1959.

Pogson, Beryl. *In the East my Pleasure Lies.* London: Stuart & Richards, 1950.

Praz, Mario. *The Flaming Heart.* Garden City: Anchor Books, 1950.

Prentice, William K. *Those Ancient Dramas Called Tragedies.* Princeton: Princeton University Press, 1942.

Price, Alan. *Synge and Anglo-Irish Drama.* London: Methuen & Co., 1961.

Price, Martin. *To the Palace of Wisdom.* New York: Doubleday, 1964.

Prior, Moody E. *The Language of Tragedy.* New York: Columbia University Press, 1947.

——————. *Science and the Humanities.* Evanston: Northwestern University Press, 1962.

Pronko, Leonard C. *Avant-Garde: The Experimental Theater in France.* Berkeley: University of California Press, 1962.

Quiller-Couch, A. T. *Cambridge Lectures.* London: J. M. Dent (Everyman's Library), 1943.

Rabkin, Gerald. *Drama and Commitment.* Bloomington: Indiana University Press, 1964.

Rahv, Philip. *Image and Idea.* New York: New Directions, 1957.

Ransom, J. C. *The New Critics.* New York: New Directions, 1941.

Raphael, D. D. *Paradox of Tragedy.* Bloomington: Indiana University Press, 1959.

Read, Herbert. *A Coat of Many Colors.* London: Routledge, 1945.

Reik, Theodor. *Listening With a Third Ear.* New York: Farrar, Straus, & Cudahy, 1954.

——————. *The Secret Self.* New York: Farrar, Straus, & Cudahy, 1952.

Ribner, Irving. *The English History Play in the Age of Shakespeare.* Princeton: Princeton University Press, 1957.

——————. *Jacobean Tragedy.* New York: Barnes & Noble, 1962.

Ridley, Maurice R. *Studies in Three Literatures: English, Latin, Greek —Contrasts and Comparisons.* London: J. M. Dent & Sons, 1962.

Roaten, Darnell H. *Structural Forms in the French Theater, 1500-1700.* Philadelphia: University of Pennsylvania Press, 1960.

Robinson, Cecil. *With the Ears of Strangers.* Tucson: University of Arizona Press, 1963.

Rosenheim, Edward W. Jr. *What Happenes in Literature*. Chicago: University of Chicago Press, 1961.

Rosenmeyer, Thomas G. *The Masks of Tragedy*. Austin: University of Texas Press, 1963.

Ross, J. L. *Philosophy in Literature*. Syracuse: Syracuse University Press, 1949.

Rowe, Kenneth T. *A Theatre in Your Head*. New York: Funk & Wagnalls Co., 1960.

Rubow, P. V. *Two Essays*. Copenhagen: Gyldendal, 1949.

Rueckert, William H. *Kenneth Burke*. Minneapolis: University of Minnesota Press, 1963.

Ruitenbeek, Hendrik M. (ed.). *Psychoanalysis and Literature*. New York: E. P. Dutton & Co., 1964.

Russell, Francis. *Three Studies in Twentieth Century Obscurity*. Kent: Hand & Flower Press, 1954.

Rymer, Thomas. *Critical Works*. New Haven: Yale University Press, 1956.

Sachs, H. *The Creative Unconscious*. Cambridge, Mass.: Science-Art Publishers, 1951.

Sackville-West, Edward. *Inclinations*. London: Secker & Warburg, 1949.

Sainer, Arthur. *The Sleepwalker and the Assassin*. New York: Bridgehead Books, 1964.

Sanford, Charles L. *The Quest for Paradise—Europe and the Moral Imagination*. Urbana: University of Illinois Press, 1961.

Santayana, George. *Essays in Literary Criticism of George Santayana*. New York: Charles Scribner's Sons, 1956.

Schorer, Mark (ed.). *Criticism—The Foundations of Modern Literary Judgement*. New York: Harcourt, Brace, 1962. LiB. HAS Rev. Ed., 1958

Schrickx, W. *Shakespeare's Early Contemporaries—The Background of the Harvey-Nashe Polemic and Love's Labour's Lost*. Antwerp: De Nederlandsche Boekhandel, 1956.

Schutze, Martin. *Academic Illusions*. Hampden, Connecticut: Archon Books, 1962.

Schwartz, Delmore. *Vaudeville for a Princess*. New York: New Directions, 1950.

Scott, Nathan A. (ed.). *The Climate of Faith in Modern Literature*. New York: Seabury Press, 1964.

————————. *The Tragic Vision and the Christian Faith*. New York: Association Press, 1957.

Scott, Wilbur S. (comp.). *Five Approaches of Literary Criticism—An Arrangement of Contemporary Critical Essays*. New York: Collier Books, 1962.

Sedgewick, G. G. *Of Irony*. Toronto: University of Toronto Press, 1948.

Seltman, Charles. *The Twelve Olympians*. New York: Crowell, 1960.

Sewall, Richard B. *The Vision of Tragedy*. New Haven: Yale University Press, 1959.

Seward, Barbara. *The Symbolic Rose*. New York: Columbia University Press, 1960.

Sharpe, Robert B. *Irony in the Drama—An Essay on Impersonation, Shock and Catharsis.* Chapel Hill: University of North Carolina Press, 1959.

Shaw, George Bernard. *Plays and Players.* New York: Oxford University Press, 1958.

Sherbo, Arthur. *English Sentimental Drama.* East Lansing: Michigan State University Press, 1957.

Shirk, S. *Characterization of George Washington in American Plays Since 1875.* Philadelphia: University of Pennsylvania Press, 1949.

Shoemaker, F. *Aesthetic Experience and the Humanities.* New York: Columbia University Press, 1943.

Sievers, Wieder D. *Freud on Broadway.* New York: Hermitage House, 1955.

Simpson, Alan. *Beckett and Behan.* London: Routledge & Kegan Paul, 1962.

Simpson, Percy. *Studies in Elizabethan Drama.* Oxford: Clarendon Press, 1955.

Slote, Bernice. (ed.). *Literature and Society.* Lincoln: University of Nebraska Press, 1964.

——————————. *Myth and Symbol—Critical Approaches and Applications.* Lincoln: University of Nebraska Press, 1963.

Snell, Bruno. *Poetry and Society.* Bloomington: Indiana University Press, 1961.

Snuggs, Henry L. *The Comic Humours.* New York: Modern Language Association, 1947.

Speaight, R. *Since 1939.* London: Phoenix, 1947.

Spender, Stephen. *The Creative Element.* London: Hamish Hamilton, 1953.

——————————. *The Making of a Poem.* New York: W. W. Norton, 1962.

Spring, Powell. *The Spirit of Literature.* Winter Park, Florida: Orange Press, 1945.

Stallman, Robert W. and R. E. Walters (eds), *The Creative Reader,* New York: The Ronald Press, 1954.

Stallman, Robert W. *Critiques and Essays in Criticism.* New York: Ronald Press, 1949.

Stanford Studies in Language and Literature. Stanford: Stanford University Press, 1941.

Stanford, W. B. *The Ulysses Theme.* Oxford: Blackwell, 1963.

Stauffer, Donald A. *The Nature of Poetry.* New York: Norton, 1946.

Steiner, George. *The Death of Tragedy.* New York: Alfred A. Knopf, 1961.

Stewart, Douglas. *The Flesh and the Spirit.* Sydney: Angus & Robertson, 1948.

Stoll, E. E. *From Shakespeare to Joyce.* New York: Doubleday, 1944.

——————————. *Shakespeare and Other Masters.* Cambridge: Harvard University Press, 1962.

Strachey, Lytton. *Spectatorial Essays.* London: Chatto & Windus, 1964.

Strong, L. A. G. *The Sacred River*. London: Methuen & Co., 1949.

Studies in Speech and Drama in Honor of Alexander M. Drummond. Ithaca: Cornell University Press, 1944.

Studies in the English Renaissance Drama in Memory of Karl J. Holzknecht. New York: New York University Press, 1959.

Styan, J. L. *The Dark Comedy*. Cambridge: Cambridge University Press, 1962.

_____. *The Elements of Drama*. Cambridge: Cambridge University Press, 1960.

Sypher, Wylie (ed.). *Comedy*. New York: Doubleday Anchor. 1956.

Sypher, Wylie. *Loss of Self in Modern Literature and Art*. New York: Random House, 1962.

_____. *Rococo to Cubism in Art and Literature*. New York: Random House, 1960.

Talbert, Ernest W. *Elizabethan Drama and Shakespeare's Early Plays*. Chapel Hill: University of North Carolina Press, 1963.

Tayler, Edward W. *Nature and Art in Renaissance Literature*. New York: Columbia University Press, 1964.

Taylor, John R. *Anger, and After—A Guide to the New British Drama*. London: Methuen, 1963.

Thomas, Geoffrey. *The Theatre Alive*. London: Christopher Johnson, 1948.

Thomas, R. Hinton. *German Perspectives*. Cambridge: Heffer, Ltd., 1940.

Thompson, A. R. *Dry Mock*. Berkeley: University of California Press, 1948.

Thomson, George. *Aeschylus and Athens*. London: Lawrence & Wishart, 1946.

Tillyard, Eustace M. *Essays Literary and Educational*. London: Chatto & Windus, 1962.

_____. *Some Mythical Elements in English Literature—The Clark Lectures, 1959-1960*. London: Chatto & Windus, 1961.

Trilling, Diana. *Claremont Essays*. New York: Harcourt, Brace & World, 1964.

Trilling Lionel. *The Liberal Imagination*. New York: Doubleday, 1953.

Tunnel, Martin. *The Classical Movement*. London: Hamilton, 1947.

Tymms, R. *Doubles in Literary Psychology*. Cambridge, Eng.: Bowes & Bowes, 1949.

Valency, Maurice J. *The Flower and the Castle—An Introduction to Modern Drama*. New York: Macmillan, 1963.

Van Abbe, Derek. *Drama in Renaissance Germany and Switzerland*. London: Melbourne University Press, 1961.

VanDoren, Mark. *The Happy Critic*. New York: Hill & Wang, 1961.

Van Doren, Mark. (ed.). *The New Invitation to Learning*. New York: Random House, 1942.

Victoria University of Manchester. *Studies in Romance Philology and French Literature Presented to John Orr*. Manchester, Eng.: Manchester University Press, 1953.

Vitale, Philip H. (ed.). *Catholic Critics*. Chicago: Auxiliary University Press, 1961.

Vivas, Eliseo. *The Artistic Transaction, and Other Essays on Theory of Literature*. Columbus: Ohio State University Press, 1963.

Walker, Roy. *The Time is Out of Joint*. London: A Dakers, 1948.

Wallace, A. Dayle (ed.). *Studies in Honor of John Wilcox*. Detroit: Wayne State University Press, 1958.

Walley, Harold R. *The Book of the Play: An Introduction to Drama*. New York: Charles Scribner's Sons, 1950.

Warshow, Robert. *The Immediate Experience*. New York: Doubleday, 1962.

Weales, Gerald C. *American Drama Since World War II*. New York: Harcourt, Brace & World, 1962.

Webster, T. B. L. *Greek Interpretations*. Manchester: Manchester University Press, 1942.

Wedgwood, C. V. *Mightier Than the Sword*. New York: Macmillan, 1964.

Weisinger, Herbert. *The Agony and the Triumph*. East Lansing: Michigan State University Press, 1964.

Weitz, Morris. *Philosophy in Literature*. Detroit: Wayne State University Press, 1963.

Wells, Henry. *The American Way of Poetry*. New York: Columbia University Press, 1943.

————. *Elizabethan and Jacobean Playwrights*. New York: Columbia University Press, 1964.

Wertham, Frederick. *Dark Legend*. New York: Duell, Sloan, 1941.

West, Rebecca. *The Court and the Castle—Some Treatments of a Recurrent Theme*. New Haven: Yale University Press, 1957.

Wilcox, John. *The Relation of Moliere to Restoration Comedy*. New York: Columbia University Press, 1964.

Wilder, Amos N. *Theology and Modern Literature*. Cambridge: Harvard University Press, 1958.

Williams, Charles. *The Image of the City*. New York: Oxford University Press, 1958.

Williams, Raymond. *Drama From Ibsen to Eliot*. London: Chatto and Windus, 1954.

————. *Drama in Performance*. Chester Springs: Dufours, 1954.

Windolph, F. Lyman. *Reflections of the Law in Literature*. Philadelphia: University of Pennsylvania Press, 1956.

Wimsatt, W. K. *Hateful Contraries*. Louisville: University of Kentucky Press, 1965.

Wormhoudt, A. *A Demon Lover*. New York: Exploration Press, 1949.

Worsley, T. C. *The Fugitive Art*. London: John Lehmann, 1952.

Wrenn, C. L. and G. Bullough. *English Studies Today, First Series*. London: Oxford University Press, 1951.

Young, Sherman P. *The Women of Greek Drama*. New York: Exposition Press, 1953.

Young, Stark. *The Flower in the Drama.* New York: Scribner's, 1955.
————————. *Immortal Shadows.* New York: Scribner's, 1948. *also* mvc
Zabel, Morton D. *Literary Opinion in America.* New York: Harper &
    Bros., 1951.
                                                            checked mr

BOOKS—II

The following works have yielded no entries for this checklist.

Abel, Darrel. *American Literature.*
Adamic, Lewis. *Two Way Passage.*
Adams, James D. *Literary Frontiers.*
Adams, W. B. *Looking at a Play.*
Adler, G. *Studies in Analytical Psychology.*
Adler, Mortimer. *How to Read a Book.*
Ady, C. M. *Morals and Manners in the Quattrocento.*
Agard, W. R. *The Humanities for our Time.*
Agate, James E. *Brief Chronicles.*
————————. *The English Dramatic Critics—An Anthology, 1660-
    1932.*
————————. *James Agate, An Anthology.*
Aiken, Conrad P. *A Reviewer's ABC.*
Alcock, Richard A. *World Literature Made Simple.*
Aldridge, John W. *In Search of Heresy—American Literature in an Age
    of Conformity.*
Alington, Argentine. *Drama and Education.*
Allen, Don C. *Studies in Honor of T. W. Baldwin.*
Allen, John P. *Masters of European Drama.*
Allers, R. *The Successful Error.*
Allsop, Kenneth. *The Angry Decade—A Survey of the Cultural Revolt
    of the 1950s.*
Altrocchi, Rudolph. *Sleuthing in the Stacks.*
Alvarez, A. *The Shaping Spirit.*
Anderson, Carl L. *The Swedish Acceptance of American Literature.*
Anderson, Maxwell. *Bases of Artistic Creation.*
Andrews, Siri (ed). *The Hewins Lectures, 1947-1962.*
Angoff, Allan. *American Writing Today: Its Independence and Vigor.*
Anchen, Ruth. *The Family: Its Function and Destiny.*
————————. *Science and Man.*
Archer, William. *The Old Drama and the New.*
Armstrong, William A. (ed). *Experimental Drama.*
Arnold, Richard (ed). *Classical Essays Presented to James A. Kleist.*
Artz, Frederick B. *From the Renaissance to Romanticism.*
Aswell, M. L. *The World Within.*
Atkins, John W. *English Literary Criticism: The Renascence.*
Auden, Wynstan H. *The Enchafed Flood.*

Auerbach, Erich. *Introduction to Romance Languages and Literature.*
———————. *Scenes from the Drama of European Literature—Six Essays.*
Aury, Dominque. *Literary Landfalls.*
Austin, Lloyd J. (ed). *Studies in Modern French Literature Presented to P. Mansell Jones.*
Avitabile, Grazia. *The Controversey on Romanticism in Italy, First Phase: 1816-1823.*
Bacon, Helen H. *Barbarians in Greek Tragedy.*
Baker, Denys (ed). *Writers of Today.*
Baker, Joseph E. (ed). *The Reinterpretation of Victorian Literature.*
Baldry, H. C. *The Classics in the Modern World.*
———————. *Greek Literature for the Modern Reader.*
Barnet, Sylvan (ed). *Eight Great Tragedies.*
Barnet, Sylvan. *The Study of Literature.*
Barrett, William. *What is Existentialism?*
Bartlett, A. H. *Six Historic and Romantic Leaders.*
Bartley, J. O. *Teague, Shenkin and Sawney.*
Barzun, J. M. *Romanticism and the Modern Ego.*
Basler, R. P. *Sex, Symbolism, and Psychology in Literature.*
Basu, Nitish K. *Literature and Criticism.*
Bate, W. J. *The Major Texts.*
Bateson, F. W. *English Poetry.*
Battenhouse, Henry M. *English Romantic Writers.*
Beatty, Richmond C. *The Literature of the South.*
Beaver, Harold L. (ed). *American Critical Essays, Twentieth Century.*
Beckson, Karl E. (ed). *Great Theories in Literary Criticism.*
Beebe, Maurice (ed). *Literary Symbolism—An Introduction to the Interpretation of Literature.*
Beesley, Pat. *Revival of Humanities.*
Beljame, Alexandre. *Men of Letters and the English Public in the Eighteenth Century.*
Bentley, Eric. *A County of Hero Worship.*
———————. *The Dramatic Event—An American Chronicle.*
———————. *The Importance of Scrutiny.*
———————. *In Search of Theatre.*
Bentley, Eric (ed). *Let's Get a Divorce.*
Bentley, Eric. *Modern Theatre.*
———————. *Parables for the Theatre.*
Bergler, E. *The Basic Neuroses.*
———————. *Laughter and the Sense of Humor.*
Bergquist, G. William (ed). *Three Centuries of English and American Plays, a Checklist.*
Bernanos, G. *The Fearless Heart.*
———————. *The Last Essays of Georges Bernanos.*
Bernbaum, E. *Guide Through the Romantic Movement.*
Berne, E. *Mind in Action.*
Bethell, Samuel L. *The Cultural Revolution of the Seventeenth Century.*

―――――――――. *Literary Criticism.*
Beyer, Werner W. *The Enchanted Forest.*
Birnbaum, Henri. *Love and Love's Philosophy.*
Bittle, C. *From Aether to Cosmology.*
Blackburn, J. M. *Psychology and the Social Pattern.*
Blackmur, Richard P. *The Expense of Greatness.*
―――――――――. *Lectures in Criticism.*
―――――――――. *The Lion and the Honeycomb—Essays in Solicitude and Critique.*
Blair, Walter (ed). *The United States in Literature.*
Blake, George. *Barrie and the Kailyard School.*
Blumenthal, Walter Hart. *The Mermaid Myth.*
Blunden, Edmund C. *Shakespeare to Hardy: Short Studies of Characteristics.*
Blunden, Edward. *Sons of Light.*
Boas, Frederick S. *An Introduction to Stuart Drama.*
―――――――――. *Ovid and the Elizabethans.*
―――――――――. *Queen Elizabeth in Drama and Related Studies.*
Boas, George. *The Critic as Philosopher.*
―――――――――. *Essays on Primitivism and Related Ideas in the Middle Ages.*
Bode, Carl (ed). *The Young Rebel in American Literature.*
Bogan, Louis. *Selected Criticism.*
Borgerhoff, Elbert B. *The Freedom of French Classicism.*
Boughner, Daniel C. *The Braggart in Renaissance Comedy.*
Boulton, Marjorie. *The Anatomy of Drama.*
―――――――――. *The Meaning of a Heroic Age.*
―――――――――. *Problems in Greek Poetry.*
―――――――――. *The Romantic Imagination.*
―――――――――. *Sophoclean Tragedy.*
―――――――――. *Virgil to Milton.*
Boyce, Benjamin. *The Polemic Character—1640-1661—A Chapter in English Literary History.*
Branam, George C. *Eighteenth Century Adaptations of Shakespearian Tragedy.*
Brandes, Georg M. *Naturalism in Nineteenth Century English Literature.*
Braun, M. *History and Romance in Graeco Oriental Literature.*
Bredsdorff, Kaj. *From Bernard Shaw to T. S. Eliot.*
Bredvold, Louis I. *The Natural History of Sensibility.*
Bree, Germaine. *Camus Criticism.*
Brett, R. *The Third Earl of Shaftesbury—A Study in Eighteenth Century Literary Theory.*
Bridges-Adams, William. *The Irresistable Theatre.*
Briggs, Katharine M. *The Anatomy of Puck.*
Brome, Vincent. *Six Studies in Quarrelling.*
Brooks, Van Wyck. *A Chilmark Miscellany.*
―――――――――. *New England: Indian Summer.*

Brown, Clarence A. *The Achievement of American Criticism—Representative Selections from 300 years of American Criticism.*

Brown, Deming B. *Soviet Attitudes Toward American Writing.*

Brown, James I. (ed). *Explorations in College Reading.*

Brown, John M. *Accustomed as I am.*

————————. *As They Appear.*

————————. *Insides Out.*

Brown, Sharon (ed). *Present Tense.*

Brown, Stephen J. and Thomas McDermott. *A Survey of Catholic Literature.*

Brown, Winifred E. *The Polished Shaft—Studies in the Purpose and Influence of the Christian Writer in the Eighteenth Century.*

Browne, Robert M. *Theories of Convention in Contemporary American Criticism.*

Bruford, Walter H. *Literary Interpretation in Germany.*

Bryan, William A. *George Washington in American Literature.*

Bryant, Donald C. (ed). *The Rhetorical Idiom—Essays in Rhetoric, Oratory, Language and Drama.*

Bryson, Lyman (ed). *Science, Philosophy, and Religion.*

Bullough, Edward. *Aesthetics: Lectures and Essays.*

Bullough, Geoffrey. *Changing Views of the Mind in English Poetry.*

————————. *Trend of Modern Poetry.*

Burckhardt, J. C. *Civilization of the Renaissance.*

Burton, Kathleen M. *Restoration Literature.*

Bush, Douglas. *Classical Influences in Renaissance Literature.*

Bury, R. G. *The Devil's Puzzle.*

Cady, E. H. *Gentleman in America.*

Cairns, Howard. *Lectures in Criticism.*

Cairns, Huntington. *The Limits of Art.*

Campbell, Lily B. *Divine Poetry and Drama in Sixteenth Century England.*

Campbell, O. J. and J. Van Grundy. *Patterns for Living.*

Canby, Henry S. *Classic Americans.*

————————. *New Land Speaking.*

Cargill, S. T. *Philosophy of Analogy and Symbolism.*

Carter, A. *The Idea of Decadence in French Literature, 1830-1900.*

Carver, G. *Aesthetics and the Problem of Meaning.*

Caudwell, Christopher. *Further Studies in a Dying Culture.*

————————. *Studies in a Dying Culture.*

Cecil, Lord David. *The Fine Arts of Reading, and Other Literary Studies.*

Chandos, John. *"To Deprave and Corrupt . . ."—Original Studies in the Nature and Definition of 'Obscenity'.*

Chevalier, Haakon. *The Ironic Temper.*

Chew, Samuel C. *The Pilgrimage of Life.*

Chicoteau, M. *Studies in Symbolist Psychology.*

Church, Richard. *Plato's Mistake.*

Churchill, R. C. *English Literature and the Agnostic.*

_____ . *English Literature of the Nineteenth Century.*
Clark, A. M. *Studies in Literary Modes.*
Clark, Barrett H. *European Theories of the Drama.*
Clements, Robert J. *Picta Poesis.*
Clifford, James L. (ed). *Eighteenth Century English Literature.*
Clift, E. H. *Latin Pseudopigrapha.*
Clinton-Baddeley, Victor C. *The Burlesque Tradition in the English Theatre After 1660.*
Coggin, Philip A. *Drama and Education.*
Cohen, A. *Anglo-Jewish Scrapbook, 1600-1840.*
Coleridge, Samuel T. (Roberta F. Brinkley, ed). *Coleridge on the Seventeenth Century.*
Collingwood, R. G. *The Idea of History.*
Combs, Homer C. (ed). *A Treasury of the Essay.*
Conference on New Criticism. *The Critical Matrix.*
Connolly, Francis X. *Literature—The Channel of Culture.*
_____ . *A Rhetoric Case Book.*
Cook, John A. *Neo-Classic Drama in Spain, Theory and Practice.*
Coomaraswamy, A. K. *Figures of Speech and Figures of Thought.*
Cooper, James F. *Early Critical Essays, 1820-1822.*
Cooper, Lane. *Aristotelian Theory of Comedy.*
_____ . *Aristotle on the Art of Poetry.*
_____ . *Experiment in Education.*
_____ . *Methods and Aims in the Study of Literature.*
_____ . *Poetics of Aristotle.*
Counsell, John. *Counsell's Opinions.*
Coveny, Peter. *Poor Monkey—The Child in Literature.*
Cowley, Malcolm. *The Literary Situation.*
Craig, Hardin. *English Religious Drama of the Middle Ages.*
_____ . *Freedom and Renaissance.*
_____ . *Literary Study and the Scholarly Profession.*
Crews, Frederick C. *The Pooh Perplex—A Freshman Casebook.*
Crites, L. *Five Twosome Plays.*
Crosland, Jessie. *Medieval French Literature.*
Cunliffe, Marcus. *The Literature of the United States.*
Curtius, Ernst R. *European Literature and the Latin Middle Ages.*
Dahlberg, Edward. *Alms for Oblivion, Essays.*
Dahlberg, Edward and Herbert Read. *Truth is More Sacred—A Critical Exchange in Modern Literature.*
Daiches, David. *Literary Essays.*
_____ . *Poetry and the Modern World.*
_____ . *Study of Literature.*
Dale, A. M. *Lyric Metres of Greek Drama.*
D'Alton, John F. *Roman Literary Theory and Criticism.*
Dana, W. *Drama in War Time Russia.*
Danziger, Marlies K. *An Introduction to Literary Criticsm.*
Davidson, Donald (John T. Fain, ed). *The Spyglass, Views and Reviews, 1924-1930.*

Davidson, Donald. *Still Rebels, Still Yankees, and Other Essays.*
Davies, William R. *A Voice From the Attic.*
Daylight, London: The Hogarth Press, 1941.
Dean, Leonard F. (ed). *Essays on Language and Usage.*
Decker, Clarence R. *The Victorian Conscience.*
De la Mare, Walter. *Private View.*
De Selincourt, Ernest. *Wordsworthian and Other Studies.*
Denny, Norman (ed). *The Yellow Book.*
De Voto, Bernard. *The Easy Chair.*
—————————. *Literary Fallacy.*
—————————. *Minority Report.*
Devoto, Giacomo. *Linguistics and Literary Criticism.*
Dingle, Herbert. *Science and Literary Criticism.*
—————————. *Threefold Cord.*
Disher, Maurice W. *Blood and Thunder.*
—————————. *Pharaoh's Fool.*
Dixon, W. MacNeile. *An Apology for the Arts.*
Dobree, Bonamy. *The Unacknowledged Legislator.*
Dodds, E. R. *The Defense of Man.*
—————————. *Minds in the Making.*
Dorra, Henri. *The American Muse.*
Downer, Alan S. *Recent American Drama.*
Dryden, John. *Of Dramatic Poesy, and Other Critical Essays.*
Duckworth, George E. *The Nature of Roman Comedy.*
Dudley, Louise and Austin Faricy. *The Humanities.*
Duffy, J. *Philosophy of Poetry.*
Dufner, Max (ed). *Romanticism.*
Duncan, Hugh D. *Language and Literature in Society.*
Durham, England. University. *Essays Presented to C. M. Girdlestone.*
Durham, Willard H. (ed). *Critical Essays of the Eighteenth Century.*
Earley, Clarence L. S. *English Dramatic Criticism 1920-1930.*
Eastman, F. *Drama in the Church.*
Ehrenburg, Ilya. *Chekhov, Stendhal, and Other Essays.*
Ehrenpreis, Irvin. *The "Types Approach" to Literature.*
Eidelberg, L. *Take off Your Mask.*
Elioseff, Lee A. *The Cultured Mileu of Addison's Literary Criticism.*
Eliot, T. S. *The Idea of a Christian Society.*
Elledge, Scott (ed) and Donald Schier. *The Continental Model.*
Elledge, Scott (ed). *Eighteenth Century Critical Essays.*
Elliott, George P. *A Piece of Lettuce.*
Ellis, Havelock. *From Marlowe to Shaw.*
Ellis, W. W. *How to Write Farce.*
Ellis-Fermor, Una M. *The Jacobean Drama.*
—————————. *Masters of Reality.*
Elvin, Lionel. *Introduction to the Study of Literature, Volume One, Poetry.*
Emerson, H. O. *Comedias D'aujourd' kui.*
—————————. *Continental French Theater.*

Eng-Liedmeeir, A. *Soviet Literary Characters.*
Engel, S. Morris. *The Problem of Tragedy.*
Esdaile, Arundell. *Autolycus' Pack.*
Evans, Benjamin I. *English Literature: Values and Traditions.*
Evans, Bert. *English Literature Between Wars.*
_____ . *Tradition and Romanticism.*
Evans, Jean. *Three Men.*
Everett, Dorothy. *Essays on Middle English Literature.*
Fadiman, Clifton. *Party of One.*
Farbridge, Maurice H. *English Literature and the Hebrew Renaissance.*
Farrell, James T. *The League of Frightened Philistines and Other Papers.*
_____ . *Literature and Morality.*
_____ . *Selected Essays.*
Fast, Howard M. *Literature and Reality.*
Fausset, Hugh I. *Poets and Pundits.*
Feasy, L. *Old England at Play.*
Feibleman, James K. *In Praise of Comedy.*
Feidelson, Charles (ed) and Paul Brodtkorb, Jr. *Interpretations of American Literature.*
Feidelson, Charles. *Symbolism and American Literature.*
Fidell, Oscar H. (ed). *Ideas in Prose.*
Fiedler, Leslie A. *Waiting for the End.*
Fischer, John (ed) and Robert B. Silvers. *Writing in America.*
Floan, Howard R. *The South in Northern Eyes, 1831-1861.*
Flower, Robin. *The Irish Tradition.*
Flugell, C. J. *Man, Morals, and Society.*
Ford, Boris (ed). *The Pelican Guide to English Literature.*
Ford, F. P. *Lucifer at Large.*
Forster, Leonard W. *The Temper of Seventeenth-Century German Literature.*
Foster, Richard J. *The New Romantics.*
Fowlie, Wallace. *Dionysus in Paris.*
_____ . *Jacob's Night.*
_____ . *Mallarme as Hamlet.*
Fox, Edward I. *Azorin as a Literary Critic.*
Frank, Grace. *The Medieval French Drama.*
Frank, Joseph. *The Widening Gyre.*
Frankfort, Henri. *Before Philosophy.*
Fraser, George. *The Modern Writer and His World.*
_____ . *Post-War Trends in English Literature.*
Frey, James E. (ed). *Romantic and Victorian Writers.*
Frick, Courtance (ed). *The Dramatic Criticism of George Jean Nathan.*
Frye, Northrop. *Anatomy of Criticism.*
_____ . *The Well-Tempered Critic.*
Fucilla, Joseph G. *Studies and Notes (Literary and Historical).*
Gail, Marzieh. *Persia and the Victorians.*
Garbo, C. H. *Creative Critic.*

418   DRAMA CRITICISM

Gardiner, H. *Mysteries End.*
Garrod, Heathcote W. *The Study of Good Letters.*
Gascoigne, Bamger. *Twentieth Century Drama.*
Gassner, John (ed). *Ideas in the Drama; Selected Papers From the English Institute.*
Gassner, John. *Masters of Modern Drama.*
Gaster, Theodor H. *Thespis: Ritual, Myth and Drama in the Ancient Near East.*
Geismar, Maxwell. *The Last of the Provincials.*
————————. *Writers in Crisis.*
George, Daniel. *Lonely Pleasures.*
Gerretson, Carel. *Essays.*
Gheon, Henri. *The Art of the Theatre.*
Gibson, H. N. *The Shakespeare Claimants.*
Gide, Andre. *Imaginary Interviews.*
————————. *Pretexts.*
Gifford, Henry. *The Hero of his Time.*
Gilbert, Allan H. *Literary Criticism: Plato to Dryden.*
Gilbert, K. E. *Aesthetic Studies.*
Gildon, C. *Supposed Author.*
Gist, M. A. *Love and War in the Middle English Romances.*
Glicksberg, Charles I. *American Literary Criticism 1900-1950.*
————————. *The Tragic Vision in Twentieth Century Literature.*
Glover, T. R. *Springs of Hellas, and Other Essays.*
Gogarty, O. *Mourning Becomes Mrs. Spendlove.*
Gohdes, Clarence L. *American Literature in Nineteenth Century England.*
Gold, Herbert (ed). *First Person Singular.*
Golden, H. H. and Seymour O. Simches. *Modern Iberian Literature.*
Goodrich, Norma L. *The Medieval Myths.*
Gordh, George R. *Christian Faith and its Cultural Expression.*
Gordon, George. *The Discipline of Letter.*
————————. *More Companionable Books.*
Grant, Michael. *Roman Literature.*
Graves, Robert. *The Crowning Privilege.*
————————. *Oxford Addresses on Poetry.*
Green, Paul E. *Plough and Furrow.*
Green, Peter. *Essays in Antiquity.*
Greenfield, Stanley B. (ed). *Studies in Old English Literature in Honor of Arthur G. Brodeur.*
Gregory, Horace. *The Dying Gladiators, and Other Essays.*
————————. *The Shield of Achilles.*
Greene, G. *British Dramatists.*
Grierson, G. *Personal Note.*
Grierson, H. J. *Critical History of English Poetry.*
Griffin, Alice S. (ed). *Living Theatre.*
Grigson, G. *Harp of Aeolus.*
Grundy, J. van. *Patterns for Living.*

Gryphius, Andreas. *Herr Peter Squentz.*
Guillot, E. E. *Social Factors in Crime as Explained by American Writers.*
Gustofson, Alrik. *A History of Swedish Literature.*
Haezrahi, Pepita. *The Contemplative Activity.*
Hagstrum, Jean H. *Samuel Johnson's Literary Criticism.*
Haight, E. *Essays on Greek Romances.*
Hallen, Theodore W. *Orientation to the Theater.*
Halliday, F. E. *Five Arts.*
Hamalian, Leo and Edmond L. Volpe. *Essays of Our Time II.*
Hamilton, William B. (ed). *Fifty Years of the South Atlantic Quarterly.*
Handy, William J. *Kant and the Southern New Critics.*
Hanzo, Thomas A. *Latitude and Restoration Criticism.*
Harbage, A. *Annals of English Drama.*
――――――――――. *As They Like It.*
――――――――――. *Shakespeare and the Rival Tradition.*
Hardison, O. B. Jr. *The Enduring Monument.*
Hardison, O. B. Jr. (ed). *Modern Continental Literary Criticism.*
Harwick, Elizabeth. *A View of My Own.*
Harsh, P. W. *Handbook of Classical Drama.*
Harvey, H. G. *Theatre of Baroche.*
Hatzfeld, Helmut. *Literature Through Art.*
――――――――――. *Trends and Styles in Twentieth Century French Literature.*
Hawthorne, Manning (ed). *American Literary Scene.*
Hayden, Hiram (ed) and Betsy Saunders. *The American Scholar Reader.*
Heiney, Donald W. *Recent American Literature.*
Heninger, S. K. Jr. *A Handbook of Renaissance Meteorology.*
Herrick, Marvin T. *Italian Comedy in the Renaissance.*
Herron, Ima H. *The Small Town in American Literature.*
Hewett-Thayer, Harvey W. *American Literature as Viewed in Germany, 1818-1861.*
Hibbard, Addison (ed). *Writers of the Western World.*
Highet, Gilbert. *The Classical Tradition.*
――――――――――. *Man's Unconquerable Mind.*
――――――――――. *The Migration of Ideas.*
――――――――――. *Talents and Geniuses—The Pleasure of Appreciation.*
Hertz, R. *Chance and Symbol.*
Hildebrand, Dietrich von. *Liturgy and Personality.*
――――――――――. *The New Tower of Babel.*
Hirst, Desiree. *Hidden Riches.*
Hoare, F. B. *Eight Decisive Books.*
Hobson, Harold. *The French Theatre of Today; An English View.*
――――――――――. *Verdict at Midnight.*
Hodin, Josef. P. *The Dilemma of Being Modern.*
Hoffman, Daniel G. (ed). *English Literary Criticism: Romantic and Victorian.*

Hoffman, Frederick J. *Freudianism and the Literary Mind.*
————————. *Perspectives on Modern Literature.*
————————. *The Twenties.*
Hogrefe, Pearl. *The Sir Thomas More Circle.*
Holloway, John. *The Colours of Clarity.*
Holmes, Urban T. Jr. (ed) and Alex J. Denomy. *Medieval Studies in Honor of Jeremiah Denis Matthias Ford.*
Holroyd, Stewart. *Emergence From Chaos.*
Hoopes, Robert. *Right Reason in the English Renaissance.*
Horton, Rod William. *Backgrounds of American Literary Thought.*
Hospers, J. *Meaning and Truth in the Arts.*
Hotopf, W. H. *Language, Thought, and Comprehension.*
Hough, Graham G. *The Dream and the Task.*
————————. *The Last Romantics.*
House, Humphrey. *All in Due Time.*
Howard, Leon. *Literature and the American Tradition.*
Howarth, R. G. *Literary Particles.*
Howe, Irving. *Modern Literary Criticism.*
————————. *A World More Attractive.*
Hsiao, Chiien. *Dragon Beards vs. Blueprints.*
Hubbell, Jay B. *The South in American Literature, 1607-1900.*
Hudson, L. A. *Twentieth Century Drama.*
Humanistic Studies in Honor of John Calvvin Metcalf.
Hughes, Leo. *A Century of English Farce.*
Hunt, Hugh. *The Live Theater.*
Husik, Isaac. (ed. by Milon A. Nahm, and Leo Strauss). *Philosophical Essays.*
Huxley, Aldous L. *Literature and Science.*
Hyde, Mary C. *Playwriting for Elizabethans.*
Hyman, Stanley E. *The Armed Vision.*
————————. *Poetry and Criticism.*
————————. *The Promised Land: Essays and Reviews (1942-1962).*
Hynes, Samuel L. (ed). *English Literary Criticism: Restoration and Eighteenth Century.*
Jack, Ian R. *English Literature, 1815-1832.*
Jackson, Holbrook. *Dreamers of Dreams.*
Jacob, Ernest F. *Italian Renaissance Studies.*
Jacobin, Johan. *The Psychology of Jung.*
Jaffe, Adrian H. (ed). *The Laureate Fraternity.*
James, D. G. *The Life of Reason.*
————————. *The Romantic Comedy.*
James, Henry. *The American Essays.*
Jameson, Robert V. *Essays Old and New.*
Jarrett-Kerr, Martin. *Studies in Literature and Belief.*
Jewkes, Wilfred T. *Act Division in Elizabethan and Jacobean Plays 1583-1616.*
Johns Hopkins University. *Lectures in Criticism.*

Jones, David M. *Epoch and Artist—Selected Writings.*
Jones, Howard M. *History and the Contemporary.*
——————————. *Ideas in America.*
Jones, Robert Edmond. *The Dramatic Imagination.*
Jones, Robert Emmet. *The Alienated Hero in Modern French Drama.*
Jordan, Elijah. *Essays in Criticism.*
Julian, C. *Shadows Over English Literature.*
Jurgensen, K. *Plays and the Modern World.*
Kaelin, Eugene. *An Existential Aesthetic.*
Kane, George. *Middle English Period.*
Kaplan, Charles (ed). *Criticism—Twenty Major Statements.*
Kardiner, A. *Psychological Frontiers of Society.*
Kazin, Alfred. *Contemporaries.*
——————————. *The Inmost Leaf.*
Keller, Isaac C. *Literature and Religion.*
Kenner, Hugh. *Gnomon; Essays on Contemporary Literature.*
Ker, William P. *The Dark Ages.*
——————————. *On Modern Literature.*
Kermode, Frank. *Romantic Image.*
Kernan, Alvin B. *Character and Conflict.*
Kerr, Walter. *How Not to Write a Play.*
——————————. *Pieces at Eight.*
Kettler, H. K. *Baroque Tradition in the Literature of the German En-
    lightment.*
Kiefer, Christian (ed). *Forum.*
King, Roma A. (ed). *A Reader for Composition.*
Kitchin, Laurence. *Mid-Century Drama.*
Kiviat, Joe J. *Studies in American Culture.*
Knapp, Samuel L. *American Cultural History, 1607-1829.*
Knight, G. Wilson. *The Burning Oracle.*
——————————. *Sceptered Isle.*
Knight, Grant C. *The Critical Period in American Literature.*
——————————. *The New Freedom in American Literature.*
——————————. *The Strenuous Age in American Literature.*
Knox, Ronald A. *Literary Distractions.*
Koestler, A. *Insight and Outlook.*
——————————. *The Trail of the Dinosaur and Other Essays.*
Kristeller, Paul O. *The Classics and Renaissance Thought.*
Krutch, Joseph Wood. *Comedy and Conscience After the Restoration.*
——————————. *Experience and Art.*
——————————. *Modern Literature and the Image of Man.*
La Driere, James C. *Directions in Contemporary Criticism and Literary
    Scholarship.*
Lamm, Martin. *Modern Drama.*
Lancaster, Henry C. *French Tragedy in the Reign of Louis XVI and
    the Early Years of the French Revolution 1774-1792.*
——————————. *French Tragedy in the Time of Louis XV and Vol-
    taire, 1715-1774.*

Landstone, Charles. *You and the Theatre.*

Lane, Robert E. *The Liberties of Wit, Humanism, Criticism, and the Civic Mind.*

Lange, V. *Modern German Literature.*

Langer, Susanne K. *Feeling and Form.*

———————. *Philosophy in a New Key.*

Langner, Lawrence. *The Play's the Thing.*

Lawrence, D. H. *Pornography and Obscenity.*

———————. *Studies in Classic American Literature.*

———————. *The Symbolic Meaning.*

Leech, Clifford. *John Ford and the Drama of His Time.*

Leeuw, Gerardus van der. *Sacred and Profane Beauty.*

Legman, Gershon. *Breaking Point.*

———————. *Love and Death.*

Lehmann, Andrew G. *The Symbolist Aesthetic in France.*

Lehmann, John (ed). *The Craft of Letters in England—A Symposium.*

Lehmann, John. *The Open Night.*

Leroy, Gaylord C. *Perplexed Prophets.*

Lester, John A. *Essays of Yesterday and Today.*

Levin, Harry. *Contexts of Criticism.*

———————. *Learners and Discerners.*

Levin, Harry (ed). *Perspectives of Criticism.*

Levy, Gertrude. *The Gate of Horn.*

Lewis, Allan. *American Plays and Playwrights of the Contemporary Theatre.*

Lewis, Clive S. *The Discarded Image.*

———————. *An Experiment in Criticism.*

Lewis, Richard W. *The American Adam.*

Lewis, W. *Writer and Absolute.*

Lewisohn, L. *Haven.*

Lidstone, R. A. *Studies in Symbology.*

Lilar, Suzanne. *The Belgian Theater Since 1890.*

Liptzin, Sam. *In Spite of Tears.*

Liptzin, Solomon. *Germany's Stepchildren.*

Littlewood, Samuel R. *The Art of Dramatic Criticism.*

Livingston, Arthur. *Essays on Modern Italian Literature.*

Livingston, Ray F. *The Traditional Theory of Literature.*

Lloyd, Roger B. *The Borderland.*

Loewenberg, J. *Dialogues From Delphi.*

Loftis, John C. *The Politics of Drama in Augustan England.*

Lofstedt, Einar. *Roman Literary Portraits.* (Trans P. M. Frazer).

Lohan, R. *Living German Literature.*

Long, Valentine. *Not on Bread Alone.*

Longaker, John M. *Contemporary English Literature.*

Loomis, Laura A. *Adventures in the Middle Ages—A Memorial Collection of Essays and Studies.*

Loomis, Roger S. *Arthurian Literature in the Middle Ages.*

Lorand, A. S. *Psychoanalysis Today.*

Lovejoy, Arthur O. *Essays in the History of Ideas.*
Lowenfeld, Viktor. *Nature of Creative Activity.*
Lowenthal, Leo. *Literature, Popular Culture.*
Lucas, F. A. *Studies in French and English.*
Lucas, Frank L. *Critical Thought.*
————————. *The Decline and Fall of the Romantic Ideal.*
————————. *Euripides and His Influence.*
————————. *The Greatest Problem, and Other Essays.*
————————. *Greek Drama for Everyone.*
————————. *Style.*
Lucy, Sean. *T. S. Eliot, etc.*
Lukacs, Gyorky. *The Historical Novel.*
————————. *The Meaning of Contemporary Realism.*
————————. *Studies in European Realism.*
Lumley, Frederick. *Trends in Twentieth Century Drama.*
Lyon, Harvey T. *Keats' Well-Read Urn.*
Maas, Paul. *Textual Criticism.*
McAuley, James P. *The End of Modernity.*
McCarthy, Mary. *On the Contrary.*
McCollum, John I. (ed). *The Restoration Stage.*
McCullough, Norman V. *The Negro in English Literature.*
MacEdward, Leach (ed). *Studies in Medieval Literature in Honor of Professor Albert Croll Baugh.*
MacFarland, C. S. *Survey of Religious Literature.*
MacFarlane, James W. *Ibsen and the Temper of Norwegian Literature.*
McKean, Keith F. *The Moral Measure of Literature.*
Mackenzie, C. *Studies in French Language, Literature, and History Presented to R. L. Graeme Ritchie.*
MacLeish, Archibald. *A Free Man's Books.*
Macklem, Michael. *The Anatomy of the World.*
McLeod, Alan L. (ed). *The Commonwealth Pen.*
Madsen, Borge G. *Strindberg's Naturalistic Theatre—Its Relation to French Naturalism.*
Magill, Frank N. *Masterplots.*
Maguire, W. *Irish Literary Figures.*
Mann, Thomas. *Addresses Delivered at the Library of Congress, 1942-1949.*
————————. *Essays of Three Decades.*
————————. *Last Essays.*
Marcel, Gabriel. *Creative Fidelity.*
————————. *Philosophy of Existence.*
Marcuse, Herbert. *Eros and Civilization.*
Marshak, I. I. *Giant Widens His World.*
Martin, E. W. (ed). *The New Spirit.*
Maschler, Tom (ed) *Declaration.*
Mathews, Andrew J. *La Wallone 1886-1892.*
Matthiessen, Francis O. *The Responsibilities of the Critic.*
Maugham, William S. *Points of View.*

------------------------ . *Selected Prefaces and Introductions of W. Somerset Maugham.*

Maurois, Andre. *Seven Faces of Love.*

Mavor, O. H. *British Drama.*

Maxwell, I. C. *French Farce and John Heywood.*

May, James B. *Selected Essays and Criticism.*

May, Rollo (ed). *Symbolism in Religion and Literature.*

Maynard, T. *Humanist as Hero.*

Menezes, Armando. *Lighter Than Air.*

Mercier, Vivian. *The Irish Comic Tradition.*

Mersand, Joseph E. *The American Drama Since 1930.*

------------------------ . *The Play's the Thing.*

Meyerhoff, Hans. *Time in Literature.*

Michael, George. *Shakespeare and his Rivals.*

Miller, H. *The Wisdom of the Heart.*

Miller, James E. (ed). *Myth and Method—Modern Theories in Fiction.*

Miller, Joseph H. *The Disappearance of God.*

Miller, Perry. *The Raven and the Whale.*

Mims, E. *The Christ of Poets.*

Miner, Dorothy E. (ed). *Studies in Art and Literature for Belle Da Costa Greene.*

Miner, Earl R. *The Japanese Tradition in British and American Literature.*

Mitchell, Julian (ed). *Light Blue, Dark Blue.*

Molnar, F. *Romantic Comedies.*

Moloney, James C. *The Magic Cloak.*

Montherlant, Henri de. *Selected Essays.*

More, Paul E. *A Paul Elmer More Miscellany.*

Moreno, J. L. *Theater of Spontaneity.*

Morgan, Charles. *Dialogue in Novels and Plays.*

------------------------ . *Reflections in a Mirror.*

------------------------ . *To Writer and his World—Lectures and Essays.*

Morgan, Howard W. *Writers in Transition: Seven Americans.*

Morgan, Stewart S. (ed). *Readings for Thought and Expression.*

Morris, Wright. *The Territory Ahead.*

Muller, Herbert J. *Science and Criticism.*

Mullik, B. R. *Romantic Literature.*

Mumford, Louis. *Faith for Living.*

------------------------ . *Story of Utopias.*

Mundra, J. N., and C. L. Sahni. *Advanced Literary Essays.*

Murray, Gilbert. *The Literature of Ancient Greece.*

Murry, John M. *Unprofessional Essays.*

Musgrove, Sydney. *The Inadequacy of Criticism.*

Musurillo, Herbert A. *Symbol and Myth in Ancient Poetry.*

------------------------ . *Symbolism and the Christian Imagination.*

Mylonas, George E. and Doris Raymond. *Studies Presented to David M. Robinson,* Volume II.

Nagelberg, M. M. *Drama in Our Time.*

Natanson, Maurice A. *Literature, Philosophy, and the Social Sciences.*
Nathan, George J. *The Theatre in the Fifties.*
Needham, H. A. *Taste and Criticism in the Eighteenth Century.*
Neff, M. L. *Keepers of the Flame.*
Neibuhr, Reinhold. *Beyond Tragedy.*
Neimerov, H. *Melodramatists.*
Nelson, F. G. *Guide to American Literature.*
New York Metropolitan Museum of Art. *The Renaissance.*
Newman, James R. *Science and Sensibility.*
Nicolson, Harold G. *The English Sense of Humour and Other Essays.*
Norton, Aloysius A. (ed). *A Christian Approach to Western Literature.*
Notcutt, B. *Psychology as Science and as Art.*
Nye, Russel B. (ed). *Modern Essays.*
Nyren, Dorothy. *A Library of Literary Criticism*—Second Edition.
O'Casey, Sean. *The Green Crow.*
O'Connor, F. *Towards an Appreciation of Literature.*
O'Connor, William Van. *An Age of Criticism, 1900-1950.*
———————————. *Climates of Tragedy.*
———————————. *The Grotesque.*
———————————. *Sense and Sensibility in Modern Poetry.*
O'Hara, Frank H. and Margueritte Bro. *Invitation to the Theatre.*
Oldsey, Bernard S. and Arthur O. Lewis, Jr. (eds). *Visions and Revisions in Modern American Literary Criticism.*
Ong, Walter J. *The Barbarian Within, and Other Fugitive Essays and Studies.*
Oras, Ants. *Pause Patterns in Elizabethan and Jacobean Drama.*
Orwell, George. *Dickens, Doli and Others.*
Osborne, Harold. *Aesthetics and Criticism.*
Osgood, Charles G. *Creed of a Humanist.*
Osteriweis, R. G. *Romanticism and Nationalism in the Old South.*
O'Sullivan, Vincent. *Opinions.*
Otto, Max Carl. *The Human Enterprise.*
Overstreet, Harry A. *Our Free Minds.*
Owings, Marvin A. *The Arts in the Middle English Romances.*
Pacifici, Sergio. *Guide to Contemporary Italian Theater.*
Paine, C. S. *Comedy of Manners.*
Parker, Dewitt H. *Principles of Aesthetics.*
———————————. *True, the Good, and the Beautiful.*
Parker, Elinore M. (ed). *I Was Just Thinking.*
Parker, Marion. *Slave of Life.*
Parkes, H. B. *The Pragmatic Test.*
Parkinson, Thomas F. (ed). *Casebook on the Beat.*
Parrington, V. L. *American Dreams.*
Parrott, Thomas M. and Robert B. Martin. *A Companion to Victorian Literature.*
Passage, Charles E. *The Russian Hoffmannists.*
Pavia, Mario N. *Drama of the Siglo de Oro.*

Payne, P. S. *Great God Pan.*
Peacock, Ronald. *The Art of the Drama.*
Peers, E. A. *St. John of the Cross and Other Lectures and Addresses.*
Peter, John D. *Complaint and Satire in Early English Literature.*
Peters, Robert L. *The Crowns of Apollo.*
———————. *Victorians on Literature and Art.*
Petherick, Maurice. *Restoration Rogues.*
Peyre, H. M. *Essays in Honor of Albert Feuillerat.*
———————. *Writers and Their Critics.*
Philipson, Morris. *Aesthetics Today.*
Philosophical Essays in Honor of E. A. Singer.
Pickard-Cambridge, Arthur W. *Dithyramb.*
———————. *The Dramatic Festivals of Athens.*
Platnauer, Maurice (ed). *Fifty Years of Classical Scholarship.*
Plumb, John H. *Men and Centuries.*
Podhoretz, Norman. *Doings and Undoings.*
Pogson, R. *Theater Between Wars.*
Polin, Raymond. *Literature and Philosophy.*
Pollock, T. C. *Nature and Literature.*
Potter, Simeon. *Outlook in English Studies.*
Poulet, Georges. *The Interior Distance.*
———————. *Studies in Human Time.*
Pound, Erzra L. *Literary Essays.*
Powell, Arnold F. *The Melting Mood.*
Praz, Mario (ed). *English Miscellany.*
———————. *Studies in Seventeenth Century Imagery.*
Priestley, John B. *The Art of the Dramatist.*
———————. *Literature and Western Man.*
Pritchard, John P. *Literary Wise Men of Gotham.*
Proust, Marcel. *On Art and Literature, 1896-1919.*
Purdy, Rob Roy. *The Platonic Tradition in Middle English Literature.*
Putt, Samuel G. *Scholars of the Heart, Essays in Criticism.*
Quennell, Peter. *The Sign of the Fish.*
Quinn, Esther C. *The Quest of Seth for the Oil of Life.*
Raglan, Fitz. *Death and Rebirth.*
Rahner, Hugo. *Greek Myths.*
Rahv, Philip. *Image and Idea.*
———————. *Literature in America.*
Randall, Dale B. *The Golden Tapestry.*
Rank, Otto. *Myth of the Birth of the Hero.*
Ransom, John C. *The Kenyon Critics.*
Rauschenbush, Esther. *Literature for Individual Education.*
Ravitz, Abe C. *Clarence Darrow and the American Literary Criticism.*
Raymond, John. *England's on the Anvil!—And Other Essays.*
Read, Sir Herbert E. *Collected Essays in Literary Criticism.*
———————. *The Nature of Literature.*
———————. *The Tenth Muse.*
Reed, Robert R. Jr. *Bedlam on the Jacobean Stage.*

Reeves, James. *The Critical Sense.*
Reeves, James (ed). *Great English Essays.*
Reich, W. *Character Analysis.*
Reid, Margaret J. *The Arthurian Legend.*
Reik, T. *Psychoanalytic Studies.*
Reinhold, Meyer. *Classical Drama, Greek and Roman.*
Reynolds, Ernest R. *Early Victorian Drama.*
_____ . *Modern English Drama.*
Reynolds, George. *Freedom Speaks.*
Richard, Peter. *Britain in Medieval French Literature, 1100-1500.*
Robach, A. A. *Psychology of Character.*
Roaten, Darnell H. *Wolfflin's Principles in Spanish Drama: 1500-1700.*
Roberts, Sydney C. *Doctor Johnson and Others.*
Robertson, John G. *Studies in the Genesis of Romantic Theory in the Eighteenth Century.*
Rooney, J. W. *Problem of Poetry and Belief in Contemporary Criticism.*
Rosenberg, Harold. *The Tradition of the New.*
Rosenfield, Isaac. *An Age of Enormity.*
Rostvig, Maren S. *The Background of English Neo-Classicism.*
Roubisczek, P. *Misinterpretation of Man.*
Rougemont, D. de. *Love in the Western World.*
Routh, Harold V. *English Literature and Ideas in the Twentieth Century.*
Rowse, Alfred L. *A New Elizabethan Age?*
Rubin, Louis D. Jr. *Southern Renascence.*
Rubinstein, Annette T. *The Great Tradition in English Literature From Shakespeare to Shaw.*
Runge, E. A. *Primitivism and Related Ideas.*
Russell, T. W. *Voltaire, Dryden, and Heroic Tragedy.*
Sachs, Hanns. *Masks of Love and Life.*
Saint-Denis, Michel. *Theatre, the Rediscovery of Style.*
Saintsbury, George E. *A Last Vintage.*
Salter, Frederick M. *Mediaeval Drama in Chester.*
Sartre, Jean P. *Essays on Aesthetics.*
_____ . *Literary and Philosophical Essays.*
_____ . *The Psychology of Imagination.*
_____ . *Search for a Method.*
_____ . *What is Literature?*
_____ . *Reading Drama.*
Satin, Joseph. *Reading Literature.*
Saurat, D. *Death and Dreamer.*
Savage, Derek S. *Hamlet and the Pirates.*
Savage, Edward B. *The Rose and the Vine.*
Sayce, Richard A. *The French Biblical Epic in the Seventeenth Century.*
Scaglione, Aldo D. *Nature and Love in the Late Middle Ages.*
Scarfe, F. *Auden and After.*
Scharlemann, Martin H. *The Influence of Social Changes in Athens on the Development of Greek Tragedy.*

Scherman, D. and R. Redlich. *Literary America.*
Schiller, F. C. S. *Our Human Truths.*
Schilling, Bernard N. (ed). *Essential Articles for the Study of English Augustan Backgrounds.*
Schlauch, Margaret. *English Medieval Literature and its Social Foundations.*
———. *The Gift of Tongues.*
Schlegel, A. W. *Lectures on German Literature.*
Schlesinger, Alfred C. *Boundaries of Dionysus.*
Schneider, Heinrich. *Quest for Mysteries.*
Schoen, M. *Enjoyment of the Arts.*
Scholes, Robert E. (ed). *Learners and Discerners, a Newer Criticism.*
Schreiber, S. E. *German Woman in the Age of Enlightenment.*
Schucking, Levin L. *The Sociology of Literary Taste.*
Schutze, Martin, *Byrcliffe Afternoons.*
Scott, Nathan A., Jr. *Modern Literature and the Religious Frontier.*
Scott, Nathan A. (ed). *The New Orpheus.*
Scott, Nathan A., Jr. *Rehearsals of Discomposure.*
Selden, Samuel. *The Stage in Action.*
Senior, John. *The Way Down and Out.*
Seyler, Athene. *The Craft of Comedy.*
Seymour, Arthur J. *Caribbean Literature.*
Shapiro, Karl J. *In Defense of Ignorance.*
Shaw, George Bernard. *Dramatic Criticism: 1895-1898.*
———. *How to Become a Musical Critic.*
Shaw, Theodore L. *Precious Rubbish.*
Shelley, P. A. (ed). *Anglo-American and Anglo-German Cross Currents.*
Sheppard, J. T. *Aeschylus and Sophocles: Their Work and Influence.*
Shideler, Mary M. *The Theology of Romantic Love.*
Shine, Hill. (ed). *Booker Memorial Studies.*
Shipley, J. *Trends in Literature.*
Short, Ernest H. *Sixty Years of Theatre.*
Shrodes, Caroline. *Psychology Through Literature.*
Shumaker, Wayne. *Elements of Critical Theory.*
———. *Literature and the Irrational.*
———. *Perspectives in Criticism.*
Silberstein, Suzanne (ed). *Sense and Style.*
Simmons, Ernest J. *Through the Glass of Soviet Literature.*
Simms, William G. *Views and Reviews in American Literature, History, and Fiction.*
Simon, John I. *Acid Test.*
Sinclair, V. *Mammonart.*
Slockower, Harry. *Franz Kafka.*
———. *No Voice is Wholly Lost.*
———. *Three Ways of Modern Man.*
Slonim, Mark L. *Modern Russian Literature, From Chekhov to the Present.*

Smalley, Beryl. *English Friars and Antiquity in the Early Fourteenth Century.*
Smeall, J. *English Satire, Parody, and Burlesque.*
Smith, Henry N. *Virgin Land.*
Smith, James H. *The Great Critics.*
Smith, John J. *The Gay Couple in Restoration Comedy.*
Smith, M. F. *Technique of Solution in Roman Comedy.*
Snuggs, Henry L. *Shakespeare and Five Acts.*
Sobel, Bernard (ed). *The New Theatre Handbook and Digest of Plays.*
Somervell, D. *English Thought in the Nineteenth Century.*
Speaight, Robert. *Christian Theatre.*
Spencer, Benjamin T. *The Quest for Nationality.*
Spencer, Terence. *Fair Greece! Sad Relic.*
Spender, Stephen. *The Struggle of the Modern.*
_____. *The Writers Dilemma.*
Spiller, Robert E. *The Cycle of American Literature.*
Spingarn, Joel E. *Critical Essays of the Seventeenth Century.*
Spitzer, Leo. *Classical and Christian Ideas of World Harmony.*
_____. *Essays on English and American Literature.*
_____. *Linguistics and Literary History.*
Spring, Powell. *Challenge to Think.*
_____. *Essays on Human Science.*
_____. *The Three Crosses.*
_____. *Two Deadly Philosophies.*
Srygley, Ola Pauline. *High Lights in American Literature.*
Stallman, Robert W. *The House That James Built, and Other Literary Studies.*
Stallworthy, Jon. *Between the Lines.*
Stanford, Donald E. (ed). *Nine Essays in Modern Literature.*
Stanford, William B. *The Ulysses Theme.*
Starkie, Enid. *From Gautier to Eliot, the Influence of France on English Literature, 1851-1939.*
Starr, Nathan C. *The Dynamics of Literature.*
_____. *King Arthur Today.*
Stauffer, Donald A. *The Golden Nightingale.*
Stein, Leo. *Appreciation: Painting, Poetry and Prose.*
Steinmetz, Lee (ed). *Analyzing Literary Works.*
Stekel, W. *Interpretation of Dreams.*
Stepanik, Karel. *English Literature from the American Revolution to Chartism.*
Stephen, Sir Leslie. *Men, Books and Mountains—Essays.*
Stewart, Donald O. (ed). *Fighting Words.*
Stewart, Randall. *American Literature and Christian Doctrine.*
Stienon, M. M. *Studies in Symbolism.*
Stoll, D. G. *Doctor and the Dragon.*
Stovall, F. *American Idealism.*
Stovall, Floyd (ed). *The Drama of American Literary Criticism.*
_____. *Eight American Authors.*

Straumman, Heinrich. *American Literature in the Twentieth Century.*
Strauss, Leo. *Persecution and the Art of Writing.*
Strecker, A. E. *Discovering Ourselves.*
Strich, F. *Goethe and World Literature.*
Stroup, Thomas B. (ed). and Sterling A. Stoudemire. *South Atlantic Studies for Sturgis E. Leavitt.*
Swallow, Alan. *An Editor's Essays of Two Decades.*
————. *The Practice of Poetry.*
Swan, Michael. *A Small Part of Time.*
Swinnerton, Frank A. *Background With Chorus.*
————. *Figures in the Foreground.*
Sykes, Christopher. *Character and Situation.*
————. *Four Studies in Loyalty.*
Symons, Julian. *The Thirties—A Dream Revolved.*
Sypher, Wylie. *Four Stages of Renaissance Style.*
T'ang, Ch'ing-i. *Selected Modern English Essays for College Students.*
Tarr, M. M. *Catholicism in Gothic Fiction.*
Tate, Allen. *On the Limits of Poetry.*
————. *The Forlorn Demon.*
Tawney, R. H. *Social History and Literature.*
Taylor, Estella R. *The Modern Irish Writers.*
Temple, Ruth Z. *The Critic's Alchemy.*
Temple, W. *The Resources and Influence of English Literature.*
Tertz, Abram. *On Socialist Realism.*
Thompson, A. R. *Anatomy of Drama.*
Thompson, Denys. *Reading and Discrimination.*
Thompson, Francis. *The Real Robert Louis Stevenson, and Other Critical Essays.*
Thomson, James A. *Classical Background of English Literature.*
————. *Shakespeare and the classics.*
Thornton, Harry. *Time and Style.*
Tillotson, Geoffrey. *Augustan Studies.*
————. *Criticism and the Nineteenth Century.*
————. *Essays in Criticism and Research.*
Tillyard, E. M. *The Elizabethan World Picture.*
————. *The Nature of Comedy.*
Times Literary Supplement. *Essays and Reviews from the Times Literary Supplement.*
Tindall, William Y. *Forces in Modern British Literature, 1885-1956.*
Tinker, C. B. *Essays in Retrospect.*
Toffanin, Giuseppe. *History of Humanism.*
Trawick, Buckner B. *World Literature.*
Trevelyan, Humphrey. *Goethe and the Greeks.*
Trewin, John C. *Dramatists of Today.*
Trilling, Lionel. *Freud and the Crisis of Our Culture.*
————. *The Middle of the Journey.*
————. *The Opposing Self.*
Trory, Ernie. *Mainly About Books.*

Turnell, Martin. *Modern Literature and Christian Faith.*
Tymms, Ralph. *German Romantic Literature.*
Tynan, Kenneth. *Curtains.*
——————————. *He That Plays the King.*
United States Information Service. *American Literature Catalogue.*
Van Nostrand, Albert. *Literary Criticism in America.*
Vitale, Philip H. *Catholic Literary Opinion in the Nineteenth Century.*
Vivas, Eliseo. *Creation and Discovery.*
Vivas, Eliseo and Murray Krieger. *The Problems of Aesthetics.*
Vowles, Richard B. *Dramatic Theory: A Bibliography.*
Wagenvoort, H. *Studies in Roman Literature, Culture, and Religion.*
Wain, John. *Essays on Literature and Ideas.*
——————————. *Preliminary Essays.*
Waite, Arthur E. *The Holy Grail.*
Walcutt, Charles C. *American Literary Naturalism, a Divided Stream.*
Walker, William E. *Reality and Myth.*
Walsh, William. *The Use of Imagination.*
Walton, Geoffrey. *English Studies in the University College of Ghana.*
Warren, Austin. *The Rage of Order.*
Watson, George. *The Literary Critics.*
Watts, Harold H. *Hound and Quarry.*
Wayne State University. *Studies in Honor of John Wilcox by Members of the English Department.*
Weales, Gerald C. *Religion in Modern English Drama.*
Weber, C. G. *Studies in English Outlook in the Period Between Two Wars.*
Weber, J. Sherwood. *From Homer to Joyce.*
Webster, Thomas B. *Art and Literature in Fourth Century Athens.*
——————————. *Greek Art and Literature, 700-530 B.C.*
——————————. *Studies in Later Greek Comedy.*
Wecter, Dixon. *Literary Lodestone.*
Wedgwood, C. V. *Poetry and Politics Under the Stuarts.*
——————————. *Seventeenth Century English Literature.*
Weinberg, Bernard. *A History of Literary Criticism in the Italian Renaissance.*
Wellek, Rene. *Concepts of Criticism.*
Wellek, Rene and A. Warren. *Theory of Literature.*
Wells, H. *Where Poetry Now Stands.*
Werkmeister, William H. (ed). *Facets of the Renaissance.*
Wertham, F. *Show of Violence.*
Wescott, Glen. *Images of Truth.*
West, Alick. *The Mountain in the Sunlight.*
West, Anthony. *Principles and Persuasions.*
West, Ray B. *The Art of Modern Fiction.*
Westbrook, Perry D. *Acres of Flint.*
Whipple, T. K. *Study Out the Land.*
White, Mary L. (ed). *Studies in Honor of Gilbert Norwood.*
Whiting, Frank M. *An Introduction to the Theatre.*

Whyte, Lancelot L. *Essay on Atomism.*
Wickham, Glynne W. *Drama in the World of Science.*
Willey, Basil. *More Nineteenth Century Studies.*
——————————. *Nineteenth Century Studies: Coleridge to Matthew Arnold.*
Williams, Arnold. *The Drama of Medieval England.*
Williams, Stanley T. *The Spanish Background of American Literature.*
Williams, Thomas G. *English Literature.*
Williams, W. D. *Nietzsche and the French.*
Williams, William C. *Selected Essays.*
Williamson, A. *Old Victorian Drama.*
Wilson, Albert E. *Playwrights in Aspic.*
Wilson, Colin. *The Strength to Dream.*
Wilson, Edmund. *The Intent of the Critics.*
——————————. *Patriotic Gore.*
Wilson, Edmund (ed). *The Shock of Recognition.*
——————————. *The Collected Essays of John Peale Bishop.*
Wilson, Edmund. *The Triple Thinkers.*
Winters, Yvor. *Anatomy of Nonsense.*
——————————. *The Function of Criticism.*
Wise, Jacob H. (ed). *The Meaning in Reading.*
Wittig, Kurt. *The Scottish Tradition in Literature.*
Woodstock, George. *The Writer and Politics.*
Wordsworth, William. *The Critical Opinions of William Wordsworth.*
Worsley, Thomas C. *The Fugitive Art.*
Wright, Austin (ed). *Victorian Literature: Modern Essays in Criticism.*
Wyman, Mary A. *The Lure for Feeling in the Creative Process.*
Yates, Norris W. *The American Humorist.*
Yatron, Michael. *America's Literary Revolt.*
Young, Arthur M. *Echoes of Two Cultures.*
Zesmer, David M. *Guide to English Literature.*

BOOKS—III

Note:
The following works were not researched due to original publication prior to 1940. Each work has been published at least once since 1940. Dates following titles indicate date of original publication.

Allen, Beverly S. *Tides in English Taste (1619-1800),* 1937.
Arnold, Matthew. *Matthew Arnold's Essays in Criticism,* 1935.
Atkins, John W. *Literary Criticism in Antiquity,* 1934.
Babbitt, Irving. *The Masters of Modern French Criticism,* 1912.
Bald, Marjory A. *Women-Writers of the Nineteenth Century,* 1923.
Baring, Maurice. *Landmarks in Russian Literature,* 1910.
Bateson, Frederick W. *English Comic Drama, 1700-1750,* 1929.
Brinton, Clarence C. *The Political Ideas of the English Romanticists,* 1926.

Bullen, Arthur H. *Elizabethans,* 1925.
Burke, Kenneth. *Counter-Statement,* 1931.
Butler, Eliza M. *The Tyranny of Greece Over Germany,* 1935.
Chandler, Frank W. *The Literature of Roguery,* 1907
Cheney, Sheldon. *The Theatre,* 1929.
Chesterton, Gilbert K. *The Victorian Age in Literature,* 1913.
Connolly, Cyril. *Enemies of Promise, and Other Essays,* 1938.
Cornford, F. M. *Greek Religious Thought,* 1923.
Cowley, Malcolm. *Exile's Return,* 1934.
Craig, Hardin. *The Enchanted Glass,* 1936.
Cunliffe, John W. *Leaders of the Victorian Revolution,* 1934.
Dewey, John. *Art as Experience,* 1934.
Dobree, Bonamy. *The Lamp and the Lute,* 1929.
Duckett, Eleanor S. *The Gateway to the Middle Ages,* 1938.
Dunbar, Helen F. *Symbolism in Medieval Thought,* 1929.
Eliot, George. *Essays,* 1925.
Eliot, Thomas S. *The Sacred Wood,* 1920.
————————. *Selected Essays,* 1932.
Empson, William. *Some versions of Pastoral,* 1938.
Fairchild, Hoxie N. *The Noble Savage,* 1928.
Fairclough, Henry R. *Love of Nature Among the Greeks and the Romans,* 1930.
Farnham, Willard. *The Medieval Heritage of Elizabethan Tragedy,* 1936.
Flickinger, Roy C. *The Greek Theatre and its Drama,* 1918.
Foerster, Norman. *American Criticism,* 1928.
————————. *Nature in American Literature,* 1923.
————————. *The Reinterpretation of American of American Literature,* 1928.
Garland, Hamlin. *Crumbling Idols,* 1894.
Granville-Barker, Harley G. *On Dramatic Method,* 1931.
Greg, Walter W. *Pastoral Poetry and Pastoral Drama,* 1906.
Grierson, Herbert J. *The Background of English Literature and Other Collected Essays and Addresses,* 1926.
————————. *Cross-Currents in Seventeenth Century English Literature,* 1929.
Haskins, Charles H. *The Renaissance of the Twelfth Century,* 1927.
————————. *Studies in Mediaeval Culture,* 1929.
Hazard, Lucy L. *The Frontier in American Literature,* 1927.
Hazard, Paul. *The European Mind (1680-1715),* 1935.
Hazlitt, William. *Hazlitt on Theatre,* 1895.
————————. *Lectures on the English Comic Writers,* 1907.
————————. *The Spirit of the Age,* 1825.
Howells, William D. *Criticism and Fiction, and Other Essays,* 1891.
Hunt, Leigh. *Literary Criticism.*
James, Henry. *Literary Reviews and Essays on American, English and French Literature.*
Johnson, Samuel. *The Critical Opinions of Samuel Johnson.*

Jones, Richard F. *Ancients and Moderns,* 1936.

Kennard, Joseph S. *The Italian Theatre,* 1932.

Ker, William P. *Epic and Romance,* 1931.

Klein, David. *The Elizabethan Dramatists as Critics—Repertory and Synthesis,* 1910.

Lea, Kathleen M. *Italian Popular Comedy,* 1934.

Lewis, Wyndham. *Men Without Art,* 1934.

————————. *Time and Western Man,* 1927.

Long, Orie W. *Literary Pioneers—Early American Explorers of European Culture,* 1935.

Lucas, Frank L. *Studies French and English,* 1934.

McDowell, Tremaine. *The Romantic Triumph,* 1935.

Machen, Arthur. *Hieroglyphics: A Note Upon Ecstasy in Literature,* 1913.

MacLean, Kenneth. *John Locke and English Literature of the Eighteenth Century,* 1936.

Marriott, J. W. *The Theatre,* 1931.

Masaryk, Thomas G. *The Spirit of Russia,* 1919.

Masque, The. London: Curtain Press.

Meredith, George. *An Essay on Comedy and the Uses of the Comic Spirit,* 1897.

Monk, Samuel Holt. *The Sublime,* 1935.

Mordell, Albert. *The Erotic Motive in Literature,* 1919.

More, Paul E. *Shelbourne Essays on American Literature,* 1904.

Mumford, Lewis. *The Golden Day,* 1926.

Nicoll Allardyce. *British Drama,* 1925.

————————. *Stuart Masques and the Renaissance Stage,* 1937.

Northrup, George Tyler. *An Introduction to Spanish Literature,* 1936.

Norwood, Gilbert. *Greek Tragedy,* 1920.

————————. *Plautus and Terence,* 1932.

Oud, H. *Art of the Play,* 1938.

Owst, Gerald R. *Literature and the Pulpit in Medieval England,* 1933.

Palmer, John L. *The Comedy of Manners,* 1913.

Parrington, Vernon L. *Main Currents in American Thought,* 1927.

Perry, Henry T. *The Comic Spirit in Restoration Drama,* 1925.

Pound, Ezra L. *The Spirit of Romance,* 1910.

Praz, Mario. *The Romantic Agony.*

Quiller-Couch, A. T. *Studies in Literature, Second Series,* 1922.

Raglan, Fitz. *The Hero,* 1936.

————————. *Jocasta's Crime,* 1933.

Read, Herbert E. *Reason and Romanticism—Essays in Literary Criticism,* 1926.

Richards, I. A. *Foundations of Aesthetics,* 1929.

————————. *Practical Criticism,* 1929.

————————. *Principles of Literary Criticism,* 1930.

Rourke, Constance M. *American Humor; a Study of the National Character,* 1931.

Ruch, F. L. *Psychology and Life,* 1937.

Spector, Ivar. *The Golden Age of Russian Literature*, 1939.
Spencer, Theodore. *Death and Elizabethan Tragedy*, 1936.
Spender, Stephen. *The Destructive Element*, 1936.
Spingarn, Joel E. *A History of Literary Criticism in the Renaissance*, 1920.
Stuart, Donald C. *The Development of Dramatic Art*, 1928.
Symons, Arthur. *The Symbolist Movement in Literature*, 1899.
Synge, John M. *The Aran Islands, and Other Writings*, 1911.
Thaler, Alwin. *Shakespeare to Sheridan*, 1922.
Tilley, Arthur A. *The Literature of the French Renaissance*, 1904.
Ward, Alfred C. *Twentieth Century Literature*, 1901-1950, 1928.
Watson, Ernest B. *Sheridan to Robertson—A Study of the Nineteenth Century London Stage*, 1926.
Welsford, Enid. *The Court Masque—A Study in the Relationship Between Poetry and the Revels*, 1928.
Whipple, Thomas K. *Spokesmen—Modern Writers and American Life*, 1922.
Wilson, Edmund. *The Wound and the Bow—Seven Studies in Literature*, 1929.

Check against Periodical holdings: Date completed: 11-14-70

BIBLIOGRAPHY OF PERIODICALS RESEARCHED

The following periodicals have been researched for this checklist. Periodicals from which entries were obtained appear capitalized.

AAUP BULLETIN
A B Bookman Yearbook
AUMLA JOURNAL
Abbottempo
ABERDEEN UNIVERSITY REVIEW
Abgila
Abside
Abstracts of English Studies
Academy
Academy and Literature (London)
Acanto
ACCENT
Accento Literarios Americanos
Acme (Milano)
Acta Antiqua
Acta Classica (Proceedings of the Classical Association of South Africa)
ACTA JUTLANDA
ACTA LITTERARIA ACA-DEMICAL SCIENTIARUM HUNGARICAL

Acta Philologica Scandinavica (Kobenhavn)
Acta Salmanticensia Serie de Filosofia ye Letras
ADAM INTERNATIONAL REVIEW
ADELPHI
Aerend (A Kansas Quarterly)
Agenda
Ahil Quarterly
Ainslees Magazine
Ajax (Illinois)
Alabama Review
Albion
ALETHEIA
Alphabet
Altertum, Das
Ambit
America (Estudios Americanos)
American Benedictine Review
American Book Collector
American Bookman
American Documentations

American-German Review
AMERICAN IMAGO
American Journal of
   Orthopsychiatry
American Journal of Philology
American Journal of
   Psychoanalysis
American Journal of Semitic
   Languages and Literature
American Library Association
   Booklist
American Literary Magazine
AMERICAN LITERATURE
American Mercury
American Monthly (Chicago)
American Monthly Magazine and
   Critical Review
American Notes and Queries
   (London)
American Notes and Queries
   (New Haven)
American Notes and Queries
   (New York)
American Philosophical Quarterly
American Playwright
AMERICAN POLITICAL
   SCIENCE REVIEW
American Prefaces
AMERICAN QUARTERLY
American Review
American Review and Literary
   Journal (New York)
AMERICAN-
   SCANDINAVIAN REVIEW
AMERICAN SCHOLAR
AMERICAN SLAVIC
   AND EAST EUROPEAN
   REVIEW
American Speech
American Society Legion of
   Honor Magazine
American Swedish Monthly
AMSTERDAM AKADEMIE
   VAN WETENSCHAPPEN
   MEDELINGEN AFD.
   LETTERKUNDE
Analectic Magazine
Analyst (Northwestern

University)
Analytical Review (London)
Anarchy
Andover Newton Quarterly
ANGLIA
ANGLICA
ANGLICAN THEOLOGICAL
   REVIEW
ANGLISTICA
Anglo-Soviet Journal
ANGLO-SWEDISH REVIEW
   (Formerly DOCK LEAVES)
_____Annales Philosophie—
   Lettres (See: Saarbrucken)
Annali Di Ca' Foscari
_____Annals of Literature,
   London (See: Critical Review)
ANNIE TALBOT COLE
   LECTURES (WHEATON
   COLLEGE)
Annual Bibliography of English
   Language and Literature
_____Annual of Philosophy and
   Letters (See: Universitat des
   Saarlandes)
ANNUAL SHAKESPEARE
   LECTURE OF THE
   BRITISH ACADEMY
ANTIOCH REVIEW
Antiquarian Bookman
Anvil
Appleton's Magazine
Approach
Apropos
Ararat
Archer
Archiv fur das Studium der
   Neueren Sprachen
Archives des Lettres Modernes
Archivum Linguisticum
Arena
Ariel
Arion, Quarterly Journal of
   Classical Culture
ARIZONA QUARTERLY
Armenian Review
Arsberattelse—Bulletin of the
   Royal Society of Letters: Lund

Bulletin of Bibliography
Bulletin of Hispanic Studies
_____Bulletin of Spanish Studies
(See: Bulletin of Hispanic
Studies)
Bulletin of the Dramatists' Alliance
(Stanford University)
BULLETIN OF THE
FACULTY OF ARTS
(ALEXANDRIA
UNIVERSITY)
_____Bulletin of the Faculty of
Arts-Faroque University (See:
Bulletin of the Faculty of Arts
—Alexandria University)
BULLETIN OF THE NEW
YORK PUBLIC LIBRARY
Burke Newsletter
Burns Chronicle
CEA CRITIC
CLA JOURNAL (COLLEGE
ASSOCIATION JOURNAL,
MORGAN STATE
COLLEGE)
CAIRO STUDIES IN
ENGLIS
Calcutta Review
California Quarterly
CALIFORNIA SHAVIAN
Californian
CAMBRIDGE JOURNAL
CAMBRIDGE REVIEW
Canadian Author and Bookman
Canadian Bookman (See:
Canadian Author & Bookman)
Canadian Commentator
Canadian Forum
CANADIAN LITERATURE
Canadian Modern Language
Review
_____Canadian Philosophical
Journal (See: Dialogue—
Montreal)
Caravan
CARIBBEAN QUARTERLY
Caribbean Studies
CARLETON DRAMA
REVIEW (See also:
Tulane Drama Review)

Carleton Miscellany
Carmelitas Discalced (OCD)
CARNEGIE SERIES IN
ENGLISH
CAROLINA QUARTERLY
Carrell, The
CASOPIS PRO MODERNI
FILOLOGII
Catholic Library World
Catholic Theater Yearbook, The
Catholic University of America
Studies in Medieval and
Renaissance Latin Language
and Literature
Catholic University of America
Studies in Romance Languages
and Literatures
CATHOLIC WORLD
CENTENNIEL REVIEW
(EAST LANSING, ...
MICHIGAN)
Central Asiatic Journal
CENTRAL LITERARY
MAGAZINE, THE
CENTRAL STATES
SPEECH JOURNAL
Centro di Studi Filologici e
Linguistici Siciliani
Centro Escolar University
Graduate and Faculty Studies
(Manila)
Chapter One
_____Character and Personality
(See: Journal of Personality)
Chelsea
Chelsea Review
_____Chicago Choice
(See: Choice)
CHICAGO REVIEW
CHIMERA
CHINA SOCIETY
OCCASSIONAL PAPERS
Chinese Literature
Choice (Chicago)
Choice (The Science Press,
Pennsylvania)
Choice Literature
CHRISTENDOM
Christian Century

Forty-Eight
Forum (Philadelphia)
Forum (University of Houston)
_____Forum and Column Review
  (See: Forum-Philadelphia)
FORUM FOR MODERN
  LANGUAGE STUDIES
FOUR QUARTERS
  (La Salle College, Philadelphia)
Freeman
French Review
French Studies
Fresco
FRONTIER
Frontier and Midland
Furioso
Furman Bulletin, The
FURMAN STUDIES
G. D. R. Review (German
  Democratic Republic Review)
Gambit
Gate, The
Genesis West
Georgia Historical Quarterly
GEORGIA REVIEW
_____German Democratic
  Republic Review (See:
  G. D. R. Review)
GERMAN LIFE AND
  LETTERS
German Quarterly
Germania Romana
GERMANIC REVIEW
Go: A Holiday Magazine
Golden Goose (Formerly
  Briarcliff Quarterly)
Goliads
Graduate Journal, The
Graduate Review of Philosophy
Graduate Student of English
  (Minneapolis)
GREECE AND ROME
GRECOURT REVIEW
_____Guide (See: Guidon)
Gymnasium, das
_____Half-Yearly Journal of the
  Mysore University (See:
  University of Mysore Half-
  Yearly Journal)

Harlequin
HARVARD ADVOCATE
Harvard Library Bulletin
Harvard Studies in Classical
  Philology
Harvard Studies in Comparative
  Literature
Harvard Studies in Romance
  Languages
Harvard Theological Review
_____Harvard Wake
  (See: Wake)
Hawaii University Occasional
  Papers
HERMATHENA, A DUBLIN
  UNIVERSITY REVIEW
Hermes
Hesperia
HIBBERT JOURNAL
High Points
HISPANIA
Hispanic Review
Hispanofila
HOGARTH LECTURES
  ON LITERATURE
Hollins Critic
_____Hollywood Quarterly
  (See: Film Quarterly)
HOPKINS REVIEW
HORIZON
HORIZONTES REVISTA
  DE LA UNIVERSIDAD
  CATOLICA DE PUERTO
  RICO
Hound and Horn
HUDSON REVIEW
Huebner's Index
HUMANIST, THE
HUMANIST WAY, THE
Humanitas
Humanities, The (Boston
  College Classical Bulletin)
HUMANITIES, THE
  (JOURNAL OF THE
  YOKOHAMA NATIONAL
  NATIONAL UNIVERSITY)
HUMANITIES
  ASSOCIATION

Journal of Religion, The
Journal of Religious Thought
Journal of Roman Studies
JOURNAL OF THE
    FACULTY OF ARTS
    (ROYAL UNIVERSITY OF
    MALTA)
Journal of the Folklore Institute
JOURNAL OF THE
    HISTORY OF IDEAS
Journal of the History of
    Philosophy
JOURNAL OF THE
    PSYCHOANALYTIC
    ASSOCIATION
Journal of the University of
    Bombay
JOURNAL OF THE
    UNIVERSITY OF SAUGAR
JOURNAL OF THE
    WARBURG AND
    COURTAULD INSTITUTES
..........Journal of the Yokohama
    National University (See:
    The Humanities)
Journal of Theological Studies
Jubilee
..........Kansas City Review
    (See: University Review)
KANSAS MAGAZINE
KEATS-SHELLEY JOURNAL
KEATS-SHELLEY
    MEMORIAL BULLETIN
Kennecott Lecture Series, The
    (University of Arizona)
..........Kent State Library
    Quarterly (See: The Serif)
KENTUCKY FOREIGN
    LANGUAGE QUARTERLY
KENYON REVIEW
King's Crown Essays
Kranich, der
KWARTALNIK
    NEOFILOLOGICZNY
..........Kyushu Studies in
    Literature (See: Studies in
    Literature)
..........Kyushu University Studies

in English Literature and
    Language (See: Studies in
    English Literature and
    Language)
L E A (Librarians, Editors,
    Authors)
LANDFALL
Language, A Journal of the
    Linguistic Society of America
Language and Speech
Langue et Parole
Latinitas
Latomus
Laughing Horse
Leeds Studies in English and
    Kindred Languages
Leuvense Bijdragen
Library, The
Library Chronicle of the
    University of Texas
Library Literature
Life and Letters (Formerly
    Life and Letters Today)
LIFE AND LETTERS TODAY
Lifeline
Limbo
LINGUA (UNIVERSITY OF
    CAPETOWN)
Listen, A Quarterly Review
Listener
LITERA: STUDIES BY
    MEMBERS OF THE
    ISTANBUL ENGLISH
    DEPARTMENT
    (ISTANBUL)
LITERARY CRITERION
    (MYSORE)
Literary Era
LITERARY HALF YEARLY
    (MYSORE)
LITERARY REVIEW
Literary World
Literature
LITERATURE AND
    PSYCHOLOGY
Literature East and West
Little Review
Lock Haven Bulletin (Lock

Haven State College)
Lock Haven Review
Lochlann
LONDON MAGAZINE, THE
London Mercury
LONDON QUARTERLY AND
  HOLBORN REVIEW
_____London University
  Institute of Classical Studies
  (See: Institute of Classical
  Studies Bulletin)
_____London University Journal
  of the Warburg and Courtauld
  Institutes (See: Journal of the
  Warburg and Courtauld
  Institutes)
Louisiana State University Studies
  Humanities Series
Louisiana Studies
Lovingood Papers
Lund Studies in English
Luso-Brazilian Review
Lustrum
McNEESE REVIEW
MADISON QUARTERLY,
  THE
Main Currents in Modern
  Thought
MAINSTREAM (Supersedes
  MASSES AND
  MAINSTREAM
Makerere
MAKERERE JOURNAL
Manchester Literary and
  Philosophy Society. Memoirs
  and Proceedings
MANDRAKE
MANITOBA ARTS
  REVIEW, THE
Mark Twain Journal
Mark Twain Quarterly
Maryland Quarterly
MASSACHUSETTS REVIEW
  (UNIVERSITY OF
  MASSACHUSETTS)
MASSES AND
  MAINSTREAM
  (Becomes Mainstream)

Meanjin
MEANJIN PAPERS
MEANJIN QUARTERLY
Measure, A Critical Journal
  (Chicago)
? Measure (San Francisco)
Medieval Studies (Toronto)
Medievala et Humanistica
Mediteranean Meeting Point
Medium Aevum
Medium Aevum Monographs
MENNINGER QUARTERLY
Mesa
MICHIGAN ACADEMY OF
  SCIENCE, ARTS, AND
  LETTERS. PAPERS.
MICHIGAN ALUMNUS, THE
Michigan Quarterly Review
Michigan State University Studies
  in American English
_____Mid Continent American
  Studies Journal (See:
  American Studies)
Midstream
Midway (University of Chicago)
Midwest Journal
Midwest Review
Mind
MINNESOTA REVIEW
Minority of One
MINT, THE
Mirador
Miscellaneous Man
Mississippi Poetry Journal
MISSISSIPPI QUARTERLY
Mnemosyne (Bibliotheca
  Classica Bataua)
Modern Age
MODERN DRAMA
MODERN FICTION STUDIES
Modern Language Journal
MODERN LANGUAGE NOTES
MODERN LANGUAGE
  QUARTERLY
MODERN LANGUAGE
  REVIEW
Modern Languages
MODERN PHILOLOGY
Modern Quarterly (London)

MODERNA SPRAK
Monatschelfte fur Deutschen
    Unterricht (Madison,
    Wisconsin)
MONTH
Monthly Magazine and American
    Review
Monthly Review
Muse, The
Mutiny
Nation
Nebraska University Studies in
    Language and Literature
Nebraska University Studies in
    the Humanities
Neon (Brooklyn, New York)
NEOPHILOLOGUS
NEUPHILOGOGISCHE
    MITTEILUNGEN
_____New Adelphi (See:
    Adelphi)
New Day
New Departures
NEW DIRECTIONS IN
    PROSE AND POETRY
New England Quarterly
NEW ENGLISH REVIEW
NEW HUNGARIAN
    QUARTERLY
New Hungarian Review
NEW LEFT REVIEW
NEW MEXICO
    QUARTERLY REVIEW
New Mexico University Language
    Series
New Morality
New Olympia, The
New Plays Quarterly
New Reasoner
New Republic
New Saltire
New Statesman
New Theatre (London)
New Theatre Magazine
New University Thought
New World Writing
NEW WRITING AND
    DAYLIGHT

New Yorker
Newsletter, The
NIMBUS
NINE
Nineteenth Century and After
Nineteenth Century Fiction
Noble Savage
Nonplus
Noonday
NORSEMAN, THE
North American Review
NORTH DAKOTA UNI-
    VERSITY QUARTERLY
North Dakota University
    Quarterly Journal
_____North Dakota University
    Quarterly Review (See:
    North Dakota University
    Quarterly Journal)
NORTHERN MISCELLANY
    OF LITERARY CRITICISM
Northern Review
NORTHWEST MISSOURI
    STATE TEACHERS
    COLLEGE STUDIES
NORTHWEST REVIEW
    (OREGON)
NORTHWESTERN UNI-
    VERSITY TRIQUARTERLY
NORWEGIAN STUDIES
    IN ENGLISH
NOTES AND QUERIES
Nottingham French Studies
_____Nottingham University
    Renaissance and Modern
    Studies (See: Renaissance and
    Modern Studies)
Nottingham University Medieaval
    Studies
_____O C D (See: Carmelitas
    Discalced)
Oberlin Quarterly
Odyssey Review
Offbeat
Ohio University Review,
    Contributions in the Humanities
OKLAHOMA A & M ARTS
AND SCIENCE STUDIES:

SOUTHERLY
Southern Observer
Southern Quarterly, The (University of Southern Mississippi)
SOUTHERN REVIEW
(LOUISIANA STATE UNIVERSITY)
SOUTHERN REVIEW
(SOUTH AUSTRALIA)
SOUTHERN SPEECH JOURNAL, THE
SOUTHWEST REVIEW
Southwestern Journal, The
Soviet Literary Studies
_____Soviet Literature (See: International Literature)
SOVIET REVIEW
Soviet Studies (Glasgow)
Spectrum
SPECULUM
SPEECH MONOGRAPHS
SPEECH TEACHER
Sprache im Technischen Zeitalter
Stage
Stand
Standard, The (Becomes The Ethical Outlook)
STANFORD STUDIES IN LANGUAGE AND LITERATURE
_____Stanford University Publications in Language and Literature (See: Stanford Studies in Language and Literature)
Step Ladder
Stolen Paper Review
STRATFORD PAPERS ON SHAKESPEARE
STRATFORD-UPON-AVON STUDIES
Studi Americani
Studi Francesi
Studi Italiani di Filologia Classica
Studi Medievali
Studi Romani
Studia Germanica
STUDIA NEOPHILOLOGICA

STUDIA ROMANICA ET ANGLICA ZAGRABIENSIA
STUDIA ROMANTICA
STUDIES (AN IRISH QUARTERLY REVIEW)
Studies in American Literature
STUDIES IN ENGLISH— UNIVERSITY OF TEXAS
STUDIES IN ENGLISH (Superseded by Texas Studies in Literature and Language)
STUDIES IN ENGLISH LITERATURE 1500-1900 (RICE UNIVERSITY)
STUDIES IN ENGLISH LITERATURE (TOKYO)
Studies in Language and Literature in Honor of J. M. Hart
STUDIES IN PHILOLOGY
STUDIES IN ROMANTICISM (BOSTON UNIVERSITY)
STUDIES IN SCOTTISH LITERATURE
Studies in Short Fiction
Studies in Soviet Philosophy
STUDIES IN THE RENAISSANCE
Studies on Loch Lomand
STUDIES ON THE LEFT
Studii Clasice
Survey
SWAN OF AVON, THE
Symposium, (Syracuse University)
Talisman
Talks—A Quarterly Digest of Addresses
Tamarack Review
TENNESSEE FOLKLORE SOCIETY BULLETIN
TENNESSEE STUDIES IN LITERATURE
TEXAS QUARTERLY
_____Texs Review (See: Southwest Review)
_____Texas Studies in English (See: Studies in English— University of Texas

TEXAS STUDIES IN LITER-
ATURE AND LANGUAGE
(Supersedes STUDIES IN
ENGLISH-UNIVERSITY
OF TEXAS)
THEATRE ARTS
(NEW YORK)
_____Theatre Arts Magazine—
New York (See: Theatre Arts)
_____Theatre Arts Monthly
(See: Theatre Arts)
Theatre Notebook
Theatre Research
Theatre Survey
Theatre Today
Theatre World
THEORIA, A JOURNAL OF
STUDIES (NATAL
UNIVERSITY COLLEGE)
Thoreau Society Bulletin
THOTH (SYRACUSE
UNIVERSITY)
THOUGHT
Thought Patterns
THRESHOLD (THE LYRIC
PLAYERS: BELFAST)
Tiger's Eye
Tijdschrift Voor Levende Talen
(Becomes Revue des
Langues Vivantes)
TIME AND TIDE
TIMES LITERARY
SUPPLEMENT (LONDON)
TOPIC (WASHINGTON
AND JEFFERSON
COLLEGE)
Traditio
Transatlantic Review
TULANE DRAMA REVIEW
(Formerly THE CARLETON
DRAMA REVIEW)
TULANE STUDIES
IN ENGLISH
Twainian
TWENTIETH CENTURY
(Formerly NINETEENTH
CENTURY AND AFTER)

TWENTIETH CENTURY
LITERATURE
Twice a Year
UNION COLLEGE
SYMPOSIUM
UNION SEMINARY
QUARTERLY REVIEW
Unitas (Finland)
UNITAS (MANILA)
Universitas: A German Review
of the Arts and Sciences
Universitas (Accra)
Universite of Montpellier:
Faculty of Letters Publication
Universities and Left Review
Universities Quarterly
_____University College Quar-
terly (See: College Quarterly)
UNIVERSITY OF
ARIZONA BULLETIN
UNIVERSITY OF AUKLAND
ENGLISH SERIES
UNIVERSITY OF
CALCUTTA. BULLETIN
OF THE DEPARTMENT
OF ENGLISH
UNIVERSITY OF CALI-
FORNIA, PUBLICATIONS.
ENGLISH STUDIES
University of California Publica-
cations in Classical Philology
UNIVERSITY OF CALI-
FORNIA PUBLICATIONS
IN ENGLISH
University of California Publica-
tions in Modern Philology
University of Ceylon Review
UNIVERSITY OF
COLORADO STUDIES
UNIVERSITY OF
DENVER PUBLICATIONS.
STUDIES IN HUMANITIES
University of Edinburgh Journal
_____University of Edinburgh
Scottish Studies (See: Scottish
Studies)
University of Florida Monographs

Views
Vinduet
VIRGINIA QUARTERLY
  REVIEW
VISUABHARATI
  QUARTERLY
Vivarium
Voices (England)
VOICES (MICHIGAN)
Voprosi Litoratura
_____*Wake* (Harvard) (See:
  Wake, New York)
WAKE (NEW YORK)
Wales
Walt Whitman Review
*Washington State College
  Research Studies*
*Washington University Studies
  in Language and Literature*
Weimarer Beitrage
WELSH FOLKLORE
Westerly (Perth)
WESTERN FOLKLORE
WESTERN HUMANITIES
  REVIEW (FORMERLY
  UTAH HUMANITIES
  REVIEW)
_____*Western Review* (See:
  Rocky Mountain Review)
WESTERN SPEECH
Westminster Review
Whetstone
William and Mary Quarterly
WIND AND THE RAIN
WISCONSIN ACADEMY
  REVIEW: PROCEEDINGS
  OF THE ACADEMY OF
  SCIENCE, ARTS, AND
  LETTERS
WISCONSIN STUDIES IN
  CONTEMPORARY
  LITERATURE
WISEMAN REVIEW
Word (New York)

Worker (Karachi)
_____*World Liberalism* (See:
  Pall Mall Quarterly)
World Report (Merged into
  U.S. News and World Report)
WORLD REVIEW, THE
WORLD THEATRE
Wort in der Zeit
Writer
*Wroclawskie Towarzystwo
  Naukowe Prace*
XAVIER UNIVERSITY
  STUDIES
  (NEW ORLEANS)
Yale French Studies
YALE REVIEW
YALE STUDIES IN ENGLISH
YALE UNIVERSITY
  LIBRARY GAZETTE
YEARBOOK OF
  COMPARATIVE AND
  GENERAL LITERATURE
YEARBOOK OF
  PSYCHOANALYSIS
Year's Work in Classical Studies
Year's Work in English
Year's Work in English Studies
Year's Work in Literature
*Year's Work in Modern
  Language Studies*
*Year's Work in Modern
  Languages*
Yugen
ZAGADNIENIA RODZAJOW
  LITERACKISH
ZEITSCHRIFT FUR
  ANGLISTIK UND
  AMERIKANISTIC

_____
*Indicates that title of periodical appears capitalized because it is an abbreviation — not because it yielded entries.

APPENDIX

I

The following compilation ranks periodicals from which entries were obtained for this Checklist by the number of periodical pages of criticism appearing herein. Only those periodicals falling in the top 50 positions are shown below.

Pages	Periodical
3,000	Shakespeare Quarterly
1,542	PMLA
1,427	Studies in Philology
911	ELH
817	Stratford-Upon-Avon Studies
808	Journal of English and Germanic Philology
793	Philological Quarterly
786	Review of English Studies
709	Modern Language Quarterly
684	Modern Language Review
683	Modern Drama
673	Sewanee Review
633	Essays in Criticism
629	Essays and Studies
617	American Imago
550	Shakespeare Survey
535	College English
508	Shakespeare Association Bulletin
504	Columbia University Studies in English and Comparative Literature
482	Notes and Queries
456	Modern Language Notes
449	Studies in English Literature 1500-1900
410	Huntington Library Quarterly
409	Kenyon Review
404	Drama Survey
398	Makerere Journal
379	Carnegie Series in English
353	Scrutiny
348	Shakespeare Jahrbuck
311	Studies in English (University of Texas)
305	American Literature
302	University of Toronto Quarterly

299	Modern Philology
296	English Studies
293	Illinois Studies in Language and Literature
280	English Institute Essays
271	Hudson Review
270	University of Missouri Studies
266	Review of English Literature
265	Anglia
213	Norwegian Studies in English
204	Boston University Studies in English
203	Educational Theatre Journal
198	The City College Papers
195	Renaissance Papers
172	Studia Neophilologica
169	Baconiana
167	Centenniel Review
	Washington State College Research Studies
158	Literature and Psychology

II

The following compilation ranks periodicals from which entries were obtained for this Checklist by the number of periodical entries appearing herein. Only those periodicals falling in the top 50 positions are shown below.

ENTRIES	PERIODICAL
.375	Shakespeare Quarterly
197	Notes and Queries
150	PMLA
127	Studies in Philology
119	College English
117	Modern Language Notes
112	Review of English Studies
111	Modern Language Review
94	Philological Quarterly
77	Journal of English and Germanic Philology
75	Explicator
	Tulane Drama Review
74	Essays in Criticism
	Modern Language Quarterly
73	ELH
71	Essays and Studies
67	The Shakespeare Association Bulletin
61	Shakespeare Survey
57	Stratford-Upon-Avon Studies
54	Modern Drama

53	Shakespeare Newsletter
44	Studies in English (University of Texas)
43	American Literature
42	Sewanee Review
	Southern Speech Journal
41	Educational Theatre Journal
	Modern Philology
40	Drama Survey
39	Encore: The Voice of the Vital Theatre
37	Review of English Literature
36	Shakespeare Jahrbuck
34	American Imago
	Huntington Library Quarterly
	Literature and Psychology
33	Studies in English Literature 1500-1900
32	University of Toronto Quarterly
30	English
	English Studies
29	Baconiana
28	Catholic World
27	Scrutiny
26	Anglia
	Kenyon Review
	Revue des Langues Vivantes
25	Twentieth Century
24	Carnegie Series in English
	Renaissance Papers
21	Critical Quarterly
	Hudson Review
20	English Institute Essays
	Quarterly Journal of Speech

III

Of the periodicals appearing in Charts I and II, 40 appear in
both lists. These 40 are shown below in the order of their
COMBINED rank.

Shakespeare Quarterly

PMLA

Studies in Philology

Review of English Studies

Journal of English and
   Germanic Philology
Philological Quarterly

Modern Language Review

ELH

College English
Notes and Queries

Modern Language Quarterly

Stratford-Upon-Avon Studies

Essays in Criticism